ALICIA LEFANU, STRATHALLAN (1816)

TITLES IN THIS SERIES

Alicia LeFanu,
Strathallan (1816)

EDITED BY

Anna M. Fitzer

Routledge
Taylor & Francis Group

LONDON AND NEW YORK

First published 2008 by Pickering & Chatto (Publishers) Limited

Published 2016 by Routledge
2 Park Square, Milton Park, Abingdon, Oxfordshire OX14 4RN
711 Third Avenue, New York, NY 10017, USA

First issued in paperback 2016

Routledge is an imprint of the Taylor & Francis Group, an informa business

BRITISH LIBRARY CATALOGUING IN PUBLICATION DATA

Lefanu, Alicia, fl. 1812–1826
Strathallan. – (Chawton House library series. Women's novels)
1. Women – Great Britain – Social conditions – Fiction
2. Parent and child – Fiction 3. Women – Education –
Fiction 4. Great Britain - Social life and customs –
Fiction
I. Title II. Fitzer, Anna M.
823.7[F]

ISBN 13: 978-1-138-23604-2 (pbk)
ISBN 13: 978-1-8519-6960-9 (hbk)

Typeset by Pickering & Chatto (Publishers) Limited

CONTENTS

ACKNOWLEDGEMENTS

I am grateful for the support I have received in the preparation of this edition, particularly from Catherine Noblet and Rowland Cotterill who generously helped out with matters of translation. Thanks are due to Stephen Bygrave and Stephen Bending for their enthusiasm for the project, to Chawton House Library, the Bodleian Library, and to Elaine Doobary, and staff at Special Collections and Archives, the University Library, University of Sheffield. As ever, I thank Mary Fitzer for her continuing support. My greatest debt is to Charles Mundye, for the help and encouragement he has given me throughout this project.

INTRODUCTION

In 1825 Thomas Moore claimed that the talents of Alicia LeFanu were 'another proof of the sort of *gavel-kind* of genius allotted to the whole race of Sheridan'.[1] Though his expression is oblique his point makes one thing quite clear: Alicia LeFanu's contribution to her family's literary history was as significant as that of her better-known relations. Moore's allusion to a system of property succession in which all descendants inherited equally comes in his biographical study of LeFanu's famous uncle, the dramatist and Member of Parliament, Richard Brinsley Sheridan, and reaffirms the acknowledgement he gives to LeFanu in his preface. Moore's biography appeared a year after Alicia LeFanu published her own family history entitled *Memoirs of the Life and Writings of Mrs Frances Sheridan, Mother of the Late Right Hon. Richard Brinsley Sheridan* (1824). Moore was indebted to the assistance afforded him by its 'highly gifted' author[2] and LeFanu remains very much at the centre of what is known of this distinguished line. That by 1825 LeFanu had also published two lengthy poems and five novels is more extensive proof of her talents. As the first of six novels LeFanu completed between 1816 and 1826, *Strathallan* demonstrates, for the first time, the ingenuity and versatility of a writer whose professional career established her as a significant contemporary of Austen and Scott.

Born in Dublin in 1791, Alicia LeFanu was the daughter of Elizabeth 'Betsey' Sheridan, who was Richard Brinsley's sister and the youngest of the four surviving children of Frances and Thomas Sheridan. Given the Sheridan family's tradition of passing on names as well as genius, a brief sketch of its most prominent members clarifies the personal and professional legacy to which Alicia LeFanu contributed her own 'first attempt'.[3] LeFanu's grandfather, Thomas, earned renown as a lexicographer, but his early career as an actor and manager of Dublin's Smock Alley theatre had been encouraged by his father, the poet Dr Thomas Sheridan, and fostered in the company of his godfather Jonathan Swift.[4] In the 1750s Thomas Sheridan became involved with Drury Lane and he and his wife moved to London where they became active in a distinguished literary scene which included Frances's mentor, Samuel

1   Thomas Moore, *Memoirs of the Life of the Right Honourable Richard Brinsley Sheridan*, 2nd edn, 2 vols (London: Longman, Hurst, Rees, Orme, Brown, and Green, 1825), vol. 2, p. 159.

2   Moore, vol. 1, p. vi.

3   *Strathallan*, The Preface, p. 2.

4   For further biographical details see *The Poems of Thomas Sheridan*, ed. Robert Hogan (Newark, DE: University of Delaware Press; London and Toronto: Associated University Presses, 1994).

Richardson. Dedicated to Richardson, Frances Sheridan's extraordinarily successful first novel *Memoirs of Miss Sidney Bidulph* (1761) was published in Dublin and
London and ran to two editions in its first five months.[5] It at once invoked and complicated his exemplary models of virtue and sensibility, and Alicia LeFanu's account
of its being written in secret as a means of paying off Thomas's debts belies its literary
ambition.[6]

By the time Alicia was ready to follow in her grandmother Frances's footsteps,
her mother Elizabeth's first novel *Lucy Osmond* had been published anonymously in
1803, and she had completed two more by 1810.[7] Alicia's father, Henry LeFanu, was
the second youngest son of the respectable Dublin Huguenot family into which her
aunt, also named Alicia, had already married.[8] This Aunt 'Lissy', as she was known in
the family, was celebrated in Dublin circles for her private theatricals and would later
enjoy some success on the professional stage.[9] In drawing on this family background
for inspiration, Alicia LeFanu became the most prolific of its authors. *Strathallan* is
LeFanu's first novel, but not her first publication. Her poem *The Flowers; or, The Sylphid Queen, a Fairy Tale in Verse* (1809) had impressed her uncle Richard who, upon
receiving a copy from Elizabeth read it immediately 'with the greatest attention, and
thought it showed a great deal of imagination'.[10] LeFanu returned the compliment
with her next poem, *Rosara's Chain; or the Choice of Life. A Poem* (1812), by signing
herself as 'Niece to the Right Honourable Richard Brinsley Sheridan'.[11] It was of
course not uncommon to summon such a virtual chaperon in pursuit of what could

5   Three further editions of *Memoirs of Miss Sidney Bidulph* were published throughout the
eighteenth century, with the last in 1796. The Abbé Prevost's adaptation, *Mémoires pour servir à
l'Histoire de la Vertu*, was published in 1762, the same year as a French translation, *Mémoires de Miss
Sidney Bidulph* attributed to J. B. R. Robinet.

6   This was fulfilled in part when Sheridan's plays, *The Discovery* (1763) and *The Dupe* (1764),
were staged by Garrick at Drury Lane. But her career was cut short. Sheridan's oriental tale, *The
History of Nourjahad*, and a two-volume sequel to her novel entitled, *Conclusion of the Memoirs of Miss
Sidney Bidulph*, were published a year after her death in 1766, aged only 42.

7   Writing as Mrs. H. LeFanu, Daughter of the Late Thomas Sheridan, M.A., Elizabeth is also
the author of *The India Voyage* (London: G. and J. Robinson, 1804) and *The Sister; A Tale* (London:
Richards and Co., 1810).

8   The cross-generational doubling of first names favoured by the Sheridans is complicated
by the sisters Elizabeth and Alicia having married LeFanu brothers, Henry and Joseph: Mrs Alicia
LeFanu (1753–1817).

9   Her five-act play, *Prejudice; or, Modern Sentiment* began its professional run at Dublin's Lyc-
eum Theatre-Royal in 1812. Under its revised title, *The Sons of Erin*, the play ran in Dublin until June
1812, before transferring to London's Drury Lane, and to theatres from Edinburgh to Exeter. It was
published in London by John Ridgeway in 1812.   In true gavel-kind tradition, the surplus of her
literary talents would be passed on to her grandson, the novelist Joseph Sheridan LeFanu.

10   Quoted by Moore from a letter written by R.B. Sheridan's first wife, the famed Eliza Linley, to
Elizabeth LeFanu. See *Memoirs of the Life of the Right Honourable Richard Brinsley Sheridan*, vol. 2, p.159.

11   Illustrated with six engravings *The Flowers; or, The Sylphid Queen: A Fairy Tale in Verse*, could be
had for 3 shillings from J. Harris. Having taken over Newbury's premises on the corner of St Paul's
churchyard, Harris was the purveyor of an 'unparalleled Assemblage of Articles for the purpose
of Education.' See *Jackson's Oxford Journal*, Saturday 23 December 1809. Although at double the
price, *Rosara's Chain* was at the more expensive end of a range similarly intended for 'the rational
instruction of the rising generation', it proved popular and two further editions were published by

still be deemed an improper profession for a woman, especially one who was, according to *Strathallan*'s preface, 'unfriended and unpatronized'. But though LeFanu invokes the authority of her grandfather on its title page, *Strathallan* continues to acknowledge her dramatist uncle, as well as other members of the familial canon, on its pages. Indeed, one of *Strathallan*'s most striking features is its negotiation of a variety of narrative and dramatic styles, wrought together in a comic-satiric prose narrative which is at once inventive and experimental rather than simply imitative.

In many respects *Strathallan* is a book about other kinds of writing, and one in which the events are predicated on various pretensions to literariness. The action coincides with the participation of the eponymous Strathallan and his younger half-brother, Spencer Fitzroy, in the Peninsula War between 1808 and 1812, but is mainly confined to the domestic life of Woodlands, the Derbyshire estate of Strathallan's father, Lord Torrendale. His wife, Lady Laura Torrendale, is a specimen of London 'Society' who, on account of her expenditure, has been retired against her will to the country by her husband. As her bibliophobia is marginally less chronic than her addiction to the latest fashion, Lady Torrendale indulges her latest *penchant* for literary parties with invitations to local poets, Mr 'Alcæus' Spring and Miss 'Sappho' Swanley. At around this time, the arrogant and selfish Fitzroy returns from Portugal as the darling of his mother's uncritical eye. It is for his sake that Lady Torrendale borrows money from her neighbour Mrs Stockwell, the widow of a Kidderminster factory owner who has considerably more money at her disposal. Lady Torrendale guarantees her loans from Mrs Stockwell with an open invitation to her home, suffering her company as well as that of Stockwell's boorish son, Sam, and her nieces the Misses Ferrars, and Hautenville. When Lady Torrendale discovers the clever and beautiful Matilda Melbourne living nearby with her parents in rural seclusion, she takes her in as the perfect ornament for her parties. Upon the introduction of Miss Hautenville's friend, Miss Sophia Mountain, LeFanu completes her feminine quartet of young readers by turns astute, fraudulent, discerning and misguided.

Throughout the novel LeFanu sustains a coherent and serious insistence upon her heroine Matilda's 'uniform dignity, propriety, and decorum' of conduct,[12] contrasting it with the fashionable society of Lady Torrendale and her pernicious crew of hangers-on. But the main romantic trajectory of *Strathallan*'s heroine, Matilda, and her involvement with Strathallan, is side-lined by a confusion of 'under-characters' which LeFanu considered essential to 'the effect and symmetry' of the novel form.[13] This process of shifting the interest from the central romantic plot underlines the displaced condition of many of LeFanu's characters. The eponymous hero Strathallan is a much talked of, but mostly absent figure who, when he does appear, is mistaken for an apparition. Though opposite in nature, both Matilda and Lady Torrendale are

---

M. J. Godwin, at the Juvenile Library, before 1818. See *The Morning Chronicle,* Thursday 26 February 1818.

12 *Strathallan*, vol. 4, p. 408.

13 Alicia LeFanu, *Memoirs of the Life and Writings of Mrs. Frances Sheridan* (London: G. and W. B. Whittaker, 1824): 'the reader must be aware that in a novel perfectly well contrived, the under-characters and incidents cannot be sacrificed without "curtailing it" of its "fair proportion," and injuring the effect and symmetry of the whole' (p. 188).

engaged in a process of reconciliation and adaptation to their new circumstances. Their displacement is reflected in that of the various orphaned women to whom they play host, and the novel is, at an abstract level, interested in the issues of inheritance, estrangement and reconciliation consequent upon a sense of (be)longing. At the level of events, Matilda is also the means through which Lady Torrendale hopes to ensure that the Scottish estate after which her stepson Strathallan is named, will be passed on to Fitzroy. Combining the dangerous charms of R.B. Sheridan's Joseph Surface with the fecklessness of his brother Charles, Fitzroy ultimately demonstrates none of the latter's redeeming features. But LeFanu is, like R.B. Sheridan, interested in the ambivalent exploitation, for good, or ill, of familial bonds.

That LeFanu does achieve symmetry in all this owes much to her ability to treat serious concerns with comic inventiveness, and the simmering romantic attachment between the two ostensible leads complements the additional fare of posturing, pseudo-intellectual poetasters, and women prone to misplaced self-identification with heroines in books. Though not guilty of this herself, Arbella Ferrars is an ironic embodiment of this confusion, for while one might trace her show of vanity to Pope's model for *The Rape of the Lock*, LeFanu has her function more exactly in the manner of the outspoken and subversive narrator Arabella Fermor in Frances Brooke's *The History of Emily Montague* (1769). Arabella's question in that novel as to just 'how entertaining and improving would be the history of the human heart if people spoke all the truth, and painted themselves as they really are',[14] is one Matilda strives to answer. The still centre of a garrulous group of under-characters variously stimulated by vanity, hypocrisy and prejudice, Matilda is, like LeFanu, a reader of human nature in all its variety.

Arbella makes the mistake of misreading Fitzroy's apparent charm, but this too pales into insignificance when it comes to Matilda's rival in love, Miss Mountain. The very antithesis of Matilda in point of character and education, Sophia Mountain is a veritable female Quixote. Brought up in the seclusion of her father's mansion and mostly confined to the library, she understands the world primarily in terms of the fictional chivalry of her favourite Arcadian knights. Her reading of social situations is no more sophisticated; the 'ponderous formality' she adopts in the company of women, gives way to male-inspired 'airy graces of coquetry, in the perplexing mazes of which the stately Sophia gambolled with all the ease and frolic sportiveness of an elephant'.[15]

LeFanu was in her mid-twenties when *Strathallan* was published in the autumn of 1816, and a good ten years younger than Frances Sheridan upon her debut. For the single, inexperienced and ambitious young woman, however, success was as immediate. *Strathallan* ran to a second edition by the end of the year, at least matching the sensationally short period in which Sheridan's novel had sold out. The pattern continued, a further edition being published in 1817 with a French translation – the translator identified only as Ch. – H. de J*** – published by H. Nicolle in Paris the

14   Frances Brooke, *The History of Emily Montague*, ed. Lorraine McMullen (Ontario: McClelland and Stewart, 1995), p. 250.

15   *Strathallan*, I pp. 51–2.

following year. An early notice had predicted that the novel was 'likely to prove most popular', and gave as much credit to the author's unique achievements as it did to her consistency with the 'polished style and taste' of her family.[16] There is a sense in which LeFanu had been wise in stalling her career long enough to avoid attracting the contempt Hannah More reserved for girls who, having 'been accustomed to devour a multitude of frivolous books, will converse and write with a far greater appearance of skill as to style and sentiment at twelve or fourteen years old, than those of a more advanced age who are under the discipline of severer studies'. Unlike such spurious prodigies who 'become stationary', LeFanu could count herself amongst that 'quietly progressive' number who pass 'through just gradations to a higher strain of mind'.[17] Yet, her first outing in prose, for all its derision of frivolous reading practices, is radically inclusive of the 'multitude' in a way which is as indicative of LeFanu's specific background as it is of the broader ideological context in which a woman writer of her generation was expected to perform.

II

If Alicia were ever in danger of running before she could walk, her mother, Elizabeth, offered the steadying hand. Having moved from Dublin to England in the 1790s, Alicia and her younger sister Harriet spent their early childhood in Kingsbridge, Devon. It was from there that, in 1804, Elizabeth wrote a letter to her cousin, William Chamberlaine, extracts from which he included in an article submitted to the *Gentleman's Magazine* shortly after. Entitled 'Anecdotes of Miss LeFanu and of Mrs. Jordan' it interpolated Elizabeth's prognostic of Alicia's 'literary eminence', and was published, in accordance with the request of its author, only when 'she arrived at celebrity as an authoress'.[18] Elizabeth's letter gives assurances as to the propriety of her encouraging Alicia in this pursuit:

> Her memory was early exercised on subjects generally tending to some useful object; her taste for reading has been constantly indulged, yet no book has ever met her eye, that could injure her principles, or lessen that delicacy of mind which, next to religious principles, I consider as the surest protection to a woman.[19]

16 *Jackson's Oxford Journal*, Saturday 26 October 1816. The reviewer adds: 'The Character of *Lady Torrendale*, in particular, is one of the most perfect portraits of a showy, attractive, and deceitful woman of fashion, that we have ever seen. The Dialogue is sustained with theatrical art; and the whole might, with little labour, be converted into an admirable Comedy. We wish, indeed, the elegant Authoress would write for the Stage.'

17 Hannah More, *Strictures on the Modern System of Female Education*, 9th edn, 2 vols (London: T. Cadell, 1801), vol. 1, p. 206. This work was first published in 1799.

18 On these terms, LeFanu was officially afforded celebrity status in 1824 when the article was published in *The Gentleman's Magazine: The Supplement to Vol. XCIV Part I.*, pp. 582–3. This coincided with a favourable review of her *Memoirs of the Life and Writings of Mrs. Frances Sheridan* in the *Gentleman's Magazine*, 94 (June 1824) pp. 532–4.

19 *The Gentleman's Magazine: The Supplement to Vol. XCIV*, pp. 582–3.

There is a seeming confluence of opinion on reading practices in this letter and in the writings of Hannah More, and Hester Chapone, whose *Letters on the Improvement of the Mind* (1773) typically cautioned against novels.[20] Alicia was supplied with 'works of taste and information' – Godwin's *Life of Chaucer*, William Cowper's *Letters* – which were 'more delightful to her than the most highly wrought Romance would be to most girls of her age'.[21] This left Alicia well disposed to one day distinguish herself from those 'ever multiplying authors, that with unparalleled fecundity are overstocking the world with their quick-succeeding progeny'.[22]

Alicia's mother had been in her early twenties when she began accompanying her father Thomas on his lecture tours on education and lexicography. For the modern reader, Elizabeth's letters reflecting on her experience of the fashionable milieu of London, and of the spa towns Bath and Tunbridge Wells in the 1780s, are perhaps the most familiar of her writings, having since been published as *Betsey Sheridan's Journal*. In some respects, LeFanu's own situation, and the motivations of Matilda's mother in *Strathallan*, Aspasia Melbourne, can be traced to Elizabeth's reflections upon the kind of social purgatory experienced by an unmarried but still dependent woman. In 1785, Elizabeth had attended a reading party at the home of the bluestocking Elizabeth Vesey, at which More herself was present. It was a far cry from the modest and provincial reading parties hosted by Lady Torrendale, and the company was eminently fashionable. But Elizabeth had felt that 'there can be no true pleasure derived even from the most delightful society unless you feel you have a right to your place in it. I cannot make my Father feel the difference the world makes between a man of talents and the women of his Family unless these are at least independent.' Then, she aspired only to step out of the shared limelight and into 'that middling state of society where people are sufficiently raised to have their minds polish'd though not enough to look down on a person in my situation'.[23] It was perhaps with this in mind that Elizabeth embarked upon her own career and encouraged the natural abilities of Alicia which she considered 'much superior to my own'.[24] Unlike the have-a-go writers described by Hannah More, the careers of Elizabeth and Alicia LeFanu were directed by necessity as well as impulse, each dem-

---

20   Editions of Chapone's *Letters* were published throughout the first decades of the nineteenth century, as were other eighteenth-century advice manuals such as James Fordyce's *Sermons to Young Women* (1765) and John Gregory's *A Father's Legacy to his Daughters* (1778). For a discussion of the complex responses to reading, see Jaqueline Pearson, *Women's Reading in Britain 1750–1835: A Dangerous Recreation* (Cambridge: Cambridge University Press, 1999).

21   *The Gentleman's Magazine: The Supplement to Vol. XCIV*, p. 583.

22   More, *Strictures on the Modern System of Female Education*, 9th edn, vol. 1, p. 219. More (undeservedly) earned a reputation for dry didacticism in her later career. Her vision of the dawn of the dreaded female novelist registers a consensus of distrust of women keen to follow a trend, but her hyperbole here is typically ironic rather than seriously alarmist.

23   *Betsey Sheridan's Journal: Letters from Sheridan's Sister 1784–1786 and 1788–1790*, ed. William LeFanu (Oxford: Oxford University Press, 1986), Letter 7, London, 8th to 14th March 1785, p. 44.

24   *The Gentleman's Magazine: The Supplement to Vol. XCIV*, p. 583.

onstrating the pragmatism of women distinguished yet insufficiently financed by a family line seemingly congenitally incapable of actual prosperity.[25]

Recent attributions of *Lucy Osmond* to Alicia LeFanu look to be a mistake (the novel was published when she was in her thirteenth year). Chamberlaine had identified Elizabeth as 'the elegant authoress of "*Lucy Osmond*," and "*The India Voyage*"', shortly after its second edition,[26] and this was confirmed in advertisements for the novel in 1805. But, as an example of an early novel which addresses women's reading practice, it provides a useful point of departure for a consideration of *Strathallan*'s negotiation of this complicated issue. *Strathallan* dramatizes the importance of practising discrimination, whereas *Lucy Osmond* is more explicit in its prescription of suitable kinds of reading material. Alicia's mother had been an avid consumer of fashionable fiction and memoirs in her youth but her published writing, like her epistolary confidences as a mother, show due circumspection. Lucy Osmond suffers no less than the fatal consequences of learning from her 'favourite authors [...] contempt of the world, and toleration of every error that did not amount to positive vice'.[27] The novel is inflected with the educationalists' stance against the adverse side-effects of sensibility as associated with the author of *Emile* and *La Nouvelle Héloïse*, Jean-Jacques Rousseau. As an ideal, feminized state of delicacy, sensitivity and compassion, sensibility also engendered what was arguably 'a facile emotionalism that placed feelings above duty'.[28] *Lucy Osmond*'s author is not as pronounced as More in her contempt for Rousseau's 'destructive politics, deplorable profligacy and impudent infidelity',[29] but Lucy succumbs to the passions excited by her reading of him 'and all of those sentimentalists who, without his genius, have adopted his faults; [...] their maxims are baneful to society in general, but to women absolute destruction'.[30]

Like *Strathallan*'s Miss Mountain and Miss Hautenville, Lucy was bereft of maternal guidance at a young age, which Lucy's friend describes as that

> most dangerous period, when your understanding had not reached its strength, and the imagination began to reign. Your taste for reading, which, if well-directed, would have proved an advantage, was to you a source of error, as authors that fell in your way were such as no prudent parent would ever have suffered to meet your eye.[31]

25 Alicia's other maternal uncle, Charles, bucked this trend in his private affairs, but 'there was a good deal of personal bitterness within the family' when Elizabeth's marriage 'was being held up by his failure to release money owed to her.' See Fintan O'Toole, *A Traitor's Kiss: The Life of Richard Brinsley Sheridan* (London: Granta, 1998), p. 189.

26 See *The Gentleman's Magazine. The Supplement to Vol XCIV* pp. 582–3. Chamberlaine completed the article some time after 25 December 1804, in which year *Lucy Osmond* was published in New York by John Swaine. A surgeon, and Fellow and Secretary to the Medical Society in London, Chamberlaine was a relative and friend well placed to authenticate this detail.

27 Anon., *Lucy Osmond. A Story* (New York: John Swaine, 1804), p. 63.

28 Anne Stott, *Hannah More: The First Victorian* (Oxford: Oxford University Press, 2003), p. 84.

29 Hannah More, *Strictures on the Modern System of Female Education*, 9th edn, vol. 1, p. 34.

30 *Lucy Osmond*, p. 72.

31 *Lucy Osmond*, pp. 121–2.

But, obnoxious as they are, LeFanu spares Mountain and Hautenville the same fate. This is because *Strathallan* is less concerned with what they read than it is interested in their interpretation, and use of reading matter.

LeFanu resolves Elizabeth's example of prudent parenting into *Strathallan's* portrait of Matilda's mother, Aspasia Melbourne. The reader is told that Aspasia Melbourne, née Villiers, 'was forced, by the death of her mother, at an early age to do the honours of a house, the centre of all that was distinguished in the world of taste, of rank, or literature'.[32] When her father died leaving her without a penny, she was set to suffer the ignominy of being at once too accomplished and too poor to satisfy any young marriageable man. But having met the older, wiser Mr Melbourne at a private play in which he took double delight in her performance as Cleopatra and the rural beauty Rosina, she left London for the provincial pleasures of his modest country hideaway. Alicia's parents had met at one of Lissy's theatrical parties and when they married in 1789, Elizabeth was a bride of 31 and Henry, a former army Captain and half-pay officer, was eleven years her senior. LeFanu's biographical allusion to her own attentive mother resounds in Aspasia's determination that 'during the first years of youth, no novel, however interesting its story, however elegant its language, however unexceptionable its tendency, should ever meet the eye of her daughter'.[33] Mr Melbourne supplements this select diet of language, literature and history with science but as Matilda grows up his wife recognizes the strategic importance of also seasoning it with a 'little of the *ton*, the polish'[34] that can be derived from an introduction to society.

In her memoir of Frances Sheridan LeFanu would go on to recall how, upon discovering aunt Lissy reading one of his *Rambler*s, Samuel Johnson had recommended to Sheridan that she be turned '"loose into your library: if she is well inclined, she will choose only nutritious food; if otherwise, all your precautions will avail nothing to prevent her following the natural bent of her inclinations."'[35] When Aspasia defends the entertainments of Society against Melbourne's scepticism, she adopts a similar line of reasoning: 'I have always been of the opinion of an elegant friend of our's, that "to indulge young people with a peep into in the show-box of fashion," is the surest method to prevent that restless curiosity and feverish thirst for amusement, which is too often produced by exaggerated descriptions'.[36] In these ways, Alicia LeFanu negotiates a different way around *Lucy Osmond*'s subject, but at the same time that *Strathallan* comically distorts Lucy's tragic frailty, it also takes, through Aspasia, a serious and enlightened view of the earlier novel's example: why should a young girl wish for more than her 'books, friends and rational occupation?', asks Mr Melbourne. Aspasia's reply coincides with Elizabeth's expectations for her little girl: because '*I* wish it for her'. Matilda's is 'not a mind for which we need fear the conta-

32 *Strathallan*, vol. 1, pp.17–18.

33 *Strathallan*, vol.1, p.149.

34 *Strathallan*, vol. 1, p. 22.

35 *The Lives and Writings of Mrs. Frances Sheridan*, p. 196. Johnson's advice is treated as reckless; LeFanu adopting in her non-fiction (as her mother did in her correspondence) discretion in matters of adolescent female choice.

36 *Strathallan*, vol. 1, p. 21.

gion of society' but 'the romantic tenderness of her disposition, rather points to the danger of absolute solitude'.[37] Unlike Lucy, Matilda is released into the Woodlands' society of valued friends, rivals and the simply deluded; a library of characters to stack alongside the books that she learns how to read.

III

As a romantic novel, *Strathallan* involves its heroine Matilda and her love interest Strathallan in the kind of entanglements experienced by Frances Sheridan's Sidney Bidulph, and her 'first love', Orlando Faulkland. LeFanu inverts the order of those events, and in her version it is filial duty on Strathallan's part which obliges him to forgo his love for Matilda and marry another woman. But Matilda, like Sidney, makes her own pledge. For the sake of her mother she will exert every power her mind possesses 'to war against the weight of woe that still oppresses it. I will remember,' she adds, 'that, though contentment be removed far from me, the reward of virtue may still be mine'.[38] When Strathallan is released from his marital ties, Matilda at first refuses him on a point of principle and, like Sidney Bidulph, surrenders to 'the evil star' which prevails over her fate.[39] But, whereas Sheridan, in ruling out the happiness of her lovers, eschewed poetical justice in favour of due reward in heaven, LeFanu applies it liberally. Strathallan returns unscathed from his business abroad, and Matilda is ultimately conscience-free. Indeed the extent to which LeFanu implicitly endorses *Sidney Bidulph*'s moral and sentimental strains is influenced by her prioritization of 'the uncommon powers of wit and humour' which 'enliven and diversify' its execution.[40] *Strathallan* is characterized by a similarly shrewd and terrifically wry observation of contemporary manners, as well as by dialogue which has the kind of dramatic quality which stands in no need of further narrative explanation. Alicia was not the first of her line to look back. R.B. Sheridan had indeed borrowed from his mother's work for his first play, *The Rivals* (1775). While for LeFanu's readers recent memory might place Mrs Stockwell in a line of direct descent from R.B. Sheridan's Mrs Malaprop, this character in turn inherits the misuse of words which resemble the ones she is aiming for from Mrs Tryfort in Frances Sheridan's play, *A Journey to Bath*.[41]

There are other relics of this comic dramatic tradition waiting in the wings. But for every allusion to a 'Mrs Goodbody', 'Doctor Doldrum' or 'Mrs Lackwit' there are more sustained references. *The Rivals*, for instance, yields another type in the form

---

37 *Strathallan*, vol. 1, p.22.

38 *Strathallan*, vol. 2, p. 232. Sidney Bidulph similarly trusts to a divine reward for her wilful supervision of the more immediate struggle in which her heart and mind are engaged. Her protestations of victory are, though, all too frequently inflected with doubt and resentment, and it is part of Sheridan's more subversive point that she convinces neither herself nor her reader that such a model of virtue is in any way edifying. As Johnson joked with Sheridan, "'I know not Madam, that you have a right, upon moral principles, to make your readers suffer so much.'" See James Boswell, *Life of Johnson*, ed., R. W. Chapman, rev. J. D. Fleeman, 3rd edn (Oxford, London & New York: Oxford University Press, 1970), p. 276.

39 *Strathallan*, vol. 4, p. 469.

40 *Memoirs of the Life and Writings of Mrs. Frances Sheridan*, p. 157.

41 See Fintan O'Toole, *A Traitor's Kiss*, p. 87.

of LeFanu's Miss Langrish. A former music teacher, she is miscast as a governess on Lady Torrendale's expedient assumption that there is an equivalence between reading music, and an understanding of history and geography. Semi-literate in both, it is little wonder that Miss Langrish shares Lydia Languish's tendency to read the incidents of popular fiction as all too credible. That other conspicuous influence upon dramatic dialogue, *The School for Scandal,* informs the staging of Lady Torrendale and her cabalistic conspirators but extends to LeFanu's interest in the tensions of fraternal love and the dynamics of marriage in which age is as disproportionate as fortune. At the same time, other scenes signify the intersection of influences. The defamation of Matilda's character over a card party at Lady Torrendale's house is, for instance, undertaken with all the skill of a scandal-school graduate, at the same time that it recalls Lady Blast's making and breaking of reputations in Frances Brooke's *The Excursion* (1777). Published a year before Frances Burney's *Evelina* (1778) *The Excursion* follows the fortunes of the disingenuous Maria Villiers as she too makes her entrance into the world. As one of the earliest examples in women's writing of a female 'genius' who prioritizes literary ambition over romantic fulfilment, Maria is the vehicle for Brooke's satirical challenge to the limiting terms of a woman's engagement in the market-place. Downsizing this 'ever-varying region' of self-interest, prejudice and fashion to the Woodlands estate, LeFanu presents a similarly derisory rendition of its caprice and vanity.

Whereas Maria Villiers is a *bone fide* would-be writer, Matilda Melbourne is unwittingly subjected to the inferior capabilities of her reading, writing, and relentlessly reciting companions. The self-referential irony which underlies Miss Hautenville's pretending to 'a literary character', nicely distinguishes LeFanu's talents from her woeful inadequacy: 'sprung from a family which had made some figure in the world of letters', Hautenville's only truly creative move is to determine that 'a portion of the same ability her ancestors so eminently possessed, was hers, by hereditary and indefeasible right'.[42] The apt quotation with which she is armed for every occasion has no further substantiation. She is, 'a bag of bones'[43]; a flunkey to Miss Mountain, where the hard currency of her inheritance makes the indignity almost worthwhile. Both confuse the boundaries of fact and fiction, and exemplify a kind of wrong-headed application of learning. Hautenville gives Miss Mountain a belated education, but she remains proof of the maxim 'too little too late'. The poetry, history and biography she reads, so 'well whipt together in her poor brain, it produced a fine froth at top', gives only 'a degree of shew and pretension to her discourse'.[44]

In this respect LeFanu takes her place in a tradition one might trace from Charlotte Lennox's *The Female Quixote* (1752) to Jane Austen's parodic *Northhanger Abbey* (1818), though, for her part, *Strathallan*'s heroine is immune to the literary mania which afflicts its supporting characters. She is not gullible, but naïve and in society meets with the condescension experienced by her fellow 'rustic', Burney's Evelina. In a world preoccupied with money, status and appearance, neither is equipped to interpret social etiquette, particularly given that its rules are often bent in the service

---

42 *Strathallan*, vol. 1, p.45.

43 *Strathallan*, vol. 1, p.61.

44 *Strathallan*, vol. 1, p. 52–3.

of egotism rather than honour. Both heroines become more discerning, but their private distrust of a world in which the uninitiated are liable to err, is combined with a very real fear of its dangers. That Evelina is exasperated in her need of 'a book, of the laws and customs à-la-mode, presented to all young people, upon their first introduction in public company',[45] is a telling if ironic indictment of the inadequacy of the conduct literature which exists for this very purpose. *Strathallan* further dramatizes the implausibility of a seamless transition between the imaginary realm conjured by literature and the "realities" of the society such heroines face in occasional narrative interventions. In the manner of Brooke in *The Excursion*, LeFanu's ironic and omniscient narrator now and then suspends and elides action, drawing attention to the very conventions of whichever comic, sentimental or dramatic form she inhabits.

In the last of the generic influences to be considered, *Strathallan*'s invocation of the gothic is complicated by its dual function. Firstly, the narrative takes a strikingly gothic turn when, upon the death of Matilda's father, her cousin Harold inherits the Melbourne estate, the Rocks. There, Harold develops an irrational obsession with Matilda, and resents her attachment to Strathallan. In this part of the novel, LeFanu plays out the rarefied feelings and ostensible mysteries associated with Ann Radcliffe's *The Mysteries of Udolpho* (1794), amidst the pseudo-Gothic architecture of the Rocks's winding pathways and hidden grottoes. Matilda is terrorized by her cousin Harold and is held to ransom by his murderous threats. In due course, Harold's deranged behaviour is explained by the burden of his secret, which comes to light when he is suspected of hiding someone in the estate. Idly speculating that this is a young woman, rescued by Harold from her Italian convent, Arbella works the idea up into an elaborate tale of romantic fixation and kidnap. But, instead, Harold is trying to care for his mother, the famed Lady Julia Melbourne who, for years, had suffered the fate of Edgeworth's Lady Rackrent and her real-life counterparts[46] by being locked away by her husband in a disused wing of Harold's former home, Mosscliff Abbey. Like everyone else, Harold had assumed his mother was dead, and had only discovered her fate upon his father's deathbed confession. It comes as something of a shock to all readers when Harold's retrospective narrative interpolates a history of domestic tyranny and violence; of Lady Julia's adultery, and of the death of her lover at the hands of a husband who then arranged for her public 'death' and private incarceration. Harold's desire to preserve Matilda's celestial perfection had, it transpires, offered respite from his own feelings of guilt and fear.

The transgressive and irrational impulses which would later characterize the madwoman motif are here dignified in a story of female frailty and mutual devotion of mother and son. But there is a second perspective on the gothic genre which draws attention not only to its 'worst' excesses, but also to its effects on the undiscerning reader. LeFanu objectifies the gothic story in the entertainment Miss Mountain provides in reciting from a gothic repertoire ranging from Horace Walpole to Charles Maturin. Though it includes Radcliffe, it also incorporates Matthew Lewis, whose

---

45 Fanny Burney, *Evelina*, ed. Edward A. Bloom (Oxford: Oxford University Press, 1982), p. 83.

46 In Maria Edgeworth's *Castle Rackrent* (1800) Sir Kit keeps his wife locked away upstairs, and details of the imprisonment of Lady Cathcart, upon which this treatment seems to be based, are sketched in a footnote.

own more macabre take on the genre is reflected in the lesser progeny of 'modern "Horrors"' to which Miss Langrish has become addicted.[47] In Mountain's hands, the potentially sublime terrors of the gothic novel subside in the wake of the horrible stories she is inspired to invent, and, joined by Lady Torrendale, she persecutes Langrish with tales unsweetened by Radcliffean sentiment or morality.[48] In this light, Spencer Fitzroy's decision to lock his new wife Miss Hautenville away at Strathallan, the remote Scottish mansion his brother magnanimously gives to him, enacts an ironic subversion of those earlier gothic tendencies. As if avenged for crimes against literary genius, Hautenville must settle for the novel's other 'Strathallan' where, with only the servants' talk of banshis, ghosts, witches and warlocks for company, she is subject to a narrative of unsophisticated superstition, and stuck with comparing 'herself by turns, to every heroine, ancient and modern, celebrated in mournful story as a victim to the perfidy of man.'[49]

IV

The creative range of *Strathallan* is in part established in the sheer scope of its references. Behind the scenes which make for what Arbella calls 'a pretty moral dissertation entitled, "Advantages of Circumspection, or Dangers of Coquetry"',[50] LeFanu hosts a backstage gathering of writers from whom she variously derives epigraphs, authorial quotations, and quoted matter for her characters. Shakespeare, Milton, Pope and Thomson can be name-checked against the kind of standard line-up favoured by Radcliffe. But there are more unusual suspects, whose insidiousness (Rousseau) or notoriety (Byron) challenges the assumption that mapping these choices against an approved list is especially pertinent. Rather *Strathallan* is a barometer of reading practices in a period of improved book-circulation and book-borrowing activity, written by a woman who avidly and intelligently engages with a diversity of literature. There are in excess of one hundred male and female writers, performers, composers, musicians, theologians, naturalists and enlightenment thinkers drawn to these pages from Britain, Ireland, France, Italy, Germany and Spain. Some, though not all, are rendered in translation, and LeFanu's proficiency in French at least is evident from her ability to deliberately render the bad French of certain affectedly Francophile characters. Sources range from the works of classical antiquity – from the writings of Terence, Martial and Plutarch – to those of LeFanu's more immediate contemporaries, Joanna Baillie, Maria Edgeworth, Sydney Owenson, and Walter Scott; and the

---

47 *Strathallan*, vol. 1, p.33.

48 In her memoir of Frances Sheridan, LeFanu comments that 'there has of late subsisted among writers of fiction, a kind of emulation *which* shall outdo his predecessor in terrifying and heart-rending delineations' (pp. 120–1). She adds, 'there is a certain point at which the bounds of terror and pity are – fixed; whenever those bounds are overpast, disgust and horror usurp their place in the mind. The reader turns shuddering from the spectacle forced upon his view, and both the picture and moral are lost alike in the eager desire to forget' (pp. 121–2).

49 Strathallan, vol. 4, p. 449.

50 In this LeFanu has Arbella take an extradiegetic step to consider how her own, and Matilda's experiences as told in *Strathallan*, might indeed make for a good story. See vol. 4, p. 409.

catalogue of genres is similarly broad. In addition to the novel, the short story, the oriental and the national tale, *Strathallan* incorporates opera libretti, poetry, ballads, songs and glees; satire, epic, comedy and tragedy.

LeFanu's liberal application of 'apt quotation' is very different from Miss Hautenville's surface gloss. Epigraphs and quotations are discerningly relevant to the mood, situation or tastes of a particular character, while Italian sources such as the seventeenth-century poet Tasso and eighteenth-century librettist Metastasio more generally invoke images of romantic chivalry and 'the spectacle of virtue' respectively.[51] Some sources remain in the novel's dialogizing background, but there are others, such as William Collins, who find their reputations the focus of more sustained debate. At the centre of the competitive tug-o-war in which the amateur bards, 'Sappho' and 'Alcæus' are routinely involved, Collins is exploited for comic effect. On the other hand, the pseudo-Gaelic bard Ossian, and the poet, James Beattie, are summoned to stage serious emotion. For both Strathallan and Matilda these writers, along with other texts as diverse as Surrey's Elizabethan love poetry, and *Atala*, by the French Romantic Chateaubriand,[52] serve as palimpsests upon which the lovers reciprocate their forbidden desire. When alone, Matilda retreats to the Ossianic landscape of the Rocks to indulge in the bard's style of mournful contemplation. There, the poet becomes substitutive of Strathallan, and the 'companion' with whom Matilda indulges in 'a rarely permitted pleasure', steeping 'her eyes in the dews of pensive transport'.[53] LeFanu's grandfather Thomas Sheridan would have read Matilda's sublime sensibility as a positive recommendation. According to Boswell, he not only 'talked well upon the poems of Ossian' whom he 'said he preferred to all the poets in the world', but 'said Mrs. Sheridan and he had fixed it as the standard of feeling, made it like a thermometer by which they could judge the warmth of everybody's heart; and that they calculated beforehand in what degrees all their acquaintance would feel them, which answered exactly'.[54]

Strathallan's prioritization of *Ossian* suggests how its influence on Romantic literature had segued into a renewed contemporary interest in Scottish literature following Walter Scott's *The Lady of the Lake*. Published in 1810, 'its effect on the public [...] was to turn a partiality for Highlanders, currently in action in the Peninsula War, into a national craze'.[55] The hazy landscape of the Strathallan estate is picked out in references to Burns and Ramsay, and LeFanu was fluent in more recent Scots

51 For a consideration of Metastasio's significance, see Susan Staves, *A Literary History of Women's Writing in Britain 1660–1789* (Cambridge: Cambridge University Press, 2006), p. 317.

52 This is also amongst the novels Horatio presents to Owenson's wild Irish girl, which were 'all precisely such books as Glorvina had *not*, yet *should* read, that she may know herself, and the latent sensibility of her heart.' See Sydney Owenson, Lady Morgan, *The Wild Irish Girl*, ed. Kathryn Kirkpatrick (Oxford: Oxford University Press, 1999), p. 144.

53 *Strathallan*, vol. 1, p. 72.

54 James Boswell, *Boswell's London Journal 1762–1763*, ed. Frederick A. Pottle (New York, London, Toronto: McGraw-Hill, 1950). In addition to family favourites, LeFanu alludes to the writings of less familiar members of the extended family, such as Thomas Tickell and William Linley.

55 Peter Garside, 'Popular Fiction and the National Tale: Hidden Origins of Scott's Waverley', *Nineteenth-Century Literature*, 46:1 (June 1991), pp.30–53, p. 45.

literature by Elizabeth Hamilton, author of *The Cottagers of Glenburnie* (1808), and Jane Porter, with whose sister she enjoyed an epistolary friendship.[56] These splashes of Celtic colour are, however, also consistent with LeFanu's yoking together old and new trends. It was a practice in which Scott himself indulged in *Waverley* (1814), casting his own auburn-haired heroine in what was possibly an ironic response to 'the sentimental heroine' Peter Garside also acknowledges as having made 'a flamboyant comeback with the translated fiction of Madame de Staël'.[57]

V

In the three years following *Strathallan*'s appearance, LeFanu published two more romances, *Helen Monteagle* (1818) and *Leolin Abbey. A Novel* (1819).[58] At three volumes per title this was a phenomenal rate of industry by any standards and by 1821 LeFanu was engaged in her next project, *Tales of a Tourist. Containing The Outlaw, and Fashionable Connexions*. As it turned out, events conspired to upset the direction and circumstances in which LeFanu planned this next move. In August, within little over two years since the death of her younger sister, Harriet, LeFanu was mourning the death of her father. Shortly after, Longman's decision not to publish her next novel compounded the sense of disorientation consequent upon loss. As part payment of her profit, Longman had kept its author in books. In the space of three weeks, LeFanu had lost a parent, the income against which she had incurred debts, and a regular supply of the very means through which she fulfilled her personal and professional interests. For her to emerge from this crisis must have taken tenacity, self-belief and something like that 'combination of Hibernian ingenuity with English patience' with which LeFanu credits O'Hara in *Strathallan*.[59] Certainly, by May 1822, *Tales of a Tourist* was advertised as going to press for Newman and the spring of the following year saw the publication of *Don Juan de Las Sierras, or, El Empecinado. A Romance*. These novels develop *Strathallan*'s extremes of interest in literature, and military action. The 'tourist' is the reclusive author of

56 Jane Porter's *Scottish Chiefs* met with some success when it was published in 1810. Her sister, Anna Maria Porter (1778–1832), was also a novelist, and the most intensive period of her career coincided with the beginning of LeFanu's own, with Porter writing five novels between 1809 and 1817.

57 Garside, 'Popular Fiction and the National Tale: Hidden Origins of Scott's Waverley' p.38. A translation of *Corrina, or Italy* was published in 1807. Garside also considers Scott's deliberations on a suitable subtitle for *Waverley*, in which he declares '[...] if I had rather chosen to call my work "Sentimental Tale," would it not have been a sufficient presage of a heroine with a profusion of auburn hair, and a harp, the soft solace of her solitary hours, which she fortunately finds always the means of transporting from castle to cottage, although she herself be sometimes obliged to jump out of a two-pair-of-stairs window, and is more than once bewildered on her journey, alone and on foot, without any guide but a blowzy peasant girl, whose jargon she can hardly understand?' See Walter Scott, *Waverley*, ed. Andrew Hook (London: Penguin, 1972), p. 34.

58 Both novels reflect LeFanu's residual interest in military action. The Welsh heiress Helen Monteagle elopes with, and marries in secret, her officer lover, and her estrangement from her family is a theme to which *Leolin Abbey* returns. Notwithstanding its detours to the Mediterranean, the action of this novel shifts from Ireland to England.

59 *Strathallan*, vol. 3, p. 346.

the ensuing Irish and English 'tales', with which, under the female patronage of the countess upon the edges of whose estate he lives, he aims to redeem his ruined literary reputation. In *Don Juan*, the Celtic inflections of the earlier writings give way to a story loosely based upon Spain's guerrilla patriot, Don Juan Martin Diaz, and in its styling of the romantic hero, LeFanu remains agile in her response to her particular historical moment.

At around this time, Alicia moved with her mother to Leamington Spa, and it was there that she completed her first work of non-fiction, the biography of her grandmother. It enacts a realignment of familial, and also national, identity at a crucial point. Since *Strathallan* LeFanu's relation as the 'Grand-daughter of the Late Thomas Sheridan, M.A.' had disappeared from her title pages but by the early 1820s, her 'unpatronized' status had taken on a devastatingly personal dimension. From a professional viewpoint, changes were also occurring which, for a woman dependent upon her writing income, demanded a refocusing of literary ambitions. According to Garside, during the first half of that decade, greater cost-efficiency and an increase in the number of male-authored novels led to 'evidence of women being edged out from mainstream fiction into alternative channels. Equally there are signs of resistance to the three-decker formula in several attempts to promote single volumes containing full-length texts at a cheaper price.'[60] Given that Newman was at that time still the 'leading bulk producer of fiction',[61] LeFanu approached Whittaker, who published the *Memoirs* as a single volume in 1824. Sometimes, perhaps too often, aiming for distinction is paradoxically reliant upon being already part of an influential circle but LeFanu's astute reading of the market does not detract from the integrity of a work at once unique in its focus upon the family's matriarch and wide ranging in its intertextual engagement with the reported lives of other eminent Sheridans.

The *Memoirs* incorporates the state of invention and reinvention which, throughout her career, LeFanu kept in perpetual motion. Through her portrait of another woman writer, she demonstrates her signature versatility, executing the business of a faithful historian with the practised art of a polymath storyteller; by turns informed, judicious, dramatic and, often suitably, sardonic. The year in which LeFanu published the novel acknowledged as her last, the *Waverley* inflected historical romance *Henry IV of France* (1826), has routinely marked the point at which LeFanu also runs out of steam.[62] What emerges is a far more interesting picture of renewed ingenuity and sheer determination. In various contributions to *The Court Magazine and Belle Assemblée* throughout the 1830s, LeFanu turns her hand to history, the short story, and literary anecdote. Of these none showcase her intelligence, wit and self-deprecating irony more than a piece which, in a kind of natural order, takes her back to her heritage. Focusing on Jonathan Swift and her great-grandfather Dr Thomas Sheridan, LeFanu offers a prefatory lament for the 'Craft of Authorship', wrecked on the swelling tides of have-a-go writers 'laying their *annual* offerings at the muse's shrine, or giving their

---

60 Peter Garside, 'The English Novel in the 1820s', in *Literatur und Erfahrungswandel 1789–1830*, ed. Rainer Schöwerling, Hartmut Steinecke & Günter Tiggesbäumker (München: Wilhelm Fink Verlag, 1996), pp. 231–47, p. 187.

61 Garside, 'The English Novel in the 1820s', p.186.

62 *Henry IV of France* was also published by Newman and Co.

experiences of life and manners in goodly volumes, of the prescribed number – three.' The 'Belgian romance', 'Peninsular recollections' and 'historical tale',

> [a]ll this must produce a wonderful competition in the market; but, as if that were not rivalship enough, the noble army of ghosts are in full march upon us in the shape of posthumous remains, family papers, and reminiscences *sans fin*.[63]

As a professional writer, LeFanu had inhabited many of the popular generic forms to which she refers. In taking this seemingly counter-intuitive position, she was playfully reflecting upon what had been her own contribution to the shifting demands of the market. But she was never simplistic in her response, and *Strathallan* is characteristic in the way in which it both invokes, and to varying degrees maintains an ironic distance from, a number of generic styles. Indeed, this is the kind of attitude which brings LeFanu Janus-face to face with Matilda on one side, the critical and detached outsider looking in on the fashionable world and, on the other, the debt-ridden Lady Torrendale who is resourceful in meeting its shifting priorities. The ultimate irony in all this is that LeFanu was most likely an unpaid contributor to the journal. These were certainly the terms in place when, in 1832, the editorship was taken on by the granddaughter of Richard Brinsley Sheridan, Caroline Norton.[64] With her own celebrity in the ascendant, Norton could call on her friends to contribute, but the favour may well have been all on the other side. Within the next ten years, Norton begrudgingly used her influence to secure some funds for LeFanu; a woman whose career reflects the vicissitudes of the literary market in the first decades of the nineteenth century. Alicia LeFanu was boarding with a family in Chipping Norton when she died from an effusion on the brain, paralysis and exhaustion on 29 January 1867. Such details of the end of LeFanu's personal life have remained obscure until recently;[65] *Strathallan* renews the opportunity to explore the beginnings of her assured and complex life as a writer.

---

63 Alicia LeFanu, 'Swift, Sheridan, and Delany', *The Court Magazine and Belle Assemblée*, Issue 5 (Wednesday 1 May 1833), pp. 220–3, p. 220.

64 See Alan Chedzoy, *A Scandalous Woman: The Story of Caroline Norton* (London: Allison & Busby, 1992), p. 88.

65 See my 'Relating a Life: Alicia LeFanu's *Memoirs of the Life and Writings of Mrs Frances Sheridan*', *Women's Writing* 15:1 (2008), pp. 32–54. See also General Record Office Civil Registration Index of Deaths for England and Wales, "Le Fann, Alicia", and 1861 Census "Le Fenn, Alice" (http://www.1837online.com) Accessed 24 October 2005.

SELECT BIBLIOGRAPHY

Aiken, A. L. and J. Aiken, *Miscellaneous Pieces in Prose* (London: J. Johnson, 1773).

Aiken, J., *General Biography; or, Lives, Critical and Historical of the Most Eminent Persons*, 10 vols (London: G. G. & J. Robinson; G. Kearsley; R. H. Evans; J. Wright, 1799–1815), vol. 8 (1813).

Anon., Notice of *Rosara's Chain, The Morning Chronicle,* Thursday 26 February 1818.

Anon., Notice of *The Flowers; or, The Sylphid Queen: a fairy tale in verse, Jackson's Oxford Journal*, Saturday 23 December 1809.

Anon., Review of *Strathallan, Jackson's Oxford Journal*, Saturday 26 October 1816.

Boswell, J., *Life of Johnson*, ed. R. W. Chapman, rev. J. D. Fleeman, 3rd edn (Oxford, London & New York: Oxford University Press, 1970).

—, *Boswell's London Journal* 1762–1763, ed. F. A. Pottle (New York, London, Toronto: McGraw-Hill, 1950).

Brooke, F., *The History of Emily Montague*, ed. L. McMullen (Ontario: McClelland and Stewart, 1995).

Burney, F., *Evelina*, ed. Edward A. Bloom (Oxford: Oxford University Press, 1982).

Chamberlaine, W., 'Anecdotes of Miss LeFanu and of Mrs. Jordan', *The Gentleman's Magazine: The Supplement to Vol. XCIV Part I.* (1824), pp. 582–3.

Chandler, D., 'Swift's "Violent Hatred" of William III: The "Paraphrase of Prior's Epitaph" and its Provenance', *Notes and Queries* (Sept. 1999), pp. 348–50.

Chedzoy, A., *A Scandalous Woman: The Story of Caroline Norton* (London: Allison & Busby, 1992).

Chesterfield, P. D. S., Earl of, *Lord Chesterfield's advice to his son, on men and manners: or, a new system of education*, 3rd edn (London: Richardson and Urquhart, 1777).

Disraeli, I., *Curiosities of Literature. Consisting of Anecdotes, Characters, Sketches and Observations*, 4th edn, 2 vols (London: Murray and Highley, 1798), vol. 2.

Dryden, J., *The State of Innocence, and Fall of Man: An Opera. Written in Heroic Verse* (London: J. Tonson, 1721).

Elegant Epistles: or, a copious collection of familiar and amusing letters, selected for the improvement of young persons (Dublin: Chamberlaine and Rice [and eight others], 1790).

Fitzer, A. M., 'Relating a Life: Alicia LeFanu's *Memoirs of the Life and Writings of Mrs Frances Sheridan*', *Women's Writing* 15:1 (2008), pp.32–54.

Garside, P., 'Popular Fiction and the National Tale: Hidden Origins of Scott's Waverley', *Nineteenth-Century Literature*, 46:1 (June, 1991), pp.30–53.

—, 'The English Novel in the 1820s', in R. Schöwerling, H.Steinecke & G. Tiggesbäumker (eds), *Literatur und Erfahrungswandel 1789-1830* (München: Wilhelm Fink Verlag, 1996), pp.231–247.

Home, J., *Douglas: A Tragedy. As it is Acted at the Theatre-Royal in Covent-Garden* (London: A. Millar, 1757).

La Baumelle, M. de, *Memoirs for the History of Madame de Maintenon*, trans. Charlotte Lennox, 5 vols (London: A. Millar, and J. Nourse; R. and J. Dodsley; L. Davis, and C. Reymer, 1757), vol. 2.

Le Mesurier, T., *Translations Chiefly from the Italian of Petrarch and Metastasio* (Oxford: J. Cooke, 1795).

LeFanu, A., *Memoirs of the Life and Writings of Mrs. Frances Sheridan* (London: G. and W. B. Whittaker, 1824).

—, 'Swift, Sheridan, and Delany', *The Court Magazine and Belle Assemblée*, Issue 5 (Wednesday 1 May 1833), pp.220–223.

[LeFanu, E.], *Lucy Osmond. A Story* (New York: John Swaine, 1804).

Macpherson, J., *The Poems of Ossian*, 2 vols (Edinburgh: J. Elder and T. Brown, 1797).

Macy, L., *Grove Music Online* http://www.grovemusic.com.

Maintenon, Madame De., *Letters of Madame Maintenon. Translated from the French*, 2 vols (London: L.Davis and C. Reymers, 1759), vol. 1.

Mason, W., *The Works of Thomas Gray. Containing his Poems, and Correspondence with Several Eminent Literary Characters*, 3rd edn, 2 vols (London: Vernor, Hood & Sharp [and five others], 1807), vol.1.

Metastasio, P., *Demetrio: An Opera, as performed at the King's-Theatre in the Hay-market. The music by Signor Pietro Guglielmi, [...] The poetry by the celebrated Metastasio, altered by Giovan Gualberto Bottarelli. Most of the translation by Mr. Carara.* (London: W.Griffin, 1772).

—, *Il Re Pastore Dramma Musica. Pel Teatro di S.M.B.* (London: G. Woodfall, 1757).

—, *The Works of Metastasio*, trans, John Hoole, 2 vols (London: T. Davies, 1767), vol.1.

Molière, *Molière: The Misanthrope and Other Plays*, trans. John Wood (London: Penguin, 1959).

Moody, E., *Poetic Trifles* (London: Cadell Jun. and Davies, 1798).

Moore, T., *Memoirs of the Life of the Right Honourable Richard Brinsley Sheridan*, 2nd edn, 2 vols (London: Longman, Hurst, Rees, Orme, Brown, and Green, 1825).

More, H., *Strictures on the Modern System of Female Education*, 9th edn, 2 vols (London: T. Cadell, 1801).

O'Toole, F., *A Traitor's Kiss: The Life of Richard Brinsley Sheridan* (London: Granta, 1998).

Owenson, S., Lady Morgan, *The Wild Irish Girl*, ed. Kathryn Kirkpatrick (Oxford: Oxford University Press, 1999).

Pardoe, J., *Louis the Fourteenth and the Court of France in the Seventeenth Century*, 2 vols (New York: Harper Brothers, 1847), vol. 1.

Pinkerton, J., *Letters of Literature* (London: G. G. J. & J. Pinkerton, 1785).

Pope, A., *The Poems of Alexander Pope*, 3 vols (London: n.p., 1779), vol.2.

Ramsay, A., *Tea-Table Miscellany; or, A Complete Collection of Scots Sangs*, 3 vols (Dublin: E. Smith, 1729), vol.1.

Seward, A. *The Poetical Works of Anna Seward. With Extracts from her Literary Correspondence*, ed. W. Scott, 3 vols (Edinburgh: J. Ballantyne; London: Longman, Hurst, Rees & Orme, 1810), vol.1.

Scott, W., *Waverley*, ed. Andrew Hook (London: Penguin, 1972).

Seymour, G., *The Instructive Letter-Writer, and Entertaining Companion: Containing Letters on the most Interesting Subjects in an Elegant and Easy Style*, 3rd edn (London: W. Domville, 1769).

Sheridan, E., *Betsey Sheridan's Journal: Letters from Sheridan's Sister 1784–1786 and 1788–1790*, ed. W. Lefanu (Oxford: Oxford University Press, 1986).

[Sheridan, F.], *Memoirs of Miss Sidney Bidulph*, 3 vols (London: R. and J. Dodsley, 1761), vol. 1.

Southey, R., *Letters Written During a Short Residence in Spain and Portugal*, 2nd edn (Bristol: Biggs and Cottle, 1799).

Staves, S., *A Literary History of Women's Writing in Britain 1660–1789* (Cambridge: Cambridge University Press, 2006).

Stott, A., *Hannah More: The First Victorian* (Oxford: Oxford University Press, 2003).

Tansillo, L., *The Nurse, A Poem. Translated from the Italian*, trans. W. Roscoe (Liverpool: [printed]; London: Cadell and Davies, 1798).

Tasso, T., *Jerusalem delivered: an heroic poem. Translated from the Italian of Torquato Tasso*, trans. John Hoole, 2 vols (London: J. Johnson; T.N. Longman [and 9 others], 1797).

Taylor, W., *Historic Survey of German Poetry*, 3 vols (London: Treuttel and Würtz, Treuttel Jun. and Richter, 1828–30), vol. 1.

NOTE ON THE TEXT

For this volume, I have used the Chawton House Library copy of the first edition of *Strathallan* (1816), intervening as little as possible. Two further editions of the novel were published in London in 1816 and 1817. The second edition has an additional Preface, substantive changes and corrections to spelling and punctuation. The third edition, with minor exceptions, is the same as the second. Substantive textual variants across the editions are listed in this volume and indicated by superscript letters in the text.

In preparing this volume, the punctuation, capitalization and spelling of the first edition, including variations, have been retained. However, obvious errors, some of which were addressed in the second and third editions, have been silently corrected. A list of substantive silent corrections is also included.

Original page turns of the first edition are indicated throughout this reset edition.

STRATHALLAN.

BY
ALICIA LEFANU,

GRAND-DAUGHTER TO THE LATE THOMAS SHERIDAN, M.A.

IN FOUR VOLUMES.

VOL. I.

Quando scende in nobil petto
E compagno un dolce affetto
Non rivale alla virtù:
Respirate, alme felici
E vi siano i Numi amici
Quanto avverso il ciel vi fù.

Metastasio – Demetrio.[1]

London:
PRINTED FOR SHERWOOD, NEELY, AND JONES,
PATERNOSTER-ROW.
1816. /
R. and R. Gilbert, Printers, St. John's Square, London.

PREFACE.

DESIROUS of holding a medium both in principle and language, between that severity which forbids the existence of passion, and consequently prevents the merit of overcoming it, and that enthusiasm, which, dazzled by its wild and fitful splendors, mistakes, or wilfully confounds, in every page, its destructive fires, with the awful and lovely lights of virtue, the author has found difficulties in the execution of her work, which may not, perhaps, be accepted as a sufficient apology for its many imperfections. / Conscious, however, that they are not the result of presumptuous negligence, she ventures, with trembling diffidence, though unfriended and unpatronized, to meet the eye of candid criticism: assured, while her first attempt is read, it will be remembered, that there is a difference between the errors of inexperience, and the sins of incorrigible stupidity: and that the bird, who begins by trilling its wild strain, uncertain, faint, and low, may, if those notes are encouraged and well-directed, burst forth, at some future time, in all the clear and varied cadence of full and grateful song.[a]

CHAPTER. I.

Meglio è morir che trarre
Selvaggio vita in solitudin, dove
A niun sei caro, e di nessun ti cale.

ALFIERI.[2]

'GOOD heavens,' cried the lovely Lady Torrendale, as her woman was putting the last finish to her dress for a dinner party in the country, 'how long is this life to last? I have tried it but a fortnight, and I am already completely sick of it. If my Lord Torrendale finds it necessary to spend some time at his Derbyshire estate, why cannot he leave me at Bath, or at Rose-villa – One could pass an Autumn so pleasantly at Rose-villa – Or if he must insist on my accompanying him here, why not suffer me at / least to fill the house with decent people from the land of the living? If Strathallan were returned 'twould make some difference – But to carry me down to a desert with no other companions than my little, unformed girl, and her sickening, sentimental governess – Really my dear Floss,' she continued, caressing a little silken haired spaniel that lay at her feet, 'as I am now situated, you are, I think, the only rational creature I have seen this some time past.'

'Very complimentary,' exclaimed Lord Torrendale, who entered her dressing-room at the moment her attendant had quitted it, 'Yet there are ways, Lady Torrendale, by which a few month's residence in the country might be rendered not only bearable, but productive of the most lasting and well-grounded satisfaction.'

'What are they my Lord? I should be very glad to know them.'

'Have you not your elegant domestic resources, the amusement of books, the cultivation of the society around you, and the pleasures of benevolence?'

'Benevolence! you know how many experiments I have tried in that way already. I came down to the country, glowing with the romantic hopes inspired by the fine description given in novels, of rural innocence and sensibility, and for the first days, Miss Langrish and I did nothing but work, and talk of them. We resolved to make petticoats and gowns sufficient for some pretty little children, who had attracted my notice on our first arrival, and who did not appear to me very well clothed. I anticipated a delicious surprise, on the part of the mother, by stealing to the cottage in her absence, and dressing the little things myself in their new array – But as soon as I took one upon my lap, it began to cry; its sister, a girl, a little older, began to beat it for being so noisy – in the midst of this "horrid stir" comes the mother herself, all in a heat from her work, and in no very gentle temper towards the strangers, who had disturbed the "sweet children." She started, indeed, as if she had seen a ghost, when she found the disturber was my Ladyship's Ladyship, and dropping a / low curtsy, begged ten thousand pardons, and made ten millions of apologies. "Children would be rude; they did not like strange faces; they did not, poor things," she continued, soothing the little sobbing urchin on her breast: and, treated as little less than an invader, I found that I had created only confusion and disturbance, where I expected the most lively demonstrations of joy, and the most pathetic expressions of gratitude. Not discouraged with the failure of my first attempt, I resolved to inform myself of the real state of the peasantry, and entered unexpectedly another cottage – it belonged to an old woman. She was in the height of business, washing her house, and altogether so strange and dirty a figure, that if I had not been the most exemplary of women, I could not possibly have refrained from laughing. Instead of which, I made the most condescending enquiries respecting her prospects, her wants, and those of her family. But she would never answer me by any thing but awkward apologies for the appearance of her house, which, she assured me was, in general, the neatest in the village, and the money I slipped into her hand seemed hardly to compensate the mortification of being, as she termed it, caught "in such a pickle," and her "*place*" in "such a mess".'

'These disappointments,' Lady Torrendale, 'have resulted from ill grounded expectations, and hasty conclusions; and rather prove the propriety of your remaining some time longer in the country, than the necessity of your quitting it. It is not by unexpectedly rushing into the cottages of the poor, that you will meet with either welcome or respect; previous good offices must justify the intrusion. When you are better acquainted with them, you will find that sentiment and impassioned gratitude are not their characteristics, particularly in England. Familiarize them to you first by a course of active and useful benevolence, and then, depend upon it, your appearance among them will be hailed, (not, perhaps, with transport) but sufficient testimonies of that solid regard, which generally arises from benefits received, and the expectation of farther advantage.' /

'I am surprised you can think,' resumed her Ladyship, 'that I have taken as yet but little trouble. Did I not put my name at the head of the list of Lady Patronesses for the School upon the new plan? But, I don't know how it is, it requires so much attention, and fuss, and exertion, and you must visit and inspect it yourself; and there is really so much to do at home, one cannot go early, that is, before breakfast time; after breakfast, one must walk: then after walking it is the hour for luncheon, and after luncheon you lie upon the sofa, and you have to dress for dinner, and, in short –'

'In short,' interrupted Lord Torrendale, 'Half an hour in the week is too much to be resolutely devoted to the purpose of benefiting your fellow creatures.'

'Now you are severe. Then, as to cultivating the society around us, I *did* patronize the monthly Assembly, when first I came down. On a most disagreeable night, with "my coachman in drink and the moon in a fog,"[3] I sacrificed myself without a murmur for the good of the community. I endeavoured to lead the way to something of a better taste among the girls, and to make them uncover their backs and shoulders, so as to look a little decent; I even tried to introduce waltzing, for which I am sure I had all the young men on my side, but still, some stiff, upright sticks, persisted in preferring to be set opposite to one another, in the straight lines of a country dance, like cabbage stalks.'

'While you thought such sticks would appear to so much more advantage, surrounded by the twining scarlet-runner; to return your gardening simile.'

'Then,' continued Lady Torrendale, taking no notice of this last observation, 'as this country is unfortunately quite hilly enough, I brought forward our Brighton diversion of Donkey-riding, which, from sympathy, or some other reason was better received by the natives; 'till one of the little animals happening to disembarrass himself of his heavy burthen, fat Mrs. Rumble-tumble, by setting her down, without any previous hint of his intentions, in a quag-mire, her husband has utterly discountenanced the amusement ever / since – I still, however, tried to fill up my time, and even in spite of nature and inclination, sometimes hunted with odious Lady Dare-all.'

'Let me entreat you to recollect,' said Lord Torrendale, looking at his watch, 'that we are out-staying our appointment, and defer the rest of your philippic 'till our return.'

'Now are you quite out of patience, and in a few moments more, you would be ready to ask yourself Lord Townley's wise question "Why did I marry?"'

'No madam,' answered his Lordship, with something of a bitter smile, 'I too well remember the only cause.'

'Of that effect, pray let me finish the quotation for you "my beauty" was it not? My goodness too, I hope, had some share – it really has been of late pretty severely tried. What do you think of having invited a pleasant party to spend a few of the dull weeks at one of the most delightful villas in the world, and being suddenly told the carriage waits, and that one has but two hours to prepare to leave them all, and to set off for the Peak of Derbyshire?'

'You know I could not keep Rose-villa, I have sold it to Lord Lyndhurst.'

'Yes, but I know that Lord Lyndhurst was not to have entered into possession 'till the beginning of spring, when I should have completely done with it; for I never wish to see the same place twice – and to leave so charming a party, and in so sudden and strange a manner –'

'Lady Torrendale, I will be very frank with you; it was to break up that very party, that I availed myself of an unexpected circumstance, that made my presence necessary in Derbyshire, to insist upon your accompanying me there. – It was to take you from the attractions of play, from those Leysters, those Pleydels, the worthy successors of your favorite Lady Julia Melbourne – that –'

'O now I see the cause of all this confusion, 'tis the ghost of the knave of clubs that arose in all his terrors. Well, as he certainly *is* a very formidable gentleman, perhaps it will give you pleasure to hear, that / notwithstanding your suspicions, I never had the slightest flirtation with him: or, to speak seriously, that I never, in my life, risked the chances of a game of hazard; or even, at a game of skill, ventured more than the most rigid prudence might sanction.'

'Ah, Laura, could I believe you were in earnest,' said Lord Torrendale, with a look in which confidence struggled with doubt, 'then would my mind feel indeed relieved.'

'Then, if that is all that is wanting to relieve your mind, be happy,' returned the Lady half laughing, 'for here, in the most solemn manner I assure "your gravity", on the word of a Countess, I never did, nor never will.'

'Then those money difficulties must have been of much less consequence than you represented them to me, and I need not have sold Rose-villa.'

'Oh yes you must have sold Rose-villa.'

'Laura you trifle with me,' resumed his Lordship gravely – 'If you have indeed escaped the dangerous fascinations of play, what source of expence?'

'Would you give any thing to know?'

'I confess, after the sacrifice I have made, I think I deserve your confidence.'

'And if I tell you, will you let me invite some civilized persons from town.'

'Yes.'

'Lady Leyster and Miss Mountain?'

'Yes.'

'And modernize the house?'

'Yes.'

'And turn it out of the windows?'

'Yes, any thing – every thing.'

'Why then set your heart at rest; for never, no never will I tell you how that money was spent.'

Seizing his arm, she ran down to the carriage with him, as she uttered these last words; and, as she gracefully stept into it, Lord Torrendale, contemplating with habitual admiration, her still lovely figure, seemed, for a moment, to lose the impression of the recent scene, in distant, but more agreeable recollections. /

CHAPTER II.

For sanctity of place or time, were vain
Gainst that blind archer's soul-consuming power,
Which scorns and soars all circumstance above.
                    LORD STRANGFORD'S CAMOENS.[4]

LORD Torrendale had entered life with good principles and respectable abilities, unaccompanied by those keen sensibilities and perceptions, which, according as they are directed, lead their possessor to glory and happiness, or to misery and disgrace. Having been commissioned by his father, to fall in love with a young lady, whose estate was near his own of Strathallan, in Scotland, he had complied with the injunction, so far as making formal proposals, which were as formally accepted; and he found himself the unconscious possessor of a treasure, in the person of a lady, whose mind was of that superior temper, which he could not appreciate, and whose form, though lovely, was not the 'kind of loveliness calculated to touch his heart.'

Some unforeseen losses, and a dispute concerning a considerable part of her property, which altogether made her possessions fall much short of what was supposed to be its original value, were the causes to which, some grave enquirers ascribed the increasing indifference of her lord. But, though not splendidly liberal, he was far from a mercenary character. Be that as it may, the lovely Rosa of Strathallan (for that was then her title) fell a victim to that general neglect, of which she hardly knew how to complain, though she suffered so exquisitely from its effects. Knowing that her malady was seated in the mind, she declined to avail herself of the vain privilege of rank and wealth, of rambling in search of that health, which happiness alone could restore; and breathed her last at the northern seat, of which her husband left her such undisturbed possession; leaving her resemblance in a lovely boy, then four years old, for whose / sake his Lordship determined to keep free from any other engagement.

Having little that was prepossessing in his appearance, and being naturally of a disposition cold, timid, and reserved, the Viscount (now Earl of Torrendale) was suffered to keep his resolution, without being much molested by the snares of high-born beauty. Yet was the year, devoted to ostentatious grief, scarcely expired, when, upon an accidental visit to Bath, he found himself assailed by a species of fascination, against which, being totally unprepared, he was the less able to guard his heart.

On the occasion of a sermon being preached by one of the most popular divines of that city, for the benefit of some charitable institution, it was proposed among the visitants from Ireland (who always form a considerable part of its company) that the practice, which had been followed up in their own country, with such universal success, should be adopted, instead of the usual mode of making collections: and that, among the ladies who constituted the ornament of the scene, a certain number, conducted by gentlemen of rank, should present themselves as the receivers of the contributions. It was at a crowded and fashionable chapel, where this new plan had been embraced, that Lord Torrendale found himself among the numerous and delighted auditory. The preacher was eloquent, even to draw tears. But his Lordship, who, hating any thing that bore the appearance of an appeal to the feelings, stigmatized the most decent and temperate use of the powers of countenance and gesture, with the appellation of grimace and stage effect, and entertained a laudable prejudice against the use of pathos, sentiment, imagery, in short, of any of Heaven's gifts, to Heaven's immediate glory, slumbered very quietly through the sermon; and when the cessation of the voice awoke him, determined fully, in his own mind, not to give more than absolute necessity required; when the plate was presented to him, not by a meagre, bowing, snuffling clerk, in his best Sunday garb, not by a good substantial church-warden, in his new coat and wig; but by a lovely young / female, glowing in the first bloom of beauty, and drest in all the bewitching elegance of fashion. Her dazzling eyes were turned on him with an expression of earnest, yet modest supplication. The dimpled smile upon her lips, seemed that of the angel of charity. Her form, the waving curls of her light brown hair, her hand, the most beautiful in the world, were all in unison to complete the charms of her appearance. Lord Torrendale deposited five times the sum he had originally intended, and added his heart to the gift. As he returned home, he discovered that the presence of a mother would add greatly to the comforts of his little boy, the young Lord Strathallan, for whose happiness he suddenly became more than usually solicitous.

Laura Granville, the inspirer of this new passion, was the reigning beauty of Bath. She had been less favoured by fortune than by nature; and her birth, though respectable, was not such as to entitle her to hope for so splendid an establishment.

The idea, that his prudence might be called in question, by an engagement for which, passion could be alone alledged as the cause, was terrible to Lord Torrendale. So terrible, that, by an effort of desperate resolution, he tore himself from the scene of attraction; and as he rolled along from the dangerous spot, and its white squares and crescents gradually assumed the appearance of a little model in card of the most elegant city in the world, congratulated himself, every mile he passed, upon his fortunate escape. But the charms of the conquering Laura had made a deeper impression than he imagined. He went to court, to the theatres, to the parks, still it was the same scene of insipidity; still he missed something which alone could make life delightful. Her graceful form, her pleading look at the moment she presented the plate, were ever before him; while the sophisticated attractions of fashionable beauty made him still more regret the perfection of the blooming and natural charms he had left behind. In short, finding himself unhappy, while absent from Miss Granville, or rather, in love's official phrase, 'that he / could not live without her,' his Lordship once more ordered his horses, but with a much lighter heart than when he had prepared for his former journey; and, arriving at Bath, enquired for Miss Granville, found she was still there; and, oh, wonderful! still disengaged; wooed her with the ardour of the most impassioned attachment, to which perhaps the secret vanity of carrying off the most beautiful girl at Bath, and introducing her at the ensuing drawing-room as his bride, contributed its unacknowledged, but due proportion; and partly with the eagerness which an infant feels to get some beautiful toy 'in its own hand,' the sort of pleasure which the full-grown child experiences upon exhibiting a rare and splendid trinket; sought and obtained the consent of his fair lady, or, as the newspapers have it, permission to lead her to the hymeneal altar.

Now, to prevent its being supposed out of nature, that a man of a disposition cold and unenthusiastic, as Lord Torrendale's; one who was alike insensible to the charms of eloquence, or the arts, should suffer himself to be thus suddenly and irrevocably captivated by the attraction of feminine graces, it is only necessary to ask one question, and to request it may be answered sincerely: is the gentleman to be found, however distinguished either by years, gravity, or wisdom, who does not, in a degree, acknowledge the influence of beauty, particularly when presented to his imagination in a manner unexpected and advantageous? Not content with confining her triumphs to the young and susceptible, it is her boast to subdue the heart, however guarded by the frost of pride, experience, or indifference. She knows a thousand avenues, by which to address the most inaccessible breast, and in this sense may be truly said alone to possess what has been so long sought for as the grand desideratum, the 'universal language.'

Like many a plain, but well meaning lady, who, seduced by the persuasions of an eloquent millener, hastily consents to buy some tempting article of finery, which she finds, too late, totally mismatches with her figure / or time of life; Lord Torrendale quickly discovered he could not have made a more useless purchase than the beautiful Laura Granville. The disparity in their years, though he was past thirty, and his blooming consort had numbered but sixteen, was only such as the world admits to be the proper difference; but the diversity in their dispositions rendered them utterly unsuited to each other. Though not of an amiable character, *he* had proper ideas upon all the duties of his rank and station. Given up to amusement and flattery, *she* exhibited an utter contempt for those of her's. He was naturally silent, fond of the pleasures of domestic intercourse, and of retirement. She, was never happy but in a crowd. The first deed of her reign, was to pass a general act of oblivion upon all her Bath friends, those who had been either the guides or companions of her youth; the second, was to send the young Strathallan, as soon as he had attained an age at which it was possible for him to be admitted, to a public seminary, on the pretence that it was the most advantageous mode that could be adopted for his education.

Poor Strathallan! for whose sake Lord Torrendale tried to flatter himself, that he had ventured again upon the cares of domestic life!

Being thus relieved from every incumbrance, she gave the reins to her prevailing inclinations; and even the birth of two children, a son and daughter, at a considerable interval from each other, did not seem to diminish her taste for pleasure and dissipation.

It was now above twenty years since Lord Torrendale had made this imprudent choice; and his disappointment preying upon his spirits, increased the natural harshness and reserve of his character. Time had a different effect upon his lively Countess:

while it impaired the graces of her form, it only augmented her opinion of the power of those of her mind; though her understanding had always been as much below, as her person was above, mediocrity. But she had in her favour, spirits, rank, prosperity, and boundless confidence. In conversation, she ventured every thing; and it would have been surprising / indeed, if success had not sometimes attended the venture.

During the first years of their marriage, she had induced her husband to give up, for her sake, his favourite plan of residing, some part of the year, upon his Derbyshire estate; but when her influence began to decline, this idea, which he had relinquished with discontent and self-reproach, was resumed by him with all the ardour which the attractions of duty and inclination united, could inspire. At first, he suffered her to spend the time he passed in Derbyshire, at a distance from him, and in what manner she thought proper. But latterly, her expences exceeding what he considered it possible even the demands of her rank and situation could require, and forcing him to submit to serious inconveniences to supply them, he began to fear, that during his absence, she might have been drawn, by the allurements of play, into some dangerous imprudence.

It has been seen, at the beginning of this Chapter, that his Lordship was capable of taking a sudden resolution. He accordingly announced to her, in the unexpected manner before described, the absolute necessity of his departure for Derbyshire, and of her leaving her fashionable friends, to accompany him. When convinced, by the explanation he had with her, that his fears upon one subject were ill founded, he was still far from satisfied with her conduct. Where no error was, where was the necessity of mystery? On the whole, he felt happy to have her once more restored to the tranquillity of domestic society, some time before her gay friends would come down from London, to visit their country seats. With very different feelings, Lady Torrendale found herself the unwilling inhabitant of a beautiful mansion, a hundred and fifty miles from London, with none but her husband or her daughter, to look to for society or support. /

CHAPTER. III.

Deh! mira egli cantò, spuntar la rosa.
Dal verde suo modesta e verginella;
Che mezzo aperta ancora, e mezzo ascosa
Quanto si mostra men, tanto è più bella.

TASSO, GERUSALEMME LIBERATA.[5]

THE day after the conversation we have already related, Lady Torrendale informed her husband, that she had discovered a treasure.

His Lordship, delighted at any thing that could relieve *her*, and consequently *himself*, from the languor of discontent, kindly demanded what it was?

'You have heard of the Melbournes of "The Rocks?" – I was determined to know them; first, because they were hundred and twentieth cousins to poor dear Lady Julia Melbourne, who, but that is no recommendation to you; – secondly, because they were the only family of any consequence in the county who did not make advances to our acquaintance.'

'Or for any other good female reason?'[6] interrupted his Lordship, with a sufficiently apt quotation.

'But how to accomplish it was the difficulty.' –

'That indeed did not seem easy.'

'No, for *he* is reckoned the strangest old dragon; and from his singular pursuits and hatred of society, has obtained the name of the Hermit of the Rocks. – You will laugh to hear that I have invaded those peaceful rocks. This is the way I managed it. As they are but a four miles drive from Woodlands, and through a delightful country, I proposed to Miss Langrish to make that our airing, as a variety from our usual drives. When we got near The Rocks, my intention was, to break down.'

'To break down! – Lady Torrendale, I am surprised that' – /

'Yes, my Lord, I knew you would be surprised; but how else draw the Recluse from his cell?'

'And do you think, Madam, such a plan very consistent with the dignity of your character?'

'Oh very dignified; – Let me go on. Leaving to our right a little straggling village that bears the same name as Mr. Melbourne's seat, we proceeded along the road 'till it began to grow irregular and rocky; we were suddenly startled by the coachman's crying out – "There, my Lady, there be Squire Melbourne's house, – down yonder in that hollow." The descent was truly terrific; it was through two meeting rocks that almost closed above our heads. But, as there appeared to me just room enough for a carriage, I resolved not to give up the adventure; and spite of Miss Langrish's entreaties, and affected screams, through the tremendous defile we drove. I anticipated the moment when we should emerge from this narrow passage, and was very tranquilly preparing myself for the expected overthrow, when Miss Langrish exclaimed, we could positively go no farther, for that the way was choaked up. Some pieces of the rock, already loosened by time, I suppose, had not been able to resist the violent storm of last night, (we never have such terrible storms in London,) and they now lay strewed in the pathway, so as to make it indeed impossible to get on. As I did not feel quite the dignity and *sang froid* of the great Duchess of Northumberland,[7] to sit quietly in my carriage, and order them "to be removed," I was thinking of turning back, quite mortified with the failure of my scheme, when it occurred to me, that as we had gone so far, we might break down as we originally proposed, and then send one of the men round to find, if possible, a more practicable entry into the enchanted castle; – he was to mention the accident that had happened in this drive, which I took for amusement, without knowing it brought me near Mr. Melbourne's domain. This message, which passed from the coachman to the footman, and from the footman to the awkward country boy, who for the moment supplies the place of poor / Williams, was conveyed; but not exactly in the manner I intended: for a few moments afterwards, the animal came back grinning, and saying, that he had found out a circuitous path, or as he phrased it, "a round-about way to the house", where he had met some of Squire Melbourne's folks, and told them "as how his Lady sent her service towards Mr. and Mrs. Melbourne, and she had driven in the coach from Woodlands, and had the linchpin taken out on very purpose, when she came near their house, that they might ask her in." This you will allow was a *contre-temps*. I did not suffer it however to disconcert me; I come into the country to *give* laws, and teach life and manners to the recluses, not to suffer myself to be discomposed by *them*. The arrival of two men from Mr. Melbourne's to enquire into and repair the damage we had sustained, interrupted these reflections. They brought Mr. and Mrs. Melbourne's compliments and entreaties, that I would alight and walk into the house. My Ladyship suffered herself to be intreated; and, leaning on Miss Langrish's arm, I let them point out to me a path, at a little distance, which led through meeting trees, directly into the grounds, much wondering at my own stupidity, which had prevented me from discovering it sooner. I arrived at the bottom of a grassy lawn, and was looking around for some one, before I exclaimed, "Where have you brought me? I fear I am an intruder!" when we perceived the loveliest little sylph coming down to us from the house, and inviting us by her smiles and blushes, (even before her voice could be heard), to approach. Her hair, of a golden auburn, waved upon her neck; her colour, heightened by modesty and exercise, had that soft, yet beautiful glow, which it is impossible, by words, to describe; her address had something singularly fascinating; it was free; yet it was like the freedom and innocence of a child, or of a little sportive animal that confides its life and safety fearlessly into your care; it was united to the most scrupulous propriety, and a dignity and retiring delicacy of manner, the most interesting. She seemed overjoyed at the sight of strangers, and fearful that we should / withdraw again. She said, her mother was hastening to meet us, and her father she would seek immediately. We understood, by these expressions, that the person who spoke to us, was Miss Melbourne, the only daughter of the family, whose privacy I had so presumptuously invaded. Her father was soon found. He was employed setting his watch by the sun-dial, and his grotesque appearance, contrasted admirably with the simple elegance of Matilda. He wore a furred cap and night-gown, and was exactly what I can figure to myself, one of the French philosophers, the *Hommes des Champs* to have been.[8] His address was, however, polite and gentleman-like, though a little singular, and I am sure he has once been a man of the world; he enquired anxiously about my "*accident*;" and when I condescended to acknowledge that I believed I had been more frightened than hurt, he pressed me to rest and take refreshment. – "If Lady Torrendale," said he, "will honor my *cottage* with a visit." I was surprised at the expression; but the house, at the first glance, really answers the description. The grounds about it are noble; not that there is much of what we call pleasure-garden, for Mr. Melbourne, with all his perfections, is no florist I believe. But all that nature can supply in rocks, in wood, and water, is here in grand profusion: and the whole of this sylvan residence is so fortified and surrounded by barriers impassable, but by one particular path; that it has the air of a delightful solitude, selected for the abode of domestic peace and – Oh! Lud! I am going to be sentimental! What I was observing before was, that the house does not, in any respect, answer to the grounds, being low, and thatched in part, and only rendered considerable by the extent of its wings and offices; but when I had got within – Oh, my Lord! prepare yourself for Aladdin's palace – trees of gold! fruit of jewels! I never met with a more agreeable disappointment in my life! The room in which I was received, half grotto, half palace, combined the beauties of both, and yet was, in fact, only an elegant and ingenious way of disposing of a collection of natural curiosities. It was rather small, the roof arched, / which was[a] favourable to the manner in which it was decorated; and the Gothic windows, of stained glass of every different colour, gave it, on the first entrance, an agreeable coolness and gloom, which set off the brilliancy of the various lights produced by the reflection of mirrors, and the refraction of crystals, – (now don't laugh if I do not express myself quite scientifically,) which struck the eye on looking around. Disposed upon slabs of different kinds of marbles, were specimens of every curious sort of ore, spar, or petrifaction, that I believe ever was found in this or any other place. These were alternately diversified by tablets on which were arranged the most rare and beautiful shells, branches of red and white coral, and other marine productions. Mirrors, placed judiciously behind these collections, and which reached from the ceiling to the floor, doubled their effect. The pannels between these mirrors were adorned with stuffed birds; not stupidly arranged in glass cases, as you have seen them at museums, but perched on branches proceeding from the wall, and made in such a natural imitation of different trees, that nothing but motion was wanting to persuade you their inhabitants were alive and happy in their native groves. There were – let me see now – for a list of the company, a greater variety of beautiful Indian paroquets, parrots, macaws, than Lady Oriole ever had in her possession. The beautiful halcyon birds of paradise, every bird of gayest plumage, from the size of the peacock spreading his glorious fan, to the little humming birds that shone in groups, forming constellations of rubies, emeralds, and topazes, were here to be found in all the smoothness, the freshness, the vividness of life. Mr. Melbourne must certainly have some secret for preserving them, for never did I see any thing so perfect. We had seats enough, though in no very common taste. Ottomans, sophas, chairs, covered with the skins of the leopard, panther, tyger, zebra, formed a set of furniture not only rich and shewy, but, I should imagine, unique; and to complete the whole, (now I am sure I shall almost make even / *you* laugh), instead of lustres or candelabras, little stuffed monkies of different species were dispersed about the room, holding golden branches. When looking at the birds and beasts, I thought myself at Parkinson's again. When I turned my eyes on the various ores, the various coloured crystals, the stalactites, and natricles,ª as Mr. Melbourne taught me to call them, which glittered round the walls, or depended from the roof; (for even the roof was fretted and adorned with those sort of ornaments), I could fancy myself in the caverns of Staffa, or the grotto of Antiparos.[9] From the divinity of the grotto, Mrs. Melbourne, I met a reception at once the most graceful and cordial. She is an elegant creature, quite in the bloom of life, not older than I am, I should think; and, though so long buried in that solitude, quite with the *ton du monde* in every thing she says and does. How she came to marry such a queer old philosopher, it goes beyond my penetration to conceive; but she is not the only woman that is mismatched.' A heavy sigh.

'A truce with moral reflection, Lady Torrendale, what farther did you see at Mr. Melbourne's.'

'During a delightful repast served up in China, adorned with the most beautiful botanic patterns, which I was *ignoramus* enough to admire, without being able to name or understand, we talked upon a thousand subjects, and spent two hours so pleasantly, we hardly thought it was two minutes. I apologised for my UNINTENTIONAL intrusion, and introduced myself as a friend to the late Lady Julia Melbourne, and well acquainted with the whole of that branch of the family. I immediately perceived, by a momentary silence, and a certain timid glance my little favorite Matilda threw at her mother, that was (for some reason), a forbidden subject. This was rather unfortunate; but, no way abashed, I turned the discourse upon music, and observing Mrs. Melbourne's harp, (which is a very fine one, with a glass frame, shewing the mechanism) I asked her if she did not cultivate that charming talent; and found by her answers she was a very superior musician; she is, indeed, highly accomplished / in every respect. I think I now remember all her connexions were remarkable for it. You must have heard of her – she was a Miss Villiers –'

'Never in my life.'

'Now I am sure you only say that to contradict me. Well – after I had paid my compliments to the lady, I thought it time to make the old gentleman talk a little philosophy. So I set him upon botany, and chemistry, and natural history, 'till he was quite entertaining. He taught me more of it in one conversation, than I ever knew before in my life, and gave me quite a clear idea of experimental philosophy.'

An incredulous smile from his Lordship was the only reply he made.

'Here,' the Countess resumed, 'my little Matilda shone too – I could positively spend whole days with Mr. Melbourne and his daughter, looking at their experiments, and hearing them discourse about them.'

'With the addition of a morning concert, an evening promenade, and half a dozen beaux to flirt with during the intervals.'

'You may laugh; but I declare I found Mr. Melbourne's conversation very amusing, as well as instructive. He has given me quite a taste for science, and I have gained such a general idea of Conchology – Ornithology – Mineralogy – O how I admired the beautiful specimens of every kind that he has amassed together! But still it was on the productions of his native country that he was most eloquent. Did you know that Derbyshire produces marbles and alabasters, as well as the most beautiful spars, topazine, amethystine of the most curious varieties and colours? I am really delighted with the riches of the country. 'Tis natural it should be the nursery of philosophers – Then if you had heard the number of other minerals he named to me. Toad-stone and and swine-stone; amazon-stone, and blood-stone; eagle-stone, soap-stone, chertz, quartz. Then as for shells, univalves, bivalves, multivalves' –

Perceiving that her lord, at this most dreadful and portentous display of learning in his wife, seemed disposed to stop his ears, / to prevent any further communications, the lady checked herself, in order to proceed with her narrative in a less alarming strain.

'After he had talked sufficiently of Derbyshire petrifactions, and crystallizations, and strata, and all that, Mr. Melbourne took me to his observatory; for he is a great astronomer, and has an orrery, the finest I ever saw – and thence to his laboratory – and thence' –

'To his oratory, no doubt,' interrupted Lord Torrendale.

'His oratory – no – what is that?'

'A place I believe you seldom visit.'

'Well you are the last man I should ever have expected to hear speak in praise of oratory – Oh, now I know what you mean, but I am determined not to be affronted. No – then he shewed me his camera obscura – the room as large as the one at Bath, and the picture it exhibited of the surrounding scenery, the trees, rocks, and waterfalls, truly delightful. We could see from it a tame Llama and Alpacha, with their young ones feeding upon the lawn (for nothing at the Rocks is in the common way.) I also observed several sheep and lambs with foreign looking faces. Dear Matilda told me the whole principle of the camera obscura. It merely consists in contriving to have the light thrown on the surface of the – superficies of the – somehow with a spring – I could tell it you exactly, if I could but remember it. We next visited the aviary, and then the apiary, where we saw the bees work under glasses; and she told me such wonderful stories of the sagacity of the bees, and of the houses built by the wasps, houses with stories, and pillars my Lord – and as for the bees, she put a book into my hand, which I laid down again, written by Huber I believe;[10] and another about ants, which says they have jealousies, and animosities, and feelings, and affections, and passions, just like us; and that they not only lay up stores as we were always told, but that they plant, and work, and make war, and peace, and –

'Oh spare me, spare me Lady Torrendale, and tell me what is to be the end of these building wasps, and fighting ants?'

'The end is, that I have taken a prodigious / fancy to the whole family – to Matilda in particular – she is the most sweet-tempered – clever – accomplished – dear little soul.'

'Is she pretty?' asked Lord Torrendale yawning.

'I think I told you so before – if you had thought it worth while to attend to me.'

'Yes, but my dear Laura – you know, a lady's beauty – "is seldom one who has the good fortune to be an equal favourite with the gentlemen"' – 'Well, so I grant you in general; but you ought to know me above such prejudice. Take my word for it Matilda has *real beauty.*'

Lady Torrendale always laid a marked emphasis on this expression; by which she often indirectly designated her own more decided pretensions in opposition to the claims of the croud of barely pretty women.

'I am glad of it,' resumed his Lordship, 'I thought you had said something about her being clever.'

'Clever! no – I only[a] meant she had a facility of expression, and a knack of explaining any circumstance connected with facts in science, which she learnt – as a matter of course you known – *as* one learns – but trust me, Matilda Melbourne is not one of our *wise ladies.* She has not the slightest grain of pride or pedantry; but on the contrary a desire to oblige in all she says and does; and an uncommonly happy manner of rendering the dryest and most difficult subjects clear, by an elegance, a choice of words – a certain peculiarly distinct, deliberate manner of utterance, which has a singular charm with her sweet, rounded voice – and then she pauses and fixes those soft eyes on you to see if she is perfectly understood, with a gentle earnestness – a look of interest.'

'Here,' continued Lady Torrendale taking from a port folio a coloured drawing of Hebe, in the attitude of pouring out nectar, 'as she helped to do the honors of our 'sparkling feast', she reminded me very much of that figure – the same oval face, turn of head, and clustering hair; but her eyebrows are black and Grecian, and her eyes, which are blue, have something more of languor in them, a something persuasive – in short / like what mine were when you used to think me handsome.'

'I never thought you handsome.'

'Oh yes you did, and you used to be ready to comply with every whim of mine.'

'Never, that I recollect.'

'Then I must remind you of it – and my present whim is that you should like old Mr. Melbourne very much; and admire his wife, who has promised to visit me with her charming daughter, and very soon – So if you will visit, and invite them, and have them very often at the house, I give you my word of honour, not to torment you any more the whole time we stay in Derbyshire.' This overture was too unexpected and important to be treated with neglect; and Lord Torrendale, on the express condition that the Countess should fulfil her engagement, readily consented to cultivate the acquaintance of the Melbourne family.

CHAPTER IV.

But this is worshipful society.

SHAKESPEARE.[11]

THE captivating manners and unassuming beauty of Matilda Melbourne, had so far won upon the affections of the volatile Countess, as to make her lay aside her usual aversion to female merit, in the correct and animated description she gave of her attractions; but her Ladyship, when she had, as she supposed, overcome every difficulty, by prevailing on Lord Torrendale to seek the acquaintance of her family, did not advert to a still greater obstacle to any farther intimacy, in the reserve and reluctance of the recluse of the Rocks. While the preceding lively debate had passed between her and her Lord, a family council, no less divided, had been / held at Mr. Melbourne's; which to understand, it may be necessary to explain something of that gentleman's situation and history.

Passionately devoted to study, from his earliest youth, Mr. Melbourne's life had been past in seclusion. He had received a liberal education, of which he could never be persuaded to avail himself, in the choice of any profession: and the patrimony of a younger brother was expended by him, in the purchase of a little estate, or rather farm, where, surrounded by the favourite objects of his pursuit, and divided between his books and rural cares, he found every day new reason to exclaim, with the conscious exultation of the contemplative bard:

'How many *his* employments, whom the world
Calls idle!'[12]

Ten years had glided placidly away since first Mr. Melbourne had declared, at the age of twenty, his determination to adopt a retired and rural life; when a law-suit, which required the presence of the whole family in town, drew Mr. Melbourne from his beloved retreat. He took up his residence at the house of his brother, who was married, and settled in London; and who, from the difference in their pursuits, had been, till now, almost a stranger to him. Here he met, for the first time, his cousin, Sir Reginald Melbourne, of Moss-cliff Abbey, the son of his father's elder brother.

The estate of the Rocks, which was at that time in Mr. Melbourne's family, came by a grandmother; and thus rendered the younger branch of the family as opulent as the elder. Here he was also introduced to the lady, who was destined, at a future period, to be the charmer and enlivener of his solitude.

Aspasia Villiers, was the only daughter of a gentleman who possessed a high situation under government; and was forced, by the death of her mother, at an early age to do the honours of a house, the centre of all that was distinguished in the world of taste, of rank, or literature. Admired for her beauty, but still more for her wit; highly accomplished, at a period when accomplishments were not so generally cultivated, her conversation / had been the solace of ministers, her talents had delighted princes, at an age when few girls begin to emerge into notice. Still however, Aspasia was the lovely and accomplished, but portionless child of a man, whose income, dying with him, left him no resource to provide for her future establishment. Her high pretensions, and the splendid sphere in which she constantly moved, made her generally looked upon as a mark too elevated for modest merit to hope to reach; yet not sufficiently distinguished by the favours of fortune, to be an object of competition among the great and powerful.

Sir Reginald, however, and his cousin, Mr. Melbourne, were struck by her charms almost in the same moment. The latter, prudently determined not to expose himself voluntarily to the fascinations of a woman, who, whatever might be her merit, lived in a style of gaiety and dissipation, which made it impossible for him to suppose she could consent to renounce the world, in order to share a retirement, which his circumstances and his taste induced him equally to embrace.

Sir Reginald, on his part, proud and secure, did not allow himself a moment to doubt his success.

The heart of Aspasia, mean time, had made its election, and it was in favour of Mr. Melbourne. 'Wisdom and worth were all he had;' but these were not lost upon a mind so discerning. A certain diffidence of manner, which was found to conceal superior talents and information, a striking figure, and an interesting and manly countenance; these were the characteristics which she had distinguished in the unpretending recluse, and distinguished with fond partiality. Where the sympathy that attracted was mutual, the resolution to fly the danger, could not be of long duration. Frequent meetings increased the prepossession, and an accidental circumstance finally unveiled their minds to each other.

At a private play, to which all the Melbournes had been invited, Miss Villiers, after charming the spectators in the part of Cleopatra, no less by her talent than by the alluring beauty of her countenance, and the majestic / graces of her person, evinced equal, though different excellence in the entertainment, where she represented the innocent and interesting Rosina.[13] Mr. Melbourne happened to be placed next to her at supper; she still wore the dress in which she had so captivated his heart. To see her in this rural habit, was soothing to his fancy; never, he thought, had she smiled so sweetly on him: it seemed to bring her nearer to his wishes; and, inspired with an unusual degree of courage, he complimented her upon the versatility that could so well sustain a character, so different from that, which birth and education had made her own. She replied, that the part she had that evening supported, however ill it accorded with her present situation, was most congenial to her taste; and that she found the dress of the simple village maid, more in character with her feelings, than when, adorned as an empress, she had worn the splendid trappings of a court. Was it love that inspired this wonderful magnanimity of sentiment, at the moment the beauteous Aspasia believed, in its fullest extent, the truth of what she said. Mr. Melbourne felt convinced she did; and a delightful and confidential conversation ensued, in which he discovered, with equal surprise and pleasure, that she possessed a heart which beat in unison with his own, and a mind formed to relish all the simple and domestic pleasures.

Nothing now remained to check the hopes of Mr. Melbourne, but the preference Mr. Villiers openly gave to Sir Reginald. A sudden and violent illness, however, shortly after deprived Aspasia of her only remaining parent; and, for some time, plunged her into a state of dejection, which refused to hear either the voice of consolation, or of love. When she at length consented to let Mr. Melbourne renew his suit, he, without difficulty, prevailed on her to quit a world, that, to her mind, already softened by affliction, no longer offered the same enjoyment; and to retire with him to that beautiful spot, to which he had added every circumstance of rural comfort and convenience, and which her taste and judgment soon rendered a *ferme ornée*. Here, in the society of a wife / so lovely and beloved, and the additional happiness which the birth of a daughter, after some years of anxious expectation, conferred on him, Mr. Melbourne felt less than ever the want of any other intercourse. At his leisure hours, he cultivated an intimate acquaintance with the families of ferns, heaths, mosses, and grasses; but forgot, at the same time, equally to cultivate the living families the neighbourhood afforded.

In this love of solitude, he was unintentionally seconded by his Aspasia, who, though she had given up the first society for him she loved, could never afterwards find attractions in any other. Sometimes, when gazing on the infant beauties of her daughter, a vague wish would cross her mind, that they could at once expand to womanhood; that the sensibility of that heart could already respond to her's; the intelligence of those eyes express themselves in the intercourse of mind to mind. But soon remembering how short is the portion allotted to life, and how much the happiest were those years claimed by childhood and youth, she blushed at the selfish thought. 'Am I not a mother!' she exclaimed; 'Oh I am surely, even now, sufficiently happy!'

But, as years advanced, and she saw her own perfections revive in the young Matilda's excellence, in every elegant and feminine accomplishment, she found, in storing her opening mind with useful and ornamental knowledge, ample and interesting employment; at the same time Mr. Melbourne took care to remedy in his daughter the defect he had often secretly deplored in his wife. For, though her acquirements in history, in languages, in general literature, far surpassed what is usually attained by a female, she was not a woman of science; and sometimes, with harmless playfulness, rather laughed at her husband's endless and grave dissertations upon blades of grass, and butterflies' wings, or the still more learned discourses upon hydrogen and oxygen, which were delivered by his friend, Mr. Sowerby, the only visitor who ever disturbed his solitude.

On these occasions, his only resource was to retire with his daughter Matilda, to his laboratory or his study: and, while amid his / books and philosophical apparatus, he beheld her lightly flitting around him, with the obedience, and almost the intelligence, of a little attendant spirit, ministering to the operations of the parent sage, or gazing with mute wonder to see him.

   – 'Mark with magic art profound,
   The speed of light, the circling march of sound.'[14]

imprison the boundless air, or ascertain the movements of the unnumbered host of heaven; he felt almost indifferent, whether she was informed or ignorant of what was passing, or had passed, in this sublunary sphere.

The acquisition of the estate of the Rocks, by the death of his elder brother, made no alteration in his way of life. Sir Reginald, though he had married almost immediately after his cousin, had never forgiven the injurious preference shewn him. There was no intercourse between the families; and Mr. Melbourne, who saw no company, hardly ever looked at a newspaper, and by degrees almost prevented one from entering his peaceful habitation, was ignorant of events and changes in the situation of those relatives, which had long been the subject of discourse among others, who might be supposed less interested in their causes.

This was not the only peculiarity in which Mr. Melbourne gradually indulged; an increasing reserve, and a singularity of habit and address, made the difference of years (though not too considerable) between himself and his lovely partner rather more than less perceptible, as they advanced in age. An innate elegance, a mind perhaps more formed to attend to the minutiæ of life, and, above all, the desire, supreme in every female breast, to be pleasing in the eyes of him she solely loves, preserves, in woman, an attention to the forms of life, even without the checks imposed by mixed society: but man requires the collision of general opinion, the spur of vanity and emulation, to enable him to impose on himself, constantly, those restraints, which, to a mind intent on greater objects, may appear of trifling import, and importunate recurrence.

Thus, while Mrs. Melbourne retained as / much of the fine lady as it is possible to do without the least tincture of impertinence; her husband, happy, and sufficing to himself, without being naturally either proud, narrow, or unsocial, had gradually reduced himself to an almost anchorite state of simplicity and of solitude too, which, it never once occurred to him, while immersed in his favourite studies, the ladies of his family might begin not to relish quite so well as he did.

The 'sensation' created by the unexpected appearance of Lady Torrendale among them, brought these opposite dispositions fully into light.

In her first address. Mrs. Melbourne acknowledged a tone of manners more congenial to her own, than any thing she had met with, since she had quitted the world of gaiety and fashion.

We have already said, this lady's exterior was prepossessing: and the circumstances of alarm and suffering under which she was introduced, had naturally excited an interest in her favour; which a languishing, sentimental air, in all her looks and actions, aided by eyes that had been once the finest in the world, tended, at a first interview, not a little to increase. The deceit she had practised to gain admittance, with the ridiculous mistake that ensued, had not yet reached the heads of the family. The desire she had expressed for their acquaintance, was flattering; and it was under this impression, that Mrs. Melbourne, speaking to her husband of the recent visit, observed to him, 'I hope you like our new neighbour, I think her a pleasant woman, and shall not delay, longer than to-morrow, my promised call.'

'You are right, my dear,' he replied, 'and there, you know, the thing may drop.'

'But I do not see why it *should* drop,' returned Mrs. Melbourne. 'Here is a woman of elegance, and apparently pleasing manners, whose acquaintance it may be of advantage to us to cultivate, and at whose house we may meet with some agreeable society.'

'Society!' cried Mr. Melbourne, suddenly starting as if out of a dream; 'I am sure I feel no want of it.' /

'No; but Matilda might, my love,' said his lady, smiling. 'When she was a child, I found, like you, every pleasure in retirement; but now she is arriving at an age, in which her fortune and pretensions entitle her to an introduction into the world, I must no longer consult my own feelings alone, but renew, for her sake, the long-forgotten labours of company, balls, and parties.'

'What can she possibly want with balls,' replied Mr. Melbourne. 'I always found them very tiresome things.'

'Perhaps so might she; but I have always been of the opinion of an elegant friend of our's, that "to indulge young people with a peep into the show-box of fashion," is the surest method to prevent that restless curiosity and feverish thirst for amusement, which is too often produced by exaggerated descriptions. They afterwards turn with redoubled pleasure to the refreshing calm of domestic society, when convinced of the fallacy of every other promise of enjoyment. For that reason, though I should be very sorry to see Matilda a slave to dissipation, I own I could wish, that by being present at a concert or an opera, she should be able to form some idea of the miracles of an art, in which she excels so much; that she should see an interesting play, a pleasure in which, you know, she has never yet been indulged; that –'

'She has no great loss,' interrupted Mr. Melbourne, who, having got hold of a large Encyclopædia, had suffered his wife to go on thus far, while he was hunting for an interesting article. 'Formerly the theatre was called a rational amusement; but now, as I hear from the best accounts, for I have not visited it myself these twenty years, noise, shew, and spectacle, entirely usurp the place of sense and nature.'

'Surely not entirely,' cried Mrs. Melbourne. 'She would see some examples of the power the theatric art possesses over the passions, of which she can now form no idea; and as for noise, I hope you do not give that name to music.'

'She has music enough in her own house,' / replied Mr. Melbourne, turning over the leaves of his Encyclopædia very fast.

'Come you are not attending to me; let us spare a few moments to discuss this subject, which may be of importance to the future prospects of our child, and lay aside that great book; I am sure you never got any good by your philosophical pursuits.'

'Good! Mrs. Melbourne, – did not I get the thanks of the Royal Society for my communications?'

'Yes, but I want to get the thanks of another "Society," for mine,' returned his lady, half laughing. 'And I doubt, if grace, beauty and talent like Matilda's, will not, when communicated, entitle me to as warm acknowledgments, as the most singular grass, or curiously formed shell, ever was the means of obtaining. By "*good*," I mean of course, connection, advantage; I have the greatest respect for your studies, my love;

but how would all the knowledge she could acquire in them tend to her establishment without a little of the *ton*, the polish, the *usage du monde*, which,' –

'And what is there pray in that world beyond what she now possesses? – with books, friends, and rational occupation, how can she wish for any thing more?'

'She does not, and for that very reason, *I* wish it for her; – hers is not a mind for which we need fear the contagion of society; the romantic tenderness of her disposition, rather points to the danger of absolute solitude in nourishing such a tendency to the destruction of her future peace.'

At this moment the interesting subject of their dispute entered the room, eager

'Soon as the morning wreath had bound her hair,'[15]

to relate the little incidents of her walk, and to enjoy again the unbounded freedom of social intercourse, in her domestic circle. She was accompanied by a gentleman, whose presence was always welcomed by the family with smiles of the most cordial friendship: though several years younger than Mr. Melbourne, a similarity of pursuits had rendered / Mr. Sowerby, of Clifden-down, a companion peculiarly acceptable to him. His visits were received with pleasure at all hours, and at all times. Nothing was concealed from him, and he was considered by Matilda, from her infancy, as her friend and preceptor.

Miss Melbourne, advancing lightly towards her mother, shewed her with pride and pleasure, a bird of extraordinary beauty, and singular plumage, which he had just knocked down among the rocks, and presented for her inspection.

Mr. Sowerby, – 'but he shall speak for himself.' – 'What's this I hear,' said he, his countenance changing from the expression of joyous friendship, to the gloomiest discontent, when he understood what had been the subject of the recent conversation. – 'This fine lady, with her balls, and her fêtes, and her dashing, not contented with turning the heads of the whole county, has turned your head too, my good Madam, I see.'

'Not exactly that my dear sir, only pleased us, as the French say, "*Cela fait evenement.*"'

'How I hate the French, and every thing that is French,' said Mr. Sowerby, turning ten shades darker at this expression of Mrs. Melbourne's, who, to confess the truth, had made use of it, from pique, aware that her cynical neighbour (from some unknown cause), could not endure the name of that obnoxious nation. 'I have just discovered,' pursued Mr. Sowerby, 'that the overturn was a mere trick, concerted between her and her people, to force herself into this family.'

'Well, then the compliment was the greater, that you must allow.'

'I have done, Madam, I see plainly how it is; – levity and dissipation, when graced by title, is a recommendation to all. I had hoped to see one family safe from the contagion of fashion, and folly, and frivolity, and vice; – but 'tis over, and I have done.'

'Come, come, dear Sowerby,' returned Mrs. Melbourne, with that playful superiority she knew so well at times how to assume. 'You mistake this lady's character – don't begin to be cross; – don't be unreasonable.' /

'But I will be cross, and I will be unreasonable,' cried Mr. Sowerby, his voice rising with increased passion, at what he probably deemed an infringement on one of his privileges:– 'Is it not enough to set a man mad to see one woman driving to the devil, and her neighbours all, all following her example.'

'You are too severe upon this unoffending lady,' said Mrs. Melbourne. 'As Matilda is the person most interested in this question, we will refer to her opinion as to the impression she has made.'

'I think her a charming woman,' said Matilda, while, as she met the stern glance of her preceptor, timidity struggled with the rising glow of youthful and ingenuous feeling.

'We do not yet know whether she deserves that title,' said Mrs. Melbourne, looking, in her turn, with anxiety at her innocent and enthusiastic daughter.

'But she is certainly pleasing; her husband is a character of the highest respectability; and since she has been among us, (turning to Mr. Sowerby,) she has surely done nothing to reflect discredit on her own.'

'She is going as fast as she can the road to ruin,' pursued that gentleman, whose general custom it was to follow the current of his own reflections, without disturbing himself to attend to the observations that might, from time to time, be made by others.

'Or, admit her to be a mere fine lady, what do you hope to gain by an intercourse with her? – is it to meet other company at her house? – To form an acquaintance with those trifling people, whom your sense and good taste, taught you formerly to despise? Is it to have the pleasure of paying an annual visit to my neighbour Sapling, where the good lady is always in such a bustle about her house and her family, that she is invisible to your enquiries – "where the men are all working out in the fields," so that you are ushered by a dirty, half-asleep maid, with her hair in papers, into the front parlour, and then begged to go into the back drawing-room; which, being unswept, and the shutters / shut, is thought unworthy of your reception, and you are once more requested to move into the front drawing-room; – there you find all sort of litter and lumber that the children have left, and are intreated to walk from thence into the back parlour. You may then begin an animated conversation with the china cat on the mantle-piece, or the time-piece on the table, only interrupted by the occasional opening of the door, by some little urchin who peeps at you, laughs, and runs away; 'till at last down comes Miss, and despairing of mama's good behaviour, takes you round the grounds to amuse you during your visit. – The family are what is called making improvements; that is to say, spoiling and breaking up every thing, and you are dragged about with "here's to be a shrubbery – and there's to be a lake – and here we will throw up a Chinese bridge – and there we are planning a gravel walk" – 'till, half dying with heat and fatigue, you are meditating a retreat, on any terms, when it is cut off by the good lady herself, who, all bustle and civility, is, "quite sorry she had not the power of seeing you sooner" and intreats you will not "think" of going away without "taking something." And something you must take, under the penalty of having it forced down your throat. And "this is worshipful society?" This is what you like, hey?'

'No my good Sir,' said Mrs. Melbourne, taking advantage of an interval of silence. 'but there are others.'

'O yes there are others and blessed ones too – you like better the patrician civility of the stately Crossbrooks I suppose, where there is indeed no bustle of family management to be seen; where the mistress of the house receives you, sitting in state at the end of a long, lofty room, whose silent echoes seem awakened by your tread. There you find good Mrs. Crossbrook, surrounded by her daughters; prim, formal damsels who, if they look off their work for a moment, to gaze on the stranger, resume it again with a gravity worthy of an Archbishop, or a Lord Chancellor. Whether 'tis netting, or knotting, bobbin or bilboquet,[16] no matter – the seriousness / and perseverance with which it is continued, are equally worthy of admiration. Meantime you make an abortive attempt at a languid conversation with the lady of the house, in which each observation seems half frozen in its passage to her ears, while the lady herself, if she now and then opes her marble jaws to deliver some remark, with a slowness and precision, that would do honor to a pupil of the instructors of the deaf and dumb, shuts them again with a manner that appears to say

"Now my weary lips I close

Leave me, leave me to repose."[17]

and it is for that society you would exchange our pleasant solitude! That is your taste in forming acquaintance.'

'You mistake me,' replied Mrs. Melbourne, who began to be tired of this harangue, 'Such company is not what I prefer, but if one mixes with the world –'

'You do, you do,' continued Mr. Sowerby as usual, not attending to any one's remarks but his own. 'You like it, and why should you not? You have a right to chuse for yourself, and to finish your daughter's education your own way – It's all over with her I see very plainly. Once she has got balls, and parties in her head, where will be our instructive evening conversations, where our pleasant morning walks? Exchanged for senseless gaiety, all rational employment will be neglected, and idleness perfect idleness,' he continued, violently jerking the end of a piece of muslin which Matilda was quietly sprigging, 'will succeed to her former interesting occupations.'

'You see things in too serious a light Sowerby,' said the placid Mr. Melbourne, who by this time began to suspect that his friend was getting into an ill-temper; 'you should not always anticipate the worst, my dear fellow, indeed you should not.'

'It is nothing to me' resumed the amiable visitor, with that affected calmness which always announced, in him, that his displeasure had reached its greatest height. 'I think young ladies should certainly amuse themselves / if they like it, and amused, no doubt, your daughter will be, very much amused. 'Tis all very delightful, and if some old-fashioned people should venture to observe that they had hoped better things of Matilda Melbourne, she may very fairly reply that, with her youth and spirits, it is but natural, serious and sober avocations, should be looked upon with contempt, and their place supplied by gaiety, nothing but gaiety.'

As he pronounced these last words, in that smothered tone of bitter and cruel irony, in which he particularly excelled, he fixed his eyes on the interesting girl, who was at this moment the subject of it, and whose countenance expressed so completely the reverse of the idea which his concluding reproof conveyed, that even the sternness of *his* censure gave way to softer feelings.

'Have I deserved this?' she said, looking at him with eyes swimming in tears.

All his harshness vanished at these words. Conscious he had been wrong, the excess of his regret was in danger of leading him into an extreme of indulgence equally unnecessary, for his heart was naturally as good, as his temper was clouded and unamiable.

'You never could deserve reproof from me' he said, assuming his mildest and most affectionate manner. 'I alone was to blame, in letting myself be betrayed, by a too anxious solicitude for your welfare, into hasty and intemperate expressions. Go fearlessly into that society you are so well fitted to adorn; with your principles, and your acquirements, I would not hesitate to trust you among all its dangers and allurements.'

Then apologising to Mrs. Melbourne for the warmth into which he had been unintentionally surprised, he took leave; and Matilda, soon after, retired to her own apartment, to calm the agitation into which her spirits had been thrown by behaviour so unexpected and distressing.

'I am glad he is gone,' said Mrs. Melbourne, as soon as the satisfactory sight of Sowerby striding across the lawn, secured her from any fear of being over-heard; 'What can be his motive for wishing to withhold my daughter from the circle in which, / sooner or later, she must move, I cannot divine. Be it what it will, you must allow the bear grows every day more intolerable. None but Matilda can tame him.'

'Then she had better marry him,' Mr. Melbourne replied, as if he was not thinking of what he was saying.

'No my dear,' returned his wife with earnestness; 'estimable as Sowerby is in his character, and independent in his fortune, worlds would not tempt me to trust the happiness of my gentle, generous girl, to the caprice of a temper, gloomy, peevish, and discontented as his.'

'Nor me neither I assure you my dear. I think Matilda far better as she is, for these twenty years to come. But as Sowerby's society is to me not only a resource, but an advantage, I beg you will not, by betraying your dislike to the uncouthness of his manners, render his visits less frequent.'

'On the contrary I esteem him and do all in my power to like him; when he is absent I almost succeed; but, in his presence, my aversion sometimes rises to a degree I can scarce suppress: there is a something about him that repels the good will, his merits tend to inspire; a kind of atmosphere of hatred that surrounds him, and that makes me breathe more freely when out of his sight. His causeless severity against the whole present system of things, prevents one's attending to his objections, even when they may be reasonable. In Matilda's case, you must perceive their absurdity. At Lady Torrendale's she may not meet with every thing I could wish united; but I look on such an introduction, as a discipline, a kind of preparatory school to initiate her a little into society, before she is herself called on to play her part in the great world.'

'Well my dear, it shall be as you please. You know the coachman will be absent for a few days, as I could not refuse him the pleasure of a visit to his relation from Devonshire, whom he had not seen for so many years. As soon as he returns, you may pay this cursed visit.'

With such friendly and disinterested sentiments to actuate their decision, these neighbours / determined to seek each other's society: and, after all the different interests were finally adjusted, in the debates that we have seen agitated at both houses, a frequent and agreeable intercourse was at length established, which appeared at first productive of equal advantages to each. The polished manners, and amiable, and intelligent mind of Mrs. Melbourne, always made her company peculiarly acceptable at Woodlands; and when Lady Torrendale wished to charm her *ennui*, among the various objects of curiosity, that art and nature afforded, at the Rocks, she generally gave pleasure to the recluses, by the occasional liveliness of her conversation, and the novelty that the trifles she communicated, in their eyes, possessed. Mr. Melbourne, as yet not quite reconciled to the charms of female society, only desired to be warned of the approach of the 'petticoats,' as he concisely denominated the Countess of Torrendale and Miss Langrish, that he might retire to his pipe, his coffee, and his book. With Lord Torrendale he was obliged to be a little more ceremonious; and their meetings were not unlike the description of those that took place between two much greater men.

'A while they on each other look,
Then, different studies chuse'.[18]

Mr. Melbourne turned to some work of scientific information; and his Lordship amused himself, in a manner equally satisfactory, by studying, for the three hundred and sixtieth time that year, the list of both houses of parliament. /

*   Swift to Pope.

CHAPTER V.

Non sai ben dir, s'adorna o se negletta
Se caso od arte il bel volto compose;
Di natura, d'amor, de' cieli amici
Le negligenze sue sono artefici.

TASSO. GERUSALEMME LIBERATA.[19]

Mais ne nous flattons point, et laissons le mystére,
La sœur vous touche ici beaucoup moins que le frere.

RACINE. BRITANNICUS.[20]

NOTWITHSTANDING Lady Torrendale's real or affected contempt for the neighbourhood that surrounded her, yet, as her's was one of those minds which demand a constant supply from without, she generally contrived to have a pretty numerous circle, to enliven her retirement at Woodlands.

To these, Matilda, till then almost unknown, formed a most welcome and pleasing addition: while, in the mixture of more general society, she lost that timidity which absolute solitude always creates, and every day disclosed some new charm of mind or disposition.

Her's had never been that excessive and distressing bashfulness, which rather argues a sense of defect, than a modest uncertainty of deserved success. This, her own inherent dignity and elegance of mind, and the education she had received, from a woman once familiar with a court, would have equally rendered absurd and misplaced. The diffidence of Matilda, was of a character more interesting and more true. It was the soft mist of a vernal morning, that increases the loveliness of the objects it covers, and which the first sun-beam of kindness easily dispels.

All her modesty was requisite to prevent the dangerous effects of the flattery, that was now poured in upon her, on every side, and / which was encouraged by the prevailing suffrage of Lady Torrendale.

The Countess, as her husband had predicted, soon lost her taste for stuffed birds, and Derbyshire petrifactions; not so her predilection for Matilda, which seemed to increase with indulgence. For Mrs. Melbourne, her affection did not advance in an equal ratio. Without exactly allowing herself to think that lady excelled her in any thing, still she felt they differed, and that, in every point where a difference existed, the advantage was not on her side.

The eyes of the deity that presides over wit, are represented as possessing something at once bright, and terrible. Mrs. Melbourne, under an address the most feminine and insinuating, concealed a quick perception of the faulty and ridiculous in others; while a consciousness of her own mental superiority, gave to her manners an unbidden grace, and a dignity which commanded, without appearing to exact respect. Lady Torrendale in the midst of the airs of beauty and high-bred elegance, which she had practiced so often, and with success, was sometimes surprised to find herself disconcerted and put out of countenance, by a glance of the eye from the recluse of the Rocks. It has been said of the superior divinities, that they can conceal themselves from the inferior ones at pleasure; but that the latter are not endowed, in return, with a similar privilege. Lady Torrendale would often fix her piercing eyes on Mrs. Melbourne, with an expression that indicated the consciousness there was something in her mind she could not fathom; while all her own frivolities, follies, and weaknesses, lay exposed, and at the mercy of that lady's remark.

But with Matilda, the innocent, the cherub Matilda, no such severity or animadversion was to be feared. With all their added elegance, her manners possessed an artless frankness, and the observations she made, an originality, an air of freshness and vivacity, which she owed to her secluded life, and singular education; and which had an inexpressible / charm, in the eyes of one accustomed to the vapid affectation, and monotonous sameness of the often repeated copies from fashion's unvaried standard. Fearless, alike, of deceit or change, and delighted with the preference she had excited, Matilda returned her Ladyship's demonstrations of kindness with that confiding, that partial and warm affection, with which ingenuous youth is apt to look up to its superiors in age or knowledge, even more readily than to companions, and contemporaries.

Not content with enjoying her society whenever she could draw the family of the Rocks from their retreat, the Countess made frequent appointments with her young friend to ride or walk. If these excursions continued 'till late, she was often pressed to take a bed at Woodlands, and her return was deferred till the following day. Whenever any accidental or domestic occurrence prevented the frequency of these meetings, elegant little billets written on pink paper, or in blue ink, where weeping figures, or emblematic flowers, on the embossed borders, denoted the grief and desperation of the forsaken Lady, were sure to pour in at the Rocks, and be the faithful messengers of her feelings.

Much, however, as Matilda valued and loved Lady Torrendale, she was sometimes when in conversation with her, obliged to acknowledge she discovered a mind that did not understand her's, and tastes in opposition to all those she had been taught to cultivate.

To a person accustomed, as she was, to find a pleasure in employment, the almost total idleness, to which every one was condemned at Woodlands, was in itself a drawback on the pleasure she enjoyed there. To take up a book, in the presence of Lady Torrendale, was high treason. Work, and all the other usual feminine resources, were equally prohibited. Music she could not bear; 'she had so much of it with her daughter Emily and Miss Langrish.' And if Matilda ever attempted to listen to that young lady, who really played very finely, her noble friend, though, perhaps, she had not spoken for some time before, immediately began buzzing in her ear, upon some uninteresting / topic; 'the sound of an instrument' (as she observed) 'always putting her in mind of a thousand particular things she had to say.' Her time was usually divided between the period she devoted to the glass,

'A' misteri d'amor ministro eletto'[21]

eating, or driving out. The second was indeed an object of great importance with Lady Torrendale; and she contrived to make her meals of such frequent recurrence, and long duration, that the intervals between them were short; and these were filled up with lounging on the sofa, while she languidly listened to Matilda reading to her the letters of her London correspondents, which she was too indolent to look at herself; made corrections and alterations in the visiting book for the ensuing season; or amused herself, talking an ingenious kind of rhodomontade, principally composed of invective, castle-building, extravagant fancies, and vain regrets: to which, for want of a term more exclusively appropriate, we must be content for the present to give the general name of – Nonsense. But, when the appearance of visitors at Woodlands roused her Ladyship from this last and favorite employment, the elasticity of her spirits was delightful; and, to introduce Matilda to the greatest advantage, seemed one of her principal and highest pleasures. On these occasions she was 'the most enchanting, the most fascinating girl that ever existed.' Whatever Miss Melbourne said and did was, of course, superior to what any body else could have said or done; and, in imitation of the '*Padrona*,'[22] it was echoed around by the admiring circle, that 'nothing could be so charming as Miss Melbourne.' Two dissentient voices amid the general hum of applause, served as the music masters tell us of discords, only to make the according harmony of flattery 'more sweet and beautiful.'

To Miss Langrish, the governess, the youth and loveliness of Matilda were, (for some unacknowledged reason), particularly offensive. To Lord Torrendale, her imputed acquirements in science, though never ostentatiously brought forward, were equally the subjects / of disapprobation. Having once taken it into his head that she was, as he termed it, 'clever,' and that she would therefore indubitably lead his wife to make herself, in some new manner ridiculous, all her respectful attentions, and elegant gaiety, were equally unavailing, to conquer the haughty and repulsive coldness that was, in him, the consequence of this preconceived opinion.

'Indeed, my Lord, you should love Matilda,' said Lady Torrendale, 'she is the little bird of paradise, that comes spreading her gay wings over me in this solitude; the halcyon that brings a calm after the storm of my vexations.'

'She has made you as romantic and fanciful as herself. This is one of your "hobbies" at present, Laura, and will soon go to the tomb of the Capulets with your former successive predilections, for Madame Recamier, Kosciusko, the young Roscius, and the Persian Prince.'[23]

'Ah! no,' replied her Ladyship, with a look which she meant should express sensibility, and which was really rather sentimental, 'those were transient fancies; this, an attachment in its nature durable, as delightful.'

'Will you venture a wager that no accident will have disturbed your sublime friendship before this day twelve-month?'

'Any you please. If I waver in my affection to my fair friend, I consent to spend another Christmas with you in this odious country.'

'Agreed,' replied her husband; and departed, very well satisfied with the morning's arrangement.

As the increasing severity of the season confined Matilda when at Woodlands more to in-door amusements, she often found a resource from the sameness of Lady Torrendale's conversation, in the intelligence and animation of Lady Emily Fitzroy. This amiable girl, now nearly twelve years of age, was peculiarly fascinated by the unassuming manners of Miss Melbourne, and spent every hour she could spare from other avocations in her apartment. One day, looking very earnestly at her, she suddenly exclaimed, 'Will / you tell me truly, do you like Miss Langrish?'

Matilda, surprised at the singularity of the question, hesitated a moment for a reply; when Lady Emily continued very fast, 'She is a good creature I believe, but not very wise. Nay, I know you will blame me for saying so,' she added, with that frank and inoffensive vanity, sometimes so striking and amusing in very early youth; 'you will think me unjust, because I am, myself, clever of my age: but all I ever knew in any branch of learning, I owe to my brother Strathallan. I shall never again pass such summers as we used to spend in Derbyshire together. Dear Strathallan, you are now far distant, and know not how I wish for you in all my walks and studies! When he was first in Spain,' continued Lady Emily, after this little natural apostrophe, 'he used to write to me; I think I will shew you some of his letters; they are so interesting, and contain such beautiful descriptions. No, I won't, they praise me so much; but there is one which does *not* praise me; and yet which I love above all the rest. I had written him something, I do not now remember exactly what it was, but that it was complaining of my mother; and, as she never was very kind to him, (for you know he is not *her* son,) I thought he would, of course, agree with me; see what he says in return.' As she spoke, Lady Emily put into Matilda's hand a letter, which, among much fraternal and affectionate advice, had the following sentence:–

'You were unhappy, you thought yourself ill-treated, my Emily, at the moment you let the expressions I have noticed escape from your pen. How often must you since have wished the transient dictates of vexation, or ill humour, unwritten! You have the happiness of possessing your parent's warmest affection. Cherish it my dear girl as your most invaluable treasure. When Lady Torrendale is displeased with you, think you are unjust; think she is in error; think any thing but that her love can suffer a moment's diminution; or if accidentally any real cause of complaint should arise, balance it with her thousand kindnesses, and let it remain buried / in your own bosom. I never knew the happiness of a mother's care; but I can fully conceive the charm it gives to the early part of our existence. How often, in your childish days, have I envied you even the reproofs that proceeded from a relation so dear!'

'Poor Strathallan!' said Lady Emily, as Matilda stood with her eyes fixed mechanically on the letter; 'He says true, or perhaps he would not now be in Spain. No matter, every thing is for the best; is it not, Miss Melbourne? How often have I kissed and wept over this kind, this disinterested advice! It was, besides, the last letter I received from him. It is now long since we have heard from him, and I fear he has far different subjects to interest his thoughts, than the grief, the anxiety of his poor little Emily!'

Matilda had often heard Lord Strathallan mentioned as an officer of merit who had served with distinction in the Peninsula.

This interest was now encreased by the anecdotes she was thus unexpectedly made acquainted with, of his domestic character and disposition. This amiable Strathallan had then been her neighbour, had spent more than one summer at a spot so little removed from her residence; and yet, only his name had reached her till now; happy and contented, and having scarcely a wish to pass the bounds of her beloved retirement, she for the first time questioned the advantageousness of the perfect seclusion in which she had been bred up, and felt an undefined wish to extend the limits of her observation. Unconsciously charmed by the candour and artlessness of the detail she now heard, she gave a sigh for Lady Emily, who lost so much in losing the society of such a brother; but cautioned her against the habit she had acquired of attributing all her improvements to his kindness and instruction before Miss Langrish; 'she encourages me, and likes me to do so,' was the young lady's reply; and Matilda soon had a proof of the truth of the assertion.

On one occasion that Emily was expatiating on her favorite theme, 'Oh, Miss Melbourne,' / said she, (turning to Matilda) 'I am sure you would like my brother; he is all that is great and noble, united to a winning softness. You are the only person that reminds me of him.'

'You are right, my dear,' said Miss Langrish, 'to cherish the remembrance of merit so distinguished; though, I confess, I cannot perceive the conformity of character you mention between Lord Strathallan and Miss Melbourne.' 'Alas!' she continued, in her most sentimental manner, 'how much more must his absence make you feel the value of such a brother! He is a superior young man; a very superior young man indeed. Were I to draw an assemblage of all that is most exalted in nature, most refined by education; all that dazzles in the hero, all that captivates in the man, I should chase for my example, and my model of united excellence, the character of Lord Strathallan.'

Matilda gazed with surprise at Miss Langrish while she pronounced this animated panegyric, in a style so unlike her usual affected languor.

She had now sunk into her wonted attitude of pensive meditation; her eyes cast on the ground; her head resting on her hand; and her whole appearance awakened in Miss Melbourne's mind, a momentary suspicion that she was one of those fair and conscientious instructors of youth, who think it much prettier to fall in love with the brother, than to attend to the improvement of the sister; but, when she considered the rank, merit, and pretensions of the object to which she must, in that case, be supposed to aspire, the surmise yielded immediately to the very slender claims to admiration possessed by the young lady. Miss Langrish, joined, to a little insignificant figure, a round, pale, unmeaning face, rather marked by the small-pox, and which would have gone decidedly under the head of *une de ces figures dont on ne dit rien;*[24] but for a pair of grey eyes, which she forced into notice, by the persevering affectation of languishing softness with which they for ever rolled. Yet, still the animated and enthusiastic expressions she made use of on one subject, regardless of her situation; one that called for double caution and circumspection / of manner, rather favored the first idea; and it was still farther confirmed by the observation, that the time she allotted to practising music, (which was enormously disproportioned to her other studies, amounting to not less than six hours in the day,) was devoted, when she thought herself alone, to the indulgence of a sentimental melancholy; and that the brilliant difficulties of

Steibelt, or the laboured intricacies of Von Esch,[25] were exchanged for the easier and lighter charms of '*Ah perdona a primo affetto;*'[26] or

'Felice quel core;
Che langue d'amore.'[27]

Once, Lady Emily had excited a blush on the cheek of her young governess, by artlessly exclaiming, after she had finished an air which she was very fond of repeating, 'That was a great favorite of Strathallan's before he left England.' The sneer that a little discomposed the usually indolent countenance of Lady Torrendale, shewed the remark did not pass unobserved; and it was at least so far of use, as to make Beethoven and his learned brethren for a time resume the places which had been usurped by *Innocenza's, Veneziana's*, and *Francalanza's*.[28]

But, however Miss Langrish might excel in music, Matilda had soon reason to suspect she was not equally a proficient in other studies. Having risen early one morning, after spending the evening with her friends at Woodlands, and finding occasion to seek for a book which she had left the preceding night with Lady Emily in the apartment called, emphatically, the school-room, her ear was struck, as she passed along the corridor which led to it, by the murmur of a low voice, which she soon discovered to be that of Miss Langrish, reading or repeating something to herself. Matilda would have been surprised if she had known the subject of these early studies. They were notes 'painfully' collected, to furnish replies to some of the numerous questions, which Lady Emily was in the daily habit of asking; some were for the improvement of the pupil, a great many to rectify the ideas of the much more ignorant governess. Here were some of the principal ones: /

'Memorandum. – To look into the dictionary for the meaning of the word "Oblivion;" also for the difference between the words Armistice, Amnesty, and Amity.

'Mem. – (For Geography). Tartary and Tartarus are two different places. The latter, I believe, fabulous. The former somewhere near Spa. Also St. Helen's, and St. Helena, not synonymous.

'Mem. – To look in the Biographical Dictionary for lives to correspond to the three names so often mentioned, Tamerlane, Tamarisk, and Tamarind.

'Mem. – (For History.) Heptarchy means seven kingdoms, and not five; heptarchy, being the old English word for "seven."

'Mem. – To call William the Second, William Rufus, not "Rueful," as I did by mistake the other day. It was he, not William the First, that was killed by an arrow in the *New* Forest, as it is still called; though I should think it must be, by now, near a hundred years old.

'Mem. – It was Mary, Queen of Scots, whose head was taken off, not bloody Queen Mary; whose name seems to import she had undergone such a fate.

'Mem. – The Rye-House plot does not mean a combination against the dealers in rye.

'Mem. – Algernon Sidney, Sir Philip Sidney, and Sir Sidney Smith, are three different personages.'

Miss Langrish had committed the whole of these valuable and miscellaneous remarks to memory, as far as the preceding sentence; and how much farther still she might have advanced, must for ever remain unknown, for the entrance of Matilda, at this moment, put an end to her studies, and forced from the young lady, a faint scream of surprise and terror, upon the appearance of a visitor at so early and unexpected an hour; while some well studied volumes of modern 'Horrors,' which peeped from beneath the huge quartos of English, French, and Italian literature that covered the table in the shape of grammars, histories, and dictionaries, accounted for the extreme susceptibility of her nerves to impressions of sudden alarm. /

'Have I disturbed you?' said Matilda, as she advanced seraph-smiling, and turned upon Miss Langrish a look, which another might have died to obtain, but which in her bosom excited only suspicion and dread.

'Nay, am I then so very alarming?' continued the lovely girl, endeavouring to calm the agitation of her companion. 'Believe me, I did not mean to intrude.'

'I trust you did not,' said Miss Langrish, by a great effort, recovering herself, and darting at the unwelcome visitor, a glance that seemed to wish to penetrate her inmost soul. 'I trust Miss Melbourne is incapable of prying into the secrets of others; or, if chance should discover them to her, of revealing them to their disadvantage.'

Matilda, who had not distinguished one word of the precious notes Miss Langrish had been scanning, preparatory to her morning's lesson, assured her with great simplicity, that her coming was quite accidental, and that she was still ignorant of the reason why it should cause so much perturbation.

The young lady paused a moment; doubts of the sincerity of this statement, struggled with resentment and dislike. At length, believing it most politic to secure the friendship of Matilda, she said to her, in her softest and most conciliatory tone, 'the fears I may naturally experience from the effects of Miss Melbourne's superior penetration are *vanished*, when I reflect on the benignity, the condescending sweetness with which it is accompanied.'

'Pray, Miss Langrish, do not think yourself obliged to address such praises to me,' said the ingenuous Matilda, disgusted with flattery from one who, she felt assured, had never viewed her with kindness. 'If this is meant to prevent my telling Lady Torrendale that I found you employed here at this early hour, you may depend upon my discretion, though ignorant of the reason why it should be necessary. I have found the book I was looking for. Permit me to wish you good morning.'

Fearful of the dangerous effects of a half confidence, the young governess thought it best, since she had gone thus far, to trust / herself entirely to Matilda; therefore, stopping her as she was leaving the room, she added, 'You cannot but have observed, Miss Melbourne, the nature of the employment you allude to; but I know you have that indulgence which is ever ready to excuse those deficiencies in others, which you, could never have experienced in yourself. Can you blame me for endeavouring, though late, to improve myself during those hours that I can steal from my daily duties?'

'You are certainly right,' replied Matilda, 'is there any thing in which you wish my assistance? if not, you must permit me to retire.'

'Will you really assist me?' said Miss Langrish with eagerness; 'and will you promise faithfully never to tell again; then there *is* a doubt which I will confide to you, and which has been for a long time an obstacle to my improvement; look at these three crabbed words,' she continued, pointing to a grammar that lay on the table. The words were Participle, Preterite, and Preposition. 'They are my constant torment, you see they all begin with the same letter, as if on purpose to puzzle people. Yet I should think there must be some difference between them. Can you explain it to me more clearly?'

Matilda hesitated a moment, hardly believing the request could be seriously made, but on its being repeated, with earnestness, she complied; endeavouring to make herself understood by the choice of the clearest terms she could select.

'Now that was very prettily said, my dear young lady,' cried Miss Langrish, 'and if you would favor me with the same explanation once more, I am sure I could retain it.'

Ever ready to oblige, Matilda consented. When she had concluded, her companion declared if Miss Melbourne would allow her to trespass so much upon her kindness, she felt herself assured that the third time she should understand the distinction completely. To this Matilda agreed.

'Well Miss Melbourne,' said the young / lady, gazing on her with an expression of unfeigned, and hopeless admiration, 'you are very happy, in that clearness of intellect, which enables you to comprehend these things. For my part they quite go beyond me: but for God's sake don't tell Lady Torrendale, and I am sure she will not find me out. You know it is not intended I should teach without the book, and with the book in my hand I do as well as another.'

Rather amused than burthened by this strange confidence, Matilda found, in the preceding scene, sufficient matter for wonder and reflection – She would have been still more surprised, if she had heard, that Lady Torrendale, too indolent to examine and enquire herself, and too vain to refer to the opinion and judgement of another, had at once accepted Miss Langrish at the hands of her intimate friend Mrs. Murray; who did not think it necessary to mention she was the daughter of a favorite servant. That, with hardly any other advantages of education, she had been instructed in music; a talent in which her voice and ear qualified her to excel, with a view to produce her acquirements on the stage. That her deficiency in genius, and in that most powerful apologist for the want of it, beauty, making her prospect of success more than dubious, she had adopted the idea of applying the only accomplishment she possessed to the purpose of private tuition; but Mrs. Murray, knowing her noble friend was at this time in want of an instructress for her daughter, and thinking such a situation still more eligible for her *protegée* had assisted her with her warmest recommendation, and thus transformed an indifferent music-mistress into a very bad governess. /

CHAPTER VI.

– Avea
Bionde le chiome, oscuro il ciglio. i labbri
Vermigli sì: un arossir frequente.

***** Metastasio.[29]

Bruno sei tu, ma bella
Quel vergine vïola; e del tuo vago
Sembriante io sì máppago.

Tasso.[30]

L'amitie' disparait où légalité cesse.[31] Matilda had reason soon to acknowledge the truth of this remark. There was too little real sympathy between the feelings of a coquette and fine lady of eight-and-thirty, and an innocent, unconscious charmer of eighteen, to allow the name of friendship to be given to their now habitual inter-course. With the young ladies whom she met occasionally at the house, she found it equally difficult to form a pleasing intimacy. In default of the *fashionables* to whom Lord Torrendale had, in a manner, forbidden the house, her Ladyship was obliged to content herself with a set of second-rate, well-meaning damsels (the best the country afforded) who found no other consolation for their own mediocrity, than in setting themselves violently against every thing that presumed to rise, though in the small-est degree, above their most moderate standard of excellence. The dazzling effect produced by Matilda's appearance among them was over; and now, one ventured to hint a fault; another, to whisper a mistake, secure of its being received, if not with an approving smile, at least without any violent expression of indignation on the part of the Countess. Of such cabals Matilda felt the oppressive influence, without being able exactly to define in what it consisted.

Conscious of no intentional impropriety, she had entered life, expecting to find, in society, that openness, that mutual confidence and simplicity, which form the charm of domestic intercourse. To keep a constant / guard upon her looks and words, to check the exalted sentiment, to curb the spontaneous burst of feeling, lest it should encounter the cold sneer, or suppressed smile, with which it was sure to be received by the well-bred circle, was most painful to her. The desire to please, with which she had at first been animated, was fast changing into solicitude to avoid censure: and her mind, in acquiring firmness and experience, was in danger of losing some of its most touching charms and graces. The country that is put under a state of defence, must submit to see some of its natural beauties defaced, and its finest edifices destroyed, by those very precautions which are taken to secure the safety of the whole.

A circumstance in which the Countess preferred applying to Matilda, to having another, less indulgent, the witness of her embarrassment, recalled her from her temporary estrangement. One day in talking over her plans for the morning, she said she should alter the course of her usual airing, having some purchases to make, and a visit to pay in the neighbouring town. 'You did not know, perhaps,' (she observed archly smiling) 'that I had connexions there to keep up; but I assure you I have more acquaintances than you dream of – or than I wish for.' In a lower tone the sentence was concluded.

They drove up straight to a handsome brick-built house, which appeared to belong to a person of considerable consequence in the town. Lady Torrendale pulled the check, and enquired if Mrs. Stockwell was at home. Being answered, by a powdered footman, in the negative, 'never mind that,' exclaimed her Ladyship; and springing from the carriage, she desired Matilda also to alight. They passed into a very elegant parlour; and the Countess ordering the housekeeper to be called up, asked her, with the air of a person enquiring into the state of the larder of an Inn, if there were nothing to eat in the house.

'Your mistress has gone out,' said she, 'but she cannot have left it unprovided – Let's see your bill of fare.' /

The obsequious gentlewoman seemed too well used to such arbitrary mandates to be surprised by them, and quickly obeyed, by serving up an elegant collation. Her Ladyship, after she had partaken of it with much apparent appetite, turned to Matilda, and said, in a laughing tone, 'You think me a strange mad creature; but I know what I do, and where I do it –,' she leant over to finish in a whisper the last words. Then, flinging herself on a sopha, she exclaimed fretfully, 'very odd this creature don't come home – I have but half an hour (looking at her watch) to stay – she should not have gone out.'

'She did not know, perhaps, she was to except the honor of your Ladyship's company.'

'She did not know it – but every fine day she knew it was – possible, and therefore it was her duty to wait for me.'

Having pronounced, with a conclusive nod, this decision, which Matilda (being unacquainted with the merits of the cause) did not attempt to controvert, the Lady amused herself for some time in silence with her own reflections, till they were suddenly interrupted by the return of the mistress of the house. Running up to her with all the demonstrations of the most cordial friendship, Lady Torrendale advanced to Mrs. Stockwell with open arms, passed her pretty head across her shoulder, and continued for some moments in that attitude, in a long, whispering embrace – Their harmony, however, was near having been disturbed by an unfortunate error.

Mrs. Stockwell, after properly expressing the delight she felt at seeing her dear Countess, added, as she turned to Matilda, 'and this, Mem, I suppose is your Ladyship's eldest daughter.'

'You remind me of my error' (said Lady Torrendale, drawing up with some disdain) 'in not introducing Miss Melbourne before – Yet I should have hardly imagined you could have mistaken her for Emily.'

'Bless me, true! what a clumsy creature I was to do so. I that is so *intimate* too with your Ladyship' continued Mrs. Stockwell, in a kind of coaxing tone. 'How could I think you had a daughter so old, / when I know Lady Emily is not more than thirteen.'

'Twelve' said Lady Torrendale.

Mrs. Stockwell, by redoubling the most fawning servility, endeavoured to efface the impression her error had unluckily made; but she found it was not so easy to remove the cloud that had gathered on the brow of the Countess. On Matilda's being introduced to her, she presented, in return, a young lady who accompanied her, and whom Lady Torrendale seemed to have known before: 'I hope my neice, Miss Ferrars, will be great friends, Mem, with Miss Melbourne,' she said.

The young lady bowed in silence to Matilda, and then took her station as close to her aunt as possible. If the countenance be a true index to the mind, few could boast of one more interesting. It was clear, open, and ingenuous, yet had a depth and penetration very uncommon in early youth; it was like the calm bosom of some rich and lovely stream, the surface of which is smooth and beautiful, but which betrays, through its crystal medium, that treasures more rare and precious are below. Such at least was the language of a pair of the finest dark eyes in the world, which a quantity of ringlets, almost flaxen, contrasting with a complexion smooth, delicate, but of a clear brown, rendered still more singularly impressive and striking. Her figure was tall, slender, and finely formed; and if her features had nothing in them particularly to attract attention, still, a general elegance of contour made the best apology for the absence of positive beauty.

While Matilda was endeavouring, but in vain, to draw this young lady a little into conversation, Mrs. Stockwell was, on her part, busily employed in paying her compliments to the Countess: and was so delighted, so overwhelmed, with the honor of her visit, that she found it perfectly impossible to divide her attentions, at the same time that she thought it her duty to notice Miss Melbourne, as the friend of Lady Torrendale.

The latter, who had not forgiven her unlucky mistake respecting the age of Lady Emily, delighted in pointing out to Matilda / the awkward attempts she made to that purpose, by a stolen look, which, often put her gravity to the utmost proof. Mrs. Stockwell had been lately at Cheltenham, and Lady Torrendale asked her if there was much company when she was there.

'O no your Ladyship – stay, I'll tell you who there was – dear me, I'm so bad at recollecting people's names, when they have not some sort of a title before them. All I can assure your Ladyship is, they was a set of despisable creeters, as seemed people of no account, or edication whatever. Bell and I, and your son Captain Fitzroy, made one party all the time we staid – as to the rest – Pray Miss Melbourne do you read much?' Before Matilda had time to reply to this abrupt question, which Mrs. Stockwell, from the character she had heard of her, thought she had addressed with the discrimination and appropriateness of an experienced Minister at a Levee, the lady had turned again to the Countess with a continuation of her account of Captain Fitzroy.

'Has not he written your Ladyship word the Cheltenham waters did him all the good in the world? When he first drove Bell in his tandem there, he looked so pale, and so pensive like – it was plain to be seen the wars had taken away all his fine complexion, and I declare I could not help piping to think –' a pause, from some unknown reason, unless it was an imperceptible hint from the young lady who sat next her, reminded the company that a slight error of expression had been committed – but Mrs. Stockwell recovering from this momentary check continued – 'When I used to play cards at their parties and dances, (take care of Miss Melbourne, Bell, my love) – and he used to lean over the back of my chair in his way, for he was too ill to dance, a lady at the table whispered to me one night, "I can't mind my game for the countenance of that young Officer; it is so *interesting*". And to be sure it *was interesting:* so like your Ladyship's, and yet so marble pale – which his black eye-brows, and whiskers, don't you call them, strait things on the upper lip.' /

'Very like my Ladyship,' interrupted Lady Torrendale, with a toss of her head and half laughing; while Mrs. Stockwell made a sudden digression from the dark whiskers, again to address Matilda, with 'pray Mem don't you find it very lonesome at the Rocks?'

'No Madam,' said Matilda, a little provoked, 'I never am so happy as when I am there.'

'True, I had forgot,' resumed Mrs. Stockwell, in a sentimental tone; 'As the Poet says, *One is never so much alone as in a croud.*[32] – Reading is every thing as I take it, for my part I doat upon study. When Captain Fitzroy used to get the novels for Bell at the Library – (addressing Lady Torrendale) by the bye Mem (turning again to Matilda) could you have imagined, to look at this lady, that she could be the mother of a son old enough to be the darling of all the Cheltenham Belles?'

'No, indeed, and I hate to think of it,' cried the Countess, interrupting her.

'Apropos,' resumed Mrs. Stockwell, with an air of greater familiarity than she had yet assumed, 'when are we to see our dear little Fitzroy?'

'Captain Fitzroy' replied Lady Torrendale, rather haughtily, 'gives us hopes of seeing him towards the latter end of this month; and then' (she continued in a lower and more subdued tone) 'he will settle every thing.'

'Ah, Lady Torrendale, so you writ me when you was at Rose-villa, and yet nothing was done.'

'Rose-villa was sold, and I was carried off suddenly from it – so I had not time to give you a meeting there, or –'

'You were carried off suddenly,' (said Mrs. Stockwell in a tone of sympathising condolence) 'and I am sure I would be the last person in the world to add to your Ladyship's inconveniences, but' – Here another long whispering conversation ensued; and Matilda being left entirely to herself again, attempted to engage the attention of the young lady by some general observations; to which she replied, with politeness indeed, but as concisely as possible: and then sunk / again into silence: yet, to judge by the intelligence and vivacity of the eyes, that spoke through those long, dark, silken lashes, Miss Ferrars was far, indeed, from being to be ranked with that class so admirably denominated by Madame d'Arblay,[33] the 'Sullens' – Forced to give up the idea of entering into conversation with this young lady, Miss Melbourne was obliged to content herself with such fragments of Lady Torrendale and Mrs. Stockwell's discourse, as happened to reach her ear; but it was carried on in so low a key, that she could distinguish little more than the words, Duke, Earl, Countess, General, Admiral, Court, and Park, frequently repeated; particularly on the side of the lady of the house; whose appearance did not quite justify her evident familiarity with such exalted subjects. Her eyes were always what first struck the observation of a stranger; there was a deceitfulness, a *feline* watchfulness in their slow, treacherous roll, which warred most completely with the affectation of sensibility she tried to throw into them; and which would have inspired a feeling resembling terror, if an expression of meanness, that mingled with it, had not changed it to contempt. For the rest, her short squat figure made the most perfect contrast to the airy elegant form of Lady Torrendale: her features were bad, her complexion coarse, and her whole appearance and contour sufficiently indicative of vulgarity.

At length, Lady Torrendale, suddenly appearing to recollect herself, started up, saying, 'I must not let this foolish little affair make me forget the principal object of my visit, which was to secure your company my dear Mrs. Stockwell, and that of Miss Ferrars, (bowing to the young lady who stood beside her) for to-morrow, at Woodlands.'

Mrs. Stockwell looked confounded – 'Positively no, my dear lady, it can't be tomorrow; for my companion, Miss Hautenville, (and I never goes any where without my companion) is engaged on a dinner party at Farley, and the next day she wants the carriage to go to her friend Lady Bunbury's, and the next she has planned a little, 'excrescence' / to Stanmore vicarage; a relation of her's having married Dr. Hartley, the gentleman, as was "indited" into that living after the death of Dr. Waring, the late "Incumbrance."

Lady Torrendale gave Matilda one of her wicked conscious glances; and she, to avoid noticing it, turned her eyes towards Miss Ferrars.

That young lady had often before given symptoms of fretful uneasiness; but now, her large dark eyes were cast upon the ground, as if she could wish to forget the presence of all around her, and her cheeks glowed like crimson. 'You teach me something new every time I visit you,' cried the lively Countess.

'I thought the very words "my companion," implied a person whose company I was to command; but I find that in Mrs. Stockwell's dictionary it means "any one's companion but one's own." 'Oh, you know, I cannot contradict her,' resumed the good lady, with great gravity, 'for she is of a very good family, and had very good prospects, 'till she was unfortunately reduced, and that – and she never lived but with very high people; Lady Bunbury – and the great Miss Mountain, 'till she "done" me[a] the honor to come "and stay with me"'

'Then you certainly do right, my dear Mrs. Stockwell, to make her descent from the "Mountain," as easy as possible,' resumed Lady Torrendale laughing.

'But after that little "excrescence," you mentioned, if Miss Hautenville should happen to be disengaged, may I hope for the pleasure of *her* company, *with* yours and Miss Ferrars.' The affair being thus adjusted, her Ladyship and Miss Melbourne, soon after, took leave: and the former was hardly well-seated in the carriage, when she burst into a fit of painfully suspended laughter, in which she indulged both 'loud and long.' Young as she was, and new to the world, Matilda could not avoid suspecting that her noble friend endeavoured to hide, under the appearance of boisterous mirth, a degree of shame and uneasiness she could not repress, at having made her the / witness of an intimacy so disproportionate. Why she had voluntarily submitted to this mortifica-tion, she was unable to guess; but that it was in order to gain some favourite point, she was by this time, too intimate with Lady Torrendale to doubt for a moment.

'You must let me go on,' said her Ladyship, after she had indulged for a few moments in this extravagant humour – 'what mortal gravity could sustain what I have endured this half hour? but it was for your sake, Matilda,' she continued, with a condescending nod. 'I wished to introduce you to that sweet girl, Arbella Ferrars, and you shall meet her again on Thursday; she is amiable, though an heiress – has been very genteelly brought up, though early left an orphan under the care of her aunt; and can be very agreeable, though not quite so communicative as the said Aunt Stockwell. There, have I not drawn you a very good impromptu character, made up of opposites, like a French *Portrait*?'

Matilda well knew that all this rattle was only meant, like the action and volubility of a slight-of-hand man, to turn her attention from the simple fact, that Lady Torren-dale wished her company on the day the Stockwells were expected, to take off from herself part of the weight of a kind of duty, which her Ladyship always denominated a 'bore,' or, in her still more favorite phrase, a '*Corvée*.'[34]

Appreciating her Ladyship's disinterested kindness, therefore, at just as much as it deserved, she did not on that account, the less readily accept her offer, which the desire she had to be farther acquainted with the amiable, though reserved Arbella, rendered peculiarly agreeable. Triumphant, at having gained her point, Lady Torren-dale announced it at dinner, when, mentioning her visit, 'we shall have a beau for Matilda, I hope,' (she continued) 'for I have made it a point with Mrs. Stockwell that her son should join the party if he should arrive in time from Worcestershire, whence he is daily expected, to spend the Christmas holidays. What say you child to the rich Sam Stockwell? I assure you he is mama's only pet, and is now by the / death of his father, master of a very large fortune, which those eyes can, if you please, assuredly make your own, instead of the fair, or, I should rather say, the brown Arbella's.'

Matilda, in order to parry this raillery, took the first opportunity to make some enquiry respecting Mrs. Stockwell and her family.

'She is a very good woman,' observed Lord Torrendale, drily. 'Her mother sold apples.'

'Oh you ill-natured creature!' cried the Countess, putting her hand upon his mouth. 'You do not mention that her husband, (which is Arbella's side of the family, by-the-bye,) was a very respectable man, a blanket merchant, or a carpet merchant: or, I protest I don't know exactly what, and that though she confesses she was raised by marriage a little above her actual situation, she says her grand-father was a general, and her great-grand father an archbishop. "Let Bourbon or Nassau count higher."'[35]

'Lady Torrendale, you know that is one of poor Mrs. Stockwell's manias. Enquire a little farther, and she will probably make out the reigning family allied to her own.

How you first became acquainted with the Scythian, or how you can endure her, it passes my penetration to discover.'

'Oh, *that* you must ask Spencer,' replied her Ladyship, with a mysterious smile. Then turning suddenly to Matilda, 'did she not launch out finely in his praise to day?' she said, 'It was little, compared to what Spencer Fitzroy deserves,' she added, in a more tender tone. 'He is a young man, in this age, I believe, seldom equalled.' At first, Miss Melbourne was not aware that Lady Torrendale, alluded to her son Captain Fitzroy; and even when she had discovered her friend's meaning, she did not immediately reply, owing to a slight confusion she felt at so pointed a reference.

'Do you not know who I am speaking of? Have you not heard of him before?' continued her Ladyship impatiently.

'Excuse me, Madam, I have often heard Lady Emily speak of her brother.' /

'Oh! by *her brother*, Emily always means, *that* Strathallan – he is the chit's brother *par excellence*. Yet Spencer excels him as much as –. Well we expect him here soon, and then you shall judge for yourself.' Thinking it necessary at length to finish this '*aside*' conversation, the Countess said aloud, with her usual attention to truth, 'I have been recommending to Matilda seriously to think of the merits of Sam Stockwell. Like the dear father, he deals a little in carpetry, or *Marqueterie*, or whatever it is, and he jobs in the stocks; and, in short, does every thing that turns money; so she *shall* have him in spite of your uncivil insinuations, you wicked aristocratic man!'

CHAPTER VII.

–, From worldly guile,
From Folly's mask, from Cunning's wile,
Keep thy generous bosom free,
And cherish sweet Simplicity.

'Tis Wisdom's guard, 'tis Virtue's friend,
On it a thousand goods attend,
A thousand goods in store for thee,
Thou favorite of Simplicity.[36]

ON the day appointed, at exactly half-past six, arrived at Woodlands, Miss Hautenville 'and suite,' consisting of Mrs. Stockwell, her niece, Miss Ferrars, and her son Mr. Samuel Stockwell. The moment the carriage was seen driving up the avenue – Lady Torrendale, who had been the whole morning doing nothing, said to Matilda, 'now I must run and dress myself for these good folks; and do you entertain them 'till I / return; – how kind it was of you to come so early!' Scarcely had her Ladyship escaped, when in bustled Mrs. Stockwell, almost 'standing on end' with finery. She was followed by Arbella, drest with a united richness and elegance well suited to her youth, her figure, and pretensions: while Miss Hautenville, who was enabled, by the generosity of her friend, to make a display of almost equal expence, if not equal taste, seemed by her air to think she did her too much honor in accepting her benefits. This lady was to be introduced to Matilda, as well as Mr. Stockwell, an ugly, conceited young man, with the pride of wealth written on every feature. This business over, the next great difficulty was to get Mrs. Stockwell, and consequently the rest of the company, seated. Her town vulgarity, transplanted into the country, had flourished into a kind of double blossom, of superfluous politeness, which was sometimes rather troublesome. It was to be feared, that neither persuasion nor threats could shake her unalterable determination to remain next the door.

'No, Mem, I thank ye, I set very well here,' she obstinately replied to every endeavour to make her go up higher; and would thus have reduced the two ladies with her, to the alternative of committing the dreadful indecorum of taking place above her, or staying outside the room, had not Matilda 'with sweet violence,' at length almost compelled her to go to her only proper seat.

Sam Stockwell, to mark that he had been hurried, and was just arrived, had thought proper to come in boots, which did not augment the natural gentility of his appearance. Displaying the airs, without the elegance, of a fashionable lounger – he, with dull, sullen coldness, which he mistook for languid ease, sauntered about the room in silence, often looking around him with fretful discontent, or only testifying his existence by a yawn.

The company at length being seated, the first quarter of an hour was employed by Mrs. Stockwell in apologies, which she might have perceived, by some circumstances, were very unnecessary, for the lateness of her arrival. / Miss Hautenville, she said, had wanted the 'Brush,' and pair, that morning, to visit a friend, who had detained her rather longer than she expected; and to be sure, if it was a brush and four, Miss Hautenville had a right to be served first.

The lady, in reply, looking at her with an air of sovereign contempt, said 'she was sure nobody could complain, with less reason, than Mrs. Stockwell, of not being indulged in the use of her carriage. That, for her part, she hardly ever took it; and that there was not a person in the world, she believed, whose wishes and convenience were less considered than hers'.

Her wealthy friend humbly recanting what she had before advanced, gave a full assent to all that was asserted by the vain and assuming companion.

Designed, originally, to move in the humblest sphere, Mrs. Stockwell, after a fortunate marriage with a wealthy tradesman, found her happiness still incomplete, because, that very marriage removed her from the scene of her earlier connexions, to whom she was desirous of displaying her newly acquired opulence and finery. Immediately on finding herself a widow, she laid out part of her very ample settlement in the purchase of a handsome house in her favourite neighbourhood; and soon after prevailed on a lady to take up her abode with her, whose advantages of birth and education, would, she thought, atone for any deficiencies in her own. Miss Hautenville, who had never been handsome, and was now no longer young; her temper soured by the disappointment of her early expectations, and her taste refined by the long habit of company rather above her, proved a most troublesome household divinity; and after making some vain attempts on the heart of Mr. Stockwell, revenged herself by behaving with the most constant and marked impertinence to his mother, and to Miss Ferrars, whom she considered, and not without reason, as, in part, the cause of her failure. This young lady, whose mother was sister to the late Mr. Stockwell, had been left, on the death of her parents, under his guardianship; a trust which he, from the undeserved / affection and confidence he reposed in his wife, made over to her, at his decease, with a clause in his will, that his niece should reside with her, till she became of age, while the management of her pecuniary affairs devolved, till that period, upon his son, Mr. Samuel Stockwell. This young man, though still possessed of a considerable interest in his father's carpet manufactory, at Kidderminster, did not think so close an attention to business either necessary or becoming, and rather preferred acting the part of a gentleman at large at his mother's, who encouraged his frequent absences from his settled abode. If she had ever ventured to form a plan, it was that of securing Arbella's fortune, to her son, by marriage; she therefore wisely consoled herself by observing 'that when Sam seemed to be most neglecting his interest, he was in reality following it up to the greatest advantage.' Matilda was glad when the entrance of some more company relieved her from the task of entertaining this ill-assorted group.

After dinner, the Countess, who had heard that Miss Hautenville made some pretentions to literature, and hated her for it, whispered to her young friend, 'have you no new music my dear; play, sing, do any thing that may hinder the wise lady from talking. I hate those sort of women. I don't know what to do with them, unless I mortify them.'

Matilda, unwilling to comply with a request for which such a motive was avowed, yet thought it better to consent, than to resist the reiterated entreaties of every one present. While she charmed, and Miss Langrish astonished, their little auditory, by the talent they displayed, Miss Hautenville, seated apart from the rest of the group, appeared perfectly absorbed in looking over a book of classical drawings, she had probably seen a hundred times before; but which, if one might judge by the noise and pertinacity with which she hastily turned over the rustling leaves, she found at this moment particularly interesting. With eyes obstinately rivetted to the book, she sat the picture of malice and discontent, till her features, naturally sharp, absolutely assumed the sharpness of a well-mended / pen. Her vexation nearly arose to a crisis, when Lady Torrendale, determined that no pause should be left for conversation, proposed looking over Emily's port-folio of drawings, as soon as the music was over: but scarcely were they produced, when her lively Ladyship joyfully exclaimed, 'Oh! here come the gentlemen at last, just in time to save us from hanging!' – 'And drawing,' Miss Hautenville muttered, finishing the sentence for her more truly.

These were some neighbouring squires whom Lord Torrendale had invited; and who, after coffee, again got together into a knot, which Sam Stockwell, rather than approach the ladies, was willing to join.

One or two of the youngest of the party, attracted by the 'soft and shaded eyes' of Arbella, had endeavoured to engage her attention; but with the same ill-success Matilda had experienced. In modest silence, she had seated herself at one end of a sofa, below every other woman, and seemed to have no wish but to remain unnoticed; yet in her the charms of countenance, of form, and air

'Et les graces encore plus belles que la beauté,'[37]

pleaded so strongly, that she pleased without speaking, and all the gentlemen, at least, were unanimous in the opinion, though they knew not exactly what made them form it, that she certainly was agreeable. On her cousin, Sam Stockwell, the judgment they pronounced was not so favourable. He was generally voted to be a 'stupid, conceited prig;' and he, surprised to find himself in a society where his money did not make him of consequence, returned their dislike with interest.

Their conversation, which chiefly turned upon country matters, was to him nearly unintelligible. The birth and breeding of a pointer, and the life and death of a pheasant or a hare, were equally subjects of which his habits made him an indifferent judge. Hardly knowing what it was to enjoy the pleasure of a day's shooting, the varied tale of each triumphant sportsman was as uninteresting to / him, as the language in which it was conveyed was new. The words 'Pop!' and 'Bang!' carried with them no gladness to his heart; neither did it beat with anxiety at stories of the invasion of manorial rights, by tremendous captains or riotous esquires. He was not of that consequence in the county to make his opinion a reference, whether Lord P –, or Lord C –, had the greatest influence in the borough of Addleham, or whether the present sheriff was likely to be as much respected as his predecessor. While these discussions were going on, he sat looking as discontented as the united powers of mortified pride and ill-humour could make him, till, at last, abruptly rising, he strolled towards his cousin Arbella, and seemed going to place himself next her as a matter of right, when she, with a 'withering look,' made him step some paces back; and Miss Hautenville, spinning the little gentleman round with an arbitrary twirl, sent him over, with the impetus of a te-totum, to Miss Langrish; at the same time whispering him, that 'if he knew any thing of life, he would perceive it was one of the young ladies of the house he ought to entertain.'

Sam looked at the lady assigned to him, and then – very deliberately walked to the window.

Miss Hautenville having now disposed of the company to her own satisfaction, began the design she had long meditated upon Matilda; which was to astonish her by bursting upon her at once in her literary character. It was one which she had acquired with some difficulty; for, not being possessed of genius, either active or passive, it had appeared at first, a hopeless attempt. A fund of vanity compensated for these deficiencies: and, being sprung from a family which had made some figure in the world of letters, and having made her entrance into life in a literary circle, she had set it down as a maxim, that a portion of the same ability her ancestors so eminently possessed, was hers, by hereditary and indefeasible right. She soon discovered, that if she could not talk, she could listen, and that many had made a reputation by listening alone. Hence when two wise gentlemen / were engaged in a learned dispute, or one still wiser gentleman favored the company with a solo, in the form of a dissertation, it was her custom to sit with her head inclined on one side, and her eyes raised up, in an attitude of admiring attention, that often gained her the name of a most 'sensible, modest, discriminating young woman;' till, emboldened with success, she was not content with solitary adoration, but ventured to arraign all those as rebels to her literary tribunal, who, possessed of more independance, vivacity, good taste, or good sense, refused to hang their heads on one side, turn up their eyes, listen, and admire, in token of similar devotion.

Having thus gained over the elder and graver on her side, her name so far intimidated the younger fry of authors and poetasters, that she was sure of obtaining from them attention and respect; and often levied on them contributions of unpublished essays, and suppressed copies of verses, which she afterwards passed off as her own.

But with Matilda, the few commonplaces with which she had armed herself, as quite sufficient to silence a young lady, of whose mental acquirements, from the extreme beauty and modesty of her very youthful appearance, she had augured but unfavourably, were soon found to be worse than useless; and the failure was the more perfect, as Matilda, in whose character the absence of pretension formed the principal charm, never once, in their conversation, suspected her design.

Miss Hautenville, like an experienced general, having chosen an advantageous post, by placing herself on an Ottoman next Miss Melbourne, who was flanked on the other side by Arbella, to secure her from intruding beaux, began a disquisition equally novel and edifying, on the smoothness of Pope, and the fire of Dryden.

'This, if not very new, (thought the innocent Matilda,) is very good, and shews at least a mind desirous of improvement.' So after correcting a few mistakes made by the learned lady, respecting translations and originals, she continued the conversation, which / soon turned upon style in general, and Miss Hautenville made haste to inform her, (as she truly might, from the most indubitable authority,) that 'those who would wish to attain a pure English style, should give their nights and days to the volumes of Addison.'

On Matilda modestly venturing to give an opinion in a point of criticism 'my dear madam,' said Miss Hautenville, 'read Burke, Beattie, Blair, Johnson, Lord Kaimes, Alison, and Knight, on the principles of taste.[38] They have said all that ever was, or ever can be, advanced upon the subject.' A remark so conclusive, effectually prevented any farther debate; till, happening to observe the *Lettere d'una Peruviana* upon a table, Miss Hautenville renewed the conversation, saying, 'you read Italian, Miss Melbourne, I presume.'[39]

'A little; but I have not read that book, either in Italian or French.'

'Oh! then you have had a great loss!' exclaimed Miss Hautenville enthusiastically. '*Aza, mon cher Aza!*'

It must be remembered, that this lady had had the prudent foresight to assure herself of Matilda's ignorance of the work, before she ventured even this slight and safe quotation; for had Miss Melbourne read enough of it to have been able to reply by a single observation, she would have found that '*Aza, mon cher Aza!*' was the extent of her companion's knowledge. For every author, whether foreign or English, Miss Hautenville had an appropriate and distinguishing epithet always ready.

Matilda, who was a passionate admirer of nature, mentioned with enthusiasm the works of St. Pierre.

'The pathetic St. Pierre,' repeated Miss Hautenville, with a look of intelligence, and then turned to another subject; denominating different authors as they occurred; 'the sublime Corneille, the classic Fenelon, the refined Florian;'[40] but, beyond these general expressions of admiration, she was rather shy of giving instances in which they appeared to her most sublime, classic, or refined. Several times, during these elevated / and interesting discussions, the silent young lady, looking through her fair locks, with an expression which it was not very easy to understand, appeared as if on the point of making some observation which she as suddenly checked; and cast her eyes on the ground. She declined cards; and by the placid smile on her countenance, appeared satisfied with her unpretending situation; while to Miss Hautenville's repeated sarcasms on her taciturnity she only replied, with a modesty which appeared to Matilda a little assumed, 'Oh, Madam, I do not aspire to what is beyond my reach.' 'Aspiring to what is beyond their reach, is not confined to those who wish to shine on literary topics;' resumed the first lady. 'Whether a woman neglects her appearance, to study a science she can never attain, or a plain worthy lover, for the chance of being noticed by a man of fashion, who contemns her, she equally leaves a solid good, to grasp at a phantom which is beyond her.'

The approach of Lady Torrendale, who at this moment had risen from cards, fortunately put an end to this *sparring* kind of conversation, which had begun to be very disagreeable to Matilda. Miss Hautenville, finding this young lady far surpassed her in information and powers of expression, had suddenly changed her former contempt for her abilities, into that last resource of expiring vanity, the most excessive admiration of them. To conclude that the talent and knowledge which eclipsed her own, must be great indeed, was some consolation. We do not like our neighbour's house should out-top ours; but we cannot feel envy at the superior height of a church or palace. She expressed her admiration in the warmest terms to Lady Torrendale.

' 'Tis a little prodigy, madam,' said she; 'I have had the pleasure of a long conversation with her, and have found her perfectly versed in all literature, ancient and modern.'

'Indeed!' cried her Ladyship, indolently stretching, 'Matilda child, why did you never tell me you were versed in all literature ancient and modern?' /

Miss Melbourne blushed deeply at this sudden appeal, but before she could frame a reply, Miss Hautenville had resumed.

'Never but in the delightful conversaziones at Lady Lyndhurst's, did I meet with such taste, such knowledge – at Lady Lyndhurst's where the brilliant Sappho, the divine Alcæus –.'

'Alcæus and Sappho! I think I have heard of them,' exclaimed Lady Torrendale; 'who are they? I know Lady Lyndhurst patronizes them.'

'Mr. Spring; or Alcæus, as he is called in that circle,' resumed Miss Hautenville, 'is really the most promising young Poet of his time. His Ode to a Grasshopper, under that signature, would be positively the finest thing that ever was seen; if his Ode to the Gossamer, which appeared the next month, had not as far transcended even the promises that his earlier production had given.'

'Oh, Mem,' interrupted Mrs. Stockwell, 'you may take Miss Hautenville's word for Mr. Spring's abilities. "Set a thief to catch a thief." You know she is well read; but you have no notion what a famous good hand she is herself at poetry writing. Now my Grandfather who was a judge of them sort of things –.'

'My dear Mrs. Stockwell,' cried Miss Hautenville, with a look which said 'I will be obeyed,' and, turning the discourse quickly to Miss Swanley, the literary lady continued, 'What she wants in solid acquirement, she makes up in shewy talent. To hear her recite Collins's Ode, is the divinest thing.[41] Two candles are set upon a table; a curtain draws up, and discovers the Derbyshire Sappho in the costume of a Muse: a flourish of flutes, or some other soft music, precedes the commencement of the poem, a prelude is played, there is a dead silence, and Sappho begins.'

'La! now,' cried Mrs. Stockwell, 'I remember it was just so, when I were at the Ditchess of Albemarle's'.

A second exclamation of 'Dear Madam, you have no idea of what we are talking about,' from the arbitrary companion, at / length effectually checked the good lady's spirit of observation; and Lady Torrendale, whose indolent curiosity was at length a little roused, deigned to observe, 'I should like to hear Sappho repeat the Ode to the Passions; could not one get her from Lady Lyndhurst's?'

'Certainly, if – '

'Oh, I understand what you mean; and it is as you suspect – there has been a sort of coolness about that house you know,' turning to Matilda. 'Or rather, I believe, you do *not* know; but the truth is, (in a lower key) I was sorry to part with Rose-villa at that time.'

'I am sure,' said Miss Hautenville, 'if there should be any misunderstanding between your Ladyship, and Lady Lyndhurst, I should be most happy to be the means. – '

'Not absolutely a misunderstanding,' interrupted the Countess, 'but since she returned to the Country, there has been some nonsense about a visit; I did not call on her, or she did not call on me, I protest I forget which; so that she may have thought something – and I confess I *do* feel a little awkward. Those wise ladies are such stiff, unpleasant – I beg your pardon, Miss Hautenville, but, I assure you I do not reckon you a wise Lady,' she concluded; with a most gracious nod.

Miss Hautenville, smothering, or rather postponing her resentment, recollected the consequence she would add to herself if she could forward the plan she had at first hinted, and returned the obliging compliment by a curtesy; while the two ladies looked at each other, with an expression of countenance which seemed to say, they fully appreciated the value of the polite offers, that could on either side be made.

'I invest you, my dear Miss Hautenville,' said the Countess, gaily resuming the discourse, 'with full and unlimited powers to treat on that important subject: and, when it is finally adjusted, we will have Lady Lyndhurst, and her two charming little cygnets, and all the other clever people we can collect. Miss Mountain is coming down to spend some time with me, and she delights / in such parties. A conversazione is positively the very thing I want to waken me, for I am literally fatigued to death, (she concluded, looking round on the company) with every thing in the way of amusement, I have yet tried. Lord Torrendale, would you not be delighted with a conversazione?'

'You know my opinion, Lady Torrendale, of those sort of parties.'

The lively Countess flirted her fan at him, but was obliged to be content with this oracular answer.

'When we meet, we will begin, if you please, Madam,' said Miss Hantenville (affecting already to regulate the order of the evening's amusements) 'with Miss Swanley's charming recitation: and then, (pretending modestly to hesitate) there is a little Treatise I have attempted on the revival of the Italian Drama, which I shall submit to your Ladyship's inspection. Have you not read it, Miss Ferrars?' (formally addressing Arbella.)

'*Et vous Madame?*' demanded the young lady; wittily adapting to this literary pretender, the well known answer of Piron, to the French Prelate, on his asking the poet a similar question, respecting one of his own Pastoral Letters.[42]

The aptness and suddenness of the retort, by which Miss Ferrars only revenged herself for the repeated and cruel sarcasms she had endured in silence through the evening, struck every one with surprise. The perfect reserve she had till this moment kept up, set off to still greater advantage, this sudden sally, and Arbella after several hours of apparent mortification, took leave with triumph and applause.

Lady Torrendale, after indulging in a hearty laugh, (her usual custom at the conclusion of a visit from the Stockwells) began rallying Matilda on the failure of her projected conquest. 'What think you of Sam Stockwell, Cherub? the bachelor would not bite, hey? (as an old quizzical acquaintance of mine used to say) Well, you must stay till Spencer and Strathallan return, they are men more in your style, particularly Spencer; but,' continued her Ladyship, without allowing / time for an answer, 'will not this literary party be delightful? And I shall have such pride in producing my little Matilda, who I am sure will as far surpass odious Lady Lyndhurst's fantastic Sappho, as she does poor, stiff, tiresome Miss Hautenville.'

To Matilda, who felt too easy in the possession, and too happy in the use of knowledge, to think of taking to herself any more merit from it, than from the enjoyment of health, spirits, or any other advantage of nature or fortune; the idea, that her acquisitions were intended to serve the purposes of vanity and display, and, in short, the whole system of 'producing' was perfectly new. She was, however, obliged to this lately adopted whim, which was the only thing that prevented her noble friend from resenting her involuntary treachery, in not having discovered to her that she was 'a wise lady,' before.

'How I long for Miss Mountain!' resumed the Countess, 'and, flattered with the idea of being a literary patroness, anticipated the glories of her Derbyshire night's entertainments, while Miss Melbourne only interrupted her to ask, who Miss Mountain was? 'In the first place, she is my daughter-in-law, that shall be. In the next, did you ever see Mr. H – 's statues with coloured eyes? no – *Tant pis pour vous, Mademoiselle;*[43] for if you had, you would have only to imagine one of those, of colossal dimensions, and Miss Mountain stands before you. But,' continued her Ladyship laughing, 'you do not tell me what you think of Mrs. Stockwell; she improves vastly upon acquaintance, does she not? Poor dear old soul, she is one example among a thousand, of the misery to which people expose themselves, who insist upon having every thing in a style above their pretensions. She is not only tormented with a fine companion, but has been successively plagued with fine governesses, fine masters, and fine servants. She insisted on Arbella's learning for a season, of Tramezzani, only because he taught Emily to sing. She would rather endure the greatest delays, inconveniences, or impertinences, than employ any other but the tradesmen of people of fashion, / though while they are working for Lady Amabel, or Lady Barbara, her own dress cap or her niece's ball shoes must be the sacrifice. She has a fine housekeeper at double the usual salary, who possesses no visible superiority, but that of having lived at the Duchess of Albemarle's, of whose four tables, and superb establishment, she takes care to remind poor Mrs. Stockwell once a day at least; and she keeps two ladies' maids for herself and Arbella, delicate sickly girls, who must not be annoyed with ringing the bell; and who seem engaged, less for the purpose of attending their respective mistresses, than for that of extolling, on every occasion, the superior elegance, taste, and fashion of their late ones, Lady Sophia, and Lady Anne. Then, is it not entertaining to see the good lady propose herself as a model to her niece, and at any active feat or lively sally of Arbella's, which it is impossible she should imitate, reproachfully exclaim, fie Niece! Did you ever see me do that? But, to ask you a much more important question: what do you seriously think of Arbella?'

'I think nothing,' said Matilda, turning on the Countess her intelligent eyes, 'or rather, I know not what to think.'

'Well, she is a charming girl, and shall come again very soon to visit you.'

'As your Ladyship pleases; but since you honored me so far as to ask my opinion, I confess I should be nearly as much entertained by a visit from the silent woman.'

'I thought she would strike you so; but Arbella Ferrars can talk upon occasion; and – good night, I'll leave you to find her out.'

'To find her out,' this was a phrase on which Matilda meditated as of dubious import. It long haunted her waking imagination; and, when she slept, her fancy still dwelt upon the dark-glancing eye, of the interesting, the singular Arbella. /

CHAPTER VIII.

– Many books
(Wise men have said,) are wearisome; who reads
Incessantly, and to his reading brings
Not spirit and judgment, equal or superior,
Uncertain and unsettled still remains:
Deep versed in books, and shallow in himself;
Crude or intoxicate, collecting toys
And trifles, for choice matter.[44]

THE arrival of the great Miss Mountain at Woodlands, enabled Matilda to convince herself, by actual observation, that the Countess had not exaggerated in the description she had given of her. Indeed, with Miss Mountain, the use of that figure in rhetoric was almost impossible. She was, herself, the very personification of Hyperbole. Her features, form, and mind, seemed all, from nature's hand, exaggerated. Her figure rose above the size of most men; and her carriage was lofty; but owed its dignity more to a certain squareness and undeviating erectness, than to the graceful easy line of real majesty. Her eyes which were large and very dark, gained much in animation, if not in fierceness, from the extreme vividness of her complexion; a vividness that excited, in most who saw her for the first time, the suspicion – more than the suspicion, of art.

Those who were anxious to defend Miss Mountain, alleged the purple hue which exercise, or cold was sure to give, as a proof that it was natural; but she had many enemies among the fair; and they used often to give a more satisfactory solution of the difficulty. 'There are so many different sorts of rouge,' Miss Langrish observed with a lisp. 'It is a pity some one does not tell poor Miss Mountain not always to chuse that which, in some lights, looks purple!' If Miss Mountain's person was striking, her manners / were no less remarkable. Of her it might be said, that she had the highest opinion of her own charms, without vanity; and of her rank and pretensions, without pride; for she exacted nothing – preserved always the same unruffled serenity of temper, whether allowed the first place, or not; and, so far from depreciating the merits of others, was always ready to join her tribute of admiration to the general voice. It must be observed, however, that with her own sex this condescension never led to familiarity, or friendship. On the contrary, she had something stiff and repulsive in her manner, that seemed doomed to keep them for ever at a distance; while the neighbouring beaux found all this frost melt away at their approach, when this ponderous formality was exchanged for the airy graces of coquetry, in the perplexing mazes of which the stately Sophia gambolled with all the ease and frolic sportiveness of an elephant.

To a character composed of such apparent contradictions, Matilda was some time in finding the clue. By repeated conversations with the Countess, she learnt a little more of Miss Mountain's early life. Her father, who had acquired a noble fortune as a wine-merchant in London, having determined, when rather advanced in years, to retire into the country, was looking out for an estate to buy, when he found that a property in Derbyshire, long in his family, was just going to the hammer: he became the purchaser, and shortly after allied himself to one of the most distinguished families in the county; and obtained at the same time, a young and amiable bride. Miss Bishop, the daughter of Sir Effingham and Lady Caroline Bishop, of Craig Castle; was induced to overlook the disparity of years, in consideration of the immense wealth offered to her acceptance by Mr. Mountain; but did not live long to enjoy the splendor it afforded. She died a few years after the birth of a daughter, who became by that means heiress to the whole of his immense property. Mr. Mountain was a good man, but he had his singularities. He would neither have a governess, a species of / inmate, which he always designated by the denomination of a domestic pest, nor send his dear Sophia to school where he was sure she would be tormented with masters. If ever she had a curiosity to read, he desired her to go to the library, where there were the plays of Dryden and Lee, the Romances of Sidney, and Orrery, and Scudery, and La Calprenède, which had descended, like heirlooms, from one generation to another, 'till bought up with the rest of the fixtures by her father. Among all these works, the quaint reveries of the amiable, but rather tedious Arcadian Knight, most fixed Miss Mountain's fancy. Pyrocles and Musidorus took possession of her early admiration, and the stately Pamela and beauteous Philoclea kept her thoughts in perpetual fluctuation between the opposite merits of affability and pride.[45] These were the only two qualities she ever thought of exercising in society; that which surrounded her consisting chiefly of dependants. The age and increasing infirmities of Mr. Mountain soon called all her attention to himself; and at three and twenty she was left an orphan, possessed of immense riches, but without either education or knowledge of the world, equal to what might be expected from her rank and fortune.

At this critical juncture, happening to meet with Miss Hautenville, the ladies were mutually pleased with each other. She appeared to Miss Mountain a paragon of learning, and the reading lady was forced to confess that, if the stately heiress had some of the defects, she had also the merits of an ancient brocade, being rather stiff, but at the same time very rich; in short they agreed to live together. Miss Hautenville enjoying all the advantages of Miss Mountain's house, carriage and servants, and administering, in return, the more subtle but nobler treasures of intellectual wealth, for which task she was as well qualified, as any of those adventurers in the newspapers, who advertise every necessary information in all the branches of belles-lettres, to any lady or gentleman, whose education may have been neglected. Had it been necessary that Miss Mountain's mental / physician should take every thing she herself prescribed, the case might have, perhaps, been otherwise; but as it was, Poetry, History, Biography of every age and every nation, was, under Miss Hautenville's direction, successfully administered, and in an incredibly short time, to the patient; 'till being all well whipt together in her poor brain, it produced a fine froth at top. The removal of Miss Hautenville, who quitted her former friend, to live with Mrs. Stockwell, produced no interruption in her studies; they were pursued unremittingly; but this taste for reading, infused into her mind at too late a period, only gave a degree of shew and pretension to her discourse, which being destitute of any inward stock of ideas to supply it, resembled those gardens, which thoughtless childhood delights to make, of the refuse of the bouquet or green-house. Flowery indeed in appearance, but wanting the root, and consequently the nourishment, which alone could give their productions durability or value. All Miss Mountain retained of her chivalrous reading, was, an expectation of general gallantry and deference, which, as she did not always immediately receive, she applied herself to obtain by a variety of means, that (without disturbing the general serenity she derived from a fixed conviction of her own excellence) gained her often the imputation of coquetry, while it was in fact only an ill understood pride.

Such a character could not appear to Matilda, a great addition to her usual society; but even at the moment when her pedantry and affectation excited in Miss Melbourne's bosom, the greatest disgust, fate was providing for her a more agreeable companion. She had not forgot Lady Torrendale's promise, that Arbella Ferrars should some day pay her a visit. In one of those long days which Matilda was invited to spend at Woodlands, she was surprised, as she entered her Ladyship's favorite sitting room, to hear a female voice (which was not that of the Countess) warbling in a sweet clear strain, apparently from the fulness of a pleased and happy heart. The room opened into the garden, which was, on that side of the / house, raised to a level with the first floor, and from this it was one of Matilda's pleasures to invite the shivering robin from his shelter on the leafless spray. The notes, however, that now attracted her attention, were not those of sweet robin; and she experienced a still livelier sensation of delight, to discover, in the unknown songstress, an unexpected agreeable visitor, her new acquaintance, the dark-eyed Arbella. To an exclamation which involuntarily escaped Miss Melbourne, as to the manner of her *entrée*, 'I came in at the window, my dear,' Miss Ferrars said, as she turned quickly on Matilda her animated glance; then, advancing and fondly taking up her little hand, as if she would examine the separate beauty of every finger, 'My sweet girl,' she cried, 'did you ever read David Simple?'[46]

Before Miss Melbourne could reply to so abrupt an interrogatory, the lively visitor continued, 'Because I feel myself just in his situation. I have long wandered in search of a friend, and never found one. Will you be mine? Nay I will not ask you to engage yourself so suddenly. You would take me for a fool, which I am not, though Miss Hautenville often makes me appear so. To tell you the truth, I have vowed never to speak more than is absolutely necessary in her presence, because she takes up and misrepresents every thing I say. Other reasons kept me silent the first time I saw you; reasons which – I cannot tell you now – I may say more of them hereafter. But my eyes were not idle, and I remarked in your countenance a something softly winning; a something which seemed to say, "Come vain perturbed soul, come calm thy restless flutters in this placid, yet feeling breast." Did I guess right?'

Matilda, who had been as much charmed by the animated graces of Arbella, as that young lady had been by her softer captivation, accepted her proffered friendship with a cordiality, of the force of which, she was herself scarcely sensible; and Miss

Ferrars, gaily looking round her as she pressed her hand, exclaimed, while a tear of sensibility dashed the / rising smile of joy, 'let this dear favoured region be ever sacred, where I have given and received the pledge of the first attachment that ever promised true happiness to my heart. You will think me strangely capricious and unceremonious,' she added, alluding to the manner of her visit; 'but I really wish for a little, quiet, uninterrupted chat with you, which it is impossible to have below; they are always so busy, or so dull. What would Spencer say if he saw the multitude his mother receives! Well we shall soon have Eyes I hope, and that will make us gay again.'

'You will soon have Eyes!'

'I perceive you are still unacquainted with our "gipsy jargon." There is one for Lady Torrendale's *boudoir* as well as for lower places; and there, that gentle youth is always denominated "Eyes," who, to vulgar mortals is commonly known by the appellation of Spencer Fitzroy.' There is a certain retarded accent, a lowered tone of voice, by which the magical name of the favored swain, whom a lady regards with peculiar interest, may be known from every other, in the Red-book, Directory, or Army List;' and it was with this soft hesitation, this unwilling pleasure, that seemed to chide its own indulgence; a sigh, almost imperceptible, dividing the Christian from the surname, that the words 'Spencer Fitzroy,' were now pronounced by Arbella.

'I know who you mean now,' said Matilda, 'he is –

'In the Dragoons, the Light Dragoons I believe,' replied Miss Ferrars, anticipating her question.

'I need not ask that of a lady's favorite in these days,' resumed Miss Melbourne, smiling archly. 'Favorite! Spencer is no favorite I assure you. Quite the reverse. But to speak impartially, and you know that is the only way to judge; he is really the most elegant young man we have, at this moment. To all his mother's beauty, he joins that playful wit, that enchanting gaiety, which, when tempered by good breeding, is so irresistible; and the whole is set off by that noble and graceful address, *cet air distingué*[47] – In short, / Spencer Fitzroy is a man whom it is impossible for a stranger to look at without demanding "who is that?" Now do you comprehend? do you see him?'

'Perfectly.' But still you have not told me why you call him 'Eyes.'

'Oh! that I leave you to find out.'

'To find it out,' Matilda murmured, this seems to be the watch-word at Woodlands.

Their conversation was at this moment interrupted by the entrance of Lady Torrendale's woman, who, all 'blushes and blooms,' advanced to them, quite out of breath, with 'Young Ladies, Madam, Miss Ferrars, my Lady bids me say you have been closetted together, chattering long enough; and it's a shame, and a mop-molly, (those are the Countess's very words) to keep Miss Melbourne up stairs any longer, when there's so much company below; and Captain Fitzroy, and Captain Lionhart arrived.'

'Captain Fitzroy!' exclaimed Arbella in a tremulous tone, while the colour with which Merriton's cheeks were overspread, seemed by some magic transferred to her own. Grasping Matilda's hand with a little more violence than friendship required, she whispered, 'hold me, or my head will grow giddy; these old stairs are so very steep,' and the two young ladies descended together. /

CHAPTER IX.

– A me lo scuopre
Il girar de' suoi sguardi
Lenti e pietosi – placidi al moto
Il soave parlar.

METASTASIO.[48]

MATILDA and her friend found a numerous circle, assembled round Lady Torrendale, among whom it was easy to distinguish Fitzroy, and his friend Captain Lionhart; a gentleman who appeared already known to the Countess, and whom her son mentioned as having kindly postponed for a few days, the object of his journey (which was to see some friends in Wales) that he might have the pleasure of paying his compliments to her. Captain Fitzroy, after having bowed slightly to Miss Ferrars, seemed anxious to approach Matilda, and the manner that accompanied the first words he addressed to her, which were indeed of the most flattering kind, put an end to the surprise she had expressed respecting the denomination he had received in their society; but, whether it arose from blindness, obstinacy, female contradiction, or the obscuring effects of fatigue, and a rather neglected travelling dress, she could discern but little of that family beauty with which Arbella's partiality had so liberally endowed him.

Captain Fitzroy appeared to her a pale, genteel-looking young man, with a person and address which could certainly boast an air of fashion; but whose countenance, which bespoke the languor of evident and recent ill-health, was no otherwise particularly interesting. Arbella, on her part, (though at no loss to divine the cause,) felt mortified at being treated with such marked and haughty coldness in the presence of her friend, by one in whose praise she had recently and in such lively terms indulged. A secret consciousness, hardly confessed to herself, that he did / not, at least at that moment, quite answer the flattering picture she had drawn, mingled with her embarrassment; and she silently wished she could have retracted a few of the encomiums she had so lavishly bestowed.

'He never looked so ill as he does today,' she whispered Matilda, as she glanced at Spencer an anxious look of fretful fondness and partiality; a partiality which she felt it was necessary others should experience, before they could view him in the light she desired. 'He has not been the same since his wound at Vimiera; but to-day he looks remarkably ill. I wish he'd talk; then you would forget every thing but his voice and manner. If he would but begin and "*deploy*" as the military say. I wish he'd talk.' Wishes were vain.

Captain Fitzroy, silent, languid, and apparently exhausted with his journey, con-tinued, after his first animated address to Matilda, completely cruel and deaf to the murmured reproaches and expectations of the fair. To the questions that were poured around him, he replied only in monosyllables, till Mrs. Stockwell, having appeared very desirous to know how he liked his last quarters, which were near a considerable town at no very great distance from London, he condescended to reply a little more at length; and assured her, in general terms, that he had found every thing very agree-able. Miss Melbourne, was amused at the distinction with which he thus honored this lady; and could not help observing, at the same time, that something between a smile and a sneer disturbed the elegant regularity of his features, as he pronounced this faint and forced eulogium. 'Never was in such a confounded place in my life,' cried Lionhart, who thought it necessary to dilate a little upon his friend's reply. As for the country gentlemen, they kept so close in their "*Quinta's,*"[49] or whatever they call their lumbering old-fashioned-looking houses, that we saw nothing of them, except when they came across us to deprive us, if possible, of our poor little amusement of shooting.'

'Really that was very wrong; particularly / to you and your friends, Captain Lion-hart, who had so bravely exposed your lives a shooting of the Frenchmen abroad,' observed Mrs. Stockwell, attempting to say something obliging; 'I am sure it was but fair in return you should have liberty to shoot the birds if you liked it at home; wasn't it now?'

'Oh! Madam, that is nothing to the purpose,' cried Lionhart, hastily interrupting her, 'I was only giving an instance of their unsociable disobliging temper. There was one fellow – he was not a gentleman, but a yeoman, or great farmer, or something of that kind, whom we took particular delight in mortifying, because he was so sulky; and I'll tell you how we managed it. He had a great deal of land on which he never would let any one kill a bird, though they might ask him ever so civilly. I said I'd get a day's sporting out of him. So I never let out about having heard of this little particular-ity of his, but one morning took my dog and gun, and presented myself in one of his fields; met my farmer – he asked me what business I had there? I said none, if he chose to warn me off; I'd take leave, and only ask permission to call him a very unsociable fellow: he muttered civilly enough, that as I had come there a stranger, I might take my diversion for that day on his grounds. I gave him the produce of my day's sport to shew him the amusement was all I wanted; and left my honest friend, I believe, very well content to have got rid of me with so little trouble.

'The next day that elegant gentleman who won't speak for himself, (designating Spencer) appeared on the ground. He had his cart with him, so he brought up his dogs in the finest style imaginable, and quite fresh; had his shooting jacket on too; no one could know him to be of the same regiment, or of any regiment at all. Honest Diggory warns him off. "God bless my soul, sir, I beg your pardon! I was certainly informed that shooting was allowed here; but since it was otherwise, of course I shall make my bow and retire." He did so; but not till he had induced the old dog to / give him some sport for that day at least. On the next, another of our lads tried his fortune. My gentleman farmer thought the deuce was in the strangers, that none of them knew of his determination. The following morning, a fourth presented himself. All of the same regiment, and so on; through the whole season, there never passed a day that he had not some one or other of our fellows on his grounds; and yet we kept within the letter of the law; for no one returned, after being duly warned against trespass.'

'Oh, you wicked creeters!' lisped Miss Langrish; 'how is it possible to defend oneself against your contrivances!'

'So much for the neighbourhood,' resumed Lionhart, who had told this story with great vivacity of action; then, as for the town itself – not a family, not a house, where you could get a lounge, or a feed in the whole place; never saw such a cursed crew.'

'Hush, hush, Lionhart,' said the elegant Spencer, mildly, 'when you are offended, you are always violent; you exceed – indeed you do; for my part, I did not find it so very unpleasant; my mornings were always sufficiently filled up with engagements; and I am sure, on the part of the ladies, at least, we had no reason to complain of particular shyness. You could not go into a shop without meeting several who –' 'Oh, yes, deuce take them, they were obliged to venture there, to purchase their riff-ruffs, frill-fralls, laces, and –'

'Not always to purchase,' resumed Spencer, calmly.

'The little Welchman seems choleric,' whispered Arbella, laughing.

'You were always the defender of the ladies,' cried Lionhart, once more addressing his friend; 'but you will allow me to say, that the principal men there, were a pack of the strangest animals that were ever assembled together since the creation of colours. The first families consisted of a heterogeneous collection, (continued the captain more slowly, as if proud of bringing out so long a word) of retired drysalters, tobacconists, / pin-makers, buckle-makers, ginger-bread-bakers, slop-sellers, fish-mongers, tallow-chandlers, coal-heavers, green-grocers, tailors, and travelling tinkers.'

The company laughed at the climax; and Fitzroy, who never did more than discover his beautiful pearly teeth in a graceful smile, interrupted him with – 'Surely my dear Lionhart, you are severe, you exaggerate – they were not quite so bad.'

'But they were,' resumed his friend, who seemed determined to prove what he had asserted.

'You will not deny, I suppose, that the assemblies, as they called them, (though they were more properly '*Assemblages*' of queer beings), were not quite the thing. Do you remember the young lady you danced with?'

Here Fitzroy interposed to 'beg,' with an air of authority, 'that they might have no more parish business;' but Lionhart, who was not to be so put off, continued

'She was a pretty girl faith; and he flirted with her, and was quite 'attached' to her for the evening; 'till, at last, upon his offering to get her some lemonade, or wine and water, she answered, "No, I thank ye sir; but I should feel quite 'comfortable' if you would get me a posset of sugared ale." If you could have seen the start my gentleman gave!'

'I confess,' said the Captain, 'I had once the honor of assisting at a ball where the ladies did not appear perfectly aware of the little etiquettes that –'

'How mildly he pronounces sentence on the "ladies." Dear creatures! there is not one of them will ever want an advocate, or a lover either, while the "gentle Spencer"'is in existence.'

At length, Captain Fitzroy succeeded in what he wished, which was, to turn the conversation to more general topics. The desire of pleasing, by degrees gave animation to his manner; at first so languid; and lit up a countenance, not deficient, either in variety or expression; even Matilda, at first so difficult, was obliged to allow him the correct and regular profile of the beautiful Lady / Torrendale, to whom he bore a resemblance, the most striking that could exist in a person of a different age and sex; and the advantage of features was farther set off by the eloquence of eyes, which, if not absolutely fine, were at least of that sort, which seem so perfectly satisfied of their own power, that others, concluding there must be some foundation for such a confidence, give them the credit of being so. To every female he had something agreeable and flattering to say; but she was particularly struck by the attention and deference with which he distinguished Mrs. Stockwell.

'Then his crest fell, and all his pride was gone;
He drooped the conquered wing.'[50]

That his manner, even to this lady, should be expressive of peculiar respect and interest, was, however, in Spencer Fitzroy, nothing very remarkable. It always changed, whenever a woman was to be addressed. Whether young, handsome, fashionable, it mattered not. An altered and more tender tone of voice; a look, soft, engaging, that insinuated itself into the soul, bespoke at once his ascendancy over, and his submission to, that sex, which it was his pleasure to please, but his glory to subdue.

Lady Torrendale had only seen her beloved son for a few days after his return from the Peninsula; for he had been ordered almost immediately to Cheltenham, to recover from his wounds; whence he had joined his regiment, then quartered in the vicinity of the Metropolis; she was, therefore, not sparing of her enquiries, either to him, or his soldier friend respecting their adventures abroad; but, from him, she could draw only very brief replies, and from Lionhart, who had served with distinction from the age of sixteen, in most parts of the globe, absolutely nothing. Yet even the slight sketch that Spencer gave of the hardships and sufferings to which the army was exposed abroad, so far worked upon her Ladyship's tender feelings, as to give rise to an idea which superseded for the present the interest she had been beginning to take in literature and literary parties. To make up articles of warm / clothing to defend our troops from the rigours of the season, would be not only very meritorious, but very fashionable. The beautiful Duchess of D – had been once much admired for being the first mover of such a plan. Why should not the Countess of Torrendale? Many of the men of the regiment in which Strathallan served, were the sons of the neighbouring tenants and peasantry, who had enlisted out of preference in that to which he belonged; how charming, how sentimental, for the fine ladies at home to think of administering to the wants and comforts of their defenders! While these thoughts rapidly crossed her mind, the probability that the subjects of her solicitude might return before she had time to put them into effect, suddenly occurred to damp the rising glow of benevolence. No matter, it would then do for Spencer's regiment, or for Strathallan's; still winter was always hard to be endured; or perhaps affairs might change; they might stay, and then what she prepared for them might be forwarded 'somehow,' her Ladyship's favorite method of doing every thing.

This was about the time the English army under Sir John Moore was on the retreat towards Corunna.[51]

Lord Torrendale, who hailed with pleasure every thing that bore the semblance of benevolence in his wife, seconded the idea with more warmth than he commonly showed; while Lady Torrendale, as usual, undecided, applauded and dissented from her own proposal twenty times in a minute: 'Poor Strathallan! how this will gratify him! – this will be quite in his way. Poor fellow! – he may not be there to receive them! Good heavens! we may have a battle from one day to another – isn't it shocking – that is a very pretty chain you have got, Arbella; is it from London? – we certainly may.'

Lord Torrendale looked as if something was rising to his lips, but said nothing.

At supper, her Ladyship laughed, and talked, and ate, and surmised, and wept whenever the idea of Strathallan (recalled more forcibly to her mind by the presence of her military visitors) returned; and then resumed / her conversation with Captain Lionhart – ate, and talked, and wept again.

Lord Torrendale made no complaint, spoke little, ate nothing, and retired early. At length, the animated discourse the Countess had held with her guests, degenerated into a long conversation, aside, with Spencer; in which (if a judgment might be formed from the glow that sometimes stole across his pallid cheek, and the suppressed eagerness of his agitated whisper) both were considerably interested. The name of 'Strathallan' frequently occurred; and Fitzroy once, while a heightened colour for a moment crimsoned his features, repeated, 'No, that is a circumstance which I never even allow myself to imagine.'

Except when thus engaged with his mother, his attentions, during the evening, were pretty equally divided between Miss Melbourne and Miss Mountain; and the former, who felt how small her claim was to such a distinction, and remembered her late conversation with the Countess, concluded, by the whole of his behaviour to the 'SUPERB' Sophia, and by the manner in which that behaviour was encouraged, that he was, without doubt, the happy man, on whose account, she was saluted by Lady Torrendale, daughter-in-law 'that shall be.' /

CHAPTER X.

D'Amori un nido
Stranamente fecondo
D'Irene è il core. Un s'incomincia appena
Su l'ali a sostener; l'altro s'affretta
Già dal guscio a spuntar –

* * * * *

Ve n'ha d'ogni colore, un le vïole.
Par che spieghi nei vanni; un altro i gigli
Ve n'ha bruni e vermigli.

METASTASIO. IL NIDO DEGLI AMORI.[52]

NOTHING appeared more clear to Matilda, than the indifference of Captain Fitzroy to Miss Ferrars. The lively yet tender Arbella felt equally persuaded, that the clearing up a recent and slight misunderstanding, was all that was necessary to restore the amiable Spencer to her chains. Of this misunderstanding, as ridiculous in its cause as serious in its effects, she soon related the history to Matilda.

'I have a very unfortunate habit,' she said, 'of suddenly saying whatever arises in my mind, without always considering the circumstances or situation of the persons present, which may sometimes make it awkward; for which reason, when I want to appear particularly discreet, I have no other resource than condemning myself to absolute silence, as I did in our first visit to Woodlands, before Miss Hautenville. Now one day, at Cheltenham, talking of some of the military in the neighbourhood we had left, I happened to observe, in a mixed company, of which Spencer was one, that in a country town, one might always guess the approaching departure of a regiment, by the wailings of the damsels, and the bustle among the taylors. At the moment, he did not appear to hear what was said; but, during the rest of our stay at Cheltenham, he never forgave me.'

Astonished at the frank and unasked acknowledgment of indiscretion and flippancy / so gross, in one whom she had accustomed herself to look upon as a model of elegant reserve, Matilda, whose own words and actions were ever bound 'in the silken fetters of decorum,' remained uneasy and uncertain what to reply, while her lively friend continued – 'This is not the only distress into which my unlucky "readiness at remark" has brought me; do you know, the whole of Miss Hautenville's envenomed hatred to me arises from as trifling a cause. A gentleman was one day complimenting her upon her literary talents, which, God knows – however, we must allow every one to have his taste – let it suffice, he *was* complimenting her. "Yes," she replied, drawing up her scraggy neck, and mincing in her odious affected tone of voice, "if I have any merit, I flatter myself it consists in the power of distinguishing and appreciating works of real genius; as for the rest –"

'"'Tis all but leather and prunello,"'[53] I interrupted, – irresistibly impelled to the quotation of Pope's well known line, by the aptness of allusion it afforded to the yellow leathern case that enwraps the bag of bones, she has the effrontery to call a person. Another time I affronted her terribly by happening to compare her poor thin arm, in the middle of a long, clear, muslin sleeve, to the worm sometimes blown in glasses: but the greatest storm was when I called her a Bookbinder.'

'And why did you call her a Bookbinder?'

'Why, you must know, she has a very impertinent way of lording it over my poor aunt, and ridiculing her for foibles that at least *she* has no right to take notice of: so one day, she was going on in this strain, and terming my aunt's attachment to Lady Torrendale "Quality-binding," – I took fire – "And pray, Miss Hautenville," said I, "what do you term your own literary mania – your devoted admiration of every thing in the shape of a poet or poetaster? that, to adopt your own phraseology, might be styled 'BOOK-binding.'" It is really ridiculous to see her, when in company either with some / of her clever people, or with her Kite, Miss Mountain.'

'Her Kite!'

'Yes: have you never observed some women, possessed of neither merit, beauty, or fortune, attach themselves to another, distinguished by one of those requisites; and, rising with her, like the bits of paper fastened to the tail of a kite, derive a degree of fancied consequence by exaggerating the importance of their principal, to the undue depression of every one else? Now, Miss Hautenville acquired that habit when she lived with Miss Mountain, and continues it whenever they meet; and I take care to notice it to her.'

'But these are all heinous offences. How can you wonder she sometimes retorts?'

'Ah, but the difference is, that any little pleasantry of mine, is but the scratch of a kitten, which, even if it does hurt, is meant only in play; while Miss Hautenville's malice, like the sting of a serpent, is always intended to produce a deep and envenomed wound.'

'And why do you, my poor little kitten, venture to play with a serpent that may wound you so fatally? You see, a similar heedlessness had nearly lost you the good opinion of Captain Fitzroy.'

'Then you allow that Fitzroy's opinion is something?' interrupted the volatile Arbella. 'I always said you would like him, though I was sorry to observe he did not immediately make a very favourable impression.'

'On the contrary, from the first I thought him agreeable.'

'There you are wrong again, my dear. He ranks above the Agreeables, and below the Adorables, such as his brother Strathallan, – he is Interesting.'

'You seem to have a perfect scale for your beaux.'

'Exactly so. I separate them into the four great divisions, or classes, of Adorables, Admirables, Interesting, and Agreeables; to which Insupportables may, if you please, be added as a fifth. These you may again subdivide into the Wits, Bearables, Insufferables – But I must take another time to explain to you my system at length; at present / an example or two will suffice. I have instanced an Adorable: the Admirable is one, who, possessed of a vast deal of mere personal beauty, thinks he has nothing to do but to shew himself to be "admired," – whence the name; while your elegant, languid, fashionable-looking man, like Spencer, with expressive eyes, and an honourable wound or two, received at Vimiera or Roleça, has a fair claim to the Interesting. Nothing can be more opposite than the Elegant and Admirable. The Elegant, at a public place, takes care never to drive out without a fair or titled companion; is never seen walking, except attending, at a late hour, on some fashionable and distinguished group; and, though really engrossed with himself, always endeavours to make them believe that *they* are the principal objects of his homage. The haughty Admirable, on the contrary, likes as well to be alone; and if he *does* meet you, stares you in the face with his fine eyes, on the first *rencontre*, as who should say, "What the deuce do I care for your beauty! I think myself as well worth looking at as you!" Lastly, the Wit, or Agreeable, is one who, perceiving that nature has denied him all pretensions to set up for an Adorable, an Admirable, or even an Interesting, quietly gives up the plan of setting hearts palpitating and eyes sparkling, and wisely contents himself with laughing at all three; while by constantly telling good stories, and saying smart things (or things meant to be smart), he gets the reputation of "a vastly clever young man," and "the pleasantest creature in the world." You must observe, that the ugly Wit is the natural enemy of the stupid Admirable. *Comprenez vous?* And now, will you deny the title that "Eyes" has obtained to the rank of "Engaging, Fascinating," – Heavens! that such creatures, that such "Detestables" as my cousin Stockwell should be suffered to walk upon two legs, and call themselves of the same species as Spencer Fitzroy!'

'To be sure, it is very impertinent.'

'I offended him grievously on one occasion, that he came up to me just going to a ball, all drest in his best, by telling him, / Spencer looked a thousand times better in his shooting jacket.'

'You must have intended to offend him. My dear Arbella, were I as fond of quotation as you are, how often should I be tempted to say to you, in the warning words of Sterne, "Trust me, this unwary pleasantry of thine – "'[54]

'Oh yes, that has been already often said to me; but –'

'You wish, at all events, to dismiss Mr. Stockwell?'

'No, no, not absolutely dismiss him; he is very well as he is – I would not inflict unnecessary pain; as my aunt says, when Spencer torments Floss, "It is not right to make the poor dumb creeter suffer." If I ever do so, to tell you the truth, it is to revenge on him what the more agreeable creature sometimes makes me endure.'

'And why do you endure it?'

'Why! Ah, Matilda! have you yet to learn that those very manners, which in an ugly disagreeable wretch excite our scorn and aversion, in a more amiable person, if they do not absolutely destroy, only increase our partiality? I never see Spencer Fitzroy and Sam Stockwell together, without applying to them poor Phœbe's expression in Shakespeare, "I'd rather hear you chide than this man woo."'

'Well, it may be so; but I own I could not discover in Captain Fitzroy's conversation any of that superiority – marked mental superiority, that could justify –'

'Why, I do not say you could quite make a Spenceriana from attending to him,' interrupted Arbella, rather piqued at her friend's slowness in approving her choice; 'yet still there is a way, there is a manner, which is every thing. If Stockwell gave himself airs indeed, 'twould be different. *'La fatuité ne convient qu'à la jeunesse militaire;'*[55] that golden axiom of Marmontel's explains my meaning better than –'

'Ah! *"La jeunesse militaire!"* nothing else can hope to succeed, where one of that body has made so deep an impression.'

'Deep! no, no, not so far gone as that, / neither. He knows I make myself very easy about him.'[a]

'Then, if that be really the case, I wonder you, who study so much to please, ever run the risk of losing any other conquest by the flippancies you have mentioned to me.'

'And who told you those flippancies *never* pleased? As I said before, manner is every thing: that is one of our little secrets; you must allow coquetry to have its freemasonry.'

'I do, indeed; and acknowledge you Grand Lady of the order if you please; for I do not understand a system so complicated.'

'You shall understand it another time,' resumed Arbella gaily: 'I am a good witch, and engage to put you in possession of all my knowledge; but at present weightier business calls. I see Lady Torrendale already armed with her scissars and fleece, preparing the charitable work, and chiding our dull delay; let us not wait her call – away, away, away!'

With these words, Arbella hastened to join the Countess; and Matilda, stunned with the torrent of eloquence she had heard, resolved to be more careful in future, before she gave any lady the title of the 'Silent Woman.' /

CHAPTER XI.

Non eres palma
Eres retaina
Eres cypres
De triste rama
Eres desdicha
Desdicha mala.
Do esta tu escudo?
Do esta tu lanza?
Todo do acaba
La mala adanza.

SPANISH SONG OF PERAZA.[56]

AND now we must behold the Countess presiding over a different scene, interesting at least from its novelty; and, while she sat at the head of a large table covered over with flannels and other materials for her benevolent work, apportioning out to each of the blooming damsels that surrounded her, their share in advancing its progress. Every morning her Ladyship was encircled by a little levee, united by the hopes and fears that they felt in common; and who discoursed on little else than the interesting events that from day to day might be expected to take place. Strathallan, the centre of every one's solicitude, was the theme of every tongue. His safe return was the constant subject of the audible wish, or the low-breathed prayer; and every circumstance of his character, disposition, and former life, perpetually discussed by those who, knowing him best, could best appreciate his value, rendered his image so familiar to Matilda, that she could hardly still believe it was that of one unknown to her. She went easily along with the detail given of his former merits, and the praises he had received; and, when contrasting them with the perils to which he might that moment be exposed, her cheek often became blanched with terror, and her respiration suspended, while

'Her fancy followed him through foaming waves
To distant shores; and she would sit and weep
At what a 'SOLDIER' suffers.'[57] /

'You must get on with that work in "double quick time," Countess,' (said young Lionhart to Lady Torrendale, who, possessing more vanity than pride, encouraged the familiarity;) 'that is to say, if you mean it to be of use to our brave fellows this winter.'

Spencer then gave his opinion. Miss Mountain said something about Hercules wielding the distaff of Omphale:[58] but in the mean time the work proceeded rapidly.

It was not to be supposed, however, that Matilda could be often of these parties. Sowerby, who affected to treat the whole plan as a whim that would never last till its object could be put into execution, alternately laughed, and railed, and seriously reproved her for joining in it.

'I wonder, Mr. Sowerby,' said Mrs. Melbourne, 'that you can disapprove of an undertaking which has humanity for its basis. For my part, I feel so interested in the poor victims of war –'

'Curse 'em, why do they make war? The victims of war are the encouragers of it too; and, in the eyes of a philosophical observer, are the least deserving of compassion.'

'Nay, my dear Sir, I did not expect to hear from you such a "tirade" against war. I am sure there was one in which you would have served with distinction.'

'What was that pray?'

'*La guerre de la Fronde*, in France;[59] for such a complete *frondeur* of every thing, whether innocent, laudable, or blameable, I never had the pleasure of meeting with before.'

'Oh, Madam! once you refer me to the French, I have only to make my bow, and wish you a good morning.'

'I am happy by any means to have induced the philosophical Mr. Sowerby to make a bow.'

To relieve the tediousness of the long winter evenings at Woodlands, it was the custom of the great Miss Mountain, who, since she had put herself under the tuition of Miss Hautenville, had "crept into favor with herself," as a literary genius, to amuse the company with some book of entertainment, which / she read aloud. In point of declamation she would not have yielded up her claim, even to the famous Miss Swanley; but, in the thrilling, the soul-harrowing style of poetry she thought she excelled the most.

'They drink out of skulls newly torn from the grave,
Their liquor is blood; and this horrible stave
They howl, to the health of Alonzo the brave,
And his consort the fair Imogine – '[60]

This she was repeating one night, in a cadence which the bell-man might have envied, and with an 'unction' to which the muscular strength and size of her tall, bony form, thrown partly into the shadow by the manner in which the lights fell, and the horror that was expressed in her red rolling eye, imparted additional effect; when, a faint shriek, from one corner of the room, arrested the attention; and it was found that poor little Miss Langrish, who had sat an almost unobserved listener, had dropt her work, and, overcome by the force of the description, was near sinking under the violence of her emotion. This new weakness, in the chosen preceptress of Emily, was a delightful discovery to Miss Mountain; who, under pretence of teaching her to conquer it, made her, from that time, constantly endure all the imaginary, but dreadful sufferings, it produces, while she herself, when she had accomplished her purpose, would look down upon the poor girl, with her accustomed smile of conscious superiority, and kindly taking her trembling hand, ask her what was the matter; then, looking round her, complacently appeal to the company if she had done any thing but what was the general desire? As soon as the candles were lit, and the work, on which every one was now employed, was begun, Lenora, Donica, the Grim White Woman, the Little Grey Man, the second book of the Last Minstrel, the Eve of St. John, the Haunted Beach, selections from Otranto, Udolpho, Montorio, whatever was calculated to inspire, on the timid or imaginative, the deep, nameless feeling of terror, unfounded, undefined, always formed a part of the evening's entertainments.[61] When most of the family were withdrawn, and / the ladies had assembled in conversation around the fire, it was the custom of the Countess, who thought this '*mystification*' of poor Miss Langrish a delicious amusement, to continue it, by vying with Miss Mountain in recalling all the horrible stories, with which her memory could supply her from her youth; while the latter, though at other times she hated to talk to Lady Torrendale, seconded her admirably, with tales, for which the vastness and solitary situation of Vinesbury (an old mansion in the family, though re-purchased by her father) furnished ample materials. A few hints, respecting the antiquity of the manor-house at Woodlands, and the reports that several of the rooms were haunted, particularly that one in which Miss Langrish slept, generally closed the kindly-meant dialogue; and the poor governess was not dismissed to her chamber, till her pale countenance and shivering limbs announced her unwillingness and almost inability to leave the scene, where, at least, if she encountered mortification, she had the advantage of light, noise, and society.

One night Matilda met her passing the long dark corridor, which she was obliged to cross to reach her apartment.

'For God's sake, Miss Melbourne,' said she, seizing her hand with a firmness which seemed to request, and almost demand support; 'have the goodness to accompany me, if it is only for a few moments, to my room. Lady Torrendale and Miss Mountain have been telling ghost stories 'till I am ready to sink and faint away with terror: and do you know, these dismal December nights, when I lie quaking in my bed and hear the hollow moaning of the wind swinging the great oaks, or rattling the casements at this end of the old house, I fancy it into the cries and groans of the wounded, and think that every blast brings me tidings of the death of Lord Strathallan. Heavens what have I said! what might lose me my situation in this family! I have only to throw myself upon your humanity, Miss Melbourne, as I once did on a former occasion.'

It was a reliance in which Miss Langrish was not mistaken. Matilda not only kindly accompanied her to her chamber, but staid / with her, till, by the amenity and soothing charm of her animated and polished conversation, she had dispelled the gloom of those terrors that hung about this unfortunate girl, and restored her mind to something of a chearful and collected tone. When she retired to rest, after the performance of this act of charity, though she pitied the weakness of Miss Langrish, Matilda gave her credit for the possession of feeling. She much more severely blamed her persecutors; and, on the whole, did not think the young lady so absurd and unreasonable as usual.

Time passed on; and, in order to assist in finishing the grand work in which Lady Torrendale was interested, Matilda was engaged to stay for a week at Woodlands. At night, when Miss Mountain began to read, her Ladyship who always dearly loved to interrupt whatever was going forward, with an 'aside' of her own, suddenly turning to Miss Melbourne, said in a low voice, 'My dear creature, I know your father is an excellent Astronomer – is he not something of an Astrologer too? I wish,' she continued, obtaining no immediate reply to this incomprehensible question, 'that he could draw Spencer's Horoscope.' A second whisper, 'a kind of presentiment I have, tells me he was born for something great.' 'Dear Lady Torrendale' – 'Nay, nay, forget what I have said, you know I have frequent occasion to demand that indulgence from you. I am a trifling ridiculous creature,' she resumed, attempting to laugh off her former remark. Then after a pause – 'I wish,' she cried, 'that Lionhart was returned.'

Lionhart, who seemed to have given up, for the present, all idea of his Welch journey, and was 'attached,' as Spencer termed it, to the society at Woodlands, had gone, with that ready officiousness, which is so well rewarded by the smiles of a fine woman, to inquire among the families in the neighbourhood if any rumours of later date than the news the public prints afforded had reached them. At this moment he appeared, and every one crowded round him, for it was evident the intelligence he brought was of more than / usual importance. It was the report of a general engagement, said to have taken place at Corunna between our troops and the French; in which the former were victorious, but no particulars were yet known.

'Happy Strathallan!' exclaimed Spencer. 'How many glorious affairs he has been in, I wish I had been with him!'

Lionhart said nothing.

'I wish I had been with him,' repeated Fitzroy, with still greater vehemence, on receiving no answer.

'I am quite as well satisfied you were not,' said Lady Torrendale, looking at him, with a tenderness, which, in this instance, she tried rather to repress than to exaggerate.

Absorbed in his own reflections, Spencer was silent; except that he at intervals continued to exclaim 'I wish I had been there; and then perhaps (he added in a lower voice) there would have been an end of it all.'

'They know more in town,' observed Lady Torrendale, 'We may know more tomorrow – 'till then –'

'That my life could ensure his,' cried Lord Torrendale, bursting suddenly from a depth of abstraction, that rendered him unconscious of the presence of those around him. 'That I could once more see him, be near him, be his protection; but he has a better. God will protect and restore him to me; he will in mercy spare the excellencies of my brave, my noble son.'

'Torrendale is distracted I believe,' said the Countess, looking at him with a mixture of shame and resentment, (which was hardly deserved,) while her lord, apparently unconscious of having uttered any thing, had sunk into his former gloomy and agitated silence. 'How like a methodist parson he spoke,' she continued.

'He spoke like a father,' thought the innocent and sympathizing Matilda; 'like one from whose character, deep, soul-felt anguish and anxiety have torn the artificial veil, by habit drawn over feelings naturally affectionate and warm.'

And now the guests, with hardly power to exchange a mute and mournful good night, had each departed; and the family, gliding / like ghosts, separated to pass in impatience and anxiety, the hours till daylight should return.

The news of the following morning brought a confirmation of the evening's report; but nothing yet, either to justify or dispel the agonizing apprehensions of the suffering friends of Strathallan. This gloomy calm was not of long duration. Their most dreadful fears were too soon fully justified; his name stood among the first of those who gallantly fell fighting on that memorable day.

Never[a] had Matilda beheld real grief till now; that of Lord Torrendale mocked description: while the Countess, forgetting all low-thoughted jealousies and animosities, yielded to her better feelings, in a tribute, late, but sincere, to the virtues of the amiable being thus lost to them for ever. 'Oh! he possessed the gentlest, noblest nature!' she exclaimed; while, weeping in the arms of Matilda, she gave way to the various and contradictory emotions that swelled, almost to bursting, her weak, but not corrupted heart. 'Who will now defend me from the effects of Torrendale's resentment? Who will interpose to obviate the imprudences of Fitzroy? You look surprised, Miss Melbourne; that man, so cold, so calm, apparently; that proud, silent Lord Torrendale, has moments of rage which nothing but the persuasions of Strathallan could appease; Strathallan, whom nothing bearing a human heart could long resist or refuse. 'Twas when Fitzroy laboured under his father's severest displeasure, that generous brother undertook and succeeded, in being his advocate.'

In the course of this conversation, Matilda gathered, from the broken sentences of the Countess, that the beloved, the lost Strathallan, was the bond of union, which had alone cemented the jarring interests of a family, where such different views and dispositions prevailed; that to her he had been ever a generous and respectful friend; to Spencer, a brother the most liberal and kind; and to the little heart-struck Emily a protector, guardian, guide; the companion of her youth, the brother of her love. /

'You must leave us, my sweet girl,' said her Ladyship, looking through her tears, at her sympathising young friend; 'This is no house for you. It would destroy your spirits, without consoling us.'

'Leave you, Lady Torrendale,' exclaimed Matilda, in a voice she meant should be calm, while, as she bent over the Countess, her swimming eyes expressed the soul of pity, descended to whisper peace to the wounded heart. 'No,' she continued in a firm collected tone, 'you may drive me from your presence, but you cannot from your house while I can be any relief to you; and as you flattered me once that you considered my society as such. I will not leave you, at least not till you tell me it grows painful to you.'

'Angel girl! this is indeed a kindness above your age, above my hopes,' she had nearly added; – but, fearful of wounding a mind delicate and grateful, as she had discovered Matilda's to be, the Countess contented herself with pressing her hand in token of pleased assent, to her friendly and truly welcome proposal.

CHAPTER XII.

With eyes of genial fire to light the morn,
Yet soft, when kind, as evening's dewy ray:
Brows, that proclaim a soul for empire born,
And smiles, to bid the enamour'd world obey.

J.[62]

On the following day, Miss Melbourne found her Ladyship in no disposition to renew the conversation of the preceding evening. The composing effects of sleep, her usual morning's refreshment, and half an hour spent with Fitzroy, had so far restored her to her ordinary train of feelings and reflections, that she seemed enabled to bear her share of the loss the family had sustained, with all due philosophy; and even inclined to retract a few of the praises that sorrow and unavailing regret had, in the first moments / of surprise and anguish extorted from her. Before her young friend had left her chamber, she had consulted her as to the most becoming mourning to be procured on account of this 'melancholy business,' as she termed it; and Matilda found, upon the whole, that the Countess had left upon her mind an impression of Lord Strathallan's merits, much deeper than what she at this moment herself experienced.

Their conference was interrupted by a bustle in the hall, which was plainly heard by Lady Torrendale; who, turning pale exclaimed: 'for heaven's sake send those people away; and don't let Lord Torrendale see them, I am sure it is some of the tenants; they were so fond of that Strathallan.' Her Ladyship was not mistaken. Several of the villagers, apprized, by general rumour, of the loss they had sustained, had assembled at the mansion, with a faint hope of hearing it contradicted; and on its mournful confirmation, filled the scene with their well-intended, but piercing expressions of sorrow. One old man in particular was deaf to all comfort. 'He was such an angel to me and mine' he said. 'When he went abroad, my two poor boys, as fine lads as ever handled a plough, would follow him for love; and after he had done every thing he could, to overpersuade them to stop with their poor old father, he bade me not to be cast down, he said, for that they were good lads, he said, and he would have an eye to them; and so he had; heaven bless him for it, and never wrote to his own father at Woodlands, but he sent me word how they were, and if they were doing well: and now my good old master himself will never hear from him more; but will have some one writing to him how his dear son fell.' 'So young to bear so kind a heart!' was repeated by several voices at once. 'There was not a tenant's son but would have wished to follow him; and not

– 69 –

one that did, but he gave them money for their friends, and wrote with his own dear hand to comfort their parents after the battles, as he did to old Robin yonder.'

Matilda, while she tried to console and dismiss these simple people, found the prevailing / tide of regret infectious; and the servants, who felt like them, had no heart to answer or to send them away; when suddenly, the appearance of an unexpected visitor in the hall recalled them to the command of their feelings, and the remembrance of the respect they owed to those of their lord. Lady Emily Fitzroy, her countenance all marked with the traces of recent tears, but with a dignity of deportment and serenity of voice, beyond what could be expected at her early age, glided in among the mournful groupe; approaching several of the country people, who were each of them personally known to her. She kindly praised them for the interest they took in the family misfortune; but remonstrated with them for indulging it to such excess. 'You do not wish to distress my father,' said she, 'consider, in the state in which he now is, how it might affect him were he to find you thus assembled?'

The sensibility, that imparted dignity to the still infantine graces of her form and features; the pleading earnestness of her voice and manner, to which grief repressed, yet evident, gave added interest, had an irresistible effect on the hearts she addressed. Convinced of the impropriety of thus giving a loose to inconsiderate sorrow, they departed, not without each having received a soothing and affectionate word from Lady Emily, and invoking in return every consolation and blessing on the remaining branches of the house of Torrendale. Till they were gone, this amiable girl preserved her apparent serenity; but, when the occasion for exerting it ceased, it yielded to the prevailing feelings of nature; and, throwing herself on Matilda's bosom, she gave vent to a torrent of tears. 'Oh! Miss Melbourne, my brother; and such a brother!' was all she could say; and Matilda, her heart already softened by the sorrow that prevailed around, was hardly in a state to afford her any consolation.

At the close of this mournful day, she felt herself nearly exhausted by the variety of painful scenes she had gone through. Sitting down by the light of a single taper, in the lately cheerful, but now deserted drawing-room, / her spirits sunk for a few moments, under the pressure of such repeated trials. Her tears flowed in silent, and almost involuntary abundance; and from these tears, her oppressed and feeling heart derived the first relief it for some hours had experienced. She had continued thus for some time in melancholy, and almost unconscious meditation, when a figure, scarcely discerned in the gloomy, partial light, passed by her, and she was startled, when she perceived it was Lord Torrendale. Her first idea was the fear of giving offence to grief solemn, sacred, fixed, as his; but the expression of his countenance soon made her forget her apprehension.

'Are these tears indeed for us,' he said, in a voice which she never thought capable of tenderness before. 'How sweet is the expression of sympathy, even from a stranger; but to think perhaps it is only a stranger bestows it;' then, as if repenting of what he had said, and resuming all his native pride, 'It is kind of you, Miss Melbourne,' he continued, 'to stay with Laura at this trying hour; her spirits cannot bear the sight of affliction, even when' –

Matilda endeavoured to speak, to express the feeling with which her heart was touched; but the effort only served completely to overcome her, and she sobbed aloud.

'Amiable creature!' cried Lord Torrendale, wholly softened, and every prejudice vanishing before the enchanting tenderness he beheld. 'You are indeed worthy to weep for Strathallan! Yet do not weep for him. Like the proud father of the noble Ossory, I can truly say, my son, though dead, is dearer to my memory, than living merit could ever become to it. But one mind on earth resembles his. Why could I not hope for such a daughter; surely you were intended for the bride of Strathallan!'

Matilda startled; was she then wedded to the grave? Often in the hour of despondency and gloom, often, when mournful forebodings overshadowed her after life, the words of Lord Torrendale struck with prophetic terror upon her soul.

Three days had now passed, since she had / been confined to Woodlands in the performance of her self-imposed duties; duties in which she did not fear any controul or opposition from Mrs. Melbourne; who, herself, bore at once 'Too tender, and too firm a heart,' not to witness with delight, in her daughter, that well directed sensibility, that correctness and justness of feeling, which made her seek, instead of shrinking, from the scenes where it could be exerted with advantage to those, who had a claim upon her gratitude or affection. On the afternoon previous to the day fixed for her intended departure, she had left the family, in whom an apparent degree, at least, of restored composure, seemed to have rewarded her attentions, in order to pay a last visit to some of the villagers, who had been occasionally the objects of her bounty. She could not enter a cottage where Strathallan was not the subject of discourse.

' 'Tis a sad thing, Madam,' said a poor countryman, 'to think we should lose our dear young Lord, and have the 'Squire Captain put over us for our master. We used often to think how happy we should live under the one that's gone, whenever it should please God to take away our good old Lord; not but that he is very charitable too, but then he is a stern sort of gentleman; now Lord Strathallan was all kindness.'

'He was indeed a gracious creature,' said his wife; 'and when after a day's shooting, he has stopt and rested himself in our cottage, and taken such notice of the children, and asked after me when I've been bad; well to be sure, though I loved him so much, I never could get it out of my head that I was talking and looking at a crowned king. They may say what they will of the beauty and the grandeur of your princes and your great folks, I am sure I would not walk to the end of the village to see them all assembled, in comparison of one glimpse of his lovely countenance.' The poor woman could hardly refrain from weeping; and her daughter, who had listened in silence, no longer repressed her tears.

'Lord Strathallan was very well known among you then,' said Matilda. /

'Known! Lord bless you, yes Miss. He know'd every one of us, and all we wished and wanted, when his father was with his fine lady far away; but now I am sure we must pray for Lord Torrendale to last long, for heaven help us when the Captain comes to rule over us.'

'You are not yet so well acquainted with Captain Fitzroy, or perhaps –'

'Yes, yes, we know'd he well enough too; and don't like him the better for that – egg and bird a wickeder, wilder, nice young gentleman,' (concluded the woman, recollecting it was a visitor at the mansion-house she was addressing,) 'could hardly be seen; and not so handsome neither to my thinking. I am sure you will repeat no harm of me Miss,' (she added,) 'I only say the same as every one else; that when the young squire came among us, every one was frightened, and looked to their own; but when Lord Strathallan came down it was a day of rejoicing throughout the whole village; but we shall never more rejoice at Strathallan's return.'

'And wert thou then indeed so much beloved, and yet beloved in vain!' thought Matilda, as slowly retiring from the rustic group, she indulged in the reflexions so naturally excited by the preceding scene. 'In vain thou wert the theme of the aged, the model for the young. An early tomb was with thee the reward of so much virtue, spirit, valour; but no, he will not wholly die; when the pride of victory is past, when the visions of glory are no more, thou shalt live in the fond hearts of those who with unavailing prayers and wishes have broken the silence of night; the grateful thoughts of nature's simple children, will ever hold thee dear, Strathallan! such is the prevailing, the surviving power of goodness!'

Desirous of concealing from the family at Woodlands, how much she had been affected, she a little prolonged her walk by the road that led from the village. She feared she had too much neglected Arbella. A slight indisposition confined her to the house, and she had requested to receive daily accounts of the state of the family, in whose concerns / she felt so interested. Matilda thought she had now an hour she could spare her friend. It was a melancholy walk; haunted by reflexions similar to those, to which she had just given vent, the oppression they caused was painful, and she only felt, as a refreshing breeze, the piercing coldness of the biting blast. Arbella was from home; feeling herself better, and tired of the confinement of the house, she had strolled to a little distance: but which way she had taken, her aunt was unable to tell. Matilda had determined to seek her in one of her most usual walks; and struck into a romantic winding road, terminating in a retreat called the Fountain of the Rocks. A few moments brought her to the spot; but her friend was not there. Fatigued and disappointed, she yielded to a sensation of dejection and weariness, that tempted her to rest a few moments, and contemplate this scene, in happier days, a favourite haunt. A clear spring rushed from beneath a cavern formed by two meeting rocks. Trees planted near the entrance, added, in summer, to the coolness and shade. The walk was not one of above two miles from her own house. Thither she had often stolen, to indulge in a rarely permitted pleasure; and, with no other companion than her Ossian, to suffer the sublimely mournful strains of the bard of Selma to steep her eyes in the dews of pensive transport. Now, the wind whistled shrill in the bare and leafless branches; but its dirge-like sound accorded better than summer lays with the present tone of her feelings. A passage in the poem she had last read there, involuntarily arose to her mind, with a train of attendant images with which before it had never been invested: it was in 'Dar-thula,' where the grey-haired King of Selma desires the bard to welcome the spirits of the departed warriors back to their native land. – 'Ghosts of my fathers, bend – receive the falling chief; – whether he comes from a distant land, or rises from the rolling sea. Let his robe of mist be near – his spear that is formed of a cloud – place a half-extinguished meteor by his side, in the form of the hero's sword; and oh! let his / countenance be lovely, that his friends may delight in his presence.' [63]

This passage she had always read with a feeling of mournful pleasure; but never had the exquisite tenderness and delicacy of the last sentiment struck so forcibly upon her mind; never had the scene and every circumstance appeared appropriated before. As she recalled it, her bosom swelled with an irrepressible emotion. She tried to give utterance aloud to the concluding words, but something checked her voice; and she continued absorbed in soft and not unpleasing reverie, till interrupted by the sudden appearance of the person of all others the most calculated to dissipate the illusions of tenderness or sentiment. Smiling, in real or affected pity and astonishment, Miss Mountain stood before her. Never had that lady's presence been more unwelcome. The stoical composure she had assumed, since the first tidings of the family misfortune, had rendered her an object of complete dislike to Miss Melbourne. Scarcely able to conceive a female character in the composition of which the softer feelings had been omitted, she gave her credit for an affectation, of which, in this instance, she was not guilty.

'Always at your meditations, Miss Melbourne,' she exclaimed; 'or rather, I fear, yielding to a melancholy, excusable indeed in the present posture of affairs, but assuredly not laudable. I walked out to meet you,' she continued, 'at the request of the family at Woodlands, by whom your presence is much missed. The day is closing, and they say they cannot lose a moment of the last evening you promised to spend with them. You see, I knew where to find you. You have surely to thank Mr. Sowerby and your father, for the philosophical and hardy education which makes you, like a true mountain-nymph, fond of being

"Rock'd by the tempest, nurtur'd on the wild."[64]

But are you not afraid, Miss Melbourne,' (in that affectedly sententious tone Matilda most dreaded) 'of increasing by solitude a tendency to the sensibility which it is our first duty to repress? I myself felt in danger / of giving way to the "torrent softness," till completely consoled by that divine letter of Sulpicius to Cicero, which I read seven times over, and which fully demonstrated to me the unreasonableness of indulging in grief for the loss of any human being.[65] Taking occasion to illustrate his thesis, by the desolation which had ovewhelmed, not individuals only, but whole cities once the most flourishing in Greece, – "Remember then, oh, my heart," continues the philosopher –'

'You are happy, Miss Mountain,' interrupted Matilda, drily, 'in being able to check the feelings of unavailing sympathy or regret, by considerations so consoling and satisfactory: but, as it is getting late, and really cold, I will, if you please, with the assistance of your arm, return to our friends, and we will defer the dissertation on Cicero till we are together.'

Miss Mountain, who made it a principle never to let the appearance of displeasure disturb the placidity in which she had arranged her features, smiled, with her wonted serene complacency, at the weakness which could not enter into her exalted reasonings, and led the way back towards the mansion.

The reappearance of the two ladies was truly welcome to the melancholy family group, who were assembled round the fire at that dull hour, which, between morning and evening, partakes of the pleasures of neither. It was after a pause in the conversation, now of no unfrequent recurrence, that Lady Torrendale, fancying she heard a sudden noise, started up; and, a moment afterwards, the door was thrown open, and a young man, of a countenance the most charming, a figure the most striking and noble Matilda had ever beheld, entered the room, and advanced, with all the eagerness of anxious affection, towards the Earl and Countess.

Miss Langrish, with a shriek, exclaimed, 'It was Strathallan's ghost!'

Lady Emily, springing forward, with the instinct of warm and sisterly attachment, cried out, 'It was Strathallan!'

Lord Torrendale, his spirits too weak from the indulgence of sorrow, to bear the admission of happiness so unexpected; scarcely / believing what he so ardently desired, gazed for a moment in fixed astonishment, neither understanding or almost hearing what was said around him: but when convinced, by the voice of his son, that he was indeed not a second time deceived, his joy could be only equalled by the sufferings he had previously endured.

The Countess mingled her congratulatory embraces with his; while the soft eyes of Matilda overflowed at the scene. A thousand questions, prompted by eager joy, curiosity, and surprise, were at once put to the thrice welcome stranger.

'Do we not see him, possess him? – is he not once more among us?' said Lord Torrendale, in a voice scarcely articulate, from the excess of too delightful emotion. 'What more can we desire?'

'Heavens! did you not expect me?' exclaimed Strathallan, surprised in his turn; while the instant alteration in his countenance evinced the pain he endured at the idea of being the cause of it to those who were so dear.

Miss Mountain, who alone had preserved her sweet serenity undisturbed, undertook to explain. 'I assure you, my Lord,' she observed in conclusion, 'your supposed loss was not regretted by your family only; strangers added the tribute of sympathy for so tragic an event. There is a young lady, who might at this moment stand as a model for a figure of Thanksgiving, in an allegorical piece on the cessation of the calamities of war.' As she spoke, she pointed to Matilda, who, retiring from immediate observation, and unconscious how much she excited it, stood, her eyes involuntarily cast upwards, her whole countenance and figure beaming with pleasure, while an emphatic 'Heaven be praised!' seemed just bursting from her lips.

Turning, for an instant, from the friends that surrounded him, Lord Strathallan looked at her; – and Miss Mountain felt sorry she had made the observation. The Countess took this opportunity to introduce Miss Melbourne to her son-in-law.

Matilda's cheeks glowed with painful confusion, / at her emotion having been made the subject of remark; and she experienced a relief when Lady Torrendale turned the attention of the company, by anxiously demanding of Strathallan, if he could explain the cause of a mistake which had been the source of so much suffering to all.

'That such an error should find its way into the public accounts, transmitted at that period, was not surprising,' he replied, 'when we consider the degree of unavoidable irregularity introduced into them, by the death of our general, and the dangerous wound received by the second in command: that it should not be contradicted in

England, I can only attribute to the circumstance, which happened to me in common with many others, of my having been separated from my regiment, by embarking in a different vessel from that in which it sailed.'

'And what was the reason of that confusion?' was the universal question.

'Must I tell you a romantic story?' he returned, forcing a smile; while a momentary agitation, he could not suppress shewed the pain this recollection excited. 'You remember, my Lord,' (addressing Lord Torrendale), 'the mention I made of the hospitality and kindness of the Spaniard Verdinha. Some time after the period when I had known his family, and when we were on our retreat, we were joined by a very fine youth, who requested to be allowed to serve among us, expressing a desire to act as a volunteer, and under my command. He said, he had caught his enthusiasm from his father, whom he hoped I still remembered. I did not know before that Verdinha had a son; but the young Antonio soon proved himself worthy of his parent. He bore all the fatigues and privations of our retreat without a murmur; but he was not destined to survive the fatal day in which our general gave battle at Corunna. In that battle he never left my side. In the moment that a French officer of cavalry aimed a stroke at me with his sabre, Verdinha advanced, and received it on his breast. A second blow having stunned me, so that for some minutes / I was thought to be dangerously wounded in the head, I was unable to afford him immediate assistance. My faithful Francis, seeing me unhorsed, carried me off the field: I was some time before I recovered; but the plumes and crest of the cap had broken the force of the stroke, so that I received no material injury. When I came to myself, the day was fallen, and the engagement over. The first object that met my eye was Antonio Verdinha, lying mortally wounded. I was entirely taken up with his situation, at the moment that our regiment, which was among the first that embarked, was already in all the bustle of departure. I imagine, that, in the hurry and confusion attending a night embarkation, I was at first supposed to be with them. The attention of every one was fully employed upon his own share in the important events that had passed, and were still taking place. The mistake was probably not discovered till it was too late; and some one who saw me fall might have recalled that circumstance to memory, and, on his arrival in England, have confirmed the erroneous statement that at first appeared respecting me. Meantime, I could not leave Verdinha; whom, for his father's sake, I considered as a deposit peculiarly recommended to my care. I afforded him every assistance the time and place would allow; but it was in vain. That night he died in my arms; and it was breathing his last wishes that –'

'Doubtless, 'twas some very important communication,' interrupted Lady Torrendale, in a tone which she meant should express friendly interest, but which had really more of petulant curiosity; 'otherwise I shall never forgive the little creature the anguish and anxiety he has caused us.'

Strathallan seemed to struggle for a moment with strong and inward emotion; and then replied, in a composed voice, 'It was.' He then added, as if anxious rapidly to bring his narrative to a conclusion, 'I embarked with the rest of the troops on the 17th, anxious to rejoin those friends who were already on their way to England; and, from the moment her white cliffs appeared in view, I could scarcely restrain my throbbing / impatience to embrace those dearer ones, from whom I anticipated so fond a welcome. From the hour of my landing, I travelled with a haste, which, while it prevented my hearing any thing till now of the reports that have prevailed, rendered a letter equally unnecessary. How well is it rewarded,' he continued, looking round him with affectionate joy, since I find myself once more encircled by this dear group – this centre, from which my thoughts, during my long absence, have so seldom wandered.'

Bending forward, in breathless attention, Matilda had listened, 'all ear,' to the narration of Strathallan. The subject itself, to her, possessed an interest; but when he spoke, 'twas that voice that caused the scarce-perceived, involuntary start; – it was one which seemed in every heart to find its echo: deep, sweet, and penetrating, it commanded that its owner, once known, should be loved – once loved, should never be forgot.

Lady Torrendale and Miss Mountain kept up the conversation, and indulged their curiosity in a thousand questions, which were answered with readiness and grace by Strathallan. Miss Mountain talked of the ancient Iberians and Lusitanians, of Sertorius and Viriatus;[66] and Miss Melbourne wondered that the pedantry which had disgusted her but an hour before, should now appear so easy to be endured.

Whatever Strathallan related seemed placed before the eyes of his hearers. Where he described scenery, it was picture; – where action, it was nature, life, and motion. The various adventures and sufferings of the companions of the scenes he had gone through, were so faithfully painted in the changes of his expressive features, that it was impossible, at the first moment, for any one to remark the first moment, for any one to remark the perfection of their regular and pensive beauty. The mind that beamed from the eye, the soul that flashed from that countenance could alone be regarded; it was one that could never be beheld without emotion, nor recalled without regret.

It is not surprising that where so much was to be asked, and so much to be related; where the enquirers were so anxious, and the narrator / so beloved, morning should peep in upon their vigil, and find the animated and happy circle still unsatisfied! At length, they broke up; but Oh! with what different feelings from those with which, some days before, the party had separated.

After a few hours rest, to recover from the effects of this tumultuous but pleasing occurrence, Matilda announced to Lady Torrendale the necessity of her return to the Rocks.

'Indeed you shan't, my little Matilda,' replied her Ladyship, 'you have shared in our dismals, and do you think I shall permit you to run away from our gaiety? I already meditate great designs; you must help me to mature them, and perhaps, we may yet astonish the world!'

'Not yet, dear Lady Torrendale,' returned Miss Melbourne, in the same playful tone; 'you, who have just had a son restored to you, must enter into the feelings of my mother, who may begin to regret my absence.'

Spite of the entreaties of the Countess, Matilda's resolution was unalterable; and she departed, followed by the regrets of all, particularly of Spencer Fitzroy, and Strathallan. The latter lamented that his presence had driven away the 'Nymph of the Woodlands.' Yet, perhaps, she was not secure from his image, amid the romantic solitudes of the Rocks. It was one that could not be contemplated without danger. She, now, dropt the tear of pity at the distresses of his gallant friends; now, saw him mournful and deserted, guarding, by his fading watch-fire, Verdinha's pale remains. Now, hurrying on board, divided from the loved companions of his perils,

'A lonely traveller on the moon-light sea.'[67]

Yet still, the look of checked but delighted surprise, of gratitude and interest, he had turned upon her, at the remark made by Miss Mountain, was that which most captivated her fancy, and played about her heart. And, while she found it impossible to banish its intrusive remembrance, was it to be wondered that Mr. Sowerby, for the first time, had reason to complain that 'Matilda was not so attentive as usual to her studies.' /

CHAPTER XIII.

Guerrier terrible,
Dans le fort du combat,
Quoiqu' invincible,
Souvent le cœur lui bat,
Car ce cœur sensible
Souffre pour le soldat.

CHEVALIER DE BOUFFLERS,
au Prince Henri de Prusse.[68]

MATILDA had an additional motive for wishing to return to the Rocks: she was recalled there by an uneasiness, the extent of which she would hardly own to herself, and yet that filled her affectionate heart with the most painful apprehensions. She had, for some time past, observed her father's health beginning to decline. A cold, caught by imprudently staying out too long on a botanical ramble, had brought on an attack on his lungs, attended with a most distressing cough. Though the most alarming symptoms were now all removed, his strength, from that time, had visibly decreased; he could not take the long walks in which he used to indulge; and was sometimes for whole days confined to his couch: during this period it was Matilda's delight to relieve Mrs. Melbourne from the fatigue of incessant attendance. She read to her father, from such books as she knew were to his taste, the passages in which he particularly delighted. She arranged, and kept in order, the various collections, of which he was no longer able to make the daily review himself. Or, if she was ever from his side, it was when, bounding through the rocks and glades, with the grace and activity of a wood-nymph, she brought him home such specimens of plants and mosses as even winter could afford, and such as she knew he would have selected.

Sometimes she felt her spirits droop, from the excess of her filial anxiety; but, more frequently, hope presented her with the bright side of the picture; Mr. Melbourne / had got through the severe illness that had attacked him in the beginning of the winter, though of a nature, at once, irritating, and dangerous. Why should not the same temperance, and extreme serenity of disposition, which had been said so greatly to have contributed to his recovery before, now bear him up against this slight relapse, 'till the return of of summer should completely restore him?

During this voluntary seclusion, Lady Torrendale often visited at the Rocks, to have the pleasure of complaining to her, and the livelier Miss Ferrars, as she termed it, 'to rattle her up.' But, on the whole, Mrs. Melbourne who had been pleased with that young lady, since the first moment of her introduction to her, thought she had no reason to repent the general invitation she had given her. Strathallan now was sometimes added to the groupe, and with respect to him (as was usually the case at the Rocks) opinions were divided. Mr. Melbourne thought him 'an amiable, unassuming, well-informed young man.' Mrs. Melbourne 'the most interesting creature she had ever beheld since her retirement into the country.' Mr. Sowerby 'the most odious, unpleasant, impertinent fellow that ever presumed to make himself agreeable to the women.' A shade of pensiveness that occasionally obscured the animated brilliancy of his conversation, only rendered him an object of added interest, at least, in the eyes of the ladies. He had been placed in a situation that peculiarly called forth all the energies of his heart and mind. An actor amid scenes the most awful and important, he had witnessed, with the deep sensibility of a soul yet unhacknied in calamity or guilt, the outrages of the oppressor, the sufferings of the oppressed; had shared in the struggle of a generous people, and had lamented the fall of valour; merit, too often alike beloved and exerted in vain. To a mind of a common mould, the miseries of the past would have only been recollected, amid the restored gaiety of the social circle, to add to the happiness, and enhance the sense of security the present moment afforded: but Strathallan's was not that mind. /

Meantime, Lady Torrendale did not long delay putting the grand design she meditated into execution. It was from Arbella that Matilda had the first intimation of it.

'Her Ladyship,' said she, 'has disposed of the clothing she has been making up this winter, so much to her satisfaction, and has met with so much gratitude from the soldiers' families she has relieved since their return from abroad, that it has converted her taste for charity into a passion; and she means to extend it, by a subscription ball to be given at S –. All the families of any consequence, who came down to spend the Christmas, approve the scheme. The money for the tickets is to be appropriated for the benefit of the widows and children of those soldiers in Strathallan's regiment, that fell at Corunna. The Countess is, of course, Lady Patroness – your mamma is named for another – Spencer and Strathallan are to be two of the stewards. In order to draw more attention it is given out that the poet Alcæus will, in the course of the evening, deliver an address suitable to the occasion. He is to speak it standing between two of the most interesting of the sufferers, with their children in their arms. We are sure they will be two of the handsomest women in the regiment, for Spencer is to chuse them.'

'But all this time you do not know whether we shall go.'

'O you certainly go – Spencer has said it, and Lionhart has sworn it.

Poor Lionhart! he has had but a dull Christmas. We must not let February pass without his having some amusement.'

'All these are very cogent reasons, yet still I may hesitate.'

'No, no – Eyes must never be contradicted; he is absolute – by the bye he has taken upon himself to pass the tickets among the ladies, and we have little fear for his success in the cause of melting charity. You know it is a trick in the family – did Lady Torrendale ever tell you that old story? Then you would laugh to see the importance he assumes, (continued Arbella with increased volubility,) while determining our dresses for this important occasion. Did I / tell you he was to fancy the dresses for you, Lady Torrendale, and me? She chuses we shall be alike – see what it is to affect youth! Every morning we have consultations, in which Spencer has the casting voice; from his infallible judgment there is no appeal. Oh if you could imagine the 'airs and graces, and doubts and disdains' he treats us with, while the respective merits of silver gauze, and gold muslin, and prince's plumes, and wreaths of roses are under consideration. – Miss Mountain, who has lately acquired or recovered a quantity of precious French, compliments him on this attention to our *attire*, and says we shall be '*Les Graces* ATTIRÉES *par l'Amour*.'[69] At length it is determined we shall figure in Spanish dresses, as the most appropriate, and we are to be as fine as pink puffs, slashed sleeves, and silver trimmings can make us – the hair in a net *à l'Espagnol*, the net of silver like the trimmings; and it is to be fastened in front with a plume of bird of Paradise feathers. – Is not that pretty? Fantastical. These are the last orders in council, but I cannot be quite positive with respect to their execution, for Captain Fitzroy changes and determines, and hesitates, and retracts "so" often, as poor Miss Langrish says, that it is impossible to know whether he will be of the same opinion to-morrow.'

'And you like all that?'

'Why, truth to say, 'tis not *le genre sublime,* but it is very pretty.'

However she might trifle with Arbella, Matilda felt an unconquerable repugnance to the idea of mingling in a scene of festivity while her father's health continued in its present uncertain state. When pressed by Lady Torrendale for the cause of her refusal, she thought she owed it to the general kindness and friendship she had met from her, not to treat her with common-place evasion, but to allege her real reasons. Matilda would have disdained to make a display of her filial anxiety to any indifferent person; but she thought that, in such frankness, she paid the highest compliment to her noble friend; who would require only to be informed of them, / to enter immediately into the nature of her feelings – she little knew Lady Torrendale.

'I am so vexed for Strathallan's sake,' she said, after listening with great signs of impatience to Matilda's detail. 'He is such a charming waltzer, and had made himself so sure of the honor of –'

'I am sorry to disappoint Lord Strathallan' replied Miss Melbourne laughing, 'but –'

'Oh child,' interrupted Lady Torrendale, with a toss of her head, 'I did not mean that. Your fine men now may be piqued, offended, but can never be *disappointed*.' Matilda felt hurt in her turn – the Countess did not give up her point, and on the very day of the entertainment called with Captain Fitzroy, resolved to make her give up her design or repent her determination. Perceiving that Matilda, who began to see into her intention, listened with great indifference, Captain Fitzroy, who had been, till now, stationed in the reserve, thought this the moment, with most effect, to bring up his force. With all that persuasiveness of address which he had been taught to think resistless; he urged the disappointment the whole party would endure on her refusal; the brilliancy of the expected *fête,* which was given partly on account of his brother Strathallan's return; and concluded,

'Consider how much I have desired; I have "ambitioned" the honor of your presence, when it leads me thus repeatedly to solicit you to change your cruel resolution. I ask it, Miss Melbourne, as a favour; and you must be aware that in general – I have not been used to entreat.'

A suppressed smile, which slightly played about the lips of Matilda, did not prevent the firm refusal she still persisted in giving, from being couched in the politest and most obliging terms. But the haughty Spencer, whom nothing less could satisfy than unconditional submission, turned proudly from her, and, during the rest of the visit, never addressed another word to her.

Her Ladyship stayed on, apparently for / no other purpose than to make Matilda regret the pleasure she had just refused.

'We shall be a great crowd,' said she, 'and we have therefore laid out a suite of four apartments. A ball-room, promenading-room, card, and supper-room. The supper-room will be the most delightful; for as we are to be all *à l'Espagnol* it will be lined, on each side, with orange trees, in boxes, intermingled with which, will be our trophies and colours. The famous man from London, the only man in the world who does those things well, will give the strains of every bird from the redbreast to the nightingale, from a place where he will be perfectly concealed from view; while artificial birds, hopping from branch to branch, will assist the illusion. This, I think, is new, and was quite my own idea. But it is impossible, by describing a part, to give you any notion of the whole effect. It will be one scene of fairyism, of splendor, of perfumes, of music; you have, no doubt, some more '*rational*' amusement in view with your 'FRIEND' Mr. Sowerby; some phantasmagoria perhaps, or magic lantern, or –'

'Pray Lady Torrendale,' interrupted Spencer, 'remember to give Miss Hautenville notice she must not appear in that blue muslin, it misbecomes her complexion so much.'

'Certainly child, but what reason can I give?'

'That I cannot bear blue and buff: tell her so with my compliments. And I wish to Heaven you could as easily persuade Miss De Courcy never to appear in pink again. I affect nothing when I declare that, at the last ball, her pink gossamer made me suffer cruelly, yet she will not leave it off.'

'Well, if it hurts your nerves, you had better tell her so.'

'Gad so I will. If she would but dress in white, she would be the handsomest woman I ever saw – as it is, she is the handsomest woman (looking round him) that I have met since my return to Derbyshire.'

The Captain rose; and Lady Torrendale, after paying her parting civilities to Mrs. / Melbourne, turned back on the staircase to exclaim to Matilda, 'So you won't be one of us; adieu, my soul, I leave you to read Zimmerman upon Solitude, or some such pretty, tender, sentimental amusement.'[70]

Taking her son's arm, she departed; leaving Miss Melbourne no other uneasiness than that which arose from the discovery, in her noble friend, of a pleasure (an incomprehensible one to this child of the woods and mountains,) in trying to inflict unnecessary pain.

Scarcely was Lady Torrendale gone, when a new visitor, in all the pleasing hurry and flutter of preparation appeared. It was Arbella Ferrars.

'My dearest creature,' she said, 'I am come for the sole purpose of trying to shake your inflexible resolution respecting this ball.'

'I am sorry,' said Matilda, 'it is taken, and that I must content myself with making you the same excuse I have just given Lady Torrendale and Captain Fitzroy.'

'Fitzroy! what business had he – that is to say, he knew I meant to speak to you,' continued Arbella, recollecting herself; while the assurance, from Matilda, that she would not go, restored to her features that serenity of which a slight shade of discontent for an instant had robbed them. 'Certainly my love, if you had good reason for not going, you were right to be firm; and I am sure you would not let any thing Spencer could say influence you.'

'Certainly not,' repeated Miss Melbourne, with a look, which, though mild, open, and satisfied as usual, yet possessed an expression that brought the colour into Miss Ferrar's cheeks, and forced her to take refuge in acknowledging the second 'whole and sole' purpose of her visit. She had not been able to procure a bird of Paradise plume that pleased her, and, recollecting that Matilda, who often received, from her father, presents of rare and beautiful feathers, might have a larger collection, she had come to request she would let her select some for the evening. Her friend, too happy to oblige, laid open her store to her inspection. Arbella, when she / had suited herself, said, that if Matilda would admit the trespass, she would dine and dress at her house – 'that at least, if I do not see you at the ball, I may enjoy, 'till the last moment, your sweet society.'

After dinner, the candles being set, and Arbella placed before the glass, she began that sort of discourse, between conversation and soliloquy, in which young ladies, suffering under a perturbation of mind, sometimes like to indulge.

'So! we shall be rather dashing, rather out of the common way. Miss Mountain is to be the third grace for want of a better. What a buzzing there is in my poor head – I suppose it is all the noise I shall hear to night.' Then, humming part of a tune – 'Fitzroy's waltz, did you ever hear it? it is by Krumpbh;[71] and is the sweetest thing of the kind, that ever was composed – I shall see him waltzing to night – see him! I shall. It is impossible to give an idea of his figure, of his attitudes; grace, and flexibility were never seen before. Indeed I think the last word was expressly invented for him. Now Strathallan is a charming figure, but Spencer is such a dear fellow, he is the exact waltzing size.'

'That is very good of him.'

'Good! nay now you are laughing.'

'No indeed; you praised him for it as if were a voluntary merit.'

'Did I! I only meant that Strathallan waltzes very well, but he is a little too tall, and besides he – You'd like Spencer better; that man, that eldest son of Lord Torrendale's, is a heart of rock, of adamant, of perfect adamant; admires nothing on earth but himself. Would not waste an hour's attention on an angel. No, not on an angel,' continued Arbella, considering herself more attentively in the glass, and fixing the plumes among her clustering tresses. 'To attempt him is mere loss of powder and shot.'

'Perhaps you have tried,' said Matilda.

'Perhaps I have,' Arbella replied. –

'There now I think that will do pretty well; I must be going my dear girl.'

All this time her friend had assisted with her usual obliging sweetness at the operations / of her toilet. As she was standing behind Miss Ferrars, to arrange a part of her hair, Arbella caught a glimpse of her lovely blooming features, that appeared in the glass just above her own. 'O that will never do,' she exclaimed, hastily rising, 'for you know it is not for me to say with truth,

"Mine's the prettier shadow far than thine Matilda"."[72]

and, perhaps, at that moment, she did not very sincerely regret, that, she was not, at the ball, to endure a comparison with the perfect and eclipsing beauty of her friend.

A message from Mr. Melbourne, requesting to see the fair visitor before she departed for the Assembly, delayed her for a few moments.

'I am glad my father will see you,' said Miss Melbourne, 'it will raise his spirits which have not been so good since his last attack.'

'Aye, I always said how it would end,' interrupted Miss Ferrars, shaking her head. 'I always said how it would end. There's Sir Edward Meadows who caught his death the other day, hunting for glow-worms in the dew, and Mr. Peak who broke his neck in a botanizing ramble to –.' Matilda's eyes filled with tears.

'Arbella, I am ever ready to listen to your anxieties, but for mine you have no consideration.'

'Bless me how thoughtless I am! Can you forgive me? I have a mind to force you to the ball to dispel the ugly phantoms I have so unfortunately raised – you will have such a loss in not seeing the Shears!'

'The Shears!'

'O, I had forgot – That sublime poet, known to the world by the name of Mr. Spring, to the Muses by that of Alcæus, is, I understand, in Lady Lyndhurst's circle, familiarly designated by the name, style, and title of the Shears – from a certain habit he has of cutting across whatever people are saying with as great a promptitude, and as little remorse, as that most useful weapon of industry. Alcæus is a wit, fancies himself a genius, and / the whole time you are speaking to him, instead of attending, is deliberating in his own head, what he shall say when it comes to his turn; then, if he happens to have a brilliant conception, bolts it out, totally regardless whether it forms a suitable answer or not to the preceding observation. There is a piece of literary anecdote for you, to amuse the tea-table; wish me in return good luck, and plenty of conquests; for oh my dear! sometimes one's evil star prevails; and then, when you begin to feel the night wearing away, and the entertainment drawing to a close, yet all your pleasure still to come, and the dear object of your hopes as far distant as ever, what a dreary, what a frightful solitude a ball room becomes! I cannot imagine a more truly pitiable situation; and, I know not how, I feel a kind of foreboding – but no, it cannot be,' continued the lively Arbella, whose mind

'Quick as her eyes, and as unfixed as those;'[73]

had already seized another leading idea. 'Spencer, dear Spencer, cannot, will not change; how well he begins to look! such a countenance, such eyes, such teeth, and such beautiful mustacioes – oh! I wish he were here; but I am keeping your father expecting me,' she resumed, after this curious climax, '*Allons donc!*' for the dear invalid.

Though stretched on a couch and visibly ill, at Miss Ferrars' approach, Mr. Melbourne languidly smiled with benevolent pleasure; 'Why now I declare,' said he,

---

*   Dryden's Arthur and Emmeline.

'those bird of Paradise plumes look very well; but, perhaps, my dear young lady, you would have liked a plume of heron's feathers, or some other bird's better. Why did you not freely apply to me? I should have offered, but that I thought you young ladies might require something more to be done to them, than I do; something that Matilda knows, with your Carbery or your –'

'Oh Sir,' said Arbella, 'I am already made rich with gifts, your daughter is so generous, that if Miss Mountain were here, she would compare her to Venus, helping to endow and adorn Pandora.' /

'But really my love,' turning suddenly to Matilda, 'why don't you go?'

Her friend had too lately received a lesson upon ingenuous simplicity and confidence, to be easily inclined again to suppose that others thought and felt like herself, she therefore replied by some general and polite evasion, allusive to her health and various avocations.

'Well I declare I am so sorry that – if it were not all settled, I believe I should be tempted to –'

'Oh don't think of such a thing, what would Spencer say,' interrupted Matilda, archly smiling, and applying a favorite expression of Miss Ferrars.

'Spencer! I assure you he is the last person, at this moment, in my thoughts. There, you have made me forget my fan; and now where are my gloves? Adieu, I must leave you, I ordered the carriage should come for me rather early because I have to help my Aunt to receive the party from Woodlands, who call at our house on their way to the Assembly. Expect me to-morrow with a lachrymatory full of the tears of the despairing beaux.'

'Arbella is a good girl,' said Mrs. Melbourne, 'and, I truly believe, would prefer Matilda to any thing in the world, except her last admirer, or her diamond necklace.'

'They are all very good-natured,' replied Mr. Melbourne, 'and though I think Matilda was wise not to go; yet, if ever young people were inclined not to grudge the trouble and loss of time such amusements cost, it would be on an occasion like this. Where the object is benevolence, even a ball may be rendered interesting. We have taken care they should be no losers by our non-attendance. But, however, it was very kind and polite of Lady Torrendale to take the trouble to come and be so pressing with Matilda, and that pretty young man her son too. As far as I can judge, he has not as much in him as his brother, who is really a fine fellow; but he is equally pleasant, and, I believe, very good natured and charitable; for when I used to walk about more, I often met him coming out of the cottages.' /

Matilda, smiling at her father's unconsciousness of the little sacrifice she had made him, enjoyed it, in secret, the more perhaps on that account: and the tumultuous throb of expectation, in the bosom of Arbella, could hardly equal the serene satisfaction she experienced when Mr. Melbourne, delighted with her innocent and companionable gaiety, fondly called her his little reader, his nurse, and secretary; and declared it impossible to remember his illness or infirmity, in the company of such a child.

The entrance of Mr. Sowerby interrupted effusions of parental tenderness, so deep-felt, and so well deserved. Conceiving it impossible his young pupil could resist the repeated solicitations of her titled friends, he had come to spend an hour with his deserted neighbour, as he imagined him to be. He had just exclaimed, with the lengthened emphasis which he knew so well how to give, 'And so Matilda is gone to this a-bom-in-able ball,' when the sight of his fair pupil, seated by her father's couch, and engaged, at that moment, in sketching some botanical drawings, under his inspection, a little disarmed his wrath. He had scarcely taken a chair when it was near being roused again, by the appearance of a servant who said a person waited to speak to Miss Melbourne.

'What person, what messenger?' cried Sowerby, 'send him away.' But, before he could be obeyed, a boy, with a basket in his hand full of dried plants, presented himself, and said to Matilda, 'Here be the roots of the odd shaken heath that your Ladyship said you wanted to get for your father, and couldn't; and hearing as Squire Melbourne was so main poorly, and didn't go out as he used to do, I thought I go myself and try to get some from my aunt, who lives at Ridgefield, six miles off; for I remembered as she used to say she had'em; so I got up yearly, and ax'd her.'

'And pray, who may you be? my good boy,' said Mr. Melbourne.

'Lord Sir, doesn't your honor remember little Tommy Leaves as you gave the bark and port to, after the favors, and was so kind to. / To be sure I be growed, and handsome, since that time, but I shall never forget.'

'I never gave you any thing,' returned his honor, whose memory did not appear to be so extensive as his generosity.

'O surely, you sent every day Sir, and mother says as how –'

'Well, well – may be so,' said the placid Mr. Melbourne, resuming his studies, and concluding with a very favorite expression of his; by which if he could not immediately call to remembrance a circumstance, he, at least, signified his assent by giving up the point. Matilda received, with one of her sweetest smiles, this welcome attention to her father, while Mr. Melbourne observed, after the boy was gone 'well, it was truly obliging of Boughs, was not that his name? to go so far to get me those specimens, particularly as I could not send my servants, for Robert is gone to see his wife, John is sick, and Thomas does not like taking long walks.'

'Humph!' said Sowerby, 'they never do any thing over and above for me at Clifdendown.' In spite of his peculiarities, and habits of almost utter seclusion, a disposition gentle and indulgent to an extreme, a great liberality to all who depended on him, and a benevolence mild, and diffusive, though silent as the streams that flowed from his native Rocks, had endeared Mr. Melbourne to his humble neighbours, who were all eager to testify their good will by any little service it was in their power to perform: while to Sowerby, on the contrary, his servants and tenants rather paid the worship of fear than love. However different their characters, both seemed at this moment as if they were vying with each other who could most compensate to Matilda, by their affectionate praises, for the absence of gayer society. When her merits were the theme, Mr. Melbourne was ever eloquent; but Sowerby went beyond a parent's praise in his affectionate partiality. Mrs. Melbourne's playful wit enlivened the social group, over which the genius of domestic happiness seemed for the moment to repose. Leaving therefore Miss Melbourne, between two beaux, whose / attentions, however sincere, will not, I fear, be envied by any of her youthful competitors, we will go back to the beginning of this eventful day: and endeavour to trace some scenes that had passed at Lady Torrendale's, and that may afford matter of conjecture whether all within was so serene, as it outwardly appeared, from the triumphant gaiety of her Ladyship, and the fascinating ease of Captain Fitzroy.

CHAPTER XIV.

O thou, the friend of man assigned,
With balmy hands his wounds to bind,
And charm his frantic woe:
When first distress with dagger keen,
Broke forth to waste his destined scene
Thy wild unsated foe!

Come Pity, come, by fancy's aid
Even now my thoughts, relenting maid,
Thy temple's pride design;
Its southern site, its truth complete
Shall raise a wild enthusiast heat
In all who view the shrine.

COLLINS. ODE TO PITY.[74]

'IT's a folly to talk, Lady Torrendale,' were Mrs. Stockwell's first words in their morning *tête-a-tête*, 'I've advanced more than I can afford, and I'll advance no more.'

'But, my dear Mrs. Stockwell, is this the moment to stop, when Spencer has set his / heart upon following up the plan with spirit? I dare not face him without the promise of this thousand pounds. Indeed I dare not; no one has any idea of his temper, who only knows him – as you know him. Surely you would not prevent his making an advantageous arrangement with his creditors for such a trifle; and if he has been a little imprudent this last year, and reduced me to some difficulties, would you increase them when you could so easily' –

'Lady Torrendale,' said Mrs. Stockwell, in a tone that she meant should be solemn; 'I have borne a great deal, and concealed a great deal, and I never let Lord Torrendale guess.'

'Oh! if you still allude to the sum you lent me, to make up what I wanted to advance him before I left Rose-villa, you were certainly very good; but consider it is all for your own Spencer – your dear Spencer, who came into Derbyshire for the sole object of seeing you;' (and recruiting his finances a little at your expence,) she might have added, aside. 'He has applied to me; but, I declare I am at this moment so in want of money.'

'Ah! that is so like me,' resumed Mrs. Stockwell, 'I am in sad want of money too, I assure you.'

'Pray, pray, my dear Mrs. Stockwell,' interrupted Lady Torrendale, forgetting her former request, in the habitual dislike she had to this assimilation to herself, a figure of speech in which her less genteel friend was very apt to indulge, but then resuming her former manner, she added 'Come, there's a dear soul, I know you will listen to reason; and I have very little time to waste in argument. In short Spencer has taken it into his head, and it must be done.'

'Well then, if Spencer has taken it into his head,' returned Mrs. Stockwell, with a mixture of bitterness and familiarity, 'Spencer must put it out of his head again, that's all. You know, Lady Torrendale,' she pursued, suddenly assuming a whining tone of sentimental reproach, 'while I thought Captain Fitzroy had any regard for me or mine, there was nothing I would not do for / him: but now, I see he does nothing but make gibes and jeers, and turn me into ricadool; I should be a fool, so I should, to go on as I have done. I'll not be duped; I'll tell Lord Torrendale, so I will; I don't forget his saying, when I wished my niece Arbella could appear at Lady Lyndhurts's, that there was ne'er a shabby room for her; as if *my* niece was to be put off with a shabby room, at any Countess's in England; when, I am sure, I spared neither pains nor cost in her edication, and sent her to the very same school with the Honorable Miss de Courcy; for all I wished was to make a true bred lady of her.'

'And she is so,' interrupted the Countess obligingly. 'You must have forgotten your French, my dear Mrs. Stockwell, or you would perceive my son must have meant *Chaperon*. Miss Ferrars could not appear, without one, in a manner suitable to her station and fortune; and, as you do not know Lady Lyndhurst, and at that time I did not visit her, he could not immediately fix upon one he thought eligible. Is that all poor Spencer's offence? then I think he does not deserve such resentment.'

'All his offence! I wish I could number his offences. T'other day, at dinner, he asked me if I didn't like blankets; deluding plainly to the business poor Mr. Stockwell used to follow: and, on some one's mentioning my son's reproaching marriage with his cousin, he turns quick upon me, and asks me how long that affair had been upon the "Carpet." If 'tis the most melancholious subject in the world; it's enough that I should open my mouth to set him laughing. It's all one what I say. When I consoled with him about his poor brother's being "macerated" by the French, I could see he could hardly keep his countenance. But, what I take as the cruellest and most ill-naturedest, and most treacherousest thing of all is, his coaxing and wheedling, (flurting I suppose he calls it) with my poor niece Arbella, to induce her / to forsake her true lover, and so get possession of her and her fortune.'

'And so get possession of her and her fortune,' repeated her Ladyship, haughtily drawing up, and all the *engrafted* pride of the house of Torrendale and Strathallan expressed in her countenance. 'Did I hear right? are you conscious Mrs. Stockwell, whom you are addressing? Have a care of what you advance; do you think it possible *my* son could for a moment have a serious thought of *your* niece? It shall be my care that he shall perfectly undeceive you, and prove to your satisfaction, that he has no intention of rivalling Mr. Sam Stockwell in her good graces.'

'Dear me, I'm sure I never thought he had,' resumed the good lady, frightened at what she had said, and desirous if possible to retract, 'and for that very reason I tried to break the neck of the thing in its first beginning; and your Ladyship is aware I miscouraged it as much as possible; and so long as a matter of three years agone, when Arbella was at school, and I found he had contrived to make acquaintance with her in the holidays, and was a coming down to Woodlands about her, I never, from that blessed time, let her come home to her "vocation," and afterwards when he and his brother still used to call, and Captain Fitzroy expressed himself surprised that she should be always away, I imbuked him severely, and approached him as the sole cause: but it seems the nature of all the young gentlemen to withstand my "approaches." I put the case most pathetically to him, and represented as such persecution, was ill-using any Lady. "Now suppose Captain Fitzroy," says I, "you was in love with me." –

'Enough, enough, dear Mrs. Stockwell, you have quite convinced me that you see the thing in the light I wish it. And now nothing remains but that you should consent to oblige me in the little arrangement I mentioned. Spencer, I am certain, could never have intentionally offended you. If you examine into the slights you fancy you have experienced, you will find they originated in something as trifling as the offer he unfortunately / made you, of veal blanquets at dinner; and as to carping at "carpets," I only wish, for your sake, he had said on the *tapis*. Then remember, dear Madam,' continued Lady Torrendale, alternately soothing and dictating to her, 'that on my introducing Miss Ferrars to-night, depends her being brought into fashion.'

'Fashion's a good paper substitute,' observed Mrs. Stockwell, with more shrewdness than the Countess fancied she possessed; 'but I own I am one of them that's for the bullion. What security pray have I, that I shall be ever paid my money?'

'The best security in the world, the estate of Strathallan.'

'I beg your pardon, Lady Torrendale; but that's not your son's; it's the young Lord's.'

'I beg your pardon, Mrs. Stockwell, that's not the young Lord's, as you are pleased to call him, but the old Lord's; and can, and *shall* be given to my son whenever he pleases. Did you imagine that because Strathallan liked to spend his time at it as a hunting seat, and perhaps because he took his title from it, that it was his? Far from it; so now having proved clearly Spencer's power of satisfying any future demand, I am sure you will consider the urgency of the case, and' –

Mrs. Stockwell reflecting that if she *did* play her cards genteelly, and sometimes accommodate her more fashionable acquaintance, it was in fact her only ticket of admission to that society of which she was so ambitious, resolved, after a short debate with herself, to do what she had often done before, put her affronts in her pocket, and take her money out of it. 'Well, since it's for the last time, and your Ladyship's so very anxious, though they *do* say that you should not sell the skin of the bear 'till he has been killed. – I don't care if I –'

'That's my own Mrs. Stockwell! I knew it would come to this: I may tell Spencer you are all adorable; may I not? I must break up congress now, for I have to plague Miss Melbourne, and to quiz Miss de Courcy, / and half a hundred more things to do before I dress for this teazing ball.'

After this unpleasant conversation, the result of a long postponed *eclaircissement* with Mrs. Stockwell, which that lady, who conceived herself much neglected by Captain Fitzroy, had often demanded in vain; we must behold Lady Torrendale all brilliant with jewels, and redolent with sweets; and retaining apparently no trace of the disagreeable occurrences of the morning.

The appearance of the graces, the lovely birds of paradise from Woodlands, at the assembly at S – seemed to be all that delayed the expected pleasures and festivities of the evening. The rooms, devoted to the purposes of promenading and dancing, were adorned with a taste, an attention to embellishment and effect, which showed that no provincial hand had directed the arrangement of the whole. Captain Fitzroy, whom it cost nothing to promise to repair any damage he might occasion, had exercised a little of the transforming power of fashion, in extending, beautifying, throwing down partitions, and raising up platforms, as additional ideas presented themselves to his fertile imagination. Every thing was gay, airy, simple, yet appropriate and elegant. The Temple of Pity, in perspective, surrounded by lights, flowers and fragrance, formed a pleasing termination to the whole. This little edifice, raised by several steps, and composed entirely of transparencies, partook much of the nature of theatric illusion. The poem of Collins suggested the hint; and such was its beauty, its 'Truth Complete,' that, could the second bard of Arun have viewed the warm creation of his fancy thus happily realized, he would surely have afforded it a languid smile of pensive pleasure.[75] The paintings in the different compartments of the temple represented some of the scenes that most interest and affect in history's various page:

> 'There pictures toil shall well relate,
> How chance, or hard involving fate
> O'er mortal bliss prevail;'[76]

and in the centre of the figure of the presiding deity, her /

> 'Sky-worn robes of tenderest blue,
> And eyes of dewy light'[77]

were seen, in all their enchanting and aërial splendor. Beside an altar, so contrived that he could, at once command the whole circle, appeared the poet. In the address, which he immediately began, the young bard Alcæus well knew how to take advantage of the enthusiasm of the moment; pointing to the two victims of the recent struggle, who were distinguished by their beauty and youth, and drest with a simplicity that was rendered at once modest and becoming, he now called on the tenderness of the patriotic females of his country, to feel for their sex's distresses in an humbler sphere; now directed their attention to the unconscious innocents that sported in their arms; and, all unknowing of the fate from which charity had rescued them, played with the fragrant sweets and blossoms that surrounded them, or smiled in sweet security on the festive group. His exertions were rewarded with success. The soft contagion of pity was caught with resistless force; the feeling of regret, excited by the fate of our country's brave defenders, was converted into a principle of active benevolence, the effects of which did not expire with the illusions of the night.

The Ode being finished, most of the company now crouded round Lady Torrendale to express the pleasure they had enjoyed, or the interest they experienced; receiving each with unembarrassed ease, she performed the pleasing duties of her situation with grace and applause; and it was considered as an exclusion from all pretension to fashion not to be presented to the lady patroness of the evening.

But Strathallan, the lost, the restored Strathallan, was, from the moment he appeared, the centre of universal attention. He arrived later than the rest of the party; and was instantly surrounded by friends and acquaintance, each endeavouring to surpass the other, in the sincerity of their welcome and in the warmth of their congratulations. Those who had been introduced to him before at Woodlands, were glad again to express the joy they felt at seeing him once more restored to / their circle; while others, who had not seen him since his return, were equally pleased with this opportunity of advancing their claim to his notice. Strathallan felt these unbidden testimonies of the general sympathy and interest he had excited, with that deep yet dignified sensibility, which so peculiarly marked his character. Looking round on the gay crowd, where every countenance beamed with kindness, and every hand was stretched forth in friendship, he yielded without reserve to the delicious illusion of the moment, and the grateful pleasure, which spoke in those gentle eyes,

'That seem'd to love whate'er they look'd upon,'[78]

pourtrayed the genuine overflowings of a soul, where manly fortitude and every soft and kindlier affection were sweetly blended.

The company had now begun to catch the gaiety and spirit of the scene. The sprightly notes of the bands engaged for waltzes, Spanish dances, and country dances, were rung in alternate murmur of trial and preparation; and the light of the lustres around could scarely equal the blaze of jewellery, or the more captivating brightness of the sparkling eyes and blushing cheeks, overspread with the gay hue of expected pleasure.

Lord Strathallan opened the ball with Miss Mountain; and already was each lady engaged, save Miss Ferrars (who, for her own reasons, discouraged every address) and Miss Hautenville, who stood, her rigid features and thin spare form adorned with a net of becoming yellow, her countenance composed into a smile, and her fan employed in gaily beating time, till the happy moment should arrive, that should bring some enamoured youth to her feet.

Arbella, ignorant of the implied compact of the morning, between her aunt and Lady Torrendale, had contrived to keep herself disengaged, in order, as she said, that she might not disappoint dear Fitzroy, when he asked her. 'Dear Fitzroy,' however, did not seem in haste to claim the honour she designed him. Independently of the reason above alluded to, it was sufficient / for the vain and capricious Spencer, that Miss Ferrars was at the ball, and Miss Melbourne was not, for him to wish her away, and her friend in her place. Not that he had any preference to Miss Melbourne. That very morning, had he been asked, which of the two he would rather see at night, he would have been probably much perplexed to make his election. But then, Matilda 'ought not' to have been equally indifferent to the idea of meeting him: 'she ought' to have known he was the best dancer in England, and to have been desirous to see him to such an advantage: 'she ought' to have shown a readiness to comply with his request, when he had condescended to acknowledge such a compliance would give him pleasure; and to have felt anxious to witness a fête that was planned partly under his inspection. He was also displeased, though he would scarcely own it to himself, at the universal attention his noble brother engrossed; and these various causes having contributed to the discomposure of his temper, he revenged it all on the innocent

Arbella. Instead of dancing, he continued walking up and down the room, arm in arm with his friend Lionhart, occasionally looking at Miss Ferrars, sufficiently to mark that she was the subject of their conversation. 'Now do, pray, Lionhart; don't you see the tender, drooping fair one is waiting your approach? Did not I bring you down for the express purpose of "superseding" me?'

'Nonsense! – I won't be refused – I won't be laughed at – I know it is you she expects.'

'Me! I did not intend to dance to night; but if I do, I believe it must be with Miss De Courcy: she is the most tolerable woman in the room, since Miss Melbourne is not here. There – make no more delay – I commission you – represent me.'

'That is very easy! You know, it is in vain for me to attempt to please any one who has seen you first.'

'Oh, you flatter! – surely it is not so,' resumed Spencer: and then, leaning towards him he whispered something in his ear, at which Captain Lionhart laughed heartily; / while poor Arbella, who could not hear what was said, but was conscious it related to her, sat in silent vexation, uncertain whether it was best to conceal her mortification, or give way to her displeasure. At length, not to afford Spencer an additional triumph by sitting out, she suffered herself to be led, by a partner of very high rank, to join the festive scene; at the same time that the inconstant Fitzroy conducted the fair Miss De Courcy to her place. This young lady, who was her intimate friend, took occasion to trip up to her, and just whisper – 'Lord! my dear, what did you do to your drapery? it sits quite ill: you certainly caught it going out of the carriage. Never mind,' she continued, observing Arbella looked a little alarmed, 'you can't possibly alter it now. I only thought it right to tell you of it:' and, satisfied with this exertion of friendship, she ran back to rejoin her partner.

Meanwhile, Lady Torrendale, observing Stockwell was disengaged, advanced towards the unemployed youth, who having frizzed out his hair in the form of a powder-puff, and shortened his legs to the size of those of a duck, imagined himself an Adonis, and stood, negligently quizzing the ladies, and expecting universal admiration. On her Ladyship's asking him, if he did not chuse to dance? 'No, ma'am,' he answered indolently, 'I never dance unless I can get the handsomest woman in the room for a partner.'

Her Ladyship bowed acquiescence to this sensible and modest reply; and, leaving the young gentleman to the 'handsomest woman in the room,' moved to another part of it.

To the waltzing, Spanish dances had succeeded;[a] and the gay foreign strains of the Fandango and Bollero were introduced by Captain Fitzroy, in honour of his brother's return.[b] Spencer distinguished himself in the management of the Castanet; but all eyes were fixed, in preference, on Strathallan.

'Is that Lord Strathallan?' whispered a young lady, who had just arrived; 'that elegant young man, who is so attentive to Lady Torrendale?'

'No; that is her Ladyship's own son, / Captain Fitzroy. Lord Strathallan is just crossing the room this moment – that fine figure decorated with a foreign order; you know, he is a Knight of the Tower and Sword – "*La Torre y Spada.*"'

'Yes, I know him now; I shall never mistake the other for him again. How I longed to see him, after that strange report that he was dead!'

Such were the whispers that surrounded the welcome wanderer.

'To him each lady's look was lent,
    On him each *warrior's* eye was bent.'[79]

Yet still some secret dissatisfaction seemed, after the first, to prevent his wholly enjoying the pleasure his presence inspired. He spoke little; and after dancing with Miss Mountain preferred taking out Miss Ferrars to any of the other ladies who hoped, from the privilege of acquaintance, for his notice. But, alas! this was only to have the power of talking of her lovely absent friend; a circumstance which, notwithstanding her affection, mortified her exceedingly.

'Both the brothers are bewitched tonight, I think,' cried Arbella, as she at length poutingly seated herself at a little distance from her aunt; who, standing in the middle of a very fine gown, and 'over that' a still finer 'Indy shawl,' was pouring her complaints to 'the idle' Sam Stockwell, upon her niece's 'unaccountable sort of behaviour.' In her most pathetic and querulous tone, she began, 'Now, if I was to set my eyes upon sticks, I declare I can't conceit what upon earth it is ails Arbella. It's quite nonsical of her for to object to you, Sam, and this person, and that person, and keep on a wherretting of me and herself, as she has done all night. I'm sure, she's had plenty and choice of nice partners.'

Sam, who was a little, or (as he thought himself) *not* a little genteel; and who had often entreated his mother to change her favorite phrase of 'worretted,' or 'wherretted,' to more fashionable 'worried,' or still better, 'annoyed,' now signified his displeasure at so improper an expression, by a dignified silence; while Mrs. Stockwell continued / in the soliloquy to which she was thus condemned: 'There's Lord Kilcare that she's had, who is better than Lord Strathallan, being an Earl in his own right, whereas t'other is only a Viscount by courtesy: and then she has had Strathallan himself, who is still better than his brother, Captain Fitzroy, who, let him give himself what airs he will, is no more than honourable: and the vulgarest partner she has had all night is Sir Maurice Milward, K.B.'

Mrs. Stockwell, as may have been observed, was, in her ideas of rank, rather Russian. It always required title, of some kind, to attract the honour of her notice. With her, a Colonel was somebody, a General was somebody, a Lord possessed her highest respect, and a Duke was almost above her veneration. But, low-born and low-bred herself, she had no idea of respecting the influence of birth or riches independently of title and station; and the whole race of Esquires were, without exception, the objects of her most unqualified contempt. She was also perfectly ignorant of that imaginary equality which the customs of society create in good company. To hear her discourse, one would suppose that each of her distinguished friends moved in a little separate sphere or orbit of his own; in which the Duke might look down upon the Earl; the Earl might return the compliment to the Baron; while the Baron might revenge himself, by annihilating, with the most killing contempt, the poor Baronet, who should dare to approach him. 'I assure you, Mem,' said she to Mrs. Harley, a lady who happily at this moment came within reach of her communications, 'if my niece Arbella don't dance, it's not for want of partners. I'm sure, Miss Mountain would have been happy to have received half the attentions she has, from Lord Strathallan.'

Mrs. Stockwell, in thus expressing herself, mistook Miss Mountain. It was not the attention of one, or of two persons more or less, that could disturb this lady's good opinion of herself, or the complete satisfaction with which she contemplated the plenitude of her own perfections. Her's was not that uneasy and tormenting thirst for applause, / which requires perpetual food to be administered to it from the admiration of others; it was rather that perfect complacency, that beatitude of vanity, which rests contented and all sufficing to itself. Miss Mountain was proud of her riches; she was proud of her birth (particularly by the mother's side); she was proud of her beauty; she was very proud of her learning; but, above all, she was proud of that dignified serenity and unruffled self-possession, which enabled her, as she imagined, to keep all this pride to herself.

Stockwell, determined to exchange his mother's lamentations for the company of his cousin Arbella, suddenly strutted close up to her, and said, 'I hate these great assemblies, dear Coz – I'm not fond of the company of your fine people – they never know where they ought to bestow their attention, and nobody's comfortable. Oh, after all, a little snug party of friends is the thing; don't you think so?'

Arbella, roused by these observations from a deep reverie, in which far other objects than her cousin had taken possession of her mind, started, looked at him from head to foot, and returned no answer; but perceiving that Sam, who thought he had made a great effort in putting so many words together, had taken his station behind her, silent and immoveable (the usual way in which he expressed his admiration), she sought refuge by the side of Mrs. Stockwell, whom she endeavoured to persuade to leave the ball-room for the card or supper-room. But to attract Mrs. Stockwell's attention was at that moment impossible. Her whole heart and soul were absorbed in her 're'el Indy shawl,' which she had just missed, and which she was sadly 'afear'd some awkward parson would set upon. Bless me! I can't conceive what I have done with it! Captain Fitzroy – Lord Strathallan – now do'ye look for my shawl – It's re'el Indy. I would not lose that shawl for more than I can say – I'm sure it cost me pounds and pounds, though I got it at the cheap shop.'

Lord Strathallan (a thing very uncommon with him) was absent, and really did not hear her. Captain Fitzroy heard, but did / not think it necessary to give any indication that he did so.

'Arbella, my love, did you see it?' continued the good lady, turning at length in despair to her niece.

'Oh! madam, you may depend upon it 'tis perfectly safe,' Miss Ferrars replied, with a sweet smile, and the air of one who had given the most satisfactory answer in the world, while, in reality, she had not the slightest idea of what her aunt had been talking about. Fortunately Mr. George Spring, the brother of Alcæus, the poet, came up, at this moment to Mrs. Stockwell's relief. This young gentleman, who has not yet been introduced into notice, was far from partaking of his brother's celebrity. They were the sons of an eminent hop-merchant in the neighbourhood, and owed their introduction into more fashionable circles to the amusive talents of the poet; in these scenes George merely served as a foil to Alcæus, being one of those mild, inoffensive, civil youths, alike destitute of conceit or consequence, who are suffered, by the ladies, to glide unnoticed round a room, very quiet, very harmless, and very dull; their services neglected, and their observations, if they ever venture to make any, unanswered. Some trifling civilities Arbella had shewn him during the course of the evening, had made him the most humble and attentive of her slaves. He had fluttered about her chair, had flown to procure her refreshment, spilt lemonade and orgeat upon her dress, and had in short done every aukward thing it was wrong for him to do, in the humble but heartfelt expression of the gratitude it was right for him to feel. With what readiness then did he offer his services in answer to Mrs. Stockwell's eager exclamation of 'Oh George! now do, there's a good creature, go and hunt about this room, and the sup-per-room, and the promenading-room, and see if you can get tale or tidings of my re'el Indy shawl; for I'm very afraid some of them giddy girls or fellers have set upon it, and rumpled it.'

George followed the route prescribed, brought back the shawl in triumph, and then asked, as a reward for his gallantry, the / honour of Miss Ferrars' hand the next time she should be inclined to dance. Arbella only replied by again urging Mrs. Stock-well to leave the room. – The company was beginning to move, but, by the injudicious haste with which all advanced towards the centre of attraction, the rush in the pas-sage, to the supper-room, rendered unavoidably narrower by the odoriferous exotics that lined it on each side, was so great, that, for some moments it was very difficult either to advance or recede. This difficulty was increased by the *sang-froid* of Alcæus the poet, who, having picked up a *programme* of the *fête*, stood very quietly reading and commenting upon it, in the very midst of the crowd, unmindful of the efforts of those who, on either side, attempted to move or pass by him.

'For the love of goodness sake, Mr. Wholl-see-us,' cried Mrs. Stockwell, 'don't ye think of stopping of us now, with the progress of the *fête*, or whatever it is you have got. Sure you can read it in the supper-room.'

Vain were her angry remonstrances, vain were Miss Langrish's screams, and equally vain were Spencer's repeated and pressing instances that he would move 'a little to his left,' and 'suffer them to extend their front;' or, his pathetic lamentations, as he was '*arming*' along his blooming partner, that he had no *guastadors** to clear the way for her. Absorbed in his studies, the immoveable bard kept his post; while poor Arbella found herself, by this means, squeezed in between Alcæus and her former admirer, and an unwilling spectator of the attentions he lavished on her rival. Really suffering beneath the effects of the increasing heat and pressure, Helen De Courcy was just able languidly to exclaim as he was busily employed sprinkling the fainting fair one with *Esprit de Rose*, 'Enough, enough, Captain Fitzroy, I am almost drowned with sweets.'

'Rather say refreshed – could I have foreseen what you were to endure,' he con-tinued in that tone of sportive tenderness / which often blended so pleasingly in his manners, 'instead of one scanty *flacon*,[80] a rill of perfumes should have run through these flowery shades for your sake.'

'Could you do that too? – There I should doubt even Captain Fitzroy's magic.'

* Pioneers.

'Did you never hear of the oriental princess, who, in an entertainment she gave her lover, contrived that a rivulet of rose water should sport in mazy windings through the grounds in which it took place?'

Romantic trifler! thought Arbella, as she again attempted to pass by him, but the sound of her own name, repeated by Miss De Courcy, arrested her attention, she listened, in breathless expectation, for the answer. "Pretty!" repeated Fitzroy, as if in reply to some observation of Helen's, and casting on Miss Ferrars a cold and careless glance, which strongly contrasted with the mingled softness and vivacity that marked his address to his partner; 'That I cannot allow – *Une assez jolie mine de fantaisie* at most.[81] My brother's attention to her this evening, to be sure, will give her a little fashion, but –'

'And what will Miss Melbourne say to that?' interrupted Helen, laughing maliciously; 'I thought Lord Strathallan was marked down as one of her host of adorers.'

'Oh! no, no,' returned Spencer carelessly, 'my brother does not absolutely *belong* to the Melbourne service. Only *attached* for the present. Spencer loved to employ, in its tenderer sense, this phrase which his military habits rendered familiar to him. As for Arbella,' he continued, 'she took my mother's fancy, who is always ENGOUTÉE; but I assure you, upon my honor, at Cheltenham, she was not at all admired – quite gone; extinguished, '*trailed off* before we left that place.'

'Gone off! impossible; she is so young!'

'Excuse me, not so young, according to my calculation. Arbella Ferrars must be four-and-twenty at least. "Rising" four and-twenty I mean.'

At this moment a party, conducted by Lionhart and a tall captain of grenadiers, / seemed determined to get on, in defiance of all the poets in the world. An opening in the crowd was forcibly effected; and the indignant bard finding himself obliged to give way, exclaimed,

'Enough for me: with joy I see
The different doom our fates assign.'[82]

Darting a fierce look at the triumphant heroes, he proceeded to the left, while they took the right, and hastened to cool the irritation this disturbance had excited, in draughts – not of pure Castalian dews, but of more inspiring Burgundy.

'Come on now, Arbella,' cried Mrs. Stockwell, 'I did verily believe that little gentleman meant to have kept us here, poetizing, all night.'

'And what matter if he had, Madam?' returned Miss Ferrars very heroically, as she '*trailed*' after her aunt to the supper-room.

Spencer was in uncommonly brilliant spirits. He had, or (what was the same thing with him,) he imagined he had turned another female head that night; and, on those occasions his own was never perfectly composed. He found a delightful variety to his amusements in the gravity of Stockwell; and, whispering Miss De Courcy that 'he would make him speak,' he immediately began the attack. Though no great votary of the Muses, he mentioned a poet of the present day with the most enthusiastic praises, and asked his silent neighbour if he had read any of his works.

'No sir,' Sam answered sulkily, 'I never read any such stuff.'

'Ask him if he has seen the new novel,' said Helen, naming a popular romance; 'no' – he 'never looked at romances.'

Miss De Courcy, who never liked the attention to be long taken from herself, attempted again to attract it by still affectedly complaining of heat and oppression.

'Surely 'tis the sound of these invisible choirs, amid groves and vernal airs,' said Spencer, (alluding to the imitative strains of the concealed musician,) 'that makes you almost fancy yourself under a July sun.' /

'A July sun when the thermometer is at 32; that's a good one,' cried Sam.

'Oh now I have found out your studies,' resumed Spencer, who well knew his friend's exactitude in trifles: 'you read the Meteorological Report, and the Agricultural Report, and the Price of Stocks, in the newspaper. And the Kalendar, and the Gazetteer, and Moore's Almanack also, I make no doubt. Well, I am very fond of that sort of thing too, and have myself made a little Meteorological Journal for my own satisfaction.'

'Indeed sir,' said Stockwell, looking at him with an expression of more respect than he had hitherto shewn.

'It is not, however, suited to you, I believe,' continued the Captain, 'it is only an account of the meteors or stars of fashion, as they appear or set in the horizon. I have also framed a little thermometer upon it, to ascertain the state of my own heart. At the sight of a meteor of moderate pretensions, it rises to gentle blood-heat: but on the appearance of a blazing beauty –'

'Oh! you dear meteorological creature,' cried Miss Langrish, affectedly interrupting him, 'you must shew me this journal and thermometer of yours.'

'Assuredly, but I have promised it to Miss De Courcy first. You will not be offended, I hope,' he continued to that young lady in a whisper, 'at the name I have placed at the head of my last observations.'

It was soon Arbella's turn to triumph. – Just as they left the supper-room, Stockwell approached her, and requested, in a whisper, the pleasure of her hand for the two next *dances*. The two next, Arbella slowly repeated, looking at the unfortunate youth with the most killing contempt;

'Whilst I with Mab my partner DAUNCE
Be little Mable thine.'[83]

Spencer, who happened to overhear the dialogue, exclaimed with delight, 'Good, good! excellent upon my soul,' and, repenting, or, as he phrased it, relenting with respect / to Arbella, he resolved, (to use his own expression,) 'to reward her for quizzing that solid blockhead, and to punish Helen De Courcy for triumphing so much over *his* Arbella.'

The amusement, however, in which the company was at present engaged, was of a nature so common and easy, that he would have thought his fine person quite thrown away upon it. He therefore preferred conversation; and, approaching Miss Ferrars, 'You call these country-dances, don't you?' he said to her, 'I have really been so long out of England, I hardly remember the name of them.'

'You are not so very lately returned,' replied Arbella, who began to be a little provoked, 'you might have seen them at the Cheltenham balls.'

'Oh you cruel creature, I was at Cheltenham, but then I was so ill, so very ill, I never went out at that time. Perhaps,' he continued, 'you, who are used to them, they may not strike in the same light; but, to me, with whom they have all the charm of novelty, nothing can be more amusingly ridiculous than the whole arrangement. – Observe the dancers – how dull the sets! how ungraceful the figures! Sometimes going round in a ring, sometimes standing at four corners, in which you only miss one personage to make the resemblance to a certain infantine pastime complete. Sometimes running after each other as if they had taken a hint from another of the plays among children. Surely the whole school of hop-it, kick-it, and gig-it, is disowned by the Graces.

"*Slow* melting strains *their* queen's approach declare,"[84]

And abroad it is acknowledged. But here, a Miss Hautenville's and a Miss Ferrars' figure are on a level; talent and elegance, like her's, are assimilated to the rustic agility of a dairy maid. Now there, every motion is calculated for the display of some thing of grace, dignity, or ease; every dance is a miniature ballet –'

'And every partner,' cried Arbella, soothed at length into resuming her native character, 'is a flattering Fitzroy, by whom / we feel our resentment, however, justly excited, insensibly charmed away.'

'Have a care, (said Spencer,) how you talk of flattery, lest envy, a sister vice, should start up *in propria persona*. I think I know her by the snaky locks,' he continued, directing her attention to the pretty, little, straw-coloured visage of Miss Hautenville, which being adorned with a tolerable profusion of thick, black, screw curls, formed no bad representation of that passion, as, with eyes askance, and limbs disposed into an attitude of spider-like watchfulness, she viewed the graceful easy form of Spencer, while, in animated conversation, he remained by the side of Arbella, and treasured up in her mind many particulars to relate hereafter of 'Miss Ferrars' excessively improper flirtation with Captain Fitzroy.'

'Doubtless you dance,' said the great Miss Mountain twisting round the little Miss Langrish, and fixing her large eyes upon her in expectation of an answer. Miss Langrish who, from causes over which she had no controul, had some doubts upon the subject, replied, that she had not determined. 'Perhaps Miss Langrish,' resumed Miss Mountain, with her wonted formality, 'you, as an institutrix of youth, despise this frivolous amusement, and would prefer the divine Tully's page.'

'No indeed, Madam,' returned the young lady, with great humility, 'I never knew any but one page of the Backstairs.'

'A page of Baxter's! Oh, then you read divinity, I presume!'[85]

'Madam!' cried Miss Langrish, who was now completely puzzled.

'You are aware of the author to whom I allude; you perfectly comprehend my meaning, I hope,' said Miss Mountain, smiling upon her with sweet complacency, for she was never so delighted as when by some of her ænigmas she had made herself quite incomprehensible. 'But perhaps,' she added, 'the poets are by you preferred.' 'They are indeed,' cried Miss Langrish, glad to have got, as she imagined, upon safer ground. 'That Ode Mr. Alcæus repeated, I think a sweet thing – a very sweet / thing; and the strathspey about the battle quite pretty!'

'I see, Miss Langrish, you are thinking more of strathspeys than strophes,' said Miss Mountain, and looking at her with a smile, compassionate, but not contemptuous in its expression, she left her to the enjoyment of her favorite pleasure, sitting with outstretched neck, eyes fixed, and head reclined in humble admiration of the graceful person and manly beauty of Lord Strathallan. It was just at this moment that Fitzroy had concluded his *tirade* against country dances, by requesting the honor of Arbella's hand for the next set. She hesitated, a consenting blush had stolen upon her cheek, when Miss Hautenville, who thought it a sin to neglect so favourable an opportunity of tormenting, put her head in between them, and said 'of course you remember, Miss Ferrars, that if you dance any more to-night, it is to Mr. Spring you are engaged.'

George approached; and Spencer observing how much his fair one was disconcerted by this new *contre-temps*, undertook to divert its effects from her, and turning to the docile youth, 'you see you cannot dance with Miss Ferrars,' he said, 'she has been engaged to me these three weeks; but I wonder, George, a man of your politeness did not think of asking Miss de Courcy, in preference, who, poor thing! is sitting out for want of a partner!'

'Dear heart!' cried Spring, emboldened by the notice of Fitzroy, who offered to introduce him, 'I did think that certainly Miss Ferrars had engaged herself to me; but you know better, Captain Fitzroy; and if it ought to be Miss de Courcy, I'm sure I'm quite agreeable; the young lady herself did not appear to coincide in that opinion; but just as a refusal hovered on her lips, Arbella, running up to her, whispered in her ear, 'If you refuse George Spring, my dear, his brother Alcæus will bring you into his next satire. It is no matter, you know,' she added, 'I only thought it right to tell you of it.'

When the company began to retire, several / unexpected and amusing scenes took place. To the enquiries made by many a silver voice of 'Where's my tippet? Where's my veil?' 'Bless me, Louisa, what did I do with my cloak?' no satisfactory answer was for some time returned; till, at length, all these various articles of wearing apparel were found upon the person of Captain Lionhart, who, completely disguised in the head dress of one, the veil of another, and the mantle of a third, seemed extremely unwilling to part with his trophies. Restitution at length being made, the Countess, with a graceful and somewhat *queen*-like curtesy, led the way. Captain Fitzroy saw the happy party that accompanied her safely seated in the barouche; and then, mounting the box with spirit unwearied and masterly expedition and skill, drove them back, as the sun began to rise, to Woodlands.

CHAPTER XV.

'Le plaisir de la critique nous ote celui d'etre vivement touche de très-belles choses.

LA BRUYÉRE.[86]

WELL these balls are terrible things, cried Arbella, as she woke still dizzy with the events of the evening; and the conversation of her fair visitants who met to 'talk them over,' did not much tend to disperse the chaos. 'Lord, Louisa, why did you dance with that odious man?' 'Bless me, Maria, how could I help it; he asked me half a hundred times.' 'And I would have refused him half a thousand before I would have been seen in the same set with him. I wonder for my part people are not ashamed to be so ugly.' 'Who do you mean? are / you talking of the man with the legs?' 'No, my dear, I'm speaking of the man with the head.' 'But dearest Julia why did you take ice after dancing so much?' 'I don't know; Lord Strathallan asked me to take it, and I did not think at the moment; besides, we should really not have been warm, but for that old cross dowager Lady Pthisick, who quarrelled with Lionhart for opening the windows.' 'Yes, and with de Millefleurs for having perfumes.' 'And with Sabredash for making a noise; though I am sure he did not make as much as she did with her cough.' 'No, indeed, if instead of shutting the windows, he had thrown her out of them, he would only have served her right, and Mrs. Early, Miss Gaylife's chaperon after her.' 'One might as well stay at home as go out with such a woman.' 'Instead of keeping it up, the moment one has begun to get into the spirit of it, she rises with her odious, "don't you think it is growing late?"' 'But why did not Bellairs dance all night?' 'How could he when he never asked any one?' 'Did he expect us to ask him?' 'I really believe he did; and I do think we did not pay him sufficient attention.'

With such conversation they endeavoured to recal the fast-fading pleasures of the evening, while Arbella, who at once gave into, and despised, the nonsense that surrounded her, occasionally threw in a word; secure that even in her sleep she could talk at least as well as the busy and wakeful tongues that hummed about her. 'After all, ladies,' she interrupted indolently, 'you must allow that every thing went off vastly well,

> "Want, with her babes,
> Round generous valour clung."[87]

in most affecting style; and Lord Strathallan "all delighting and delighted," was quite in his element.'

'Lord Strathallan was not so attentive, I think, as his situation required,' replied one young lady; who, though she had not quite taken in the force of the first allusion, perfectly comprehended the observation that followed it, 'had he remembered the rules of politeness.' /

'Rules of politeness!' exclaimed an enthusiastic fair one, who had till now been silent, 'he needs them not. Strathallan, the lovely Strathallan, is alone beyond them all, and pleases most when most transgressing them! he is the Shakespeare of love's legionaries; but Miss Ferrars,' she continued, after this eloquent apology for his Lordship's negligent discharge of the duty of steward for the evening, 'how polite his brother was to every one, and how I pitied you when, instead of him, Miss Hautenville brought up dear little master Spring. Excuse me, but I cannot help laughing to think of it; and really the look with which you seemed to implore her to take it away, was enough to have disarmed a savage! and Miss Ferrars, when you *did* stand up, how could you be so unthinking as to call '*The Old Woman behind the Fire*' when Lady Kilcare and her son were dancing in the same set?'[88]

Rather piqued at the pertness of these remarks, Arbella was not sorry the entrance of Mrs. Stockwell put an end to them. The Misses primmed up, for they perceived that this lady, angry and wearied with having 'stopped up all night,' as she called it, was prepared to regale them with one of her pathetic lamentations, which they were not just then in a humor to hear, they therefore soon after took leave.

A few days had passed, and Matilda wholly engrossed in the performance of her filial duties, had almost forgotten the ball, when it was recalled to her remembrance by a visit from Lord Strathallan. He had been some time with Mr. and Mrs. Melbourne, before she appeared. It was with an alteration, an added tenderness of voice and manner, (she in vain tried not to remark) that, turning to her, he inquired after her health, and expressed the disappointment, that on the night of the ball he had experienced. He had been absent from home the whole of that morning; and had, therefore, to the last, flattered himself with hopes that Lady Torrendale might have prevailed on her to change her mind. /

'She might have gone,' said Mr. Melbourne, who had by this time been made to comprehend that young ladies *liked* balls, 'I was rather desirous that she should; but I do not know how it was, she really preferred staying at home with me.'

Lord Strathallan gazed upon her as her father spoke; it was not that glance of quick, yet soft surprise, which, at their first meeting had communicated itself like lightning to her heart; it was a look tender, long indulged, of the fondest interest, and admiration. Strathallan had never appeared so amiable to her before, yet she felt that she never had less regretted not meeting him at the ball. Two hours had passed, and to the peaceful group, had hardly appeared so many moments. It was not that any thing of importance had been discussed, but every thing that was said derived a charm from the consciousness of each, that it was heard with interest, with sympathy, and friendship. This intercourse of the heart, this perfect confidence, this feeling of given and received delight, possessed a soothing, a tranquilizing sweetness, which more extended or brilliant societies, can never boast. It was, indeed, the music of the mind; one of those golden hours of life, when, for the moment, every wish is satisfied, and no fear, no regret intrudes, but that it cannot last for ever. 'Twas thus Matilda thought, 'twas thus she felt, when at that instant, the charm was broken; Strathallan rose, and resuming the subject that had been the cause of his visit, he turned to Mrs. Melbourne with persuasive grace, 'Am I the bearer of good news to Lady Torrendale?'

'Such a party would be peculiarly agreeable to me, but –.' She looked at Matilda, and Matilda, at the mention of another invitation, with anxious solicitude at her father.

'You must go my love,' he said, 'I may be considerably better by next week. This is nothing of late hours or gaiety to make you unwilling to leave me, and yet I think it would be a thing highly improving and amusing to Matilda.'

This last consideration determined Mrs. Melbourne; and, it was at length agreed, that / if Mr. Melbourne's state of health did not grow worse, the ladies would certainly attend on Tuesday, or as Spencer phrased it, 'assist' at Lady Torrendale's literary party. Lord Strathallan took leave, very much pleased with the success of his mission, which had been partly forced on him by Lady Torrendale. The history of this conversazione 'threatened oft, and oft deferred,' was sufficiently curious.

The jealousy of rival wits is more cruel than the enmity between courtiers, lovers, or even, beauties. 'Alcæus repeats nonsense so well, that people mistake it for sense,' was Sappho's obliging remark, when she heard of the applause the young poet had obtained by his Ode, at the subscription ball. To this Alcæus had, with equal politeness and readiness, replied that Sappho, on the contrary, repeated sense in such a manner that every one took it for nonsense. The observation of the bard, as alluding to her famous recitation of the Ode on the Passions, piqued the vanity of the poetess, and she defied him to prove his charge. She urged Lady Lyndhurst to remember her promise of introducing her to the Countess. Lady Lyndhurst who equally patronised these rival sygnets, consented. At Lady Torrendale's they were to meet, and there Alcæus was to be convinced, that Sappho could do justice to her author. Great interest was made to prevail on Mr. Sowerby, (whose literary and scientific reputation had reached the ears of the Countess) to honor the proposed assembly with his presence, but without effect.

At this party Lady Lyndhurst took the opportunity of introducing her own daughter, the honorable Miss De Courcy. The young lady from the celebrity of her mother, was already considered, by the profane, as a candidate for literary honors, or, in more familiar language, as a blue-elect. If the initiated, on the contrary, did not perceive in the lovely Helen any remarkable tendency that way, still they were forced to acknowledge she was very pretty, very modest, and cast up a pair of blue eyes, (which possessed every charm, but meaning) in rapturous admiration, whenever Lady Lyndhurst, or Mrs. / Melbourne spoke. To the manners and conversation of that lady and her daughter, she was exhorted to pay particular attention. A recommendation that was, to Matilda, the only disagreeable circumstance in her occasional intercourse with Miss De Courcy; as it laid the foundation of a jealousy and ill-will, which, though it did not break out till afterwards, was not the less deep-rooted in her bosom. In other respects, Helen was a most docile scholar; though, perhaps, had she felt courage honestly to avow her inclinations, she would, at any time, have preferred to a literary circle, the amusement of playing domino, or even push-pin with Lady Emily; or coronella, (she was too indolent for shuttle-cock) with her more fascinating brother.[89]

Miss Hautenville, proud of the share she had in promoting the party, 'had brought' Mrs. Stockwell, on a whispered injunction, that she should not 'Speak, to expose herself.' Miss Ferrars, though disdaining thus to appear in Miss Hautenville's train, could not resist the prospect of amusement such an assembly afforded; and joined the party prepared, as occasion should serve, equally to shine, to be silent, or to laugh. Alcæus, himself, was not without a *protegée*; having begged leave to introduce his younger brother George Spring. In Mrs. Melbourne, the vivacity and talent of Aspasia Villiers seemed only to wait calling forth in order to revive: while the warmth and ingenuousness of Matilda, alive to every new impression of improvement or delight, formed, in itself, a different, yet, perhaps, equally pleasing recommendation. To settle the different pretensions of her visitors was not found, by the Countess, so easy a task as she had, at first, imagined. Lady Torrendale, who at a ball, or a dinner party, valued herself upon assorting her guests, and who really excelled in the little observances that impart to such meetings their gaiety and ease, thought she could not do better than place the two poets, Sappho and Alcæus, next to each other. Now, beside the grievous subject of complaint that the wit of Alcæus, in conversation, had recently given her, it happened that, but two months before, / he had, in one of the Magazines, attacked the grammatical accuracy of an elegy of Sappho's; and that Sappho, in the ensuing number, had designated an Ode of Alcæus by the unparliamentary term 'said stuff.' Her Ladyship, who never looked either into Magazine or Review, was surprised and disconcerted to see the two Luminaries, on a near approach to each other, turn pale in their orbits, and then, alternately, flash fire. Miss Langrish, the gentle mediator, at length succeeded in separating them, yet still the ease that should have prevailed in such a meeting was not restored. The Countess felt ashamed to lead; and those whose habits better qualified them for such a task, seemed to fear nothing more than to 'commit themselves,' by saying something which their wiser companions would have disdained to utter. Such was the state of parties, while tea and refreshments were handed about.

At length Arbella, creeping over to Matilda on tip-toe, as if afraid to disturb the horrid silence, whispered 'An't we very dull? I had something very brilliant to say just now; but it could not stand this dreadful atmosphere. It was frozen, like the words spoken by Sir John Mandeville[90] and his crew, before it could reach you. Oh! I see what we want; Miss Mountain, the soul of our miniature world, is not here; and Miss Hautenville has set her neck on one side in the Alexandrian twist, and given her eye the admiring roll in vain. There is nothing to admire!'

The entrance of the lady, thus regretted, formed a pleasing break in the formality of the circle. She slightly apologized for the lateness of her appearance, declaring that she had been so engaged, in her own apartment, with 'a Tome of Bacon,' that she knew not how to quit it.

'Bacon!' cried Mrs. Stockwell, 'why mine has been all saved a month ago.'

'My dear Mrs. Stockwell, did not you promise me,' whispered Miss Hautenville, gasping for breath.

'I usually breakfast on a page of Young, / and sup on a Tome of Bacon,' resumed Miss Mountain, with great *sang froid*.[91]

The restraint, in which the company was held, being once broke through, each began to speak freely of the pleasure they expected to receive; and to hope Miss

Swanley would not long delay the promised recitation. Miss Mountain talked of the *Melopée* of the ancients, (as she called it)[92] and then said she trusted Miss Swanley would add the charms of appropriate music, at intervals, to her declamation.

'The Ancients Madam,' interrupted the Poet Alcæus, 'I hope they are not to give rules to us. They knew little of the resources of Poetry; still less of the secrets of the Arts.'

'Yet you must allow that, in most branches of literature, they are our masters,' said Lady Lyndhurst, 'in the drama, particularly the Greeks.'

'Surely Madam,' resumed Alcæus, 'you do not think we derive any advantage from the unnatural plots, cold monotonous scenes, and tiresome declamations of the Greek stage! take my word for it, were they to write now, Æschylus, Sophocles, and Euripides are fellows who would not be so much as heard of.'

'Certainly,' observed Lady Lyndhurst, 'they knew little of the art of moving the passions, compared to our own dear Shakespeare.'

'Shakespeare,' interrupted our young critic, 'has some fine scenes, and was fortunate in the conjuncture in which he lived: but Shakespeare, with his nonsense, his puns, and his anachronisms; his blunders, historical, geographical, and chronological, together with his vile mixture of tragedy and farce, would, in these days, be absolutely hissed off the stage. Otway sometimes commands our pity; Rowe's language is harmonious; but he is cold, affected, and declamatory; besides that the tone of morals is so low you really hesitate whether to laugh or cry.'

'The times in which Otway and Rowe flourished,' said Mrs. Melbourne, 'seemed more favorable to the cultivation of wit, than / the expansion of genius and sentiment. In the days of Charles and Anne –'

'Wit!' exclaimed Alcæus, who could not bear longer to be silent; 'there was an absolute stagnation of it. Dryden himself, whose name appears, at first, the most conspicuous, what did he write, but bombastic plays, or forgotten satires; and every one knows that his Æneis, as he calls it –'

'Æneas!' cried George, eagerly; 'if that's the Æneas that wrote Virgil, I'll answer, for one, that *he's* not forgotten. – Many's the good –'

A look from his brother silenced him; and Alcæus proceeded – 'And what, I beg, was that celebrated constellation of wits, in Queen Anne's time, that they should arrogate to their æra the title of the Augustan age of England? Gay wrote an opera, that is not fit to be read; Pope published translations; and Swift, political pamphlets: the rest, not worth a thought, a name.'

'My dear little Alcæus,' cried Miss Mountain; looking down "from her amazing height," with an air and voice of very pardonable apprehension and pity, at the juvenile critic.

'I have often thought,' said Mrs. Melbourne, who really considered it as charity to turn the attention from his absurdity, 'that the present period affords a richer poetical harvest than that of which we are speaking; and that when my Lord Oxford is supposed to ask of Swift,

"'Have you nothing new to-day,
From Pope, from Parnell, or from Gay?" [93]

we could fill the spaces they now occupy, with at least equally illustrious names.'

'Why, there I must beg leave to differ from you again,' resumed the inexorable bard. 'We have some poets, to be sure, that are popular; but none, in my humble opinion, that deserve to be so. Those ballad-romances, for instance, that you ladies like, really to a classic ear –'

'Classic!' cried Sappho; 'I thought, Mr. Spring, just now you disowned that school. But perhaps 'tis to the splendor of the modern fictions you object, and you prefer those / poets whose genius can embellish the humblest scenes in real life.'

'Real life! Oh, detestable! Pray do not bring us back to the Seasons and the Deserted Village.'

'Ah, that was a charming thing! – written by Goldsmith, you know,' said Miss Hautenville, looking round to be applauded for the discovery she had made.

'No, no,' continued Alcæus, 'give me none of your Georgics, nor Cowper's Task; – I'm sure it's a task to read them' – (here he laughed very loud); 'nor metrical imitations of the Arabian Nights; nor itineraries of travels put into verse; nor songs, nor sonnets, nor modern odes – I'm sick of modern odes; nor –'

'Any thing, in short, but the works of Alcæus,' murmured Arbella.

'I think you mentioned sonnets, Mr. Spring,' said Miss Mountain, turning to the poet with great solemnity: 'I hope you mean to except from your wide-sweeping censure the Sydneys and Surreys, the charming sonneteers of Elizabeth's time. The modern writers, I will admit, may have degenerated; but there is, in all the works of those bards, a refinement and intricacy of expression, a delicate and elegant mysticism in the ideas which is, in my opinion, very charming. There is a poem of Sir Philip's, "Astrophel and Stella sweet," which would perfectly illustrate my meaning. If I recollect right it is not above a hundred and fifty stanzas: but as that might possibly be considered rather too long, I shall for the present content myself with repeating the eight first lines of his "Dactyls," another exquisite performance:–

"Who hath his fancy pleas'd
With fruits of happy sight,
Here let his sight be rais'd
On nature's sweetest light.
A light which doth dissever,
And yet unites the eyes;
A light, which, dying never,
Is cause the looker dies."[94]

I am far from wishing, however, to depreciate the efforts of later bards. That divine poet, whose finest ode Miss Swanley will / favor us with to-night, is a proof how far genius may soar. There is another ode of his, that on the poetic character, which I always thought unequalled. Are you not of my opinion, Miss Melbourne?' turning suddenly to Matilda, who had, till now, modestly refrained from joining in the conversation.

'I – I – yes, Madam – I certainly think it a very fine thing,' she replied, after a moment's pause, and with an air of constraint and coldness, rendered more remarkable by the spirit and ingenuousness of her usual manner.

'I believe I can explain that start – that charming hesitation,' Strathallan whispered to Matilda. 'You really admire that beautiful poem, which is one of the touch-stones of true taste; and, for that very reason, on suddenly hearing it warmly commended by one you suspect to be incompetent to appreciate its real merit, you experience, for your favourite author, the sentiment expressed by the Portuguese bard for his mistress;[95] when he declares he prefers his secret adoration, to the danger of suffering even praise, that might be unworthy of her, too lightly to trifle with that sacred name.'

Matilda made no other reply than by a look, bright with sweetness and intelligence, a look that seemed to say, '*Vous m'avez deviné*.'[96]

Strathallan, encouraged by that look, proceeded – 'I observed you smile too at some extravagant encomiums that were bestowed upon our earlier poets; yet, believe me, they are not unworthy of your attention. They often possessed the language of nature more than their successors. Surrey was at once a poet and –' (he sighed) 'a lover. I wish you were acquainted with his works.'

In this manner, Strathallan, charmed to discover in Matilda a character that was equally, in trifles and matters of importance, in unison with his own, applied himself to draw out the latent feeling and intelligence that adorned the mind of this amiable girl; till, finding himself but too successful, and that her conversation was in danger of taking him completely off from those claims that he too / painfully felt might be urged by others, he suddenly checked himself, and gazing with passionate earnestness on her enchanting face, 'Cease! Nymph of the Danube!' he exclaimed;[97] and, abruptly turning from her, left Miss Melbourne in a state of uneasiness she could hardly moderate or conceal, at the strangeness and apparent caprice of this unintelligible expression.

Miss Ferrars, who had not been so interestingly engaged, and who regretted the impertinent conversation that seemed destined to supply the place of her promised amusement, could hardly refrain from whispering, 'What nonsense! – how insupportable Alcæus is to-night! What would Spencer say?' – when the beloved hero himself made his appearance.

Sappho, who had, for her own reasons, purposely delayed the recitation till that moment, now required but few entreaties to begin. A short prelude from the flute was heard. Lady Torrendale, by a sign, commanded silence; and in a moment all was mute attention, except on the part of Lionhart, who having, as well as his friend, spent the day abroad, and returned without knowing what was to be the order of the night, seemed absolutely terrified by this exordium; 'Hey! what have we got here? – a conversation party! You did not tell me of that, Fitzroy!' he continued, turning reproachfully to his friend. 'We must be all very wise, must not we?'

'No, not all,' returned Spencer in the same under-tone. 'Come, come, Lionhart, we must have you one of us; upon my soul, my dear fellow, we must. I long to enrol you among the Royal Derbyshire Blues – Lady Lyndhurst's own.'

Alcæus, perceiving symptoms of discontent on Lionhart's countenance, thought this a fine opportunity of making him an unconscious abettor of the design he meditated; and began whispering in his ear a series of criticisms on the poem, which he thought would end in turning the repeater of it into ridicule. She had just arrived at these two lines –

'Exulting, trembling, raging, fainting,
Possess'd beyond the Muse's painting.'[98] /

when he exclaimed, 'Was there ever, in such a small compass, crowded together such a quantity of bombastic frenetic stuff? But Fear, it seems, when he tried his hand at it,

"Back recoil'd he knew not why."

Oh, truly, Mr. Fear, I could tell you the why and the wherefore, if it were not already much better explained; it was

"Ev'n at the sound himself had made;"

and really, if poor Fear had had any modesty, such sounds were enough to have terrified any body. But some people' (glancing insolently at Sappho) 'think their own music must always be delightful.'

By this time, the suppressed smile and smothered laugh, produced by these remarks, which, though contemptible enough in themselves, were received with pleasure by some, as flattering the favourite propensity in the human mind to bring down superiority, of whatever description, to its own level, began to be very distressing to poor Sappho. Spencer perceived it; and, actuated partly by his general gallantry to the sex, partly by his own turn for elegant raillery, resolved, that if Alcæus was determined to continue, it should end with his completely exposing himself. Whispering Lionhart (to keep him quiet) that he meant to quiz the poet, he turned to Mr. Spring, and, professing himself much informed and amused by his criticisms, complimented him on the courage that could venture to oppose such generally received prejudices.

'Why, yes, Sir,' returned the juvenile bard, swallowing the bait with prodigious complacency, 'I flatter myself, I am not one of those who can be daunted by the splendor of a name: and I will engage to prove, to any one who will take the trouble of listening to me, that a more contemptible cento, under the name of a poem, was never palmed upon the indulgence of the public.' He then continued, giving his little nose, as he went on, the true Zoilus curl:

' 'Twas sad by fits, by starts 'twas wild;'[99]

a most exact definition, in one line, of this / absurd farrago, miscalled an ode; which is not more defective from the variety of subjects it embraces, than from the eternal changes in the metre. For where is the pleasure of discovering the resources of the poet's art – the *difficulté vaincue*, if he may swim, hop, or jig it away, just as he finds it convenient?

" 'But thou, O Hope! with eyes so fair.'"[100]

Alcæus had almost run himself out of breath, yet was proceeding, in the same strain of remark, upon this stanza, without observing that Lionhart, till now one of his most attentive listeners, had turned from him, and was whispering his friend, in apparently great agitation, 'Oh, Spencer! it is all over with me. Going, going, going; in a moment or two it will be gone!'

'Nonsense! what will be gone?'

'My poor heart.'

'Pray, pray,' resumed Spencer, in the same under-tone, 'do not let me have a love-fit. You know I shall have to nurse you, and I really have not time. There – turn your eyes in some other direction, and do not stand gazing (transfixed like a statue) at a girl who is not thinking of you.'

The object that had given rise to this singular dialogue was Matilda; who, all unknowing of her charms, and thinking of any thing rather than securing a conquest, bent forward, rapt in listening, mute attention, by the beauties of a poem, which she had often perused in private, with renewed delight; but which she enjoyed still more, when set off with those graces of delivery that Sappho knew so well how to give it. But when the glowing Sappho, with all the energy inspired by the subject, repeated the last line in that beautiful personification –

'And Hope, enchanted, smiled, and wav'd her golden hair,'

Matilda caught her enthusiasm; and, involuntarily imitating the action described, gracefully raised, with her white hand, the flowing ringlets on her neck.

'Fitzroy! I can resist no more,' whispered Lionhart. 'What beauty! what elegance! / Heavens! what a neck! and how those waving curls, that seem powdered with gold, increase the vivid glow of her cheek, and the charm of that dimple that sinks into its crimson surface! Deep, rich carnation – how does its changing, increasing beauty, deaden the effect of Miss Mountain's confounded paint!'

'Well, don't grow so loud – Upon my soul I won't allow it, Lionhart – I'm quite ashamed of you.'

While that passion, which inspires the slowest with eloquence, had betrayed poor Lionhart (who was, of all heroes, the most susceptible) into this rhodomontade, – very different were the feelings with which the poet Alcæus, who conceived that the hour of his complete triumph was arrived, in the remarks that he was about to make, commented upon the passage he had just heard. 'Now, I should be glad to know the opinion of the company with respect to the expression

"Eyes so fair."

Fair is white; so it comes to the same as if he had said,

"O Hope, with eyes so white."

Now white eyes were never particularly admired, that I heard. I have seen a notable poem, on the death of a great person, which says –

"The aldermen with fair eyes
Followed him to Mary's."

But whether that is a precedent, or that the writer borrowed the hint from Mr. Collins, I cannot determine.

"And wav'd her golden hair."

What cursed nonsense! he might say, that she had wavy hair, or that her hair had a wave in it; but that she waved her own hair! – he might just as well say "waved her golden wig;"' nobody joining in the laugh, he would have been quite discouraged, but for the approving nods and smiles of Spencer; who, while he dexterously contrived to expose, to all around him, the vanity and inability of the little critic, encouraged, / him, every moment, still more conspicuously to display his folly. He was now arrived at the personification of melancholy.

'Well done Mrs. Melancholy! I have heard lately of ladies playing the flute; in the last generation, your Euterpes excelled on the viol.[101] I have heard even of women fiddlers. But my poet here determined to out-Herod Herod, makes you

"Pour through the mellow horn the pensive sound."[102]

I congratulate you Mrs. Melancholy upon your proficiency in blowing the French horn. Never heard before of such an instrument for a lady; never did, may I be shot! did you, Captain Lionhart?'

'Ask Fitzroy,' said Lionhart, who began to be a little tired, 'it may be very pretty, and very right, for aught I know, I am no judge of poetry and that sort of thing; Fitzroy, I believe, has all the books that are in the regiment.'

'For shame,' replied his friend, 'you know I never have a moment's time to read. Besides reading is quite unfashionable, and I think it the greatest bore upon earth, except for such a thing as this, or POUR PASSER LE TEMPS.'

'Don't believe him,' resumed Lionhart, addressing himself to the poet, 'trust me he knows more than either of us, and could cap Latin with you as fast as –'

'What do you think of this passage, describing Chearfulness,' said Spencer to Alcæus, desirous of turning the discourse; for, though really an elegant scholar, such was the frivolity he thought proper to assume, that he had a vanity in avoiding the imputation of knowledge. 'Think sir! Oh I can only think to be sure that chearfulness, with

"Her bow across her shoulder hung,
Her buskins gemmed with morning dew."

is a fine bouncing lass. Perhaps no one has ever reflected that all this dew and jemmy boots only means, in plain English, that she got her feet wet, or was wet-footed as they say in Sussex.'

'Admirable sir! You make me see the passage quite in a new light.' /

The bard was not a little elated by the elegant Fitzroy's praise: but, perceiving it was not followed by the universal applause he expected, he turned somewhat more sourly to his task, and, at length, exclaimed, 'Oh here comes "something pretty," as the ladies say,

"Last came Joy's extatic trial."

And really, master Collins, so we come to the last of it, in any shape, I believe there is nobody who cares much, how.

"He with viny crown advancing,
First to the lively pipe his hand addressed,
But soon he saw the brisk awakening viol."

What does this mean, but that Joy, having got very tipsey, sent for a blind fiddler, gave him sixpence, and then danced, while he played him a tune.' Nothing is so flat and abortive as ridicule, which is not immediately taken as it is meant. Where others do not feel inclined to sympathize, it recoils with double force upon itself. Alcæus found he was deserted, one by one, by his whole auditory, who had crouded round Sappho, to whom they were now pouring forth praises on her performance; every one of which acted as a sting upon the irritable vanity of the poet. As he was, however, one of that happy class of beings, denominated self-listeners, and could always supply to himself, in a degree, the admiration which he might want from without, he continued his harangue, with tolerable complacency, 'till Spencer interrupted him, exclaiming, 'Bravo! you have completely opened our eyes as to the absurdity of the piece we have so long foolishly admired; but, poet, your work is but half done. To make the lesson useful, you must, after demonstrating in what the ridiculous consists, also give us an example of what constitutes excellence: and of this, if I am not much mistaken, your own Ode to the Gossamer affords the most perfect model. Let any one only repeat the second stanza, and I think, my assertion will be put out of doubt.'

'Agreed,' returned Alcæus, delighted with the proposal; 'let any one of these ladies,' he continued triumphantly, 'repeat / the second stanza of my ode, and then I submit myself, without fear, to the decision of the court. Miss Hautenville, perhaps you will favour me so far.'

'I – me!' said Miss Hautenville, vexed that her own work on the Italian Drama had never been called for. 'Mr. Spring I always admired your charming Ode to Gossamer, and all your odes; but I don't know how it is, I have been so much engaged of late that at this instant it is not very present to my mind. Miss Mountain, I dare say you could.'

'My memory is, I am sorry to say, the pitcher of the Danaides,'[103] replied the stately lady, 'but, I doubt not, Lady Torrendale could.'

'Lady Torrendale,' turning formally to her, 'you subscribed to Mr. Spring's poems; surely you can remember his Ode to the Gossamer.'

'I – yes,' replied her ladyship, suppressing a yawn, 'I did subscribe to them.'

'But she did not think herself obliged to read them,' said Arbella, in a half-whispered ASIDE.

'I beg you will not call upon me,' continued the Countess, 'my poor head retains nothing.'

'But it did contain the whole ode;' pursued the indefatigable Arbella, heedless of Mrs. Stockwell's repeated 'nudges,' and the apprehensive tone in which she whispered, 'for shame, for shame niece, to tell. Did you ever see me do so.'

'Last night,' she continued, to her next neighbour, 'the little smartly bound volume was promoted, from its post in the window, where it has been tost about this month, to have its nice foolscap pages converted into PAPILLOTES for her ladyship's hair.'[104] [*A pause ensued.*]

'Deuced unlucky – no one able to repeat my Ode to Gossamer – confounded awkward, may I be shot!' muttered Alcæus, ending with a wish, which was a favourite one with him, perhaps, from the little probability of its ever being realized. /

'Really very extraordinary,' continued Spencer, affecting surprise, 'that no one should remember this charming ode, nor the Ode to the Grasshopper, that would do just as well. – Miss Hautenville, Miss Mountain, perhaps you could repeat me part of the Ode to the Grasshopper.'

'Pray Miss Hautenville repeat some of the Ode to the Grasshopper,' said Miss Mountain, 'I cannot remember it.'

'Pray Miss Langrish do you,' whispered the lady, sending the commission round.

'Dear me ma'am! I know nothing about it I am sure,' returned the young governess, 'Miss Ferrars can you?'

'Who, I?' answered Arbella aloud; 'I never heard of it.'

The conclusion to be drawn from this experiment was obvious. The boasted triumphs of modern wit were unknown and disregarded, even by the small circle that effected to patronize them; and the laugh, that Arbella began, extended itself, like electricity, along the line, 'till even the marble muscles of Miss Mountain threatened to give way. Spencer, satisfied with what he had done, took no share in the general mirth; but, retiring to a window, at the end of the room, with his friend Captain Lionhart, stood, with him, (while it continued,) in a graceful attitude, apparently engaged in the most interesting and animated conversation. Poor George Spring, on the contrary, who had sat, in admiration of his brother's wit, 'till he was more tired than he chose to acknowledge, was only roused from the stupor into which it had plunged him, by a call to supper. While Fitzroy secured a place next to Matilda, Lionhart consoled himself for the past, by some plentiful slices of a wild-fowl pasty; after a proportionable number of libations of champagne, to the goddess of his soul, he thought himself a match, even for the conquering Captain, and determined not to leave the field entirely to him.

He began by lamenting, 'she came so little among them,' and declared that he had found the ball the cursedest bore on earth / without her. 'I am beginning to like reading a great deal better,' he said, 'for I have not seen you, a whole evening together, for an age before. I thought it would have been something very stupid; but, wherever you have good company, and good supper, and fine women, call it a rout, or an assembly, or a *conversazione*, or what you will, it is equally good I think.'

He then poured forth a volley of compliments, which, however exaggerated, were not the less sincere. But Spencer, who secretly smiled at his confidence, in venturing to cope with him, and was resolved to point out his friend's prevailing foible in its most ridiculous light, said to Matilda, 'You must know, Madam, this gentleman is sadly subject to the malady of falling in love. I call it a malady, because it is a kind of flying pain, an uneasiness that comes upon him by fits, so sudden, yet so transient, that it would be vain to listen to his suit; for, before the lady could possibly have settled her mind, he would, most indubitably, have changed his, at least a dozen times. For instance, in the last town where we were quartered, he had, to my certain knowledge, four *grandes passions*. The first was for a lady's Turkish slipper – "Oh Miss Wingfield's Turkish slipper!" – Cinderella's was but a *sabot*[105] compared to it. He was just going to take the leap, when, *heureusement* he met a lady, in the public walk, moving gracefully along. She had a ridicule – poor Frank had a heart – you may easily suppose they were soon exchanged; or rather, I should imagine, she popt his heart into her ridicule; for, certain it is, for a week it was gone astray. We advised a cry, as the only thing. You remember Miss Dashwood's crimson and gold ridicule, hey Frank?'

'Well,' interrupted Lionhart, half angry, though pretty well accustomed to his friend's raillery, 'When I *do* fall in love, at least it is sincerely, not like –'

'The next *belle passion*,' pursued Spencer, thinking it better not to let his friend conclude the sentence, 'was excited by harmony, heavenly harmony. He was with me at a party; a young lady was singing – Oh / why will ladies sing? or why will officers listen? – Poor Frank's heart was not proof against Miss Poyntz's singing Robin Adair.[106] The last, and most serious of his passions, was raised by a hat and feather, at a review. The lady was very pretty – the wind was very high – it blew her white ostrich feather over her face, so that she could not see any thing. She put it back, with the whitest hand, and discovered beneath it the finest eyes: to replace a wandering curl, or a waving feather, with a fair hand, is a most graceful action,' (he continued, turning on Matilda a penetrating glance,) then pursuing his story, 'Lionhart felt it so. – In the evening he attended her to the ball. The figure of the first dance was difficult; it could not be, you know, that the young lady was stupid – Lionhart had the pleasure of being her instructor; and she looked down with a modest blush, for she blundered through the whole set; only think how pretty! she blundered through the whole set. Now, had she danced tolerably, it would have been nothing. But this pretty ignorance and confusion was so "in-te-REST-ing," it banished the Turkish slipper, the Ridicule, and Robin Adair, from his heart, or his head, for ever. I have known him, upon my soul, fall in love with a Spanish girl, or a Jewess, I declare I forget which, for her false English; and with a nun, for the elegance of her cross and rosary.'

'I should think such attachments not very dangerous,' said Matilda, smiling at the ludicrous point of view in which the Captain had placed the "PASSIONCELLI" of his friend.[107]

'I do not know,' returned Spencer in a softened voice; and instantly assuming a milder air, 'in my opinion, a man is happy who can thus lightly receive, and lose an impression;' then, sighing, and after a pause, in which he seemed to have called up at once into his eyes and countenance, all their most expressive and dangerous power, he turned to her, and added, with earnestness, and in a still lower tone, 'for my own part I *feel* it is not a passion to be trifled with; and that an attachment, excited in a moment, / by a charmer, perhaps unconscious of her power, may decide the happiness or misery of my whole future life.'

Matilda looked down, the Captain withdrew his eyes, quite satisfied that they had done their duty: and the young lady smiled to think how little was supposed sufficient to ensnare her. Meantime Lionhart, who, as the night advanced, had only become disposed to be more communicative, took advantage of Fitzroy's attention being called off, to open to his fair lady the whole of his mind and thoughts. It was now Spencer's turn to be described: and the kindness with which the friends spoke of each other, at least, was mutual. 'Don't believe that young fellow,' he whispered to Matilda, 'though he says the finest things in the world; for he has a tongue that would deceive an angel. But you must not mind a word of it; for its all hollow; he is the greatest Philanderer in the regiment, and that is saying more than you may suppose,' continued the Captain looking very significantly. 'It would take the whole night to tell you the number of ladies he has flirted with, though he never had any intention beyond the amusement of the moment; and yet, because he has a smooth tongue, and dresses well, he is to be preferred before an honest fellow, who never says more than what he thinks, and what he would.'

'Lionhart, Mrs. Stockwell would thank you for some of that fowl, but you had better let me assist you,' said Spencer, most opportunely for himself, breaking in upon the conversation.

'Yes, I must have some of the fowl, if it is only for the jelly,' said the lady; 'but now, do ye Captain Lionhart let Captain Fitzroy help it; for you know as you will keep niggle naggle, niggle naggle all night; and I always like a good slice of breast with my wing; but I don't say that as any way to disparage you Captain, for I respect you the more for the cause.'

'– Take the old witch and her cause, will her tongue never stop?' muttered Lionhart, quite out of patience at the interruption. He, however, insisted upon helping her himself; / and, with some difficulty, accomplished his task; while Matilda observed, for the first time, that he had almost lost the use of his right hand? and recollected having heard of its being caused by a severe wound he received abroad, which, though dangerous, he had not esteemed of sufficient consequence to mention, 'till a second rendered it necessary for him to return home to try the effects of his native air towards his recovery. This she had learnt from Arbella Ferrars; for, from his own discourse, she would never have imagined that he had even been in the Peninsula. He resumed the conversation, lamenting the necessity he was under to begin his Welch journey, (which had been too long postponed,) on the following morning, and seemed anxious to secure every moment of Matilda's attention, while she staid.

This was a short-lived pleasure. Mrs. Melbourne, who began to be uneasy at being so long absent from her husband, rose to depart; and the company, as if by one consent, soon after broke up; with many congratulations on the 'delightful evening' they had spent, and many hopes of meeting to enjoy the same again – hopes in which Lady Torrendale politely joined, while she reserved to herself the privilege of prorouging, for an unlimited term, this sitting of *beaux esprits*;[108] in which, it did not appear to her, that she made the conspicuous figure she ought to have done. Matilda seized the first opportunity to ask Arbella the meaning of the title of Nymph of the Danube. She doubted not it alluded to some work, with which she was unacquainted; and her friend's knowledge of general literature, and foreign languages, made her always a desirable reference.

'The Nymph of the Danube – the Danube,' repeated Arbella, 'aye now I recollect, among my uncle's old German plays there was a piece with such a title.'

'And what was her character?'

'Why, if I mistake not, she was some goddess, or sea-nymph, (not much better than the Neapolitan syrens,) who allured a poor mortal to become desperately in love with her, and when he afterwards married a / good every day sort of body, like myself, *par example*, haunted him with the image of his lost happiness, by the perpetual miracles, with which she pursued him, of her genius and power. What's the matter with you? don't you like that description? You look like the governor in the Critic, it seems to have "touch'd you nearly!"'[109]

Matilda did not tell Arbella the reason of her question; but she still continued to repeat to herself, with a degree of painful perplexity. 'It was strange that he should call me the Nymph of the Danube!'

CHAPTER XVI.

With thee conversing, I forget all time;
All seasons, and their change, all please alike.
                                        * * * * *

But neither breath of morn, when she ascends
With charm of earliest birds; nor rising sun
On this delightful land; nor herb, fruit, flow'r,
Glitt'ring with dew; nor fragrance after show'rs;
Nor grateful ev'ning mild; nor silent night,
With this her solemn bird; nor walk by moon,
Or glitt'ring starlight, without thee is sweet.

MILTON. PARADISE LOST.[110]

THE circumstances of surprise and interest, under which Matilda had been first introduced to Strathallan, had led him, perhaps, to notice with more attention than he
otherwise would have done, her singular and captivating style of beauty. Her behaviour, when the Ball was in agitation, had convinced / him that she had a heart, which
corresponded with the charms of her countenance: but to discover that she had a mind
which in its minutest emotions sympathized with his, harmonized in every taste, and
agreed in every feeling – was reserved for him in the too short and delightful evening
he had passed with her, at his mother's *Converzatione.* He could not resist seeking
soon to renew a gratification so great. Matilda's timidity, that had at first thrown a
veil over all her perfections, wore off by degrees; and, as Mr. Melbourne's continued
indisposition prevented their intercourse from being so frequent as Lord Strathallan
wished it, he enjoyed in those meetings a pleasure, perhaps the more exquisite from
its being rare.

Mrs. Melbourne, for a different reason, was charmed with her evening. She was
fascinated by the talents and conversation of Miss Swanley; and amused by seeing
something resembling a society to which she had long since bid adieu. 'Sappho is
really as interesting and agreeable,' she said, 'as her little rival is the contrary.'

'Sappho, by all I hear, is the reverse of every thing a rational man should value,'
growled Mr. Sowerby.

'Well, my dear Sir, you will allow, at least, she is not one of the hum-drums; and,
you know, *Tous les genres sont bons, hors le genre ennuyeux.*'[111]

Mrs. Melbourne knew the way to silence her old friend; and, it must be confessed, was rather unmerciful in the use of her power.

Lady Torrendale was the least satisfied of the party. 'Those clever people are the greatest bores on earth,' she said one day to Matilda. 'One cannot put any two of them together – I wonder what possessed me to collect so many of them. I had a recollection that reading parties were agreeable things – I am sure they were so at dear Lady Julia Melbourne's; but then Sir Harold was the soul of her theatricals, and her reading parties, and her suppers – Oh, those suppers! / where I have heard the charming ***, and where –'

'I know nothing of Lady Julia, or Sir Harold,' said Matilda, as she looked down, and sighed.

'Not your cousin, Sir Harold? – Mr. Melbourne he was then. Oh, no, I had forgot. Well then, you knew nothing of a most captivating creature. With just a tinge of romance, sufficient to make him interesting, he had all the ease and gaiety of a man of the world; and that at an age when most boys are at school with their tutors. Lady Julia was the dearest friend I had in the world. Old Sir Reginald was nobody, you know – always at the club; and this young Melbourne was –'

'An old flirt of yours,' said Lord Torrendale, quietly finishing the picture.

'I own the soft impeachment; Lady Julia Melbourne applied to me, to produce him and shew him a little of life. I would have done any thing for dear Lady Julia. – Then, suddenly, her wise husband chose to carry her into the country, away from all her friends; as gentlemen will sometimes do,' (looking at Lord Torrendale); 'and we – somehow, we – new objects, you know, will – But I was really very sorry for her, at first. The next thing we heard was, that after lingering there some time, her health had obliged her to go abroad in search of a milder climate: and there she died. Sir Harold was on the continent, when the event took place; and I lost sight of him when he returned, which was on the death of his father, that happened soon after. He has lived ever since at Mosscliff Abbey, a magnificent place they have in the north; and, since his travels, has been entirely given up to study. But whether he draws plans, collects medals, or writes poems, I really cannot tell.'

Strathallan exactly guessed Matilda's feelings at this little account of relations so near, and that ought to be so dear to her, as it was unfeelingly rattled off by Lady Torrendale; and endeavoured, by a redoubled portion of attention, and the resources of his ever soothing and animated conversation, to / banish from her memory every unpleasant feeling.

Matilda found, with surprise, that Strathallan was more the companion of her mind than even her mother. Accustomed to the habits of ingenious and polished society, and endued with every grace and talent that is calculated to adorn it, Mrs. Melbourne was too much a woman of the world to be able to enjoy, in their fullest extent, the sweet illusions of the imagination. Her education, while it tended to give to wit its finest edge, and most complete perfection, was perhaps of that sort, which rather prevents than encourages the expansion of genius. That temporary inaction of the soul, by which it alone is qualified for the admission of deep and lasting impressions; that keen perception of the great and beautiful, that power of wholly embodying abstract ideas, and living amidst the world of shadows, which gives the mind its poetical and romantic cast, is incompatible with an early mixture in society. Solitude is required to develope those finer emotions, those ideas evanescent and delicate, which shrink from the collision of general conversation, however intelligent and refined.

Mrs. Melbourne, who conceived this turn of mind in her daughter to be a defect, had ever applied herself, by a gentle, almost imperceptible, and delicate raillery, to repress every thing bordering on enthusiasm and romance: and Matilda, so far from priding herself on the possession of a soul superior to others, used every effort to conceal the excess of a sensibility, which she found it impossible to destroy. How great then was her surprise to find, that by Strathallan, a man used to the bustle and the pleasures of the great world, it was felt and cherished as her highest charm. He often caught her animation when the tear of sympathy trembled in her eye; the smile of pleasure played upon her lips, if she could persuade him to talk of the distant scenes he had witnessed. The subject, at first, seemed painful to him: and he could never be brought to mention any circumstance of the engagements he had witnessed; but, respecting the country, or its / inhabitants, he was less uncommunicative; and, when he made her, in imagination, the companion of his former excursions, or breathed the accents of that lofty tongue which was preferred by the Imperial suppliant when addressing his God, the landscape derived a new beauty, the language a new charm from his lips. When he described an early walk, or moonlight ramble, to visit some monument of barbaric splendor or modern piety, the moorish fort, the gothic tower, the ruin or the palace rose on the mind, clad in those mellowing tints, which imparted to them their romantic and magic grace. She followed, with him, the shivering goatherd to his cottage on the cliff; or listened to the song of the muleteer, in the valley below. Of the higher orders of the people he spoke with more reluctance; and on that fruitful theme of eloquence, the beauty of the Spanish women, was utterly silent. While thus conversing with her, he seemed to lose the melancholy with which he had at first been oppressed; but another of a different sort appeared to have succeeded it, and he had fits of abstraction, which filled those whom he most interested with surprise and alarm.

The fondness of the Countess for her two young friends daily increased; and she contrived to have one or other constantly at Woodlands.

One cold, stormy evening, in the month of March, when the favorite groupe happened to be assembled round Lady Torrendale within doors, Arbella, observing on their happiness and tranquility, while the elements were busy without, continued – 'Are you of Gray's opinion, Matilda, that the pause – listen to it – between the more violent gusts of wind, and the sound that gradually rises again with a shrill note upon the ear, exactly resembles the voice of a Spirit?'[112]

'Matilda and Gray must be both good judges,' said Lady Torrendale. 'That is like the description Dr. Darwin gave of a flower – "precisely the colour of a seraph's wing."'[113]

'Well,' resumed Arbella, 'it certainly is like the voice of a ghost.' /

' 'Tis like the plaintive moan of a dying female's voice,' said Strathallan, who had not appeared to be attending to the conversation before.

'Why a female voice? – what put that in your head, particularly?'

Observing in the countenance of Strathallan a degree of painful confusion, which it had never on any other occasion betrayed, Matilda, with a watchful tenderness, that seemed instinctively to point out to her whatever might be distressing to him, checked the voluble Arbella, and contrived so dextrously to turn the discourse, that during the rest of the evening, the subject never again came in question.

'There is something very singular about Strathallan,' Miss Ferrars afterwards observed to her: 'I wonder he keeps his looks so charmingly; for, do you know, he never sleeps – never, or hardly ever – I know it; for his apartment is just over mine, and all night he is walking up and down there, or in the library. I joke him about it, and say it was the terrible things he saw abroad "won't let him sleep o'nights;" and do you observe he never will talk of any thing that happened there: I really believe something affected him. – Then, did I ever tell you the story of the ring; he had one that he never would show me, he said it contained Verdinha's hair, so one day I contrived to snatch it off his finger, and look at the chrystal. There was a little ringlet so bright and soft, I could hardly conceive it to have belonged to a boy, and a Spanish boy too. I overwhelmed him with questions, and if you could have seen how distressed he looked! I am sure there is some romantic tale we ought to know. I only wish whatever it is he would forget it, for it makes him very bad company and I am getting very tired.'

Arbella was not the only person who was getting tired; Lady Torrendale confessed, now the bustle of the Christmas festivities was over, and now the country was thinned of visitors of consequence, and now that – a – Captain Lionhart was gone, she began to feel it intolerably oppressive; yet without the sinews of war, (she significantly observed) / she could not follow the fashionable swallows in their flight to London; and those Lord Torrendale would not supply. Matilda alone, amid the discontented circle was perfectly satisfied with her situation; and though arrived at an age when most young ladies think their attractions should be brought forward to more public notice, felt not a wish beyond the society with which she was at present surrounded. She wondered to find herself, in this respect, so superior to so great a lady; and, perhaps, indulged in a little secret self-applause at the reasonableness of her conduct in the very moment that reason's most insidious foe was stealing, unperceived, into the heart. Mrs. Melbourne was not so contented; she loved her husband, but she lamented his peculiarities. And when, just before Lady Lyndhurst's departure, she happened to see on her table a number of cards, with her daughter's name, that had just been struck off for the honorable Miss De Courcy's 'first winter,' she felt a mother's throb of regret in the reflection that charms and talents, in her opinion so much superior, should not be produced to the world with equal advantages. All that Lady Torrendale's influence in her immediate circle could do was already effected. Her two young favorites, Arbella and Matilda, had, under her auspices, risen rapidly into fashion, and were already considered as stars of the first magnitude in the Derbyshire world; with this difference, that the introduction of the fashionable Countess, brought Matilda's advantages of birth and connection into more general remark; while it secured from malignant observation Arbella's deficiency in both. Could the vanity of giving the *ton* to the surrounding neighbourhood have sufficed for Lady Torrendale, she might indeed have been completely happy. *La cour et la ville*[114] in old France, were not supposed to convey more different ideas than any fashion in language, dress, or manners, that had only general practice for its support, or that had received the sanction of the happy few admitted to Woodlands; and, indeed, when Miss Melbourne, by a few visits to Miss Ferrar's home, became more acquainted with the manners of *la ville*, she became less surprised / at her friend's fashionable enthusiasm, or that she endured a few mortifications to partake of more polished society. Arbella had often entreated she would spend with her some of those days she herself was condemned to pass at 'aunt Stockwell's;' but her father's indisposition took up most of Matilda's time, and Lady Torrendale claimed, as her right, the few hours she could spare to friendship.

As the advancing season brought on an amendment in Mr. Melbourne's health, which enabled her to leave him more frequently, she no longer resisted her friend's invitations, and those of Mrs. Stockwell, uttered in that tone of extreme softness, which she imagined to be most insinuating.

When Matilda arrived, the house seemed to be in a degree of commotion; there was nobody to announce her, and she at length took the liberty of running up to the drawing room, where she expected to meet Arbella: her attention was arrested at the door by the sound of loud voices and altercation within; and by hearing Mrs. Stockwell, in no very gentle tone, reproving one of her attendant damsels, and after cordially consigning her, before she dismissed her, to the escort of all the subterranean powers, concluding with, 'saucy minx! do you think this is the way for me to give you a character?'

'I don't know,' some one replied in a muttering voice, 'but I shall take care to give you one.'

At this moment the door burst open; Martha sobbing, and with her handkerchief in her hand, bolted past Matilda, while Mrs. Stockwell, quite ashamed to be discovered in one of her morning exercises, was profuse of her apologies. 'Bless me Miss Melbourne, I did not expect to see you so soon, and I am afraid *as* there was no one to denounce you properly. For to say the truth, I have been making a little house-clearing, as one must sometimes do. Not that I was saying any thing to Martha, farther than a little remonstrance; but I am glad you came in, or it might have come to high words – she's a good girl, and knows I hardly ever give her a / jobation.' Matilda begged her polite hostess would not think any apology necessary: while she secretly smiled at the contrast afforded by the sickening affectation of softness Mrs. Stockwell had already resumed, to receive her guests who soon came pouring in. All *top* men, or *top* women, or, at least, very *imminent* men, in town or country; and one top gentleman, who was an *imminent* farmer and grazier, was the top man of the whole county; and, to judge by the manner his friends spoke of him, Lord Torrendale was nothing in comparison to him.

In this circle, Matilda was amused to observe the degree of deference and respect Miss Hautenville (who, at Woodlands could sometimes hardly command common attention) received, as the chosen friend, or rather *kite*, of Lady Torrendale and Miss Mountain. Her first display of power, or rather tyranny, was, chusing to have the headache, instead of appearing at dinner; and Mrs. Stockwell, after many enquiries and messages, was obliged, with a most lamentable face of distress, to seat herself at table without her. 'Arbella my dear, do you take the head, I always set on one side – the Ditchess of Albemarle does so.' The second course had come on when Miss Hautenville deigned to make her appearance; but it was only to sit down with her hand applied to her head, in silence, and in an attitude of suffering; instantly a number of voices assailed her with so many compliments and enquiries, of what she would chuse, that, though she had at first refused to touch any thing, she at length suffered herself to be intreated; and a dish of wheat-ears being near her, she soon demolished the whole.

'Poor thing!' whispered Mrs. Stockwell, 'she has *such* a delercate appetite! She can never touch a bit but wheat-ears, or sweet-breads; or drink any thing but soda water, or Pyrmont water, or them sort of exotics; and I get her Iceland moss for fear of consumption, and sometimes a little arrow-root; but I fear it won't do.'

Arbella, disgusted with this assumption of consequence, could hardly conceal her feelings; and, at the tea-table, where she, of / course, supplied Miss Hautenville's place, threw out so many *piquanteries* against would-be fine ladies, that Mrs. Stockwell, surprised at her recreant niece, undertook the defence of her friend; and then, diverging a little from her subject, continued to urge, in whispers, the necessity of enduring a few inconveniences, for the advantage of forming fashionable connexions. 'It is the same in all the relations of life,' she said, 'and thats what I have taken care to conculcate to my niece Arbella, and to my son too, if he would but mind me; a young gentleman has plenty of ways of pushing himself in the world; and, as for young ladies, from a partner at a ball to a partner for life, rank is the only thing should be considered. Yet how many do we see,' she continued, turning to one of her cronies, and with a pathetic tone of voice, 'who neglect it, both in the one and the other! I had a young friend once, (Arbella don't bite your lip, I'm sure 'tis full red; did you ever see me do so?) a sweet pretty creeter she was, and her parents very credible people too, I can tell you; had a capital iron foundery, kept their coach, a country house, high life all over. (Arbella love, don't laugh so loud, you'll disturb Miss Hautenville, did you ever hear me do so?) Well Mem, before she was twenty she had four very good offers. The first drove a gig; the second a tandem; then, a chariot and pair made a proposal, and lastly a coach and four. My young relation had objections to them all; the gig she said was old; the tandem crazy; the chariot and pair was impertinent; and the coach and four was a free-thinker. Well Mem, some time afterwards I saw by the newspapers – I saw – (Bella my love, do mind the urn – you have let the water run all about – did you ever see me do so?) that this young creeter – Miss Araminta Ferrars (this infamous creeter I must call her) after refusing a gig, a tandem, a chariot and pair, and a coach and four, had gone at last, and married a serjeant, a common serjeant Mem, as sure as I'm alive. I was very sorry for her, but, of course, even if I had been inclinable myself, could not, for Arbella's sake, keep up any acquaintance with such a sort / of person. When, would you believe it – she had the assurance to write me a letter, and it was all about her husband. She praised him, and called him a prime serjeant: but, in my reply, I made her to know her distance; and told her, she might have what opinion of him she thought proper; but, if he was the primest serjeant ever bore a halberd, still a serjeant was but a serjeant, and must be a low fellow, and one as I could not associate with no how. Never heard from her again, so I hope and trust I made her ashamed of herself.'

While Mrs. Stockwell was clearly proving that she had not been able to distinguish between a serjeant at law, and a recruiting serjeant, Matilda was meditating her escape before the card-tables should be set; and great indeed was her joy to see her father's carriage draw up to the door. Though it was quite early, she immediately took leave; and was so delighted with the idea of her release that she hardly perceived the dangerous situation for which she had exchanged the safety of Mrs. Stockwell's drawing-room. She was awakened from this careless reverie by the coachman begging of her (with a face of dismay) 'not to be frightened!' and found herself in the midst of a very uneven road, in turning which, one of the horses had began kicking and plunging, and at length became so unmanageable, that the man, after having in vain attempted to quiet him, was obliged at length to own his young lady had better get out. Scarcely had she done so, when the animal, happening to strike his foot violently against a piece of broken rock, fell down; and, getting entangled in the traces, hurt himself so much, that it was impossible for her to think of returning home in the carriage. Less alive to her present perplexity than to her recent escape from a greater danger, Matilda inhaled the cool evening breeze, as it was wafted from the Fountain of the Rocks, which was within a few paces of her; admired the rich foliage with which it was surrounded, and the extent of lawny prospect, that stretched beneath one side of the road. A moment after, the appearance / of a man ascending the eminence arrested her attention. She felt she could not be mistaken; it was Lord Strathallan. The delight pictured in her countenance was more than reflected, in the animated joy that beamed in his. Behold her from below, her white dress floating on the wind; the radiance of an evening sun, tinging its folds with a wavy line of golden light; while, reflected from the pointed rocks around, it lent added beauties to her blooming countenance, her flowing hair, and the wild graces of her form; he could have adored her, amid these sequestered shades, as the tutelary Deity of the fountain. Never, to his ardent imagination, had she appeared in such dazzling, such captivating charms.

'There seemed a glory round him, and "Matilda"
The angel of that vision.'[115]

He was soon made acquainted with the subject of her distress, and offered to accompany her home; in the course of their walk, he could not forbear expressing his admiration of the scene in which he had happened to meet her: 'what a romantic spot!' he said, 'have you not yet given it a name?'

'My mother calls it, Sybil Gray, from the diamond clearness of the spring that flows into the bason below:[116] and sometimes you may see me, like the Nymph in the Eastern tale by the waters of Oblivion, seated, in a pensive attitude, or with my book in my hand, within the cavern.'

'Oh, who can think, who can wish for oblivion,' exclaimed Strathallan earnestly, 'when you are near?'

Matilda tried to consider this as a common-place compliment; she had herself spoken playfully. They were, however, for some moments, both silent; she walked on, her heart swelling with a tender exultation, to which she durst scarcely assign a cause; she reflected on the past; she compared it with the present; she remembered her visit to that fountain, when the fate of Strathallan had, though he was unknown to her, called forth the sign of pity from her breast; then, all was bleak, cheerless, desolate like the / feelings of those who mourned his loss. Now, nature blooming in the full luxuriance of renovated spring, seemed to have waited to burst forth and blossom into beauty, to welcome his return.

If the chance, that made Matilda the companion of his walk, was pleasing to Strathallan, to her it was an equal gratification. His conversation she found ever delightful; but now it had a peculiar charm. Oh, it was after the sickening frivolity, the impertinence, and affectation, she had just escaped from, that she felt how grateful, how refreshing, was the intercourse of a mind regulated like her own! Turning the discourse to a subject on which he always seemed, when with her, to dwell with peculiar pleasure, 'You can just see the tops of the trees at the park at Woodlands; it now hardly deserves the name,' he continued with a smile, 'I wish to extend the plantation to the right. Woodlands could be greatly improved. I would have clumps of trees on every naked and barren spot; and cut down those that bound the view at the end of the lawn, and shut out from the prospect that bold chain of hills to the South – But (after a sudden pause) the romantic beauties of Derbyshire are nothing in comparison to the wild Ossianic scenery of Strath-Allan in Scotland – I wish you could see Strathallan.'

This, though said without design, was not heard without emotion. Matilda did not immediately reply to the wish, and a second silence ensued; a silence, perhaps, more interesting than any discourse could have been. Still, whether engaged in converse or reflection, so many charms surrounded their walk, so fragrant was the air, so delightful the stillness of evening, so perfectly did all nature seem to accord in tasting the happiness of the moment; from the sheep and cattle that reposed in groups on the herbage, to the glittering insect that hummed and fluttered along their path, that they could each have wished to prolong, to twice its extent, a ramble so delicious, and to admire, while time fled unperceived away, a view so rich and varied. Above, a bold extent of woods / and mountains, stretched as far as the eye could reach, and was lost at last in the gathering mists of evening – below, meadows and corn-fields, waving in every luxuriant tint of vivid green, afforded a different, but equally pleasing landscape. The road that wound between these lovely prospects, at length opened to a view of Mr. Melbourne's retirement; and, in a few moments Matilda was restored to her parents, who began to be alarmed at the length of her stay. Mrs. Melbourne thanked Lord Strathallan for his attention to her daughter; but he thought he perceived a degree of constraint and uneasiness in her manner, unlike the frank and graceful cordiality with which she usually received him: and, observing a similar anxiety in Mr. Melbourne's countenance, he guessed that some unexpected circumstance had disturbed the tranquility of the family, (something they perhaps wished to communicate to Matilda,) and therefore almost immediately took leave. He was hardly gone, when Mr. Melbourne mentioned, with a composure that was evidently assumed, the necessity of his setting off the next morning to London.

'Going to London!' Matilda repeated, astonished at a determination so sudden.

'Even so my love,' said Mrs. Melbourne, 'and I must accompany him. – Dear Lady Torrendale has kindly undertaken the charge of you in our absence, which you may be sure, will be as short as possible. Necessity can alone detain us. You do not fear,' and she attempted to smile, 'that your father will become a Bond-Street lounger!'

'But mamma, in my father's weak state of health – indeed, indeed he will want his little nurse.'

'While I am with him!' with a glance of playful reproach, 'Matilda, Matilda, he must prove to you that he can live some days without you.'

Mrs. Melbourne appeared so determined, that it was useless to press the point. She seemed equally unwilling to give a reason for this sudden resolution. Matilda spent a night in tears and anxiety, which was encreased by the obscurity in which this unexpected / communication was involved; that Mr. Melbourne should, though scarcely recovered from a dangerous illness, undertake a journey of such a length, and with so little previous preparation, had to her something surprising and mysterious. Solicitude for that parent's health and safety, was mixed with her feelings of curiosity and alarm: there was, however, in the morning no time to remark the effects of this painful night upon her countenance. Mr. Melbourne, anxious to escape from the kind wishes and adieus of his servants and tenants, who crowded round the carriage, prepared for an early departure. He strained Matilda fondly in his arms: 'Bless you, my darling,' he said, 'may the exertion I am going to make, terminate in your happiness, and I am more than repaid.'

Scarcely comprehending the meaning of these last words, his daughter only remarked the weakened voice, the trembling hand that still held her's, and the enfeebled frame of her father, as he was supported by two of his faithful domestics into the carriage, and felt that she was wretched. Mrs. Melbourne's manner, at parting, was most affectingly and even prophetically solemn. She could hardly be prevailed upon to tear herself from the treasure of her heart. She repeatedly embraced her daughter, and endeavoured, in vain, to acquire strength for the separation, by anticipating the moment which should restore her to her arms. – 'Of Lady Torrendale's kindness,' she said, 'I can entertain no doubt – she is not all we could wish, but she has obligingly stept forward on this occasion, and we had no other alternative. Your prudence and discretion, my love, will, during this short interval, best supply the place of a mother's care.'

'Oh do not make it necessary,' said Matilda, who felt all her assumed courage give way as the moment of separation arrived – 'Let me follow you, I will serve you, attend you, I can still go, I will not take a moment for preparation, only do not, do not leave me.'

Finding all attempts to change her mother's resolution vain, Matilda's only resource / was acquiescence, however painful to her heart; and Mrs. Melbourne employed the short time that remained for them to be together in a few admonitions respecting her daughter's future conduct, and in speaking to her on a subject which had lately caused her some concern. 'You have gained a great conquest over Mr. Sowerby's prejudices,' said she; 'he has so far waved his antipathy to fine ladies, and, above all fine ladies, to Lady Torrendale, as at length to reply to the advances of her family, for your sake; and to consent to call sometimes at Woodlands, to communicate any letters he may receive from us, and to prevent, (as he expresses himself,) a total suspension of your former habits of study and application: you see,' she continued, with a penetrating smile, 'how anxious he is for your improvement.'

'Yes, indeed, he becomes quite like papa,' returned the artless Matilda, with great simplicity.

'No, not at all like papa,' replied the anxious mother. 'When a man, without the right that relationship gives him, assumes, with a woman, the commanding tone of an adviser and monitor, and thus by degrees gains an encroaching influence over her conduct, it is, almost always, a proof, that he thinks he has an interest in the mind he is forming, and that the lover is to reap the fruits of the virtues that were sowed by the friend.'

'A lover!' cried Matilda, starting with undisguised horror.

'Nay my dear!' said Mrs. Melbourne, 'I only wished to caution you; tell me, would it really pain you were he to think of you in the light I have mentioned?'

'I cannot even imagine, it Mamma: how could I hope to console him for such a woman as he has often described his first wife? and so young as I am, I should be quite lost at the head of such an establishment.'

'But suppose he waved your inability to emulate the late Mrs. Sowerby, or to do the honours of Clifden-down, and seriously wished you for the wife of his bosom – Oh Matilda, Matilda!' continued Mrs. Melbourne, / dropping her tone of attempted irony, while an expression of anguish and solicitude, which seldom dwelt there, suddenly overcast her features, 'do I deserve to be treated with concealment, or evasion? Would that his virtues could indeed make sufficient impression on your heart – but fear nothing my love; 'twas an unreasonable wish, and no advantage this world could afford should ever tempt me to force your inclinations, unless you could bring yourself to love him.'

'Oh! mamma,' interrupted Matilda, blushing, 'I have, as yet, hardly thought of love, nor do I believe I ever shall; for they say it has its principal source from want of employment: but if I do, I am sure it will be a feeling quite different from any I have experienced for Mr. Sowerby.'

'Then you know what love is *not*, though so unacquainted with what it *is?*' cried Mrs. Melbourne; her countenance resuming its former expression of good-humoured raillery. 'May you long continue so, my child,' she added, tears of maternal tenderness starting into her eyes – 'but if it should be otherwise, remember your first, your best, your only counsellor, ought ever to be, your mother.'

The entrance of Mrs. Melbourne's woman, (who travelled in the carriage with her) to receive some orders, interrupted this affectionate conversation; a moment afterwards, a barouche drove up to the door, and Mrs. Melbourne resigned, into the hands of Lady Torrendale, the object of her fond anxiety; and, hastily stepping into the carriage, hardly trusted herself with another look, while it remained in sight. Matilda's tears, 'till now with difficulty suppressed, flowed abundantly. The Countess did not endeavour to check this necessary relief: but, while she received them on her bosom, endeavoured, by every gentle and feminine soothing, to mitigate the violence of her emotion; and, with a kindness which Miss Melbourne never afterwards forgot, cheered and supported her during the whole of their way / to Woodlands. At length the venerable mansion appeared in sight: and the poor drooping traveller, her heart bursting with the first real sorrow she had ever known, was consigned to that solitude and repose which her state OF SPIRITS[a] made so necessary to her recovery.

CHAPTER XVII.

But if, at first, her virgin fear
Should start at Love's suspected name,
With that of Friendship sooth her ear,
True love and friendship are the same.

THOMSON.[117]

THE grief of Matilda, on this first separation from all her heart held dear, was violent beyond even what the cause might be supposed to demand. The parting words of Mrs. Melbourne respecting Sowerby, the wish implied in them, so different from the former expressions of avowed dislike, in which that lady had frequently indulged, affected her painfully. She feared some mystery was concealed beneath them; yet, finding it vain to attempt to fathom it, relapsed into a dejection from which she was only roused by the receipt of a letter, informing / her of Mr. Melbourne's health and safe arrival.

It was the attentions of Strathallan that first reconciled her to the aspect of gaiety, and the sight of strangers; and in this trying moment, he added the dangerous character of consoler, to his former title of friend. There was, in the manner of this amiable man, a melting tenderness, more captivating, in the end, than the most brilliant spirit and vivacity. Alive to the slightest sufferings of others, he seemed to insinuate, to infuse himself into the very soul of those he loved; and he seemed to love whoever excited in him the smallest degree of interest. His style of countenance was analogous to his character; though regularly beautiful, still it inspired in whoever first saw him, less the idea of beauty, than of love; it was one which would have communicated the knowledge of such a passion to a heart till that moment ignorant of its existence.

Matilda had another consolation in the society of Miss Ferrars, who was invited to pass some time at Woodlands. When a passion for fashionable celebrity or personal admiration did not interfere, Miss Melbourne found this young lady's understanding solid and penetrating, her judgment discriminating and correct. She possessed many languages, and spoke them all, even better than she could write or read them. The warmth and quickness of her disposition always qualifying her to excel most in what demanded readiness and decision. Besides her amiable qualities and talents, there was one point of union between them, which (though Matilda was unconscious of it,) drew them to each other. All the lively and partial esteem that was dawning in Matilda's heart for Strathallan, was experienced by Miss Ferrars at the same moment for his brother. Yet it was not, as in Matilda's case, a parity of manners and character that attracted the lively Arbella towards Fitzroy. Neither Spencer nor Strathallan were blessed with those wearing, TEARING spirits, so delightful to the possessors, so painful to every one on whom they are inflicted. Yet though the manner of both had a softness which bordered / upon pensiveness and melancholy, this characteristic was, in the two brothers, the result of very different causes. In Strathallan it arose from reflection and sensibility, heightened and concentrated by the operation of singular and unexpected occurrences. In Spencer it was the consequence of an habitual languor, which, to be dissipated, required the excitement of gaiety, society, and applause. Spencer, to be seen to advantage, must be animated with the desire of pleasing – Strathallan with that of making happy. Spencer was delightful when any plan of amusement was to be promoted – Strathallan all amiable, where benevolence or generosity was the object. To both, the behaviour of Matilda was polite and obliging; but she reserved for the favoured Strathallan, the riches of her mind; and he felt the proud distinction; not so the ungrateful Spencer, who seemed anxious to prove to Arbella, on every occasion, how unworthy he was of the partiality she lavished on him. His behaviour to her one evening, when they were all met in the Caverna d'Aurora, filled Miss Melbourne with indignation. It may be necessary to go back a little and explain what the Caverna d'Aurora was.

Lady Torrendale, who was cold and stately in general society, piqued herself on acting the lively and elegant hostess in her *boudoir*, as she styled a little favorite apartment, where the productions of every climate seemed assembled, and which, for richness and elegance united all Lord Torrendale's taste, to his Lady's love of magnificence; there, retiring with her chosen few, she loved to be styled Calypso, surrounded by her Nymphs;[118] and received the incense liberally offered by the Poet Alcæus, who had been established by his friend Lady Lyndhurst, before she left the country, in that agreeable situation; and maintained by flattery, the post he had acquired by favour. Here, every evening, he was sure to be encountered by the brilliant Sappho, whom the Countess, from vanity, chose also to patronize; and amused herself with seeing these obstinate enemies, impelled, by an invincible attraction, to a / scene where they were sure of meeting each other, and yet where they must dissemble their hate, in contributing to the enlivening of the party. Here, by universal consent, every troublesome form was banished, and every one bore the characteristic or romantic appellation by which, as a kind of watch-word, they were known to their intimates. The names of Miss Swanley and Mr. Spring were so completely merged in those of Sappho and Alcæus, that they were constantly designated by them, except indeed when the less courteous cognomen of the Shears, given by Arbella to the unlucky Bard, was sometimes remembered to his no small mortification. She herself, and her fair inseparable Matilda, obtained the denomination of Celia and Rosalind. It was difficult, when in his company, to forget Spencer's surname of Eyes; while his brother, from his partiality to his Scottish residence, and Miss Ferrars having once, in her rattling manner, declared he was the only man whose personal appearance exactly gave her the idea of Leyden's 'Lovely Lord of Colonsay,'[119] was never addressed by any other name: and Miss Mountain, whose coldness might have better qualified her for the character of the Mermaid*, was, from the loftiness of her port, and the stateliness of her dignified

* Minstrelsy of the Scottish Border.

charms, always styled Sacharissa.[120] Here, all seemed to partake of the happiness and freedom of the scene, from Lady Emily, who danced, in fairy rounds, to Miss Langrish's magic music; or, far happier, sat nestled close by her brother Strathallan, looked in those gentle eyes, and in silence blessed his return; to Spencer, who, lounging on a sofa, amused himself with talking brilliant nonsense to Sappho, a species of accomplishment in which that young lady was fully his match.

Of Sappho, it was not easy, immediately, to form any decided opinion. That numerous body to whom Miss Seward has so happily given the appellation of the Prosers,[121] would have determined the question in one word, by saying, Miss Swanley was 'not / like other people:' but as this charge, besides being too vague and general, has the additional disadvantage, that it may be applied, for different reasons, to several very different objects; such as the Venus de Medicis, a modern Esquimaux, or an ancient Pigmy; it may not be unnecessary, in order properly to appreciate her character, which was an energetic and singular one, to be, at some future time, somewhat more detailed and particular. Without having Sappho's eccentricities, the little stranger from the Rocks found the agreeable ease that reigned in this society peculiarly suited to the innocence and candour of her disposition; yet it was to one mind alone that her's felt pleasingly and powerfully attracted. Matilda feared not to unfold every good and generous emotion of her soul in the presence of Strathallan; and when Strathallan, seated between her and Lady Emily, said, 'now I have my two sisters,' he seemed as if nothing need be added to complete his felicity.

'Come, shut the door, and draw round, all ye that are initiated,' said Alcæus, with exultation, one evening after they had dismissed a formal party, whom they had determined to exclude from their laughing supper; 'Thank heaven we are clear of the humdrums! For my part, when I am seated in this dear apartment, and see you, Contessa, "*Les jeux, les graces, et les ris,*"[122] attending your steps, I have a mind, as priest of this sacred region, to consecrate it to social pleasure, and write in golden letters on the enchanted portal,

"Lungi ah Lungi ite O profani."

'That was the inscription,' said Sappho 'to the entrance of the Caverna d'Aurora, mentioned in Tasso's Aminta.[123] It was well known he meant by it Leonora of Estes's[124] boudoir. It was a pretty compliment to an Italian Princess.'

'And why not to an English Countess – Gad I've a mind I'll give names to every room in the house.'

'That will be new; it is mentioned, I think, as far back as the time of Madame de Maintenon, that the apartment in which she / generally received her visitors, was called, in allusion to her birth-place, America; the King's was named, as more suitable to the theatre of his empire, Europe; while Asia and Africa were allotted to other intimate friends.'[125]

'No quarter, my "fair enemy!" Now would you fain say of me what was said of Voltaire, "What is good of his is not new, what is new is not good."'[126]

'Certainly. I am equally struck with the resemblance Alcæus bears to Tasso, and to Voltaire.'

Alcæus, who was lodged, *secundem artem,*[127] in a garret, immediately began by naming his air-built citadel, Belrespiro. The room in which Lady Emily received her *no*-lesson from Miss Langrish, and her various more important lessons from Italian, French, and German professors in music, drawing, dancing, &c. where she was permitted to keep her pet lap-dog, who was not allowed to share the honours of Floss; and where she kept, without permission, two dormice, a squirrel, a marmoset, and a rabbit, the poet wisely denominated Noah's Ark; while, to Lord Torrendale's study, where none, under any pretext, were ever admitted, and which was said to be begirt with the head of many a grimly sage and old philosopher, he gave the terrifying appellation of the Blue Chamber.[128] The Earl heard the sarcasm unmoved; content if, amid the lively group, he was allowed to remain silent and unobserved.

'My dear he is a *slate*,' said Arbella, in reply to some remark made by Matilda on his Lordship's want of conversational talents; 'The man is a slate, and nothing better nor worse.'

'You have such strange names for every thing! Pray what am I to understand by a slate?'

'A slate, my dear, is that, which, if it happens to be among the coals, will neither burn itself, nor let any thing that is near it burn – *or comprenez vous?*'

To return to Spencer. The usual party were assembled in the dear boudoir, now never called by any other name than la Caverna d'Aurora. Miss Mountain, the divine / Sacharissa, was seated at the piano; Lady Emily accompanied her on the tambourine; Strathallan stood bye, attending, or appearing to attend to her peacock-tones and abortive execution; and Miss Hautenville, who recovered from her fine lady-like transformation, appeared in this region, in her true character of *Kite*, acted convulsionary to admiration; with eyes cast up, and breath suspended, she made as many contortions as an ancient Pythia,[129] or a modern disciple of Mesmer, to express the delight with which the performance overwhelmed her; occasionally interrupting herself to exclaim 'Dear, how great Miss Mountain is in those Aria's since Trasimani has *made her a voice!*'

Spencer, with his back to the group of ladies, was teaching, or trying to teach, poor Miss Langrish, Trou-madame; while Lady Torrendale, reclining on a sofa, in conversation with Arbella, sighed, shook her head, turned her fine eyes, full of softness, upon her, and tenderly pressing her hand, seemed to wish it were possible to fix that wandering fancy.

Matilda, who knew that all these blandishments were designed to draw this amiable unsuspecting girl into some unguarded confession, to be repeated, perhaps, to the unworthy object of her partiality, that he and his mother might smile together at her expence, was anxious to interrupt the dangerous *tête-à-tête*, and approaching with her work, 'What do you think of it, Miss Ferrars?' she said, 'is it not beautiful?'

'Beautiful!' Arbella repeated, 'but you did not do that, it was by Miss Crossbrook; I know her hand; Lavinia Crossbrook does every thing by a thread.'

'I should detest a woman who did every thing by a thread,' cried Sappho.

'You must not detest Lavinia Crossbrook, dear Saph,' said Spencer, suddenly turning from the Trou-madame table 'for she has just now the honour to stand very well in my Imperial Highness's good graces. A sweet innocent creature – lovely blue eyes,' looking at Arbella, 'clear fair blushing complexion, and the figure I particularly admire; rather under than over-size;' still / looking at Arbella, 'exactly the slight yet beautiful form of the little girl who acted first Sultana in *Les noces Persanes*, at the Opera.'[130]

'Surely you are not serious in your admiration, 'tis such a piece of affected insipidity.'

'Excuse me – there is, in my opinion, a great charm in that elegant *nulleté* of character.[131] In her manners, a woman should have nothing *salient* – I hate a dasher' – again he looked at Arbella.

'The Scotch expression 'drumlie,' ' said she, 'is one that I have often envied them, and wished to apply to those dismal insipids – now Lavinia Crossbrook, with her rolling eyes and her nun's face, is what I call a drumlie girl.'

'And she is what I call a charming girl' – resumed Spencer warmly. Arbella turned from him – Miss Mountain had quitted the instrument, she walked up to it, and, while her hand wandered rapidly over the keys, endeavoured to conceal the anguish and perturbation of her feelings. An extremely pretty French air lay upon the music desk – she tried it, and then accompanied it with the words –

'De mon Berger volage
J'entends le flageolet,
De son perfide hommage
Je ne suis plus l'objet.'[132]

Her voice faltered, as she repeated the last line, and her eyes fell upon Spencer's – his expressed, at that moment, the perfection of careless indifference.

'Is not that the air in the Devin du Village,' said Sappho, 'in which Madame de Pompadour drew tears from the eyes of the most volatile and thoughtless court in the world, when she represented the character of the lovely and forsaken Colette? I think I see her in her white dress, adorned with blue ribbands, her straw hat and crook enwreathed with the same.'

'Drew tears!' cried Spencer, who, like his Lady-mother, could, when he had any object in view, lay aside the excessive gentleness and refinement of his usual manner, / 'I never heard such cursed nonsense in my life. Do you think that in a court where gallantry was so universal, and inconstancy, of course, so impossible to be avoided, so simple a circumstance as a young peasant's ceasing to pay his devoirs to his mistress, when he became tired of doing so, should excite such violent emotion – Come, come, let's have no more of this. Who brought it up? Celia, Miss Langrish,' he continued, in a half laughing, half decisive tone, 'never as you value my displeasure, sing another French song while I stay; they are my aversion.'

'And yet,' said Miss Langrish, in a tone that she meant should be interesting, 'several of them express so well the artless language of affection.'

'Affection! O horrid! if ever I have a wife, (and his eye glanced at Arbella) the first thing I shall do will be to desire her to erase that word from her vocabulary. Nothing can be so preposterous, so absurd, and so teazing, in the present state of society; and if I suspected it before-hand – Oh! by Jove, I think the greatest preservative against the fatal noose would be the knowledge, that the lady was one of those tender – dying – mournful – reproachful fair ones, (he dwelt with marked emphasis on every separate word) who are always complaining, and always forgiving their dear – false – Damons.'

'Miss Langrish, Miss Langrish,' said Lady Emily, who had waited with impatience for the conclusion of this speech, of which she little guessed the intention, 'Do pray tell me what is the meaning of Devin du Village'. In vain the governess tried to nod and wink her into silence; even her usual never-failing resource 'that is not a proper question,' was now, from the publicity with which it was made, of no avail. Lady Emily, with true infantine pertinacity, as yet uncorrected by the studied politeness of Lady Torrendale, reiterated her demand; till finding evasion useless, the young lady replied to the question, now for the sixth time repeated, 'Miss Langrish pray what is Devin du Village?'

'Devin – a hem – Devin du Village means / – means, my dear – you are very inquisitive. Why don't you look into your dictionary? You will find it means the Divine of a Village – a Village Divine – in short, in our language, a Country Parson.'

'Is that reading sanctioned by the Academy, Madam?' said Alcæus, with affected submission.

'It is, I assure you, Sir – at Miss Moffat's academy.'

The laugh which, at this reply, could be scarcely suppressed, for a moment turned the attention from the subject which had been so painful to Arbella; but Spencer was determined not so soon to give up the dear delight of trifling with, and torturing a heart too fondly devoted to him. He renewed his critique upon the languishing shepherdess, as he called her, and seemed to study, by every look and word, how best to convince his Celia of his complete indifference, and of her folly in having mis-construed any former attention of his, into an opposite sentiment. Arbella looked down, fearing every moment, her vexation would betray itself in tears. Spencer saw his power, and had the cruelty to make use of it to the utmost.

'I do not remember the air Celia just played us in the music of the "*Devin du Vil-lage*," said Matilda, taking up some remark of his, to which her friend was unable to reply: 'but in the scene with the Conjuror (*le Devin*), where Collette consults about the means to recover her lover's heart, there is a song equally worth attending to; and which is said to contain good advice –

"L'amour croit s'il s'inquiète,
Il dort s'il est content,
Et la Bergère un peu coquette
Rend le Berger constant."[133]

Arbella tenderly pressed her hand; – a look of gratitude showed how she valued this well-timed interference. From that moment, rallying her spirits, she addressed all her discourse to the poet Alcæus; would touch no refreshments but what he brought her; made him write verses on her, the principal merit of which consisted in their being handed across the table with great mystery, / and shewn to her alone; extolled him beyond all the French *poétes de societé*, placed him before the graceful Bernis, *le gentil* Bernard, Nivernois, Chapelle, Chaulieu, and La Fare;[134] asked him some questions respecting an opera he was composing; offered to set some of the songs: from thence returned to the subject of the French operas; drew a rapid sketch of their progress from Quinault[135] to Rousseau; digressed from the lyric to the pastoral poets; praised the 'Jardins' of Delille, and the Idylls of Deshoulieres.[136]

Miss Hautenville put her head on one side, repeated '*L'aimable Delille!*' and thought she had given an opinion: while Miss Mountain stared even wider than usual, to perceive herself forsaken by her bard, of whom she had been the earliest patroness. He seconded the efforts of Arbella to admiration: and, setting down all her attentions to the account of his own merit,

'For ne'er
Was flattery lost on poet's ear,'[137]

sportively reproached her with having drawn him away from the centre that usually attracted him.

'If you mean the Loadstone Mountain, my poor Sindbad, I sincerely pity your involuntary inconstancy; but what shall I do for you? – Believe me, when I compare Miss Mountain to a magnet, I recollect it has two powers; and the attractive one I do not find to-night with her.'

Animated with the desire of pleasing, and with the success it had met, Arbella soon in reality acquired the spirits she had at first assumed. Meanwhile, it was observed that Spencer appeared disconcerted; that he refused to take any thing; and every moment looked graver. On his loss of appetite being remarked, Lady Torrendale (who, with all her tenderness, sometimes did not dislike a laugh against Joseph)[a] observed in a whisper that he did not like his '*sauce piquante.*' –

'She is a charming lively creature,' said Fitzroy to himself, on reviewing the behaviour of his fair mistress that evening; 'and I must not lose her for a trifle. What a pity / she is not born in a certain sphere, and has not certain connexions! – Even as it is, if her old aunt continues unreasonable, and if Lady Almeria D –, and Miss P –, and Miss C –, and Miss De V –, should fail me – I think after all, that may be – I may take her.'

CHAPTER XVIII.

– As she liv'd peerless,
So her dead likeness, I do well believe,
Excels whatever yet you look'd upon,
Or hand of man hath done.

SHAKSPEARE. WINTER'S TALE.[138]

ONE day, that Matilda entered Lady Torrendale's sitting-room, rather unexpectedly, she found her engaged in conversation with Lord Strathallan; in which the Countess seemed to be remonstrating on some subject that deeply interested her, and his Lordship with equal eagerness attempting to justify himself. 'I hope I have given proofs of the sincerity – the warmth with which I –' He stopped, without concluding the sentence, as Matilda appeared. Both paused, and then attempted to turn the conversation, with the / air of persons who had been interrupted in discussing a subject of importance.

Lady Torrendale, who was the first to recover herself, begged she would stay. 'We have been talking of something not very material,' said she. 'This gentleman, though he will soon perceive the reasonableness of what I say, is troubled with an unfortunate delicacy which makes him unwilling even to oblige, lest the favour he confers might lessen the disinterestedness of the attachment he inspires. No one can be more jealous of the nature of that attachment. It must be unmixed with interest's more base alloy. But *consolez vous*,[139] my dear exceptious knight; the advice I give you is as much for your advantage as mine.'

Lord Strathallan, who did not seem to like raillery on that head, soon took an opportunity of leaving the room; while the lively Countess carelessly repeated

'That still the grateful youth might own
I loved him for himself alone.'[140]

I have been giving my opinion to Strathallan upon a subject,' she said, 'that is at present a matter of some consequence to us all.' Then drawing her chair closer to Matilda's, and taking her hand in all the friendly confidence of a *tête-à-tête*, she continued – 'Though there are not above eight or ten years between us, yet even this slight difference gives something more of authority to that I can suggest, at the same time that we are sufficiently near in age to prevent a little friendly counsel and interference on my part from appearing to have the harshness of a parental command. His sex is later in acquiring a knowledge of the world than ours, and the wisest of them may consult us with advantage on a question in which it is required.'

Her Ladyship concluded this irrefragable maxim with an approving toss of the head; and Matilda soon found, that this disinterested and friendly advice was to persuade Lord Strathallan to agree to his father's disposing of the Scottish property, which she had often heard mentioned, in favour of his son Spencer. This Lord Torrendale could / not do without his eldest son's consent; and it was what he had often declared he *would* not do, whether his son consented or not. – 'I have endeavoured to persuade Strathallan,' she said, 'of the evident advantage and utility of this. Lord Torrendale talks of not alienating an estate that gives a second title to his family – of not impoverishing his eldest son: that son, whenever he has the misfortune to lose his worthy parent, will find himself possessed of an ample, too ample fortune; while poor Spencer is utterly unprovided for – for you do not call his commission, and what personal property Lord Torrendale may be able to leave him, any consideration to a man in his style of living. Spencer has talents, has ability, that might one day give lustre and support to the house from which he sprung: but what can a man without property, without influence, do? All this I have fairly represented to his brother, with the coolness and impartiality of a third person, equally anxious for the welfare of both. But then – "I do not love him," – nor "Spencer does not love him" – never asks his advice – "He cannot bear to load a brother who dislikes him with unwelcome obligations" – "he cannot bear to owe that to his gratitude, which he strove in vain to obtain from his affection." – Indeed, he 'wishes Spencer well; but he fears his imprudence would prevent even this last sacrifice from being of essential benefit." Oh, that false delicacy! how easy it is to see through it!'

Matilda could not compliment herself on being as clear-sighted as her Ladyship. She remembered the obligations, both of a pecuniary, and a much more valuable nature, which the Countess, in the first hurry and surprise of grief, occasioned by his supposed loss, had once acknowledged to have received from Strathallan; and she could not persuade herself that a brother so generous and affectionate should refuse to step forward when any real exigence demanded his assistance. The present communication only confirmed to her the remark of months:– she had observed, that in his family, Strathallan was not happy; that the excessive regard and attention he seemed to have for his / beautiful mother-in-law, was, if not a little affected (a term she could not bring herself to apply to any thing in his conduct), at least rather constrained; and that Spencer appeared more his companion, than his friend. From the Countess he had never experienced, in childhood, those attentions which could have supplied the place of the mother he had lost; and whose image, though so early torn from him, was fondly impressed on his infant mind. Lord Torrendale, indeed, had early discovered the superiority of his eldest son; but, cold and austere from nature, his manner had involuntarily checked the first ardour of affection, that expands in early youth; and when, at length, he would have tried to alter it, and sink the father in the friend, the time was past when he could have read the secrets of that heart and commanded its every delightful emotion. That such a heart should suddenly change, and be closed against the powerful claims of blood and friendship, Matilda found it impossible to believe.

Happily her Ladyship was one of those convenient discoursers who, so they can find one in whose ear they may murmur a complaint, or expatiate in self-commendation, never require the interruption of an answer; and think a good hearer by far the most agreeable figure in a conversation-piece.

After a great deal of buzzing, to which Matilda listened, and a great deal, to which she did not, the Countess summed up the whole with a hope that when they next met she might find her son-in-law more reasonable. 'He might conclude,' she said, 'that, where we happened to differ, he was probably in the wrong; and that if I may pique myself upon any thing, it is some knowledge of life, and a little experience in matters of business. – I believe it is time for our airing, Matilda; are you for the dust, or the pallet? For the pallet, I suppose; so I will leave you a quiet hour to enjoy yourself.'

Matilda had obtained permission from Lady Torrendale to take possession of a small room commanding a northern light, where she might sometimes amuse herself in / painting, uninterrupted by the various and distracting occupations of which the general sitting-room was the scene. This apartment communicated with two others, which had been formerly allotted to Lady Emily, as play-rooms, and which were now totally neglected; their style of decoration not being sufficiently modern to please the taste of the mistress of the house; they contained nothing of any value, except a few old family pictures. Matilda had seated herself at her desk; and taking out a drawing that Lady Torrendale had recommended to her to copy, had just sketched a figure, which, for airy lightness, almost emulated her own, when her occupation was suspended by the appearance of Lord Strathallan; he begged she would resume it, and bestowed the highest commendations on the drawing.

'You often promised to give me a lesson,' returned Matilda, 'but you must not begin by praise. – I assure you, my Lord, I am patient of reproof, and any improvements you suggest will be thankfully adopted.'

Lord Strathallan sat down, made a few trifling corrections; then throwing aside the pencil – 'Shall I acknowledge Miss Melbourne,' he said, 'that I think myself fortunate in finding you alone; I have wished to speak to you upon a subject in which my feelings, my heart, are concerned. Affectation is unworthy of you, as it is, I hope, undeserved by me; you are not ignorant, I am sure, of the subject of my recent conversation with Lady Torrendale, and I may appear, in your eyes, a hard, unfeeling brother;' he paused, a thousand expressions came to Matilda's lips in reply; but none with which she felt completely satisfied. She was shocked he should believe her prejudiced against him – she wished to assure him of her good opinion, but how sufficiently to measure the terms in which it was to be expressed, was the difficulty.

'Believe me, my Lord, I never imagined – believe me, I never supposed you capable, I never wished for any communication that –'

Again she was silent, and Lord Strathallan proceeded – 'I know that is the light / in which I am often represented – to the world I am content to be so – I value not the opinion of the world – but your opinion I value; and in trying to rob me of your esteem, she does me an injury, of which a mind like her's, is incapable of conceiving the extent.'

Matilda made no reply. Why should Lord Strathallan be so very anxious to excuse and justify any thing that might hurt him in her good opinion? This was a perplexing question: but it was a perplexity which, though it prevented her immediately answering to this appeal, was not unattended with pleasure.

'I love my brother,' he continued, 'none know how much I love him; and could what is demanded of me contribute to his real advantage, I should not hesitate a moment; but shall I, to enable him to supply the demands of present extravagance, deprive him of all resource in his future life? Spencer has fine talents (he spoke with a tenderness of which Matilda at that moment thought Fitzroy unworthy,) he has virtues that I hope will yet expand; but he is still very young, and is not aware of the value, the importance, of independence. My father has been careful, but too careful to secure to me a load of useless wealth,' here some painful idea seemed, for a moment, to intrude, but, (soon resuming the subject of his discourse,) 'I never wished to increase it; I consider him and myself as holding Strathallan in trust for Fitzroy: to be his as soon as –' Distrest that he should think it necessary to enter into such a detail, Matilda would again have interrupted him: but he prevented her, adding with increased emotion. 'Am I wrong Miss Melbourne in the conduct I have thus far pursued? is this friendly interest in his real welfare to be confounded with the selfish policy that seeks its own advantage at the expence of others?' A look from Matilda, full of esteem and confidence, convinced Strathallan, that at her tribunal at least he had nothing to fear. He apologized for the interruption his entrance had occasioned, and entreated she would allow him the pleasure of seeing her / continue the charming study upon which she was engaged.

'No, no more drawing for me to-day,' said Matilda, concealing by an affected gaiety how much her heart and soul were absorbed in the communications he had just been making. 'I am like the bird who deserts her nest the moment any intruder has approached it.'

'Would I could stay near it for ever,' murmured Strathallan: 'perhaps though you do not chuse to paint any longer, you would have no objection, Miss Melbourne, to have some subjects recommended to you for the future exercise of your pencil. I assure you, in those deserted apartments there are forms and countenances not unworthy of Matilda's touch. If you would permit me,' he continued, with a smile, 'to be your Cicerone, – '[141]

Matilda rose. – Owing to the gloomy and neglected state of the adjoining rooms, she had never thought of examining the pictures they contained; and now, with a little more perturbation than was desirable for a connoisseur, she prepared to have their beauties pointed out to her by Lord Strathallan, 'and why were these apartments deserted?' she enquired.

'Look,' said his Lordship, opening the shutters, by which means a full light was thrown upon the portrait of a lady opposite to them, 'did you ever remark the expression of that face?' The picture represented a young lady, still in the bloom of youth; the elegance of her form, the exquisite fairness and beauty of her neck and bosom were remarkable; but nothing could long attract the attention from the liquid softness, the heaven of countenance her blue eyes expressed, to which the delicate bloom spread over her features, and the mild regularity of the features themselves, seemed to contribute, but could not be said to form her principal charm: a pensive smile sat upon her lips; it was a smile of repressed sensibility, and one which seemed to say the mind from which it emanated was not happy. 'That is my mother's picture,' said Lord Strathallan, 'it was / taken in that distant land, where she drooped, languished, and died. She was beloved, but she was not long lamented. Had she lived –' then turning quickly to another, as if fearful of pursuing the subject, he recommended it as more worthy of Miss Melbourne's attention. It was a whole length figure of a boy of about four or five years of age, who seemed guarding, with jealous watchfulness, a favorite bird, which he kept nestled close to his bosom, from the gripe of a cat, which appeared ready to spring forward and devour it. The inbred, habitual cunning and cruelty expressed in the looks of the cat, formed an admirable contrast with the momentary caution and suspicion which had stolen over the soft and infantine features of the boy; while the flow of health spread over his cheek, the mild sweetness of his eyes, and the rich luxuriance of his clustering curls of a golden brown, made the picture altogether as pleasing a study as could be desired by the amateur or artist. 'Could you trace any likeness in those mild features and that rosy cheek' (said Lord Strathallan, turning round with a forced smile,) 'to that excessively fine man, Captain Fitzroy?'

Matilda confessed she could not; 'yet such he was; and, as youth advanced, his mind promised to equal the graces of that form. Active, penetrating, and inquisitive, nothing seemed too high for his comprehension, too laborious for his perseverance, to attain. With a soul ardent, and thirsting for every species of knowledge, he seemed one of those favoured beings whom nature has marked as destined to rise above the crowd, in whatever walk of life her gifts may be employed; but society, early and frivolous society, destroyed the work she had so well begun. Happy if even his heart had escaped the contagion! what would I not have given to have touched that heart, to have obtained its confidence, but that was impossible. Yes, I would have given up Strathallan, the seat of my early pleasures, the favourite abode of my mother! more would I have sacrificed could it have purchased friendship;' he paused, and then fixing on her those blue eyes which, whether / in joy or anguish, alike pleaded to the heart they addressed, he continued, 'in my family, in the world, I have sought, vainly sought, for that affection, the wish of my heart, the dream of my soul; once, only once I met it, and then, too late discovered –' This last broken sentence he uttered in a hurried voice, and tone scarce audible. 'Forgive,' he resumed, 'this wandering of a heart too severely tried. Oh Miss Melbourne, Matilda, consoler, gentlest friend, to you alone I would dare to speak those feelings, you, you alone can allow for, can understand them.' The emotion with which Matilda heard these words is not to be described. Never had Strathallan addressed her by that appellation before. Matilda, HIS Matilda, it seemed that, by this expression, he had brought her nearer to him; this trifling circumstance, which Matilda would have scarcely remarked, sunk deep into her heart; 'can you forgive me,' he cried, 'for unintentionally paining a bosom gentle and indulgent as yours: believe me –'

'Very pretty indeed,' a voice exclaimed, which seemed to be that of a person just entering the room, 'I hope we do not intrude;' turning round they beheld Miss Langrish and Miss Hautenville at the door of the apartment; it was the former young lady who made the exclamation, and who, advancing towards Matilda, with eyes in which jealous rage attempted in vain to assume the appearance of contempt, she said, 'I am surprised Miss Melbourne that you could have amused yourself, as you formerly did, prying into my studies, you who have found out such useful ones for yourself with Lord Strathallan;' but irony being a figure which requires calmness of mind to be kept up with consistency, she dropped the attempt, and continued, in a voice trembling with passion, 'I see now why you withdraw yourself from the general society: but Lady Torrendale shall be informed of it; I assure you Ma'am, Lady Torrendale shall not be duped any longer.'

Matilda who, feeling perfectly innocent, had none of that aukward confusion and want of presence of mind, which often gives the appearance of guilt, replied very coolly, / 'my dear Miss Langrish you need not give yourself the trouble of informing Lady Torrendale; for as I shall see her Ladyship in a quarter of an hour, the circumstance (how ever insignificant in itself,) of my having examined some family pictures in company with her son, will probably furnish (for the want of something more interesting,) matter for conversation: if, however, you pique yourself upon telling a story well, or think it of importance that her Ladyship should be informed of it still sooner than I have stated, I beg you will hasten to her with the news, for fear I should anticipate it.'

Miss Langrish coloured, and seemed not to know how to look, upon receiving this calm reproof. Miss Hautenville said 'hem.'

'I hope Miss Langrish,' said Strathallan, who seemed excessively hurt at this scene, 'that you will not employ so very trifling an incident as my pointing out to Miss Melbourne some paintings, which, however injured by time and dust, I think worthy to be rescued from oblivion by her pencil, into an engine to give pain to her feelings; and, through her, to hurt me, who must consider her, while remaining in this house, as claiming a different treatment from our kindness and hospitality.' These words, from Lord Strathallan, with the accompanying expression of resentment, which so seldom passed over his gentle countenance, completed the confusion of Miss Langrish; she looked down, and stammered out some apology for her imprudent warmth. Matilda, extending her hand to her, assured her with a smile it was already forgotten. Miss Hautenville, who all this time had been hanging on her companion's arm, repeated her oracular 'hem,' an observation which, as it can neither be replied to nor controverted, is found particularly useful by those ladies, who wish to cast a reflection on the conduct of another, without hazarding the chance of any remark being made in return upon their own.

As Lord Strathallan had foreseen, Miss Langrish was too wise to risk her present tranquillity by disclosing her suspicions, whatever / ever those supicions might be; and even Miss Hautenville, for once, thought it better to be silent. A sneering demand from that lady, 'if she had DRAWN lately,' a formal request from Miss Langrish that she might not interrupt her 'STUDIES,' and a witty remark from the poet Alcæus, that the DRAWING-room was, after all, the only place for a young beauty to shine in, were the only penalties Matilda had to pay for an hour the most charming she perhaps had ever spent; the hour in which Strathallan had unveiled the emotions of his heart to her; in which he had called her his consoler – his friend – depository of the secret thoughts of Strathallan! How many proud, how many delighted feelings mingled with this consciousness! pity added its charm to the sentiment of admiration, of esteem, with which his image was ever surrounded. He was not happy – happy as he deserved to be: and, if a starting tear would surprise her unawares upon this conviction,

'A sigh, a tear so sweet she wished not to restrain.'[142]

Having once spoken to her with the openness of friendship, Strathallan now communicated to her every feeling, every opinion as it arose. He took a peculiar delight in discoursing with her on those benevolent plans in which he was sure that she would sympathize. Matilda who had been used to be her father's almoner at the retirement of the Rocks, missed, at Woodlands, the pleasure attending that daily occupation, and found nothing so much compensate for the want of it, as the contemplation of the still more extensive exertions of Strathallan. She perceived that, though he never reflected upon the line of conduct his father had pursued, he regretted the period in which he had absented himself from the abode of his ancestors, and did every thing in his power to remedy the evil this neglect might have occasioned.

Alive to 'every want and every woe,' the poor had, in him, at once an advocate, a benefactor and friend.[143] 'Strathallan has a fund of *unappropriated* tenderness;' Lady Torrendale one day carelessly observed, 'take / care, Matilda, he does not give it into your keeping.' At this indiscreet sally, both coloured and seemed to suffer, but were both in equal danger? While the innocent and ingenuous Matilda was gradually, under friendship's guise, allowing an attachment the most exclusive to take possession of her heart, Strathallan, with the advantage of being many years her senior, and in habits of a much greater intercourse with the world, was, perhaps, only seeking an amiable and sympathizing friend, who could sooth the sorrows of his. We will not absolutely deny that he loved; but, though capable of passion to its utmost excess, and its most exalted refinement, certain it is that it was not necessary, with him, as with most others, to be under the dominion of a sentiment, tyranical, engrossing, and often selfish, in order to shew sympathy, interest, and attention. Of a nature composed of all the softer, kindlier elements, he could give much without breaking in upon his heart's sacred store: and that was what rendered his intercourse imperceptibly, yet ever, dangerously, attractive; Sappho had once, with her glowing pencil, most truly touched his character. 'As colours appear invested with added brightness when seen beneath the rays of the sun, every affection seemed as if it assumed a warmer tint, a livelier glow, as it passed through the mind of Strathallan; and, in return, whatever is the species of interest he inspires, it always partakes of the nature of enthusiasm.'

Yet, though adored by his inferiors, the idol of his sister, and his father's pride; though the object of imitation, of esteem the most marked, and regard the most flattering, with his own sex; of jealousy, competition and the most passionate admiration, with the other, still he feared he had never yet met with that pure, disinterested, tenderness, independently of every adventitious circumstance, which his ardent and romantic mind alone could value. The friendship of Matilda appeared the nearest substitute for it – the Countess, easy, careless, and unconcerned, seemed not to perceive, or not to heed its progress.

'O nól véde, o non s'avvéde.'[144] /

Lord Torrendale, indeed, though he treated Matilda with uniform kindness, and even distinction, seemed to view his son's increasing partiality with some uneasiness; and never saw them engaged together in conversation, without appearing to regret his having been so communicative of his opinion on the subject of the Duke of Ormond and Lord Ossory in a certain *tetê-à-tête* he once had with her.

Strathallan was scarcely ever from her side in those walks that were become more attractive than any in-door employment, as the beauties of the country gradually unfolded themselves, beneath the genial influence of the advancing season; a season which seemed, as it approached, to bring a fresh influx of joy and gladness into every heart, and to impart even to Spencer's languid cheek a portion of that vernal bloom, of which sickness and fatigue had nearly robbed it.

'He grows handsomer and handsomer every day,' said Arbella, 'but not more agreeable I can assure him – and so I shall tell him when next we whisper "soft and low." Did you ever observe, Matilda, the difference of Fitzroy's and Lionhart's voice? Poor honest Frank's is rough and boisterous – Spencer's sweet, low-toned, like that of a man in the habit of saying things he wishes to be heard but by one alone – Poor Lionhart! It is not for thy worth which is superior, nor thy talents which are inferior, that thou art constituted the illustrious Fitzroy's chosen "Amigo." It is that manly plainness of appearance, so well contrasting with the elegant beauty of thy friend that has promoted thee to the honor of accompanying him every where, apparently in the character of his "Fidus Achates",[145] but really in that of his Foil.'

After the first unpleasant sensations were over, Matilda saw no reason why she should suffer the silly sarcasms of persons she despised to prevent her having recourse to an employment which had charmed the impatience of many a weary hour; and, determined to sketch some of the figures that Strathallan had pointed out more particularly to her / notice, she once more established herself in her little painting-room. Hither she often invited Arbella, Lady Emily, or even Miss Langrish, to inspect the progress of her work. And here, Strathallan had too much delicacy ever again to intrude. To chuse among these family groups was not so easy a task as she had at first imagined. That of the youthful Spencer and his bird was a pleasing study; but then, besides the awkwardness of sitting down to copy a picture intended for a very vain young man, who was of her daily acquaintance, the piece contained too many objects, and was too complicated and difficult, she feared, for her execution: others there were; but then they were formal wigs, or stiff ungraceful heads of the Lady Bettys and Lady Dorotheas of the last generation; it would be absolutely no improvement to paint them. At length, after much deliberation, nothing was found to suit her purpose so well as the portrait of the late Lady Strathallan, which, besides being the best designed and most exquisitely coloured, had the great additional recommendation of 'not being like any body living.' 'She was beloved,' she often repeated to herself these words of Strathallan during the progress of her pencil; and, uniting them in idea to the name and the fate of this early victim of sorrow, the train of reflections they suggested gave rise to a little fanciful design and inscription, with which she adorned the sketch she had just completed; it represented a rose broken from its stem, the legend '*elle fut aimée.*'[146] The recollection of a French device, with something of a similar inscription, had tempted her to give it in that language. When she contemplated this tribute to the memory of a beautiful young woman, torn from the most endearing ties in the bloom of youth; she felt satisfied with its execution, and anticipated the praises of Sowerby in the next visit he should pay her. The pleasure she promised herself was, though unknowingly, perhaps heightened by the consciousness that he could not praise a line in the delineation of those beautiful features, that lovely countenance, without at the same time praising the resembling features of Strathallan. / Nothing is so bold as the heart of a lover, at a distance from the accomplishment of any of its designs; nothing so timid, upon approaching the completion of the slightest of its wishes. Matilda, who, during the progress of the work, had secretly enjoyed the ingenuity which enabled her, unsuspected, and with impunity, to indulge in some of her feelings, no sooner saw the portrait in the hands of her rigid censor, than the most painful and extravagant apprehension seized her; and she thought the feminine dress and form scarcely sufficient disguises, to conceal that in them she had pourtrayed the soft smiles and love-breathing looks of Strathallan: her agitation was so great as even to attract the notice of Sowerby, no very accurate observer of the variations of countenance in those he addressed. He interrupted some admiring comments he had been making upon the picture, to exclaim 'why Matilda, what's the matter? you are nervous I believe: the hurry of this dissipated place don't agree with you, child.'

'Oh, no,' she replied, her eyes filling with tears, 'it is not that, I am perfectly composed; but these praises, so great, indeed I cannot bear them – from you,' she paused: and Sowerby, betrayed for a moment, by her ambiguous expressions, into an error the most delightful he had ever indulged in, was nearly surprised into an avowal, which would soon have brought on the destruction of all his hopes; but a timidity foreign to his usual dogmatic character, seemed suddenly to have put a seal upon his lips; and, a moment afterwards, a circumstance catching his eye, which excited at once his surprise and displeasure, his lovely pupil was soon roused from imaginary terrors, to the real uneasiness produced by his serious reprehensions: 'Matilda what's the meaning of all this,' in the voice which always announced 'this,' was something excessively wrong, proceeded an exclamation of 'why child you have forgotten your French! in the inscription underneath the picture, you have put the masculine for the feminine pronoun.' Matilda looked at the drawing, which he turned, or rather pushed towards her, and read with dismay and astonishment, / instead of *elle, il fut aimé*. She had hardly apologized for this unaccountable oversight, when she was alarmed by a second exclamation of 'Matilda, what's all this,' her inexorable tutor had been looking over the remarks he had desired her to make upon her last astronomical lesson; and had already discovered two mistakes in the first page, and that, out of four problems he had left her to resolve, three were done wrong. Listening with a look of contempt and incredulity to the excuses she attempted, in palliation of her accidental inattention, he replied to them in that tone of irony, which was still more painful to her feelings, than serious reproof, 'really Madam, I congratulate you on the accuracy of your calculations. Your talent for observing is equally wonderful; and I doubt not, in time, you will know the pointers from the pleiades. How I shall applaud myself for having had some share in the education of a young lady, who, threatens to rival Miss Herschell, and surpass Miss Smith!' As Matilda turned away to conceal the tears she could no longer suppress, Sowerby continued resuming the severity of his usual tone. 'Look'ye child, this may be all idleness and folly for aught I know, occasioned by the frivolity of the society in which you have lately lived; but if it has any more serious foundation, beware how you listen to any nonsense; how you enter into flirtations, (I think you call them) with strangers. Trust me, such conduct will be productive of nothing but sorrow and disappointment to yourself, and anger and regret to your truest friends.'

He was silent from resentment, Matilda from vexation. When, at this critical moment, the door was flung open, and George Spring advancing up to Miss Melbourne with a face full of officious joy, abruptly cried, 'Miss Melbourne, don't you want some wentle-traps?'

'Wentle-traps, Sir!' thundered Sowerby, provoked past endurance at this ridiculous interruption.

'I say Madam,' resumed George, turning with a little less confidence to Matilda, / 'Didn't you say you wanted some wentletraps to complete your Papa's collection, because if you do,' he continued hesitating, 'I have just got a present of some of those beautiful shells, and I am sure I should be very happy –'

'Officious monkey!' murmured Sowerby, while Matilda, knowing the poor boy, who constantly paid her every attention in his power, meant a civility, felt hurt at the ungracious reception he must think they had given him. George, awkward and unwilling to retire, though conscious he was an intruder, began humming an air *par countenance*. Sowerby caught some of the first verse.

'By the side of a murmuring stream,
As an elderly gentleman sat,
On the top of his head was his wig,
And the top of his wig was his hat.'[147]

The philosopher darted a look upon him that seemed to say, 'do you mean to affront me, Sir?' But George proceeded, satisfied and unconscious of giving cause of offence, through one or two stanzas more, till having arrived at those important words –

'Cool reflection at length came across,
As this elderly gentleman sat;
He resolv'd to put up with his loss,' –

– human patience could bear no more – Sowerby rose up, threw down, with a tremendous noise, a chair and table that stood in his way, and casting a terrible glance upon the unintentional offender, darted out of the room. George, perceiving this was no time to think of entertaining Matilda, followed his example; and this innocent and amiable girl was left to herself, or rather to misery.

However hurt she might feel at the harshness that appeared in the manner of his interference, she had that habitual respect for Sowerby's superior knowledge and experience, that any insinuation of his, had weight with her; and his parting words sunk deep into her mind. 'And can it then be so?' she cried. 'Can all this friendly interest, this tender, this delicate attention to relieve the sorrows of a drooping heart, be meant as so many snares, to dazzle and deceive? / Yet such indeed, I have heard, is often the conduct of those who move in the world of fashion – that world, in which I am a stranger, but with which he has been acquainted. Ah, no! I'll not believe it; the noble Strathallan is too good, too generous.' And with that name of Strathallan, as by the magic spell that stills the murmuring ocean, the tumult in her bosom was appeased. A thousand soft and endearing images crouded in upon it, to supply the place of those painful ones, with which it had till now been haunted. Sowerby and his reproaches were banished in a moment from her mind; for it was the privilege of Strathallan, whatever scene he occupied, to reign alone.

Too much agitated with the events of the day, to like the noisy society of the general room, she sought, in her music, a resource against the return of unpleasant thoughts. Enjoying the evening breeze which blew from an open window, and seated alone at her piano, she had just touched the first notes of a melody which she always found soothed and tranquilized her spirits; – it was at that soft, dubious hour of sunset, when approaching evening, sheds over every object her own harmonizing tints. Scarcely had she begun to sing, when the sound of another voice united to her own, surprised her – it was Strathallan's. How did her lately tightened and oppressed heart expand and swell, with unbidden transport, as those tones, deep, rich, and powerful, mingling thus unexpectedly with her's pleaded to its inmost feelings. She pretended not immediately to perceive his approach, that she might prolong the pleasure it inspired. Never had any circumstance presented to her, the image of a union so intimate with the only mind that corresponded to her's. Breathing together those soft languid notes, to the rich balmy air of a declining summer's day, it seemed as if their souls were mingled and borne away to some blissful isle, where melody and love alone might mark the lapse of time.

At the close of the song, Strathallan entreated she would let him hear her in another; a gratification, he said, which he so / seldom enjoyed in the general circle, where obtrusive noise and shew, were too apt to usurp the place of expression, sensibility, and taste.

Matilda, when wearied with singing, played him several of his most favorite pieces, with that unbidden grace, which waits not to be told, when it can confer a pleasure. She had a talent, possessed by but few, of producing from the subject of any music, however new to her, the most beautiful variations – running through every combination of harmony, with a rapidity and brilliancy which rendered the expression of 'flying fingers,' when applied to her light, feathery touch, no longer a poetical common-place; but in reality the only manner of appropriately describing the perfection of her skill – and then, returning to the original air, in a strain so soft, so sweet, and plaintive, as finally to establish the touching triumph of nature over the most dazzling exertions of art.

'I am not surprised,' said Strathallan, (alluding to a passage they had lately been reading together in the life of Alfieri), 'that our favourite Italian poet should describe himself as composing most of his sublime pieces during, or immediately after, the performance of music.[148] While you play, my soul is filled, my heart oppressed, by the variety and number of the new and exalted emotions it experiences. Images of virtue, of heroism, and tenderness, beyond what this world can afford, arise within my mind, and seem only to require embodying, to start up in forms of more than mortal beauty. But when you have ceased, the illusion vanishes; my enthusiasm is extinguished, and I feel I never was designed for a poet.'

'You were designed for more,' said Matilda; and a conversation, thus begun, continued with its soothing spell, to render imperceptible the lapse of time, and to banish every painful and intrusive recollection.

Had Sowerby been able to conceive how much his ill-judged severity at this moment weakened his cause, even he, little as he had been accustomed to restrain his feelings, would, in this instance at least, have checked / the expression of his impatience. Exposed to the daily, the hourly fascination of converse such as Strathallan's, it was when contrasted with the unmerited harshness she had just before experienced, that it appeared invested with its most dangerous and seductive charm; it was when, dejected and mortified, she looked around for consolation and support, that its engaging tenderness, its insinuating softness, stole upon her wearied spirits, and, while it won her soul from sorrow, won it from itself.

The serenity inspired by an hour thus spent, extended its influence to the rest of her evening; and Matilda was retiring at night, her fancy filled with a number of gay and pleasing ideas, too flattering to be distinct, when, just as she was preparing to undress, she was alarmed by a sound at the other end of her apartment, like a groan; and, advancing with trembling steps towards the spot from whence it proceeded, she perceived her friend Arbella, stretched upon the sofa, which filled an alcove in her apartment, apparently in an agony of sorrow. All the delightful visions that had, a moment before, floated on Matilda's fancy, vanished on beholding the real affliction of her friend. Arbella's face was almost entirely hid by a handkerchief she held in her hand; but the moment she perceived Matilda's approach, she sprung from her couch, and throwing her arms around her, burst into a fresh torrent of tears. 'It was you I wanted to consult,' said she, in a voice interrupted by rising sobs.

'For heaven's sake, dearest Arbella, what is the matter?' cried Matilda; alarmed beyond measure at this violent display of grief, in one who had almost obtained the appellation of the laughter-loving queen. 'Is your aunt taken dangerously ill? or –'

'No, no, no; that would be no matter at all, you know – or – I don't absolutely mean no matter, but nothing compared to –'

'Well, is it any thing about Lady Torrendale, then?'

'Lady Torrendale!' exclaimed Arbella, starting, as if her indignation kindled with the name – 'A wretch! who can sentimentalize, / and toss her head about – and smile – and smile – and deceive – and betray and ruin you!'

'But still you do not tell me what it is you complain of. At first, you said I could be of use to you, Arbella. Celia! do you mistrust the friendship of your Rosalind?'[149]

This appeal seemed to rouse Arbella: it was always easier to touch her fancy, than her heart. She at length consented to disclose in intelligible terms the mighty secret. It was no other than the discovery that the mischievous little poet, Alcæus, in a novel ushered into the world under the auspices of the Countess of Torrendale, had, in the character of 'Arabella, the Female Quixote of Fashion,' made very free with Miss Ferrars name, her relations, and connexions; and, availing himself of its similarity to the title of another romance, had represented in a very ridiculous light, all the little extravagancies into which her attachment to Lady Torrendale had occasionally led her.

Extremely relieved by finding the evil was of no greater magnitude, Matilda endeavoured to reason with her friend, who seemed bent on quitting the house that moment; but in the course of their conversation, she could not help suspecting, that something more than the gall of Alcæus's pen must have envenomed the shaft that so rankled in the bosom of Arbella. At length she confessed, while burning blushes crimsoned her cheek, that it was the part Spencer had in this affair, that went most cruelly to her heart. 'I found the novel, among a heap of similar trumpery,' she said, 'on Lady Torrendale's toilet: and, while looking through it with that avidity which, as it were, possesses us sometimes to seek what is disagreeable, a pencil dropt out. I had observed several of the most provoking, severest things, had marks of approbation in pencil. I picked it up, but could hardly believe what I saw – it was Spencer's – I had remarked the case a hundred times; it was a gold one Miss De Courcy gave him.'

'Still, I am unwilling to think Lady Torrendale can have any share in this business. *She* may not have read the book; you know / she reads very little. It may have been dedicated to her without her permission.'

'She! she knows it well enough: and now I can guess the meaning of the smiles, and nods, and whispers, that have been going on for a month past among the cabal, as we call the set below stairs. And this is what the world styles a SWEET woman! and a most in-te-REST-ing woman!'

'But still you acknowledge the pencilmarks were Captain Fitzroy's, not her's.'

'No, they were not – were they? How could you remind me of that? Aye, there's the sting!'

Matilda saw how deeply her friend's peace of mind was concerned in putting an end to a partiality which had as yet produced nothing but mortification; and for her sake determined to disclose a circumstance which, though not communicated to her under the absolute seal of secrecy, she had always considered as a kind of confidence that she had resolved not to betray. She related to Arbella the conversation she had with Lady Torrendale a few days previously to the arrival of Miss Mountain; in which that lady had styled her 'my daughter-in-law that shall be.' She added the observations she had herself made respecting Spencer's attentions to Miss Mountain, on his arrival, and at the very time he was shewing the most marked coldness to Arbella. She added to this many circumstances she had afterwards observed. 'O, I see it all!' exclaimed Miss Ferrars: 'but you must decide for me, my friend – I shall suffer, but obey.'

At length it was agreed between the two young ladies, that Miss Ferrars should, on the following day, announce that her aunt could no longer dispense with her society; and thus withdraw herself without animadversion from a scene rendered hateful to her, by the petulance and malice of one individual, and the encouragement he received from the rest: and that, without absolutely breaking with Lady Torrendale, she should gradually slacken the bands of her intimacy with one who had proved herself unworthy of her confidence. 'How many thanks I owe you, my dear little Prudence,' she said, / 'for restraining my headstrong turbulence, which would have given such a triumph to the prosers. "There is the end of the *belle amitie* between her and Lady Torrendale," they would say. For I assure you, the privacy and distinctions of the favoured region, and the fashion enjoyed by those who visit at the *Residence*, as it is called, have excited great jealousies among those who are not of the chosen few. What I wish,' she continued, 'is to get away without seeing Spencer again; for his idea is hateful to me.'

'That you can easily manage; for you can take leave of Lady Torrendale at her toilet, and he always rises late.'

'I long to put your plan in execution.'

'You see the delay I required did not make much difference; the clock has already struck three, and the birds are beginning to chirp under our windows.'

'Yes – the little unfeeling wretches! But though it is so late, or rather so early,' continued Arbella, 'I have no inclination to sleep;' and, without inquiring whether her friend might not possibly have some, she continued the recapitulation of her wrongs: she had just began the third edition, with additions of the ever-interesting history of the dressing-room and the gold pencil-case, when suddenly interrupting herself, she exclaimed 'This is very wrong! I should not keep you up to listen to my nonsense. You are very good, very patient; but you must want to sleep.'

This was true. The tumults and perplexities of the day made rest more than usually necessary to Matilda; and she suffered herself to be prevailed on by her friend to undress; Arbella continuing the whole time, while she assisted her, to harangue upon the cruelty of the Countess, and the perfidy of her son. 'Good night, sweet Patience!' she said, as she at length prepared to leave the room.

'Good night!' Matilda echoed.

'Arbella retreated a few steps towards the door; then returning – 'But isn't it peculiarly provoking,' she resumed, 'that my prophecy to Helen De Courcy should exactly / come true against myself: I told her, at the ball, Alcæus would hitch her into a satire; and you see he has brought me into a novel. – Very provoking! – Good night.'

Matilda endeavoured at length to compose herself to rest. Arbella put her head in between the curtains – 'He mistook in the use he made of my name, which is not Arabella, but Arbella. Go to sleep, my love; it quite pains me to see you losing your rest. – It is the same as the Lady Arbella Stuart's the female Pretender mentioned in Hume;[150] if the little wretch had had any knowledge of history, he might have remembered that – But don't let me prevent you from sleeping.'

'You do not, indeed; I am quite awake. What I have heard will I fear keep me long awake,' replied Matilda; whose innocent and ingenuous spirit was surprised and pained to excess by the discovery she had made.

'That's my own Matilda,' cried Arbella, embracing her with tenderness, before she concluded her audience of leave. 'Give me a friend, who will thus soothe every sorrow, share every joy; – prove that little Pope's maxim should not be confined to the superior sex alone; but in every trial act up to its noble spirit.

"One should our interest, one our passions be;
My friend should hate the man who injures me."[151] /

CHAPTER XIX.

L'onda che mormora
Tra sponda e sponda,
L'Aura che tremola
Tra fronda e fronda
E' meno instabile
Del vostro cor.

METASTASIO. SIROE.[152]

ANXIOUS to support her friend in the last trial she had to go through, Matilda rose early and sought Arbella, whom she already found tolerably composed. We are told by a pleasing author, '*La jeunesse dort bien sur une resolution;*'[153] and with that which she had taken Miss Ferrars had reason to feel satisfied. 'I hope I shall not see Spencer,' she repeated.

'I hope I shall not either,' said Matilda 'for I shall never be able again to look on him in the light I formerly could.'

As Arbella did not wish any explanations with Lady Torrendale, she altered her first plan to that of announcing her intended departure when they should meet at dinner. She was prevented however from putting this design in practice by the absence of the Countess, who, whenever attacked by slight illness or caprice, ordered her dinner up to her own apartment; and who, suffering under one of those two complaints, took it by herself that day. It was necessary, therefore to wait for her appearance in the Caverna d'Aurora, where the circle generally retired to take coffee. Its usual inhabitants dropped in, one by one, and a kind of constraint and melancholy seemed to reign over all.

The appearance of Lady Torrendale was a welcome relief. 'Eyes,' apparently unconscious in what manner he had offended, was quietly sunk, (beside Floss) in repose upon the sofa – Arbella, with her back to him, sat in silence at a window, obstinately admiring / the prospect. Lionhart, too happy to have got possession of Matilda's ear, was whispering to her, 'You see I did not forget my promise to make Woodland's my way back, unless I could get out this summer.'

'Apropos, Lord Strathallan,' said Alcæus pertly, 'When do you think of getting out?'

'Oh,' cried Lady Torrendale, 'he must not think of it till then,' looking down and laughing. 'Bless me, what an indiscreet creature I am!'

'I do not know what you mean to do, gentlemen,' exclaimed Spencer, stretching himself, and opening his languid eyes, 'but I am cruelly tired of this inactive life, and, I really believe, must soon assume the sword and plume again – why, do you know how long I have been here? It is, I assure you, more than six months already.'

'Oh, what delightful things are those unlimited leaves of absence!' said Arbella, looking disdainfully at him. 'I really do not know what a man of fashion could do without them. How charming, while lounging negligently on a sofa, to look through an eye-glass at the rural prospect, and sing the "Soldier tir'd."'

'You may rally as you will, Miss Ferrars, but I declare to-day, when attempting to resume my helmet, I was shocked at its insufferable and unusual weight – You see,' he continued, shewing the table on which it lay, 'I have been trying to accustom myself to it.'

' 'Tis a ponderous helmet,' said Miss Mountain, holding it at an awful distance, in her giant grasp, while she gazed on the shadowing plumes, 'but not so huge, I doubt, as that which proved so fatal to Otranto's Prince.'

'It presses cruelly upon me, I know,' resumed Spencer, as he fixed it on his graceful brow; 'but you, ladies, so much surpass us in every thing,' he continued, affectedly, 'how I envy your superior strength. In hunting, Miss Mountain is more active than I am: in dancing we are always the first to give in: and I doubt not this cap, which gave me such an excruciating head-ache' – /

Here Alcæus cut across to make some foolish sarcasm about brains; and Arbella remarked, 'There are some gentlemen who find the slightest inconvenience intolerable: I am sure it is not so heavy –'

'Will you try?' said Spencer.

Arbella, not aware of the forfeit sometimes incurred by such a compliance, heedlessly consented. The adventurous youth did not delay to urge his claim. Surprised and offended, Miss Ferrars haughtily drew back; Spencer insisted, but Arbella, favoured by the whole of the female group, pushed open a glass door that led into the pleasure-grounds; and, light as a nymph, escaped from him.

'A race, a race,' cried the poet Alcæus, 'Captain Fitzroy, Miss Ferrars has won if she reaches the end of the walk first;' and up he skipped, as he said, to measure the distance. Spencer began the chace –

Arbella's agility long kept him at a distance; nothing was an obstacle to her speed – the love-lorn lily drooped its head, the dusky myrtle shook from its leaves the dew as she carelessly brushed by its blossomed sweets. Weary, out of breath, she still continued at full speed; her companions, who had followed her with their eyes almost to the end of the gravel walk which stretched before them, were near crying *victoria* to the swift and spirited Arbella, and insisting on the return of her persecutor; when, just as she thought herself secure, fate presented an obstacle in the officious little poet, who, starting up and spreading his arms declared she had no right to proceed any farther. Vexed at the unfair interruption, she tried to dart past him; but before she could effect this Spencer had come with her, and redoubling his speed was the first to reach the end of the course. If the pursuit thus terminated in his favour, it was more owing to the address of the bard than his own. It however procured for him the pleasure of returning with Arbella, at rather an easier rate than that at which they had set out;

and he took the opportunity to demand an explanation of her, which turned out, as such explanations generally did, to his advantage. Perhaps Miss / Ferrars found the Captain a more ingenious commentator on the story of the gold pencil-case than Miss Melbourne; or, perhaps she was herself one of those students who always think the last reading the best – be that as it may, they were remarked as they approached the house to be deeply engaged in apparently earnest and pleased conversation; while Alcæus, who formed the trio, hopped along repeating.

'Zephyr whither art thou straying,
Tell me where?
With prankish girls in gardens playing,
False as fair.' [154]

Matilda, though not aware of this new league of amity, observed, that Miss Ferrars made no farther mention of departure, and therefore thought if most prudent to be silent on the subject. She could not, however, so far conquer the usual frankness of her disposition, as to treat Spencer with the same good humoured freedom she had formerly done, in the little pastimes in which they spent the evening. He perceived the change, and affected to be offended at it.

'What is the matter with you Matilda,' said Arbella, in a whisper to her, 'Do treat my poor little Fitzroy kindly, he is quite mortified, he says, with your sullen cold looks.'

'I know not, Miss Ferrars, in what I have had the misfortune to displease your fair friend,' Spencer resumed, 'but I am sure you will plead for me, that I may obtain forgiveness.'

'Arbella, the intercessor for Fitzroy,' Matilda murmured, 'I thought, my dear, your opinion of him had been different.'

'So it was last night, my dear, but he is quite altered since; altered within this hour, I assure you.'

Meantime, Lionhart wondered to see Fitzroy bestow so much time upon a girl of such moderate personal attractions, compared to his Matilda; but, as he never questioned the wisdom of any of his friend's proceedings, he contented himself with concluding that she was possessed of some charms above his humble comprehension to discover. What it was attracted Strathallan so irresistibly to / Matilda, was considered as an equal enigma by Miss Langrish; who, however desperate her case might have ever appeared in the eyes of others, always ascribed to Miss Melbourne's arrival at Woodlands, the total over-throw of all her plans. Lord Strathallan's behaviour to her was indeed the same as it had ever been. In it there was none of that common place and unfeeling gallantry in which, as a young man of fashion, he might have thought himself authorised to indulge towards a dependant, but too ready to misconstrue his slightest attention; none of that haughty freedom or cold neglect, which, from the Countess, so painfully marked the difference of rank that existed between them. His manner, to her, respectful, considerate, and most scrupulously polite, was calculated, in the most effectual manner, at once to raise her consequence and to depress her hopes; but nothing could entirely check the romantic forwardness of this misguided young woman, and his cheek was sometimes suffused with the glow of confusion, for the unthinking folly of her conduct, while conscious there was nothing to cause him self-reproach or regret in his own.

Spencer, to do him justice, would not have willingly suffered the damsel to endure the mortification of neglect; but, when he found Matilda unwilling to attend to him, or Arbella otherwise engaged, would, if she had permitted it, rather than not keep himself in practice, have gladly flirted with the governess. But this young lady, whose passion, however absurd, had, at least, the merit of constancy and devotion to its object, regularly repulsed all such advances; and, in her heroic and decided preference of his brother, Spencer's vanity received a blow from the quarter whence he least expected it.

To see Matilda and Strathallan enjoying a species of happiness, of which she had no idea, and which she had no pretext for disturbing, oppressed her with a consuming envy, which destroyed her spirits, and threatened to undermine her health: the hope that some imprudence, on the part of one or the other, might enable her to prove this mutual friendship not so disinterested as was / supposed, was alone what supported her spirits; and a trifling circumstance aided by the sagacity of her good friend Miss Hautenville, soon afforded her the wished-for opportunity to communicate to the heart of the innocent Matilda, a part of the anguish which corroded her own. Matilda, left to herself one evening in the drawing-room, had taken up a book that she found under one of the pillows of the sofa from which Lady Torrendale had just risen. Though she had no great reverence for her Ladyship's taste in reading, she was surprised to find, in the guise of what she had hastily deemed a flimsy French novel, eloquence that captivated and entertained every feeling of her fancy and her heart. It was Chateaubriand's *Atala*; the book opened at the description of her flight with the American chief, whom she had delivered from the dreadful fate, that, a few hours before, awaited him. – '*Notre promenade fut presque muette. Je marchais a coté d'Atala.**** *Un regard tantôt levé vers le ciel, tantôt attaché a la terre, une oreille attentive au chant de l'oiseau, un geste vers le soleil couchant;* *** *un sein tour à tour palpitant, tour a tour tranquille. Les noms de Chactas et d'Atala doucement répétés par intervalles. Oh! premiere promenade de l'amour il faut que votre souvenir soit bien puissante,* ***[155] she had read thus far when she perceived, for the first time, that she was no longer alone.

Lord Strathallan was near her; and by the manner in which he stood, his eye must have gone along the page with her's; she paused; in a bosom so completely devoid of art as Matilda's, it was easy to read every emotion that arose, as on a stream's limpid surface. It was easy to perceive that the passage she had been reading was associated in her mind, with some suddenly suggested and pleasing remembrance; but one which she feared distinctly to recal. His Lordship did not follow up the advantage that memory or imagination seemed to be preparing for him in her heart. On the contrary, a slight shade of displeasure passed over his expressive features. 'Are these your studies Miss Melbourne?' he said. /

Matilda assured him, with equal truth and simplicity, she had but that moment taken up the volume, which was new to her, and had fascinated her attention. She suffered him gently to take it out of her hand; and, restoring it to its place on the sofa, 'as Lady Torrendale is reading this,' he continued, 'if you are fond of French literature, I will look among her books if I can find any thing equally attractive. Are you acquainted with the works of St. Pierre? You would be enchanted with his *Paul et Virginie*. Or no,' replacing the book and taking down *Caroline de Lichtfield*, 'here is a work, which I am sure you would like better.[156] It is by a lady, and does honour to your sex and the age in which it was written.'

Matilda, who had waited patiently during these doubts and hesitations, and submitted with the most passive acquiescence to his final decision, felt instantly assured she should like it better than any other book she could have chosen. The disparity of years between her and Mr. Sowerby was such, as to preclude a possibility of a conformity in their tastes and pursuits; but Strathallan possessed just that superiority in age which gives an amiable man a pleasing ascendancy over a woman, young, ingenuous, and anxious for improvement. An involuntary deference to his opinions, a reliance on his experience, which she could not perhaps with sincerity have yielded, to one who was exactly her equal in age, blended a feeling of diffidence and timidity with the tenderness she felt only to render it more enchanting.

It was with such sentiments that she entered with avidity upon the perusal of a romance, that still perhaps, derived its principal recommendation from its being associated, in every page, with the idea of Strathallan. By those who have been accustomed to unbounded indulgence in this species of literature, it will hardly be believed that it was the first work of that description which Matilda had ever been permitted to read. It had been one of Mrs. Melbourne's decided resolutions that, during the first years of youth, no novel, however interesting its story, however elegant its language, however / unexceptionable its tendency, should ever meet the eye of her daughter; and with a resolution of Mrs. Melbourne's, it had always been Matilda's custom to acquiesce without a murmur, or a regret. What was then her pleasure, when, with feelings unhacknied, emotions keen and pure as sensibility and the first morning of youth can give, she entered into the interest of a story in which she found sentiments and opinions, so often congenial to her own.

She closed the volume, her mind filled with a variety of sensations equally new and indescribable. The fascinating Caroline was the only subject on which she could willingly discourse. She admired the conduct of the story, she rejoiced in its happy termination; she envied the heroine – no, she did not envy her, for she did not know Strathallan, and with this idea, that of the book became comparatively insipid; she only wished to think of it that she might seek him, to know his opinion respecting it. In conversation with him, however, all Matilda's enthusiasm revived. She could not express the anxiety she felt at the moment when the too generous Walstein, under the mistaken idea of ensuring his Caroline's happiness, hastened to complete the sacrifice, which would have rendered them both miserable for ever. 'I assure you, my lord,' she said, 'I found it impossible to tear my eyes from the book during the time that cruel application for permission to part with her, was made by the Count to the great Frederick. The moment was so critical; the chances that many persons should be made unhappy, so great – my breath became suspended – I read with a degree of palpitation – if novels are sometimes blamed for not sufficiently engaging the attention, do not you think it is also a fault, when they are too – too interesting?'

Lord Strathallan smiled, 'I wish Miss Melbourne I could read a novel as you do.'

'Yet in this charming work,' she continued, 'there is, I own, one improbability that shocks me. It is that Caroline should, in Lindorf's society, almost forget the existence of Walstein, and suffer the stranger to gain such a hold over her affections, before /

she discovered to him she was married to the Count. That any circumstance should banish from her mind a solemn engagement.'

'Oh it was unpardonable,' interrupted Strathallan, and again a slight cloud of discontent overshadowed his countenance. Matilda now, too watchfully attentive to its slightest variation, immediately turned the discourse to the character of Lindorf. – 'I cannot forgive,' she said, 'his often-changing loves – who could value a heart that had first been offered to Louisa, then to Matilda, then to Caroline, then at length to Matilda again?' 'Yet he acknowledges that in Matilda was centered all that was necessary to make him happy.' 'But what assurance have we of the continuance of these sentiments?' 'The best in the world; his own acknowledgment that he felt for her, the most fervent, fixed, and purest passion. You forget, I believe, his concluding words. I think I can repeat them, *J'ai été épris de Louise; J'ai adoré Caroline. Mais j'aime ma chère Matilde et je sens que c'est pour la vie;*[157] his Lordship had concluded this sentence with an animation into which he had been gradually led by the subject, and an energy still farther enforced, by the expressive sweetness of a voice which, whether in speech or music, ever thrilled to Matilda's heart, before he recollected the accidental resemblance of the name to that of the person he addressed; the blushing confusion with which he was heard, first reminded him of this coincidence; and her eyes, quickly averted, told him that, in the earnestness of discourse, his had been imperceptibly suffered to indulge in too fixed, or too fond a gaze. Agitated beyond what she had ever before experienced, it appeared to Matilda that at this moment she heard Strathallan vow eternal love. The perturbation of her feelings seemed contagious. He caught her embarrassment and found it impossible to continue his discourse. Ashamed thus to act the novice where he had committed no intentional error of expression, Lord Strathallan was the first to endeavour to recover himself, and resume the topic that had so interested them the moment before. But the thoughts of each appeared so much / to wander; the sentences were so broken, so interrupted, and, at length, degenerated into such absolute nonsense, that it was found both more pleasant and more improving, to seek the society of the general circle; or, each separately to try to rally their spirits among the magic bowers, the grottoes and fountains of Woodlands, where it might be truly said in the language of the Italian bard:

'Odi l'aura che dolce sospira,
'Mentre fugge scotendo le fronde,
'Se l'intendi ti parli d'amor,
'Senti l'onda che rauca s'aggëra,
'Mentre geme radendo le sponde,
'Se l'intendi ti lagna d'amor.'[158]

CHAPTER XX.

Oh maraviglia! Amor ch'appena è nato
Già grande vola, e già trïonfa armato.
TASSO; GERUSALEMME LIBERATA.[159]

The keenest pangs the wretched find,
Are rapture to the dreary void,
That leafless desert of the mind,
That waste of feelings unemployed.

LORD BYRON; THE GIAOUR.[160]

THE next morning Lady Torrendale, who dearly loved what she called a little mystification, sent for Matilda early to her chamber, and accosted her with 'How now my
little gipsey witch, what have you been doing to cause such a hurly-burly in the middle
region of the air! Lionhart swears the candles always burn blue when you are in the
room, and I begin to believe it. Yet I warn you, despise not the counsel of a more excellent / witch than yourself; beware of the light wings of Miss Langrish's eyes, dread the
thunder-bolts of Miss Hautenville's tongue, and as for the Mountain, take care it does
not turn out a Vesuvius.'

Though used to a good deal of similar rhodomontade, in the pleasantries that each
individual allowed themselves almost perpetually to act upon the others, at Woodlands; there was a laughing malice in her Ladyship's eyes, which seemed to announce
to Matilda, that something more than common lurked beneath this violent shew of
spirits: her nerves were not as strong as formerly, and rather startled and distressed,
by the number of unpleasant images her livelier friend had huddled together in this
strange address, she answered,

'I am surely a very insignificant object for indignation, so great as your Ladyship
alludes to.'

'Oh no – certainly Miss Melbourne is the most insignificant creature in company, whereever she appears. She never attracts the gaze of the most humble swain, or
brings home from the field a single prisoner; but at the same time, if ladies will listen,
and if gentlemen will declare themselves –'

'I assure you Madam,' said Matilda, filled with an uneasiness and alarm that she
had never experienced before, 'you are misinformed if you imagine that –'

'Nay, you will not deny that Strathallan has more than once declared himself –'

'Permit me to assure you Madam –'

– 151 –

'Dissatisfied with Spencer, and *ennuied* with his present situation – I mean, has he not said so to you? Come, own the truth.' Her Ladyship, after enjoying the perplexity into which her ambiguous phrases had thrown Matilda, and having sufficiently diverted herself with her heightened colour and increasing perturbation, continued, 'and now as I take your silence as a confession of his misdeeds, I will, in return for this amiable candour, reveal what has been plotting against you below stairs in "the cabal." You remember Miss Mountain's praising the last sketch you made from those old family pictures, with her stately grace.' /

'Well, well, extremely well indeed.'

Here her Ladyship suddenly rose from her sofa, assumed Miss Mountain's stiff erectness, and looking down upon Matilda, mimicked her air so naturally, that it was impossible to repress a smile at the ill-natured correctness of the imitation. 'The moment you left the room, poor Miss Langrish, who, for this last month I believe, has felt all the inclination of Midas's wife, to whisper, if it was only to the reeds of the brook, some mighty secret with which she had been occupied, said, "Oh Madam you would admire those pictures much more, if you knew the pretty scene that first gave occasion for their delineation." Upon being desired to explain herself, however, it only appeared that she and Miss Hautenville had one day found you and Lord Strathallan in the north parlour; that he had said nothing she could distinctly hear, but that she did not doubt he *had* said something; and Miss Hautenville was of the same opinion. At this moment in runs Miss Hautenville, quite out of breath, with a second edition, later than the Langrish Gazette, containing overtures of accommodation that had actually been made by the enemy, and though the terms had been proposed in French, yet as that is the general language of congress, there was little doubt but that they must be understood. You, my little friend, had not noticed her being deeply engaged with Lord Strathallan, discussing the merits of Caroline, (*apropos* why did he give you that old stuff?) he might have found Werter or Oberon[161] – did you ever see Oberon? – they are both upon the same line. "However," as poor Miss Langrish says, he did not – and you thought Caroline a very fine thing, I suppose, and were just telling him so, for I am sure I have heard of nothing else these two days, when poor Miss Hautenville, who knew of no Matilda in the world but Miss Melbourne, interpreted the words Strathallan used in reply, into a most formal declaration to said Matilda.'

'You are very good Madam, so immediately to advert to what must have been the origin of this ridiculous mistake. I did not indeed perceive Miss Hautenville was so near / us, but whatever might have been her conjectures, why should they affect Miss Mountain?'

'Why? because,' to give you a lady's reason – 'but to reply to your question more seriously, for my charming Matilda should not be put off with a "because," is it necessary that she should ask whether Miss Mountain can find it agreeable, that the general conversation should run upon the attentions received by another from the man to whom she is engaged.'

'Engaged!' Matilda repeated, scarce conscious of what she said.

'Yes, she chose it should not be talked of, and made that, a condition of her visit to me this summer – but you may remember I made one exception in your favour,' continued her Ladyship, nodding with an air of assumed friendliness and confidence, 'I could conceal nothing from my Matilda.'

'You surely never told me Madam that –'

'Indeed I did my dear, in this dressing-room, when I announced her expected arrival. I called her "my daughter-in-law that shall be."'

This could not be denied. Yet Miss Melbourne thought she saw at that moment a something in the countenance of Lady Torrendale, that shewed she noticed her confusion, and enjoyed her mistake. Was it possible? Could she be one of those whose delight is to betray the unsuspecting; one of those malignant and misleading spirits, that

'Palter with us in a double sense,

That keep the word of promise to our ear,

And break it to our hope.'[162]

She would not admit the idea; and listened in a silence which had hardly the merit of being voluntary, while her Ladyship continued, 'Miss Mountain, in every thing truly original is, though a tremendous flirt in her peculiar manner, in some circumstances full as great a prude. That Lord Strathallan should be known to the whole circle of giddy young people assembled round me, to be on the terms of an accepted lover, was, in her opinion, a thing the most highly indecorous that could be imagined. She insisted on our / observing an inviolable silence to every one on the subject, till the happy event should take place; a discretion in which she herself led the way on the most trying occasion you know, Matilda; and it must be owned, that since his return, she has been admirably seconded by Strathallan, who has forborne to assume any of the privileges of a lover, particularly lately, with a self-denial truly edifying. Fearful, if she made no remark, of being suspected by the Countess to be too much interested in this communication, Matilda observed, 'Miss Mountain's fortune certainly made this a most desirable connection.'

'Certainly, my dear, for she unites in that little person of her's, the possessions of her own family, and of Strathallan's – I will tell you how. You have heard, I dare say, once or twice of Miss Mountain's estates "on the maternal side." Now the late Lady Strathallan's father married a Bishop – no that was not it, the late Lady Strathallan's mother was a Dean. I must begin again, I am certainly the worst person in the world to tell a story about "Sir Archy's Grandmother."[163] In short, Lady Strathallan and Mrs. Mountain were cousins. Mrs. Mountain who was, you know, one of the Bishops of Craig Castle, was as poor as a church mouse, till by the caprice of a whimsical grandfather, a fortune which passed over the head of Lady Bishop her mother, became eventually her's, to dispose of as she pleased. Now, if things had been properly arranged, this fortune would never have been either Lady Bishop's, or Mrs. Mountain's; but Lady Strathallan's; because – if the estate had been left to Lady Strathallan – Lady Strathallan would have had the estate. I hope you perfectly comprehend me – No? – I am certainly the most unlucky creature – no woman in England has a clearer head for business, and yet I never can make myself understood. I am sure it was as plain as possible, as I have heard Torrendale explain it to me.

'Mrs. Mountain and Lady Strathallan had been bred up at school together, and loved each other more as sisters than cousins. Mrs. / Mountain was desirous of making Lady Strathallan amends for the injustice in the disposal of the fortune, which, as the daughter of the eldest sister, she might suppose herself to have suffered; and it was agreed, that if Strathallan married – that if Miss Mountain married – that is to say if Strathallan married Miss Mountain, it would settle every thing to their mutual satisfaction. This plan which had amused the mothers, during the infancy of their children, was, after the death of Mrs. Mountain, seriously taken up by the old Don, who was anxious to secure a noble alliance for his daughter; and Torrendale, who had been rather disappointed in his wife, in the article of fortune, readily, after he became a widower, entered into the schemes of the old gentleman, an engagement took place between the young people when they were sixteen, but the marriage was, on account of their extreme youth, deferred: and owing to Strathallan's going early into the army, and his father's strange whim, of letting him pass a great deal of time at his Scotch estate, he saw little of his fair cousin; so I invited her down to the country, that he might get a little more familiarized to her idea. She is, at first, rather alarming; but that is all *écorce*; and we shall accustom him to her ways, as he accustoms his horse to stand fire, by snapping a pistol at his ear every day, till he learns to bear it without starting.

'Now, though I have entered into this detail with you,' continued her Ladyship, taking Matilda's hand with a friendly familiarity, 'because I abhor concealments, and like above all things, to be open and direct in every thing, do not think, my dear Miss Melbourne, that I imagine you require the least hint respecting the manner in which, as to an engaged man, you ought to conduct yourself towards Lord Strathallan; it has always been, believe me, exactly what I wished, and though I diverted myself a little this morning with the idea of throwing you into alarm, I knew perfectly well that you had no real grounds for apprehension. Miss Hautenville may die for envy, Miss Langrish for love; but depend upon my authority, / and it is the only official one, there is no harm done.'

'I should be sorry, indeed,' Matilda interrupted faintly, 'to be the cause of any misunderstanding between Lord Strathallan and Miss Mountain.'

'Miss Mountain! will you never know that phœnix, that fair perfection, for whom little Sappho said the word *self-sufficient* in its most literal sense, should have been invented. Her pride would not allow her to believe a report, or even to listen to an inward whisper, of his negligence. I shall never forget the cool composure with which she heard the account of the two angry ladies, and then, observing after she had let them exhaust themselves in doubts and conjectures the whole evening, that Lord Strathallan paid the most delicate compliment to her feelings, in reining in the ardour of his passion, and bestowing his attentions, "as she had commanded" him upon indifferent objects, she lit a taper, and with a low curtsey, which put her nearly on their level, wished them a very good night. Poor girls, they looked so foolish! They were mistaken indeed in Miss Mountain, when they thought to alarm her jealousy. Jealousy supposes a diffidence of success, and she would not change places with an angel, or a Matilda. She exactly reminds me of a character in some play, that says, I would not be a bit taller, a bit shorter, a bit younger, a bit older, a bit handsomer, a bit wiser, or in short any other than what I am. She is the most eccentric creature in nature, and this self-opinion is the cause of all her eccentricities; she is a bundle of contradictions, and they all spring from the same source. She is a prudish flirt, and a flirting prude; and, while she severely censures the most innocent freedoms in others, or even imagines them where they are not, will go the strangest lengths herself, because, it is sufficient to impart to them all propriety and grace, that "'twas the great Miss Mountain did so." That every thing she does is "wisest, virtuousest, discreetest, best," is out of all question.'

Matilda would at another time have smiled / at the fidelity of this ludicrous portrait; she now only gravely replied, 'I shall soon be out of the reach of her animadversions, if she is inclined to make any;' and retired as soon as possible to hide those tears that a thousand mingled circumstances at length forced to flow. No sooner did she find herself in the garden, and at liberty, than clasping her hands together in an agony, till now faintly repressed, she tried to arrange her confused ideas; to recover from the dizziness, the stupor into which they had been thrown, by the too sudden discovery of the precipice on which she stood. She doubted whether she did not dream; but every painful particular of the late conversation was already but too indelibly imprinted on her mind. After a long drawn sigh, at length an exclamation burst involuntarily from her lips: 'Oh, I am very unhappy!' she cried; and miserable as she had been before, this confession, wrung from her by the resistless vehemence of internal feeling, seemed to have broken down the slight barrier between her and the torrent of anguish, that now overwhelmed her soul with irresistible violence. Unwilling to attribute her present wretchedness entirely to herself, her first emotion was one of resentment against Strathallan; but repenting, in a moment, of her injustice, she recalled the whole of his conduct, since the commencement of an intercourse that had terminated so fatally to her peace; and found it equally vain to attempt to attribute to him, error, or deceit. The engagement with Miss Mountain was certainly kept secret; but had be not repeatedly given her to understand, that from the perfect confidence Lady Torrendale seemed to repose in her, he was sure she was acquainted with every circumstance relating to his family; and could he be supposed to except one so intimately connected with his future interest and happiness? Had he not always, in their most unguarded and delightful conversations, preserved the character of friend, instructor, guide, and, if any softer feeling seemed for a moment to intrude, had he not repressed it with a caution, sometimes greater than her own? Was it possible for a heart like his, to witness unhappiness, / springing from whatever source, unmoved? He had consoled her when dejected; defended her when calumniated; had encouraged her timidity, and dispelled her anxieties.

'These were thy crimes, Strathallan,' she repeated, 'these were the gentle acts which my fond forgetful folly misconstrued into love. Is he to blame if the friendship of Strathallan has a fascinating character beyond the love of other men? Ah, no! he is all excellence, and I have only myself to accuse. –'

To accuse! And was it even thus with Matilda, must she too submit to that tyranny, which, changing the whole course of the thoughts and feelings, refers every action to a different standard; bids each emotion, no longer subject to control, move round a new circle; makes virtue no longer find reward in its own approval; application no longer satisfied with its own success; but, placing its devoted victim in an unknown scene, thrown on a new earth; breathing beneath a new sky; bids every happiness depend upon the will, the wished, the feelings of another; makes pleasure no longer pleasing, unless shared with him; praise no longer sweet, unless flowing from his lips. The discovery that Strathallan was lost to her, had taught her that he was essential to the happiness of her existence. But at the same time, she had learned, that she could not with innocence indulge any longer in the delightful visions, with which, till now, his image had been invested: for a few moments these silent shades witnessed a conflict, perhaps, the most sever that human nature in youth, and without direction or support, can be exposed to. But Matilda was never without support; and recalling those sentiments of mingled dignity and resignation which had always marked her character, she felt an instantaneous calm returning to her soul. Raising her eyes to heaven in modest confidence, she preferred a short mental prayer, and pressing her hands upon her breast, now no longer tortured with tempestuous passion, she remembered, as she bent forward, the affectionate admonition she had but that day received from her beloved parent, and which she had there, as in a sanctuary deposited, to / be ever near her. She took out the paper, and bedewing it with tears of grateful tenderness; 'where were those counsels,' she said, 'when I suffered myself to be misled thus far? In what a waking dream I have lately lived! why did I not hold them ever in my remembrance? No, kindest, truest friend,' she continued, as she re-perused the lines with fond attention; 'I deserve my sufferings, for have I not broken the promise my heart made to you? In the day of surprise and affliction, that day in which I was first torn from your maternal breast, my tears silently engaged to devote the interval till your return to fond anticipation, or tender regret. But I suffered a stranger to break in upon your right. I preferred a wild delusive meteor, to the pure pleasures springing from that earliest, most enchanting feeling of our nature, in the indulgence of which alone, there is neither error nor excess; these signs, these conflicts, do they not sufficiently avenge you? Oh, let me renew that engagement that gives every future thought of my heart to you!'

While engaged in reflections thus alternately soothing and self-condemning, their course was abruptly interrupted by the sudden appearance of Miss Swanley, who advanced with a paper in her hand, on which it was evidently her intention to consult Miss Melbourne. It was a Sonnet she had just composed, and Matilda, ever averse to such confidence, was never less in train for them than now. Escape was, however, impossible; and Matilda prepared to meet her with her usual smile of cheerful benevolence, not foreseeing the pain this casual interview was soon to cause her. 'Verses I see Miss Swanley,' she said, and knowing the request that was always expected to follow this observation, added, 'may I not be favoured with a sight of them?'

'I sought you for that purpose,' the poetess replied with her accustomed frankness, 'I own I should wish Miss Melbourne's opinion before I read them to the general circle. You may remember I once said I meditated a Sonnet to the shade of departed love, and promised to repeat it to you: this / sequestered scene appears peculiarly adapted to the purpose.'

Sappho then, without farther entreaty, and with a fire and sensibility, sooner to be expected in an enthusiastic *fantastici*, than the sober daughter of a country clergyman in England, recited the following

SONNET.

I sighed for peace – mid passion's fevered heat
How pleasing seemed her long-forgotten balm!
'Return,' I said, 'this aching breast to calm
And bid my throbbing heart no longer beat.'
Such was imagination's fond deceit.
Peace came; and passion's meteor-visions fled:
Hushed was my lyre; to grief, to transport dead;
No more its chords Eugenio's name repeat.
Sick with the breezeless calm, full soon I cried,
'Fierce is the thorn of Love; but sweet the rose,
Again, sweet power, o'er all my soul preside,
Heartless I pine in languid, dull repose.'
Vain wish! the guest that once I dared to spurn,
Love, and his lovely train, will never more return.

'Am I to consider you as expressing your real sentiments, Miss Swanley?' said Matilda.

'Oh, heavens! that a person who had once experienced the dangerous illusions of passion should ever wish to renew them: I think the enviable calm you describe, no object, however worthy, should ever tempt me to renounce.'

'A worthy object! Oh, Miss Melbourne, have you already learnt to talk like a person of this world? It is the passion itself, with all its charms, its sweet illusions, I regret. That only feeling, which, in our present state, can entirely satisfy the heart, because it doubles its possession, can be experienced in all its vigour, force, and purity, but once. Do you consider it merely as an elegant common-place, and overlook the refined and too painfully important truth, conveyed in the Poet's beautiful expression:

"'Young passion's tender bloom?'"[164]

What other does it mean, than that bloom of the soul, the enchanting freshness of those first emotions, which, like the dew drops of the morning, once brushed away, can never more return. Often,' continued the fair / Sophist, after this ingenious commentary, 'would I willingly recall, if, but for a moment, those impressions in vain – like the brilliant, but evanescent colours of some early dream, they fade the more completely the more I endeavour to retrace them, and each succeeding effort but the more painfully convinces me the youth of my heart is gone.'

Matilda listened in silence, but not with perfect approbation. She admired the genius of the enthusiastic visionary maid; yet still she felt there was in its most bewitching wanderings, a something her best friends would wish altered: Sappho expressed her feelings with eloquence and grace; but there was a want of that retiring timidity, more graceful than their most eloquent expression. This deficiency could not but be remarked by one, who was herself an example of the rare and difficult art of uniting true feminine delicacy, with an unaffected nobleness of thinking, which was without effort and without pride; that dignity of sentiment and steadiness of principle which generally distinguishes matured years, or elevated station alone, breathing from the lips of cherub innocence, simplicity, and youth. Possessing that *tact* which both her Sappho and *Celia* wanted, she regretted in the character of the former, to observe that the absence of that golden quality, discretion, lessened the lustre of talents, and diminished the grace of sentiments, noble, exalted, and delicate, as her's. For still, notwithstanding all the condemning forms, and sneering whispers of grave matrons, or prim damsels, there were few minds so delicate as Sappho's. She was all passion, because she was all purity. Ever considering love under its highest, most interesting aspect, she ventured to express, respecting it, the sentiments of a soul glowing with generous enthusiasm. Believing every mind pure and ingenuous as her own, repeated disappointments had not taught her that necessary lesson of caution and reserve, which alone could make her uncommon endowments ensure respect to herself, or advantage to others. As it was, those distinguished talents were only (to borrow Madame de Staël's forcible expression) *d'une noble inutilité* – [165] or served at / most to enliven the social circle, or to contribute to the acquisition of an ephemeral literary reputation.

But a few days ago the conversation she had heard, and the picture that had been presented to her of the charms that attend even the torments of a passion such as Sappho described, might not have been without danger for Matilda; but love now appeared to her only in the form of a malignant demon, and in discovering to her the full extent of his power, had inspired her with a terror of its consequences.

'I consult you in preference to Miss Ferrars,' continued Sappho, resuming the subject of her poem, 'because there is in your manner something that more invites to confidence. She is not, like the Countess, troubled with patrician pride, it would be extraordinary indeed if she were; but of the pride of wealth and independence she has, unknowingly to herself perhaps, some small share – I mean that kind of confidence which makes her ready to give her opinion on every subject, careless whether it may soothe or hurt the feelings of others. With all her good nature I am never sure whether a degree of triumph does not mingle with her condolences on any mortification I experience; for I have often thought, even when she has praised me, there was a kind of a – you will not comprehend me, Miss Melbourne – a manner that seemed to say, it was less for the possession of – a – talent, than for the want of – other advantages that she sought and liked me. An air that expressed "Yes, you can write, that I allow. Take care how you step out of your province, and attempt to please." Now do you not think,' continued Sappho, observing Matilda was silent, 'that such praise is very insulting? I have often left her company, vexed and angry with all around me, and yet if I had repeated her conversation, nothing could have appeared more obliging, or more flattering.'

Matilda had often tried to correct this fault in her friend, and had one day asked her, in a playful manner, if it was not common with her to extol others for that in which they excelled the least, or to applaud them for / qualities they really possessed in a manner, that made them discontented with that possession; but before she had time to reply to Sappho's observations, the sudden appearance of Lord Strathallan, crossing the walk through which they were passing, startled Miss Melbourne, without awakening in her bosom an emotion of pleasure. That aspect, but lately so beloved, for the first time failed to breathe peace and joy into her heart. He glanced his eye for a moment on her companion, and his countenance exhibited an uneasy and singular expression, which it would have been difficult immediately to account for, or define. But the time was past when Matilda's heart could vibrate unreproved, to every variation in the countenance of Strathallan.

Hastening her approach to the house, she found Lady Torrendale still in her dressing room. She purposely spent a good deal of time with that lady; to efface from her mind, if possible, any impression that the too obvious agitation she had betrayed in the morning might have left there. Through the day, in an exaltation of mind, a kind of delirium, between the triumph of virtue, and the intruding consciousness of overwhelming misery, she tried to occupy herself more than usual with every thing that surrounded her. To interest herself in the conversation of the Countess, the complaints of Arbella, the employments of Lady Emily, in short, as she too often repeated to herself in the eloquent simplicity of nature and the heart; 'Any thing, every thing, but Strathallan.'

He, on the contrary, had never seemed so anxious to engage her attention; but she eluded his efforts so ingeniously, that evening was arrived, and nothing, but a few common place words, such as were called forth by the usual forms of daily intercourse, had passed between them. At length, seeing a place unoccupied on the sofa on which she sat, he approached it, Matilda arose to leave it. 'Do not let me scare you from your seat, Miss Melbourne,' he said, 'and I am gone.' She could not, in common politeness, testify any farther impatience at his presence; she let him place himself next her, but he now semed uncertain how to avail himself of the / privilege he had been so anxious to obtain, and for a few moments both were silent. 'I have hardly spoken to you, Miss Melbourne,' he said, 'since I saw you with –'

'Miss Swanley; we had had a long conversation.'

Lord Strathallan hesitated. 'You – you find her pleasant?'

'I think her a delightful companion.'

'So should I – for any one but Miss Melbourne.'

Matilda made no reply. She would have formerly felt complimented by this observation; but now – perhaps it was a snare – perhaps it was still sincere; at all events, was it not immaterial to her? The opinion of Strathallan was no longer to be of any value to her.

'I hope you understand me,' he pursued, after a pause. 'I admire Miss Swanley's genius, but it is obscured by her eccentricities. In the favoured intimates of Miss Melbourne, I should always wish to see dignity, elegance of mind and manner, like her own. I know Sappho has many pleasing qualities; but a female character, to borrow an expression in painting that you once taught me, requires "finishing off in small strokes:" it is to those finer shades, those minuter touches, it owes its distinctive charm; and do you not perceive the want of these, in your intercourse with Miss Swanley?' He looked in her eyes for a reply, with an expression of the tenderest yet most respectful anxiety in his own.

A few hours before, Matilda would have received such an intimation, with gratitude and secret pleasure. But her interview with Lady Torrendale had opened her eyes to the danger of her situation. Strathallan was nothing to her, was never to be more than he was at present; yet did not his manner suppose an influence over her conduct? – a right, or a desire, to direct her wishes and pursuits? She remembered her mother's remark to her on similar behaviour in another. She felt indignant at the idea of her feelings being trifled with; and for a moment she dared to suspect Strathallan, the noble Strathallan, of intentional deceit. 'My adviser, too!' she / proudly whispered. 'Ungenerous man! you shall know your power is not as great as you perhaps imagine:' and turning from him, she drily replied, 'that she conceived any young ladies she met at Lady Torrendale's must be proper companions for her, and that she had not observed any thing in Miss Swanley's conduct to contradict the good opinion she had formed of her.'

Strathallan looked at her for a moment in surprise – 'I have done, Madam,' he said; and rising, approached the table, where his mother and Arbella were seated.

Matilda had prepared herself for an argument. She waited a moment, irresolute, in expectation of something that should follow these words, which though conclusive, were not satisfactory. In vain; – through the rest of the evening, Lord Strathallan spoke little to her, or to any one else; but he appeared deeply hurt. She was confused; a secret feeling (it could not be remorse) mingled with her dissatisfaction. She recollected that the discovery which had made such a revolution in her own mind, could not be supposed new to her by Strathallan. *Her* conduct had changed to *him*; but *his* was only in conformity with that constant attention, that watchful tenderness, with which, like a superior, and almost guardian spirit, he had till now been ever eager to preserve her from aught that might injure, aught that might give her pain. The manner in which Strathallan received this unexpected repulse, added to the poignancy of these reflections. It had none of the resentment that might flow from offended pride; none of the submission that might bespeak a consciousness that it was deserved. The expression of injured friendship, of feelings wrung by the sudden appearance of caprice and unkindness, in her whose welfare had so warmly interested them, was all that was painted on his too eloquent countenance.

Matilda saw that she had given pain to Strathallan – to Strathallan, whose delight it ever seemed, to give joy to all. She asked her heart, in what instance he deserved it of her? – her heart acquitted him of every / crime, but that of being too much beloved. The conviction that he suffered, filled her bosom with equal wretchedness; yet what she had said was the result of principle, and she could not at the moment – no, she wished not, to retract.

CHAPTER XXI.

Two maxims she could still produce,
And sad experience taught their use;
That virtue, pleas'd by being shown,
Knows nothing that it dare not own;
That common forms were not design'd
Directors to a noble mind.
'Now,' said the nymph, 'I'll let you see
My actions with those rules agree,
That I can vulgar forms despise,
And have no secrets to disguise.'

SWIFT.[166]

'I WISH to have a little serious conversation with you, Lady Torrendale,' said his Lordship one morning, as he entered her dressing-room at an unusually early hour. 'That friendship you have formed with –'

'Matilda,' interrupted the Countess eagerly – 'Well, have I not won the wager I laid last year?' /

'That you would be as fond of Miss Melbourne as you were then, that day twelvemonth? No, Lady Torrendale; you are very far from having won the wager: it took place towards the latter end of October; – July, August, September, October – it still wants three months, three weeks, and two days, of the given time. – It was not of that I was going to speak, but of Mrs. Stockwell; that Scythian becomes every day more insupportable.'

'Is Scythian, my Lord, the best name you have for her? If you will have it my poor friend is a barbarian, it is certainly better than Parthian; for then, you know, she would wound you as she fled.'

'So she fled, I should little care whether she wounded me or not. Your attachment to Miss Melbourne at least can do you no discredit. She is a dignified young woman, a young woman such as now is seldom met with. How much is it to be regretted that many more do not resemble her. But for the other –'

'Well, enough of Matilda,' exclaimed her Ladyship. 'What is the good of recapitulating her merits, now we must lose her? For lose her we must, whether they send for her to town, or return to the country.'

'True – it was not on that subject I intended to speak. You are, Lady Torrendale – what was I going to say when you interrupted me? You are, if I may allow myself the familiar expression, extremely new-fangled in your attachments. What else can account for that little Alcæus, so lately your aversion, being now –'

'Oh, I am persuaded my patronage of Alcæus will do me honour. The young man has real genius. The last lines he wrote upon my birth-day shewed a degree of talent that – Besides, in this strange place, how could I possibly amuse myself without my Sappho and Alcæus?'

'I have no objection to Sappho; that is a harmless folly. But for that little, insufferable coxcomb, to have him calling you 'Contessa, Contessa,' as he always does, and waltzing with you every evening –' /

'He calls me Contessa to keep up my Italian, which I have begun to study with such success; and as to the waltzing, I declare I never can sleep without a few turns after supper.'

'You may treat the matter as lightly as you please, Lady Torrendale; but it is my unalterable opinion, that such familiarities lessen your respectability, and are neither consistent with the dignity of your age, or character.'

Character was very well; but the unguarded term, age, which just preceded it, undid the whole effect of his Lordship's well-intended admonition. Concealing her resentment under an appearance of well-assumed scorn, his Lady replied, 'Since you allow that my age is so respectable, it is surely sufficient to protect my character against any remarks, that the unimportant freedoms you mention might occasion: therefore, while you preserve *your* opinion unaltered, you must allow me the privilege of also retaining *mine.*'

'I see you are offended. Yet there is another subject to which I must recur – Stop, Lady Torrendale, that Scythian – that Stockwell –'

Remonstrance was vain; the Countess had already left the room: and his Lordship was obliged to defer his protest against this domestic pest, for another opportunity. Her frequent visits, and the respect and distinction with which she was often treated by Spencer and Lady Torrendale, were growing more and more irksome to him: but his deliverance was nearer at hand than he imagined; though it took place in a manner he perhaps neither wished nor expected.

After dinner, Miss Mountain happened to be haranguing, in her manner, on the excellent dignity of her family by the maternal side. Strathallan, who was himself of descent too noble, ever to dwell upon that advantage, thought to turn the stream of his fair cousin's eloquence, by jocosely defying her to prove that it was equally ancient with Lord Torrendale's. The challenge was accepted seriously by Miss Mountain; who, with all her respect for the house of Torrendale, / would not have yielded the claims or her own, to that of Bourbon.

'Come, bet on both sides, that's fair,' cried the poet Alcæus, who for the last five minutes had been kept in painful silence: 'Miss Ferrars and I for Miss Mountain – Miss Melbourne and Sappho for Lord Strathallan. Come, fair ladies, cannot you wager like the Caliph and Zobeide in the Arabian Nights; [167] your "Palace of PICTURES" to her "Garden of Pleasures,"' glancing with delighted malice from Matilda to Arbella.

'Picters and Pleasures!' repeated Mrs. Stockwell, who remarked the confusion he had created. 'Well, to be sure, Mr. Who'll-see-us, you have, as my niece Arbella says, a comical way of coming across whatever is going on, with your "two eggs a-penny."

Now, I dare say, you have made Miss Mountain forget the whole line of her pedigree. 'Tis so like a dispute I once had with the poor Dichess of Albemarle. She never would give up to me in pint of family, till I said to her one day, "Your Grace, it's a folly to talk. Your grandfeather was a Duke – very well; my grandfeather was an Archbishop – Grace for Grace." Poor woman! we never had any more dispute ever after.'

Spencer, who had listened to this illustration with an appearance of great indifference and unconcern, now began amusing himself with a table sonata, to which he hummed, as if accidentally, part of the air of 'Don't you remember a Carpet-Weaver.'

Mrs. Stockwell's eyes flashed fire; 'I expect very well what that gentleman would be at. But let him beware – he knows I'm not bound to submit either to his taunts or his tantarums.'

A sudden demand from Lord Torrendale, for an explanation of the threat contained in this remark, soon produced from the enraged lady the long-dreaded *eclaircissement*. She was too much agitated, to give the particulars of Lady Torrendale's obligations to her with great perspicuity at the moment; but his Lordship, in an ensuing conversation, learnt with dismay and astonishment, that the supposed imprudences of his Lady were / all occasioned by her false tenderness for her son. That it was on his account she had drawn upon him for those immense sums, which, before their departure from Rose-Villa, she had allowed him to think the discharge of her own debts of honour rendered necessary. That when he had refused any longer to supply her, the accommodation offered by Mrs. Stockwell had rendered her acquaintance unavoidable, and her resentment to be feared.

Lord Torrendale could not easily forgive his lady for having concealed from him an evil, which if he had been made acquainted with at its commencement might have been easily checked. He upbraided her for thus voluntarily involving him in connexions he despised, and sacrificing the peace and dignity of his family, to the false principle of postponing the acknowledgment of a painful truth; a principle which was sure to terminate in added embarrassment and distress.

To none was this degrading discovery more unexpected, – by none was it more poignantly felt, than by Strahallan. He knew his brother had been guilty of imprudences, but till now had no idea of their extent. Concealing, out of tenderness to Fitzroy, the deep wound it gave to every feeling of his lofty and delicate mind, his first object seemed to be to consult on the most effectual means to assist him to satisfy every claim that might be made upon him by his vulgar and rapacious creditor. For this important end, no sacrifice was considered by him as too great. All he intreated of his father was, to allow him to resign without delay, in favour of Spencer, every expectation, every claim, that could interfere with the interests of his honour, or his final extrication from embarrassments equally unnecessary and distressing. 'Let the estate of Strathallan be his,' he said; 'it is more than sufficient to enable him to release himself from all his obligations: or, if it be necessary, let that woman take it – let her take all, so she leaves us the possession of conscious rectitude, and self-respect.'

Notwithstanding the warmth which accompanied these generous instances of his / son – instances which were ably seconded by arguments from the Countess; notwithstanding the difficulties of the moment, Lord Torrendale preserved coolness and presence of mind enough, to declare his unalterable determination, not to sacrifice the worthier, for the unworthier part of his family.

Hurt that it was not in his power to do more, Strathallan objected to this resolution with a vehemence, and pleaded his right to a voice in the disposal of this estate, with an earnestness, which he seldom used in opposition to his parent. He and Spencer seemed to have, on this occasion, made common cause, and to have an equal interest in the sale of the lands of Strathallan.

His Lordship contented himself with telling them they were both unthinking impetuous young men, who looked not beyond the present moment: and then turning more particularly to his younger son, he set before him, in colours that would have made an impression upon any mind less light and volatile than his, the dangers into which his imprudence had led him; and told him, that he had now nothing farther to hope, but to retrieve, by a rigid economy, the effects of his former extravagance.

Spencer, after looking down in vain at his boots, and finding they would not help him out with an answer, contented himself with replying, 'that economy was a perfect bore; that he felt satisfied his Lordship, upon reflection, would be aware that a certain income was necessary to enable him to "represent," in the manner that became a branch of the Torrendale family; and that if it could not be made up in one way, it must in another.'

The ease and composure of the offending Spencer, who had heard the whole discussion with the calmness of a person wholly unconnected with it, was singularly contrasted with the agitation of his generous brother; who, convinced of the impossibility of moving Lord Torrendale, had desisted from his proposal, yet showed by his heightened colour, and the anxious earnestness that had animated his voice and manner, how much / he was pained and surprised by this refusal.

The Countess took it upon a higher tone. She urged, perhaps not without some degree of justice, that her being found innocent of the extravagance, till now imputed to her, ought to be accepted as some mitigation of the other charge brought against her – a blameable indulgence shewn to the faults of a beloved and only son. She declared she could not forget those reproaches, till Lord Torrendale made some apology for his unwarrantable warmth; and that, till he became reasonable, and acceded to *her's and Strathallan's wish*, which could alone ensure future comfort to her poor ill used Spencer, she should no longer consider herself as mistress of his house, but beg leave to remain in the retirement and solitude of her own apartment.

The family group broke up with feelings of mutual discontent. Her Ladyship, either from obstinacy or pique, maintained her resolution of remaining a voluntary prisoner, admitting no one to her privacy but Matilda; who, though she spent much of her time with her, in the hope of bringing her round to more pacific resolutions, yet anxiously awaited the moment which should recal her from a scene, that, when gayest, had failed in securing her lasting satisfaction; but which, now that it had become an abode of discord, was painful indeed. Arbella quitted Woodlands with her aunt on the night of the angry explanation, which had left Lord Torrendale in a state of such irritation with the family, that Matilda concluded her friend would not like to revive his unpleasant sensations, by too hasty a return. Accustomed as she was to Arbella's caprices, she was still therefore a little surprised to find her the following morning in her room, which that young lady had entered by her favourite leap; and approaching her with eyes sparkling with pleasure, insisted upon having, 'five minutes gossip with her.'

Without farther preface she began, 'You know, my dear, this terrible *fracas* has made me the happiest creature in the world.' Before / Matilda had time to enquire into the nature of this great felicity, she continued, 'Now my dear little charming Spencer is completely ruined – *de fond en comble –* [168] is it not so?'

'I hope not.'

'Why is it not evidently so? My aunt and her precious son have been plotting together to pursue him with the utmost rigour of their hatred; that is on one side preparing for him; on the other, his father, I hear, will do nothing for him; so is he not absolutely without resource?'

Matilda admitted the inference; yet still was at a loss to conceive how such a circumstance should cause the supreme satisfaction Arbella seemed to derive from it.

'Why there is no way of its being settled otherwise, is there?' pursued her friend peevishly, as if vexed that her position could not be made out quite so clearly as she wished.

'None, I fear, except by the sale of the Strathallan estate.'

'Pho! pho! put Strathallan out of your head for a moment, and tell me, don't you know of any other estate that might equally relieve him?'

'Indeed, Miss Ferrars, I do not,' replied Matilda; trying, in vain, to conceal the pain inflicted by this thoughtless sally of her friend, 'You must explain yourself more clearly.'

Arbella looked a little confused at this; then, raising her eyes from the table, on which she had been, for a few moments, making several very pretty hieroglyphics with her finger, she began – 'While the advantage in point either of rank or fortune is on the man's side, a woman should of course conceal, at least, as much as possible, I mean, any preference she may feel for him, until he has given her the most positive and unequivocal testimonies of his regard. But where the reverse happens to be the case, and the power of obliging devolves upon the woman, it becomes then her duty – dont you think so?'

'To do what?'

'How affectedly slow you are to-day! I / am sure I have expressed myself as intelligibly as possible – why to spare the generous delicacy of her lover to be sure, by the frank, unhoped-for offer, of her hand and fortune.'

Matilda's eyes were opened at once to the danger into which her friend's precipitancy was hurrying her – 'Stop, I entreat you, my dearest Arbella,' she said, 'and weigh well the consequences of a step, which, if once taken, you might wish to recal in vain. You talk of the love of Captain Fitzroy – tell me truly, before this unfortunate circumstance, did he ever make you any express declaration of his attachment?'

'Why I cannot say he exactly did – not exactly;' returned Arbella; who now began twisting the string of her ridicule in a brisk circular motion around her wrist, 'but a thousand and a thousand times his eyes have told me tantamount; those eyes that know so well every varied expression in love's harmonious language, from the *crescendo, forte, rinforzando,* of persuasive ardour, to the *languendo, smorfioso, rallentando, smorzando, morendo,*[169] of despair and death.'

'Treacherous indexes, my Arbella, on which to venture the honour and repose of your future life. 'Twas but lately, you force me to remind you of it, you complained, and with reason, of his conduct; and do you not perceive, that should he now, for the first time, seem grateful, as you expect, for your partiality, the real dictates of his heart run the risk of being mistaken for the result of a change of circumstance; and should he act otherwise – Oh, Arbella! can you, can I bear the idea that my friend should be rejected? –'

'I now *perceive*[a] the whole,' interrupted Miss Ferrars with warmth, 'you like him too well yourself, to wish I should be preferred. Weak that I was to imagine any one could enjoy a daily intercourse with him and escape that enchantment – that' –

'How painfully contradictory are your accusations,' resumed Matilda, turning on Arbella a look which breathed the softest expressions of injured tenderness. She would not give up the hope of saving her friend, yet where was she to find arguments sufficiently / powerful to influence her? She could not, alas! now, as on a former occasion, alledge Fitzroy's supposed engagement – 'Reflect, my generous Arbella,' at length she said, 'before you pursue the first impulses of your warm and affectionate heart, whether those it addresses resemble it. A woman trusts her happiness to a dangerous hazard, in being the first to declare her attachment, even where she is sure of meeting disinterestedness, tenderness, delicacy equal to her own. But where she is not, think what would be your sensations, if the proofs of your artless affection were converted into the triumphs of vanity; if, where you hoped impassioned gratitude, you met with coldness; if, where you expected admiration, you experienced –'

'Contempt!' interrupted Arbella, not suffering her to conclude her sentence. Then rising and suddenly embracing her, 'I owe you more than I can express,' she said; 'You have saved me from a folly to which I never could have looked back without confusion and repentance. The idea of contributing to Spencer's happiness was what seduced me, and I was nearly lost by the deceitful flatteries of my own heart. But if he is really desirous of possessing it, he knows but too well the way to it. I would not for worlds, by anticipating him, incur the danger of his neglect – his mother's scorn. So now, having settled that matter, tell me how goes on all above? Blue-beard still angry, and the fair self-immured Fatima still sullen, hey? I always said it would go hard with her when she brought matters to a crisis, for he is as determined as she is flippant – Well, well, never mind, let them fight it out,' she continued, shaking the wild roses in her bonnet as she tripped down stairs, 'the one is equally prepared for defence, as the other can be for attack. If her Ladyship is possessed of porcupine-spirit, his Lordship has as much hedge-hog valour, and that will do just as well – Don't you think so?'

Not possessing the versatility of the lively Arbella, Matilda could not consider in the same light a disagreement in which it was necessary she should bear a part, and yet / in which it was most painful to her natural modesty to seem to interfere. The interest which she really began to take in the happiness of Lord Torrendale, alone served to render this situation more tolerable, by the hope it held out to her of being able to be useful to him. Early confirmed in a habit of reserve and mistrust, by the unfeeling advantage which his lady had taken of the influence her beauty gave her, to hold up to ridicule the less obtrusive character of her lord, he had retired into himself for his resources and consolation, and was often mistaken by others, as being dull and inattentive, when nothing that passed had escaped his penetration and remark. Though devoid of that amiable charm of conversation, that *fleur d'esprit* which can give pleasure to others, his abilities were respectable, and his virtues solid.

Meanwhile, the gaiety of the mansion drooped with her who had promoted it. Those twin-cygnets Sappho and Alcæus, 'Slept with wings in darkness furled;'[170] and forgot their mutual enmity, in regret for the interruption of their mutual amusement. Arbella alone served to keep up the life and spirit of the party; for she found at Woodlands, such an attraction in Matilda's society, that however unwelcome to the master of the mansion as 'a Stockwell,' she could not refrain from at least one daily visit. Absorbed in the duties that friendship required of her, Matilda seldom saw Strathallan; and when she did, they conversed on different topics, with no attempt to renew that interchange of mind, that blameless yet tender intercourse of the heart, which had made her, in their conversations formerly, consume so many hours in innocent luxury. He seemed to retain no resentment for the past; but chilled and repelled by coldness unexpected and unexplained, he avoided exposing himself to the risk of a similar repulse. At least Matilda guessed these to be his feelings; and mourned the obligations imposed by a rigid delicacy, not by a word or look, to do away the impression one painful moment had produced. Sometimes she thought that the unpleasant circumstances which had recently taken place, filled the mind of Strathallan, and caused the / alteration of his manner; at all events she felt the change, and felt it the more, because conscious she had no right to complain.

Lady Torrendale had now been some days confined to her chamber, and began to feel extremely weary of her self-imposed penance. Matilda seized this auspicious moment of returning reason. This amiable girl had a penetration and insight into the disposition of others, which, as it was the result of intuition, not of experience, so far from injuring the bloom, only added a grace that was *piquante* to the interesting delicacy of her character. 'Twas this, that enabled her, with all those little wiles that are so blameless and so winning, when employed in a worthy cause, to adapt her arguments to the weak mind to which they were addressed; and to know the juncture at which to apply them with the greatest probability of success. However wearied with her lofty station, how to descend with dignity, was literally and figuratively, the great difficulty with Lady Torrendale. She had positively declared she would never enter a room which her Lord inhabited. nor speak to him again, unless he testified by a proper submission, his desire that she should do so – and how recede with honor from so solemn a declaration?

At length Matilda ventured to hint, that communication by letter might be productive of some change without compromising the dignity of the writer; and suggested a few topics of the mildest and most conciliatory nature, of which she thought her noble friend might advantageously avail herself. Lady Torrendale listened, or rather seemed *not* to listen, with her usual languid toss of the head; but the next day, she took an opportunity to tell her, that she had been thinking it would be no unbecomming concession on her part, to address a few lines to her Lord, if it were only to justify her own conduct, and disclaim any intention on her part, of bringing affairs to the present violent issue; and the Countess accordingly presented her with a paper all fragrant with musk and rose-wood, in which Matilda found all her own arguments made very honorable use of. She felt delighted that her Ladyship should have the / entire credit of them, so they were found useful in forwarding the reconciliation she so much desired. Miss Melbourne undertook to deliver the letter to Lord Torrendale, who had felt miserable since the interruption of his usual domestic habits, and only wanted a decent pretext to give up his resentment; but Miss Ferrars, whose imprudent vivacity it was impossible to restrain, had nearly ruined every thing, by snatching the precious billet from Matilda, whom she met upon the stairs, and declaring she would present it herself, with – 'To your pomposity, these are humbly sent by your afflicted wife, &c.'

Matilda with difficulty got the manuscript out of her hands, and seized a favorable moment of solitude and *ennui*, to offer it to his Lordship. It was not difficult to bring Lord Torrendale to terms. He had from the first rather wished to alarm than to punish Spencer; and he now readily came to a composition in which it was agreed, that his Lordship should, without disposing of the long-contested estate of Strathallan, satisfy all the present demands upon his younger son out of his own private fortune; on condition that that son should give him his word of honor not to contract any more debts without his knowledge, and that he should immediately join his regiment, which was now returned and quartered in the North. That Lady Torrendale should be given all due credit for not having involved herself on her own account, in the embarrassments that had proved so distressing to the family, and for being guilty of nothing farther than – encouraging Fitzroy in every folly. A separate article which there was great reason to suppose was not read by Lord Torrendale, left the ports open to Mrs. Stockwell, at Woodlands, and Fitzroy Square. Some, recollecting his Lordship's sagacity, which was equalled by his hatred of this lady, declare he could not have overlooked a clause that so materially concerned his future tranquillity; and scruple not to whisper, that there were two copies made of the treaty, in the second of which alone, this secret article was surreptitiously inserted. Her Ladyship, perhaps, had a secret whispering that she should still have / occasion for the visits of her old friend; or perhaps she did not wish the history of her former obligations to go farther. Be that as it may, Mrs. Stockwell was obliged to be both more sparing and more circumspect in her ensuing visits to the mansion. Every thing was now arranged to the satisfaction of the countess, except the approaching departure of Spencer; which was to take place the ensuing week. She, however, statesmanlike, comforted herself with the idea that even that small portion of time was something gained; and during that interval, a circumstance occurred, as if contrived to her wish, which suggested to her ladyship's fertile brain, the hope of fixing him near her, by a brilliant and permanent establishment. Matilda meanwhile tasted the delight of a disinterested and ingenuous spirit, in seeing domestic happiness and tranquillity restored by her exertions; while in the eyes of an indifferent observer, she acted on this occasion the only part her youth and character made becoming; that of an unmeddling, though not unfeeling, spectator.

CHAPTER XXII.

Ecco dirò quel fonte
Dove avvampò di s'degno
Ma poi, di pace in pegno
La bella man mi dié.

METASTASIO.[171]

WHEN no longer called upon to interest herself in the concerns and distresses of others, Matilda looked around, and could not conceal from herself, that the prospect offered nothing but misery to her heart. In her former vexations she had accustomed herself to look to Strathallan as her consoler. How doubly painful, then, was an affliction, of which Strathallan was the source and cause. As for him, he was not so completely unhappy, as his conduct might have led her to believe. However hurt, at the first moment, at the only instance of want of confidence she had / ever shewn him, it was difficult for the penetration of a lover long to confound resentment with contempt; it was impossible for him not soon to perceive, Matilda could not have thus treated one who was indifferent to her, and the altered conduct which had begun in pique, was continued from a persuasion of its being the only course he ought to pursue – A lover! must he own himself one? a feeling of self-reproach, unusual as severe, mingled with the unwelcome conviction. Valuing himself upon that high-souled delicacy of honor, that forbade alike in every relation of life, whatever bore the least appearance of duplicity, he found he had been led by a concurrence of unforeseen circumstances into a situation, in which it might, perhaps, with apparent justice be imputed to him. Yet was it so singular, that two hearts, which, from opposite causes, the world could not make happy; his, because he had proved its deceitful flatteries too early and too long; her's, because secluded from its influence in opening youth, she shrunk dispirited and dismayed from the rigid caution, and heartless observances it required, should, as by a natural sympathy, find their repose and level in each other?

The discovery of the sensibility of Matilda, a discovery which his peculiar tone of character, a native diffidence and elegance of feeling, not incompatible with a high consciousness of worth, made him slow and reluctant to admit, filled him with that shame and regret which a generous mind feels, at the acknowledgement of even an involuntary error. He judged of her sufferings by his own; and knowing himself capable of an enthusiasm of passion, which the extreme mildness of his manners, perhaps, only concealed, to concentrate with force more intense; he could not forgive himself for introducing a guest so painful, into a bosom, late the mansion of purity, innocence, and peace.

These were not, however, his constant reflections: the heroism of the moment often yielded to the natural and involuntary pleasure that arises, even under the most opposing circumstances, from the consciousness of being beloved. As for his gentle mistress, / now Woodlands was become, for so many reasons, unpleasant to her, her only recreation was a ramble with Arbella to the beloved Fountain of the Rocks, their most favourite walk; where, at a distance from the scene of her disquiet, she could just get a glimpse of the sylvan wildness, and picturesque grandeur of those natural barriers that surrounded her once happy home; and, while her eye watched the tops of the tall trees that guarded its approach, recall the hours of peace and innocence she had spent within its bosom. Such a situation was, for both parties, a state too forced and violent to last; and while Miss Melbourne and Strathallan would both have given worlds to taste, for one hour, that tranquillity with which Miss Mountain, though so intimately concerned in them, seemed to view the agitations and commotions around her, accident revealed their mutual feelings to each other, in a manner which Matilda had long reason to doubt, whether she most regretted or rejoiced at.

Taking the arm of Arbella, who gave her friend her sympathy, without enjoying her confidence, she had proceeded on her usual melancholy stroll to the Fountain of the Rocks. – Arrived there, Arbella, to whose activity it ever appeared but a trifling walk, amused herself, with the gaiety of a careless, if not a happy heart, in seeking wild plants for her friend, among the recesses of the rocks beyond them, bounding with aërial lightness from cliff to cliff, or displaying her agility by her rapid yet safe descent, down the narrow and precipitous paths into the road below. Matilda, on the contrary, whom dejection now always inclined to lassitude, found herself already in need of repose, and seating herself on a little stone bench within the cavern of the rock, indulged in the luxury of melancholy which that scene, with its attendant circumstances, was, always sure to inspire. 'Happy Arbella!' she sighed, 'why am I not like you, possessed of that gaiety which rises elastic from the pressure of disappointment or misfortune. Yet no – I would not, for your enlivening gaiety, exchange the thoughts that sometimes steal in to gild my / hour of grief. And am I then so lost! Is wretchedness, connected with his idea, preferred by me to happiness without him? Why am I not as I was but a few short months ago, when gay and innocent as the bird of spring, every flower that expanded, every breeze that blew, could swell my heart with grateful pleasure? What right had you to disturb happiness so blameless and so perfect?'

Then, fixing her eyes upon that fountain which was connected with a thousand different recollections, 'Twice-lost Strathallan!' she exclaimed, 'was it pity caused me once to shed those tears for you; was it not presentiment of the misery you were still reserved to inflict upon me. How much less bitter were they, than those that now will fall. Yes, soft, gracious, relieving to the heart, they proved their worthier source; while these, the offspring of a more selfish feeling, avenge with their corrosive bitterness the weakness that encourages them to flow. I will return to my native rocks; with the employments, I shall perhaps resume the serenity, of my former life. I will quit this fatal scene; I will quit that dangerous abode, where every object reminds me – breathes of love; surely there is some magic in this place.' She rose as she spoke;

but felt as if still rooted to the spot, on perceiving two persons approaching it whom she soon discovered to be Lady Emily and Lord Strathallan. The brother and sister appeared fondly engaged in interesting conversation. Lady Emily was relating to him something to which he listened with evident pleasure. As she drew nearer Matilda, 'This is the place,' she thoughtlessly exclaimed, 'this is the very spot where Miss Melbourne so lamented for you Strathallan, when we all thought you lost to us.'

'Lady Emily,' interrupted Matilda, colouring, 'you surely do not think of what you say.'

'You know you did,' continued the young Lady; 'are you going to impeach the veracity of Miss Mountain? And you may recollect, when she told us of it, were marked that all the feeling she should have shewn, was expressed by you.' /

'When you remember, that I had not even seen Lord Strathallan at that time,' said Matilda gravely, 'you will feel conscious, Emily, how little ground there must be for this discourse, which, however amusing to you, I must beg, on my account, may not be continued.'

'Don't mind her,' said the little girl, again addressing herself to her brother, 'she knows what I say is true – and she knows I could tell more, and that often since that time –'

'I shall believe nothing but what Miss Melbourne allows,' interrupted Strathallan, and, thrown off his guard by the delightful communications to which he had been listening, he added, as he approached her, in a hurried whisper. 'Dearest, loveliest creature, is this slight confirmation too much to demand, in return for all that for this last week I have suffered?' She turned from him to hide her emotion. He mistook the action for indifference. 'Oh Matilda,' he resumed, with that accent of plaintive tenderness which always penetrated to her heart, 'will you make me regret my return?' In these words he had involuntarily resumed that tone which she had not heard him use for many days. It spoke the more dangerously to her feelings, and conscious of the necessity of firmness, she replied with affected calmness:

'Impossible. You have every thing that attaches us to life. Friends, father, an expectant bride,' she had nearly added, and this indiscretion of a heart too little accustomed to the blandishments of love, would have too surely revealed the nature of its emotions to Strathallan – but it was lost by the impetuous vehemence with which he interrupted her, exclaiming:

'Heavens! how a few days have altered you – to what am I to ascribe this change?'

'To what you please,' replied Matilda, who, trembling at the greatness of the error from which she had just escaped, thought it necessary to call in the aid of all her self-command in her answer.

Strathallan walked a few steps from her in silence. 'Come, come,' cried Lady Emily, who began to be frightened at what she had done. 'You know, you used to call yourselves / brother and sister. Brothers and sisters should not quarrel. Strathallan, Miss Melbourne, give me each a hand. You must, you shall be reconciled.'

He could not long retain displeasure where he depended so much for happiness. He advanced towards her. The momentary resentment his eyes had expressed, only rendered their returning tenderness more resistless, as they were now bent upon her face, beaming once more with looks of love. To Matilda's young heart their silent language was all-powerful. It yielded after this short estrangement, with added pleasure to the charms of reconcilement. He advanced – Lady Emily took Matilda's unreluctant hand, and it had fallen into Strathallan's before she recollected that hand was plighted to another.

END OF VOL. I.

STRATHALLAN.

BY
ALICIA LEFANU,

GRAND-DAUGHTER TO THE LATE THOMAS SHERIDAN, M.A.

IN FOUR VOLUMES.

VOL. II.

Quando scende in nobil petto
E compagno un dolce affetto
Non rivale alla virtù:
Respirate, alme felici
E vi siano i Numi amici
Quanto avverso il ciel vi fù.

METASTASIO. – DEMETRIO.[1]

London:
PRINTED FOR SHERWOOD, NEELY, AND JONES,
PATERNOSTER-ROW.
1816 /

R. and R. Gilbert, Printers, St. John's Square, London.

CHAPTER I.

'Je n'examine point ma joie ou mon ennui,
J'aime assez mon amant pour rénoncer à lui.'

RACINE. – *Bajazet.*[2]

ON the day succeeding the scene that had passed near the Fountain of the Rocks, every thing seemed to wear an aspect of unusual gaiety and content. The countess was more kind in her manner than ordinary, and the looks of Strathallan expressed a soft and delighted triumph; Matilda alone could not forgive herself, and was even inclined to be angry with that appearance of satisfaction in her lover, which she felt so little disposed to share. The soft illusion to which she for a moment had yielded, was succeeded by the / bitterest repentance. For the first time she experienced the sting of self-reproach; and its power was, therefore, the more painfully strong upon her young and ingenuous mind. She had been led, though unintentionally, into an imprudence, in which her heart could not wholly acquit her of all blame; and after having passed a sleepless night, reflecting how best to repair it, it appeared to her that nothing but a frank confession of the whole to Lady Torrendale, could restore her to that peace and serenity of mind, without which she felt so completely unhappy. But how to make this confession, without leading the countess to suspect a partiality, which, under the circumstances of Strathallan's present engagements, would be most painful to the delicacy of her feelings, was the greatest difficulty. Lady Torrendale, however, soon gave her the opportunity she desired. The character of this lady was so habitually DOUBLE, that though really fond of both Arbella and Matilda, she never could refrain from blaming the one to the other, when engaged with either in confidential discourse. She was, according to this laudable custom, expressing to Miss Melbourne her disapprobation of Miss Ferrars's coquetry, and her perpetual anxiety lest Spencer, (though incapable of entertaining a serious thought of one so much below what his pretensions entitled him to aspire to,) might be drawn by such arts into some imprudent declaration.

'How happy would it be for her,' she added, 'did she more resemble my charming Miss Melbourne, in whom every look and action is guarded by that high sense of honour, which is equally removed from artifice or imprudence.' As the countess concluded this sentence with that condescending nod, with which she generally accompanied praise bestowed upon those whom she thought of less consequence, or who were younger than herself, the heart of Matilda burnt with the most painful emotion; it seemed as if suddenly too / large for her bosom, her temples throbbed, and a feverish feeling ran through her whole frame, while she listened with a sort of sickness, to praises, and received proofs of a confidence, which appeared to her at that moment so undeserved. In what respect was she superior to the unhappy Arbella, whom she heard so severely condemned? If her friend was to be blamed for engaging the affections of one brother, was she more innocent with respect to the other? Could Miss Ferrars feel for Spencer, an emotion which was not reflected in her own bosom, and to a greater excess, for Strathallan?

While these thoughts passed rapidly in her mind, she exclaimed in a tone of anguish, 'Ah! Lady Torrendale, why did you not tell me some months sooner of Lord Strathallan's engagement?' 'Why, how could it interest you?' returned the countess, with a look in which some surprise was expressed, but in which she could not trace any mixture of displeasure. Matilda saw that the time for concealment was over, and making one great effort, she related, with timidity indeed, but with the most perfect simplicity and candour, the circumstances of her late interview with Strathallan; not without throwing the greater part of the blame where she thought it could very well be supported, upon Lady Emily.

When she concluded, she cast her eyes on the ground, and awaited with blushing cheeks and palpitating bosom, some of those haughty glances and disdainful sarcasms, for which she had reason to suspect Lady Torrendale could occasionally exchange her fond expressions and dove-like looks. She was most agreeably surprised by that lady's saying, with a smile of encouragement, while she kindly tapped her on the shoulder, 'And is that all? well, I positively see nothing so terrifying in Strathallan's choosing to *make the agreeable* to you a little; though to do you justice, you have taken a great deal of pains to convince me, that Emily is more in love with her brother than you / are. Nay, do not start so at that word love, I know it is a very ugly one, but it makes you look very pretty; so pray go dress, and put on again those little cherub smiles which make you so dangerous, for I assure you there is no harm done.'

This *quietus*, which her ladyship so constantly applied to any thing that alarmed the prudence of Matilda, contributed greatly to puzzle her, but at this moment it certainly afforded her consolation. She felt as if a mountain had been removed from her breast; and relieved from the fear of having acted with impropriety, the rebound of happiness was so great, that it produced an elasticity of spirit, and a lightness of heart, to which for some time past, she had been almost a stranger.

In this state of mind she passed the greater part of the day; but in the evening, when retiring to rest, she was surprised by a visit in her dressing-room from Lady Torrendale, her countenance all radiant with affectionate pleasure. 'Joy, joy, my dear girl!' she said, while she warmly pressed her hand in token of gratulation, 'we triumph! every difficulty is removed, and Strathallan may follow the bent of his own noble, affectionate nature, in offering his hand where his heart has been so long fixed. Give me leave,' she continued, 'to be the first to salute my dear Viscountess on the change I have had the happiness to be instrumental in bringing about.'

Matilda, pleased, surprised, but scarcely able to believe the intelligence thus suddenly conveyed to her, looked at the countess in silence, as if waiting a farther explanation.

'I perceive,' said her ladyship, 'I must be more explicit. Strathallan we, of course, allow to be *le premier des hommes;* but this Strathallan has a brother. Now I would not say any thing to detract from your matchless hero, but certainly, without absolutely deciding that 'the younger brother is the prettier gentleman,' it must be acknowledged that / my Spencer has, when he pleases, a manner still more insinuating. In short, there is no disputing ladies' tastes; and we have just made a discovery which is no more than what I have long suspected – that Miss Mountain is decidedly in favour of Fitzroy. Strathallan had been convinced of the coldness of his stately mistress, from the period of her strange reception of him after his return from Spain – that time, you know, when we were all so disappointed – agreeably disappointed. Well, as nothing is so mortifying to our lords and masters, as the idea that their dear persons can be absolutely and positively indifferent to us, this discovery led Strathallan to seek in some other prepossession, a less offensive cause for Miss Mountain's dislike, and he thinks he has at length found it out in her apparent preference of Fitzroy. "Upon this hint I spake," or rather I set to work; and you will feel inclined, I trust, to make me your confidant again, when you find how warmly I have been engaged, like a little mole in the dark, in forwarding your interests.'

Her ladyship then unfolded her plan, which was no other than to substitute her son Spencer in Strathallan's place, as a suitor to Miss Mountain. 'He will declare himself,' she said, 'as soon as his brother has smoothed the way for him. She may stand a little upon punctilio at first, but in her heart I am sure she will be delighted; and I am much mistaken, if the animated attentions of a man like Spencer, do not soon make more impression on the lady, than the cold and constrained homage of a heart prepossessed like Strathallan's.'

'But are you sure, madam,' demanded the still-doubting Matilda, 'that Miss Mountain can – that she does, I mean – prefer Captain Fitzroy to Lord Strathallan?'

'Positive, my dear; and a number of little circumstances, which I did not before remark, now serve to make this *penchant* / quite clear to me. Don't you remember, she used always, when we walked out, to allow Spencer to carry her handkerchief? – and have you forgot how fond she was of his great poodle dog, and what care she took of it in his absence?'

Obliged to be satisfied with the conclusive evidence of the handkerchief and the poodle dog, Matilda listened in silence to the countess, who continued: – 'The great difficulty was, to get Spencer to admit the idea of addressing one, who had once consented to be united to his brother, for his delicacy on that subject is extreme. Affection for Strathallan, however, in the end got the better of his scruples, and he has at length consented.'

Glad that the captain's delicate scruples were conquered in any manner, Matilda now ventured to contemplate the happiness that was offered to her; it delighted, but did not dazzle her – for it was Strathallan only, and not his rank, she loved.

She now listened with eagerness to those details which the countess was equally pleased to give. Proud of her achievement, as any French *intriguante*[3] under the old government could have been, of having effected a revolution in the cabinet, she alternately dwelt upon her own ability in carrying on the negotiation, and the striking instance given by Spencer of fraternal affection, in thus sacrificing to it the refinement of his feelings.

Matilda, considering only the happiness which she thought she owed entirely to Lady Torrendale's active friendship, saw nothing but the kindness that appeared on this occasion to have influenced her feelings and actions; and while she contemplated her with a mixture of gratitude and delight, whispered to herself, – 'How is it possible I ever thought this amiable woman indolent, selfish, and incapable of taking a generous interest in the concerns of others!'

Lady Torrendale was eloquent in removing any doubts with regard to the compliance of Miss Mountain. 'Though / glad at heart to be released,' said she, 'and though she does not care a straw for Strathallan, she will, besides the other motives I have given for her conduct, feel a pleasure in making what will appear a generous sacrifice, while her feelings will be in reality about as acute as those of Mrs. S – when, in the representation of some fine tragic character, she buries a dagger in her breast. Such a piece of easy heroism will be quite to her taste.'

After spending a delightful hour in such conversation, Lady Torrendale hastily rose, crying, – 'Adieu, my dear Viscountess! I must recollect that indulging you in these new *veilleés du chateau*,[4] is not the way to make you appear to-morrow with those fresh roses, that should adorn the bride of Strathallan.'

With a heart too full for language to express its feelings, Matilda threw herself into the arms of her noble friend, and burst into tears.

'For shame! for shame!' cried her ladyship, laughing; 'consider I am not Strathallan. – Farewell! I will not depart with our vulgar English Good night – the more animated Italian salutation, *Felice notte*, will, I think, better suit with the nature of your present feelings.'

Sylph that presidest over dreams, accomplish the countess's wish! be not in haste to rouse thy lovely charge from her slumbers of felicity; for well thou knowest, that the fulfilment of all her dearest hopes cannot impart to her waking hours happiness so exquisite as it is the airy province of imagination to bestow!

Delightful as had been the company of her 'lovely, lively' countess, Matilda felt, in the return of silence and solitude, a grateful change, as it enabled her more fully to indulge the overwhelming, yet charming sensation of unexpected bliss. She did not attempt to analyze the visions that presented themselves to her fancy; she feared too much to diminish any of their softness, brilliancy, and richness; she awoke with a confused, but soothing / sensation of inward satisfaction; she was conscious HE had been with her in her dreams, but the images they had presented she could not recal. It sufficed that, like a perfume which remains after the flower that gave it birth is gone, they left an internal spring of joy in her heart, which it would have been difficult for any outward circumstance to disturb. The happiness arising from the sensation of a half-forgotten dream is, in itself, of a purer nature than that which can spring from any more substantial reason; for as the latter acknowledges its earthly origin, by having necessarily some positive pleasure or advantage for its source, the former, in the very circumstance of its having no immediate cause, partakes more of the nature of the immaterial and invisible world, and seems to originate from the excursion of the free spirit which, while the body is weighed down by sleep, takes a momentary flight to a higher region, from whence it returns, bearing a foretaste of purer joys, and breathing the airs of Paradise. What a pity that from such exalted contemplations, the breakfast bell should summon Matilda!

It was not without emotion, that she heard Lord Strathallan, who always rode out in the morning, order his groom to lead back his horse; and when she heard he was actually engaged in private conversation with Miss Mountain, her uneasiness became great, as the stake, for which she now ventured, was important; and a few doubts, she had before resisted as importunate intruders, now forced themselves upon her mind.

'His power is great, indeed, but can he persuade her to resign him with indifference? Ah, there alone I doubt it!' But again recalling the communication of the countess, which agreed so well with the observations she had made in the early part of their acquaintance, she rallied herself upon the absurdity of suffering such a suspicion to disturb her mind; and reconciling herself at length to the conviction, that there could be one woman / blind and unworthy enough to prefer Fitzroy to Strathallan, she allowed herself to give the reins to hope, delightful as unbounded. 'Yes,' she exclaimed, while a tear of rapture fell upon her cheek, 'this explanation will clear up all; Miss Mountain only waits for it, and we shall yet be happy.'

These reflections were on a sudden interrupted, by the entrance of Miss Hautenville, accompanied by the officious, and ever busy, Mrs. Stockwell; who, with her favourite exclamation, of 'Lord bless my heart and soul! Lord bless my soul and heart!' cried out, 'has nobody never a *romantic* vinegar-bottle for poor Miss Mountain, who went into an *historical* fit, at something my Lord Strathallan has been a telling of her, and has now fainted quite dead in the dressing-room?'

Though the first part of this account may, by some, be considered as nothing very uncommon in this lady, Matilda felt otherwise, and with an emotion, almost resembling the trepidation of conscious guilt, she followed her informant and her companion; who, by her haughty and reproachful looks, appeared as if she would willingly have struck the beautiful culprit dead, could a blasting glance have done it. They reached the room, where it was said the

'Giant statue fell.'[5]

There, surrounded by Miss Langrish, and three waiting women, Miss Mountain lay extended 'long and large;' and, but for the unchanging brightness of her colour, looking, indeed, as Mrs. Stockwell represented her, inanimate. Matilda, approaching, took her by the hand, as it lay dead and motionless, but the extreme weight of the arm she had raised, soon obliged her to put it down again. She then began chafing her temples from her vinaigrette, and soon had the satisfaction of seeing Miss Mountain first open a little of one eye, and then (perceiving she was surrounded only by the female attendants, into whose hands Lord Strathallan / had consigned her, as the most capable of administering relief) gradually extended them both 'wild and wide.' Then, heaving a deep sigh, she faintly murmured, 'Oh, Miss Melbourne, you have robbed me of my love!'

The surprise and emotion with which Matilda heard these words, was rather lessened by observing that they were repeated with a calmness of countenance and manner, which gave more the idea of a lesson, than of a natural burst of the heart. Miss Mountain, having now reared up her enormous bulk, and appearing pretty well recovered, motioned with her wonted dignity, for her attendants to withdraw; which they did, with many a whisper of commiseration for the sweet sensibility of the young lady, and many an indignant and suspicious glance at Matilda; then, turning towards her, and looking down with that gracious bend, which her great height had converted into a habit, she, with much formality, thus addressed her. – 'I have had an explanation with Lord Strathallan, which discovers to me, that our situations, Miss Melbourne, might aptly be compared to those of Roxana and Statira, in ancient story.[6] The more so, as his lordship is, I think, not unlike what historians have handed down to us as the description of the person of Alexander, except that he is somewhat taller; which, as I am myself above the common size, is no objection. As to the idea, that I preferred Captain Fitzroy to him, I have already convinced his lordship, as I am ready to convince you, that it is one of those unfounded reports, which rumour, with her hundred tongues, is always delighted to circulate. Captain Fitzroy, compared to Lord Strathallan, is indeed Hæphestion to Alexander; not but that Lord Strathallan might say, as that monarch did of Diogenes, if I were not Strathallan I would be Fitzroy.[7] Yet, still, that he should wish to change places with his brother, would be the eagle desiring to be the goldfinch, the lion to become the lap-dog. Perhaps, you think, that as / Octavia pursued the faithless Antony to Athens, I will seek him round the world; and wherever I discover him, maintain my claim; or again, you may imagine that I will consent to give him up for his own advantage, as Berenice did Titus;[8] which suppose you that I will do?'

Then, perceiving that she waited in vain for an answer, she pursued with inimitable complacency. 'My preference for Lord Strathallan did not originate in one of those caprices of the heart, by which meaner souls are united; it was my father's wish that I should be his, and as such, I hold it a sacred duty not to suffer resentment, or wounded delicacy, on my part, to prevent the execution of his intentions. Lord Strathallan has seen (here she appeared to weep) the affection I bore him, by the immense effect his communication had upon a frame, ever too delicate to endure the vicissitudes of the passions. He has observed the dignity with which that affection was accompanied, in the noble self-possession, which, in the most trying situations, I have till now, ever preserved; and he may perceive the generosity which is added to crown the whole, in the dispassionate manner in which I, at this moment, discourse with you, my rival. Having then no doubts of Lord Strathallan's character, as a man of honour, a man of delicacy, and a lover, I no longer feel any uneasiness as to the manner in which he will choose to act, when once he knows it is my unchangeable resolution – never to resign him.'

Having said these words, Miss Mountain, with a low courtesy, the manner in which she generally concluded any declaration she thought remarkably impressive, sailed out of the room, leaving Matilda to reflect upon the strange situation in which she was placed. She remained for some moments in a sort of stupor, occasioned by the shock of surprise, and the contemplation of the extreme waywardness of her fate; she was obliged at once to bid adieu to all those flattering hopes she had so fondly cherished. But one / short night was past, and she had been saluted the bride of Strathallan! She must now relinquish those gay visions, for the severe and stern realities of life. That this compound of affectation and simplicity had no real love for Strathallan was, she thought, apparent – yet her obstinate resolution to keep him firm to his first engagement, rendered her as great an obstacle as if she had. Nothing therefore remained for Miss Melbourne, but to urge her lover, if such a step should be necessary, to the only part that honour dictated, and that could save him from the charge of perfidy, and her from that of deceit.

In the Caverna d'Aurora (oh! with what different sensations she entered it than those which at other times she had there experienced!) she met Lord Strathallan, more fully persuaded of Miss Mountain's indifference, and still more unwilling to listen to her arguments, than she expected – perhaps not more so than she wished. He had in youth, and before his heart had made any other choice, consented to an engagement by which his father hoped to make him amends for any disadvantages, of which his second marriage might be the cause; but having now freed himself from those chains by an explanation which he thought Miss Mountain's pride would make her consider as just cause for a final dismission, he could not prevail upon himself to resume them. If he had been led into an error in supposing Spencer attached to her, we must refer to that gentleman's general gallantry of manner, and ambition to appear well with every lady as his excuse; while Fitzroy's vanity, which led him to admit the idea of the lady's partiality, the moment it was suggested to him, had tended to confirm Strathallan in his mistake; but though obliged to acknowledge himself wrong in his first supposition, he was equally unwilling to believe he could be mistaken as to the perfect indifference of Miss Mountain to himself, and he entreated, with all the earnestness of a first and / fervent passion, that Miss Melbourne would not suffer any needless scruple to make her retract those proofs of regard which to remember would form the happiness of his future existence.

Matilda, who having experienced the weakness of her own heart upon one occasion, was now afraid to trust to its flattering suggestions, only pleaded Miss Mountain's cause more warmly; and with that beautiful earnestness, in which self seemed for the moment annihilated, represented the proofs the young lady had that day given, of affection; and urged that they ought to be considered as the rule, that should guide a mind like Strathallan's in the only course it ought to pursue. 'We have been in error respecting her,' she said, 'and we owe her reparation.'

'But how can you suppose we have mistaken her? How can you think that she cherishes an attachment, which every look, every action, denies?'

'Why should I not? Has not poor Miss Mountain's love led her to take the most distressing step, to which pride, like hers, could descend? – its frank avowal! We once, indeed, thought otherwise; but let that moment pass, like some tale, related of the hopes and fears of a person distant and unknown to us; to act generously, to act like yourself, you must forget it – banish it!'

'How easily you can talk of considering the hope of my life as a dream! You are anxious to spare the feelings of Miss Mountain,' exclaimed his lordship resentfully, 'while you need not how you torture mine.'

'I had thought,' said Matilda, 'that in shewing myself anxious for the preservation of that high honour which I had persuaded myself would sooner have endured any privation, than the slightest stain, I was shewing the consideration – the interest with which I was inspired, in the most flattering manner; I am sorry I was mistaken.'

The colour of Strathallan, which had / frequently varied during this conversation, now assumed the brightest and most animated glow. 'I yield,' he said; 'I will do any thing, every thing that Matilda and honour require of me; yet by that very action to sacrifice my hopes in such a heart! – to relinquish my right even to ask that you should not forget me!'

The tears of Matilda declared, but too well, how unnecessary was such a request.

'Reflect, I intreat,' he pursued, 'my dearest, my only beloved, before you hurry me to this resolution, that you are perhaps sacrificing our mutual happiness to a vain punctilio. I am persuaded, notwithstanding her violent demonstrations to the contrary, that I am to Miss Mountain, an object of indifference.'

'Ah, Strathallan!' exclaimed Matilda, no longer able to control her feelings, 'can you think that possible?'

This expression, which, in a woman of a character less free from art, might have been blamed as an encouragement to the passion which she professed to wish subdued, spoke so perfectly the struggle of that delicate and generous heart, that it conveyed more than a thousand arguments to Lord Strathallan's. 'Yes,' he exclaimed, while the emotion of his voice bespoke his inward conflict, 'angelic creature! I will pursue the path which alone can render me worthy of such virtue! Cruel thought! that I can only do so, by adopting that conduct which will forbid me for ever to aspire to it!'

The effect of Matilda's counsels was soon perceptible in the reconciliation of Strathallan and Miss Mountain. A heart so severely tried as his, required, however, some interval of reflection to recover its tone; and unable to live in the daily contemplation of loveliness, which he was no longer to hope could be his, he suddenly recollected an engagement to a friend in a distant part of the county, secretly resolving never to return to that dangerous scene, till the enchantress, who had disturbed his peace, had quitted it. /

A day or two afterwards, the term of Miss Mountain's visit being expired, she took leave, while Spencer, inexpressibly chagrined and disappointed at the recent check his ambition and vanity had received, and having no longer any pretext for absenting himself from his regiment, prepared to rejoin it; suffering under a state of depression not easily to be imagined; but which he had the art, in a parting interview with Arbella, to lay entirely to the account of his attachment to her, and his fears respecting the opposition it might encounter from his father.

Matilda did not receive from Lady Torrendale the applause she expected for the generosity of her conduct. When that lady was informed of the share she had had in recalling Lord Strathallan to a sense of the obligations incurred by his first engagements, she expressed more surprise than pleasure, and coldly observed, that she thought it was for Lord Strathallan himself to judge, what was most calculated for his own happiness.

'I should have thought so too, madam,' said Matilda, modestly but firmly, 'nor should I have presumed to interfere in any case in which my interests had not been so mingled with his.'

'Then why not let them be mingled?' interposed her ladyship, fretfully. 'I put you in the track to attain to distinction and happiness; I could do no more.' But then, as if ashamed of her injustice, she begged of Matilda to excuse a warmth which originated in her anxiety to see her dear young friend established in a manner suitable to her merit; praised the part she had acted, and requested she would not mention her name as having been adverse to it.

In the mean time Lord Torrendale, divided between the plans of personal aggrandizement, and real benevolence, which engrossed his whole attention, had no suspicion how nearly the immense possessions of Miss Mountain had been transferred from his eldest, to his youngest son. While county meetings, proposed improvements / on his estate, tolls and turnpikes, boroughs and barracks, charters and charity-schools, by turns claimed his time and thoughts, the ingenious cabals of his active and restless countess were about as well known to him as the secret designs of the court and cabinet of Japan.

It was some days after the departure of his two sons and that of his fair visitant, that he began to perceive something of a change. Having made enquiry, in his absent way, why he did not see Strathallan and his brother as usual, – 'You forget,' said his lady, peevishly, 'they went away from us the beginning of this week.'

'Indeed! and Miss Mountain, where is she?'

'She is gone too. Surely you remember, my lord,' returned the countess still more impatiently, 'she took leave of us yesterday.'

'Gone!' repeated Lord Torrendale, with a look of astonishment; 'I thought they had all spent the day with us!'

CHAPTER II.

Playful and artless, on the summer wave
Sporting with buoyant wing, the fairy scene
With fairest grace adorning; but in wo,
In poverty, in soul-subduing toils,
In patient tending on the sick man's bed,
In ministerings of love, in bitterest pangs
Faithful and firm; in scenes where sterner hearts
Have cracked, still cheerful and still kind.

COLERIDGE, *Remorse.*[9]

THE serenity which Matilda experienced as the reward of the painful sacrifice she had made, though deep, heartfelt, and beyond what can be conceived by those, who, living only for the moment, know not what it is to yield up inclination to the more imperious call of duty, was not, however, of a nature to allow her to enjoy, with her former relish, the trifling pursuits of the circle in which she moved; and to this distaste was soon added another, and a more serious cause. Anxiety respecting / her parents now began to make every pleasure of Woodlands insipid; a considerable period had elapsed beyond the time originally fixed for their return, and yet she had not lately received from them, any letter to account for this unforeseen delay. She determined at length to write, requesting that she might be no longer kept in this torturing state of suspense; and was just sitting down to execute her intention, when she was startled by the sudden entrance of her own maid, who addressed her with – 'Ma'am, a gentleman in black, who waits below, says he wants to speak to you.'

Matilda was in that state of mind, which the smallest circumstance is sufficient to agitate and alarm. Not immediately recollecting that the girl, (who was the daughter of one of the neighbouring cottagers, lately hired to attend her) was not acquainted with Sowerby's appearance; nor adverting, at the moment, to the circumstance of his having, since the death of his wife, constantly dressed in black, a thousand vague and agonizing apprehensions assailed her, as to the name and business of the ominous stranger. Her old friend's first approach was not indeed calculated to dissipate them. He met her at the parlour door, his countenance pale beyond its usual sallow hue, his eyes wild, and lip quivering. 'Do not be alarmed, my dear Matilda,' he exclaimed as she entered; but his looks and manners so decidedly contradicted the words he uttered, that they only increased the perturbation they were meant to allay.

'For God's sake, do not conceal any thing from me!' she exclaimed, 'You have heard from my father and mother! – He is ill – they are both ill – too ill to return perhaps – tell me, I entreat you – tell me the worst!' – 'You distress yourself unnecessarily, my dear girl,' said her considerate friend, who had now in a degree recovered himself; then pausing, as if seeking for terms in which most gently to convey the intelligence, 'I have heard from your mother,' he said; / 'she is well, quite well; but your father has had a slight return of his former complaint, a very slight one; but as his physicians have, for the present, forbidden his travelling, he has expressed a wish – nay, do not turn so pale, my love, – not to be longer deprived of your society.'

'I understand you, my best, my truest friend,' said Matilda, with a look in which she endeavoured in vain to stifle the anguish that was rising at her heart, 'and I will try to prepare myself with serenity for whatever –' Here her voice lost its assumed firmness, and Sowerby taking occasion to interrupt her, said, 'Do not, I entreat you, so fatally misconstrue the meaning of a communication, by which I intended to save you from suspense and alarm, and not to increase them. I am going to London to be with your father, as I think, in his situation, the presence of a friend is the best medicine that can be administered. My sister accompanies me, and if you have no objection, we shall be happy to take you under her care.' He turned, as he spoke, to a lady, who bowed in silence as he presented her. Matilda had never heard that Sowerby had a sister, but on his introducing the stranger, she contemplated her with some curiosity. Apparently absorbed in her own thoughts, and not wishing to be called from them, she occupied one corner of the window, yet hardly seemed to perceive the objects that passed before her; her face was veiled, but the light that fell full upon it, still partly discovered a countenance that was most engaging and interesting, but touched with a degree of sadness, which appeared to the distressed Matilda in unison with the melancholy circumstances of the moment.

This lady had certainly something singular, both in her dress and manner; her eyes had an expression almost plaintive, her air was dignified, though mild. What was remarkable, her brother never introduced or mentioned her by any but her Christian name of Clara.

'As I suppose,' continued Sowerby, / forcing a smile, 'that you have not many very important preparations to make, we shall, with your permission, call for you in a couple of hours.' Matilda signified her assent by a motion of the head, for she was unable to speak. She felt, by the hastiness of this summons, how much more urgent the necessity of her presence must be, than Sowerby's friendship chose to represent it. 'Farewell, dear amiable child!' he said, as he took leave; and while he gazed on her, his stern countenance assumed an expression of interest the most painfully anxious; his eyes filled with tears; he attempted to say more, but something appeared suddenly to interrupt him, and again recommending her to lose no time in preparing for her journey, he hurried out of the room.

When the countess was informed of the necessity for her young friend's departure, she expressed the warmest sympathy in her distress, kindly took her hand, and regretted much that she was not then going to London, that she might herself conduct her thither: and here followed a pathetic digression on Lord Torrendale's cruelty in having kept her so long in the country; from which Matilda with difficulty brought her back to the purport of her present communication, which was, to thank her lady-ship and Lord Torrendale for all their former kindness, and to mention the necessity of her being in readiness to attend the summons of Mr. Sowerby and his sister, in two hours at furthest.

When the moment for Miss Melbourne's departure arrived, Lady Emily clung to her arms, and would hardly by force be separated from her. It seemed to her, that she was at once deprived of her companion, guide, and instructress. 'I shall be lost, Miss Melbourne,' said she, while the tears ran down her blooming cheeks, 'I shall become the poor, little, idle, untaught creature I was, when first you knew me. Who will encourage me to be otherwise, now I have lost both you and my brother? Indeed, I can hardly / wish it. No, I am determined I will not do any sort of good till you return.' – 'Then I hope I shall return soon, Emily,' said Matilda, forcing a smile, which gleamed like a rainbow through a fast-dropping shower. The little girl then bending forward, in a whisper added, 'Ah, Miss Melbourne! what shall I say to Strathallan?'

Matilda started: it seemed as if the trifling sorrows of love were a profanation to the sacredness of her present grief. She was not sorry the impatient voice of Sowerby prevented the necessity of any reply; and again waving her hand, and kissing it to the friends she left behind, she soon found herself again with him who had been her first, and perhaps her sincerest friend; and his sister, who seeming hardly desirous to be observed, sat silent, and still veiled, in one corner of the carriage.

Each of the travellers being absorbed in melancholy reflections which they could not communicate to each other, Matilda found little to disturb the mournful tran-quillity which had succeeded the bustle of departure. Could any thing have drawn her thoughts from the subject that so painfully occupied them, it would have been the kindness and courtesy of Sowerby, so unlike his usual harsh and over-bearing manner. He who might truly be said to prefer the house of mourning to the house of feasting, had completely dropped his wonted asperity, in apprehension for his friend and sym-pathy for his young companion. With surprise, mixed with pleasure and admiration, she beheld the man who had often damped the hour of gaiety by the most capricious and ill-founded complaints; whose fastidious delicacy the least opposition would irritate, the least inconvenience distress, now, all kindness and consideration for the feelings of his still more pensive companions.

No complaint escaped him, no dispute occurred to disturb the course of their mournful journey; at the end of two days, through which Matilda had never / bestowed one thought on Strathallan, she found herself in the arms of her mother, and had flown to her father's couch, who seemed to have recovered new life to embrace her; but this was a momentary relief, and, much as she had been prepared for a change, the total alteration in his appearance, effected during the course of a few weeks, sur-passed all that her strongest apprehensions had taught her to expect. Mr. Melbourne, in the ardent prosecution of his favourite pursuits, had, when in the country, too long neglected the frequent threatening of a pulmonary complaint, which had at length attacked him with great violence. Though he had been afterwards persuaded to use more caution, it had returned upon him in town; and a fever, occasioned by vexation, anxiety, and a total change in his habits and modes of living, being added to its slow and destructive influence, he was now reduced to a state of weakness, which left little hope that his life could be preserved. When she first saw him, he had an interval of ease; he was sitting up, supported by pillows, and as she approached, he cried 'I wished but to live to bless my eyes with the sight of my Matilda once again. She is come, and I am satisfied.'

'Oh, do not say so!' exclaimed the weeping Matilda, who felt at this moment, that if she could see her father restored to the health and vigour he had enjoyed at the Rocks, she could spend a life with pleasure at his side, nor ever wish again for any farther happiness. Next to the presence of his daughter, the arrival of Sowerby seemed to give Mr. Melbourne satisfaction. This gentleman spent every hour that he could spare, by the sick couch of his friend; and from the occasional animation, caused by the society of those he best loved, drew a flattering augury of his recovery.

Matilda listened to his prognostics, with all the sanguine eagerness of youth. Vain hope! the relief was transient, the suffering continual and intense; and Matilda had for some days the inexpressible / anguish to behold this beloved parent, whose mild commands had never been issued to her in any form but that of kindness, and whose singular sweetness of temper was such, that she had never heard from him a harsh expression, or an unjust reproof, gradually consuming away, under sufferings, of whose greatness she could judge by their visible effect on his enfeebled frame, though that same mildness of temper, and habitual philosophy, prevented a single complaint from escaping him. Sometimes, when gazing on his child, an expression of mental anguish and anxiety would pass across his features; but otherwise, ever calm, his life seemed to be ebbing away, without, on his part, a struggle, a sigh, or a regret.

One day when he was sitting up, and had been looking at her with more intentness than usual, she asked him if he wished any thing that she could do for his relief. 'Nothing,' he replied, 'but to thank you for all your kindness, my dearest girl, and to return my acknowledgments to Heaven, while yet I can, for having given me a daughter, who during the course of her short life, never willingly caused me a moment's pain.' While Matilda's tears fell, as a tribute, to the melancholy pleasure this solemn declaration afforded her; he said kindly, as in one hand he held hers, and in the other that of Mrs. Melbourne, 'I believe there are few who pass their last hours so happily in the full possession of all they hold most dear. In my plan of life, I may have been mistaken, but it has constituted my own happiness: I never sought for numerous friendships; my wish was rather to enjoy the individual tenderness of a heart that should be devoted to me alone; neither did I look for pleasures in that world, where they are supposed to be usually found, but in a few pursuits, for the success of which I depended only upon myself. I may have been blamed as retired, unsocial; but my solitary studies and enjoyments never prevented me from doing any good office in my power, / to my fellow creatures; and they were innocent, at least in the eyes of that Being, whom I never voluntarily offended, and to whom I shall soon present myself, with a heart resigned, and, though humble, yet full of confidence.' Then turning more particularly to Mrs. Melbourne, he added, after a moment's pause, 'I have sometimes reproached myself with not having studied your happiness, as much as my own gratification; and reflected, that I had not always to the utmost afforded Matilda every advantage, to which her birth and uncommon attractions entitled her; but if it was so, your conforming goodness, that ever left me in doubt, whether all my wishes were not your own, will now, I am sure, equally lead you to forgive me.'

Mrs. Melbourne, anxious to turn him from this conversation, begged he would not let a doubt disturb that composure, on which depended their best hopes of his recovery; she then pressed him to take a cordial draught, which his physician had ordered at stated hours to be administered.

'I thank you,' he replied, 'my best love,' the name by which he most often called her; 'how refreshing it is from your hands!' Then, affectionately smiling upon her, he expressed a wish for rest, and, leaning back in his chair, seemed in a few moments sunk in profound repose. Mrs. Melbourne, with an action commanding silence, retired with Matilda to a small distance, not to interrupt his slumber. At length the perfect and motionless serenity in which he lay alarmed them, and softly approaching, it was not till some moments after the event, that they discovered these grateful and affectionate words had been his last; and that, in breathing forth expressions of habitual kindness and benignity, this blameless and gentle spirit had ascended to the source from which it first derived its being. /

CHAPTER III.

The heart that sorrow doomed to share,
Has worn the frequent seal of woe,
Its sad impression learns to bear,
And finds full oft its ruin slow.
But when the seal is first imprest,
When the young heart its pain shall try,
From the soft yielding trembling breast
Oft seems the startled soul to fly.

LANGHORNE.[10]

THE faithful and persevering attachment of Sowerby, in taking upon himself the charge of every mournful office for his departed friend, deprived the unhappy survivors, at the moment, of the support his presence might have afforded; but perhaps it was compensated by the additional freedom in which they indulged together, in the first transports of a grief which the world could not have understood, and poured forth the expressions of a sorrow, so just and sincere, till by degrees it subsided into that calm melancholy, which rather cherishes than shrinks from the contemplation of the past. Sowerby had attended the remains of his friend to the Rocks, to see the last sad duties paid to them; and to watch over the interests of his family, now that place was no longer to be their abode. All Mr. Melbourne's valuable collections, his books, prints, and manuscripts, were to be sold for the benefit of his widow and daughter; and under the superintendance of a friend so intelligent and attached, they had every reason to expect the business would be transacted for them in the most advantageous manner. On the death of Mr. Melbourne, the estate of the Rocks devolved on Sir Harold Melbourne, the nearest male relation of the family; but on the change this circumstance might make in her situation and prospects, Matilda's grief had not yet allowed her leisure to reflect. Wholly occupied with the greatness of her irreparable loss, there were moments in which her young / heart, unused to sorrow, could hardly believe the extent of that which was now inflicted on her; then would the occurrences of the last weeks appear to her but as a feverish dream, and it seemed impossible that so short a period should have robbed her of so large a portion of her happiness. That time was too brief to produce any alteration in her outward form, which had caused such a revolution in her inward feelings; the aspect of every thing around her was the same, while every thing was in reality so much changed. Then, putting her hand to her eyes, as if endeavouring to exclude every thing but the past, she would say, ' 'Tis all a dream; so lately he was here; so lately could feel pleasure in my society, and thank me when I administered to his comfort, with a look that repaid every exertion! And is he no longer sensible to those exertions, and can he be gone, gone for ever, and I still bear to live and mourn him! Oh, I did not love him enough, I did not value him alone, and now I am punished for it!'

During this period of affliction, Matilda often afterwards remarked with surprise, how seldom Strathallan had been the subject of her thoughts; that image, which so short a time before had appeared to rule them with such despotic sway, now, if not wholly obliterated, had at least lost much of its force. It was then that she discovered how much the powerful ties of nature prevail, in an unsophisticated mind at least, over the fragile and fantastic bonds of love; by this, she also felt, however well grounded may be the supposition, that grief subdues the mind, and disposes it more readily to tenderness; yet, that to experience in their full force those soft but lively emotions, which grace, spirit, and loveliness, are calculated to inspire, it requires a mind comparatively at ease, a heart ready to vibrate in unison to those sweet impressions. Those gay visions of beauty and of love, which, thick as motes in the sunbeam, had danced before her fancy in the flowery arbours of / Woodlands, vanished amid the mournful duties and gloomy scenes of her town abode. New trials and new cares soon called her at once from these reflections, and from remembrances more painful; and an incident discovered to her a secret, which nothing but Mrs. Melbourne's unwillingness so soon to add to the sufferings she had already endured, had prevented her from revealing long before.

She had for some time observed that her own maid, who had been permitted to accompany her to town from Woodlands, had appeared sullen and dissatisfied with her situation, and often failed in the respect she before had uniformly shown her.

One day, when remonstrating with her upon leaving some work neglected, which she had desired her to finish, Susan answered, that she had work of her own to do, 'for if I don't finish my new bonnet myself,' she continued sulkily, 'I sha'n't have any thing fit to be seen in when Miss Mountain's woman, and all the quality folks, comes up to town: for I have not been paid my wages, to buy one, by your lady mamma, I don't know when.'

'I don't think I ever refused you a bonnet, Susan,' replied Matilda, 'but do you suppose this is the way to recommend yourself to my service, or that I shall long retain you, if you continue to treat me with this disrespect?'

'Service!' cried Susan, sticking her arms a-kimbo, 'I'll warrant there's many a prettier service going a-begging than one, where folks is all at sixes and sevens, as I may say. There's to be no more going to the Rocks, as I hear, and to tell you a piece of my mind, I'm tired of poking about in this sort of a place, where one gets no fun, and sees no company.'

Matilda, her mind painfully occupied by other and higher considerations, had hardly remarked what was now forced upon her observation, that the appearance and furniture of her lodging in town, was not equal to what she might have supposed / Mr. Melbourne's circumstances required. Her unpleasant feelings disappeared, however, almost as soon as the object which had excited them. 'That this should grieve me!' she said, smiling, as in contempt upon herself, on recollecting the maid's impertinence; without adverting to its being of any serious consequence, she yet, from her habitual care to save her mother the slightest pain, resolved against communicating the circumstance to her. But Mrs. Melbourne, who perceived something had disturbed her daughter, easily divined the cause, and said, with a forced smile, 'I guess what has made you uneasy, for I saw you in close conversation with Susan just now, and I suppose she was giving you some of the fine lady-like airs she has lately assumed.' Matilda, while she affected to treat the matter with equal lightness, confessed there was an alteration in the manner of the young woman, which made her conversation not very exhilarating.

'So, she has heard some rumours of what has happened; 'tis what I expected,' said Mrs. Melbourne, in a smothered tone, and dropping her assumed cheerfulness. 'The thoughtless scorns, and bitter slights of servants, are the first fruits of the miseries of the poor.' Then addressing Matilda aloud, she said, 'can you bear, my dear girl, a communication, which will add heavily to what you now must feel; yet, I fear 'twas only false tenderness which has till now concealed it.'

'Ah, mamma, what can add to my affliction, since' – Here she paused, observing the change in Mrs. Melbourne's countenance; and suddenly the most painful apprehensions for her health and safety, or that of some of those who were dear to her, filled her mind. Mrs. Melbourne, perceiving the excess of her uneasiness, and wishing to relieve her, at least from the torments of suspense, continued –

'But a few weeks ago you were in possession of a fortune, which was sufficient to have preserved you in affluence, / even when obliged to consider the abode of your childhood no longer as your home; that fortune, by the failure of those in whose hands it was placed, is gone; and you must, my dearest girl, by the exertion of that spirit and principle to which I have from childhood formed your mind, endeavour to conform it now to your altered situation.'

'Is that all!' cried Matilda, breathing more freely upon finding the communication so much less dreadful than she had expected.

'All! Sweet, untaught girl, you view it in that romantic light which conceals, from those unlectured in the world's hard school, that loss of fortune is indeed almost loss of every thing; of pleasure, of consequence, of friends; but why should I anticipate – I will rather, since I have thus far opened myself, treat you with that confidence your generous spirit still more than your age, should now for the future ever claim. You have heard me say that your father, in marrying me, was influenced by preference alone; his liberal spirit would not suffer him to consider my want of fortune as a disadvantage, and possessing himself at that time but the portion of a younger brother, retirement was adopted by us both, as much from necessity as choice. When, by the death of his beloved relative, he came into possession of affluence, unenvied and undesired, he was anxious to secure a part of its enjoyment to me; but as I had brought him no fortune, a delicacy, perhaps misplaced, made me ever averse to the proposal: as I knew, however, that if we were not blest with a son, the estate of the Rocks must go from our part of the family, I acquiesced with pleasure in a plan that he thought would secure to me a compensation for what I had declined, which he adopted from the moment he came into possession of it: part of the income of every year we laid by, to accumulate as a fortune for you. As we had neither of us expensive tastes and habits, this overplus would at all / events have risen to some amount; but from the increasing, and perhaps unnecessary seclusion, into which your dear father's peculiar turn of mind gradually led him to indulge, it became considerable indeed; and you were at eighteen possessed of a portion that avarice itself would not have overlooked, while taste and love –

'How often have I anticipated,' continued Mrs. Melbourne, while tears of affection sprung into her eyes, 'the hour when with proud delight I should present you to an admiring world – and must such sweetness be consigned to obscurity?'

'Why should I wish a different fate from yours?' replied Matilda; 'why, rather, dearest mother, did you not permit me to share all your anxieties, to accompany you on this cruel journey, which I am sure was undertaken on my account?'

'I hoped to spare it you all,' resumed Mrs. Melbourne. 'While yet in the country, we received private notice from a friend in London, who was anxious for our welfare, of the diminished credit and apprehended failure of that house, in which the whole accumulated sum we had so long destined for you was placed. Mr. Melbourne would not delay a moment, weak as he was from recent illness, to hasten to town, still hoping the representation of his correspondent might be false or exaggerated; or that, at all events, he might be in time to withdraw his property form it before its final ruin. Useless precaution! We arrived just in time to hear of that crush which involved us, in common with so many others, in one general destruction. Still we rejoiced you were not present, to share the first shock of our dismay. We had left you with our only Derbyshire friend, under the idea of sparing you the sight of anxieties, and the knowledge of unpleasant affairs, with which, if they terminated favourably, you need never have been made acquainted, if otherwise, were better communicated on our return. While the / Rocks were ours you would still have had the enjoyment of affluence, though deprived of your former expectations; therefore, had your father lived' –

Here Matilda, heedless of her own afflictions in the desire to console her mother, interrupted her, to profess her readiness to adopt any views which this reverse in her prospects might make necessary; and her perfect resignation to this additional weight, light indeed in comparison with the other which it had pleased Providence to inflict on her.

'I have no view, no wish at present,' replied Mrs. Melbourne, 'but to recover, if possible, that peace of which we have been deprived; and to hide myself from those who knew me in a far different situation.'

'Oh! mamma, why would you deny them the greatest pleasure they can possibly experience,' said the artless Matilda, 'that of shewing you that no difference in your situation can alter their sentiments; as it was your character, not your fortune, inspired them, surely no change of circumstances can affect them: there are the Torrendales, Miss Ferrars, Mr. Sowerby – '

'Oh, Lady Torrendale!' repeated Mrs. Melbourne, with that tone of slight and indifference which speaks but little hope; ' and as for Sowerby,' she continued, 'he was truly attached to his friend, but to me he never was kind; an indescribably irksome manner of undervaluing every thing I said and did, ran through his whole behaviour; and now the tie that cemented our intimacy is gone, it would not surprise me, if he should soon completely desert a society, to which I can no longer contribute the attention and spirits that made it formerly agreeable to him. With some good points of character, he is an egotist in the truest sense of the word, selfish – fastidious – overbearing – '

The entrance of the gentleman in question put an end, for the present, to the *catalogue raisonné*[11] that Mrs. Melbourne had been giving of his virtues. He seemed embarrassed at seeing Matilda, and / desirous of some private conversation with her mother. Accustomed to watch his looks with almost filial attention, the young lady soon took an opportunity to indulge him in what he wished; but though absent, she was not long kept ignorant of the subject of their conversation.

'We have been speaking of your virtues, my dearest child,' said Mrs. Melbourne, 'but before I tell you how much Sowerby values them, let me remind you of what my whole life has proved, – that your happiness is ever my first object, and that I do not wish any representation of mine should bear the force of a command, but rather that of the counsel of a tender and enlightened friend. Sowerby loves you, and has generously offered, upon this reverse of fortune, to share his affluence with you; now tell me truly, could you accept him without repugnance?'

Matilda looked down, and remained for a moment in deep reflection; then raising her mild eyes, in which a modest confidence and dignity were expressed, 'I think,' she said, 'that from the whole tenor of Mr. Sowerby's conduct, and the recent proofs of friendship he has given me, I could, I do not say love, but regard him sufficiently, almost to wish to give him my hand, if it could contribute to his happiness; but then my choice must seem free, my situation be what it has been. As it is, when my altered views are opposed to his wealth, his age – Oh, mamma! I hope,' she continued, casting down her eyes and blushing, 'that I do not deceive myself, but I think love, love alone, could excuse my accepting such an obligation.'

'And you cannot give him this same love!' repeated Mrs. Melbourne, thoughtfully, 'Is it so? Am I not sufficiently your friend, to deserve to know, it is because it is bestowed on another?'

'No, no indeed, that's all over,' replied Matilda, hastily; and then, upon an exclamation of surprise escaping Mrs. Melbourne, she related, with that ingenuousness / which only waits to repose itself in the bosom of true friendship, the conflicts and escapes she had gone through at Woodlands.

'You acted nobly, my generous girl!' exclaimed Mrs. Melbourne, embracing her with tears of pleasure, 'but oh! what a lesson of prudence, in this instance far surpassing my own, does your conduct give me! Misled by maternal affection, I only reflected at that time, that in my daughter I possessed a treasure which the highest might envy, and which, though it might derive from rank an added lustre, must, wherever I bestowed it, confer a greater obligation than it received. Under this impression, I rather viewed with pleasure the first dawnings of a partiality in Lord Strathallan, which I thought could only be productive of happiness to you both.

'Fortune has now placed an insuperable barrier between you, even if that engagement did not exist, which must now confine his choice. I will not remark upon the injustice, the impolicy of thus fettering the mind before it is capable of making a free election. It is but too common, where any object of interest or ambition is concerned, and to such considerations the happiness of a life is often thought too cheap a sacrifice.

Neither do I ask, if the impression made by those dangerous hours you were allowed to spend together, does not still linger about your heart. I anticipated your refusal of Sowerby, but I do not approve of your motive for it. Consider, my love, were affluence still added to those advantages, which I am sure no blind partiality tempts me to exaggerate, what right would he have to aspire to my Matilda? He himself pleads the reverse in your fortune, as the only circumstance that emboldens him to acknowledge a preference he has long in secret felt; while he declares, with a generous delicacy, it was the fear of influencing your choice by the parting recommendation of a parent, that prevented him from opening his intentions to his friend. On the whole, I am better pleased / with his conduct than I expected; but do not let the sense of obligation weigh upon your mind; neither on the other hand suppose, that a vain wish to be restored to the enjoyments of wealth, at your expense, has the slightest influence on the counsels I am giving you. Reflect before you decide; but I entreat, whatever be your final determination, that you will consider me as a person wholly unconnected with the question.'

'I will consult my pillow upon it,' said Matilda, attempting to smile, for she began to fear that the flattering suggestions of her own heart might have deceived her into believing, that that was a noble action, which was, in reality, only a sacrifice to disappointed passion.

Mrs. Melbourne having approved of her determination, with mutual expressions of anxiety for each other's happiness, and mutual endearments, which changed the hour of sorrow into one of bliss, these amiable sufferers parted from each other for the night.

CHAPTER IV.

The morn that warns th' approaching day
Awakes me up to toil and woe,
I see the hours in long array
That I must suffer lingering slow:

Or, if I slumber, fancy chief
Reigns haggard-wild in sore affright,
Even day all bitter brings relief
From such a horror-breathing night.

BURNS, Lament.[12]

THE hour of darkness, of silence, and solitude, which by the happy is consecrated to repose, Matilda devoted to serious enquiry into the nature of her own feelings. Though others may consider her as a beauty, a heroine, and till late, the object of envy as well as admiration, she was still old fashioned enough to know herself to be a poor, weak, erring creature. She did not forget that the heart is deceitful above all things, and she determined its dangerous dictates should not be substituted / for the less pleasing, but safer decrees, of reason and religion. The result of this self-examination was, a resolution at once to conquer any repugnance that might be inconsistent with duty; and by a graceful compliance, to shew her gratitude to her truest friend, and to ensure the happiness of a mother, who had ever made hers the first object of her life.

The attachment Sowerby had shewn for Mrs. Melbourne, had touched her affectionate heart beyond any thing in his former conduct; his present disinterested offer added to the esteem with which he had ever inspired her. 'I feel friendship, confidence, gratitude, towards him,' she continued, 'and after all, what is this love, without which I fondly imagine I cannot make him happy?'

At this instant, a long-forbidden image rushed before her fancy's eye, – bright, distinct, and visible, as reality could have made it. It was the beautiful form of the beloved Strathallan, which burst upon her soul, beaming in all those mild glories which had led it captive in happier hours. Turning on her those soft eyes, which had learned so directly the channel to her heart, it seemed to look at her reproachfully, and say, 'Do you still ask what is love?' 'Oh, forgive me, Strathallan, I was in error – I repent!' cried Matilda, starting up, while her voice was drowned in the tears she could no longer suppress: 'Surely you are mine, – I have been given to you, – your claim shall be admitted, – I will obey you, my gentle lord. But do not upbraid me,' she added, panting under the strong impression of terror her imagination had conjured up, and trying to banish from her mind the form which was ever before it, seen, felt in the air, chaining her to one spot, and alone illuminating the surrounding gloom with its light. It appeared to her that he implored her not to desert him, to leave him without consolation in a loveless, joyless world; not to hasten of herself the destruction of his hopes. He seemed to ask her, if a short delay was / too much for one who had shewn such love?

But soon recovering from, and ashamed of the transport into which passion had led her, 'Has he not resigned me?' she said; 'Have I not myself pointed out to him the path he should pursue? And shall I now show myself incapable of a similar effort? Shall I, while he is perhaps successfully endeavouring to banish my image from his thoughts, still cherish his, in hopeless and cowardly despair? No, let this conflict, the most violent, be the last; let me recal my former resolutions, and seek in duty that happiness, which ill-directed love can never give.'

Having composed her mind to this determination, she waited with anxiety for the approach of morning, that she might make her mother's heart happy by communicating it; perhaps that she might put it out of her own power to retract it. She met her at breakfast with a countenance serene though pale.

'I have examined myself, my dear mother,' she said, 'and I assure you, I can, with satisfaction, comply with the proposal that has been so generously made to me.' 'And I assure you,' returned Mrs. Melbourne, while she pressed her with tenderness to her heart, 'I will never consent to such a sacrifice.'

Matilda, anxious to be understood, and fearful that she was not supposed in earnest in the wish she now expressed, repeated with eagerness the arguments by which she had brought her mind to such a determination. But Mrs. Melbourne continued firm to her original resolution. 'I allowed you time to reflect upon the offer thus unexpectedly made,' she said, 'because I thought it necessary your refusal should be the result of deliberate consideration, in order to satisfy your own mind that we neither of us suddenly rejected it on rash or romantic grounds. But I was determined, even should a false generosity lead you to sacrifice such youth and merit to a temper and age like Sowerby's, under the idea of contributing / to my happiness, that I never would consent to it.'

Matilda insisted, and a contest of generosity ensued between the parent and child, most unlike those which are generally represented; but which we may surely trust to be of more frequent occurrence, than those conflicts so often described as taking place between aversion on the one side, and tyranny on the other, when we consider, that the heart, generally painted the abode of the latter, is that which in reality is capable of tenderness, generosity, and self-devotion, beyond what all other hearts conceive. Matilda was obliged, at last, we will not ask whether with reluctance, to yield.

'We cannot hope any thing from Sowerby's friendship, after this,' continued Mrs. Melbourne; 'offended pride, in a mind like his, is likely to settle deep, and to rankle long; but do not let this affect you,' she pursued, kindly pressing her hand, 'the sale of my jewels, and the various personal property your poor father left, will be enough to support us decently, though in a situation far different from that in which we have lived. Your amiable temper and merit have made you friends; you will, I hope, find more. At all events I am blest, to see in you a disposition to that contentment and resignation, which would make many, more favoured by fortune, could they look within, envy us in our humble habitation.'

Sowerby did not long delay his return, in order to know how far he might indulge those hopes which had been the delightful dream of his life, but which he had never till lately aspired to realise. Mrs. Melbourne had a long conversation with him; and Matilda almost repented that she had suffered her mother's delicate generosity to prevail, and thus expose her to the pain and regret it now might cause her.

She waited in the front room of their little lodging, in that unsettled state of mind, and agitation of spirits, common to those who are conscious that something / is taking place in which they are intimately concerned, yet over which they no longer possess any influence. The figure of Sowerby darting from the house across the street, was the first object that roused her from this reverie. She hastened to the room where her mother had been; she was at the door, her handkerchief was at her eyes: 'How I have wronged him!' she said, 'He is the most generous of beings! he was indeed the worthy friend of the best of men.'

Then retiring with Matilda, she related to her, that much as her friend had seemed to suffer from the rejection of his suit, his greatest anxiety had appeared to be, lest this imprudent disclosure of his attachment would take from him the right of being considered any longer with that confidence which he had formerly enjoyed. 'As Mr. Melbourne's friend,' he said, 'let me still be allowed to contribute to the happiness of his family, though no longer hoping to be united to it by a dearer tie.'

'I cannot repeat to you,' continued Mrs. Melbourne, 'the generosity of his offers; he seems better acquainted with the unhappy affairs of our family, even than I am myself; he talks of leaving all his possessions to you; and in the warmth of his friendly zeal for your welfare, he pressed me to let him settle upon you, entirely out of his own power, that portion of his fortune which, had you been united to him, he would have made yours.'

An expression of alarm which she could not repress, passed over Matilda's countenance, and inclined her to interrupt Mrs. Melbourne's narration; but meeting her eye, she blushed at having for a moment suspected the determination of a spirit as delicate, and as proud as her own.

'Trust me, my dear,' said that lady, answering her thoughts, 'I could not bring myself to accept of any of Sowerby's pecuniary offers; but at the same time that I refused them, I conveyed to him / the high sense I entertained of the generosity and kindness by which they were prompted. His heart felt the distinction, and I may promise you, that you have secured, for ever, a warm and steady friend.'

Matilda's tears evinced how capable she was of appreciating such an attachment; and her mother, to relieve her mind from the subject, began talking over their future plans of life; the manner in which they must now economize upon their narrow income, and the changes necessary to be made in the establishment they had formerly kept up.

'We must learn to attend upon ourselves,' she said; 'one man and a maid would, I think, have been sufficient for our small family, but that my own woman, Hanway, who has shewn herself as attached and respectful, as Susan was the contrary, has entreated not to be dismissed from a family where she has so long lived in happiness;

she offers to turn to any sort of work, rather than be sent away; and I, for my part, have been so affected by her generosity, that I would rather inconvenience myself, than either part from her, or make her suffer too much at her advanced age, by her inconsiderate kindness.'

'Faithful creature!' cried Matilda, delighted with this new proof of attachment in an old servant, who she knew had not only welcomed her, but Mrs. Melbourne, into the world. 'As to the other maid, mamma, we shall want one that will be active and clever, and I will take care it shall not be Susan.'

Pursuant to this intention, she sent up for her own maid that evening, and said to her, 'I think, Susan, you complained yesterday of wanting a bonnet?' 'Yes, ma'am – no, ma'am,' answered the girl, with a look that implied trepidation and self-reproach. 'It was never our intention, I am sure,' pursued Matilda, 'that you should have been put to any inconvenience for want of money, though the harassing events that have / happened to us in succession, might, for the moment, have made your just claim escape my mother's memory. Here,' she continued, taking out her purse, 'is what I believe will satisfy your demand, and take this in addition,' pressing on her a handsome gratuity, 'as an acknowledgement of the cheerful services you used to render me; and as I am no longer in a situation to require them – '

'Oh, ma'am,' cried poor Susan, bursting into tears, 'take back your money I beg, and forgive me, for I was a very foolish, insolent girl, yesterday, and a wicked ungrateful wretch, to speak so to my sweet young lady, who never said an unkind word in her life. Punish me, pray do, ma'am, but don't talk of sending me away.'

'But my dear Susan,' said Matilda, quite softened by the girl's repentance and confession, 'our present circumstances put it out of my power to keep a separate attendant for myself, and you are not used to any other employment.'

'Oh, yes, ma'am, I am,' cried the poor creature sobbing, 'and so you will let me be with you wherever you may go, I'll be housemaid – I'll be cook-maid – I'll wash the rooms upon my knees, or do any thing, so you will but forgive me.'

Matilda looked at her with a compassion which was evidently the precursor of pardon. She was touched by the sincere expression of shame and grief, that was betrayed alike in the words and countenance of this well-meaning, simple creature. At a loss how to proceed, she consulted with her mother; who, pleased with this artless tribute to her daughter's mild virtues, warmly counselled her to prefer the girl to a stranger, since she was so willing to repair her fault, and so desirous to be useful.

Mrs. Melbourne and Matilda, with this small establishment of three servants, and inhabiting part of a house in a genteel but retired street in London, fixed their minds to accept with thankfulness the good that remained to them, and determined, / since they had preferred delicacy and independence, to the prospect of affluence, when incompatible with those considerations, not to afford, by any future regrets, a new example in their own conduct, of the inconsistency of human wishes.

CHAPTER V.

I'll beg one boon
And then be gone and trouble you no more.
Shall I obtain it?
  Name it, fair cousin.

SHAKESPEARE.[13]

SOWERBY, in resigning the character of a lover, had resumed, with increased warmth, his former attentions as a friend. He seemed only desirous that it might be forgotten he had ever aspired to a higher place in Matilda's esteem; and so perfectly did he succeed in making her feel once more at ease in his society, that the charm of her artless manners and affectionate frankness communicated itself to him, and he dictated and dogmatized, quarrelled and asked pardon, with all his former good-humoured assumption of authority. Since his return to town he had taken a lodging near / Mrs. Melbourne, and seemed determined not to forsake her till the first shock of adversity at least was past.

As soon as that lady was able to attend to any thing beyond the afflicting circumstances of her present situation, she yielded to her daughter's persuasions in inquiring after the interesting sister of Mr. Sowerby, who had been Matilda's fellow-traveller; but nothing could conquer her reluctance to receive the visit of a stranger; and on Mrs. Melbourne's expressing to Sowerby her surprise that a woman of manners so pleasing as Matilda described hers to be, should be so devoted to solitude, and so indifferent to the interest she involuntarily inspired, he replied, in his abrupt manner, – 'It is because my sister is a nun.'

'A nun! – How singular that you should never mention the circumstance before!'

'Very singular.'

Mrs. Melbourne easily comprehended from these concise replies, that her old friend was not to be questioned on this subject; but as the curiosity of ladies, once raised, is not so easily appeased, she, by persevering attentions, at length induced Clara to make an exception in her favour from her plan of perfect seclusion, and soon learned from the fair recluse herself a little more of her history.

It appeared she had been educated in the Romish persuasion, which was that of her mother, the father of Mr. Sowerby having married a lady of immense fortune who was of that communion. She was considerably younger than her brother, and had, in the bloom of youth, voluntarily returned to the convent in France, where she had

– 199 –

been brought up, and there assumed the veil. When that country no longer offered a safe asylum, she had been conducted by her brother to a similar institution in England, where, for several years, she had remained contentedly performing the duties enjoined by her profession, till her extremely rigorous observance of them, acting on a / naturally delicate frame, brought on an illness which occasioned such serious apprehensions for her life, that she had been recommended to try the effects of a change of air, and some relaxation in the severity of her former discipline. So far her present situation could be accounted for; but the reasons that had induced the fair nun, possessed of beauty and enjoying a large fortune, originally to take such a step, were still withheld. Clara's manners were frank, even affectionate,

'And her mild eye was eloquent to speak
The soul of pity;'[14]

yet still, mingled with this softness and apparent confidence, there was a degree of reserve; and whether the veil was drawn by caution or sorrow, Mrs. Melbourne equally felt it was too sacred to attempt to remove it. It was certain that her resolution had been taken contrary to the wishes of Sowerby. His constant hatred to whatever bore the name of French manners or education, and that unwillingness to speak upon the subject, which, after an intimacy of so many years, had still made it a secret to his friends, that he had a sister, proved how much her self-devotion pained him. Even now, when in company with her, an involuntary and fretful glance, where pity and interest seemed mingled with some distressing feeling of resentment and regret, shewed that the consciousness of her situation was never absent from his bosom.

An observation like this was sufficient for prudence, such as Mrs. Melbourne's; while Matilda, enjoying the present hour in Clara's innocent and amiable society, feared, lest in attempting to know more, she should, with the indiscretion of the imprudent Psyche, suddenly deprive herself of the advantages she already possessed.[15] The fair recluse spent many hours of each day with her, and in her company she felt an ease even beyond what she now experienced with Mrs. Melbourne.

There are times when the members of / the same family, from the very excess of the affection which unites them, cannot so freely unbosom to each other, those sorrows in which they take an equal share, as to some friend who feels a kind, but less lively interest in their distress; a kind of restraint and timidity reigns over those conversations, where each is anxious to avoid some subject the most painful to touch upon, yet the most present to the thoughts. With Clara, Matilda could spend hours in a luxurious melancholy, which at all other moments she feared to indulge, and with her could pay the tribute of affection to the virtues of the parent who was lost to her on earth indeed, but whose image was seldom absent from her memory, and never from her heart.

The death of Mr. Melbourne was found to be productive of other distresses to his family, than those to which they had at first adverted. The confusion in which his affairs were left, rendered it necessary they should have an interview with Sir Harold Melbourne, the present possessor of the Rocks. It could not be supposed but that such a meeting must revive painful feelings; and it was with no great satisfaction that Mrs. Melbourne heard of his arrival in town, and saw the day approach which was to introduce to her, at once, a relation and a perfect stranger.

As if the disposition, studious yet indolent, of the late possessor of the Rocks, had been foreseen by his ancestor, he held the estate on the condition of appropriating a part of the yearly income it afforded, to the purpose of keeping the mansion in repair; and adding to it such embellishments as time or taste might suggest. This sum, though not turned by Mr. Melbourne very much from its original destination, was yet employed in a manner to which his provident and wise progenitor had perhaps never adverted. The first year he came into possession of the estate he built a menagerie; the next, an observatory; and finding afterwards that the rooms of his house / were not laid out on a plan sufficiently extensive to contain the numerous foreign curiosities of various sorts that now began to crowd in upon him, he proceeded to dismantle some of the rooms, and to take down part of the old walls, in order to convert the materials into other erections more suitable to his taste.

It was at this period that his wife had ventured to remonstrate, and to remind him, that while he was intent upon these fanciful plans, which neither added to the beauty nor convenience of the mansion, he was letting the greater part of the original building fall to ruin, and diverting the money that was destined to repair it, into another channel.

Struck with this representation, he promised immediately to attend to it; that year his museum would be finished, and he would positively make no more additions to it. In the beginning of the following, however, temptation arrived in the shape of an American bison, of a size so uncommon, and so beautifully preserved, that Mr. Melbourne, not having a corner left for it in the apartment already erected, declared he must be allowed to begin another room, or at least a boudoir, for the bison.

In the ensuing year Mrs. Melbourne still hoped some alteration in his plans; but he was then deeply engaged building a conservatory for Matilda, and after that he decidedly would think of the dilapidations the mansion had endured. The conservatory was built, and it was at length determined that the work should soon be begun of restoring the family-seat to its ancient appearance; when the slow but sure prognostics of a dangerous complaint, warned its possessor that he might not have it in his power to do his heir the justice that he meditated.

Fully aware of his danger, his intention had been to reimburse him in his will, for the sums thus appropriated, by a part of the fortune he had formerly considered as exclusively laid by for Matilda. /

The sudden stroke, which at once deprived him of this resource, embittered his last moments, by putting it out of his power to do what honour, if not justice, required; but Mrs. Melbourne, who well knew his wishes, determined to make any exertion or suffer any privation, rather than let obloquy rest upon the memory of one whose only real fault was, perhaps, a too great contempt for money matters, and a careless procrastination in the final arrangement of his affairs, increased, no doubt, by the apparent facility of retrieving them, which the probability till lately held out, of a long and undisturbed life, afforded. She had resources on which she hoped she could rely. Delay was all she required of Sir Harold, to satisfy his demands; but delay might even be considered as a favour – and a favour it was painful to ask, from one whose family had been at enmity with her late husband.

This repugnance was not lessened by Sowerby, who rather seemed to take a strange delight in adding to her apprehensions. – 'You will get no good out of Sir Harold, I promise you,' said he; 'a wild rogue, I wonder he is not here already to worry for the money.'

'I am inclined to hope better of him,' observed the lady; 'the very circumstance of his having chosen to become the purchaser of poor Mr. Melbourne's collections, argues a mind not entirely given up to dissipation.'

'Not at all. That was just in character with a hasty, feather-headed Melbourne, as they all were. He knew the collection was *unique* in England, and therefore, though he had no use for it himself, he would not let it go out of the family to those who could have valued it better. He a superior mind! There never was one among them; they are a bad breed; there was always something odd in the family – the father, old Sir Reginald, was something odd – the son is something odd – the Melbournes are a bad breed!'

'You forget, my dear sir, we are / Melbournes – at least I claim the honour of – '

'Oh, you know very well I do not mean you. – The Melbournes of the Rocks were always pure, as the healthful air that surrounded their charming retirement, – but as for the Melbournes of Moss-cliff Abbey – all I can say is, what few will feel inclined to deny I believe, – that the inhabitants of the neighbourhood of the Rocks will long have reason to regret their change of masters. Matilda, child, why do you hold down your head, and look as if you were going to cry? I am afraid I vex you – I think I always vex you,' continued Sowerby, in a half angry tone, to conceal the real repentance he felt at the thought of having given her pain.

Mrs. Melbourne took this opportunity to enquire if he had any thing, more than common report, to justify the opinion he had taken up, of Sir Harold.

'It is the result of every thing I have picked up about him since I have been in this vile place, this London, this sink of iniquity. His mother, a mere worthless fine lady, seemed to take a perverse pleasure in giving him an early initiation into all those follies by which she had rendered herself so notorious. When he ought to have been at school, she had him in company with her at balls and parties. When he ought to have been at college, he was driving barouches, acting private plays, losing his money at White's, and making himself talked of in every region of frivolity and folly. When he ought to have been in the world he was at college, beating the tutors, spending much, getting little, except the name of a ruffian, added to that of a trifler; – and when he ought to have been in parliament, he was abroad, wasting his time, confirming his follies, and neglecting his improvement. At an incredible expense and trouble, he got permission to run over the continent, merely for the indulgence of a caprice; his tour was cut short by the illness of his father, who summoned him to return: he travelled through France and Italy in / an incredibly short time, and killed I don't know how many post-horses, by which means he embarked for England, soon enough to see his father, and be with him a few hours before he died; and this was the only time in his life he was where he ought to be. After Sir Reginald's death his character took quite a new turn. He became gloomy, fond of solitude, and shut himself up like a prisoner, in Moss-cliff Abbey. Many strange stories were circulated of his way of life there, and his reasons for this utter seclusion: I see in it nothing but the natural effect of an education such as he had received, and of his being the favourite son of such a woman as Lady Julia Melbourne. He was satiated with dissipation, before he had time to lay a foundation of solid acquirements, sufficient to make him play his part on the great theatre of the world with advantage and credit, and therefore, he shrunk from the duties his station required; and though equally unfit for solitude, sought it as a refuge which would conceal at once his incapacity and discontent.'

'What a character!' exclaimed Mrs. Melbourne, as she looked at her daughter with uneasiness; 'my aversion to see this man hourly increases.'

'Could I see him for you, mamma?' said Matilda, 'and save you this unpleasant conversation.'

'*You* see him, child! what do you know about business? and we meet upon nothing else.'

'I think I could learn to say any thing you wish,' replied the affectionate girl.

Mrs. Melbourne, considering that these were affairs, in which her daughter's interests were as intimately concerned as her own, and that it might be perhaps advantageous to her, to see and converse with a relation, whose countenance would be a protection, whose enmity a source of distress, as soon as she found herself alone, turned in her mind this offer, which she at length determined to accept; while / Matilda, on her part, from the extreme love she bore her mother, and her anxious desire to save her a moment's pain, exerted her attention so successfully to become mistress of a subject, till now altogether new to her, that she was as competent as Mrs. Melbourne to discuss it, and could descant without embarrassment on debts, arrears, and repairs, long before the arrival of the dreaded Sir Harold.

He was punctual to his appointment; and it was with a beating heart that Matilda, on hearing of his arrival, prepared to appear before him. How much was she surprised then, to see in this 'ruffian,' this gamester, this solitary and savage Sir Harold, a man of the most interesting appearance, and the mildest and most captivating address. The baronet was still young – but, in his anxious and grief-marked countenance, sickness or affliction seemed to have anticipated the effects of time. His person was graceful, but tall and slight in the extreme; it seemed to bend to every passing breeze. His features were at once, marked and elegant; his smile, of uncommon sweetness; and when the hectic of a moment lighted them up with that fine but fearful glow, which so surely announces the destroyer within, the exquisite perfection of their almost feminine beauty, irresistibly reminded her of what she now recollected to have often heard as the general remark, that he was the living image of the late celebrated and lovely Lady Julia Melbourne.

Sir Harold, on his part, could not behold, unmoved, the charms of the young relative, to whom he now for the first time was introduced: the mourning she still wore for the death of her father, only shewed to more advantage by its simplicity, the graceful proportions of her form; and when, in a voice, made tremulous by painful remembrance and present emotion, she apologised for her mother's absence, on the ground of her spirits being yet unequal for the discussion of the affairs on which they met, he thought he had never heard a sound so plaintive and / so sweet. He listened with the greatest attention to the detail she gave of the late Mr. Melbourne's embarrassments; but when she came to mention the composition she had for the present to propose, and the period that she required to be granted before the final settlement of his affairs, Sir Harold interrupted her, to beg she would not think him capable of taking advantage of Mrs. Melbourne's generosity and high sense of honour to urge claims which, if ever valid, were from that moment annulled. – That if he did not regret their existence, it was solely from the consideration that they had been the means of introducing him to a family, from whom he had been too long estranged. He spoke handsomely of the late Mr. Melbourne, and expressed a hope, when her spirits would admit it, that he might be allowed to assure his widow in person, of the esteem he had ever felt for her character. Delighted with goodness and consideration so unexpected, Matilda ventured now to indulge the pleasure, (unknown to those whose families have experienced no division) that arises from the acquisition of a relative, and the removal of a painful prejudice. There was an energy, yet an artless dignity, preserved in the expressions her gratitude suggested, that charmed and surprised Sir Harold.

When every thing had been settled in the manner best calculated for the accommodation and advantage of Mrs. Melbourne; when all that could be urged and suggested on the subject, had been urged and suggested over and over, he sat silent, yet still unwilling to rise; his eyes fixed on that enchanting countenance, and apparently waiting, in hopes that some observation might fall from those lips, that might afford him a pretext for a longer stay.

At length Matilda broke up the conference, saying, 'I think, sir, it is time my mother should be informed of the result of this conversation; believe me, she will feel your behaviour as I do – as' – She was / proceeding, – her cousin again interrupted her, said he had many more things to propose, which he should reserve for another interview; and assuming the privilege of a relation, slightly to kiss her hand, withdrew; leaving her filial heart rejoiced in the consciousness, that what had passed would be productive to her mother of a peace of mind, to which she had been lately a stranger.

When Sowerby heard of Sir Harold's visit to the house, he was anxious, but with no very benevolent curiosity, to be informed of the event; for, being one of those who would

'Rather chuse that "you" should die
Than his prediction prove a lie:'[16]

he had already disposed in his own mind what it should be; and abruptly accosted Matilda with – 'So, child, you found that young Melbourne very impracticable.'

'On the contrary,' said Mrs. Melbourne, 'he is all goodness; and I congratulate myself on having acquired a valuable relation.'

'Pressing and unreasonable in his demands, hey?'

'So far from it, he has behaved with all the kindness of a brother, the liberality of a friend.'

'Ay, ay,' continued Sowerby, following the train of his own reflections, 'a man of the world, a mere man of the world! You found him very harsh and unpleasant, Matilda, did you not?'

'My dear sir, you have formed a strange idea of my cousin's manners; to me they appear to have a softness, an excess of gentleness, bordering, if any thing, upon effeminacy – they are sometimes almost dejected; but for any thing like rudeness or want of feeling, it seems the most opposite to the character of Sir Harold Melbourne.'

'At least you will not deny me,' growled the censor, glaring on her with eyes, that, at this moment, much better answered to the expression he made use of, 'that he *looks* like a ruffian, as he is.'

Mrs. Melbourne, recollecting the description / her daughter had just been giving her, of the prepossessing, but too delicate appearance of Sir Harold, could hardly suppress a smile, while Matilda ventured to express her dissent.

'I can only say then,' (concluded Sowerby) 'that he must be possessed of a cursed deal of deceit and assurance, to contrive to appear so completely the reverse of what he really is.'

The recent visit had not been productive of less satisfaction to Sir Harold, than to his fair cousin. Never (in his opinion) had he beheld loveliness till now. Bred up with the same prejudices against Mr. Melbourne's part of the family, that they had been against his, he had understood that 'old Melbourne,' who was an oddity, had educated a little daughter to be his exact counterpart, and had accordingly fancied his young relative a compound of all that was ugly, affected, and disagreeable.

Some one, whom he had met with accidentally, mentioned her as pretty, which a little softened his judgment respecting her; but for such a union of beauty, dignity, and elegance, as had burst upon his sight, he was wholly unprepared; and it had accordingly produced an impression, at once made softer by repentance, and stronger by surprise.

'Your doctor's gown becomes you infinitely, my little Portia!'[17] said Mrs. Melbourne, delighted to be relieved from the load of anxiety with which she had expected this interview, 'but have a care Sir Harold does not fall in love with the doctor, if not with the doctor's clerk, and even be induced perhaps to offer him the ring.'

Matilda, blushing, denied with eagerness the imputation, and never would allow her mother, in the frequent ensuing visits of her cousin, to hint again of such a possibility.

Mrs. Melbourne, however, preserved her opinion, and observed with a secret delight, not perhaps the less lively because it *was* secret, the growing partiality / that was expressed in every look and action of Sir Harold. In one respect, his visits were rather inconvenient; during the day they were short, languid, and uninteresting; but, if he called late, his spirits, which rose towards night, rendered him equally capable of enlivening, and unwilling to relinquish such enchanting society. From him they understood that partly for pleasure, and partly in search of health, he had visited, and made some stay in the capitals of Spain and Portugal; the opposite coasts of Fez and Morocco had been objects of curiosity to him, and he had not omitted visiting the more classical scenes of France and Italy. He had a considerable talent, without fatiguing attention, of making the scenes he had passed through, contribute to the variety of conversation; at other times, leaving the plain track of description or narrative, he loved to seize upon some argument, the more fanciful or untenable the better; and building upon it his own superstructure, would indulge in a thousand imaginations, which amused by their oddity, and sometimes even by their very absurdity; but these were only occasional starts. He would frequently entertain Mrs. Melbourne with grave plans of the various improvements he meditated at the Rocks. These he always concluded with a sigh, and an implied wish that she would witness them. Suddenly these improvements, which were to take up years, seemed forgotten, and nothing so much captivated his fancy as the pleasures of travelling; then again every thing was deemed insipid, in comparison with the advantages of reading and learned retirement. While he alternately took up or dismissed these various ideas, with a rapidity and vivacity peculiarly his own, the excessive brightness and fire which flashed from his eyes, joined to his hectic uncertain colour, and emaciated appearance, strongly realised that idea, of a mind too active for the slight frame which enclosed it, that is conveyed in the French expression, 'la lame use le fourreau.'[18] But at times this / flash and animation would fly, his eye lost its lustre, and a look of unutterable, unexplained, helpless anguish, seemed to own that all subjects to him equally uninteresting, were only the resources of a spirit 'with itself at war;' which endeavoured, in the sportive windings of fancy, to wander from some stern reality that incessantly pursued it. Still he was pleasing, and even Sowerby, who had been the most prejudiced against him, soon became reconciled to his society.

It was remarked, that however agreeably engaged before, his spirits invariably drooped after twelve o'clock; yet did he always seem more desirous to prolong his stay, the less he became capable of contributing to the amusement of the party.

'This poor man,' Mrs. Melbourne one day observed to her daughter, 'always puts me in mind of Johnson, of whom it is related that when parting at night he used to exclaim 'you go to rest, but I to misery.'

To this, Matilda could not help assenting; particularly when she noticed the intreating look, which he sometimes cast at her mother, after the forbidden time, for one little half hour longer; and the artful manner in which he would steal out his watch, put it back, and then appeal to the ladies if it did not want a considerable time of their usual hour for retiring to rest.

Sir Harold, though he had not yet declared himself, in his every look and word so much evinced the lover, that even the modest Matilda could no longer misunderstand the nature of his attentions, or the cause of his visits; and Mrs. Melbourne, though she still referred her daughter to the ultimate decisions of her own heart, yet evidently shewed that this was a prospect which she viewed with more partial pleasure, than that of her union with Sowerby. In this there appeared nothing to which a reasonable objection could be made; here was youth, worth, and honour, united to fortune and consequence, / as high as her hopes could aspire to; this union would at once cement the friendship of two branches of a family, of equal though perhaps different merit, and restore Mrs. Melbourne, in a great measure, to the peace, the affluence, almost the very situation, she had lost.

This representation Matilda made very fairly to her own heart, and asked it, if every duty, every advantage, did not conspire to command her to accept Sir Harold; that heart still replied in the negative, without even deigning to assign any reason for so unconditional a refusal. Why am I lower and more wretched, she would ask herself, at the moment that rank and fortune once more seem to be offered to my view, than many hours in which I foresaw only indigence and obscurity? I think I perceive the reason; does not the firmness, the spirit, which we sometimes feel arise within us, to meet adversity, the sinking and dejection we experience at the moment of some offered pleasure or happiness, prove that the enjoyment is not suited to our nature, and that pain and suffering are its more congenial habits?

Matilda was mistaken; the prospect presented to her, no happiness; and could she have followed the emotions of her heart unreproved, she would have preferred the humblest lot with the freedom of choice, to wealth and splendour with Sir Harold; but to sacrifice the emotions of that heart to the happiness of one, who was dearer to her than life itself, was now become her first principle. An accidental communication, however, soon made her consider her present entanglement in a different and more alarming point of view. /

CHAPTER VI.

Maiden, a nameless life I lead,
A nameless death I'll die:
The fiend whose lanthorn lights the mead
Were better mate than I.

Scott. – Rokeby.[19]

'Sir Harold stays very late, ma'am,' said old Hanway, one day, as she was dressing her lady, or rather standing, with her arms across, seeing her lady dress.

Mrs. Melbourne, who always liked this freedom of conversation in an old and worthy domestic, whom she now considered much more in the light of a friend, replied with good-humour to her remark, which encouraged her to add, – 'To be sure I'm angry with people in common for keeping up the house so late; but I think nothing of sitting up for Sir Harold, because he's a relation – and because,' she added, with a significant wink, 'it's easy to see what he comes for. Well, I hope he'll make the poor child happy,' she continued, looking with an expression of fondness and anxiety at Matilda, 'I hope he'll make her happy!'

'And why should you doubt it, Hanway?' said Mrs. Melbourne, not quite pleased with the manner in which her words were accented.

'Oh, no reason, ma'am – only Mr. Franklin, his man, *does* say he is a comical gentleman.'

'How! – comical? You must explain yourself.'

Here Hanway took a fit of wonderful discretion; but at length she was brought to own that it was said he did a number of comical things on going to take possession of the Rocks. 'You know, ma'am,' (Hanway's usual way of telling her mistress every thing she did not know) 'he sent most of his servants away before he left the Abbey; and writ to Anstey to hire new ones at the Rocks, so that they was all ready to receive him. / He arrived there himself at eleven o'clock at night, and then – Mr. Franklin says this, not I – he went directly down stairs, made a terrible to-do, abused the butler, beat the cook, and knocked the plates and dishes about their heads, and all for not having his dinner ready for him, he said. – "Lord, sir," says she, "your honour should have given orders, if you meant to have dinner at this hour of the night." However they began laying the cloth in the great parlour, when his honour threw the knives and table-cloth on the floor, and asked them how they could think of having it in such a place. – "Why where would you please to have it, sir?" said the footman. – "At the top of that rock, to be sure," said his honour; and leading the way through the grounds, he

– 208 –

clambered up to the top of one of the highest crags as nimble as a squirrel, and there stood triumphing over 'em like as if he had said – "Here am I above you all." But soon not liking such a dark, dismal place, as I take it, he ordered the dinner all back again into the parlour, and began eating, as hungry as you please. He did so; but the minute the clock struck twelve he dropped down in a sort of fit; and then, when he recovered, he says, – "Carry me away; I can't stay here," and so locked himself up in his own room, and a quiet house they had of it till morning. Well then, very early, they heard a kind of rustling and tumbling things about. This was their master running up and down stairs, and into the rooms, and looking at every thing very curious like; and then he called to him William Anstey, the old steward, that he had said he would keep on at the Rocks. – "William Anstey," says he, "you need not say any thing of my little fit last night; and now I want to see Mr. Melbourne's collection, that I ordered to be purchased for me, and the museum." – And so he looked very earnest at the stuffed beasts, and then at the birds, and afterwards opened their glass cases, – "Fly away," says he; "I give you liberty." / Then he began for to sigh piteously, and to add, – "Oh that I had the wings of a dove, and could fly away like you! but I am confined," says he, "confined to one stated round," I think he said. Then, when he went to the real birdery, where the birds from foreign parts were singing and hopping about, all alive, pretty creatures! – "William," he says, "I won't have all this waste; for you see this quantity of grains and seeds you buy for these animals, which is no use, for they're all stuffed." – "Lord bless you, sir!" cries the steward, "these an't stuffed, but as pretty little live things as your eye would wish to see." – "Are they so?" says Sir Harold, "then have a couple of them roasted for my supper."'

'Well, and what more?' said Matilda, perceiving that Hanway had stopped, feeling the symptoms approaching of another fit of discretion. It was with some difficulty she was persuaded to open her mouth again, and then she began with sundry wise observations that 'Parsons said many more things, Heaven knows, than was true,' and that "twould be better if they made it a rule to hear, see, and say nothing;' but soon proceeding with that increased rapidity which is observed in a carriage the moment the drag is taken off and it gets on level ground again, she continued, – 'they say he did still comicaler things on coming up to London. When he was to go to court, on coming to his estate, his man could not get him to put on any thing but an old shabby blue coat, and strings in his shoes. However, next Sunday he went to church in a very fine coat indeed, with diamond buttons, and said he'd no notion of being finer in the presence of a temporal king, than in that of the eternal King of the whole world. But he is a very good-natured gentleman, and a very generous gentleman, Mr. Franklin says; and so charitable that he gives to every beggar he sees; and if he meets with a poor little boy, idling, or cursing and swearing, and seeming neglected like, / he orders him to be sent home and fed and clothed at his own expense, and sends him to school.'

'Well, Hanway, that's no harm at least,' observed Mrs. Melbourne.

'No, to be sure, ma'am, no harm but good. I wou'dn't say any harm of Sir Harold for the world; though he did make me laugh, going one day to the blacksmith's, and ordering home dozens of ices; then, when he went to the confectioner's, he desired him to make him a saddle, and such like whimsies; but to be sure, a fine young gentleman, with a fine estate, does not come every day now-a-days; and he may be very wise and clever, and that, for all he's a little odd at times.'

Matilda was surprised she had not remarked, before, any great singularity in Sir Harold's general manner and conversation. She certainly remembered having once noticed the strangeness of his reply, to an observation she made, upon his telling her that he had gone one campaign with the army. She said he must have suffered great privations. – 'No,' he answered, 'it was amusing – very amusing.' But on mentioning a *fête* to which he had been invited, he remarked he should not go – for that the labour and exertion would be intolerable. These, however, might be mere singularities of expression, not very uncommon, but the account she now received, excited the most serious apprehensions.

'Whatever appearance this narration may give, of his suffering under some enation of mind,' said Mrs. Melbourne, 'as it is a misfortune from which I am certain your family is free, I am willing to believe there may be some exaggeration in these accounts; but fear nothing, my love,' she continued, observing the alarm expressed in Matilda's looks, 'Sir Harold may labour under some individual affection; and it is a point on which I would obtain the clearest satisfaction, before I would trust the welfare and safety of my child, to a man who perhaps cannot / answer a moment for his own. But how clear up the doubt?'

Mrs. Melbourne proposed that, as even considering him only as a relation, they must be interested in his behalf, Matilda should write to Lady Torrendale and Miss Ferrars, who both lived near his new abode; and mention, incidentally, the present possessor of the Rocks; which, as the newest topic, would no doubt draw out every particular that was known, concerning his character and conduct.

Matilda felt a repugnance to this step; she had written once already to Lady Torrendale, briefly informing her of her late misfortunes, and altered situation. She had received no answer; and was unwilling by another, perhaps, equally unsuccessful, attempt, to verify the fears which, from some expressions that had escaped her mother, she had been lately led to adopt. From Arbella she had less to apprehend; that young lady had already written her two letters, filled with expressions of her warm, though rather inconsiderate sympathy; to her, therefore, she first addressed herself; and then resolved, in this as in every other case, to yield up her will and wishes to those of her mother. She once more wrote to the Countess of Torrendale, and determined to wait patiently, or at least as patiently as she could, the event.

'No post to-day!' These were the words which Matilda was obliged to repeat morning after morning to Mrs. Melbourne; and which, as confirming her fears of the indifference of her late friends, struck still colder on that lady's heart, than on that of her daughter.

It has been observed that country correspondents often complain of the neglect of their friends in town, but that town friends never make the same reproach to those they have left in the country; surely this remark is not meant to apply, when the people in the country happen to be possessed of fortune or consequence, and those in town are blessed with neither. /

At length, on the same day, two packets arrived; they were from Lady Torrendale and Miss Ferrars. Matilda resolved that, on this occasion, tried kindness should have the precedence of rank, and first opened that of Arbella. The account it gave of Sir Harold exactly agreed with Hanway's statement, and even added particulars illustrative of still greater extravagancies; but the conclusion of the letter was what most surprised and affected Matilda. Much as she had avoided to hint that they now suffered any material inconvenience by their change of circumstances, enough had been discovered, by the penetration of the delicate and generous Arbella, to convince her that her friend's present situation was far from what she wished it. She inclosed a draft upon her banker, for five hundred pounds, which she entreated her to accept for her own and her mother's use; adding, that though they might have no real necessity for such a sum, upon the final arrangement of their affairs, there was always at first, upon any change in a family, debts and demands to satisfy that were unexpected, and that might make a small supply of ready money at the time more grateful than a much larger one at a future period. She observed in conclusion, lest her dear Matilda should imagine she had put her to any inconvenience, that it was a nothing, a mere windfall, to which she had herself no positive right, as it was the produce of a little sum which her cousin, 'pretty Sam,' as she often jocosely termed him, had turned for her in the stocks; and happening to be fortunate, had thought to surprise her with its amount as an agreeable birth-day present.

Miss Melbourne well knew how to appreciate the consideration that led her friend to enter into these details; and the manner in which this accommodation was offered, (for she secretly determined it should be no more than a temporary accommodation) constituted by far its greatest value. /

The letter from Lady Torrendale we shall transcribe, not so much for the intrinsic value of the matter it contained, as from its affording a good specimen of her ladyship's manner, and the qualifications she possessed for epistolary excellence.

CRESCENT, BUXTON.

'The accounts I received of my dear Miss Melbourne's sufferings, during the period that has intervened since I had last the pleasure of her society, have penetrated me with the sincerest and most poignant regret; I make no doubt, however, that she will experience relief, from that spirit of contentment and resignation, which renders even the greatest distresses perfectly easy to be endured.

I trust my dear Matilda has long ere this attributed my silence, not to unkindness, but to its true cause, illness; the most distressing, complicated, and severe. I was first seized with a nervous sickness, lassitude, and giddiness in my head, which deprived me of the power of attention, and rendered all employment impossible; an affection in my eyes attacked me at the same time, which made them wander, see every thing in a wrong light, and be perfectly incapable of fixing upon a book. Then, I was tormented with little floating specks perpetually dancing before me; and then these little floating specks were changed into diamonds; and these squares or diamonds again, into little fantastic figures, green, blue, and yellow; with a thousand other nervous appearances, indescribable and insupportable. I had an universal tremor, and a noise in my head; sometimes of people whispering, sometimes of drums and trumpets sounding, sometimes again of carriages rolling, or knocks at the door, so as to be entirely deprived of rest.

Just as I began to get the better of these dreadful symptoms, I accidentally / sprained my ancle, waltzing with that excessively handsome young Irishman Lord Kilcare, and this accident, by confining me for some time to my couch, completed the ruin of my health. I was advised to have hot water pumped upon my foot, and afterwards to try the hot springs of Matlock and Buxton; but as neither succeeded, Bath was recommended. It is my native place; and I am sure, were Lord Torrendale a man of the slightest humanity, he would consent to my going there; but he has the cruelty to urge, that, because my mind can be amused by gaiety and conversation, application, (its destruction) would be its best cure; and that, if I cannot walk, neither could I dance at those balls, which he foolishly supposes would be my great attraction to that spot: but I believe no woman has suffered in silence so intensely, and with so little pity as I have.

Lord Torrendale himself has been ill; and poor little Floss, whom you remember, has had two attacks of his old complaint. I must give you the symptoms: the first time I believe he caught cold, by running out too hastily to see a friend, just after he had been washed; he coughed twice during the night, but towards morning had a sound sleep, and seemed better: the next time he was more seriously ill; he alternately barked and coughed during the whole night, with several symptoms of high fever; which altogether made me so nervous, that I have had another attack, worse than the first, accompanied with sinkings, tears, hysterical terrors, and the most dreadful palpitations of the heart. But a truce with this unpleasant topic; you know how I detest complaining.

Buxton is very full, and we have some really fashionable people; they wear the dresses still tighter than ever in the morning, and in the evening it is quite indecent to have any clothes on; trains are shortening considerably, but a drapery may relieve the scantiness of / the general effect. I give these hints to you, Matilda, because from recent circumstances you might be less attentive to the changes in fashion.

The balls answer very well. Old Lady Kilcare, "of the hundred petticoats," (to apply the phraseology of Strathallan's favourite poet) looking as frightfully, dancing as furiously, and making as great a noise with her heels, as ever.

Arbella (mind I don't reckon her among the fashionables) is here; her present favourite, a Major O'Hara, a handsome, dashing Irishman, pleasant, easy, insinuating, like most of his countrymen; but sometimes, I think, deficient in the first polish of good breeding; and most shamefully erroneous in his taste as to female beauty: she bores me to death to *chaperon* her to some fine places; where Mrs. Stockwell, (poor silly soul! though she durst not shew her face), is ambitious her niece should appear. I am unwilling to seem an accomplice; yet I really believe I would go with her to Lord Sommerton's breakfast, if I had a dress to my mind.

By the by, Matilda, you promised to paint me a trimming like one of yours, which I admired prodigiously; if you could do it for me this *fête*, and send it down immediately, I should be greatly obliged to you; I cannot remember the pattern, or any thing about it, but that it *was* a trimming; but I dare say you will find it out – somehow.

Your letter contained several questions which I would gladly answer, but I am nearly arrived at the end of my paper. Your present situation, and the attention required by Mrs. Melbourne, (to whom Lord Torrendale and I desire to be remembered) will, I doubt not, prevent your being able to bestow so much of your time upon your friends as you formerly did. Should you, however, upon our return to town, be able to spare half an hour to Fitzroy-square, I shall always be happy to assure my / dear Miss Melbourne personally, how much I am, with the sincerest regard, Her most faithful friend, and humble servant,

'LAURA TORRENDALE.'

'P.S. I now recollect what the trimming was. It had peacock's feathers and roses in it; and I should be obliged to you, in copying it for me, to put a few more touches of gold upon the spot at the tip of the peacock's feather; and to make the green *un peu plus prononcé.*'[20]

'Here are the letters of the fine lady and her butt,' said Mrs. Melbourne, as she returned them to Matilda. 'Consider at least, my love,' she continued, answering the silent tear, that involuntarily started to her daughter's eye, 'the same change of circumstances, that has shewn us the hollowness of one friend, has developed in another those excellent qualities which, in the hour of prosperity, some trifling foibles obscured.'

The tears that she observed, had a deeper source, than this tender, watchful parent imagined. Reason can console the heart for those, that disappointed friendship bids it shed; but love alone can dry the tear, that love has commanded to flow.

On the first perusal of the letter, when the name of Strathallan had struck Matilda's eye, she had eagerly passed on to what followed, in hopes at least to receive some proof of interest and remembrance; to hear from himself of *his* health and welfare, for whose sake she had sacrificed her own. How great her disappointment then, to find that name mentioned only in association with a ludicrous and flippant parody! Through the day she endeavoured to reason herself into composure, but in vain. Every re-perusal increased her dissatisfaction. 'I desired him to forget me,' she said, 'but I did not think he could do it so soon and so completely. I judged of him by myself, and erred, in / making him an exception to all his sex, when I supposed him possessed of sensibility equal to my own: yet, was this the moment, Strathallan, to shew the self-command, with which you could banish *her* from your thoughts, who, you once declared, formed their most delightful occupation? Would one little word, one expression of kindness bestowed on me, have been too much? Should you, too, be found among the proud, the selfish, and the unfeeling? Should you, too, join to press down to the earth, a creature already bowed with calamity, by the additional weight of scorned, insulted love? But am I not unjust? – Surrounded by pleasure and prosperity, how can you spare a thought to Matilda? The world and fortune love you even as I do; and I, who behold them under their unkindest aspect, would trouble your enjoyment, by clinging to your felicity; but in vain – fear me not – for I am miserable, and misery cannot approach you. It is changed, at your presence, into joy. Joy, calm, pure, delightful, joy, such as I once have known, surrounds you, speaks in each gentle glance, and overflows from that blest countenance, all graciousness and love. How many, adorned with every advantage that beauty, wealth, and rank, can give, are at this moment disputing the empire of that heart. But it is vowed away, and may its choice be happy!'

Her tears flowed as she spoke, in involuntary and bitter regret; the more bitter, because involuntary. She had hardly wiped them away when she was startled by the unexpected entrance of Sir Harold Melbourne. 'Has any thing disturbed you? You seem ill, my lovely cousin,' he said. Matilda, recovering herself, in some confusion replied, that she was perfectly well. 'Forgive me then,' he said, 'and attribute it to my anxious tenderness, if the least change in your appearance excites my alarm.' Then gazing on her with an earnestness, at which her modest eyes were cast upon the ground, 'How / lovely is virtue,' he cried, 'when thus enshrined in beauty's mould! Oh, my fair cousin! was it nature, was it passion, that drew my heart towards you, the first moment I beheld you, with a sweet but imperious force? – I regretted the past, I lived but in the present. – I will not say I experienced happiness, – that is extinguished in my bosom; but at that mild, yet radiant aspect, my joyless deserted heart was awakened to the remembrance of the existence of such a sentiment. It started once more to the recollection of what constituted its charm. Can I do less than make an offering to you of those feelings, which you alone could revive? Oh love, I thought I had known thy power! – beauty I had seen before – but never till now did beauty arrayed in its most resistless force, in all its gentle, innocent, yet awful, pride, thus come upon my unprepared heart, commanding it in that voice which the world obeys, to yield up its every wish to her direction, its peace to her control, its very existence to a word. – Will you speak that word, fair cousin?'

Matilda looked up. She was assailed by professions of passion, of devotion the most ardent – professions to which perhaps the romantic wildness of the language in which they were conveyed, added a persuasive charm, at the moment that her feelings, outraged where they had loved and trusted most sincerely, – felt at once the ties of friendship broken, and every tenderer recollection converted to bitterness and regret. She opposed the disinterested, generous love of Sir Harold, to the coldness, the silence, of the proud Strathallan. She paused a moment – but did she hesitate? No; love, that refuses to allow any merit to her decision, dictated that constancy, which in vain aspired to be called a sacrifice, since she must be inconstant to herself, ere she could admit the idea of existing for another than Strathallan. yet that passion, which was deaf alike to the voice of interest / or resentment, must have yielded to that of duty, if the fatal objection which every word and action seemed now to confirm, had not determined her reply.

With a tenderness which she alone possessed, to soften refusal, yet at the same time extinguish hope, she professed the gratitude she should ever retain for the proofs she had received of her cousin's friendship; while she declared, that her heart had been too recently and repeatedly attacked by sorrow, to allow her to repay it with that warm affection which preference so flattering deserved.

'I hardly hope it, my lovely cousin; merit like yours can be won only by the noblest heart, not by one lost, like mine; – yet where could you find one, that would more earnestly endeavour to repay the sacrifice you made? Do you ask love? Behold me at your bidding, the creature of your will. – Would you be worshipped as some fair being, above this wretched scene? See me devoted, ready to sacrifice at your shrine!'

Alarmed by an increasing wildness and earnestness of manner, which justified her most distressing apprehensions, Matilda continued only more firm in her denial. 'I see the truth!' cried Sir Harold, his countenance suddenly changing from an expression of touching dejection, to the most furious violence, 'it is love, not grief, that keeps you from me.' – 'Oh no, no, believe it not,' exclaimed Matilda, while a fear too horrible to acknowledge, thrilled her breast with insupportable anxiety, 'there is not a being on earth whom I prefer – there is not a being in whom the interest I take – believe me, I conjure you,' she continued, interrupting herself, and scarce knowing what she said from the excess of her alarm.

'I am satisfied,' he replied, with resumed calmness, 'and after the assertion you have made, there is one slight favour, which I am sure you will not refuse me.' Sir Harold was drest for court; he had his / sword on, and he now put his hand to it. Terrified by this action, Matilda hastily ran towards the door; he bade her not be uneasy, for he had locked it. She then attempted to reach the bell; but her cousin placed himself between her and it, and completely drawing his sword, told her she was safe only on condition that she did not cry out, and placing a chair for her, he begged, and at length forced her to be seated. Then with one hand waving the sword over her head, with the other he took hers, and intreated her to hear him.

'Oh spare my life!' cried Matilda, kneeling to him. 'Compose yourself, my pretty cousin,' he said, raising her, 'why should you imagine I desired to harm you?' Then having reseated her, and observing the terror expressed in her eyes, 'What is the matter with you,' he continued, 'can you not sit quiet? Did you never sit with a sword over your head before?' – 'Kill me at once,' she exclaimed, 'but keep me no longer in this distracting state.' 'Do not be afraid, what harm can a sword do you at this distance? I intend you no harm – at least not if I know myself,' he added, putting his hand to his head. 'There – with your weakness – your woman's fears, you had nearly made me forget the purpose of all I had done; – it was only to make you swear upon this sword, that since my suit was rejected, you would never admit that of any other.'

Even in this moment of agitation and alarm, Matilda felt the consequences of an engagement so rashly taken, and with a firmness and fortitude little to be expected at her age, and still less in her present situation, she refused to comply; and endeavoured, by every argument she could devise, to make her unfortunate cousin alter his resolution. 'Take your choice!' he said, alternately presenting the sword before her eyes, and raising it above her head; 'we are alone. No mortal can hinder me from putting an end to your life. If you call out for help / you are lost. Swear or die!' At length Matilda, bursting into tears, knelt before the sword, and took the oath required.

'You are now free,' said Sir Harold, 'but remember,' he continued, turning with added solemnity to his trembling victim, who had sunk, almost inanimate, to the ground, 'if you fail in your engagement, not yours, but the life-blood that is dearer to your heart, shall flow to revenge the perfidy.'

Matilda opened her eyes, while a convulsive shudder alone showed, that though scarcely conscious of the words he had uttered, she felt they were of dreadful import. Sir Harold ran to the window, threw up the sash, and flinging open the door, in order to give more air to his fainting cousin, left her to recover, if possible, from the effects of this truly dreadful interview, and quitted the house, resolving no longer to delay his intended return to the Rocks.

CHAPTER VII.

Envy will merit, like its shade, pursue;
And, like the shadow, proves the substance true.

Pope.[21]

'When from Southampton's or from Brighton's shore,
Which charmed when London's revelry was o'er,
The fading beauty of autumnal hours,
Recalls the sportsman to his native bowers.'[22]

LADY Torrendale, who perceived she must reconcile herself to the thoughts of spending another Christmas in the country, found the constraint rendered more tolerable by the return of her London friends, who flocked around her with a vast importation of fresh fashions, fresh compliments, fresh news, and fresh scandal, particularly about the recent events, that had happened in the family of the Melbournes.

Had Matilda been concealed behind a curtain, and enabled to listen to all that / passed, she would not perhaps have been much flattered by the various opinions expressed of her, among the circle of which she had been so late the happy idol. But sentiments were changed at the residence, and it was no longer necessary to conceal the offence which her unequalled, though unassuming merit, had given.

Lady Lyndhurst, who hated her superiority, because she herself made pretensions to talent; her daughter, Miss de Courcy, who hated her, because too indolent to aspire to similar distinctions; Miss Langrish, who envied Matilda for the attention excited by her beauty; and Miss Hautenville, who envied her for exciting attention at all, now spoke their sentiments, unrestrained by the fear of giving pain to the mistress of the house, or of incurring the reproach of singularity. The conversation happening to take place shortly after the re-appearance of Sir Harold Melbourne at the Rocks, 'I think,' Alcæus the poet began, 'that we shall not be much benefited by our new neighbour. He is the most singular being; sometimes he is seen sitting for whole hours at the top of a rock, solitary and fantastic as an ape; sometimes bounding from cliff to cliff, with the agility of a monkey; or passing the day in some thick wood, without taking any refreshment, but for the attention of his servants, who know his haunts, and where to follow him on those occasions. So that on the whole, if we have lost old Sidrophel, he has at least provided a worthy successor.'

'All the Melbournes are oddities,' said Lady Lyndhurst. 'I have heard that after all Mr. Melbourne died in great-difficulties, and left his family in distress.'

'Poor man! what a pity! I always said it would come to that!' was echoed around the room, though why it was to 'come to that,' but for the unfortunate accident which overwhelmed a part of Mr. Melbourne's fortune, no mortal could divine. While some made a faint attempt to commiserate their former friends, for the reverses they had experienced, others / calling philosophy to their aid, concluded that it was useless to deplore what was inevitable: but, however divided opinions were, on the subject of their other misfortunes, it was universally agreed, that after all Mr. Melbourne had endured, his death was rather to be considered 'as a release;' that easy word, by which the world endeavours to disguise the more than cold indifference, the impatience, too often inspired by long protracted suffering; ignorant or unheedful of the nature of true affection, which clings fondly to the wreck, however faded and decayed, of what it long has loved; and dreads nothing so much as the cessation of those mournful duties, at once its pleasure and its pain.

Lady Lyndhurst, who thought it proper to affect a degree of sensibility, asked the Countess, with an appearance of becoming interest, if she had lately heard of Miss Melbourne: 'I am quite in pain about her,' she said; 'brought up with such different expectations, what do you think is now to become of her; is she to marry her cousin?'

'Positively I make it a rule to think of it as little as possible,' replied Lady Torrendale. 'Dwelling upon unpleasant subjects affects one's self disagreeably, and can do one's friends no possible good.'

'I subscribe to that,' cried Alcæus, as her ladyship uttered this praiseworthy maxim, with that self-approving not with which she generally laid down the law. 'Besides that, really to call one's friends to mind, after they have suffered some little change in their situation, requires something of Mr. Professor Feinagle's assistance.'

'Miss Melbourne had better have played her cards with a little more attention, when she was in fashion,' observed Miss Hautenville, 'for she will not find it now so easy to secure an establishment.'

'Oh!' said Arbella Ferrars giddily, 'young ladies of twenty have always / time enough to think of whom they will have; it is only young ladies of thirty, who need begin to think who will have them.'

Miss Hautenville made no reply – but she treasured this remark among the various misdemeanors of the imprudent Arbella, for which she hoped at some future period, a full and perfect revenge.

'I have it,' cried Alcæus; 'she will now marry old Sowerby, and glad enough to get him. How very attentive he used to be, teaching her all sort of things, and catching her butterflies' –

'Mr. Sowerby catching butterflies!' The laugh that was led by Lady Torrendale, was echoed by the whole company.

'I don't mean running after them,' resumed the poet a little disconcerted, 'but he had a way of catching them, sitting quite still in his study, by alluring them to some viscous matter, and preserving them, and – I can't explain it better, may I be shot; but I have seen whole folios of preserved butterflies, and dried sea-weeds, that he collected for her when he was at Swansea – and I am sure now they will make a match of it.'

'Impossible! You do not think Miss Melbourne would so little consult her heart, though you pretend to do so, Mr. Spring,' said his fair enemy, Sappho.

'Upon my honour I do; I think she is. . . .' said Miss Langrish, looking in Lady Torrendale's eyes to discover, before she ventured to proceed, what she was; but as the expression of that lady's countenance was very dubious, she thought it most prudent to drop the sentence unfinished.

'Depend upon it,' said Helen de Courcy, 'he will not marry her; those very clever women are the gentlemen's aversion.'

'True, Miss de Courcy,' observed Sappho mournfully, 'men of sense discourage and despise them; while others hate and fear them. The reputation of genius carries such a disadvantage along with it, that one would almost imagine it had some super-natural power of depriving / the woman of all personal attractions who possessed it.'

'I wish for my part,' said Alcæus, looking maliciously at Sappho, 'that because the prejudice is supposed to run, that every woman of genius is ugly, every ugly woman would not, by an inverted rule, fancy herself a woman of genius.'

'You must surely mistake,' cried Lady Lyndhurst, 'no woman ever became less charming by the cultivation of her mental powers; it is to Miss Melbourne's extreme giddiness, affectation, and coquetry, that we are to look for her failure; not to her pretensions to ability or knowledge.'

'Pretensions your ladyship justly denominates them,' replied Miss Hautenville, grinning a ghastly smile, 'for as to their solidity, it was very dubious. She boasted much of her father's instructions; but what could *she* possess of knowledge in natural philosophy, for instance, who had never read the Loves of the Plants? and was igno-rant even of Buffon, except such passages as papa selected?'[23]

'Oh, there you do her injustice, I doubt not,' resumed the wit Alcæus: 'trust me, Miss Hautenville, your young friend was better acquainted with the French philoso-pher, than either her papa, or her still dearer tutor, supposed. A forbidden study is always the sweetest; and the Italian inscription for the violet, *Nascosta ma dolce,*[24] might, I doubt not, have been chosen very appropriately by Miss Melbourne, for her "*devise.*"'[25]

Arbella, indignant, was again going to speak, when the entrance of Lord Strathal-lan and Major O'Hara diverted the attention from her. The gay, the handsome, Major O'Hara, though now her professed admirer, could hardly obtain a word or a look from her, while, eager in the cause of friendship, she was only vexed at the interrup-tion occasioned by his presence. Not so the rest of the ladies, who anxiously applied to him, as the umpire to decide their dispute.

'Oh, major, you are just come in time,' said Lady Torrendale, 'we have been dis-cussing / Miss Melbourne's fortune – have you any *sortes Virgilianæ*[26] to determine it? With us nothing has yet come up but Mr. Sowerby.'

'For Matilda Melbourne! Oh, by all that's beautiful, that is a little too bad. I cer-tainly cannot pretend to be better informed than Lady Torrendale, but I will tell you what, when I was last in town, was generally believed.' The major then began with the air of one who was accustomed to an admiring auditory; 'The story, that generally prevailed in the world, that is to say, in a certain circle, was, that her cousin Melbourne had fallen suddenly and passionately in love with her, and the way of it was this: Old

Melbourne had some debts, which his heir, Sir Harold, who is a very good fellow, was in a much greater hurry to claim; than his widow was to pay. So she arranged it that he should have an interview with her daughter instead of herself.

'Miss Melbourne met him, still in mourning for her father, and looking most interestingly beautiful. She was at first all tears, timidity, and sensibility; he all attention, politeness, and compliance. In short, he was by far too much *épris*[27] to think of demanding his debt; and, contrary to the usual course, they were given to each other by mutual engagement; even before the world, so apt to be liberal in those cases, had thought on whom to bestow them: a promise passed between them, which only waits to be ratified when Sir Harold returns from the Rocks, where he is at present to adjust some final arrangements. The equipages are ordered – the dresses ready for inspection, at Madame R – 's – and Mrs. Melbourne is complimented by all her acquaintance as she ought to be, for a devilish clever woman.'

Lady Torrendale gave Strathallan a look which seemed to say, 'There – I said it was so!'

'And pray, major,' said his lordship, turning to O'Hara, 'what is your authority for that report!' /

'My authority! Oh, faith, my lord, you must ask half the world for that; I only repeat what others say; and yet I believe I am pretty correct too; and by Jove, I don't see how she could do better. It is plain he thought of her from the first, by his complimenting the family in purchasing all the collections. For what use upon earth could they be to him? It was a great loss to the public though: the sale would have been such an excellent lounge. I was told I should see more curiosities than ever were collected together, since Sir Ashton Lever's museum was sold.'[28]

'Or Nicholas Gimcrack's,' said Alcæus.

'I never was at that,' replied the major, 'but I really did think of the disappointment of Lord N –, or the Marquis of D –, and some of those gentlemen with the bibliomania, when I heard of the books and manuscripts. Such a feast of black letter, and illuminated scrolls as they would have had: the loss was less to me, who never admire any page so much as that which a pair of lovely eyes illumines,' bowing politely to the ladies. While the major paused to receive that applause, which his eloquence, or his fine teeth, could always command, and Miss Langrish whispered 'what a complete ladies' man he was,' Alcæus, who thought this a good opportunity for what he called a little quiz upon Lord Strathallan, resumed, 'No, no, trust me, major, you are all in the wrong; quite out, my dear fellow; you may depend upon it, Miss Melbourne will marry no Sir Harold. She will bring forward those bright talents, that astonished us all, upon the stage. 'Tis the only way now, and my life for it,' glancing maliciously at Strathallan, 'a coronet will, in less than a season, replace her pasteboard crown.'

'Excuse me, Mr. Spring,' said Miss Hautenville, 'universal as were Miss Melbourne's talents, it is not likely she / could have learnt much of the business of the stage at the Rocks, with old Prospero, who lived there like a wizard in his cave.'

'If you style Mr. Melbourne Prospero,' observed Sappho, 'you must at least allow the sweet, innocent, Matilda to have been his Miranda.'

'And we need not look far for a Ferdinand,' continued Alcæus, again glancing at Lord Strathallan.

'And if ever there was a Caliban,' cried the major, 'it was that Sow – Sow – Sow – '

'Sowerby,' said Miss Langrish.

'Well, Sowerby might perhaps be the name. He encouraged old Melbourne in all his singularities, and taught him to make such an anchorite of himself. Why, think of his having three companies of our fellows quartered within a mile of him for a summer, and never inviting one of them within his doors – and where would have been the great favour, pray, if he had given them a dinner once a month, once a week, ay, or every day in the week? Who'd have thanked him if he had?' continued O'Hara triumphantly, 'I say, who the devil would have thanked him?'

'If no one would have thanked him – ' interrupted Alcæus, with a pertness perhaps more allowable than usual, 'I think Mr. Melbourne was not so much to blame, in keeping his good dinners to himself.'

'I had once the honour of a *rencontre* with that Squire Sowerby,' resumed the major, turning from the poet with the most sovereign contempt; 'and though it originated in a mistake, I think he might have conducted himself with more respect. I understood that when Mr. Melbourne was out, one might see the collections and walk over the house. So one day as I was on horseback, reconnoitering the country a little – happening to pop upon it rather suddenly – purely *par hazard*[29] I give you my honour; I thought I'd just ask the question, and I called out to this Sowerby, or whatever / his name is, whom I mistook for one of Melbourne's people, to know if I could get admittance; he made me no answer at first, till I, (recollecting he might possibly be the old fellow who helped Mr. Melbourne to stuff his birds and preserve plants and shells,) asked him more civilly if he would be my Cicerone. He looked at me for a minute, as if he wondered how I had contrived to get within sight of the mansion, and then, putting on a more forbidding countenance than he had got already, he said, I must be misinformed, for the curiosities were never to be seen; and at any rate, the ladies of the family were, at that very moment, drinking tea in one of those apartments.'

'Well, major, and what did you answer to that very civil repulse, after your very accidental wandering through the *only pass* to the Rocks?' interrupted Alcæus maliciously.

'I answered,' replied O'Hara, addressing himself to the countess, 'that it was never my intention, nor was it often my misfortune to displease ladies; but as to himself, whom I presumed by his appearance to be some domestic of the family, (I knew by this time who the cunning old fox was perfectly,) I begged to know by what right he kept sole guard over fine women, as he would over a preserved pheasantry. He said, still more sulkily, that he was no servant, but a friend of the family, and muttered something about taking offence without cause. I said, he had his redress – that if any thing I had said gave him offence, I was easily to be found; my card was at his service; my name was major O'Hara – and I was ready, at any time he should call upon me, to give him whatever satisfaction he might require. Rode off; and never heard more of Mr. Squire Sowerby from that time to this.'

'Oh, he was afraid for Matilda,' said Alcæus, 'he kept watch over her like a dragon. I heard he used to make her study astronomy with him night after night, like the lady Pekuah.[30] But it / didn't do. Did he think she was to stay with him for ever, counting the satellites of Jupiter, or watching for the star Benemasch, in the tail of the great bear? He was educating her,' continued the poet, 'as a little learned wife for himself. She knew the whole theory of comets, from Aristotle to Tycho Brahe – [31] and before she left this could as well describe one of their transits – '

'And when she left this, it was a transit of Venus by Jove!' interrupted O'Hara.

The poet cast on him a look of scornful reproach. Miss De Courcy bit her lip: 'Miss Melbourne was certainly pretty,' said she, 'it was a pity she was so very affected' – 'Yet so ignorant,' cried Miss Hautenville. 'And so confident,' added Miss Langrish. 'Oh no, deucedly awkward and bashful,' said Alcæus.

'Really now, you have been all too hard upon the poor young thing!' exclaimed Mrs. Stockwell, rolling her eyes, and drawling in her whining tone of affected commiseration. 'Though she is not, to be sure, of the consequence she have been – and though she has not as many advantages as you, Arbella, for instance, (don't look so cross at the major, you know he's a field-officer, love) yet still she is a gentlewoman – and birth is every thing as I say – I am sure my grandfather the general – ' 'I thought he was an archbishop,' interrupted Alcæus. 'So he was!' resumed Mrs. Stockwell, thankfully accepting the correction, 'he was an archbishop.'

'My dear Mrs. Stockwell,' cried Sappho, (who thought her good nature deserved that she should help her out of this difficulty,) 'I agree with you perfectly in the opinion you have expressed of Miss Melbourne, and hope no idle sarcasms will ever be suffered to reach her ear, and disturb her recovered tranquillity; if they should, she must only remember that

'Sweet are the uses of adversity,'[32]

and that showers as well as suns are / necessary to bring the charms of the rose to perfection, and to expand to full beauty its loveliness and bloom.'

'Miss Swanley,' replied Mrs. Stockwell, 'do you know, the whole time you was a talking I have been admiring of the pattern down the front of your gown; 'tis so sweetly pretty? Is it a lace pattern, pray mem? – Did you get it at the shop, or did you do it yourself?'

Sappho, who, when she paused, with perhaps a little allowable vanity, at the conclusion of her well-rounded period, had flattered herself with having made a convert of Mrs. Stockwell, and roused the latent spark of benevolence and good nature she had discovered, into a flame; turned from these multiplied interrogatories with a degree of impatience, which was not lessened by the remarks of Miss Mountain, who, taking up her observation, and quibbling as she was wont, in imitation of her favourite Arcadian knight, exclaimed 'Sweets to the sweet – [33] Miss Melbourne's sweetness might well entitle her to the parallel, so ably instituted by Miss Swanley, between her and the rose; yet much I fear she is not unsurrounded by thorns; and that those sweets would be soured, if the union with her sour tutor Mr. Sowerby, which some of the company seem to expect, took place. For that reason, I rather hope that Sir Harold, her kinsman, as more congenial in years and disposition, may transplant that sweet rose into his garden,

'For earthly happier is the rose distilled
Than that which, withering on the virgin thorn,
Grows, lives, and dies, in single blessedness.'[34]

Are you not of my opinion, Lord Strathallan?' she continued, turning to him, with her accustomed low bend and gracious smile.

'Well now, I think, say what you will, Miss Melbourne is a very nice lady,' said a voice, issuing from a distant part of the room, which was soon recognized to be Mr. George Spring's. 'And though she knew the stars and the books, and was / well read and accomplished, and could tell about the plants, and the knuckles of comets – '

'Nuclei, *Sirrr!*' cried Alcæus, with an emphasis upon the last letter that seemed to say, 'Will the earth never open to receive this Goth, that pretends to call itself my brother? – '

'Well, though she knew about the Nuclei, and was a fine lady, and a clever lady, and above all things cried up for her beauty, she never was saucy and impertinent as some misses are. I am sure I have cause to say so, for she was always very obliging and kind unto me. – '

'Very kind to you, that's good, faith,' cried the major – 'that's very good – stick to that, George – Miss Melbourne was very kind to you, and no doubt you are very grateful in return. Gad! that's the best thing I ever heard in my life.'

Arbella, who had been in vain waiting for the end of a conversation, in which she who had been so lately 'the most charming, the most fascinating' girl in the world, was thus wantonly loaded on all sides with the imputation of almost every fault and folly – at length exclaimed, 'I own I have listened with surprise to charges, so various and contradictory, preferred against one whose only crime was the possession of perfections, employed so pleasingly, borne so meekly. Her virtues, distinguished as her talents, artless as her beauty, were, I thought, beyond the reach of malice itself to attack. – I, for my own part, have contemplated her character with a delight, beyond what any success of my own could have excited – a feeling as distant from envy as from emulation – one which convinced me of the reality of that friendship in a female breast, whose existence' (looking disdainfully around her) 'I might otherwise for ever have doubted.'

'My dearest Miss Ferrars,' cried Strathallan, snatching her hand in a transport of which he instantly repented, 'how I adore you for that sentiment!' Then, relinquishing it in some confusion, he / added, 'how pleasing it is to find one whose feelings are so much in unison with our own!'

'On that subject, my lord, I trust we shall never disagree,' Arbella replied; 'it is not for those who have seen her, to be reminded of her various charms and talents.'

'No indeed, she was a charming creature, if I may say so,' cried George Spring. 'Don't you remember, my lord, when she sung or repeated any thing, she had such a look with her eyes – stay now, I'm bad at expression, but I know what I mean myself.'

'You mean,' interrupted his brother Alcæus,

'Her eyes' blue languish, and her auburn hair – '[35]
that was what charmed you, George, hey?' It was always poor George's fate to be told what his meaning was. He on this occasion, however, sturdily maintained his opinion against his brother, who continued to reply to his praises of Miss Melbourne's various accomplishments, 'Nonsense, nonsense – cursed affectation – abominable squalling – You're wrong there, George – Depend upon it you're wrong. – '

'However Mr. Spring may mistake in particular instances,' observed Arbella, 'no one will, I fancy, feel inclined to deny the truth of his assertion in general, that art and affectation were, by Miss Melbourne, equally unknown and unrequired; and that in whatever way she exercised her talents, whether she read, sung, or recited, she followed nature, passion, and feeling, as her only guides.'

Arbella's beauty depending less upon regularity of features than upon the soul that informed them, and which imparted animation and variety to her every action, always appeared to the greatest advantage when any circumstance called forth the innate spirit and generosity she possessed in such a high degree; but the graceful earnestness of her manner, the beautiful openness of her countenance, / were disregarded, while it was only remarked that she had expressed herself with a warmth unusual in very young women.

Lord Torrendale coldly observed that the less young ladies had to do with 'nature, passion, and feeling,' the better. The major, as he leant over the chair of the half-encircled Helena, whispered – 'feelings in unison – poetry and passion – very pretty indeed!' and both continued laughing and sneering at they knew not what, while Miss Hautenville, who perceived that Miss Ferrars, as was often the case, had, from an advantageous beginning, got upon dangerous ground, made no remark, but 'hushed in grim repose,'[36] awaited the issue of the conversation.

'Am I wrong,' exclaimed Arbella, looking around her, 'in making use of terms which express only a laudable sensibility, a feeling of all that is good and great? If we are forbidden all the finer energies, all the stronger emotions of the soul, where is the field for the exertions of genius, the triumphs of beauty? – For what does Shakespear write, but to excite an exalted pleasure through his magic power over the passions? to what does he address himself? is not nature his archetype – feeling his tribunal?'

'I agree with you perfectly, my dear Miss Ferrars,' said Major O'Hara, 'wherever pleasure is, as you justly observe, there can be no harm imaginable.'

'No, not exactly that,' said Arbella, who now begun to grow confused in her turn; 'you mistake me. I fear I am not perfectly understood,' she continued, looking from her favourite resource, the table, to the company for assistance, but in vain; many had not attended to what was said, but hearing the words 'passion, beauty, emotion of the soul,' uttered by the dashing Miss Ferrars, concluded there was something wrong. Two very good ladies, Mrs. Sagely and Mrs. Rueful, who did not understand one word of what had passed, but who would not have 'committed' themselves in such a manner for / the world, looked at each other in silence, and shook their heads most ominously – the major laughed – the fair Helen tittered – while the satanic sneer diffused over Miss Hautenville's features, evinced her satisfaction was complete.

Unable to endure their triumph, Arbella took little Sappho under her arm, who, for her defence of Matilda, was suddenly become her friend, and rising hastily, walked with her into an adjoining room, where a sober party were assembled at whist. The perturbation excited by the late circumstances still remained in Arbella's features, and Sappho, who had been told that in complexion and features she resembled the best descriptions of her illustrious namesake, adopted a good deal of the costume she is usually represented to have worn, in order to favour the illusion – so that she was altogether a most extraordinary figure – we will not say that the appearance of these two luminaries united, absolutely blinded the party assembled, as owls blink at the sun; but certain it is that their entrance did excite a degree of emotion, in which Mrs. Goodbody forgot to win a trick she might have secured, and for which, being severely reprimanded by her partner Doctor Doldrum, she cried out, 'I beg your pardon, but I was really startled, – surely there is Arbella the wit, and Sappho the poet together.'

'So much the worse, so much the worse,' growled the doctor, 'the world was never the better since women for-sook their tent-stitch to turn wits and poets.'

'But what's the meaning of that petticoat she has got upon her head,' said Mrs. Lackwit, turning round to look at Sappho.

'Oh, Ma'am, you know she is a genius,' yawned Mr. Drowsy, 'geniuses never wear their clothes like any body else.'

'Well, I thank my stars, I am no genius!' resumed Mrs. Lackwit, raising her eyes to heaven in pious gratitude. /

'Nor I,' cried Mrs. Goodbody – 'nor you, my good Doctor,' nodding sympathetically to Doctor Doldrum, 'you are no genius neither; so let them walk about and amuse themselves, while we count how many we have by honours.'

CHAPTER VIII.

Tu que la dulce vida en tiernos años
Trocaste per la vida trabajosa
La blanca seda, y purpura preciosa
Por aspro silicio y toscos paños
Canta la gloria immensa que se encierra
En el alma dichosa ya prendada
Del amor que se enciende en puro zelo.
Que se el piloto al divisar la tierra
Alza la voz de gozo acompañada
Que deve hazer quien ya descubre el cielo?

JUAN DE TARSIS.[37]

A SEVERE illness, the consequence of the dreadful scene she had recently gone through, left Matilda in a state of weakness and depression, which rendered her recovery at once slow and doubtful. The idea of the obligation imposed by her vow, even if one, taken under such circumstances, could be supposed binding, was not what could materially affect her spirits. Was not Strathallan already dead / to her? He was – and in that reflection, at once her consolation and despair, the loss of all that in this world she valued seemed included.

But though his fate was no longer connected with hers, this did not prevent the idea of his possible danger, from darkening her imagination with vain, yet insupportable terrors. She reasoned, she struggled against this impression. She set before herself the absurdity, the improbability of the supposition, that a tenderness, known to so few, scarcely acknowledged but to be checked, should reach the ears and excite the vengeance of an offended lover.

That impaired state of health, which prevented the admission of pleasurable impressions, rendered her susceptibility to distressing images only more painfully acute. The recollection of the sad, solemn, interview with Lord Torrendale, in which the afflicted parent pronounced her alone worthy to be the bride of his lost Strathallan, recurred to her imagination, and roused that latent spark of romantic superstition, which solitude, and her singular education, had contributed to foster in her mind. 'It was in death alone he would have united us,' she said; 'and am I at length to bring round thy destruction, to be the cause of evil to thee, who hast been to me, till now, the source of happiness? Is my fatal love to be thy bane? Must I, who would die to ensure thy safety, be the worthless cause that shall endanger it?' These feelings she was obliged, however, carefully to conceal; for Mrs. Melbourne, who had indulgence for every other form of suffering, mental or corporeal, was deaf alone to the forebodings of fancy.

This restraint, which Matilda felt at the time as painful, was in fact of use to her; and by not speaking of her apprehensions at all, she learnt to think of them less. But this forced tranquillity was in nothing allied to happiness. She neglected no duty, she omitted no employment; but occupation and amusement were alike / vapid, tasteless, and uninteresting: every pursuit, in which she was engaged, was rendered unpleasing, by an overpowering languor, that seemed to promise, but that never brought repose. Dread, deep, and silent, it had all the gloom and stillness without the advantages of rest.

Deprived alike of health, of appetite, and gaiety – she arose, but it was not to hope; she read, but not for improvement; she lay down, but not to sleep. Of all the pleasures she had formerly tasted, one only was still a solace to her mind: it was, when, alone and undisturbed, she dedicated to harmony that solemn twilight hour, in which her ear had once drunk with such deep delight sounds unexpected and thrilling – sounds attuned by love and Strathallan. Then recalling his air, his voice, his look; figuring to herself the very spot on which he stood – at that moment she felt, indeed, a transient respite from her sorrows.

While thus nourishing a melancholy, which, because unacknowledged, she thought innocent, an accidental conversation with the interesting recluse, whose company, since her illness, was become more and more dear to Matilda, induced her to look with more care into the movements of her own heart, and to dread the encroachments of a selfish indulgence, which might, if not checked in time, swallow up all her better feelings.

Though considerably Matilda's senior, the slenderness of her form, the delicacy of her features, on which no trace of emotion seemed to have ever rested, and a certain peculiar and beautiful transparency of skin, through which the liquid current of her 'pure and eloquent blood'[38] was seen in each slightest variation, continued to the countenance of Clara some of the graces of youth. Moving with the freedom from care, and almost the lightness, of a disembodied spirit, no anxiety appeared to have power to reach her, no accident to ruffle the undisturbed serenity she enjoyed. 'How I envy you!' said Matilda, pressing the hand of the gentle / nun, while an involuntary tear sprung into her eye, 'Still an inhabitant of this world, you seem already disengaged from its pains and pleasures. Here you have already a taste of that hereafter, the happiness of which we are told is to consist in an eternity of rest. Oh! what would I not give to have attained to your blissful state!'

Clara smiled, and turning on her those dove-like eyes that ever beamed with a chastened and saint-like light, 'I have often observed,' she said, 'that you, who still set a value upon what this world has to give, never seem to view with such envy, even those, who are in the fullest possession of all its advantages, as those who completely and contentedly resign them. I own it has always struck me, as a strong argument against the satisfaction they are supposed to afford.' 'There is but one my heart refuses to resign,' Matilda resumed, 'but I am ashamed to intrude upon the sainted calm of a soul like yours, with sorrows to which you must have ever been a stranger.' 'What!'

exclaimed the nun, with momentary emotion, 'do you believe my mind is content from insensibility, – that I attained to my present state without a sigh, without a struggle? No, I rather thank that merciful power, that never chastens but to correct and bless, for teaching me to turn the feelings that consumed me, into the channel in which alone they could be productive of lasting joys. He gave me time to repent of the dreadful blindness in which I had wandered, and to atone for the past, by devoting the rest of my life to his service.'

These expressions excited Matilda's curiosity in a more vehement degree than she ever had experienced it before, and though internally convinced, the fair nun could never have been guilty of any error, for which, in a worldly sense, she had cause to reproach herself, yet still the idea of a picture of sorrows and conflicts, perhaps like her own, was soothing to her mind; and she intreated Clara, if / the recollection of the past were not too painful, to explain to her, some of the circumstances, to which she alluded.

Clara looked fixedly at her. 'I will comply,' she said, 'the more readily, because I see it is not an idle, inquisitive, spirit that dictated your request; and my simple history contains a lesson that may be useful, my sweet girl, even to you. I am glad we have an hour alone, for your mother has a manner, which, though it invites confidence, yet chills enthusiasm; and enthusiasm was the master-spring of my destiny.

'You have heard of my having been sent to a convent in France for education. There, thrown among a number of young people who were of a different country, and put under the superintendance of strangers, the gratitude I felt to my superiors for their care, did not prevent the friends, from whom I had been separated, from being the first object on which my feelings, even in childhood ardent and enthusiastic, rested, with the longing aspirations of impassioned attachment. My parents were indeed to me but a name – but it was a name in which, to my youthful imagination, was centered all that is venerable, sweet, and holy. I pictured the transports of my return, I anticipated a father's blessing, a mother's smile, till fancy, wearied with her own exertions, seemed to droop, dispirited, at the long interval that must elapse before the delicious indulgence of feelings, so long repressed, could be permitted. A part of their energy found employment in friendship, and Constance de Louvigny was my sister in mind, in thought, and sentiment.

'I had just attained my sixteenth year, and my parents, impatient to embrace me, had written to give me notice that my brother would soon arrive to conduct me back to my native country, when the sudden and unforeseen decease of my mother defeated all my hopes, and taught me to mourn in death, a blessing which, in life, I had scarcely ever enjoyed. Observing that this event delayed his departure / from England, and that the double disappointment preyed heavily on my spirits; Constance prevailed on her mother to invite me to her house at the same time that she herself was to be removed from the convent, and, my father's consent being obtained, we soon found ourselves beneath Madame de Louvigny's hospitable roof.

'The mansion was within a few leagues of Paris; and the amusements, of which I occasionally partook, tended to remove the dejection into which I had sunk; and had perhaps additional fascinations for a heart new to pleasure, and accustomed previously to the most absolute seclusion. But it was soon decreed that her house, in the country, was to be the centre from which I was to date all my enjoyments.

'The countess lived on ill terms with her eldest son; but her second, the idol of his mother, the favourite brother of Constantia, was daily expected from the army. He arrived, and day seemed too short for the happiness of relatives so long divided – it closed in the midst of pleasing pastime, or affectionate discourse. Oh dangerous nights! – nights passed at Vezelai, nights marked by the enchanting presence of Volange! why is not your short and fatal course for ever blotted from my memory? To the lively glow of youth and gaiety he united a depth, a refinement of feeling, a susceptibility of strong and romantic attachment, which is supposed more peculiarly to distinguish our country. A shade of impetuosity, with which it was accompanied, I viewed with thoughtless admiration, not foreseeing the excesses it might lead to; my heart exulted in a vain presumptuous pleasure, to see that haughty spirit cower in its proudest flight, before a look, a tear of mine.

'My brother still did not come, and I no longer accused time, as formerly, for retarding the object of my wishes.

'I imagined I was growing resigned, when in reality, a culpable indifference to all that had the worthiest claim on my / affections, was stealing over my heart. Confining to the narrow circle around it, all its hopes and wishes, it still palpitated; but it was for a new object; it still formed vague dreams of happiness, but those dear and absent relatives, whose image had so long soothed the languor of my secluded life, were no longer their centre. One passion gaining upon me with rapidly increasing force, made me forget my friends, my country, and my God.

'At length my brother came; I gave him a reception I thought kind, but which was cold, compared to the fraternal delight he expressed upon embracing me: but when he talked of leaving Vezelai, my bosom could not vibrate in unison with the feelings that hastened his return; and tears alone betrayed I left all my heart had learnt to value within those walls. My brother viewed Volauge with a jaundiced eye; and his distinguished endowments seemed to him crimes, since they had turned me from my dearest duties. Madame de Louvigny was our friend. She pleaded our mutual attachment; asked if a father, whom he represented as so fondly partial to his children, could refuse his consent to a union so desirable? – My brother vented his rage and disappointment, in all that violence of invective in which, even in youth, when carried away by gusts of passion, he too frequently indulged. The great superiority of his years gave, to his reproaches, the force of those coming from a parent. I could only weep and promise to submit. He desired to be left alone with me.

"You feign submission, Clara," he said, in a hurried voice, "but it is to gain time." Shocked at the imputation of treachery being added to that of weakness, I disavowed the meanness he attributed to me, with an eagerness which seemed to make some impression on him.

"You have it in your power," he said, "to atone for the past – Volange is absent from Vezelai – This will spare you the great danger of a parting scene. – Write to him with your own hand an eternal / farewell – and be in readiness to depart with me to-morrow." Ashamed of my weakness, which he had set before me in its strongest light; anxious to justify the good opinion of a parent who, he assured me, would never consent to my union with a foreigner, I found no argument strong enough to oppose to the pressing instances he used; and, with a trembling hand, and a heart that bled at each line that it traced, I wrote to Volange the mandate of cold prudence, that forbade him to think of me more, in language that my brother himself suggested, or rather partly dictated to me as I sat. The next day, when the hour arrived which was to bear me from the scene of all my pains and pleasures, he saw how unable I was to make the exertion his sudden summons required; all his harshness vanished in a moment, at the sight of the bodily and mental sufferings I endured, his natural goodness of heart gained the ascendancy, and his countenance expressed the alarm and pity that he felt.

'"I have been harsh to you, Clara," he said, "when my only wish was to promote your real advantage. The hope of my life was to see you fortunately established in our native country. Perhaps I view it with too proud and exclusive a partiality; I am an Englishman; and I own I glory in the title, and to see my sister wedded to an alien – Yet still I am your brother, not your parent. I feel I was wrong in attempting to control your inclinations. Those were most to blame who placed you in a scene, where such connections were the only ones you could form. If your happiness depends upon a union with Volange, I no longer oppose myself to it; I will do more, I will endeavour to obtain our father's consent."

'What could I say? I wept, I kissed the hand of that dear brother who, for my sake, had consented to sacrifice the prejudices inwoven with his existence, the wishes most dear to his heart. Overcome with excess of joy, I knew not what steps were most proper to be taken; I could / fix on no plan; when my brother, lamenting his past violence, told me I must again write to my lover. "Though grievously offended no doubt," he said, "his must be that kind of resentment which finds its happiness in giving way. Nay write," he continued, forcing a smile, "it is fit that the hand which gave the blow should also apply the cure."

'I obeyed; – still let me dwell upon that moment – the last I ever enjoyed of worldly pleasure; that moment in which I said, with timid haste, "Return, Volange, return to thy Clara, for now her duty and her passion are reconciled."

'The letter reached its destination – one hour sooner, and it would have been the bearer of peace and joy. – It arrived too late. The wretched Volange was no more. The coldness and unexpected change of a woman he had so fondly adored he could not survive. In the brilliant circles of Paris he had imbibed, in all their fatal extent, those pernicious principles, which give to each individual a power over his own existence; and that spirit, which was alike unable to brook neglect or control, had voluntarily burst its bondage, and carried its proud, vindictive passions, uncalled, before the throne of the Most High.'

Clara paused – and Matilda, shocked at the communication she had drawn forth, still more shocked at the idea of the pain she must have inflicted, endeavoured in vain to conquer her own emotion, in order to soothe that, which she conceived, must be the pain of her friend; but she remarked with surprise, that though the nun's voice trembled, and her countenance was pale, no trace of passion passed over it – it rather bore the meek expression of saint-like pity, such as might move an angel's breast at a mortal scene of woe. Matilda entreated her not to continue her history.

'Shall I have survived the reality,' said Clara, faintly smiling, 'and tremble after a lapse of years at the picture? The bitterness of my sufferings is past; and I / shall soon hasten to relate to you the mercies by which they were followed. I was hurried away from the lamentations of my friend, from the sufferings of her mother, in a state of delirium or insensibility, I know not which, that was the only thing that preserved my life. But on my arrival in England, neither the change of scene, nor the affectionate solicitude of a parent, who had been so long the object of my thoughts and wishes, could for a moment rouse my mind from the gloomy torpor, which had succeeded the first paroxysms of despair. Remorse added its sting to affliction – I considered myself as the murderer of Volange – as the murderer of his soul; and in the short and hurried slumbers that broke the misery of the day, his unforgiven spirit, reproaching me for the penance it endured, was ever before me. These harrowing ideas, which the belief in which I had been educated, forbade me to banish, poisoned every source of pleasure, and rendered even the exercises of that holy religion, once my sweetest solace, distasteful to me. – I prayed without hope – I arose without relief. I thought myself too unhappy to look for consolation in that resource which afforded it to others. It was for those who were still in possession of some valued blessing, to return thanks – for those who looked forward, at least, to some mitigation of their sufferings, to put up prayer. I looked upon life with more than indifference, – with disgust; and considered death as the termination of a dreary journey, in which I was useless to others, and hateful to myself. Sometimes, roused by a human feeling of impatience from the gloomy resignation, or rather despondency, into which I had sunk, I would endeavour to shake off the load of sorrow, that, like an enemy pursuing me, seemed to press, to weigh down, to overwhelm my heart. The fanciful and the happy, talk of the joy of grief, the luxury of woe; but the very terms they use, shew that it is not cherished in the bosom, till it has lost its name and character. No – against real, / long protracted grief, we feel an impatience, a weariness, almost a resentment, which proves it an alien to the natural feelings of our souls, formed to aspire after a felicity, which it only forfeits by error; and recovers, never again to have it endangered, in an eternal world. – This happiness I was nearest enjoying, at the moment I thought myself abandoned to despair. In an illness brought on by the dreadful sufferings of my mind, a vision was graciously vouchsafed to me, which opened my eyes to my real situation; and showed me its dangers, only that I might avoid them. It seemed to me, that my disembodied soul was released from its frail and suffering tenement; and that, surrounded by myriads of spirits, it was awaiting the decision that should award its final doom. A door was opened in the heavens, which discovered to me a blaze of insufferable brightness; and those happy spirits whose deeds were approved passed me in multitudes, celebrating their joy in the sweetest harmonies, as they advanced to plunge and lose themselves for ever in that sea of light. Others filled the air with cries, as they heard themselves condemned to inexpressible torments, the just reward of their crimes. I shuddered to hear their hopeless lamentations; but all sympathy and curiosity was soon swallowed up in anxiety on my own account; and I demanded, with tears, to know my fate, amid this general and awful distribution. At that moment I heard a voice say, in a low, mournful tone, "Poor wayward creature! Thy life was not stained by any crime – not marked by any exertion of active virtue. The sufferings by which an eternity of happiness might have been purchased, thou hast neglected to improve. Given up to passion, with a soul wholly bent on the contemplation of an earthly object, thou hast lived in the forgetfulness of that source, from which at once thy blessings and thy woes have flowed. Innocent of intentional crime, thou shalt escape the tortures of the guilty – Unworthy of the crown of virtue, / no punishment awaits thee but to be excluded from the sphere of that perfection to which thou hast never aspired." The voice ceased, and a cloud – a veil – a curtain – thick, dark, impenetrable, appeared between me and all my soul loved, to remain, I was conscious, for ever. I found myself alone, at a distance from the confines of our world, in a vast region of uninhabited air, without boundary, form, colour.

'The sensation of darkness and solitude, which, at that moment, struck upon my heart, carried with it a feeling of misery, of which I should in vain endeavour to give you the slightest idea. Let it suffice that what I suffered when first deprived of Volange, was bliss compared to it. Conceive the impression of dismay, of anguish and repentance, with which the intelligence would be received that we had, by our own folly, missed the greatest earthly good, the highest possible exaltation; some good that might but a moment before have been secured, but which was now irreparably, irrecoverably gone. With a sensation something resembling that, but as far surpassing it in degree as the object that had escaped me surpassed what this world has most glorious, I heard my righteous doom. With the sense of my loss came that of the meanness of the object, which my mad passion had magnified into importance sufficient to enter into competition with my eternal bliss; and it was to this I had sacrificed the short hour allotted to me.

'One day was past, and I might have lived for ever at the fountain of those perfections, have tasted at their spring those pleasures ever renewing, which overwhelm without oppressing the heart; and now I was exiled for eternity from the vision of that divine and glorious presence, the end and object of my being; that unknown good to which, through life, my unsatisfied aspirations had, though unconsciously, tended; that beauty, of which all that is great or lovely upon earth, is but the faint and feeble representation. With / faculties enlarged beyond measure, those faculties only served to shew, to my still increasing anguish and confusion, the immensity of the loss I had sustained. I endured no pains – no penance was inflicted – the sense of privation – of eternal privation and banishment from *his* sight, in the love and contemplation of whom is bliss supreme, included within itself the bitterness of every other torment.

'It was not for a soul still imprisoned in mortal mould, to endure it long: I started wildly from my couch, my frame trembling, my heart panting, my eyes pouring torrents of tears, exclaiming in grateful ecstacy, as I gasped for breath, "It is yet time!" The attendants that surrounded me were alarmed, and thought my intellects were still disturbed by some horrid dream. Alas, it was the first time I awoke from a dream, in which, for many months, I had been lost. It was soon perceived, by the alteration in my conduct, that some revolution had taken place in my mind. The desire I had to recover my health, and the willingness with which I adopted every means to attain that end, contributed to its speedy re-establishment. My mind was now the abode of peace and thankfulness; and, oh! in this, the beginning of my conversion, how soothing was the thought – more than the thought – the conviction with which I was often filled, that at length Volange was happy; happy in consequence of my repentance and mental devotion, which had atoned for his presumptuous crime. By degrees, though he never ceased to have my pity, his image no longer mingled with my prayers; one object possessing every thought, wish, and affection of my soul, swallowed up all others in its superior claims. I began to be impatient of the forms of common life, which still prevented me from giving myself entirely up to them.

'The rest of my history you know. In that convent where I had been brought up, two years after I quitted, full of youthful hope, its peaceful walls, I took / the vow which was to confine me within them for ever. But it was otherwise decreed; and Heaven is my witness that when anxiety for my safety conducted once more to my convent grate the beloved brother, to whom I thought I had bid an eternal adieu, my own distresses less engrossed my mind, than the change my peculiar situation had wrought in his. I was struck by the strange and singular contrast. The settled sadness that now dwelt on his countenance shewed to the most careless observer, that he never ceased to regret my imaginary sacrifice; while mine expressed that content, which I had never tasted, till I made the election he deplored.'

'And were you as happy in England?' enquired Matilda.

'No,' replied Clara, 'for I was less useful. You smile, but surely our recluse life did not prevent us from being in many ways beneficial to our fellow creatures. Ours was not one of those orders to whom is assigned the sacred charge of soothing the last hours of the sick, and preparing the winged spirit for its ascent to Heaven. Yet, though denied that satisfaction, I found one inferior, but still grateful to my feelings, in contributing to impart the advantages of the education I had received, to those who yet might be in need of instruction. It is only in being useful that we can be happy. Yet still I am content; and every day I bless that gracious Power who enlightened me on the subject of my destiny, and who granted to me the only means of obliterating the past – a life devoted to his praise and service.'

Perhaps the perfect self-devotion of Clara, the effect of an imaginary warning from Heaven, acting upon a heart too tender and afflicted, a spirit too enthusiatic and susceptible to resist its influence, was a sacrifice rather to be lamented than applauded. Yet still, was there not something in the sentiments she had expressed, which Matilda might apply as a guide and rule to herself? The last words of / the recluse, upon the subject of the necessity of active virtue, particularly struck her.

'Yes,' she exclaimed, 'it would be little if the whole of my unvalued life were one long prayer for thee, Strathallan. If my days were consigned to the hopelessness of despondency, my nights to the tears and the phantoms of despair, it would be little thus to mourn thee, if I lived for myself alone; but when I think on her, whose widowed heart turns to me alone on earth for consolation, that indulgence which before was scarcely innocent, becomes, indeed, a crime. Sweet Clara, your greater sufferings shall teach me to blush for the weakness, which made me yield so easily to mine; and you, my mother, shall find your counsels have not fallen on an ungrateful ear – have not been bestowed on one, who shrinks from the occasion which should put their value to the test. For your sake my mind shall resume its energies; for your sake it shall exert its every power to war against the weight of woe that still oppresses it. I will remember, that, though contentment be removed far from me, the reward of virtue may still be mine; and when tempted to murmur at my trials, will recall the words of Clara, that, "to be useful is to be happy."' /

CHAPTER IX.

I wander through the night,
When all but me take rest,
And the moon's soft beams fall piteously
Upon my troubled breast.

Miss Baillie. *Ethwald*.[39]

MATILDA had hardly time to strengthen herself in these praiseworthy resolutions, when she was called upon to try their force in action. On being summoned the following morning to attend a visitor in the parlour, she was startled at seeing her cousin, Sir Harold: the servant had not named him to her, or she had not caught his name. Her mother's presence, however, abated the involuntary terror with which he would otherwise have inspired her. But it was not easy long to retain terror, or even to harbour resentment, against her unhappy cousin. There was something so helplessly interesting in his wildly mournful wanderings, so attaching in the affectionate earnestness of his look, whenever he addressed her, that it was impossible, when in his presence, to recollect he was the fatal obstacle to her most distant hope of happiness; – the evil genius that threatened with destruction the opening bud of promised joy, even if it should dare to expand, after the storm that marked its early morning.

Sir Harold looked ill and fatigued; but his manner, now singularly calm, if not collected, contrasted, in Matilda's mind but too forcibly, with the terrific violence, which in their last interview had given her peace such a fatal blow. 'You are surprised, my fair cousin,' he said, 'to see me so soon returned, and it is true I must not long remain with you; they already begin to murmur at my stay. But though not free often to move, I must indulge sometimes in a short wandering from the circle where I am bound. It is now a month since I have seen you, and / in that space of time I have traced a thousand miles.'

On Mrs. Melbourne's expressing her surprise at what she heard, for she did not know of his having been any where but in Derbyshire, he explained that the constant exercise he took, both day and night, around the spot that he inhabited there, was alone what he alluded to.

'Yes,' he continued, 'since I must not rove from place to place, it is that shall be my abode. If I must be chained, let me be chained to my rock, for enchantment marks the scene; and sure some blessed spirit embalms the air, where once it wandered through those green recesses.' He looked wistfully at Matilda. 'In the wild walks and winding groves I trace the steps of beauty, but no where can I trace the haunts of love. My servants follow me,' he added, 'and when night comes on would persuade me to return: they sometimes use submissions, and sometimes' (his countenance changed) 'even threaten violence to their lord. Poor silly souls! They know not that they would rob me of the sweetest, most balmy hour; and that, sleep I believe you call it, on which they set such value, I never get – I never need!' and he uttered the last expression with an air of wild triumph. Then, as if suddenly recollecting the purport of his visit, he turned to Miss Melbourne, and said, 'I wished to prepare you, my dear cousin, for presenting you to-morrow with a gift, the most precious I could possibly bestow. Will you receive it at my hands?'

'We must know what it is first,' interrupted Mrs. Melbourne, with a good-humoured smile.

Sir Harold shook his head, changed the subject, and conversed for an hour so agreeably, upon indifferent topics, that he would have pleased and prepossessed any one in his favour, who had not been acquainted with his unhappy derangement. Before he took leave he promised, on the following day, to return with the treasure, / and left his fair relatives rather curious to know of what it might consist.

The next day at an early hour Sir Harold called; he had in his hand a little girl, who appeared hardly ten years of age, of a countenance prepossessing in the highest degree, and the most angelic beauty. Sir Harold looked earnestly at Matilda, 'I would have given you my own soul,' he said, 'but you despised the worthless gift. I know I have nothing to offer that is worthy of you; but what is dearest to me on earth I will give you: take her – she is yours. Had I aught more precious it should be added to it: but she is the sister of my soul: the orphan child of my mother.'

Matilda kindly spoke to the little girl, who stood trembling and dismayed on hearing this singular address. The sweetness of her manner seemed a little to dissipate the alarm of her young cousin. She then turned to Sir Harold, hardly knowing how to understand conduct so singular and unexpected; but before she could ask an explanation he had arisen to depart. Julia Melbourne threw herself into his arms, bathed in tears, 'Oh, do not you too abandon me, my brother!' He was deaf to the piercing cry which sensibility seemed to have attuned to tenderness, to foreboding anguish, beyond what her years should have known. 'Turn to that lady,' said he: 'you are no longer mine; she is in future to command you.'

'I accept the trust,' said Matilda; and, taking the interesting little stranger by the hand, she retired with her to her own apartment. Left to herself, Julia threw herself upon a bed, and gave vent to a torrent of tears.

Matilda tried by every gentle art to sooth and console. 'Do not grieve so, my love,' she said. 'I hope you have not been taught to fear your cousins? – '

'No, no,' replied Julia, sobbing, 'it is not that – but to see my brother so strange – so very strange. What a sad / misfortune has befallen him! he that was so gentle – so good.'

At length Miss Melbourne succeeded in a degree in calming the agitated spirits of the little girl, and learning from her some of the particulars that had preceded this singular scene. Julia Melbourne was but recently out of mourning for her father; she had been left since the death of her mother, which had taken place about three years before, under the care of a worthy woman, who acted in the capacity of house-keeper at Mosscliff Abbey; but who remained with her more in the character of a governess than a domestic. Her original prospects had been better, and her education qualified her in a great measure to supply the place of a parent to the young orphan.

'She said she had promised mamma to do so,' Julia continued. 'Mrs. Carlyle was a good woman, and I never regretted our solitary life at the Abbey. After we lost my dear father, my brother kept her on at Moss cliff. He had only me with him when he went to take possession of his new house; but he soon sent for Mrs. Carlyle to stay with me while he went to town.

'He came back from London quite joyous, and said he would introduce me to my cousin, who would be a sister to me; and who, of all the women he had ever seen, alone resembled my dear mamma.'

Of her mother's accomplishments and instructions, (though she had lost her at so tender an age) Julia seemed to retain a lively and distinct remembrance; and her frequent allusions to them, revived in Matilda a curiosity which had been often excited, but had never yet been gratified. From the time she had been introduced to the circle, in which such a name excited interest, she had always understood that Lady Julia Melbourne, (who seemed to have been suddenly hurried into neglect and oblivion more complete than is usual with those who have once imparted / lustre to society), had been, at one period, considered as the 'mirror of fashion;' her taste undisputed, her beauty allowed pre-eminence, even where beauty most prevailed. The poet, the sculptor, the engraver, emulated each other in perpetuating her charms by their exertions, and referring their claims on fame to her arbitration. No novelty, from the turn of a head-dress to the composition of an ode, obtained currency till it had passed the ordeal of her decision. No young aspirant in the walks of science, of taste, or of politics, was supposed to have his claims confirmed, till he had been introduced to the lovely Lady Julia Melbourne. Her house, her equipages, her dress, her air, even her attitudes in waltzing, playing the harp, in the exercise of her theatric talent, or the more unassuming graces of private life, were the objects, among her own sex, of fruitless admiration and competition; in which might be truly applied to her Voltaire's expression, respecting the unfortunate Henrietta of England, '*Toutes les femmes l'imitaient, et nulle ne la ressemblait.*'[40]

Matilda had heard she had been educated abroad, and Julia confirmed it. 'I believe she was born there,' she said: 'she had several foreign servants. Her own woman, Lavinia, was a Florentine, and she used to shed such tears on her bosom. She promised to teach me Italian soon, that I might know what they were talking about, and she had already taught me French. She took such pains to make me recite it. I still remember the lines she loved best:' and with a sensibility and energy, as surprising as the grace and propriety of the gesture with which she enforced them, Julia Melbourne repeated out of Racine's Britannicus the four lines, beginning

'Combien de fois, hélas! puisqu'il faut vous le dire
Mon cœur de son désordre allait – il vous instruire?
De combien de soupirs interrompant le cours
Ai-je evité vos yeux, que je cherchais toujours!'[41]

Matilda, in admiring the spirit and expression / she gave them, was no less struck with the infantine innocence which accompanied that expression. Her voice was indeed modulated to the tones of impassioned softness; but it was evidently passion that the ear had caught from another, without returning its echo from the heart.

'I often saw her perform in that play,' continued Julia, 'for she acted in French quite as easily as she did in English; and she said that when I grew up I should be the Julia, for that she was a poor little interesting princess – very young – yet very hardly treated. Poor mamma! she wished to teach me every thing she could – she loved me so –.' There was frequently something serious, even solemn, in Julia's manner; though it had nothing formed or decisive, like that of a woman. Great sensibility, like grief, anticipates the progress of time. A family air of dignity and beauty, that distinguished her features, unanimated by the glow of complexion, rendered her appearance at once interesting and striking; while their extreme regularity and marked expression, would have been rather unfavourable, at such an early period, to the promise of their future perfection, but for the softness and delicacy every lineament possessed. Her air, her gestures, the plaintive sweetness of her tones, and the impressive earnestness with which she often spoke, altogether gave the idea of a matured but beatified spirit, inhabiting the infantine and innocent frame, and inspiring the countenance of a child.

Sir Harold did not return again for several days, and Julia had forgot the name of the hotel where they had stopped; so that they were unable to make any enquiry respecting him, and it remained uncertain whether he was not gone back to the Rocks.

'What an attaching creature,' said Mrs. Melbourne to her daughter, 'is your little pale beauty, your ivory maid! She is absolutely Mrs. Barbauld's exquisite personification of Pity.[42] Poor Lady / Julia! She seems, by a strange fatality, to have studied the unhappiness of her children, by too early cultivating in them both every taste that has a tendency to increase that exquisite susceptibility that nature has given them already in too great a degree for happiness. But what do you intend to do with your little charge when you see her brother again?'

'To keep her!' returned Matilda firmly.

'To keep her?'

'Yes, he gave her to me, and I have mentally ratified the engagement. Can you disapprove of it, my mother? She has experienced the greatest loss, in that of a parent: I will endeavour,' she continued with fervour, 'to supply her place.'

'But have you considered well, Matilda; have you thought of the importance – the responsibility attached to such a task? – '

'I have; but I thought also of her forlorn situation. We are her only female relatives. Who can contemplate without horror her being left to her ill-fated brother, given up to regret, to melancholy, to a sensibility, that, if ill-directed, may become the source of torments so exquisite?' Matilda paused; but her trembling lips and agitated voice, shewed the picture she had drawn was not quite from imagination.

'Amiable girl!' said Mrs. Melbourne, embracing her, 'how I joy to see you looking around amid the wreck of our own happiness, to some being more unfortunate, on whom to exert the benevolence of that kind, affectionate heart! trust me, while possessed of it, you have still a store of joy; far be it from me to oppose its dictates; much we can not do – but our time, our talents, we can still command; and, for the number of pensioners that waited at our door, if one little innocent be snatched from evils more dreadful than poverty, Heaven will not disregard the offering, however unequal to our wishes – will not despise the tribute of the orphan and the widow.' The / allusion she had made recalled a subject, on which Mrs. Melbourne had not yet learned to speak without tears; and Matilda mingled her sorrows with those of her mother, to the memory of a parent so tenderly and justly beloved; till the recollection of the new duties, in which she had engaged, taught her to dry them, and to seek in active exertion a remedy against vain regret.

She had not devoted herself a week to her new employment, before she experienced in her amended health and spirits, the truth of the maxim which Clara had so earnestly endeavoured to enforce.

Julia and the fair nun were mutually pleased with each other. Julia found it impossible to feel timidity at the aspect of gentleness like Clara's; and Clara, who fancied she discovered in her style of beauty, a resemblance to her still beloved Constance De Louvigny, was never tired making her presents of sweet-meats and embroidery, out of the remains of her once ample convent stores. The little stranger quickly became domesticated; and the re-appearance of Sir Harold, lately so much the object of her wishes, threatened to inspire her with more terror than satisfaction. He said he had been ill, and that was the cause of his having been so long absent from his fair friends. 'It is a fever,' he said, 'which sometimes seizes me; and then in my dreams I fancied I wanted my Julia, and I could not recollect where I had left her. So I came here to look for her, and take her away.'

'You are very welcome to be here,' said Mrs. Melbourne, endeavouring to speak to her unhappy cousin with cheerfulness: 'but as to your sister, you must not take her away you know, for you gave her to my daughter.' Sir Harold looked surprised.

'Yes,' resumed Matilda with an angelic smile, 'and I have adopted her from that moment.'

Again Sir Harold paused; he put his hand to his head, and seemed to try to / recall some half forgotten images to his memory, but in vain. At length, with a deep sigh, he shook his head, and exclaimed 'it is gone; but if you say I did so, my fair cousin, I am satisfied, for your words are truth: and will you,' he continued, as if suddenly struck with the greatness of the benefit she would confer, 'will you, indeed, be guardian, friend to my more than orphan sister? Teach her to be all that is good and amiable – to be like yourself? – Will you be to her an elder sister? – ah, why not her sister in reality? Are we not already related? Matilda, lovely cousin, am I not yours; and, being so near to you, can I be indeed the wretch you think me? You complain that I pursue you with my passion. Ah, Matilda! am I to blame, in wishing to draw closer the strong bonds of nature, by the still dearer ties of love?' Though pained by the turn he had given to the conversation, what most struck Miss Melbourne in all that had passed, was Sir Harold's expression, 'more than orphan sister.' From Julia she could of course gain no elucidation; she only repeated that his manner was often strange, and that to her, as to others, he often spoke wildly and unintelligibly.

'And was he always so?' Matilda enquired.

'Oh, no – not always – but since he has been abroad!'

'And do you know the reason?'

'No; but I think it must be something that happened to him there.'

'Fatal absence!' thought Matilda.

'How often does the wanderer from his country bring back some hidden woe, which, though secret its source, poisons the remainder of his days.' She recalled the imputed dejection of Strathallan, which had always been traced to the period of his return from Spain. 'Ah, why are we tempted,' she cried 'to leave a home of love? do not the sufferings that so often ensue, seem to follow like avengers, to chide the vain curiosity, or / wasteful ambition, that won the heart from domestic pleasures?'

From such reflections she was not sorry to be roused, by another visit from Sir Harold; who came quite gay and animated, with the prospectus of their day's amusement. He made it a point that Mrs. Melbourne and Matilda should take the two vacant seats in his carriage, alleging, with a smile, that it was the only way of reconciling the little timid Julia, to venturing abroad with her violent brother. Julia joined her earnest entreaties, and Mrs. Melbourne, who thought a little recreation might be of service to her daughter's health, without much hesitation consented.

After stopping at one or two of the public exhibitions, that were open at that time, and having spent the morning in that manner, not without amusement, Sir Harold told them there was one more place, which, if they were not tired, he wished them to visit before they returned home; and pulling the check, as they arrived before the door of a house of genteel appearance, in a street in the most fashionable part of the town, he assisted the ladies to alight. He conducted them through several rooms, but still they did not perceive any thing worthy of attracting their curiosity.

'Pray, good people, what is to be seen here!' said Mrs. Melbourne, with affected spirits, to conceal a kind of vague alarm she felt, at the conduct of the eccentric baronet.

'The professor is above stairs, I believe.'

'Is he to give us a lecture on astronomy, or hydrostatics; or are we at a painter's? Do, dear Sir Harold, explain; for I think we have reined in the impatience of female curiosity for a sufficient time.'

'Look around you,' said Sir Harold. 'How do you like it all?'

'Very well. Still I see nothing but chintz curtains, and white draperies, and / Venetian blinds, and marble chimney-pieces, and Brussels carpets, and glasses, and chairs, and tables.'

'Well, and what could you see better?' resumed the baronet with great gravity. 'But I am wrong: I should have introduced you before to the mistress of the house;' and taking her by the arm, he led her to the other end of the room, where stood a large mirror: 'Look at her,' he said, 'is she not amiable? and she is, I assure you, as good as she is lovely. Am I not right in bringing you better acquainted? for you are still ignorant, I am sure, of half her merits. She has laid me under an obligation,' he continued, putting his hand to his heart, 'which, however this wandering, treacherous memory may sometimes deny, will never be forgotten here.' As he said these words he had dropt the animated tone of fanciful gallantry, in which he had begun to speak, for one of the deepest emotion.

Startled, pleased, surprised, Mrs. Melbourne hesitated before she could immediately frame an answer to so unexpected an address.

'Nay, nay, I will have it so,' he continued, anticipating the objections that she appeared about to make. 'If I am to be robbed of my Julia, I will have her in a more airy situation, near the parks, and some square, where she may inhale something bearing the resemblance of fresh air. I could not otherwise venture my little Northumbrian with you; it is to her you owe all this.'

Mrs. Melbourne easily saw through the delicacy that dictated this remark, and doubted whether the relationship Sir Harold stood in to her family, would not warrant her accepting this proof of the generous interest he took in it.

'From the moment you talked of keeping my sister with you,' pursued the baronet, 'I perceived the inconvenience she must be to you in that small lodging, and I instantly began to look about for a house which would suit you; this I found / ready furnished, and took for a year; and then (if it still pleases you) take it for ever.'

The ladies did not long delay to take possession of their new residence. Throughout, there reigned an air of modest elegance, peculiarly suited to the feelings and taste of Mrs. Melbourne. There was a pretty garden behind the house, and there, with a book in her hand, or the prattle of the little innocent Julia, she beguiled many an otherwise tedious hour. Sir Harold had promised to visit them soon, to see how they liked their new abode. They now received him with pleasure, and in the course of his different visits, he gave them his opinion with earnestness, on some subjects connected with the education of his sister. Observing with what rapt attention she hung upon Matilda's harp, and listened to her when accompanying it with her voice, 'She is tremblingly alive to the charms of harmony, Miss Melbourne,' he said, glancing a look of anxiety at the little girl. Then, after a pause, he continued, 'her talent for music is as great as her taste; I have no fear indeed of her excelling in every accomplishment under yours, as under a mother's care. But, my fair cousin, let it be your first, your greatest solicitude, to watch the unfolding bias of her mind; cultivate in her, before all things, that strict regard to decorum, that shrinking delicacy, the surest safe-guard of all true dignity, without which all female loveliness, grace, and talent, serve but to adorn a splendid ruin; the more conspicuous, to be the more deplored.' Some painful remembrance seemed to arise in his mind as he pronounced these words; and he quickly turned from the distressing subject to announce his intended departure for the Rocks. 'I ought to have been there a month ago,' he said, 'but I know not how it is, the spell that used to bind me to my rock is now transferred to this Persepolis,'[43] this fascinating city, "too guilty and too pleasing to be either / spared or destroyed." I must tear myself from it, or it will tear me from myself; and it seems my workmen are all gone mad, and want my presence; they have hardly done any thing, since I have been here, to the great bason, or towards levelling the mount, or –'

'The estate will be so much improved,' Mrs. Melbourne observed, forcing a smile, 'that if I should ever visit the neighbourhood of the Rocks again, I should hardly know it.'

'No, no, not much improved,' Sir Harold resumed, in a tone of sudden and surprising indifference. 'But one must have some object; one must do something. Adieu,

---

*   Voltaire's Novel.

Julia,' he then said, 'I shall hope to see you in the summer. Can you, do you think, remember your rambling brother till then?'

Julia looked earnestly at him, her eyes filled with tears; 'Remember!' she repeated, while an expression of infantine simplicity added grace to the artless energy of her manner – 'for ever!'

Sir Harold seemed affected: – 'and you, Matilda?' he said, – 'yet do not answer,' he continued, preventing the reply that faltered on her lips. 'I know what you would say – yet do not say it; for the conviction of your indifference does not strike so cold on my heart, as would your uttered refusal. Wherever I wander, I have one consolation – your image, which, far kinder than yourself, refuses not to accompany me. It is a talisman that keeps from me every thing wretched, noxious, or unholy. Must it not be so, for has not the Maker's hand impressed it with each different attribute of perfection?' It was thus that in his wildest bursts of passion, some expression, some allusion, in which a beam of fancy gleamed between, proved the wreck before them to be that of a once elegant imagination and cultivated taste.

It was not without emotion that Matilda received his farewell. Fixing his eyes upon her with melancholy steadfastness, 'I go,' he said, 'to my lonely / rock, to that which fronts the window where you used to sleep; and then when I sigh, and think how soon my short course was ended, the cool air speaks repose to my soul; and the darkness around seems to whisper, Matilda at that moment may think of me with pity. Adieu, thou best and loveliest! Remember,' and his countenance changed to the fierce expression that once thrilled to her heart with terror, 'though never to be mine, bonds strong as death secure thee from ever giving thy love to any other.'

CHAPTER X.

'Un beau visage est le plus beau de tous les spectacles, et l'harmonie la plus douce est le son de la voix de celle que l'on aime.'

LA BRUYERE.[44]

AND where was Strathallan while Matilda, introduced to new connexions, united by the ties of mutual obligation to that part of her family with which she had been till lately unacquainted, tasted some few pleasures, and suffered many a bitter pang, of which he was not the source? His mind had, like hers, endured a revolution since they parted; and he had become strengthened in a determination to forget her, which seemed now equally necessary to his honor and his repose. Whether it would stand the test of renewed intercourse, remained still to be decided. /

Sir Harold allowed his sister every advantage that the best masters could afford, and though averse to exposing her delicate health to the dangers of crowds and late hours, was yet so far indulgent to her favorite taste, as to request Mrs. Melbourne would in the course of the season take her to one opera; an amusement respecting which she had expressed a vehement curiosity.

The fashionable winter had set in, and Matilda reminded her mother of this promise.

'We must think about tickets,' said Mrs. Melbourne; 'the time is past since I had them pouring in upon me for Lady Such-a-one's box, and Mrs. Such-a-one's box. How many faces that used to welcome me with smiles now look on me as on a stranger! London is altered much since I lived in it at my father's house, and I am altered. The connexions I had, I neglected to cultivate. I gave up the world for one person; it is fair the world in its turn should give me up.'

It was agreed they should try for tickets at Hookham's;[45] and, taking Julia by the hand, Matilda set out, attended by a servant. She was just crossing over to the library, when she was stopped by the run of carriages, which happened at that moment to be very great, and stood fearful of venturing till she had let them pass. These crossings were to Matilda, as to every timid person unused to walking in London, a great annoyance; at the moment she thought she had found a favourable opportunity for venturing, a dashing equipage from the other end of the street suddenly appeared, driving towards her with such fury, that she relapsed into timidity and uncertainty, and holding the trembling Julia by the hand, remained, though fully conscious of the awkwardness of her situation, with her foot still lingering on the kirb-stone, when the name of Lady Torrendale caught her attention; and, turning round, she perceived a tall footman in a crimson and gold livery, / very, which she instantly recognized for her ladyship's, who was running after the coroneted equipage with almost equal speed.

'Whither away, Lawrence, so fast?' cried one of his comrades, who was passing more leisurely along.

'Oh, for the life of you, James, don't be after stopping me now! Here's my Lady Torrendale wants to pay a visit to Lady Lyndhurst.' Having just overtaken the carriage, which was empty, and chucked a visiting card into it, he rejoined his companion, who asked him, 'Are the Torrendales in town, then?'

'Yes; the old one and his lady, these six weeks and better, preparing every thing for the young lord's marriage. An ugly thing, to my fancy; but a power of money.'

'And Spencer?'

'Oh, he can't come among us – still under the hatches – in Cumberland, I think they say; but I can't be staying all day with you, or else I'll never be returning, and cook will be mad. Why don't you come see her?'

'Why, what has she got?'

'A round of beef, a pye, some veal – Come, have a snack.'

'I don't care if I do. I'll just step home and see what our people are about, and be with you again in a crack.'

Matilda had by this time effected 'a safe landing on the opposite bank,' but the intelligence, of which she had by this delay been made an involuntary hearer, was of a nature to excite perturbation beyond what rolling carriages and spirited horses, however formidable those objects, could ever create; and she had entered the shop and sunk upon a seat, before she recalled to mind the business upon which she came. A polite enquiry from the master of the shop what were her commands, and if she would have a glass of water, restored her a little to herself; and she had just enquired if she could be accommodated with three tickets for the / opera that night, when the entrance of two ladies, who were laughing and talking very loud together, excited her attention. One voice she thought she knew; but by the time she raised her languid eyes, the speaker had her back turned towards her, and was making some enquiries at the other counter. Her first motion, as she took up a book that lay upon it, convinced Matilda that she was a lady of distinction; her second, as she turned round, that it was Lady Torrendale.

'Oh, Miss Melbourne! my dear girl,' said she, with the most unembarrassed air, 'I am truly glad to see you; how are all at home?'

Matilda had begun to reply, but her ladyship was by this time deeply engaged. The words died on Matilda's lips when she found she had no longer an auditor; and having hastily put up her tickets, she was preparing to leave the shop, when Lady Torrendale, observing the paleness of her countenance, resumed, 'but how are you, my dear? you don't look well.'

'Pardon me, madam,' said Matilda, 'I am quite well, and – '

'One, two, three, four, five, – twenty on the list, I declare, already for the Missionary,' repeated the countess, looking over a paper-book: 'how provoking to be so late! I want it so much – I am dying for the Missionary. Mr. Hookham, remember to let me have that, and the Lady of the Lake, as soon as you possibly can;[46] in the mean time,

I believe, I must be content to take these,' and giving some half-bound volumes to a servant to be put into her carriage, she followed, saying to her companion, as she left the shop, without another word or even look at Matilda, 'I must make haste home, for I have hardly time to dress for dinner, and Strathallan promised to be with us today.'

The circumstances of this short and unpleasant interview, the unkind and unfeeling manner in which her ladyship had hurried in and hurried out, made a deeper impression on Matilda's spirits than it / ought perhaps to have done. Yet one great consolation offered itself – Strathallan was still expected. He had not, then, like his mother, brought himself to spend weeks in her vicinity without a message, an enquiry respecting one lately so dear. When Miss Melbourne informed her mother of what had passed, she seemed neither surprised nor offended. 'That is so like Lady Torrendale,' she said: 'I never thought her friendship of that substantial nature to resist the first storm of adversity; and, to do her justice, she never had a sincere regard for me.'

'Perhaps, mamma,' said Matilda, timidly, 'she thought we knew of her arrival, and ought to have visited her first; perhaps she – '

'Even if I had heard it, she knows I have no carriage,' Mrs. Melbourne replied; 'and I should not wish to force myself upon the notice of a woman vain and haughty as Lady Torrendale, in a situation inferior to that in which she remembers me.'

'Oh, mamma, you would always be sufficiently superior to Lady Torrendale, however differing from her in outward circumstances.'

'That was very well said, my dear, for the time of the consuls of Rome, when virtue was the only distinction, and a noble matron was sure of commanding respect from that circumstance alone. Were I to boast my jewels, like Cornelia, I think I could produce at least as good;[47] but in these degenerate days, the unfortunate, who cannot conquer an inborn pride, and a certain value for themselves, must be content to nourish it in solitude, if they would escape from contempt.'

In their conversations upon the world, Mrs. Melbourne and her daughter often differed. The younger lady was unwilling to believe it what the elder one knew it to be. This tempered 'regard for state and wealth,' which formed an ingredient in Mrs. Melbourne's character, contrasted at first rather unfavourably with the extreme openness and disinterestedness of / Matilda's disposition; who seemed to be without a thought for her future situation or a regret for her past affluence. Perhaps the difference more consisted in that of years and education, which made the daughter, if not better able to bear the slights and neglects attending upon want of fortune, at least ignorant that there were so many to be borne.

'But we must not let the overcoming disappointment of the morning make us forget the projected amusement of the evening,' resumed Mrs. Melbourne, with affected spirits.

With a little of her daughter's assistance, she had soon completed her simple but becoming toilet. Matilda's was not much longer, yet never had her distinguished loveliness appeared to greater advantage. It was the first time she had gone into public since she had left off her mourning, and she was on this occasion little tempted to it, but by the desire to give pleasure to her young cousin; they now only waited the appearance of their old friend to set forward, and Matilda was soon introduced into a scene, which, spite of her settled sadness, seemed to promise, for some moments at least, agreeably to engage her; Sowerby had taken care to place them in the centre of the pit, that they might have a good view of the house. Almost as much delighted as little Julia, with the novelty and beauty of every thing around her, Matilda was some moments without noticing that she was in the immediate neighbourhood of one of her old acquaintance; when the sound of a voice, which appeared familiar to her, exclaiming, 'Bless us! how contrary; who'd ha' thought o' them people setting of themselves next us!' induced her to remark the group nearest her, and she thought she could not be mistaken in her friend Mrs. Stockwell. Was Arbella then in town also, without seeking her? a new pang struck Matilda's heart; but she perceived her friend was not of the party; and she was unwilling to ask any question respecting her of her aunt. /

'Now, do ye Sam,' continued that lady, 'put your fashionable, large, new opera hat between them and us, that they may'nt be familiar.'

Mrs. Stockwell, who was but recently come to town to 'look after the money,' as she termed it, for her noble patroness had already contracted new obligations to her, began endeavouring to discover if any of her titled acquaintance had entered the boxes; and asked her son the names of many others, with whose appearance she was not acquainted.

Sam, who had by this time imbibed an opinion, that his mother ought to know, or to appear to know, every body, was much distressed by these interrogatories, and named them to her 'as though he named them not.' Some few she acknowledged, and was noticed by them in return, Miss De Courcy, Lady Lyndhurst, Lady Kilcare. Matilda looked the way Mrs. Stockwell's eyes directed, for she remembered the names; but no similar acknowledgment ensued. That they saw her, she could not doubt, since they used the assistance of a glass, to discover her features more clearly; but that they did not think her worth the honour of a salute, occasioned her a momentary pain, which nothing but her inexperience could justify. On the other hand, she could not be unconscious of the attention she excited among the strangers around her; and we will hope that it was pity, not vanity, prompted the smile, when she overheard a gentleman whisper Mrs. Stock-well, 'who was that beautiful girl in the white satin and net?' and remarked that lady's answer, ' 'Pon my word, sir, I don't know; how can I tell the name of every girl as gets leave of her friends to go out and see an opera!'

'What a heavenly complexion!' resumed the stranger.

'Not natural, I can assure you, sir; to my certain knowledge Miss Melbourne puts gamboge upon her face.'

'I should doubt it. You know her name, madam?' /

'Pray, Sam,' continued the lady, turning from the cross-questioning gentleman, 'isn't that there, yonder, Lady Etherington?'

As the boxes filled, Matilda for a moment recollected the triumph Lady Torrendale, in her days of kindness, had anticipated in presenting her lovely young friend, for the first time, among the brilliant circle assembled there, and a sigh would force its way: but it was stopped in its course by the notes of the first singer in the world, and, given up to the illusion of the scene, she soon sunk or forgot the little feelings of the woman, in those of the tasteful and enlightened amateur.

Towards the middle of the entertainment, the entrance of some very distinguished personages into the stage-box, attracted all eyes towards that part of the house. 'Do lend me your glass, Sam, till I make out who has got there,' said Mrs. Stockwell, on the appearance of another gentleman decorated with an English and foreign military order, 'I can't extinguish him. My stars!' (a most appropriate exclamation) 'I expect it is, yet it can't be him, neither; yes, it certainly is Lord Strathallan. Now he's speaking to the Prince of –, now he's speaking to the Duke of – ; dear me, I wish he'd look this way; dear, I wish he'd let one bow to him! Do put your large, new opera hat out of the way now, Sam, there – so; I wish he'd look – '

At length Strathallan *le desiré* turned round, and *did* look, but it was not at her; in a moment he had left the persons he was with, and was at Matilda's side, while, with the most delicate and respectful tenderness, he anxiously enquired after her health and welfare since the moment of their separation. All this was effected so instantaneously, that she could hardly believe it, but by that sweet tumult at her heart, that soft surprise, giving to each meeting the charm of a first interview, the tenderness of habitual friendship, which ever announced to her the / approach of Strathallan. Attracted towards her by an irresistible impulse, the radiant joy her countenance expressed justified to him his having yielded to its suggestion: the impression of months was done away by that welcome smile, and while gazing with renewed rapture on that enchanting face, he repeated to himself, 'She has not, no – she cannot have forgotten me!' Matilda, on her part, endeavoured to reason herself into a conviction, that she owed her chief pleasure to the contrast afforded by the kindness of one of her former friends, opposed to the neglect of the rest; and this innocent sophistry contributed to her serenity, and increased her satisfaction.

In the mean time, this girl, with whose name she was unacquainted, became a personage of vastly increased importance in the eyes of Mrs. Stockwell, now she had attracted the notice of the fashionable Lord Strathallan. She grew suddenly extremely uneasy lest she should find her seat too crowded, moved away to make more room for her, while she scolded her son Sam for not jumping over the benches to find another seat for himself rather than incommode the young lady: she then attempted to obtain some share of the notice of Lord Strathallan; but he, wholly occupied with her he adored, would not for a long time be made to perceive her existence; nor was she much more successful in her attempts to attract Matilda. Strathallan, when animated by pleasure, was irresistible, and the elevation of his spirits communicated itself insensibly to her whose presence had inspired them.

Mrs. Stockwell forgot Miss Melbourne had a book of the opera, – offered her's. – 'I've no use for it myself, mem,' said she; 'but I can't help thinking it a great inconvenience for poor people as don't understand French; but now I think of it, mem, you can't want it either.' To all these contradictory remarks Matilda replied by an assenting smile; but one which did not much encourage her to proceed. / The presence of Strathallan had indeed effected a revolution in every object around her. 'You have surely seen my mother since her return to town,' he said. Matilda hesitated; the transient interview at the library was all she had to acknowledge; he guessed the reason of that pause – that passing expression of suppressed indignation, which she had once or twice observed Lady Torrendale's conduct excite, for a moment flushed his cheek;

but instantly gave way to the habitual softness of his manner when addressing her. All about her seemed to breathe of peace, of love, and joy. A dispute between two gentlemen about places, occurred near them, and their loud and angry voices created a momentary disturbance among the company. Matilda looked up, astonished that any one could be discontented where every thing was so pleasing. The scene, at this moment, represented the Elysian Fields; graceful forms moving through beautiful landscapes, to which an interposing gauze gave a light shadowy air, represented the companies of the blest; while strains, that might rival those of Paradise, composed their choral harmonies. But she heeded not their charms; her Elysium was in her heart.

Meantime Mrs. Stockwell, who was not in love, and to whom even Strathallan was only the heir of Lord Torrendale, was extremely mortified at his neglect. She was now making efforts to obtain the attention of Mrs. Melbourne, since she was at the head of the favoured party; but it was in vain that she besought that lady to excuse her not knowing her at first; alleged her extreme blindness, 'great as the dear Dichess of Albemarle's,' which she said, 'she hoped would expatiate her fault.' To all her advances, Mrs. Melbourne replied by a quiet and cold civility, which was the last thing she understood. Resentful looks, or even smart retort, would have pleased her better, as being what she could comprehend. /

Towards the close of the ballet, Sowerby, who for some time had appeared to sit uneasily, proposed to Mrs. Melbourne to go: 'this dancing cannot interest you; indeed it cannot please you,' said he, looking at Matilda. The young lady immediately rose, and Strathallan begged the honour of attending her; but Stockwell, who thought proper to acknowledge her now as being of his acquaintance, pushed himself forward, saying, 'This lady, sir, was of our party before ever you came into the house.'

Matilda, who perceived that Sam had mistaken her forbearance, and indifference, for insensibility to his former impertinence, with a glance of contempt, such as her mild countenance hardly ever assumed, turned from him, and gave her hand to Strathallan.

'You shall answer to me for this, sir, in another place and time,' said Mr. Stockwell, growing bold as he saw numbers surrounding him.

'Why not now?' replied his lordship, who perfectly knew his friend Sam. 'I have but one objection to employing your time, my dear Stockwell, which is, that while you are bestowing it here so uselessly upon one lady, who, you see, has already got a protector, you are neglecting your own mamma,' turning to Mrs. Stockwell, 'who would, no doubt, be most grateful and proud of your attentions.' The tall martial figure of Strathallan; the good humoured triumph with which he uttered the words, and above all the gay sweetness that smiled in those rich blue eyes, 'swimming in youth and love,' so contrasted with the discomfited air, and smoked look, of the little powdered beau, that the uneasiness painted in the countenance of Matilda did not repress the envy excited in many, on account of the cause; when suddenly a figure, dressed in deep mourning, advanced between the disputants, and, taking her trembling hand in silence, led her away from both. Stockwell hastily withdrew, scared / at the glance the stranger cast on him as he passed; while Strathallan, giving way, yielded to claims he acknowledged superior – for the intruder was Sir Harold Melbourne.

CHAPTER XI.

Demetrio.
    Ah! nel tuo volto
Veggo un lampo d'Amor, bella mia face –
Berenice.
Che vuoi da me? – Lasciami in pace.

METASTASIO. Antigono.[48]

MATILDA atoned, by hours of the most dreadful anxiety, for the short-lived but exquisite pleasure of those she had passed with Strathallan. The unforeseen re-appearance of Sir Harold Melbourne, whom she believed to be at the Rocks, revived, in their full force, those terrors of which she had experienced a short suspension. As he had not attempted to accompany her home, her fears were as vague as they were terrible. They all turned upon the suspicion of his having followed Strathallan from the opera; and she was convinced, by the agonies the bare idea of his danger excited, how far she was yet from / experiencing for him only that calm friendship, which the nature of his engagements made her consider as a duty. Bitterly did she lament the fatal chance that had first introduced her to the notice of Sir Harold Melbourne. 'Unhappy man! blest days,' she cried, 'when I was ignorant of thy existence! Surely 'twas decreed my peace of mind should not survive the hour that brought me acquainted with a relative, so long unknown; and only known at length for my unhappiness!'

From these reflections, what was her delight to be aroused by the unexpected appearance of Strathallan! It was still early; and he was shewn into the room where Matilda was seated alone; for her mother, who seemed unusually flurried and fatigued with her last night's exertion, had not yet appeared below. He came full of uneasiness and doubts; but the kindling blush of glad surprise, with which she welcomed his approach, put them all to flight, and again, he only lived to love. He remembered the glance which, on his return to his native home, after the false tidings that he should never return, had first drawn his soul to Matilda. The same look, only that it expressed a more full and delighted thankfulness, now betrayed that all her thoughts had been employed on him.

'Forgive me, dearest Miss Melbourne,' he said, advancing towards her, 'if I have intruded thus early: what I have to communicate will, I hope, plead my apology. It is on the subject most interesting to my heart; and that is, I hope, not indifferent to yours.'

'You can have nothing to say, my lord, that I ought to hear, which might not be told in the presence of others,' Matilda replied. 'You must be conscious that I can make no alteration in the conduct I have hitherto pursued, while no change in your circumstances justifies such an alteration.'

'But if such a change could be hoped –' resumed Strathallan quickly. – / Matilda hesitated – A bright beam of pleasure, for a moment, lit up her countenance.

Strathallan, without waiting her reply, continued, very fast – 'I have had a disagreement with Miss Mountain, on a subject in which her pride will not permit her to yield; and on which I have a right to be equally inflexible. – I left her; I will not say in resentment, (for of that, as well as of every other passion, you know the immovable coldness of her disposition renders her incapable) but she was certainly, deeply offended; yet it was a point which neither my own feelings nor my father's would, I am sure, allow us to give up. Not to waste these precious moments on such an unworthy subject, let me rather now hope, that my Matilda will no longer refuse to hear me. I have obeyed all your just but cruel mandates! Three months, amid the wilds of Strathallan, where no human voice intruded to break the sullen stillness around me; where no intelligence from the world was suffered to reach me, I tried to bring myself back to that frame of mind, which would enable me to fulfil the dreadful duty I had imposed on myself – to return to that cold, joyless calm, which had alone induced me ever to assume such chains. I wrote to no one – I forbade your name to be pronounced – I fondly thought that, if it no longer met my ear, it might in time be banished from my heart. – In vain. – Mixed with the image of a beloved mother, whose memory, amid those sequestered shades where her latter days were past, is still adored, your idea filled the lonely scene, met me in each gloomy walk, and turned the solitude I had sought as a refuge, into an encourager of the fatal passion which preyed upon my peace. I returned to society. It was then I first learnt the reverses which my self-imposed banishment had kept from me. How doubly did I regret those bonds that, in the trying moment of affliction, prevented me from proving my truth! But with no right, no claim – every thought to be devoted to / another, the rules of that cruel delicacy, which you taught me so severely to respect, forbade me to address you, even under the name of friend; and I could only through another, breathe the feelings of a heart, that bled in every vein for your sufferings. To Lady Torrendale, to her, who, with feelings so comparatively calm, possessed the precious privilege I had resigned, I trusted the task of conveying, with all that female tenderness, that delicacy, which might make even you forgive the intrusion, the share I took – How poor those words! – How does every expression fail in describing the truth! At that fatal moment, that my whole heart and soul were yours, I thought I should rejoice in whatever mitigated your unhappiness. – I heard your marriage with your cousin talked of – I found my mistake, and how far my passion was from bearing the generous character of my Matilda's. Shall I own it, my gentle love? Should not every feeling of this erring heart be exposed to your just but pitying eye? Resentment mingled with despair. – Though I had consented to yield up my hope in you, my heart I had reserved as yours, and I could not bear you should so soon consent to devote yourself to another. The madness of jealousy, at that moment, fired my breast; – tortures that your pure and gentle bosom can hardly image urged me, by turns, against *his* life, against my own! Returning reason calmed these transports, but it was only to sink me into the torpor of despair. Again I tried to forget you. – In a degree I thought I had succeeded; but the meeting of last night convinced me it was in vain to struggle with my destiny, for that my life was bound up in yours. Listening to that voice – gazing on those enchanting features – I forgot myself – the world – every thing but happiness; – a heaven surrounded you, but with you it vanished. Watching, with strained eyes, till your form disappeared among the crowd, I seemed parted from myself, deprived of more than life; while every rumour that / had robbed me of my small remains of happiness seemed only too fatally confirmed.'

Matilda had received from Strathallan proofs of the strongest attachment: yet, well as she thought she knew him, the energy, the nobleness, the generosity of that lofty and impassioned character required, in order to be developed in its fullest extent, to be acted upon by a sentiment, of the excess of which, as it existed in his breast, she found she had still but a faint idea. He would hear of no obstacles; he would endure no repulse. He painted their future happiness in the glowing colours of youth and love: it was impossible to listen to him, and not share for a moment a similar illusion. And was it then possible? Were all her past trials, severe but short, to end in being restored to the object of her wishes, after they had served only as so many tests, to prove his pure and fervent faith? Was her patient endurance to be crowned with bliss like this? Ah, no! – The remembrance of the vow extorted from her terrors by Sir Harold Melbourne, pressed with a death-cold force upon her heart, and chilled the rising throb of hope that had just began to beat.

'Strathallan,' she said, in a solemn voice, 'it is in vain you would attempt to obviate every difficulty: I never can be yours.'

'I was right then!' he exclaimed, in an altered tone, while the animated flush of pleasure fled from his features; 'and Sir Harold – ' He looked up in expectation of her answer. Matilda was silent.

'Oh, Matilda, while I was eagerly preparing for our happiness, how could you so hastily, so irrevocably – but I deserve it. Did I not first set you the example, in voluntarily giving up a claim which love in one sweet moment had conceded to me? which nothing – not even your angel eloquence, should have induced me to relinquish. But I threw from me the precious gift, and I would in vain recal it.' /

He walked up and down, distracted by the painful variety of emotions that crowded in upon him. At length, stopping before her, with a look of mournful tenderness, 'and will you indeed, Matilda,' he said, 'can you at length be his?'

Matilda saw that he was in error, and longed, in order to relieve his heart of part of its load, to explain to him the exact nature of her engagement: but would he then admit it? Would he not rather laugh at the idea of dangers which she shuddered to contemplate, and blame her fears as chimerical, without being able to satisfy her they were ill-founded? Another reason, that may perhaps appear of less importance, yet weighed with a mind, sensible and delicate as hers – she could not find words, although she tried several different forms of expression, in which she could bring herself to convey, to a stranger, the idea of the weakness, the violence, the frenzy, of her unfortunate relative. Unable thus to give Strathallan the satisfaction he required, she again held down her head, and was silent.

'And is it thus we part – and in so short a time too – and must I believe you love him?'

'I did not say I loved him,' she replied.

Strathallan started from her in anger; 'By heavens I will not bear this; this ambiguous, cruel trifling, in return for the free offer of a heart, devoted, fond, as mine!'

'And I should, perhaps, less hesitate to accept it,' exclaimed the distrest Matilda, 'if – if – I valued it less. – '

She paused. Her expressions were hardly intelligible; yet still there was enough in them to intoxicate Strathallan with love and joy; again he was all repentance – imploring pardon for the past – the creature of her will.

'Leave me, leave me!' she exclaimed, grieved at the unguarded words that had escaped her; 'I am an unhappy creature, and carry the contagion of misery to whoever / would attach himself to me; – leave me, for your more fortunate bride: for, believe me, fate opposes to our union, a power, imperious as invisible – an influence that I dread to think of – an eye that is ever waking – an arm that is ever stretched out for vengeance!' Overcome with the picture her terror-struck imagination had drawn, it seemed as if she really saw the peril that was only the creation of her fancy: the conflict of the morning, united to the operation of habitual apprehension, was too much for her; her voice grew faint, and she was obliged to seek relief in tears.

'Let me but clasp the charming danger to my bosom,' cried the enthusiastic Strathallan, 'and I spurn at fear – it cannot harm me!' Alas! he guessed not the nature of that danger, which to contemplate, so shook the bosom of Matilda. To see that beloved being on whom, spite of herself, she doated with such fondness, exposed to the blind transports of frensied jealousy – to behold that form, on which even now, she gazed, with forbidden but impassioned delight, defaced and sacrificed to his senseless fury; these were the thoughts that, the more he was endeared to her, determined her the more to resist her too fondly trusting lover.

'What have I done to deserve so singular, so cruel a fate?' she said. 'Cease, cease, I entreat you, to tempt your own destruction. How wretched I am to be the cause of misery to all I love most on earth!' Hardly conscious of the extent of the confession she had made, the sudden revolution it effected on the too-speaking countenance of Strathallan, alone informed her that it was no longer time to retract or hesitate.

'Enchanting creature!' he exclaimed, gazing on her passionately, 'repeat, repeat those delightful words. – Yet you need not repeat them; they have sunk deep within my heart – never by any future coldness to be effaced.' It was in vain that Matilda tried to recal what / she had said; to deny that she had given such positive encouragement to his wishes, in the words she had uttered. The brilliant joy that penetrated through every look and word of Strathallan, alone formed the completest contradiction to all she would have said. The restraints of timidity were too feeble, any longer to oppose the expression of happiness like his. Unable further to repress it, he yielded to the sweet violence with which he felt it overflow and inundate his soul, and no more attempted to conceal the delightful conviction with which he was filled, that Matilda loved him. With a gentleness in which she tried, vainly tried, to mingle a degree of severity, she endeavoured to moderate those hopes, to convince him of the necessity of their parting. But Strathallan only saw in these repulses, in this eagerness for his departure, new, flattering, tender testimonies of anxiety and love. Though he forbore to press her on the nature of her apprehensions, he had heard enough to persuade him they were not of a sort to weigh with him for a moment against his happiness.

'You bid me cease to hope,' said he; 'but Miss Melbourne must borrow Miss Mountain's eyes, Miss Mountain's voice, before she bids me obey her.'

Distressed at transports that she found herself unable to share, the appearance of Mrs. Melbourne was a welcome relief to Matilda; and that lady was charmed in Lord Strathallan, with a display of vivacity, and brilliant animation, that was always in him the more enchanting, as its occurrence was rare. Gradually fascinated by his flow of spirits, though ignorant of the cause, she felt herself flattered by his prompt and early attention; by which he appeared to wish to disavow, in the most pointed manner, the selfish, unfeeling conduct of Lady Torrendale. She found the time pass with peculiar pleasure in his society, while Matilda, as every moment he unfolded some new power of pleasing, more and more bitterly deplored the cruel persecution she endured, / from one, who seemed determined to step in between her and every hope; who, when least looked for, was still found hovering around her, ready to cross her path, whenever it appeared that path might lead to happiness.

CHAPTER XII[a]

O entre tes beautés, que ta constance est belle!
C'est ce cœur assuré, ce courage constant
C'est parmi tes vertus, ce que l'on prise tant
Aussi qu'est-il plus beau qu'un amitié fidèle?

Boethius' *Sonnets.*[49]

'Arbella has not real beauty, but she'll do.' These words, pronounced with an oracular nod, by Lady Torrendale, to the select circle assembled in her dressing-room, had decided the fate of Miss Ferrars. To accomplish this prediction, she slighted her aunt, affronted her cousin, and broke with all her other relations.

'Were I possessed of Miss Ferrars's independent fortune,' said Miss Hautenville, 'I think I would not consent to be moon to Lady Torrendale.' Miss Ferrars was of a different opinion; and preferred being / moon to a more elevated sphere, to being the sun of her own.

Mrs. Stockwell, having declared she found it inconvenient, for 'peculiar' reasons, now she knew the Torrendales, to spend her winters in town, Arbella hoped to derive the greatest advantage from that circumstance: but this expectation was far from making her forget her friend; and she was extremely disappointed, not to find her at the house to which she had the direction. Arbella, though a warm friend, was a very bad correspondent; and Matilda, who had a little of the jealous delicacy of the unfortunate, had not written to her since her change of residence. Mr. Stockwell, under pretence of a visit to his mother, had followed Arbella up to town; the only unpleasant circumstance, she declared, attending her journey. How much reason had she to think otherwise, when she discovered, by the accident of her cousin's meeting Matilda at the opera, the friend, respecting whom she had made so many anxious and vain enquiries? She had staid at home that night on account of a slight indisposition; but was resolved he should make her ample amends for her self-denial.

Had Stockwell foreseen the torments that were preparing for him, he would certainly have wished the trifling sore throat, of which Arbella had complained, changed into a settled hoarseness. Miss Hautenville, as usual, breakfasted in bed, and the family trio did not assemble till a very late hour.

At the breakfast table she began the attack; 'Well, Sam, what did you see last night?'

'See!' repeated Sam, who in addition to his natural uncommunicativeness, was now just entering upon the enjoyment of a morning paper, and a mountain of butter'd muffins, from which he did not wish to be disturbed, by the flippant interrogatories of his cousin.

'Ay, see, Mr. Silence: now pray don't think the part of *personnage muet*[50] becomes / you; for I assure you, it never suits but those who can agreeably employ the eyes, if not the ears. So lay down your muffins, put your paper in your pocket, and make the *agréable*,[a] as Lady Torrendale calls it. Now begin, and tell me all you saw at the opera.'

'Why, nothing,' replied Sam, sulkily.

'Nothing! you saw Vestris surely.[51] How did he dance?'

'Hum – nothing remarkable.'

'And Catalani, was she in fine voice?'

'Pretty well, I believe: I did not attend much,' said her phlegmatic cousin, who would not, for the world, be suspected of admiring any thing.

Mrs. Stockwell, herself, was shocked:

'Oh, sure, Sam, you forget,' she said.

'She was very great in the bravado, in the first act; and so were Rovedino and Viganoni, in the recitavee.'

'And Tramezzani,' pursued the pertinacious Arbella, 'was he as interesting as ever? what a dear fellow that is! how I doat on Tramezzani!' and then unmindful of her aunt's reproachful exclamation of 'for shame, for shame, niece, to talk so of a stage-player! Did you ever hear me do so?' she continued, 'but surely there were some acquaintance of ours in the boxes – who were there?'

'In the first place, there was Lord Strathallan, as was very attentive to us,' said Mrs. Stockwell, helping out her son.

'Strathallan!' cried Arbella, eagerly, 'now tell me, Sam, how did he look? was he in high beauty?'

'I don't know. I hate that word beauty, as you ladies apply it to a man,' answered Stockwell; 'he looked as he always looks, I think; a most proud, haughty, disagreeable coxcomb.'

'And I hate that word coxcomb,' Arbella replied, parodizing[b] her cousin's expression, 'as you gentlemen "of the second table" apply it to all the dear creatures we like. I assure you, you don't follow your own interest, in doing so. *A propos*, Sam; why don't you go to Spain, to get that charming brown, which just / makes us love, instead of envying, Strathallan's beautiful bloom?'

'You are right, miss, to envy any one their bloom; but I can assure you, I envy nothing of Lord Strathallan's.'

'Not his eyes? Oh, you certainly must allow, you envy his eyes. I wish I had them here, then would I give them to you, dear Sam, to go a wooing with.' Stockwell's countenance grew blanker and blanker, and Arbella hummed *Begli astri d'amor*;[52] but recollecting this was not the way to obtain the information she desired, she suddenly extended her hand to her cousin, exclaiming, with a smile, 'Come, come, do be pleased, and look pretty, and here am I, all attention to your account of the opera; to begin like the news-papers, "Among the persons of distinction, we noticed – " Well, go on.'

'Why, there was the Duchess of Normandby, and the Duchess of Albemarle, and the Prince of E –, and the Duke of O –, and the Cossack, and the Spanish ambassador, and G – the great poet, and N – the great traveller, and C – the quack doctor; and there were some pretty women, Miss De Courcy, and Miss Mordaunt, and Miss Melbourne, – '

'Miss Melbourne! – Matilda Melbourne!' exclaimed Arbella, 'Fool! idiot! blockhead! why didn't you tell me that the first thing? Where does she live now?' And she had scarcely obtained the desired information, when starting up, heedless of a story just begun by her aunt, with 'when I were with the Dichess of Albemarle,' and letting fall her cup of tea upon Sam's leg, which forced from him an exclamation, any thing but lover-like, she hastily threw on a shawl which lay beside her, and, without hat, bonnet, or any other covering for her head but a veil, darted down stairs, and, unattended even by a servant, was hastening to the street-door, when Mrs. Stockwell bawled out from the top of the stairs, 'Niece, niece! where are you flying away at such a rate? Did you ever see me do so? In your state of health, and against my express conjunctions –' /

'Oh, ma'am, I'm quite well now,' cried Arbella, who had got to the street-door.

'Well then, if you are quite well, you can hear me.'

'No, ma'am, I'm sick.'

'But niece – '

'For God's sake, ma'am, don't keep me talking; I'm sick, I'm hoarse, I'm deaf, I'm dumb, I'm speechless!' screamed Arbella; and running out of the house without waiting for an answer, she soon reached the abode of her friend, from which she was only separated by a few streets; and was received by Matilda with the kindest and tenderest welcome.

So many events of a pleasing and unpleasing nature had occurred, since last they met, that it was impossible, by words, to give utterance to the various emotions excited by the present renewal of their friendship: tears were the only language which, for a few moments, expressed their feelings, on both sides; and Matilda experienced sincere consolation, while weeping on the bosom of her tried and affectionate friend. She did not, however, allow the pleasure this meeting afforded her to make her forget to thank Arbella for her kind and generous conduct; from the pecuniary part of the obligation, she said, she had now a prospect of soon relieving herself.

'Talk not to me of payment,' cried the vehement Arbella; 'you outrage my feelings; can I ever repay you for saving me from an imprudence? Oh, what an egregious fool was I going to make of myself then, and might again to-morrow, had I not little Prudence in London, at my elbow: surely, dear Matilda, we are quit, or rather I am everlastingly your debtor. But why did you hide yourself from us? I lost not a moment in going to the house indicated in your old direction, but you were not there; and it was only by the merest chance that booby, – oaf, – I beg ten thousand pardons, I mean that excessively elegant young man my cousin, overheard you mention where you lived, last night, / to Lord Strathallan, and retained it in his – oh, lud! I shall never get out – his head – without another epithet, and that won't be right you know, since he is my relation – and since he mentioned he saw you – and since he told me where

you were to be found, and since, as good Mrs. Hill says in the "Limerick Gloves;"[53] so
tell me, my dear, the history of your removal, to put me in good humour.'

Arbella was in the most brilliant flow of spirits, which was always the manner in
which her affectionate joy demonstrated itself, after the first emotions were subsided;
and she had hardly patience to listen to the account which she had herself requested,
and which Matilda thought due to her sincere friendship; omitting, of course, the
particular interest which her charms had excited in the hearts of her cousin and Mr.
Sowerby.

She had scarcely heard her out, when, to Matilda's great surprise, she exclaimed,
'So, it is all settled, is it not? and you are to be transported into Mr. Sowerby's museum;
the rarest treasure in the whole collection. I think I see the old virtuoso throwing you
a seal's skin and a piece of coral as a wedding gift, like the rich lover of Ajut in the
Greenland Tale;[54] no, that was a kettle and a piece of coral, I believe. Well, it's all the
same. Come, tell me truly, are not the dresses fixed on? A pair of Brazilian humming-
birds for ear-rings, and gloves of the silk of the Pinna Marina? I assure you, I shall
expect a pair. The writings are of course drawn up on a leaf of the papyrus. How I long
to be of the wedding party! Instead of dull cake and wine, we shall have, at the head,
a dish of the Chinese bird's- nest soup; the bread-tree shall supply our only loaf, while
your rosy lip shall sip nectar from the American lotus horn. The harp-shell must be
put into requisition to sound your nuptial song. The common lyre would do for an
idle thing like me; but we must have the noble harp to strike your praises, my charming Bragela!'

Matilda, scarcely able to interrupt her / friend's volubility, took the first opportunity to assure her, with a blush, that she was quite mistaken.

'No?' cried Arbella, with a look of interrogative incredulity. 'Then perhaps it is
Sir Harold after all? In the wrong box again, as Aunt Stockwell would say. Is it then
indeed to be the adorable – Really, my dear, with your three lovers, Sowerby the worthy – Strathallan the resistless – and Sir Harold the flighty, you put me in mind of the
princess in the French fairy tale, who was courted at once by as many suitors: of whom
the first was Un Prince comme il faut; the second, Un Prince comme il n'y en a point;
and the third, Un Prince comme il vaudrait mieux qu'il n'y en eut point.'[55]

'My *three* lovers!' repeated Matilda, with a look of unfeigned astonishment.

'Perhaps, my dear, you do not know that Sir Harold, like the melancholy Jaques,
or mad Malvolio,[56] muses by the babbling brook, or carves in fantastic love-knots
Matilda's name on every beech-tree at the Rocks. Then he tells every one that will listen to him that he has you fast by bonds that 'not death shall sever;' but as the knight
is rather moon-struck, we were inclined to believe he dreamt; at least such was the
opinion at the Residence, who in general gave you to Mr. Sowerby.'

'I did not think,' resumed Matilda, endeavouring to conceal, under an appearance of careless indifference, the agitation into which this new proof of her cousin's
determined persecution threw her, 'that my affairs were of sufficient consequence to
arrest your attention, among the various occupations and amusements Woodlands
used to afford.'

'Occupations, my dear! what is so delightful an occupation as the affairs of others,
to "diligent Miss Hautenville and painful Miss Langrish?" as they would certainly be

called by worthy Old Fuller,[57] or some of those queer long leathern-coated gentry, that take the dust at the bottom shelf of Lord Torrendale's library. / The trouble those poor ladies give themselves, to ascertain that you have charmed half the world, is not to be told; and what makes it the greater pity, is, that success, which is the reward of other discoverers, only makes their hearts overflow with the bitterness of envy and regret. But let us not waste a thought on them. I am distracted when I think of the time I have wasted, and the hours I might have spent with you. I regret every day, every hour, I passed without your company. Why did I not guess you were here! Why did I not go to the Opera, where I should have met you last night? I might have gone to the Opera – but really' she almost blushed as she spoke, 'just as I was thinking of going, the idea arose to my mind's eye of Sam – his face, and his opera-hat, even as he last attended me – sitting next me, leaning forward, just so – brows knit – munching the end of a stick – "for ever silent, and for ever sad." I could not stand it, and by giving way to that horrible fancy, I lost the greatest pleasure. How could I guess Matilda would be there! but I ought to have guessed it, for I have often observed, that when from caprice or any other cause, we refuse to comply with some trifling wish of our friends, or, without necessity, make some alteration in our usual arrangements, we find it productive of unforeseen inconvenience or disappointment, which had not entered into our calculation, when we yielded to the whim of the moment.'

'But you have not always the phantom of Mr. Stockwell and your aunt,' said Matilda, unable to resist a smile at her friend's ludicrous distresses. 'You have sometimes Lady Torrendale for a chaperon.'

'True, my dear, and I was just going to tell you that the great step is taken; I have made my debut. Appeared with her at one or two grand assemblies, and even endured the buzz at the Opera, and the whispers that ran round the box circle of "Who is she? What is she? She's / not one of us! Yet she's with Lady Torrendale." "She is a rich Jewess!" "No, she's the daughter of a Christian stockbroker." "Of a Derbyshire squire." "An Irish beauty from the castle, come to make her first winter campaign in London." "No – no beauty – that's the only thing that's positive." How my heart beat when the eye-glasses were first put up; and the stare, and the sneer, and the lounge, were mingled with a few glances of – admiration shall I call them – in the region of fop-alley. But, on the whole, though she took me twice last week, I have not had the satisfaction I expected on going into public with her ladyship; for, in the first place, she is too much taken up with self, and given to flirting, which is abominable in an old woman; and in the next, she is not a good *nomenclator*. Now I see by your face you, as usual, do not understand me; I will try to explain my meaning more fully. I go to the Opera, anxious to see all the lions; more desirous of knowing the fine people, than the business of the stage. A little ugly jewlooking old man enters her box for a few moments; I mechanically turn my eyes away, as I always do, by a sort of instinct, from any object not particularly agreeable. When he has left us, she says, that was the famous Portuguese Conde, [58] whom you said you wished to see so much; Don Manuel Ordognez Felipe, Herrera, D'Aveiro, y Cunha, y Torres, Vicentios y Souza. Or perhaps a strange looking woman, fantastically dressed, stays half an act with her, chatters some nonsense, and departs. As soon as the door is shut, she turns round to me and says, "that was the great Mademoiselle R –, the celebrated foreigner whom all the world is running after." Then I say "dear! why did not your ladyship whisper me that before they came in? I would have looked more at them." She replies, with that delightful toss of the head, which you must remember, "Lord, I thought every body knew them!" Then, in the coffee-room, I look about in hopes / of seeing some distinguished orator, or great military character, that is the talk of the day. Driving home with her I lament my disappointment. Surely, she replies, you must have observed that gentleman in a plain brown coat, who bowed to me as we entered the room; he was standing with several others, who were all talking to me, that was Lord –. And if by all these most distinguishing marks I do not immediately acknowledge him, she adds, "Really I cannot help it, Arbella, if your acquaintance with remarkable people is not so extensive as your excursive imagination leads you to wish it to be." You know her dear deliberate way of saying an obliging thing; though I really believe, knowing my *tic* for celebrated men, she did it once or twice purposely to vex me, in return for a terrible mistake I made the first night I went with her. I thought I could not keep too near her, to avoid falling into any impropriety, and kept my place next to her the whole evening. She was cross to me all the way home, and was talking at me, I could perceive, in her good-natured manner, about the insipidity of girls – the insufferableness of misses – and the hateful stupidity of a female party. At length I happened, unfortunately, to observe, I wondered Lord Kilcare did not break in upon ours, for I saw him opposite to us all night. Then burst the smothered flame. "How could he," she exclaimed, "when he saw his place was occupied?" I directly perceived the famous blunder I had made, and that I had been tormenting her all night without knowing it. So next time we went with our usual ladies, Miss Mountain, and Mrs. Murray, and Sappho, who has come up to learn taste; I was resolved the countess should not accuse me of keeping too near her, and sat quite in a corner at the back of the box, talking to that very Lord Kilcare all night. She often turned round and told me there was room in front, but I obstinately kept my post.

'Returning to my aunt's, she told me / it was very odd I chose to interrupt the performance with my incessant noise, and "vulgar country giggle," instead of staying by some of the ladies of my party. "Lord, madam," said I, "I thought you did not like me to take up those seats; I left that place for Lord Kilcare." She looked confoundedly vexed; but what could I do more? the man had his choice, and if he could not bear the glare of the lights, it was not my fault, was it?'

'So, Miss Mountain is as much as ever with Lady Torrendale?'

'Yes; why should that surprise you? Oh, then you have heard of the hitch there – oh, that will be easily got over. It all originated in that fertile source of pride and dissension, Miss Mountain's estates "on the maternal side." Now, as she was to enrich Strathallan's impoverished revenues with those estates, she thought it but fair Strathallan should, in return, assume the name and arms of the family of Bishop or Dean, or whatever it is that was her mother's maiden name. But the gentleman was unpersuadable; having no fancy for the church, I suppose, he would neither be Dean nor Bishop; and as pride is never so well awake, as when love is fast, quite fast, asleep, not all the estates in Derbyshire, or out of it, could tempt him to take that little name instead of his own. No, no, "the blood of the Fitzroys was up in him," as Major O'Hara would say.'

'Major O'Hara! that is a gentleman mentioned in a letter of Lady Torrendale's,' said Matilda, endeavouring to conceal, under an appearance of curiosity respecting a new subject, the interest she took in Arbella's last piece of information. 'I understand he also pretends to – '

'Oh, yes, my dear, pretends to be very fond of me; it's a long story, and I must defer it to another visit,' resumed Miss Ferrars, who, if the truth must be acknowledged, felt some confusion in speaking of another lover, after her violent professions of eternal constancy to Spencer. 'I must go,' she continued; / her hurry increasing in exact proportion as she found herself at a loss for an answer. 'Bless me!' (running to the window) 'I protest there are Lady Torrendale's liveries. She'll be up stairs in a minute. I know you have been very ill-behaved, my lady,' she continued, in a half aside, 'and I won't stay to help you out. She will be con – *very vexed*, as George Spring calls it, at not finding your mother at home; but she deserves it. Now, bless you, my love, and tell me when you will call; for I want to talk to you about Major O'Hara, and to tell you of Fitzroy's behaviour, and half a hundred more. And for Heaven's sake don't be so flurried when any of that family are named; and don't sit there, looking like the man in the story, who was obliged to eat with a drawn sword suspended over his head. There, now I see I have said something wrong again,' she continued, observing the visible emotion which these last words, that so unexpectedly and forcibly conjured up the most painful circumstance of her life, excited in her hearer. 'Yet how I have done so this time, I confess, I am perfectly at a loss to conceive.'

'And you will ever be so – kind, well-intentioned, inconsiderate Arbella,' Matilda inwardly murmured, as her friend, unconscious of the deep pang she had inflicted, lightly tripped away. 'Of all the aggravations to my sad singular fate, is there any more dreadful than that it is incommunicable?'

The absence of Mrs. Melbourne, who had gone out shortly after the departure of Strathallan, rendered it necessary that Matilda should receive Lady Torrendale. It was a circumstance on which the countess congratulated herself, as she dreaded the scrutinizing eye of her former friend. Her ladyship was accompanied by Miss Mountain, two or three inches taller than usual, by the approaching honour of being a viscountess. Lady Torrendale was in a real or affected flutter of spirits, and went up to Miss Melbourne with apparent / kindness. 'I have been expecting to see you, my dear girl,' she said; 'why did you never come near us?'

'If I had known – ' said Matilda, hesitating, but with dignity. 'If your ladyship had sent – had written a line to let us know that . . . . .'

Lady Torrendale endeavoured to cover her own confusion, by addressing her young friend with some questions about her mother; muttered some unmeaning regrets, and assurances of regard, and then added in the same breath, 'I am very unfortunate never to find her at home.' Miss Melbourne repressed a smile. The countess, only ashamed of having *appeared* ashamed of herself, and vexed to have betrayed, before this little rustic of the Rocks, an embarrassment and want of presence of mind, not uncommon in those who are conscious of having acted ill, (whatever may be their usual politeness, self-possession, or knowledge of the world) now turned to Julia Melbourne, fell into ecstacies upon her beauty; and judiciously praised, to the child herself, the touching air of sensibility with which it was accompanied; forgetting that it owed to its artless and natural expression its greatest charm; and that if sensibility in early life was interesting, a look and character of assumed sentiment was the most revolting thing to be found at that age, where every emotion is expected to bear the stamp of simplicity and truth.

' 'Tis a delicate tiny thing,' said Miss Mountain in her solemn voice, as she raised her up a little, to be able to contemplate her more at ease. 'Her mother did not long survive her birth, I believe. Tell me, my dear, can you remember your mother?' Then staring most distressingly at the little timid girl, she asked her formally 'if she was not reckoned very like the late Lady Julia Melbourne?'

The entrance of the lady of the house was welcomed by the terrified Julia, as the signal for a most grateful release. Not so Lady Torrendale; she felt no joy / at the approach of Mrs. Melbourne, and her little remaining fund of confidence was chilled and dispersed by the look of mingled coldness and surprise, with which Mrs. Melbourne greeted her approach. Her beauty, once so perfect, had been always of a nobler style than that of the countess; and though several years older than her ladyship, the retired life she had led, had preserved it in far greater perfection. The matron-like simplicity of her dress, which announced her widowed state, added to the majesty of her figure and deportment; and the quick glance of that eagle eye, which always looked as if it would pierce the gazer's soul, might well strike awe into a mind accustomed, amid all the assumed airs of wealth and consequence, to look up to hers with a secret acknowledgment of inferiority.

After the first compliments were past, Lady Torrendale tried to rally her spirits; but every look and motion was so constrained, her visit appeared so evidently to be in consequence of the suggestions and wishes of another, that she failed in either feeling, or inspiring, the ease she seemed anxious to restore. How to resume the conversation seemed the difficulty. Expressions of sympathy – condolences for the past – self-gratulations for her present good fortune – seemed likely to be all equally ill-received. A cold silence ensued; at length the countess, recovering a degree of courage, talked with rapidity of her numerous engagements, lamented the daily demands made upon her time, and concluded, turning to Mrs. Melbourne, 'I assure you, I should not have stood upon ceremony, but should have immediately done myself the pleasure of waiting on friends I so much valued, if – I had had your last direction.' This excuse her ladyship thought an ingenious one; and she uttered it with that sort of confident smile and nod, which shewed she expected no reply.

Mrs. Melbourne drily observed that it was three weeks since they had been settled in their abode; now Lady Torrendale / had their address for their former one, and had been in town exactly six. This circumstance, which she perceived had not escaped the penetration of Mrs. Melbourne, made her feel the full force of that apparently simple remark. Unable any longer to conceal her uneasiness, she looked first at Miss Mountain, then at the floor, caressed her little dog, and at length, spite of her usual volubility and boldness, pronounced only an unintelligible and lengthened 'Oh! – ho!'

Miss Mountain, seeing her noble friend thus overset, conceived herself bound to support her; and calling to her aid the French phrases, which she so ingeniously contrived not to mis-pronounce, but to misapply, began by remarking that they had certainly been misinformed; for that the countess had been told Mrs. Melbourne had left her former lodgings before she herself arrived in town, though she could not learn to what part of London she had removed. The stately lady continued to declare 'she could not guess the reason of the deceit, but that people in general were *bien imposans*; and to regret that by it she had been *déterrée* from making her purposed visit. We had no time to enquire into it,' she added. 'Pleasure, you are aware, Mrs. Melbourne, has its martyrs and its slaves, as well as business; and our chains are not perhaps the more pleasing for being made of gold. Be that as it may, on one's first appearance among them, after any thing of an absence, one's friends are very apt to interrupt and hinder what one most wishes to do, by a perpetual succession of offered amusement. Indeed such people are *très prévenans*.'59

If Lady Torrendale was silent during this harangue of her companion's, it was in utter astonishment at the superior boldness she displayed: for the peeress (who had persuaded herself that her visit would be received with gratitude, at whatever time, and in whatever manner it might be paid,) was completely disconcerted by the digni-fied coldness of the / elder lady, and the graceful but almost timid reserve, expressed in the countenance of the younger. She looked at her watch – caressed Julia anew – wisely told her she was a little beauty, and would always continue one, if she would 'look thus, and hold her head just so,' then after a little more common-place chat, reminded Miss Mountain of some engagement, that made it impossible for them to prolong their stay. The young lady rose, again praised the little Julia in flowery phrase, and promised the next time she called to bring her some French toys, which were of a new invention, and *très ingénu*. Then,ᵃ as she made her formal parting courtesy to Mrs. Melbourne, she apologised for the length of time her visit had been deferred, but added, with a gracious smile, '*Je suis sûre que vous n'êtes pas effrontée.*'60

Scarcely had this well matched pair taken their departure, when Mrs. Melbourne yielded to the inclination to laugh which she had scarcely been able to repress in their presence. '*Voilà le monde*! Matilda,' said she.61 'Who would have believed that this lady, who seems to have thought it almost impossible for the sagacity of a Bow-street officer to trace my impervious haunts, was the identical Lady Torrendale, who used to hang upon my words, and affect an admiration, as little deserved as her present neglect. Long, long ago, I knew her. Lady Torrendale is all outside. Those fascinating manners, that at first, more or less, deceive and prepossess persons of every age, (but which should be only the approach to that superior excellence, of which the mind is the proper temple,) form the whole of her character: or, if there be any thing beyond it, the building, unfurnished, dark and narrow, ill corresponds with the splendid por-tico that leads to it.'

Matilda was not disposed thus calmly to moralize. Mrs. Melbourne only saw in the countess a trifling fine lady, alike unworthy of resentment or regard. Her daughter, though their minds had, perhaps, never been in unison, remembered / Lady Tor-rendale in scenes of interest, in moments of tenderness, and mutually shared regret; remembered her, endeared by sorrow, beloved for the services, which, on more than one trying occasion, she had been able to render her: and that it should leave no trace behind! Yet, though it was evident, from her recent conduct, that Lady Torrendale did not experience the slightest wish to soften or participate in the afflictions of her former friends; it would be doing her injustice to believe her capable of intending deliberately to insult them with the insolence of prosperity. No – selfish in all her feelings, the first news of the reverse they had sustained, had been received by her with that mixture of indifference and disgust, which the bare idea of misfortune inspires in minds of a certain class. But she might, perhaps, have still continued a portion of her friendship towards them, had not reasons interfered which shall appear hereafter.

To drive away the unpleasant ideas which Lady Torrendale's visit had excited, Mrs. Melbourne turned the conversation to the other occurrences of the morning. 'You see you alarmed yourself needlessly about Sir Harold,' she said; 'Strathallan heard nothing of him, and all, as yet, is safe.'

'All, *as yet*, is safe!' Matilda repeated, with a deep, convulsive, long-drawn sigh.

'I have great hopes of our eccentric baronet,' resumed Mrs. Melbourne. 'His numerous attentions to you – the solid proofs of friendship we have received – '

'Oh, my mother,' interrupted Matilda, misunderstanding her. 'Would you sacrifice your child?'

'How the mention of that unhappy man alarms you!' said Mrs. Melbourne, looking at her with compassion. 'I only meant to say that I should never have accepted his benefits, but in the hope, that in the opportunities afforded by more frequent intercourse, I might seize one in which he would consent to release you.' / What was Sir Harold's motive for appearing, and whether he would not soon appear again, could not, from the irregularity of his habits, and general flightiness of his conduct, be with any degree of certainty ascertained; and Mrs. Melbourne contrived gradually to draw off her daughter's attention from fruitless and painful speculations, by the art she so eminently possessed, of turning the mind of those, with whom she conversed, towards the most pleasing topics their situation could suggest. The brilliant vivacity which had distinguished her in early life, was tempered, not destroyed, by time, and now shewed itself in the spirit and cheerfulness, with which, after the first shock of misfortune was past, she bore up against the minor miseries attendant in its train. Without any unbecoming pride, a consciousness of innate and superior worth contributed to the equanimity of her temper. She looked on the world with the feelings of a woman, but the discrimination of an elevated mind; and, while she pointed out with humour, devoid of asperity, its contradictions and follies to her daughter's notice, the poignancy of her wit was ever chastened by that bland and winning softness, which in brighter days had made Aspasia Villiers alike the solace of the statesman, and the soother of the student; even the care-harassed Matilda, before she retired to rest, learnt to repeat, with a great deal of self-taught resignation, and a little of her mother's gay philosophy, '*voilà le monde!*' /

CHAPTER XIII.

'Love was given us by the author of our being, as the reward of virtue,
and the solace of care: but the base and sordid forms of artificial (which
I oppose to natural) society, in which we live, have encircled that heavenly rose with so many thorns, that the wealthy alone can gather it with
prudence.'

Sir William Jones.[62]

STRATHALLAN was true to the promise he had given Matilda, to pursue to the utmost,
the interest he felt persuaded he possessed in her heart. With her he had for the first
time tasted the sweet satisfaction of inspiring a passion, in which he was himself alone
the object; and the singular ingenuousness and openness of her character, was ever
preparing for him a succession of new and delicate enjoyments, which he well knew
how to appreciate. Still Matilda, supported and encouraged by Mrs. Melbourne, persisted in her positive rejection of his suit. 'He believes it would ensure his happiness
– he believes he could win over his family to his way of thinking,' she said. 'But if once
you yielded, reason would soon tear away the veil, that passion now draws over every
other interest. 'Tis your high duty, my Matilda, to be the guardian over those interests, which he now despises and neglects; and the more he shews himself incapable of
weighing them with your attractions, the more you should steadily refuse the sacrifice
proposed by this generous young man.'

An ensuing short interview with Lady Torrendale, confirmed Matilda in her
opinion of the justness of her mother's conclusion. Nothing could exceed her coldness when they returned her visit. Mrs. Melbourne was in no hurry to perform this
necessary duty; observing that as she always made it a rule to return civilities exactly
in the manner she received them, that call 'might keep cool.' On / arriving at Fitzroy-
square, the sight of a very elegant landaulet[63] at the door announced there were visitors
within; they found her ladyship, who seemed hardly to have done breakfast, though it
was past two o'clock, in very animated and apparently interesting conversation with
her intimate friend, Mrs. Murray, the lady of the landaulet, who was of course entitled
to twice the attention her other visitors could claim. The countess slightly noticed
her once 'charming Matilda' with a muttered inquiry, and a languid bend of the head;
and paid a little more attention to Mrs. Melbourne, whom she could never see without a slight degree of confusion, but did not introduce either of them to her friend.
She rang for more chocolate, and though they assured her they had long breakfasted,
and refused to touch any thing, continued to press it upon both the ladies; seem-

ing to think that she thus excused herself from taking any other trouble to entertain them. Mrs. Murray stared at both; seemed rather displeased at the intrusion – then, with Miss Melbourne's appearance; then turned towards the elder lady, in whom she seemed to hope to find plainness more consoling; she was soon, however, glad to take refuge in the less assured looks of the innocent and unassuming Matilda; and lastly, turning to Lady Torrendale, resumed the conversation, which this slight interruption seemed only to have rendered more interesting. 'So his whole fortune is to go to his niece, Miss Luttridge.'

'No, my dear creature, I told you it was Miss Luttrell.'

'I assure you Luttridge is the name.'

'Don't you mean the lady in green that we saw at the opera the other night?'

'Well! that was Miss Luttridge.'

'Luttrell you mean?'

'Miss Melbourne, I wish you would take another cup of chocolate – another! – I mean I wish you would – Depend upon it Luttrell is the name.'

During the continuance of this unintelligible / dispute, in which the names of Luttrell and Luttridge were sent backward and forward with the velocity of a game of shuttlecock, at least a hundred times, Lady Torrendale seemed almost unable to remark that there were any other person in the room: at length, having settled that important matter to her satisfaction, she turned to Mrs. Melbourne, and had actually begun some very polite and tender enquiries, when the entrance of another visitor, who seemed to have *les entrées libres*[64] to her ladyship's morning levée, caused a new and a more serious interruption – a young man of very fashionable appearance, whose boots, whip, and general air and dress, at once announced him to be one of the heroes of Bond-street,[65] abruptly approached the countess, and accosted her familiarly with 'Lady Torrendale, you remember my little dog Gip?'

'I cannot say I do,' replied her ladyship, turning from her half finished enquiry, and replying with a complacency which shewed the new comer was a person of importance in her eyes – 'I shall, however, be very happy to hear of any thing that concerns him.'

'I have cut off both his ears, and his tail.'

'Both his ears and his tail! Poor little thing!' repeated Lady Torrendale, looking from Mrs. Melbourne to Mrs. Murray for an answering glance of sympathy.

'Are you not afraid, Lord Kilcare,' she continued, in a plaintive tone of voice, 'that in this cold weather he will suffer by it?'

'Suffer by it! no – what should he suffer? it will do him a great deal of good. Mrs. Murray, I wish you would let me cut your dog's ears for you.'

'My dog's! Heaven defend me from such barbarity!'

'And I return thanks every day,' resumed Lady Torrendale, with a look of becoming piety, 'that my poor dear little Floss is a spaniel, so that it cannot be even proposed to me – for I cannot bear / to give pain to any living creature!' and her eye, carelessly wandering over Matilda, rested upon the lap-dog.

'Only yesterday,' added Mrs. Murray, 'Lady Dareall was walking with her little Flora in the park – little Flora has had her ears recently cut, and they began to bleed again – it was a shocking sight.'

'Oh, but I have an infallible styptic to prevent dogs' ears from bleeding,' resumed my lord.

'And I can tell you that dogs' ears – ' continued Lady Torrendale eagerly.

'Come Matilda, my love,' said Mrs. Melbourne, 'I think we are outstaying our appointment.'

'My dear Mrs. Melbourne, you must not think of running away from us so soon,' cried the countess, hastily rising to stop her, 'you are always in such a hurry – I had a thousand things to say to you.'

'And I will hear them with great pleasure, dear madam, another time.'

'Well – if you must go, you must; but I am really – very – I am sure I am quite – '

'Good morning, good morning – indeed you must excuse us, but I am afraid we shall be late,' interrupted Mrs. Melbourne, as with an air of perfect good humour and self-possession she hurried away, leaving her ladyship in the middle of a speech, which she had begun without carefully considering what should be the conclusion of it; while Matilda, as the transient glow of indignation flushed her cheek, could not forbear inwardly exclaiming, 'Cruel, cruel world! why do thy rules condemn me thus to seek the most selfish, and to avoid the most generous of human beings?'

Of the necessity of avoiding that amiable being, if she wished for tranquillity, Matilda became every day more and more convinced. When she found he would not give up the pursuit, she thought it most prudent to have herself denied to / him; but she could not avoid sometimes meeting him abroad; and whenever it was possible, he renewed the subject most interesting to both their hearts, though banished from her lips. He seemed, by a sort of intuition, to be acquainted with every spot she was most likely to frequent. A morning walk with Julia in the park, a ramble towards the fields in quest of fresher air, or an unambitious turn amidst the dusted shrubs and tamer vegetation of the adjoining square, were equally sure to be intercepted by this watchful and persevering lover; who, with respectful attention that Mrs. Melbourne could not bring herself to repel, and tenderness of address that it was most dangerous for Matilda to admit, joined their party: too happy, if in the course of a lengthened walk he had an opportunity of whispering two words expressive of his unchanged devotion to Matilda.

The appearance of the ladies beyond the precincts of their own house and garden, became more and more rare; but the conduct of Lord Strathallan remained unaltered.

Suddenly, and without the least apparent reason for such a change, the behaviour of Lady Torrendale became as pointedly attentive, as it had been haughty and neglectful. Heedless of the coldness with which her civilities were received, she continued to overwhelm Mrs. and Miss Melbourne with offers of kindness and politeness. Tickets for every place of public amusement to which they might possibly wish to go, crowded in upon them every morning; and visits or enquiries from her ladyship were equally frequent.

They could not avoid being sometimes with her in return; but to her evening parties they steadily refused to go, fearing that at them they might risk meeting Strathallan.

'What can be her ladyship's motives for this wonderful reformation,' Mrs. Melbourne observed, 'is more than we can divine – all that we may be certain of, my child, is that it is for no good.' /

There was one invitation, however, that Lady Torrendale would not hear of Matilda's refusing. This was to grace her young friend Emily's birth-day, of thirteen, with her presence, at a little ball given on the occasion.

'We have included all under the head of dancers from eight to eighteen,' observed the countess, 'purposely to take in both you and Julia. She is not more than eight, is she?'

The idea of Julia's gratification determined Miss Melbourne; and the gratitude that was expressed by the whole party at Torrendale house, made her feel pleased with herself for this prompt compliance with the wishes of her friend. For the first hour, she observed nothing that should make her alter her sentiments. The room that had been set apart for the little dancers was chalked and adorned with festoons of flowers, in a simple but elegant taste.

Notwithstanding the latitude that was given, few exceeded the bounds of childhood; and the unmingled joy that diffused itself over their lively and happy countenances, while engaged in the amusement, seemed to communicate itself, by a correspondent sympathy, to the other guests. Among these Matilda was surprised to meet Arbella. When her friend gaily rallied her on the infringement of a vow she had once playfully made, 'That she would never go to a ball without a beau, or a party without a peeress – '

'True, true, my dear,' she replied, 'I thought I had renounced all such insipid affairs – "Pray, Miss Jane, take Master John, because he cannot do right hand and left, poor little dear! – But Miss Anna, as you are the tallest in the room, you shall have that little soul in petticoats; and above all things take care you do not run over Lord Skip and his partner" – but – all I can say is, I have an aunt and a cousin at home.'

'What an advantage I have over you,' said Matilda, 'in the pleasure these / scenes always give me. I cannot help fancying I share the joy of my poor favourite Edwin, when in vision admitted to the fairy revels –˙

"The little warriors doff the targe and spear,

"And loud enlivening strains provoke the dance.

"They meet, they dart away, they wheel askance;

"To right, to left, they thrid the flying maze."[66]

I almost expect those well-traced flowers and circles to assume a brighter and more emerald glow where marked by their light tread.

'Why, certainly, they can perform the figures with perhaps still more grace and perfection than we, who are "obliged" to flirt up a whole dance, and who have our attention distracted by having to mind whom we choose to dance with, and whom we choose to "stand next." And, after all, I do not know but the lightness and smallness of those little delicate creatures, is best calculated for an amusement, sportive and playful in its essence; that it both satisfies the eye of the spectator, and pleases those engaged in it, better than – '

---

*   Beattie's Minstrel.

'Pleases! They seem indeed completely, and without one drawback, pleased and happy – pleasure, pure, perfect and unalloyed, the only pleasure that deserves the name,' continued the enthusiastic Matilda, while a tear unbidden started into her eye, 'seems to dance in the gay bosom of those little innocent creatures! – happy season! how painful to think it cannot be prolonged.'

'But one would not like to remain a puppet all one's life, without a heart or a soul, though perhaps it would be very convenient,' Arbella continued, while the comparison that she made of the present amusement, with some entertainment of a different kind, seemed to strike her with painful recollection – 'but then when you envy these little souls, you must consider, *mon ange* –

"If few their wants, their pleasures are but few."[67] /

You look surprised; perhaps you do not follow the march of my ideas – So to change their course, we will, if you please, march into one of the adjoining rooms, to see what these good people have prepared for us; for when there is nothing else to be had, my veneration for cakes and custards always rises proportionably.'

After passing through one or two apartments, in which refreshments were served, Arbella led her friend on to a sort of vestibule; but Matilda started back as soon as she had opened the door – 'Why don't you come on, love? Is it that gentleman who frightens you?'

Standing alone, and in apparently deep contemplation of a picture, she beheld Strathallan. He turned towards them with unaffected ease, though the joy that overflowed his heart treacherously betrayed itself in his eyes, at the appearance of Miss Melbourne.

'That is Lady Torrendale's picture,' said he, 'just finished – by Lawrence – [68] Do not you think it does great justice to the original!'

'And so, my young man, you have been staying in the waiting-room, falling in love with "my grandmother's picture:" you will easily make me believe that,' whispered Arbella, in a murmured half-aside.

'It is an age since I have seen you, Miss Ferrars,' continued Strathallan, turning to her with a smile, 'you must favour me with a little of your reviving conversation. I long to have another battle with you;' and drawing Matilda's arm within his, and giving the other to her friend, the trio took, in that manner, several turns up and down the elegantly decorated apartments, during which Strathallan addressed the greater part of his discourse to Arbella, reserving nothing but the more dangerous language of his eyes for Matilda.

'This grows intolerable,' thought Arbella, who was too practised a coquette not / to perceive what was going on before her. 'Matilda, my dear, it is very hot – it is very cold; there is a draught of air in this room – I want my aunt – lord, what am I thinking of? I mean my shawl – Do, do, let us return to the ball-room.'

'Do not return this moment,' Strathallan whispered Miss Melbourne, in a low, persuasive tone. But Matilda followed Arbella's lead, and Strathallan entered the room with them. Matilda moved towards Lady Torrendale, and a party, who were assembled round the fire.

'I was sure, my dear,' Arbella whispered, 'you wanted to get rid of him, but did not know how to do it;' and satisfied with her skilful manœuvring, she proceeded to engage the attention of Strathallan herself; but he seemed wholly taken up with the little interesting Julia. Arbella would play with a child as she would play with a lap-dog, to shew off her vivacity or good nature; but both objects were, in reality, equally uninteresting to her; and if one of those infantine competitors, for a moment, took off the attention which she imagined always to be her due, her indifference changed into absolute dislike and resentment.

'Now come, come away, do, that's a good creature!' she cried, dragging Julia away, rather abruptly, from Lord Strathallan; 'there's a lottery of toys in the next room; and there will not be a single ticket left for you, Julia, if you do not make haste.' There were, however, tickets sufficient for Arbella and Matilda, as well as for the younger Miss Melbourne; and they came in for their share of the prizes, of which Lady Torrendale was the distributor. Never, in Matilda's eyes, had she looked more interesting. During the period of the dancing, as well as that of the lottery which succeeded, she had seemed, for a moment, to have laid aside the fine lady, and to be entirely the mother, contemplating the pleasure and improvement of her child; and when she affectionately called the little Emily to her, and anxiously took precautions against her catching / cold, or over fatiguing herself, the amiable expression of countenance that lit up her faded features, restored to them some of those graces which they might have been supposed to possess in earlier times: these traits were few and transient; her ladyship soon resumed herself, and showed that she still was Lady Torrendale.

The handsomest prize in the collection, (consisting chiefly of fans, lockets, bracelets, smelling-bottles, necklaces, rings, toothpick-cases, and a variety of toys and trinkets, in ivory and sandal-wood) was a large broach, of a beautiful composition, set round with pearls of some value. Now this broach was intended as a *galanterie*[69] to Miss Mountain; but by some mistake in the distribution of the prizes, it fell to Matilda's share. Lady Torrendale took an opportunity to inform Miss Mountain of its original destination, lamenting the awkward blunder by which it had been attached to the ticket held by 'that chit, Miss Melbourne.' She then sought out Matilda, and with one of those fascinating smiles with which she usually prefaced any of her false confidences, she in a whisper declared she congratulated herself upon her lucky mistake; by which, she said, the ornament had fallen to one, whose person was so much better calculated to adorn it; and added, 'if I must own my little malice, and I will, (for I value sincerity above all things,) I am glad you have mortified that ugly, stiff Mountain of pride; for her manners are growing insufferable, even to me.' Matilda, who by this time had learnt how to appreciate her ladyship's 'sincerity,' made no reply to this compliment: the acquisition of a prize of any value, was a matter of great indifference to her; and it was not till long afterwards that she found the circumstance productive of consequences to her, which, from its apparent unimportance, she had not anticipated.

At supper, Arbella found ample occasion to renew the lamentations excited by the superior air of joy and contentment, that appeared in every face around, from / what she had observed at more brilliant entertainments. 'How enviable,' she cried, 'the delight of those creatures! That little lord seems to have attained the *summum bonum* in the plate of trifle that is before him; and this little lady feels not a want or a wish, beyond those tempting raspberry drops; one young gentleman's whole soul is in his yellow shoes, and another young lady's whole heart in her green braces! How they eye each other! Toes turned in most pertinaciously, forming the model for Lady Spencer's correspondent designs of "new shoes," "nice supper;" and that little fellow is happier than Fitzroy, after he had turned the heads of a whole ball-room; and little miss is happier than – heigho! There are no disputes where one shall sit – and who one shall talk to; and, when tired of eating, they have only to feast their eyes on temples and sugared ornaments, and be content!'

And now the more prudent part of the company made the signal for retiring, and while each mother seemed anxiously engrossed in her darling charge, Matilda, who was truly one to Julia, was carefully securing her against any possible injury from the night air, of which the peculiar delicacy of her cousin's constitution made her more particularly apprehensive. Entirely engrossed by this object, and totally regardless of that admiration which Arbella was labouring so hard to obtain, she heeded not the enchanted gaze of Strathallan, when, hastily taking from her neck a light blue scarf, which she had worn the whole evening in consequence of her having a slight cold, she tied it round that of the little girl; discovering, for the first time that night, the ivory whiteness of her beautifully formed throat, which till then had been partially shaded. He admired the graceful turn of her form; far more the kind, the almost maternal expression that glowed in every mind-illumined feature; and only quitted his silent stand to follow her down stairs, and hand her to her chair. /

In returning her fan, she perceived he had slipped a paper, with it, into her hand. It was not long before she examined its contents.

'Time presses. – I am beset with the arguments of worldlings. – I can hardly bear the sight of a father's increasing anguish and anxiety; yet can I relieve it at the expense of my feelings – my principles – my life?

My spirit shrinks from the idea of owing a weight of obligation to one, whom I cannot even repay by the possession of my heart. That honour which once urged me to be hers, now equally whispers against our union. My hopes were unclouded, my fortune flourishing, when we were mutually promised to each other; shall I now, with fortune impaired, and all the future shaded with gloom and apprehension, ask her to share it? Still I have enough left for happiness and Matilda: – say but the word, and I am at your feet: but beware how you drive me to despair; – in one rash moment I may –

Adieu, dearest! gentlest! I will not re-read these distracted lines: trust me they give the picture of a heart which, though torn by varied sufferings, tortured by anxiety, wrung by undeserved reproach, will never cease to throb in every bleeding vein for you. Farewell, most lovely, most beloved of women!

Thine, (while he is his own,)
'Strathallan.'

The despairing earnestness with which this proposal was urged, for a moment staggered the resolution of Matilda. She could think of nothing but her noble, her suffering lover. Her heart was wholly with *his,* that was offered, so generously, so unconditionally to her. His feelings were, in hers, as in a limpid stream reflected; and, like the image in a stream, in faithful, but somewhat fainter colours; / as suited best the, if possible, still greater purity and delicacy of her timid, retiring, fearful love. Yet, when she reconsidered his letter, she saw nothing but wretchedness inevitable, and too late repentance, as the consequence of her compliance. She perceived the necessity of keeping a strict watch over passions so much stronger than her own: too conscious that it required only to meet his eyes to render vain the conflict of months.

She now confined herself entirely within her narrow domestic circle, scarcely venturing abroad, and never where there was any chance of seeing him.

'You become quite a prisoner,' said Clara: 'you will lose your cheerfulness, your health, almost your existence.'

'Fear not for me,' Matilda replied. ' 'Tis only thus I can ensure my freedom. I acknowledge no bonds but the disgraceful claims of passion, – I know no evil but weakness, – no enemy but the persevering love of Strathallan!'

CHAPTER XIV.

Dear are those bonds my willing heart that bind,
Formed of three chords, in mystic union twined;
The first, by Beauty's rosy fingers wove,
The next by Pity, and the third by Love.

ROSCOE'S Translation of Lorenzo de Medici.[70]

STRATHALLAN TO MATILDA.

'I MAKE you a prisoner. I shut you out from society. The very air is grown hateful to you, since it may be shared with me. – It is enough: – I yield. The morning has dawned upon the third day passed at a distance from – you. Days, welcomed by you as the return of tranquillity and pleasure. By me! – Oh! Matilda, you never knew the pangs of absence: – suffice it, they are past.

But I am not forbidden to write. I will make one more attempt. It is yet / time. Could I see you, I am sure I have arguments of force to move you; but, repulsed by your family, – denied your sight. – At your house I am received by your mother with a look that chills my hopes, or by that mournful nun, in whose very aspect I, shuddering, read a fearful omen of eternal separation.

Dear, dear Matilda! in adversity how doubly dear! – Yet why should I call that adversity which brings me nearer you? You say I have no right to urge my plea: – yes, loveliest, I have a right, a claim, – sorrow has made you mine; and here I solemnly swear to renounce all bonds, but those she has twined around me.

Vain arguments! – they will not change the sternness of your immoveable determination. – Yet still I write – I experience no cessation from torment, but in action. While I am thus employed, I do not wholly yield to despair. – Each plan attempted supposes possibility. When I recal the last delightful hours we passed together; when I behold your mild features beaming on others with interest or compassion, I cannot, no, I cannot believe that heart can be steeled against me alone. It is but too true; and my life, for this last year, has been a sweet, fallacious dream. Oh, had I died when report announced my death! Matilda would have mourned me, and pity would have wrung those tears that are denied to love. How fondly I believed them the sweet earnest of more precious tears! But no; – where most I seek affection, a malignant fate still delights to snatch from me the only boon I value, and I shall leave the world with the cruel thought, that by none have I been ever truly loved.

It is midnight; but rest does not suit the fever – the madness of my mind. The hour shall be given to you, – to you, cruel girl; to make you, if possible, share the sufferings I endure, since bliss, with me, you will not share. /

You will call these the ravings of passion. – You will smile, in the dignity of superior firmness, at the frenzy that dictates them. – You will despise their writer, – and you are right – for I despise myself.

I am no boyish lover. – I was not used to be the mere creature of passion – to live upon a smile; there are moments, in which my soul rises against its self-imposed slavery; and do you not fear that, in one of those moments, it may for ever burst its chain?

Matilda, it is in vain to deceive ourselves. – We were intended for each other. I have been thinking, but I can find no obstacle, such as your cruel prudence would suggest; no obstacle of force sufficient to break those bonds, which Heaven itself has formed; and should you indeed succeed, would not your heart at length confess a pang like mine? – Am I deceived? – Let me atone for my presumption at your feet. Recal me to you, – recal me to myself.'

It appeared that there the letter was meant to end; but a few more lines were added, in which the same request was still more passionately urged.

'I look every where, but in vain, to seek myself. – In these fond transports I know not Strathallan. Oh, Matilda, this subjection is grievous, even though endured for you. – My spirit spurns at once, and loves its chain.

Spurns did I say? forgive the unconscious treason, and think it only a different form of giving words to hopeless love. – Yes, weep for me, and pray that I may be restored to reason, virtue; – armed with resolution to endure my pitiless fate. – They say the prayers and tears of angels are accepted. – Restrain them yet; – I'll make one effort more: one effort upon nature and compassion. My father was not wont to scorn the plaints of a kneeling son. I will tell him the sacrifice he demands of me is beyond my power, beyond my strength. / I will tell him my whole existence hangs upon my noble-minded, my obdurate love; on her, to whose firmness alone, he owes that I have not, in despite of his ambitious views and wishes – Oh! when his heart yields, as it surely will, and admits the claim of such distinguished virtues; then, blest with a father's sanction, I shall no longer fear a repulse. – I shall no longer fear distracting doubts, and suggested difficulties, even from Matilda.'

With such letters, which he contrived, through Hanway, to convey to Matilda, Strathallan endeavoured to relieve the severity of his sufferings, when denied her sight; and, if possible, to work some change in her sentiments. – They wrung her heart; but could they alter her resolution?

CHAPTER XV.

'True filial love, like the love of God, is accompanied with an awe and reverence, which, if its object will not remit or a little abate, they may live for ever in the same room, and be utter strangers to each other.'

HERVEY.[71]

MRS. Melbourne was fully convinced of the truth of this observation; and from her daughter's earliest childhood had so blended, in her conduct towards her, the characters of parent and friend, that those delightful associations, too often irreconcileably divided, formed but one idea in Matilda's mind. In the retired life which choice and necessity conspired to make her lead, she felt the inestimable advantage of so amiable and enlightened a companion. There was no point in which Mrs. Melbourne differed from her sufficiently to disturb the intimate union and confidence that marked their little social / circle. Conformity of character is not absolutely necessary to friendship; though it is difficult for it to subsist under a perfect opposition of taste and sentiment: a degree of diversity only adds poignancy to its charms. In conversation Matilda had the most captivating flow of language, where any subject of feeling was discussed – most of the *éloquence du cœur*.[72] Mrs. Melbourne had perhaps more liveliness of remark, and brilliancy of imagination. Among the arts, drawing was that in which Mrs. Melbourne most excelled. Miss Melbourne, though she understood, and had practiced it with success, still gave the preference to music. Yet in the most unguarded moment of conversation, of sportive contest, or unbounded confidence, the manner of Matilda never had, at any time, passed those limits of deference, which no freedom should ever tempt a child, when addressing a parent, to overstep. In her respectful familiarity there was no assumption of equality, nothing that could for a moment appear, to the most superficial observer, to resemble the manner suited to a companion of her own age, welcome and becoming, when employed towards a friend; towards an Arbella.

That young lady found her aunt wholly averse to paying Mrs. Melbourne those civilities in town, which she had, with importunate servility, forced upon her in the country; and Mrs. Melbourne, who had held back very much from Mrs. Stockwell's acquaintance in her most prosperous days, was by no means sorry to escape her vulgar impertinence, when less agreeably, or, at least, less showily situated. Miss Ferrars was not, however, to be deterred, by that circumstance, from having her dear little dish of gossip with Matilda, as she styled it. Wishing to consult her upon the subject of Major O'Hara, she entered upon it at once, with 'Do you know, my dear, the major talks of getting leave to join me in town, and I mean to write to him not / to think of it. Yet still to word it in such a manner – for he is not to be despised; he is gay, handsome, polite, *et pour la reste* – Why, Lord!' she continued, answering Matilda's eyes, 'you would not have them all judges and philosophers.'

'I said nothing!'

'No, but you *looked* something. I cannot bear those eyes of yours.'

'I hope the gentlemen are not of your opinion,' replied Miss Melbourne, attempting to catch the gaiety of her friend.

'No, you know they are not – you are safe enough there. I never saw so much art with so little – : well, I'll not find fault with you, since you don't own to it, and, as the major says, *peccato celato*. You remember the rest. Apropos, do you know Major O'Hara has been in Italy? Can talk very well about the Pope, and the palaces at Rome, and the Florentine gallery, and the charms of a little Venetian Barcelone. It saves a great deal of drawing upon one's own intellectual bank, which I am afraid would sometimes protest the bill.'

'Still the major!' interrupted Matilda. 'So Spencer, I see, is quite forgotten.'

'Spencer!' repeated Arbella, starting as if thrilled by that name. 'How could you, Matilda, bring me so suddenly to the most painful part of my story? when I, like a poor giddy insect, was fluttering and fluttering around it, treating of every thing distant from it, knowing it was necessary, yet fearing to approach. Spencer forgotten!' she continued, while the alteration in her voice and countenance announced the painful perturbation of her mind. 'No, no; while one pulse that beats within this anxious frame vibrates to the voice of love or joy, thy name, dear Spencer, will never, never, be forgotten! Heigho, Matilda! there are moments, in which it is in vain to say, like La Volubile, in the Canzonet: /

'Vo' star allegramente,

'Non vo' pensar a niente.'[73]

The heart, the rebel heart, cries out, and will be heard. And then what a sudden pang, what agony, we sprightly ones for the moment endure. My only way is to run to my instrument, and rattle off a march, or a country dance, to drown its voice; or, if that won't do, rattle up my aunt, or my cousin Sam, or some wretch equally odious; or, if all is not sufficient, go and tease you, my sweet friend, who possess in your cheering conversation the only true specific against all such spasms. To-day Lady Torrendale shewed me a letter, in which Fitzroy, after a great deal of buzz, informs her of the progress he has made in the good graces of a northern heiress, whom he met accidentally at Grasmere, or Windermere, or some of those places; and he believes that he shall soon be united. Stay, no, I must give you the exact expression: surely the mother and son were formed from the self-same model. That "he believes he must soon take pity on Lady Margaret Maclean." She did so laugh when she came to that expression, and exult in the address, and the airs of her darling Fitzroy. The wretch! after all he has said and sighed at Woodlands! but I had reason to expect it. Not a line, not a word ever came to confirm those protestations, from the time he left us to join his regiment. But I would have his Lady of the Lake, his high-born Margaretta, beware how she fancies she has secured that wandering heart. 'Tis but to alarm Spencer's jealousy, and he is here in an instant. Now O'Hara will exactly answer my purpose; for, imprimis, he is the fashion, which is all in all, according to my way of reasoning.'

'In a lover? I don't admit your major.'

'But you would, my dear, if you saw him. There is not a house in Buxton that could resist admitting him while he / stayed. He is the most beautiful, admirable – quite of that species.'

'A beautiful – admirable – Indeed, Miss Ferrars?' exclaimed Sowerby, who had just that moment strolled into the room, with a book in his hand. 'May I be favoured with a sight of it?'

'Oh, lud! sir,' cried Arbella, forcing herself with the greatest difficulty to repress her laughter. 'It – it is – not here.'

'Can you oblige me then with a description of it? Is it larger than the ordinary size of that kind of Papilio?'

'Rather, sir,' replied Arbella.

'Any variation as to colour?' continued Mr. Sowerby, gravely pulling out a pencil, and beginning to write.

'No, sir, not much. The usual scarlet and black, or some dark mixture, only its two superior wings are of a bright golden colour, and – '

'My dear sir, we were not talking of butterflies; it is an officer she means,' interrupted Matilda, who did not choose the grave pursuits of her friend should expose him to the childish ridicule of Arbella.

A significant 'pugh!' from Sowerby evinced the contempt he felt upon this discovery.

'Pugh!' repeated Arbella, most highly offended, 'you shall unsay that "pugh!" again, Mr. Philosopher. I'll teach you to treat young ladies so, who do you the honour of making a rational reply to your tiresome observations.' Then approaching the window, where he still stood, affecting to be more intently engaged than ever upon his book, 'May I be permitted, sir?' she said aloud, as she archly peeped over his shoulder. 'What have we got here? Philosophical Transactions![74] I wonder, Mr. Sowerby, you can waste your time on such reading.'

'Why, young lady, do you not think it at least a harmless way of passing time?' /

'Harmless enough; but it is so stupid!'

Sowerby stared, and for some moments could not recover from his astonishment, at the unparalleled liberty thus taken with the dignity of his silent studies; a liberty, that, in the course of their long and intimate acquaintance, his gentle Matilda had never once ventured upon. This was exactly what Arbella wanted.

'You are no doubt a good judge, young lady, of the object of those pursuits you take upon you to deride.'

'Something of a judge, I flatter myself, sir. I have attended the lectures of a few professors; have gone through a course of chemistry; and since my acquaintance with Miss Melbourne, have endeavoured to avail myself of her uncommon acquirements, to – '

'Really!' exclaimed Sowerby, and condescended to enter into conversation with the fair intruder, and to examine a little into her pretensions to such universal acquirement. Arbella had some knowledge, and still more knack. What she had learnt, she could bring out immediately, and display to the greatest possible advantage; and if ever she found herself at a loss, she displayed such good humour and candour in the acknowledgement of her deficiency, that it amply compensated for the want of greater depth of information. Even the severe Mr. Sowerby could not bring himself to bear hard upon errors, which were acknowledged with a laugh, betraying two rows of teeth, like pearls for evenness and lustre, and a blush, which brought the pure blood in transparent brilliancy to animate the clear brown of her ever varying complexion. 'You will be surprised to find me so learned;' she continued, turning gaily to Matilda, after he had left the room. 'I, who before the high-priest of Apollo, Alcæus, had vowed fidelity to the cerulean symbol of Belles Lettres, and a thousand times forsworn the dirty nymphs of the mines and crucible.[75] / Well, postpone your curiosity, for I want now to talk about Sir Harold. Did you ever hear any reason assumed for his giving up his superb family residence, and pitching his tent at the Rocks?'

'Never!'

'And can't you guess it?'

'No!'

'Oh, then I cannot venture to tell you. Indeed, I don't know it myself; and it would not be right to say it. What? have you no curiosity? won't you ask? Sir Harold gets his wines from Italy, his servants from France; what if a little Neapolitan nun, or Milanese signora, had accompanied his rapid flight back to England, and declared the wilderness, and the gold fish-pond, and the camera obscura at the Rocks, the prettiest, "tastiest" things she had ever seen since she left her dear native home; and that she would not, no, she could not, leave them to return to that gloomy old mansion, among the ghosts and the goblins, and the owls and the ivy! Or perhaps some little sylph speaks peace to his wounded spirit from the groves. Some fairy strews good luck on every sacred room, or in short – '

'Arbella, that is not a subject to jest upon,' said Matilda gravely. 'Sir Harold is my relation, and as such I must be interested in what concerns him. He is Julia's brother, and I must wish him, for her sake, a man of honour and principle. If you have any thing seriously against him, say it; if not, do not, by ambiguous hints, trifle with a calamity that – '

'Nothing, nothing, but guess-work, my dear, I assure you. Sir Harold may be the very mirror of knighthood, and flower of chivalry, for any thing that I know to the contrary. Lord how she colours! I did not think it could interest you so much. To call a new cause, you see Lord Torrendale is proceeding in all his grand nuptial preparations, very much to his own satisfaction, and soon I believe somebody may sing "*Più non ho la dolce speranza.*"[76] Heavens! what have I done?' / she continued, observing the emotion her friend in vain endeavoured to conceal.

'Now I take all the powers above to witness, I meant Miss Langrish, when I rattled off that remark. One may talk of Miss Langrish, may not one? As for another dear little friend of mine, my *real* opinion is, that she has nothing to fear. The exalted Sophia must love her Strathallan; it is impossible but she must, with all her greatness and her coldness too. But I am positive – stay – I won't be positive of any thing. Yet surely, if those "Eyes, like break of day;" those "Lights that do mislead the morn,"[77] do not mislead me too, which would be a much worse thing, they tell me the bird will yet burst through his confinement. They tell me Strathallan will never consent to unite himself for money to that *mountain* of pride and paint. Excuse me, but I am positive she enamels; ay faith, and puts on a vast deal too.' Arbella noticed the expression of surprise and dislike, that Matilda could no longer restrain, at language so new and unbecoming, and which she had heard often repeated during the latter part of their conversation. 'Now,' continued Miss Ferrars, enjoying her friend's astonishment, 'she thinks me quite rusticated with my aunt, because I use a few expletives, to embroider and set off my meaning; but 'tis quite the reverse: they are fresh from the mint. Lady Dareall and Lady Barbara Montravers have made them quite the rage, and they have become the most fashionable women in the world by it.'

'Do you not rather think such language is become fashionable *because* Lady Dare-all uses it, than that Lady Dareall has become fashionable by the use of such language; and had not we better, my Arbella, who are not at the topmost round of fashion's ladder, content ourselves with imitating some of the many graceful and improving models the great world affords, than risk exposing ourselves to its censure, by following any one solitary example into dangerous eccentricity, without / possessing rank or consequence to excuse it, or make it admired?'

'Hum! there may be something in what you say: for certainly those women are of the very first dash. Now whereabouts was I when you interrupted me? O, I was saying that Strathallan – '

'Dear Arbella!'

'Well, I will not name Strathallan, if the sound is disagreeable to you. What shall I call him, charmer, charmer, charmer? We will give him the name of *le Desiré, le Bien-aimé*,[78] or whatever other *nom de guerre*, or rather love-name, you like best. By the by,' continued the volatile Arbella, overlooking, in the new train of ideas her fancy had raised, the subject which but a moment before had employed her thoughts: 'Do you not think that word *Bien-aimé* has a charm in the French language, which we would vainly endeavour to transfer into our own? In Claire d' Albe for instance, (but you would never read Claire d'Albe for me, you obstinate gipsy) it has a tenderness – an expression; and in that other novel, (by the same writer) which I call Love in the Deserts, for I always forget the name; when the dear charming three-tailed Bashaw, that Malek Adhel, says to your name-sake, "*Que crains tu, ma bien-aimée?*"[79] Oh Lord! I am sure I should have feared nothing with such a defender. Now how would you render the expression *Bien-aimée*? The literal translation is horrid. *Well-beloved!* you might as well at once say, right trusty, and well-beloved.'

'It does not convey that idea to me,' said Matilda, smiling. 'I have friends well-beloved, yet whom I would by no means trust.' In uttering this sentiment Matilda was far from meaning to insinuate any idea to the disadvantage of Arbella; though to some it might appear that, while at the same time encouraging Captain Fitzroy and Major O'Hara, she wished also to have the grave philosopher in her train. But Matilda knew her friend's principle, on those occasions. To / please was her whole design. 'You can never have too many *prôneurs*,'[80] was her maxim. 'Those who may not please, at least can praise. In this bad world success is merit. A circle of beaux is the true cestus of beauty, and attracts additional admirers to the fair one, who, if observed to be neglected by some, might be pronounced unworthy of the attention of any. The fruit that's most picked by the birds, is always observed to be the best,' says the dear countess. And with these laudable maxims, Arbella applied herself, and with success, during the frequent visits she paid her friend, to gain the 'good word' of Mr. Sowerby.

CHAPTER XVI.

'Who aims at every science, soon will find,
The field how vast – how limited the mind!'

MISS MORE. *Search after Happiness.*[81]

LADY Torrendale had not forgotten her good custom, taken up at Woodlands, of sending Miss Melbourne notes, in what she called the language of 'the dear region.' When these contained any thing that could amuse the social circle, they were read aloud; but sometimes the 'gipsy jargon' was so unintelligible, as to be evidently intended for Miss Melbourne's eye alone. One evening when the usual party, consisting of Sowerby, his sister, Mrs. Melbourne, and Matilda, were assembled, one of these rose-coloured billets arrived; and, being delivered to Mr. / Sowerby by mistake, for one he had that day expected, was read by him, with good emphasis, for the benefit of the company. It was without a signature, and the following is a literal transcript of the contents:

'My dear soul,

'We are all at sea without the admiral; are there no hopes of *Vice* or *Rear?* Above all things the Orange flag is to be preferred; but perhaps you would less scruple about the Mitre?'

Sowerby had the greatest confidence in the discretion of Matilda; but there was something in the allusions contained in this ambiguous billet, that staggered and confused all his ideas. He was aware Miss Melbourne might have met at Lady Torrendale's many acquaintance, of whom he knew nothing. But if she confided plans to a stranger, from which he was excluded; if he was to lose the character of her friend and guide, life no longer presented to him any thing pleasing or desirable. These thoughts, as they rapidly crossed his mind, betrayed themselves partly in his countenance. Miss Melbourne observed them, and the innocent and spontaneous burst of laughter, in which she so seldom indulged, instantly restored his good humour, and dispelled his fears. 'May I be entrusted then with the key to this wonderful and astonishing billet?' he asked with a smile.

'My dear sir, the key is, that Lady Torrendale is making a little museum.'

'A museum!' Sowerby repeated, with the air of a person who had at once discovered the clue to some intricate mystery; and then, knitting his brow, with an air that convinced Matilda it was in vain to urge the request that trembled on her lips, he instantly turned the conversation.

It will be necessary, in order to explain this scene, to refer to the occurrences of the preceding week. Matilda had forgotten to remind Arbella of her promise, to inform / her how it happened she had made such a wonderful progress in the sciences; when a card of invitation to a conversazione upon a new plan, at Lady Torrendale's, at once solved the difficulty. This ticket, which was of white and gold, adorned with groups of plants, shells, and foliage, on its embossed border, and farther decorated by a pleasing design, representing 'amusement lighting her torch at the lamp of science,' unveiled to Matilda the nature of her ladyship's present pursuits; and she was not slow in, herself, unfolding them more fully to her young friend. 'At length I have hit upon something, that I think will please you,' she said. 'I used to talk of renewing the literary conversaziones in London; but I find we were all wrong there. Scientific assemblies, to hear some clever man talk, are all the rage; and I don't see why I should not avail myself of the great advantage I had in Derbyshire, of an introduction to a family so much better versed in those matters, than any of our fashionable dillettanti can pretend to be. You will be the chief ornament of these conversaziones, which must be quite to your taste; and you can put me right whenever – '

'Excuse me, dear madam: the state of my mother's spirits at present prevents her from mixing in society; and I make it a rule never to leave her.'

More disappointed than the occasion seemed to require, her ladyship renewed her entreaties, and made use of every form of persuasion to gain her point; but Matilda, sometimes referring to her necessary attention to her mother, sometimes to the care that Julia required, continued resolutely to refuse going to Lady Torrendale's, or rather to the house which Strathallan inhabited; till the countess wearied out, exclaimed, 'What then am I to do? I must have these people, as I have asked them; and I hope you will give me a little assistance, though you won't be of the party. We are to begin with conchology; and that will bring my / collection into play. Now it is far from being complete, and I was quite vexed with Lady Valeria Volute, to whom I shewed it the other day, and who, the whole time, kept looking up and down, and enquiring for every thing she did *not* see, instead of admiring what she *did*. "Have not you got a watering-pot? I don't see any admirals, nor any nautili. You could surely procure some admirals, Grand, Vice, or Rear. Dear Lady Torrendale, you have been shamefully taken in; you have hardly got any thing but what a conchologist would throw aside, as only fit to make flowers, and adorn grottos in ladies shell-work!" Now I should like to shew her it is not so; yet I do not wish to go to any enormous expense neither. They say a single Admiral (the Orange Flag, I believe,) was sold abroad for a million of florins.'

'A hundred, dear Lady Torrendale.'

'Well a hundred, or whatever it was; any coin could I think be a great deal better employed, particularly when one can borrow of one's friends, who know better how to choose those things. So you know you will ask Mr. Sowerby.'

'Ask him what, madam?'

'Did not I explain myself sufficiently?' returned Lady Torrendale, a little vexed by the slowness of her young friend: then altering the mode of attack, 'I am to have a very clever man,' she said, 'on Thursday, and there's to be Lady Valeria Volute, and Lady Virginia Nightingale, and this Mr. Professor Von Krustakoat, from Sweden, will give us a dissertation upon non-descript shells; and we are to have a little mineralogy, and a little chemistry; and now if I could show Mr. Professor Von Krustakoat a specimen of the buccinum, the beautiful non-descript from New South Wales, it would greatly assist his eloquence, and make him think my collection superior even to Lady Valeria's. Now tax your memory, my sweet Matilda; do you know of any one who has such a shell?'

'Really I do not; perhaps Sir J – / B –, or perhaps your ladyship will find it at the British Museum, or – '

'Perhaps, you are a dear charming little simpleton. It is Mr. Sowerby has the buccinum in his possession; the scarlet buccinum, the most beautiful of all; and he must lend it me for one night, for my scientific supper.'

'Excuse me, dear Lady Torrendale,' interrupted Matilda, with a look of alarm. 'I dare not ask him such a thing; indeed I dare not. You know not the value he sets upon his collections.'

'Indeed I do, and I set a great value on them too, and that's the reason he must lend me some of them. The buccinum, and the mitre, and several different sorts of admirals,' continued her ladyship, enumerating what she wanted with the most provoking obstinacy, and as if she had not heard Matilda's objection. 'Why, Lord,' she pursued, 'you do not think I want to embezzle them? You know I think a piece of china much prettier, and after the evening was over would not care if all the shells that ever existed were sunk in the sea, from whence they came; only when I exhibit my cabinet of natural curiosities, let me but appear to possess them, and – '

Matilda smiled at the mingled inanity and love of vain display which this confession exhibited; so completely illustrating in another point of view her mother's observation, that Lady Torrendale was *all outside*; but she knew too well Mr. Sowerby's peculiar aversion to all such applications, to undertake a commission in which failure seemed inevitable.

'Well,' resumed her ladyship abruptly, 'I really did think, Matilda, you would have been a little more obliging. I give up the buccinum, but the other shells I positively must have, or I put off the party. To have them all coming down upon me, and find me so utterly unprovided; and after boasting so much too! Lady Valeria Volute, Lady Virginia, and Lady Chrysanthia Nightingale, Sir Haarlem Von Huyser, Sir Jacob / Thornback, Mr. Petal, Mr. Cruciform, and Mr. Professor Von Krustakoat!' But perceiving this enumeration did not affect her auditor so much as herself, she added, 'If you will not be persuaded, we will think no more of it; but there is one little favour, which depends entirely on yourself, and which I trust you wont deny me; it is to let me have some of those specimens of Indian grasses, that your –, that you promised me once in the country.'

'With pleasure, dear Lady Torrendale,' said Matilda, delighted she had it at last in her power to oblige her noble friend. 'The jatamansi I think you mean.'

'I believe I do. I don't know what I mean; you have put all my ideas into confusion. All I was thinking was, that as we may have a little botany in the course of the evening, it might be an opportunity to shew one's knowledge.'

'Certainly, madam; and you will remember,' continued Matilda, gently prompting her, 'that it is supposed to be the same with the Indian nard. Indeed, with the name of nard, spike-nard, and other Eastern perfumes,' (she continued smiling) 'we are pretty well familiarised in a book we often read.'

'A book we often read?' exclaimed her ladyship, eagerly. 'What upon earth can that be – one of Alcæus's?'

'No; an Oriental work.'

'An Oriental work! It must then be the Arabian Nights. – No? – Nor the Persian Tales!'

Matilda blushed; and after the countess had run herself almost out of breath, half through the 'Cabinet des Fées,'[82] could not bring her herself to name what the book was, to which she had alluded. 'Well, now I am ready to take my departure,' said her lively ladyship. 'I am only waiting for the Buccinum, the Mitre, and the Volutes.' This sudden attack proving as unsuccessful as the preceding ones, Lady Torrendale found herself obliged reluctantly to give up, with a secret / acknowledgment, that the quiet directness and steadiness of her young friend, was a match for all the starts and windings of her little policy. She, however, could not be led so easily to renounce her other object, which was to draw Matilda to her house; and, in pursuance of this design, continued to practise various manœuvres, many of which were as curious as the one above related. On that occasion, as in every drama where she bore a part, her ladyship, it may be observed, contrived to have an underplot (involving some petty and ridiculous interest) going on at the same time; for she really intended the scientific display, she had mentioned with such complacency to Matilda; and the note Sowerby had read, was the result of a despairing effort to obtain, from the good-nature of her young friend, the articles she so much desired.

From her varied persecutions Miss Melbourne at length was freed, by the departure of the countess.

Lord Torrendale, though he could not be induced by any arguments to change his determination with regard to Strathallan, suffered so much from the sight of, the misery he caused, and the daily increasing domestic dissensions which divided his family, that it brought on a severe attack of a bilious complaint, to which he was often subject, and he was advised by his physicians to try the Tunbridge waters for relief. His lady declared she would accompany him, at least for a week or two, and announced her intention in a take-leave visit to Mrs. Melbourne, in which she did not fail to assume some credit to herself for leaving London, though for ever so short a time, at the height of its gaieties.

'To be sure,' she said, 'I shall disappoint Lady Heathcote, and Lady Lyndhurst, and Lady Kilcare, and Mrs. Murray, and Lady Jane Murray, and Mrs. Howard; and there's Miss Mountain's grand masquerade, and poor little Miss De Courcy, that I promised to take out whenever her dear literary mother was in / the vapours or had the *blue* devils. I have engagements, three for every evening, but my duties must be preferred to them all. Sad restraints, Matilda, but unavoidable to persons of *our* way of thinking. His friend Villiers has made every thing agreeable to Torrendale, by lending him his house; yet still, as he is not well, I do not like to let him go among strangers by himself, quite at first – he might miss my attentions; and, besides,' she added in a whisper, 'to tell you the truth, I mean by this *short excrescence*, as poor Mrs. Stockwell would call it, to *cut* the scientific assemblies. You know I planned them partly for you, but as you were so disagreeable,' (how her ladyship had contrived to travel from Tunbridge to her 'disagreeableness,' Matilda could not guess – but so it was,) 'as you were so disagreeable, they have few attractions for me. The evening passed off very heavy. None of my friends made any figure. Little Sappho, whom I had desired to be remarkably brilliant, was quite the reverse. I mistook her, I find; I thought she was a – somehow you know – a genius; but at the end of Mr. Professor Von Krustakoat's discourse upon conchs, she had absolutely nothing to say; and Mr. Cruciform assured me she did not know the difference between Anthoxanthum odoratum, and Trifolium Macrorrhizum. – Arbella yawned, – Strathallen was distracted; but that is only *comme a l' ordinaire*;[83] and Lord Torrendale was, if possible, more oppressive than usual. Well, you know this cannot go on: so having given out I should have two of these scientific parties a week, I am not sorry, by going for a little time into the country, to make the whole plan be forgotten; and may be, by the time I return, something quite new will be the fashion. And now I am come to the grand favour for which, to let you into a secret, I have paid this visit: it is to request you will take charge of my little wild girl for the week or ten days that I shall be out of town. I do not want to take her down to Tunbridge with me for / so very short a time, because children are very troublesome, and I have nobody to stay with her, as I have been just obliged to dismiss Miss Langrish, for a thousand reasons that I shall tell you another time. My friends have been tearing her from one another, but I have given the preference to Mrs. Melbourne over them all, as you two are the only persons in the world I would entrust with such a precious charge.'

Though this was said in her ladyship's most obliging manner, and with a look which seemed to expect an answering acknowledgment, Mrs. and Miss Melbourne were too well aware of the predominence of self in her disposition to doubt that she studied any thing in this arrangement but her own convenience. Yet, though by no means elated, as she supposed they would be by the compliment, they made not the slightest objection to the proposal. Mrs. Melbourne's maternal good nature easily led her to enter into the anxiety of the countess; and Matilda, who saw herself an object of dislike to one part of the family, and treated with capricious favour by the other, was eager, by any service in her power, to pay off the debt of gratitude, any former acts of kindness and attention might claim;

> 'For to the noble mind
> Rich gifts wax poor, when givers prove unkind.'[84]

The marked coldness of Lord Torrendale's manner to her at the children's ball, and on every occasion in which she had accidentally met him, hurt her as equally unkind and undeserved. In the midst of many subjects of painful reflection, the arrival of a letter from the Rocks gave rather an agreeable turn to the course of her feelings. The unabated affection and gratitude it expressed, convinced Matilda, notwithstanding Arbella's random assertions, that the soul which dictated those effusions could not be the abode of duplicity or guilt.

'Flattering expressions!' exclaimed Mrs. Melbourne: 'but what do they avail, / when one unhappy circumstance forces us to view that alliance with horror which might otherwise have gratified a mother's most sanguine wishes? Birth, character, ages suitable; for the seven or eight years between you and Sir Harold make only an advantageous difference. How little do we know what is best for us! Married in the same year, how often did I envy the bride of Sir Reginald Melbourne the possession of a promising boy, while you were not accorded to my prayers till after long, long years of expectation!'

'Little indeed!' sighed Matilda, as she stood with her eyes rivetted to the letter, in fixed and despairing attention; for the concluding paragraph, at which she had arrived, damped all the satisfaction the previous part had given her.

'I sought, in London, your noble Strathallan; but he for ever eluded my search: or, if we met, your love, like a protecting shield, defended his bosom from the vengeance I prepared. But he yet may mourn the charming hours he owes you! Oh, shades of Woodlands! shades where I have learned that, which, if I valued peace, I had better have never known: not even in your retreats will I give the purposed blow – his hour approaches – I wait him at the Rocks!'

END OF VOL. II. /
T. DAVISON, Lombard-street, Whitefriars, London.

STRATHALLAN.

BY
ALICIA LEFANU,

GRAND-DAUGHTER TO THE LATE THOMAS SHERIDAN, M.A.

IN FOUR VOLUMES.

VOL. III.

Quando scende in nobil petto
E compagno un dolce affetto
Non rivale alla virtù:
Respirate, alme felici
E vi siano i Numi amici
Quanto avverso il ciel vi fù.

METASTASIO. – DEMETRIO.[1]

London:
PRINTED FOR SHERWOOD, NEELY, AND JONES,
PATERNOSTER-ROW.
1816. /

R. and R. Gilbert, Printers, St. John's Square, London.

CHAPTER I.

'Tous les défauts humains nous donnent dans la vie
Des moyens d'exercer notre philosophie,
C'est le plus bel emploi que trouve la vertu,
Et si de probité tout étoit revetu,
Si tous les cœurs etoient francs justes et dociles
La plupart des vertus nous seroient inutiles
Puisqu'on en met l'usage a pouvoir sans ennui
Supporter dans nos droits l'injustice d'autrui.'

MOLIERE *Misanthrope.*[2]

IN the first letter Lady Torrendale wrote to Matilda from Tunbridge, it appeared as
if her ladyship purposed a longer stay than she had at first hinted. The earl intended
to try the waters for three or four months, and his lady declared herself unwilling
to leave him. She, however, gave no hint of a wish that Emily should join the party,
but on the contrary seemed fully satisfied that she was better at Mrs. / Melbourne's,
without once giving herself the trouble to enquire, whether her stay was convenient
or agreeable to that lady or not. True to her own character, it sufficed that it might be
so to her; and she did not find it any thing unreasonable or extraordinary, that those,
whose acquaintance she at one time seemed almost desirous of dropping, should at
another confer on her the most important and essential benefit.

Miss Melbourne was too grateful to her, for the relief she had, by this new and
welcome employment, administered to her mind, to feel uneasy at this prospect, or to
find time to make these reflections. Lady Emily was delighted to be with her and Julia;
and in contributing to the improvement of those two amiable girls, whom she treated
with equal kindness, and in contemplating the innocent affection that was every day
increasing between them, her heart experienced a relief which no other circumstance
could have afforded it.

Strathallan had, 'in a fit of duty,' as Lady Torrendale termed it, accompanied his
father to Tunbridge, and since his stay there, he had made no attempt to renew any
application to her by letter; therefore, she might conclude that the arguments of reason and prudence had at length prevailed, and that he had given up a pursuit, which
promised, whether in success or failure, to be equally productive of unhappiness and
regret. Yet in admitting this conviction into her mind, and turning to other resources
for consolation, Matilda experienced none of that restless dissatisfaction, that void of
the heart, which more often proves the narrowness, than the capaciousness of *their*

bosoms, who most complain of it. She had heard a second time from Lady Torrendale since her little trip; in this letter her ladyship, by an unfortunate oversight, forgot to mention Emily: on other subjects she was however voluble and copious enough.

'Lord Torrendale's bile, and his vapours, and his various *ill* humours, have,' / she said, 'terminated in a pretty smart fit of the gout, upon which Dr. Milner congratulates him; but had the candour to add, at the same time, turning to me, 'but I sincerely pity your ladyship.' It would do your heart good to see how edifyingly attentive Strathallan is, watching by his couch, and walking beside his wheel chair, that belles may whisper, *en passant*, how interesting! who is that charming, fine, young man who never leaves the side of that respectable looking, cross old gentleman? The other day some one added, as we were both walking beside him, "that is Lord and Lady Strathallan attending on their sick father: what an amiable pair!" To be sure any one might make the mistake, but – that is no matter. Your Colonsay,[3] as we used to call him at Woodlands, in the delightful region of Aurora,[4] has found out another amusement for himself, in wandering among the romantic rocks near Tunbridge, which they say are a real curiosity, and which I should certainly go to see, if I could make an agreeable party. There he met, the other morning, with an acquaintance almost as romantic as himself; no less than that renowned and valorous knight, Sir Harold Melbourne, who has unexpectedly started up in this gay scene, as if on purpose to give us the pleasure of his company. He and I take many a solitary ramble and scramble together. S – says he is as mad as ever, but the baronet insists upon it that he is quite in his senses, and that it is Strathallan himself who is mad; and adds, with the greatest gravity imaginable, that there never was a man, who, wherever he went, encountered so many mad people as himself. You see I contrive to keep up my spirits; and as for Strathallan (Colonsay), what with his necessary attendance on his father, what with his unnecessary excursions with your cousin, and what with a certain little flirtation, he has taken up at the rooms with a Lady Georgina Maclean (sister to Spencer's Inamorata), he has not time to be so disagreeable as he would otherwise / indubitably be. Had I foreseen my stay would have been so long, I should have contrived to get Miss Mountain to be of the party, but as it is I feel awkward and undetermined. Have you seen her lately? With all her faults she must be allowed to be a truly interesting creature.'

Matilda knew her ladyship too well not to perceive, that the little hint thrown out about the Scotch heiress (which was most probably entirely without foundation), was merely invented from the gratuitous desire to give pain, which, with that lady, often afforded at once a motive and its reward. But another circumstance in the letter, awakened, in the most painful manner, those tumults and anxieties which all her reason had been scarcely sufficient to repress. Her unhappy cousin had written to her that he waited Strathallan 'at the Rocks.' Yet he seemed to follow his footsteps. There were other rocks than those, which had once cradled her peaceful childhood. Would that be the fulfilment of his dreadful denunciation? She shrunk from replying to this question; and flew to her only panacea from the vast unutterable pangs of thought, active exertion.

Lady Emily's mind had been much neglected, but it was one which amply repaid cultivation. 'How kind you are to me,' Miss Melbourne, she said: 'you treat me like a rational creature; mamma treats me like a child, and Miss Langrish *used* to treat me like the automaton young lady, who had no soul, nor fingers, but to play a sonata. One day I told her I wished the automaton was her pupil instead of me, for that she could listen with just as much improvement to "one and a two, and a three and a four; pray, Lady Emily, begin that polacca⁵ again. Three and a one, and two and three, and one and two, and three," and which, together with a pathetic exhortation to "play the notes exactly as they were written," was all the lesson she ever gave me.'

'What have you done with Lady Emily?' said Arbella to her friend: 'her / improvement is the conversation of all those who see her. You have certainly uncommon talents for instruction. Miss Hautenville says you make it a rule to devote yourself to the sisters of your admirers, that you may fix an obligation upon them. Miss Mountain, most characteristically and classically, compares you to those noble governesses, of whom Melmoth maketh honourable mention;⁶ and who, in Rome's golden days, voluntarily supplied, to their young relatives, the place of females less interested in the formation of their minds and manners. Some say that your present establishment is only another name for a little school, and that you know why you trouble yourself about these young sprigs of fashion; and *I* say you are very kind at all events to busy yourself about such an uninteresting pair of little tiresome puppets.'

'Some people are very good,' replied Matilda, with a languid smile. 'I own that from my childhood teaching has been my passion. I cannot flatter myself that Lady Emily has, in the course of a fortnight, made any surprising progress: if she is left as long with me as the countess in her letters seems to intimate, it may be an advantage and a pleasure to both. Having no younger sister, a blessing which I ardently desired, I tormented all the children in the neighbourhood of the Rocks to let me hear them their lessons, and I envied no heroine so much as the little princess, in the Tales of the Castle,⁷ who had leave entirely to patronize and educate the child of a poor *paysanne*. I have not lost that taste; and there was nothing I so much admired in your favourite, Lady Wortley Montague,⁸ when you gave me her letters to her daughter to read, as the declaration she makes of having desired in her youth to be a prioress, or else at the head of some institution for the advancement of female knowledge. Clara is of my opinion. She insists upon having a share in the education of my little cousin; and in the idea of once more resuming the usefulness that was attached to her / situation when abroad, I see her mild eyes light up with an expression of inward satisfaction, that communicates a similar pleasure to me.'

'Well, my dear, much good may it do you with your cousin, and your little romp Emily, who is now, I suppose, grown good Queen Emma, and your nun, and your dog, and your cat; you are all, I think, suited for each other. Heaven defend me from such a party! For my part, I never attempted the character of an instructress but once in my life, and that was to teach Spencer blindman's buff.'

Matilda soon found, that however ridiculous and absurd the rumours in circulation respecting her were, Arbella was not wrong as to their existence; and they soon procured her the favour of a visit from Mrs. Stockwell; a visit, which, but for that circumstance, she might still longer have remained without.

Many were the conjectures excited among the little party, the first time she bustled, sidled, or rather wriggled into the room, – advancing in tortuous mazes, displaying her glories to the sun; for she had at once something of the gait and the gaudiness of an Indian snake; – expectation was on the tip-toe – was it to do the honours of her handsome new shawl? or was it to become mistress of the rest of the particulars of the reason of Lady Torrendale's secession from the gaieties of the London winter? or was it to seek her niece Arbella, after some new and more alarming elopement, that Mrs. Melbourne was, after an interval of some months, thus favoured? The lady, being seated, seemed rather at a loss how to begin: though desirous to make this visit appear a voluntary one, yet it was evident some motive more powerful than mere friendliness and good-nature had prompted it, and how to account for its being delayed so long, if it were right it ever should be paid, was the difficulty. She at length determined upon the epic manner of dashing at once into the middle of the story, so leaving the first meeting at the / opera, and subsequent visits of her niece Arbella, for the subject of some future recapitulation, she began talking in general terms of her own ill health, which prevented her seeing her friends as often as she wished; and then, according to a maxim of her own, that it always made one welcome to begin with a good offer, proceeded to say, she found herself so much better she was going to the opera that evening, and if Miss Melbourne pleased, would be her chaperon.

Miss Melbourne thanked her, but 'whenever she chose to go had the use of Lady Torrendale's box.' This was naturally enough to have been supposed from the degree of intimacy that seemed to subsist between that young lady and the countess; yet it was a thunderstroke upon Mrs. Stockwell, who had never been admitted to a similar honour. Sensible how absurd and officious her tardy offer must appear, she could not refrain from committing the next moment a similar error. 'Arbella,' she said, 'had been delighted and surprised, and surprised and delighted, at meeting her young friend at the children's ball at Lady Torrendale's. Had she guessed that Miss Melbourne cared for such a thing, or had meant that night to join the votaries of the light "frantras-trick" toe, she would have made it a point to send her niece in her own coach to take her up.'

Mrs. Melbourne did not seem properly grateful for all these civilities; and the poor woman, after she had exhausted her whole store of compliments and offered attentions, without producing the expected conciliatory effect, sat down in such evident mortification, that Matilda, out of mere charity, interrupted her with some enquiry about her niece, taking care, with her usual urbanity, not to forget Mr. Stockwell.

But the good lady, who, as she afterwards declared, had 'never been so put out of her way in her life,' could not recover from her painful embarrassment; and to all Matilda's obliging enquiries, /

'Answered neglectingly she knew not what.'[9]

It was amusing enough to observe the different manner in which the same degree of confusion, occasioned by the same meanness of conduct, was expressed by the elegant Lady Torrendale and the unpolished Mrs. Stockwell. After taking in, however, with one glance of her eye, the dimensions and furniture of the room, and secretly comparing them with those of the Rocks, and ascertaining, with another, every article in the dress of Mrs. Melbourne and her daughter, the effrontery and self opinion of Mrs. Stockwell began to revive. She could not conceive why a woman who had not a better gown, nor near so good a house as herself, and a chit, whom Arbella could buy out and out, should make her feel so awkward and 'comical like;' so resolving to shake off this troublesome awe, she began by regretting she met Miss Melbourne so seldom any where. Miss Melbourne had not been well. 'Ah, that is so like me! I am never well; but, however, you was well enough to go to the opera.' 'I am so fond of music,' observed Matilda. 'That is so like me too; I do so idolotrize music!'

This passion for finding out that her acquaintance were 'just like her,' and 'so like her,' had been remarked by Mrs. Melbourne and her daughter since their first acquaintance with Mrs. Stockwell; they were content, therefore, simply to notice it with a smile, while she continued.

'But, my dear Mrs. Melbourne, you should not shut yourself up in this way, as I may say, from all your friends; now how comes it that all the time you have been in town you never once thought of ordering your carriage my way.'

'Mrs. Melbourne had no carriage.'

'Ay, so I remember now; and more's the pity that a lady like you, ma'am, should be without one. For my part, I can't imagine, never having been so myself, how people manages, as is without a carriage. I never had any acquaintance / neither that did not ride in their coach. However, I heard that there were such things as hackney coaches (not that I ever was in one), which might be very convenient to others.'

No one seeming inclined to satisfy her doubts on the subject, she appeared again uncertain how to proceed, till accidentally casting her eyes upwards, she exclaimed, looking at a large picture which hung over the chimney, 'bless me! if this isn't the very image of the picture the man done for Arbella, as I have hanging up in my house in Derbyshire.'

'I copied it some time ago to preserve the remembrance of my friend,' said Matilda.

'Oh, miss, you was always very artificial! and this reminds me of the little business I am come about, as I hear from Lady Torrendale that you keep a school.'

'Lady Torrendale!' exclaimed Matilda in unfeigned astonishment: 'believe me, dear madam, you are misinformed.'

'Oh, I knew 'tis only amongst ourselves, just a little select thing of a few girls of quality, quite snug and comfortable; now that is the very thing I want. I have two wards, nieces of the late poor Mr. Stockwell's, who are girls of very good expectations, and whom I should wish to place in something of a higher style from their present situation. They are but sixteen and seventeen, poor things, so they should not come out of the egg-shell just yet, till they have had a little finishing; now they are very well frenched, and musicked, and danced already. All I want of you, my dear Miss Melbourne, is to have 'em taught to get into a carriage elegantly, and put on a shawl prettily, and play cards well, and pick a bone the Paris fashion, and crack a whip, and manage their opera glass. And for the sciences, a little about hydras and oxen, and that sort of thing. And as for the book learning, the history, and craniology, and bible, and that, it comes naturally into young folk's heads, I take it; so, without decanting any more / on the subject, shall I send 'em up to you to-morrow?' She had come to the end of her proposal, before Mrs. Melbourne had an opportunity of assuring her, she acted under the influence of a complete mistake.

Mrs. Stockwell was very slow to admit the conviction, but when she found that her hopes of patronising (as she termed it) her former friends, must be changed into fears of appearing ridiculous before them, she thought she could not too quickly abridge a visit, which she had already pretty well prolonged. In what had dropped from her respecting 'young girls of quality,' Mrs. Melbourne discovered the whole secret of her visitor's newly acquired rage for education. But what could have been the occasion of poor Mrs. Stockwell's awkward mistake, she could not divine; nor were they likely ever satisfactorily to learn. Whether Lady Torrendale had amused herself with her friend's prevailing foible, in a little of what she called innocent mystification; or whether the officious ignorance of Miss Hautenville, or some other person, had caused her unfortunate and unsuccessful application, they were at a loss to determine.

'We must not, amidst our conjectures,' said Mrs. Melbourne, 'forget the request, which Mrs. Stockwell made me at parting; and which she assured me she made a "particular *pint* of." I really believe it was one reason for her visit. It was to have Emily to dine with her on Saturday, to meet these nieces of Mr. Stockwell's.'

'No, certainly,' replied Matilda; and while she assisted to adorn her young favourite in muslin and lace on the appointed day, she gave her a strict charge to bring her home a good account of the party; well assured that what she would have to relate must be productive of some amusement.

'I have undergone an examination,' said the lively girl on her return, 'respecting my great improvement in all the sciences; / and have been proposed as a model to the Miss Stockwells, though so much older. I have been desired to attend to my Plutarch, that I might remember all the principal events of the History of England; and have been requested to name all the suffering bishops of each archiepiscopal see. I suppose the old lady meant suffragans; however, I pretended not to take her, and said I knew of no suffering bishop, but the good bishop of E – , who has been an invalid such a long time, and is now supposed to be in such a dangerous way. Then it came to Miss Hautenville's turn, and she would have taken me on her knee, while I underwent a second cross-examination about my brother and Miss Mountain, and I do not know how many other things, to which I could not have answered if I would, and which I am sure I would not have answered if I could. "Speak up, my love," says Mrs. Stockwell, "you know you need not fear Mrs. or Miss Melbourne here." – I never liked the woman, and was provoked beyond bearing with her seeming, for a moment, to think me as mean as herself. Madam, I replied, with great spirit, Miss Melbourne's absence or presence has nothing to say to the business; any thing that was proper to be said, I should repeat in her presence; any thing that was not so, I hope you do not think so ill of me, as to suppose I should take advantage of her absence to advance. I have not the happiness of enjoying my brother's confidence; it is not to be expected that, at my age, I should: but if I did, be assured I should consider it as a sacred deposit, and the last that I should lightly tamper with, by readily communicating, what was so entrusted to me, to another.'

Emily finished this little recital with a look, that seemed to claim expected applause; perhaps there was an air too theatrical, a leaven of the Torrendale vanity, in the manner in which she pronounced this last sentence; but Matilda only saw the generous glow of her countenance, / the sweetness and animation that sparkled in those bright blue eyes, and that spoke a mind within, which spurned the least imputation of deceit. Though she smiled at this little ebullition of spirit, she could not suppress a tear of pleasure, while impressing an approving kiss upon that rosy cheek. At this moment she observed Clara's eye fixed upon them, and answered its expression. Letting go Emily's hand, she murmured with a sigh, as she cast her eyes upon the ground. 'Why that glance? is it possible to express a noble, a generous sentiment, and not look like –'

Arbella was soon with her friend to make her aunt's peace; or at least to express her regret, that the good lady had occasioned any confusion. 'How she came to take it into her head, I can't imagine,' she continued; forgetting she had herself in a great measure, by her thoughtless volubility, given rise to the report. 'I had just gone out, for half an hour that morning, and could not guess that, before my return, she would have done something absurd. I went to call upon Miss Mountain, to see how she bears Strathallan's absence. Oh! for a dose of the seraphic Sophia's opium – tranquillizing and intoxicating! What a specific against every mortification, is the perfection of vanity. Really, the resplendent contentment, that shone in that ever-blooming and self-satisfied countenance, put me out of all patience. There is no doing any thing with a woman who will not be affronted. I attempted to condole with her on the hurried departure of her swain, without even paying her the compliment of announcing it to her; but no – no – no – she would not admit the idea, that it was possible any coldness could be intended. She did not stand upon ceremony – every thing was as it should be; with an ordinary lover it might indeed be different; but, with Lord Strathallan, who, alone, realized, in his person, every attribute of the perfect and / accomplished Musidorus',[10] a little more pains might be taken without any degradation.

"Why, my dear ma'am," said I, quite worn out with her obstinate determination to be pleased; "Don't you see it is evident the man is quite anxious to get off; and that if you would give up Vinesbury to keep him, he would resign Strathallan to set himself free again?" A little impolite you will say, but I really had her interest at heart, for I think nothing promises so much misery as an ill-assorted marriage. She took me as I meant it, and thanked me for my good intentions; but added they were perfectly unnecessary between lovers, who understood each other as well as she and Lord Strathallan did. Was there ever any thing so provokingly persevering? I cannot help being foolish enough to fret a little that O'Hara has not obeyed my call, or rather has literally obeyed my prohibition. As to Lady Torrendale, though I miss her sadly, I cannot blame her so much neither, for trying the country again, as all her plans of amusement here failed. You heard how the last party went off, even with the assistance of the scarlet buccinum.'[11]

'The buccinum!' repeated Matilda.

'Yes,' replied Arbella. 'She got it at last; that is to say *I* got it; not for her, as you may suppose, but under pretence of wanting it myself. I told Mr. Sowerby I was just reading a work in which it was described, and wished to compare the original with the picture; praised his industry and research, and said – , all that *we* say you know; and so of course the old philosopher could not refuse a lady such a trifle; hey!' Miss Ferrars looked in Miss Melbourne's eyes for a reply; there was an expression in them which seemed to say 'I do not think it is *of course*.' A degree of disingenuousness, though she knew not of what exactly to complain, struck her in / the whole narrative. *She* had

---

*   One of the heroes of Sir Philip Sydney's Arcadia.

communicated to Miss Ferrars the pain that Lady Torrendale's reiterated and unreasonable entreaties had given her; would it not have been more frank and open for her friend to have consulted with her in return, upon her little meditated attack on Mr. Sowerby? She had acknowledged it was a favour she would not venture to ask on her own account. Was there not something of display in Arbella's officious information, that, on so much slighter an acquaintance, she had taken that liberty and succeeded?

'You seem displeased, my love,' said Miss Ferrars, the little flash of momentary triumph instantly changing to the mild, subdued air of repentance. 'Surely you cannot let such a trifle move you. In essentials, you know, he must always give you the preference, you are so superior!'

Matilda did not return the expected look of gratitude for the upward, admiring glance, with which her friend accompanied these words, and Arbella was not sorry to have their conference interrupted by a thundering knock at the door, and the servant announcing Miss De Courcy. 'Bid her walk up,' said Matilda, in some surprise at the visit.

'But, ma'am,' resumed the footman, hesitating, 'she says she won't walk up.'

'Won't walk up!'

'No, ma'am; if you have no objection,' answered the man, who thought it proper to insert a little civility into the message. 'She is in her carriage, and cannot stay a moment; and says it would be very convenient to her if you would go down to her.'

'Go down to her, – impossible!' resumed Matilda, with a cool dignity. 'Tell her I beg she will give us the pleasure of her company, if it be for ever so short a time. What new whim is this?' she continued, turning to Arbella; 'since I have been in town, Miss De Courcy never seemed to remember my existence.'

'Then it was not for want of being / reminded of it, by your various excellencies,' resumed that young lady; 'and you may be sure the present impertinence is the result of her wearied envy. But we must beat her down, as we would a little forward spoilt child.'

Miss De Courcy, as she ran into the room, did not much contradict that description. Too childish, and too much taken up with her own affairs, seriously to intend to be impertinent, her thoughtless rudeness produced the same effect as if she had: as she took Matilda's hand, and, with no flattering familiarity, poutingly exclaimed, 'Now was it not very ill-natured of you, when I told you I was in a hurry, to make me come up stairs? But, however, since I am come, we may as well settle it at once, for it is a thing that I don't want mamma to know any thing about, till I astonish her with my progress.'

'You have, indeed, made an astonishing progress,' said Arbella, with a penetrating look; she paused – while Matilda was utterly at a loss to know what this strange introduction was to end in.

'So just tell me,' resumed the young lady, 'what are your days, and we will take it an hour before she gets up – Mondays, Wednesdays and Fridays – or Tuesdays, Thursdays, and Saturdays; for as I merely want a few lessons on recitation – '

'Excuse me, Miss De Courcy; the world seems to have made a strange mistake with respect to me; I have no days; I give no lessons.'

'La! no lessons on elocution and grace? I am sure you schooled me enough at Woodlands; and I only want to know your terms. I have engaged in a business, but I really have no time to tell you now about it, upon my honour. I have left a young lady peppering in the coach, and we are both going on to dine at a friend's house; but in short it is a – a play – a private play. And I think we will have you down for a few days at the Duchess of Normanby's; and there we can / settle it all, and talk over it at our leisure; it is at Richmond. We are all friends, and I want your assistance of all things; and if you do not know all the people, you can spend the mornings in your own room.'

'That is what I fully intend to do;' interrupted Matilda, with a smile of mingled contempt and good humour. 'Therefore, if you have any thing to say, that it is necessary for me to hear, dear Miss De Courcy, better say it now. If, as I suspect, it is out of my power to render you any assistance, I will not trespass upon time, so very precious, by detaining you.'

'It is not out of your power, if it was not out of your will. I have undertaken a part, and it is not a very important part neither; nothing very dashing; it is only Lady Randolph.'

'Lady Randolph!' exclaimed Arbella. 'Do you think – excuse me, Miss De Courcy – but do you really think you have all the requisites for such a part?'

'All, I am certain. I have already bought forty yards of crape, and twenty yards of bombazine.'

'That is a good beginning. But don't you imagine something more is wanting?'

'Something more!' said Miss De Courcy, with a sudden start, and a look not unlike reflection. 'That is what I have been thinking of, and Miss Melbourne could assist us; for I always said she would make an excellent milliner, she had so much taste. Now you know, as Lady Randolph, I am to be a widowed wife, inconsolable for the death of my first husband, whom I have never forgot, and the supposed loss of my son: now I am doubtful whether the most absolute simplicity of dress would be becoming; or whether I shall have a trimming of set and jet ornaments; or again, a trimming of bugles would be very light and elegant, don't you think so, finished off with a small black bead at the edge?'

Miss Melbourne was silent, and Arbella, / stealing over to the young lady, said to her in a whisper, 'Don't you perceive, my dear, that you are making yourself every moment more and more superlatively ridiculous?'

'Eh, ridiculous! how?' replied Miss De Courcy, who had hardly wit enough ever to be affronted, and who was, at this moment, much too deeply engaged in the important speculation she had entered upon, to call the little she possessed to her assistance. 'I own I am puzzled; and I can't conceive why I undertook the part; except, that one day we were talking, I believe it was about you, Miss Melbourne, and that somebody praised simplicity of dress; and Lord Kilcare said he would give a hundred pounds if that old woman, my aunt, was dead, for that I should look a thousand times – , very well in mourning. Kilcare is to be Douglas to my Lady Randolph.'

'A most respectable and interesting pair,' observed Arbella.

'Yes,' resumed Helena. 'I shall look my part divinely, they tell me; and I have it quite pat, only that I wish I could catch the exact air and tone for

"Ye woods and wilds whose melancholy gloom
Accords with my soul's sadness."'[12]

Matilda smiled, as the young aspirant (who, though excessively pretty, had that extremely childish look, and baby air and lisp, which most wars with the attempt to excite a deep and continued interest), ran over these lines in a jig-time, casting her vacant light eyes round the cheerful and ornamental apartment.

'I am rather inclined to think of you,' said Miss Ferrars, directing a complimentary glance at her nymph-like figure, 'in the first line of Anna's account:
"She ran, she flew, like lightning, up the hill."[13]
I remember your races with Spencer Fitzroy in Derbyshire; were they not much more in character, Helena?'

'Now I wish, Miss Ferrars, you would disturb us with no more trifling, for I must / beg of Miss Melbourne to tell me when she can come and perfect me in this character.'

'You had better have asked her when we were together at Woodlands,' resumed the malicious Arbella. 'When Miss Melbourne produced that sweet wild melody at the piano, which you got Miss Langrish to harmonize, and then called your own; and when she copied the Hebe you were desired to draw, and wrote your Italian exercise for you.'

'Let us understand each other,' interrupted Matilda. 'Miss De Courcy will, I hope, not think me disobliging, or uncomplying, in doing what I think my duty – informing her that our circumstances, though altered, are not such as to require the exertion of any trifling talent I may possess.'

'Well, if there is any mistake in the case,' resumed Miss De Courcy, very much disappointed, 'it must be referred to Miss Hautenville; who assured me she had it from the very best authority, that you attended ladies of fashion at their houses; and gave them private instructions in reading and reciting.'

'My dear Miss De Courcy,' interrupted Arbella, 'do you not perceive that malicious Miss Hautenville has been alternately playing us both off? The hair-dressing, that you were so kind as to notice in me the other night, was a tender mercy compared to the complete hoax she has put upon you.'

'Well, I am sure it was nothing so singular,' resumed Miss De Courcy, tossing her head, and hardly able to conceal the starting tears of vexation. 'We all settled it at Woodlands, that it was the very best thing to be done.' She ran down stairs to her carriage, hoping to receive no more of her soi-disant friend's officious information; but Arbella followed her with – 'Do you know what you have done, my dear? these people will make a fine story of you wherever they go, and they are still intimate with the Torrendales, though you do not meet / them often at her evening parties; and it is said, by half the world, that Lord Strathallan will marry Miss Melbourne instead of Miss Mountain.'

'Is it possible? I thought they always gave him to me,' cried Miss De Courcy, her eyes assuming, with apprehension, an expression something like meaning. 'Dear, I should be very sorry – what shall I do? I'll go back and apologize.'

'Not for the world. That would make it ten times more ridiculous. I did not mention the circumstance to you with the least idea that you could make any amends for the past, but merely that you might avoid such little errors in future; and because,' she added in a whisper, 'because I thought it but right to tell you of it.'

'I am glad,' said Matilda, as Arbella returned, 'that my mother was not here; her proud spirit would have risen at the foolish levity and ridiculous proposals to which the undue commendation, once bestowed on the few showy talents of her unfortunate child, have given rise.'

'I rather wish she had been here,' replied Arbella, 'to have pierced her with one of those diamond glances which miss, in her days of humility, used to complain seemed to "look her through." A creature to whom you paid such attention! gave such kindness, such countenance when she was a mere chrysalis, – in the bud, – not out, as she terms it. Now she is out; and for any sense or manners she has acquired, she might as well, I think, walk in again. Then with all this shew of simplicity she has the worldliness without the wisdom of age, and the precipitancy without the good nature of early years. Helen de Courcy is as narrow as if she never ran in debt; and is always casting about how to get every thing at the very cheapest rate. Now youth ought to be generous, friendly, open, and – '

'Undesigning,' said Matilda, finishing the sentence for her with an emphasis sufficiently marked, though not intended. /

'Yes, and undesigning,' resumed Arbella, making use of her friend's word with the greatest good humour, while, bidding her farewell for the present, she rushed forward and embraced her, burying her face in Matilda's bosom in a transport of feeling, gaiety, – perhaps confusion. Yet was Arbella really without design, at least without design beyond those unhatched projects, and embryo schemes of future conquests, which, numerous as the *constitutions* that are ascribed to a Gallic statesman of our day, line every pigeon-hole of the brain of a coquette. Her heart was upright, just, sincere, as such a heart can be. It has been already shown how it swelled at the least unkindness offered to her friend by any but herself. If Matilda's was not completely satisfied with such a tribute, if it sighed for virtue more unalloyed, for a still nobler tone of feeling, in short for the living image of her own, she soon checked the romantic wish, and, with a sigh, remembered, that such a heart it had been her lot but once to meet, and that its future feelings were all imperiously claimed by another. Yet, though aware of the duty of contentment, Matilda's was not the calm of insensibility. Her heart, which would sometimes bleed afresh from the deep-fixed wound of hopeless love, was also tremblingly alive to every slight and injury that can be offered to a delicate and noble spirit, struggling with misfortune; and from the first discovery which the vulgar violence of her attendant made to her of her altered state, to the moment in which she was now left by Arbella, no mortification had for a little time more painfully affected her than the want of delicacy and kindness of a young friend, with whom she had, for the short period they had met, lived on terms of equality, excepting the unavoidable distance which the great difference in their acquirements and talents created between them. At such a moment, how dangerous would it have been for Strathallan to have renewed the tempting offers, to have recalled to her imagination the / fairy pictures of grandeur, of gaiety, and felicity, shared with him! But Strathallan did not return, nor give any indication of being desirous to renew his former intercourse with her. Lord and Lady Torrendale's arrival in Fitzroy square was, however, an agreeable circumstance to Miss Melbourne, as by restoring Emily to them she put an end to reports which were to her a source of trouble, uncompensated by the discovery in any of her friends, of either kindness, or generosity.

CHAPTER II.

Thickest night o'erhang my dwelling,
Howling tempests o'er me rave,
Angry torrents, wintry swelling,
Still surround my lonely cave.
Crystal streamlets gently flowing,
Busy haunts of base mankind,
Western breezes softly blowing,
Suit not my distracted mind.

BURNS' Strathallan's Lament.[14]

'WHAT can be the reason of the very short stay the Torrendales made at Tunbridge? They left town towards the end of May, and have returned in the beginning of June. This is not giving the waters a fair trial. It is but the commencement of the season.' To these remarks, which Matilda made to her young friend, Arbella at first gave no reply. At length she said, shrugging her shoulders, / "Tis a dangerous matter to meddle with state secrets. All I know, is, that her ladyship took a sudden aversion to Tunbridge Wells, and instantly his lordship's gout forsook him, and he was able to follow her up to town; for he accompanies her now like her shadow, and may not ill be compared to it, being much taller than she is, but slender, silent, and neither possessing her beauty, grace, or colour.' Then, after a moment's reflection, she added, 'Perhaps I am needlessly censorious. His lordship's fidgets may proceed from an idea that it is a slight to Miss Mountain; for the whole family long to remain out of town without her; and from his desire to conclude this marriage, which has been so long arranged that Strathallan has nothing to do but to hold out his hand and take her. Indeed I believe he suspects such is the plan, for you see he delays his return.'

Matilda sighed, and while her thoughts dwelt with mournful retrospection on the brother, she found it hard to receive consolation from the compliments Lady Torrendale very profusely paid after taking back the sister.

'I make it a point of conscience to hurry Emily away from you,' she said, 'for you took upon yourself, it seems, all the duties Miss Langrish was engaged to fulfil. *Yet* it is wonderful how gratefully the little soul speaks of you. She could not love you better if you had not imposed any restraint on her. She declares these three weeks have opened to her a new world. I am absolutely jealous; for it is evident which of us she prefers. Yet I am sure I never contradicted her, nor attempted to teach her any thing in my life. The least you can do is to come and witness her improvement. Nay, I will take no denial, for I have a serious design upon you. You shall go with us this evening to see the new Melpomene,[15] Miss – . Nothing ever came up to her; the first night of her appearance several ladies were carried out fainting, I understand – '

'Dead, absolutely dead!' added the / complaisant Miss Ferrars, who had accompanied her ladyship in this well-intended visit, and whose slight propensity to exaggeration has before been noticed.

'I myself was there,' resumed the countess, 'when it might be said to have rained tears.'

'Rained, madam! positively hailed – positively and literally:– the old story of the boxes being set in a float by the performance of some famous actress in Isabella, was revived in this *debutante*.'

'Come, why do you hesitate?' pursued Arbella, observing her friend still silent: 'I guess who is the cause of this reluctance; you are, as usual, afraid of papa Sowerby; but I will engage to obtain permission for you,' she continued, laughing, 'and I may boast of some interest with him.'

'You may indeed,' Matilda replied, with great simplicity; yet she thought of the buccinum.

'Now that, "you may indeed," was not quite fair. Was there not a little malice concealed under it?' exclaimed the conscious Arbella, reddening rather than blushing.

Miss Melbourne, in truth, expected Mr. Sowerby that evening; he had said he would spend it with her and her mother: an accidental circumstance induced him to call in while her friends were still with her; and perceiving that Matilda's unwillingness to disappoint him was her only reason for refusing an amusement in which she pictured to herself high gratification, he, in a momentary fit of indulgence and good-nature, insisted on her accepting the proposal. 'As her ladyship will probably come late,' he added in a whisper, 'we can have our game of chess as usual.' Arbella looked over her friend's shoulder as if her eyes could have drawn out the subject of the whisper. Matilda started, and felt a strange apprehension which almost inclined her to wish it yet possible to retract, as the countess, with an air of friendly gaiety, under which she fancied a degree of half-suppressed triumph lurked, exclaimed, / 'Ah, little timid one! have I caught you at last?'

Notwithstanding the favourable impression that had been left on Sowerby's mind by Matilda's conduct, his old aversion to every thing that bore the appearance of pleasure or recreation returned in double force towards night; and though punctual to his appointment, he exhibited symptoms that did not seem to promise a very delightful and cloudless evening. The first thing that disturbed him was being obliged to entertain Mrs. Melbourne alone for five minutes after his arrival. Now, though he had repeatedly declared Mrs. Melbourne to be a most delightful companion, it happened, most unfortunately, on that occasion, she could hit on no subject of conversation to please him. The appearance of Matilda, attired in simple elegance, and 'moving in the light of her beauty,' interrupted this languid tête-à-tête.[16] Sowerby, repressing the first involuntary emotion excited by her presence, which was one of unqualified admiration; and that sudden, almost respectful surprise, which transcendent loveliness and grace, however often seen, never fail to inspire in the beholder, roughly desired she would keep them no longer waiting for tea. With a different sentiment

Mrs. Melbourne contemplated the air of dignity and sweetness diffused over her whole person, to which it was impossible to add the slightest decoration, without immediately acknowledging in her that peculiar and distinguishing air of fashion, which, even more than the attractions of beauty, commands the admiration of those who live within its influence. She gave a sigh to maternal weakness at the thought that charms fitted to adorn a court, had, since they expanded into their fullest perfection, been either devoted in the dear delightful days of youth, to forming other youth to move in those scenes to which her contracted prospects forbade her ever aspiring; or to soothing the sorrows of *her* declining years, whose afflictions she shared without having ever tasted of similar / enjoyments to those she had formerly known. Though Werter's Charlotte[17] could hardly do the honours of tea and bread and butter more gracefully than Matilda, the countenance of the cloudy visitant cleared up but little during that short repast; and even the appearance of the favourite chess-board, immediately after it, failed to conciliate him. He was sure, beforehand, Matilda would not attend to her game; and in this comfortable presumption he indulged for some time, uninterrupted, in all the luxury of grumbling. 'He hated to see a house put into confusion, hours deranged, and habits broken in upon, on account of some amusement projected for one individual of the family. To see young ladies running about, and arranging their curls to the very last moment, was what he detested.'

'My dear sir, I am quite ready; I do not run about,' Matilda ventured submissively to observe.

'No; but you would if I had not told you,' rejoined her obliging monitor; who, having his tongue once set going on a theme so fruitful, continued, like a piece of clockwork put in motion, to mutter 'Pulling out their papers' – 'Settling their curls;' unmindful of the radiant tresses, that, almost disdaining the confinement of the comb, floated in loose ringlets on Matilda's neck, – 'Running about;' while his fair antagonist, in an attitude of fixed attention, sat with heart and looks wholly absorbed in the chequered board.

'I wonder who that fine lady and her precious confidant will get to escort them to-night? That Strathallan is not in town, I hear. Look up, Matilda; child, I want to see your face; why do you keep your eyes rivetted to the board?'

She raised them, with a smile which would have disarmed the soul of jealousy itself. 'Sir, you desired me to mind my game.'

'What are you looking about for? Your queen's in *prise*.'[18]

'Sir, you desired me not to keep my eyes fixed upon the board.' /

In addition to these various and contradictory orders, Matilda had to endure, without betraying the slightest sign of impatience, the ceaseless hum with which her old friend was apt to amuse himself during his meditations, with the accompaniment, *ad libitum*, of beating, what Arbella very unceremoniously termed the devil's tattoo, upon the carpet. His long pauses between every move; and the constant habit of taking the piece he meant to move, off its square, and flourishing it in his hand before he had determined where to lay it down, till both he and Matilda were perhaps uncertain of the spot from which it had first been moved; a habit in which, spite of Mrs. Melbourne's admonitory exclamation, 'Oh, Mr. Sowerby, is that allowed at the club?' he continued pertinaciously to persist. His countenance evidently brightened as the hour for Miss Melbourne's departure approached, without any notice from Lady Torrendale. 'You'll see she will not be punctual; you will be too late, if you go at all – '

'Oh, sir, the first act is no loss,' interrupted Mrs. Melbourne: 'merely what the French call the "*exposition*."'

'You'll be late,' he continued to growl.

'No, no, she will be in time for the grand scene in the third act.'

'Mind your game; – she'll forget you.'

'Well, sir, I shall console myself.'

'She has forgot you – mind your game. – Dum, dum, dillo – Check. She has forgot you – Dum, ti tum – Check – you may rely upon that – Dum, ti tum.'

'Mate!' exclaimed Matilda, darting with a sudden stroke upon her unguarded foe, while the animation of pleasure and surprise heightened the roses of her complexion, and gave an added brilliancy to her glancing eyes. Now it so happened that while Sowerby, entirely wrapped up in his own project,

'Long meditating, strove
To make one great decisive move, /
Whose powerful influence should subdue
Whate'er his gentle foe could do;'[19]

Matilda dexterously availed herself of an oversight, by which he left himself open to her attack. The stroke was a surprise; still he allowed it was a fair one.

'I only want you to confess, my dear sir, that I can be as attentive as other people.'

'Well, well, we will allow you were – out of the spirit of contradiction.'

At this moment a thundering knock announced the arrival of the Countess of Torrendale. Flushed with recent triumph, and impatient for expected pleasure, Matilda gaily started up, bade her mother and Mr. Sowerby adieu, and had run half down stairs when recalled by the well-known croak:–

'You have brushed down one of the men with some of the cursed trimming of your foolish gown. – Pick it up – don't you see it – 'tis on the ground – at your feet – the knight at your feet.'

Matilda hastily threw the chess-men into the box.

'That will never do,' muttered Sowerby: 'count them. I always count them myself.'

'And I wish you would do so now,' she softly whispered; as with a smile of patient good humour she began the enumeration, and, counting them carefully over, obtained his tardy and unwilling approbation; and at length took leave of him, she trusted, for a few hours at least. In a moment she forgot all these little crosses, when, seated in the carriage by the Countess of Torrendale, she returned the warm pressure of Arbella's hand, who welcomed her with her usual obliging raillery, saying, 'I had almost hoped you had meant to leave the field clear for my conquests to-night, and had repented of your consent, in pity to me; but I find you persist, and I must give up all hopes.'

'*Drest* for conquest, indeed, I see,' added the countess, in a slow, drawling / tone, as the lights afforded her a glimpse of Matilda's elegant but unpretending decoration. 'Now that work is vastly becoming, but very expensive too, I should suppose. For my part I never can afford to indulge in fancies.'

Though Lady Torrendale was never good-natured, Matilda could not help imagining something must have recently disturbed her, to induce her to make such an unprovoked attack, as this unfeeling sneer conveyed. She, however, kept her observations to herself; but her friend Arbella did not long delay an attempted apology for her ladyship's apparent ill-temper.

'My dear,' she whispered, 'Lord Torrendale has grown as cross as possible since he finds himself debarred from moving about, and watching every thing himself, as he used to do; and he objects to every soul the countess likes to appear in public with. He is so afraid of a cicisbeo,[20] that I believe on my conscience he would lay an embargo on our taking George Spring. Poor George! only the other day, he came to me, very good-naturedly, with some books I particularly wished to see; I scolded him for startling me, and was ready to twist his neck off for not being Spencer Fitzroy; that was my first impulse I mean; but I never yield to first impulses. It would not be very amusing to have him by one during a whole entertainment, and wishing him somebody else all the time.' With such discourse Arbella continued to amuse Matilda, or rather herself, while the countess continued moody and silent till they arrived at the theatre; but if Miss Melbourne had before found occasion to regret the alteration that had taken place in her ladyship's humour since the morning, she was no sooner engrossed in the illusion of the scene, than she wished it had continued, at least as far as silence was concerned. Her ladyship, after casting a fretful and dissatisfied glance round the house, was seized with a most violent fit of talking; / rather than not have a hearer, was willing to pour into Matilda's ear the various interesting circumstances that occupied her imagination. She had not yet had an opportunity of informing her young friend of her reasons for dismissing Miss Langrish, before she left town for Tunbridge; and the most interesting scene of an interesting tragedy, was the moment she pitched upon for that important communication.

'I discovered,' she said, 'even before we left the country, not only that her mind was uncultivated, but her language most shamefully incorrect. Only think of her bringing me a serious complaint one day, that Lady Emily would do nothing but run among the hay-makers and dairy-maids, and that she had even attempted to milk the kiows! Well, we forgave the kiow, as it was in the country, and there was nobody by when she said it; but it was a great deal worse when we returned to town. She committed herself dreadfully at Lady Barbara Montravers' French theatre: the play was Piron's *Metromanie*[21]; she pronounced it *Matrimony*, and matrimony she would call it all night, to the great amusement of the beaux, and my equal consternation. And I know the reason the Duchess of Normanby gave for not including me in her private theatricals at Richmond, was for fear I should take the liberty of bringing Miss Langrish. I have been told that Mr. Murray observed on the occasion, she would fill the *rôles de suivante*[22] admirably; but that I will not believe. Whatever may be her origin, I have certainly been most barbarously deceived. Do look at this man who is coming on now; he is a great favourite; I want you to attend to his first speech.' Miss Melbourne would have attended if her ladyship had given her leave; but, in order to assist her attention, she continued her incessant buzz.

'Emily was reading Robertson's Charles the 5th or 6th,[23] I forget which, and met with something about auricular / confession. She wanted to know what it meant, and

Miss Langrish told her that it was the confession of a gardener of the emperor's, who had stolen some auriculas. Another time she explained the order gallinæ, in natural history, to mean an Italian breed of poultry, introduced into England by the late Sir John Gallini of the Opera. Has not that actress a sweet voice? she is reckoned a very rising performer, I assure you. She is a lovely creature, and they say – ;' here her ladyship leant over to Matilda, and whispered her something so very low, that even she could not hear it, and being very desirous of attending to the business of the stage, did not think it worth while to ask her to repeat it. Still the countess kept close at her ear, talk, talk, talk.

'I could never tell you all the mortifitions she has caused me. Lady Evergreen Prudely gave a children's ball, for the sake of her little nieces, to which Emily was not invited. She said it was impossible she could do otherwise, for that as they were to be all attended by their governesses, she would have been obliged to ask Miss Langrish; a concession, which the young woman's former situation and connexions rendered absolutely impossible. Then her behaviour when in company with a certain gentleman, was so very – so excessively improper. In short I am told, that it is the general topic among all my friends, who either wonder, or laugh at me, for having endured it so long.'

Miss Melbourne had often observed, with surprise, that her noble friend had a habit of voluntarily making those, whom she might have reason to think she had offended, or whom she had treated, at best, with capricious civility, the confidants of whatever mortification or impertinence had at any time been shown to herself; exposing herself by that means to their comments at least, if not to a species of ill-natured triumph. She knew not how to reconcile such art and worldly mindedness, with such apparent confidence, almost amounting to simplicity. / Matilda, like many other people, sought, in some dignified and mysterious cause, the source of that which had its origin from a circumstance, which, if less noble, will at least be found, in those cases, to be the most general in its influence, though often the last that is suspected; namely, the force of that prevailing folly and absurdity, which, where-ever it pervades a character, levels the great with the little, and puts the strong in the power of the weak. Whenever there was an intermission from this sort of conversation, Matilda took all the advantage of such an indulgence the time allowed her. Giving herself up once more to the business of the stage; surrounded by the fascinations of talent, and the splendour of the arts, she forgot for a few moments that such beings as Lady Torrendale, Miss Langrish, or even Arbella existed; and was only roused from the too pleasing trance by the falling of the curtain, and her ladyship's rising to leave her box. 'I have to look in at Miss Mountain's masquerade,' said she; 'so I shall not stay the entertainment: but I can set you down first,' she continued, nodding kindly to Miss Ferrars, who she knew was dying to be present at such an amusement; 'and then, (turning to Matilda) we will proceed to Mrs. Melbourne's.'

After she had left Arbella at Mrs. Stockwell's, Lady Torrendale called at Fitzroy-square, in order to make some alteration in her dress, before she proceeded to the masquerade; and as the delay was unavoidable, she was very pressing with Miss Melbourne to alight. This offer Matilda at first declined, but the fear of appearing unaccommodating or impatient overcame the suggestions of her better genius, and she consented to leave the carriage.

'There; I told you it was better to rest yourself,' said her ladyship, 'than to sit waiting alone in the dark, for perhaps half an hour. Now, while I dress myself, you may retouch the roses, that / fatigue or something has banished from your face; or admire my bust, I believe you never saw it; or, in short – '

'I am not tired, dear Lady Torrendale, and you know I have no roses which any power of mine can recal; but I will certainly follow your lead.'

Her ladyship flung open the door of a small apartment, which, when only surrounded by a few select friends, she made her favourite sitting-room; and discovered to Matilda's dazzled sight a blaze of luxury and magnificence, under the unassuming pretext of a little retreat, sacred to the pleasures of friendship and conversation. 'It is Torrendale's taste,' she said. 'I believed he wished to make the cage agreeable to me; nothing less, you know, would be fit for the reception of the reigning divinity. He has just put the bust there, that he chose to have taken of me; don't you think it is in great glory?' She closed the doors with these words; and Matilda, impelled by curiosity, advanced with a light step, almost unconsciously, repeating part of a speech which had most imprinted itself upon her memory, in the performance she had just witnessed. Indulging but rarely in any species of amusement, with her, the attractions of talent had not lost their edge, by losing their novelty; and in giving up her soul freely to the delight they excited, she found, on the whole, the emotion they occasioned, rather pleasing and elevating than exhausting to the spirits. Her whole heart had melted and sympathised in the fictitious distress of the scene; but at the same time her imagination was filled, her reason was satisfied by a combination of genius, taste, and sensibility, such as she had never had an opportunity of witnessing before. Delighted to find that her feelings, however severely tried, were not so dead, so inaccessible to every outward impression of pleasure, as she had been led, in the hour of despondency, to imagine, she yielded to the gay and sweet illusions of the moment; which reminded her less of the habitual / tone of her feelings for some months past, than of that happy flow of spirits she had known, during some of the hours spent at Woodlands, when, new to every joy, her heart thrilled with responsive emotion, and love's 'light summer cloud'[24] was the only shadow that was suffered to obscure the sunny glow of her opening prospects. Perhaps this idea was recalled more forcibly to her mind, by the resemblance the apartment, in which she found herself, bore, to the 'dear consecrated region' she had left behind.

It was evidently Lord Torrendale's intention to restore to his lady, in this her winter palace, as much as possible, the charms of her little favourite retreat in her summer residence; and accordingly, excepting the bust, which was placed upon a tablet of verd antique, surmounted by a sky-blue drapery, studded with silver stars, and supported by light pillars of lapis lazuli, there was not an ornament which was not placed in imitation of those at Woodlands. No Turkish sultana was fonder of her own resemblance in the mirrors of Venice, than Lady Torrendale was of the repetition of her once lovely image; and the numerous and superb pier-glasses, which multiplied and reflected the ornaments of gold, bronze, and marble, consisting of classic figures, vases, and candelabras, disposed to the greatest possible advantage, on their tesselated or mosaic slabs, bore testimony to his lordship's attention to the prevailing tastes and inclinations of his lady.

'And is this the man,' Matilda mentally exclaimed, as she glanced her eye from the monument of faded beauty, which his still partial fondness had so conspicuously adorned, to the mingled richness and elegance with which every part of the room was furnished, 'this the Lord Torrendale, whom his lady, in the moment of caprice and dissatisfaction, would represent as all that is cold, selfish, narrow? Attentive to anticipate her wishes, he consults her inclinations in the manner of doing so; and seems desirous / to unite the memory of past pleasures, to the charm of present enjoyment. He little thought at the same moment of procuring me a similar indulgence; here, every thing, even to the colour of the decorations, the blue and silver paper, the silver mouldings remind me of them. The odoriferous exotics all breathe of dear Woodlands.' From these reflections she was roused by the light touch of some one as detaining her by her drapery. She started in alarm, which was not lessened, when the too faithful mirror discovered in its shadow the tall graceful form of Strathallan. Half overcome already, she was near sinking to the ground; but a slight motion, which he made as if to support her, restoring her recollection, she recovered herself so far, as not to betray to him how much she had been affected by his sudden appearance. His countenance expressed a tender joy at this meeting, but none of the surprise which was visible in hers. The idea that she had been drawn into this situation, by the consent and with the knowledge of Lady Torrendale, instantly took possession of her mind: indignant at the thought, she was again about to leave the room, when he caught her hand, and entreated to be heard. She trembled so violently that she found herself almost obliged to take a seat; yet felt hardly able to reproach him, when she perceived how completely her alarm and uneasiness had banished from his expressive features the radiant delight, with which they had at first beamed. 'Is this well, Lord Strathallan?' she faintly murmured, 'Thus to attempt to surprise me into an interview, which my better reason disapproves.'

'I acknowledge my error; you are right to upbraid me, Matilda; but I know not what I do. I have only misery, hopeless misery, and the desperate resolution of learning your sentiments from your own lips, to plead in my excuse!' Alas! he knew not that he could not have advanced a more forceful plea, to the still tender heart of his Matilda. 'Why will / you oblige me to excuse it?' continued the impetuous Strathallan. 'My mother already approves my choice, and my father is not accustomed to hold out long against her wishes.'

'Ah, Strathallan, would you oppose the authority of your mother-in-law to that of your father, if it contradicted instead of flattering your love?'

'Think then what must be the violence of that passion, which can make me even forget the leading principle of my life – the submission, the duty, such a father claims. Hear me, Matilda; before I knew you I was alone in the world; abandoned to the dark tempestuous night of my passions, neither expecting nor receiving happiness. I met you, and felt it was impossible to behold you with friendship unanimated by love; love, unsoftened by the still tenderer power of friendship; and will you, can you, for reasons to which I cannot allow the weight you give them, dissolve so sweet a tie, and throw me back to the dreadful solitude from which I had escaped? In you my heart acknowledged the best being it had ever held acquaintance with. Must it, can it, resign that sacred intercourse, after having once tasted of its charms? but I need not resign it. In the wilds of Strathallan, we shall no longer be obliged to conceal the sentiments of our hearts. There, living to love, and love alone, I shall no longer be forced to endure the presence of her I shrink from; to conceal my passion from her my soul adores. My whole life shall be devoted to the happiness of yours. Reflect, reflect, I entreat you, before you finally decide my fate.'

To waste life in a soft solitude of bliss with Strathallan; such was the picture thus unexpectedly offered to the imagination of the woman, who still tried, vainly tried, to deny, that in him, and him alone, her every wish, her every hope of future happiness was centered. Such was the intoxicating draught, prepared with all the flattering poison, and pressed on her with all the seducing eloquence, of love! She / durst not meet his eyes; she feared too much their dangerous tenderness; but she could judge by the emotion of his altered voice, by the soft violence with which he pressed the hand he held to his palpitating heart, with what trembling anxiety he awaited her decision. She would not look around – Strathallan was at her feet. 'Oh, cease to urge me,' she said, passing her hand across her eyes, as if to banish that instant from the memory of her life; while, perhaps, her heart secretly wished it could for ever endure. 'If, even when fortune comparatively smiled upon me, I acquiesced in your father's more extended views for you, and thought it a breach of hospitality to authorise your vows; would Strathallan wish me now to enter his family, a despised unsanctioned bride? Accustomed to be the pride and love of all who know you, you think not of the effect that time, the coldness of former friends, the alienated affections of relatives, once so much prized, would produce upon a mind like yours. You were not formed for obscurity,' and she sighed as she cast a timid glance on the fairy magnificence of the scene around her. 'In the calm hour of reflection you would lament the precipitate resolution by which you renounced society. You would never reproach me for having snatched you from an admiring world, – for having condemned your best years to struggle with difficulties, they should never have known. But I should read in your silent glance, that my affection was no longer sufficient for your happiness; I should see that lofty and aspiring spirit panting after more than I could bestow; and I should not long survive the silent agony of that conviction.'

'Hear me, deign but to hear me, charming model of the most noble disinterestedness,' exclaimed Strathallan; 'while I swear, that when you are near me, I feel no wish beyond what those eyes have promised me; that I desire no other happiness – feel no other ambition than – ' /

'But *I* have ambition,' interrupted Matilda, the virtuous animation of a noble soul sparkling in her eyes, and giving added energy to her utterance. 'Ambition, not for myself, but for you, Strathallan. Do not defeat the hopes of your family; be what you were intended for – alike unblamed in all the relations of social and of public life; cited in private for the graceful discharge of every virtue that distinguishes the son, the brother, and the friend; in public, as the supporter of all that is noble, munificent, and truly great. With extended influence, and powers proportioned – almost proportioned to the expansive views, the boundless benevolence, of that generous – that princely mind. Seeing you move in the sphere, which you were formed to grace, I shall not have a wish ungratified. In the privacy, which is my portion, your praises still will reach me. To that of a multitude, I will add my feeble voice, and, blessing you, shall be completely blest.' Her manner, which, when representing to him the inconveniences of a hasty union, had been mild, reasoning, and persuasive, as she pictured the future splendor that awaited him, acquired a warmth, an energy, that would have been resistless in any other cause.

Strathallan continued gazing on her with a rapture, a tender and increasing admiration, which only added force to the bitterness of his regret. 'Bewitcher! you allure while you plunge me in despair; but do not think I will obey you. Every word you utter is an argument against yourself; you shall not persuade me a second time to resign you!' He paused, and looked in Matilda's countenance, for the irresolution he could not discover in her words – in vain.

'Alas!' she said, 'it is impossible I should repent, or change my determination. I might mistrust the dictates of my judgment; but your happiness is concerned, and I cannot be mistaken in the suggestions of my heart.'

While charmed with the extent of tenderness / these expressions conveyed, Strathallan saw there was no farther hope of influencing a mind so habituated to combats, and to victory over itself: on the contrary, the only means of removing the cruel interdict which prevented his approaching her abode, was, at least in appearance, to submit. He did so – but even in the moment that he engaged not again to renew a subject so painful to her, the violence he did himself was so evident, the anguish he endured so intense, that Matilda doubted whether she had to congratulate herself on her success, or to lament that she had driven him to despair; and, more than sharing all his sufferings, she was, at the moment he left her, in a state scarce less pitiable than his own. She was roused from this painful situation by a soft hand laid on her shoulder, and a well known voice asking her the subject of her reflections. She had hardly looked up, when she started at the unexpected figure she beheld – Lady Torrendale, attired as Calypso for the chase, had once more resumed the character in which she most delighted.

'Why, how I have startled you,' exclaimed her ladyship, taking off her mask, after she had enjoyed for a moment her young friend's surprise. 'As I hope for pleasure, she had quite forgot that I was gone to dress, or that I ever was to return. Shall I explain the cause of those pretty palpitations? are they not the heralds of the last dying struggles of poor duty, against the supreme commands of sovereign love? But calm yourself, my love,' she continued, perceiving Matilda almost suffocated by rising sobs. 'To be sure, a private marriage is a terrible thing; but we will arrange every thing with your mother, and she shall sanction it by her presence, and accompany you to Scotland; and there you will all live like so many hermits, and never be heard of more. Strath-Allan is the sweetest place; they say; a perfect paradise for a fond pair to retire to, and you will be so / happy. I always sympathize with lovers, for though I never felt the passion myself, I can well imagine it to be a certain something. Heigho! my sensibility was sadly mismatched to Lord Torrendale's apathy.'

Matilda, as soon as she could command voice sufficient, answered this rhapsody with the most severe and merited reproaches.

'Why, Heavens above!' exclaimed her ladyship. 'Now, as I hope for mercy;' and here she added several pretty strong asseverations, for she was seldom sparing of them upon proper occasions. 'I did not know of Strathallan's being returned to town, till the moment that I ran up stairs, and he crossed me; or if I did suspect it,' (observing the incredulity painted on Miss Melbourne's countenance, at the palpable contradiction which her first and second address exhibited) 'I can't see the mighty harm of your seeing one you were so fond of conversing with, and drawing with at Woodlands; and how can I help it if he will be unreasonable? those men are always so.'

'I do not expect it of your ladyship,' returned Matilda. 'I have a surer pledge against the recurrence of a similar scene, in the promise of Lord Strathallan himself.'

'Impossible! can he have been such an egregious fool?' Lady Torrendale muttered, while her countenance exhibited the most unequivocal marks of ill-humour and disappointment; but recollecting herself in an instant, and resuming with those bland and winning manners, that look of persuasive sweetness, which had formerly deceived so many men, and which, even to women, she directed rather than not deceive; she assured her young friend of the unabated affection she had ever borne her, which alone made her urge a step, that she felt certain would be permanently conducive to her happiness; and pleaded Strathallan's cause, with all the eloquence of feminine / softness, aided by more than feminine art.

Matilda sighed; for she knew too well that even if the other motives, that determined her rejection of Strathallan, did not exist, there was a cause which forbade her to think of one so dear, even as she valued that life, which he fondly offered to devote to her. But this secret, which she considered as much the unfortunate Sir Harold's as her own, was not to be trusted to levity, curiosity, and indiscretion, like Lady Torrendale's; she therefore contented herself with replying to her ladyship; that as the same reasons existed, which had influenced her resolution at Woodlands, she could not, consistently with her own ideas of right, adopt any other line of conduct than that which she had then pursued: she added her earnest entreaties, that the countess would no longer detain her, and did not attempt to conceal the rising indignation she felt at the double part that lady had acted.

Amazed, confused, and disconcerted, at finding so much firmness in one so young, Lady Torrendale still affected to carry off the circumstance with a careless air, and while Matilda was speaking, continued to play with the silver javelin, which, as a huntress, she carried in her hand;[25] it accidentally fell, and caught in a part of the drapery of Miss Melbourne's muslin-dress.

'Ah! Lady Torrendale,' cried the amiable girl, perhaps warmed by the subject into a little allowable romance, 'Even as a weapon like that could inflict a personal wound, the idea I was acting wrong, would pierce my bosom with a mental pang, which no sophistry could alleviate, no time could hope to heal. If, yielding to the weak dictates of inclination, I indeed followed the plan you propose, what would you yourself, at a future moment – what would Lord Torrendale think?'

'Lord Torrendale!' exclaimed her ladyship haughtily, interrupting her. / 'What's Lord Torrendale to me?' Then, almost made to blush by Matilda's unfeigned surprise, and reflecting that perhaps she had better not be quite 'let into the baby-house,'[26] she assumed a milder air, and said 'Indeed, I could have loved him, had he not shewn in every transaction, that my interests held but a second place in his heart; and that he loved Strathallan far better than *my* child.' She looked down with bitterness, as she pronounced these last words; and all the habitual resentment, that she cherished in her heart against her lord, seemed to have resumed its place.

Matilda started, for in this unguarded sally, the secret spring of all her ladyship's machinations, since the beginning of their acquaintance, was disclosed. The thin veil of disinterestedness, which had often been partially raised, was now torn away, and for ever. Wondering at her slowness in suspecting artifice, she now perceived that the countess had uniformly acted towards her in conformity to the ruling principle, or rather no-principle, that governed her mind. When she thought that Spencer could be benefited, by his brother's forming a wealthy connection, she promoted it with all her power, to the total exclusion of Matilda's pretensions. When she thought that wealth could be transferred by marriage to her son, she as warmly espoused Matilda's cause. On Miss Mountain's resisting this scheme, she recurred to her first plan of conduct, and, delighted that chance had thrown Miss Melbourne to a distance, neither the misfortunes nor the merit of her young friend, could tempt her, by hazarding the least show of friendship, to risk the renewal of an intimacy, that she considered as most naturally and fortunately broken off. But when the apparently insurmountable aversion of Strathallan presented an obstacle to the success of her designs, she applied herself to her last resource, and by flattering his passions, and encouraging the noble-minded, generous, and till now, dutiful son, in open opposition / to the wishes of his father, she hoped to hurl him from the proud pre-eminence which he had hitherto maintained; and to secure for her own all the partiality, and perhaps most of the advantages, his brother had before engrossed.

Lady Torrendale perceived she had betrayed herself; but mistaking candour and gentleness, for easiness of temper, she thought she could still impart a specious gloss to her motives, sufficient to impose upon youth and innocence like Matilda's. In vain – the spell was dissolved; and convinced at length that it was so, her ladyship, like a disappointed enchantress, remounted her chariot, and, after restoring her young charge to her peaceful home, sought, in the pursuit of tumultuous pleasure, to banish the remembrance of the failure she had just experienced.

CHAPTER III.

'O married love, thy bard shall own,
Where two congenial hearts unite,
Thy golden chains inlaid with down,
Thy lamp with heaven's own splendour bright.
But if no radiant star of love,
O Hymen, smile on thy fair rite,
Thy chain a wretched weight shall prove,
Thy lamp a sad sepulchral light.'

LANGHORNE.[27]

THE fate of Strathallan was drawing to a crisis, and events rapidly succeeded each other, to determine the uncertainty of his wavering resolutions. A few days after the last interview Matilda had with him, Mrs. Melbourne received a note from the Countess of Torrendale, in which she invited herself (if that lady were disengaged and *quite alone* to dine and spend the day with her; as she 'wished to have some uninterrupted conversation with her, and had some important particulars to communicate.' What these / 'important particulars' might be, Miss Melbourne and her mother were equally at a loss to divine; nor were they very solicitous to fathom the mystery. Matilda felt assured that, after what had passed, Strathallan would not insult the steadiness and sincerity of her determination, by again making use of any indirect means to shake it: and respecting Lady Torrendale's secrets, as they were unconnected with Strathallan, she felt more than indifferent. Her forbearance was not however put to the trial: long before the hour appointed, a second note arrived from Lady Torrendale, written under evident perturbation of mind; which stated that she must give up the pleasure of spending the day with Mrs. Melbourne, as Lord Torrendale was taken suddenly and alarmingly ill. Mrs. Melbourne, who had desired her daughter to open and read the note, was struck with the sudden and visible emotion that its contents excited in her. Matilda looked down to hide the tears that rose to her eyes, and dropt faster than she could conceal or wipe them away. Never had she found herself so affected by any incident: she still esteemed, she honoured Lord Torrendale; yet she could not, even to herself, account for the dreadful flutter of spirits, into which she was thrown by this intelligence. Desirous of calming a perturbation, for which there appeared no adequate cause, Mrs. Melbourne rather soothed than reasoned with her daughter, and imputing the extreme sensibility she betrayed on this occasion to the frequent shocks her spirits had recently sustained, she gently suggested that the danger was probably not so great as Lady Torrendale's imagination, which was ever ready to take the alarm, might lead her to suppose; and that the morrow at all events might be the herald of better news. The morrow came, but only with a confirmation of Lord Torrendale's danger; the illness of which this sudden and violent attack was a precursor was a bilious fever. Quiet of mind was strongly insisted upon / as affording the only chance for his recovery, but how was that to be obtained? The same restless phantom that had urged him to fly from Tunbridge, before he could derive any benefit from his stay there, continued to haunt his anxious days and disturbed slumbers. To see his son united to Miss Mountain, was the point to which all his wishes tended; and which, till it was accomplished, would not allow him an instant of repose. The absolute necessity of this marriage, as the only means of extricating himself with honour from his various and distressing embarrassments, appeared to him every day more obvious; and the sight of the countess, from whose imprudent fondness for her son they had principally arisen, was now, to his proud and embittered spirit, a perpetual source of added irritation.

When Matilda considered all these circumstances, she could not forbear commiserating the fate of a man, whose recent coldness to herself had proceeded rather from his situation than his heart; and who seemed condemned, after a life of chagrin and discontent, to all the miseries of a lingering and painful dissolution. What was it that increased the bitterness of those reflections – was it a secret sad conviction, that at the moment she shed the pious drops of sympathy for another's sorrows, she was doomed to 'want the generous tear she paid!'[28] Certain it is, that as if a more affecting and mysterious sympathy was destined to regulate the life and all the actions of the lovers, in the very hour that Matilda was indulging in those reflections which presented life in its most gloomy colours; Strathallan, the victim of filial affection, and filial terror, was binding himself to offer up every other feeling of his heart at its shrine. That moment of surprise and misery, that moment in which his parent seemed between life and death, beheld this affectionate, unhappy son kneeling by his bed, in agonizing tenderness, and / bathing the hand he held with tears; his sister was on the other side. The countess, by Lord Torrendale's express entreaty, was in an adjoining apartment. Apparently convinced he had not much time to live, he exerted his little remaining strength, affectionately to address a child, whom he had always loved with as much fondness, if not with as much pride, as his son. 'My Emily,' he said, in a faint exhausted voice, 'I need not recommend you to your brother; to you he was ever kind. I had hoped I should have left him situated, so as to be still better enabled to show his friendship to you, but that is past.' Then turning to Strathallan, he continued; 'A succession of circumstances, which I have in vain endeavoured to avert or control, prevent me from leaving you as I wished; but I thought that by the advantageous alliance I had secured for you, I had in a great measure repaired the effects of the imprudence of others.'

'Do not accuse them,' exclaimed the generous Strathallan. 'Whatever may be my fortune, I shall know how to be content, nor wish to live beyond it.'

'But I shall not,' his father resumed. 'The idea will embitter my latest hour; that my son, perhaps the last of his race, will close in himself our once splendid career; or, that by some disadvantageous connexion, he will put it out of his power to preserve that hereditary dignity, which belonged to our family.' Much affected by the subject, Lord Torrendale took breath before he could proceed. 'My life has been a life of disappointment: when deceived in my hopes of Spencer, I looked to you for consolation; till now you have ever given it me, but it is fit that the last hope of my existence, like all the others, should be frustrated.'

'Dearest father, I only ask a short delay.'

'And in that delay your father expires! my honour, your dying mother's wish! Oh, Strathallan, what will not passion / do? your purposed procrastinations leave me uncertain whether those engagements will ever be fulfilled.'

'Oh, sir! if by any sacrifice I can calm your mind, point it out, and I will make it,' Strathallan said, wound up to enthusiasm by the united power of grief and affection.

'You know the only way,' his father faintly replied.

Strathallan paused; for a moment his respiration seemed suspended, and his whole frame agitated, by the dreadful conflict of his mind; at length he cried in a low, yet quick, and hurried voice, 'then let it be so!'

Without appearing to notice his visible emotion, Lord Torrendale requested he might see his lady and Miss Mountain; the countess came, leaning upon the arm of that young lady; neither the altered looks of the exhausted invalid, nor the mournful appearance of every thing around her, could in the least lessen the stiffness of Miss Mountain's proud unfeeling carriage, or the stare of affected superiority, which ever seemed to look down upon distress. Lord Torrendale beckoned to her to advance, which she did with the greatest readiness; he then called Strathallan, desirous of joining their hands. 'Let me have the satisfaction of seeing you thus united,' he said, 'before I close my eyes. My dear young lady,' addressing Miss Mountain, 'let me request a consent from you, which my son has long learnt to value.'

Strathallan offered his hand; his look was full of softness; to a woman it could not be otherwise; but more he could not affect; and, perhaps, no other but Miss Mountain would have accepted an assent so yielded. She took his hand, however, with an air of the greatest satisfaction, and turning to him, with that formal bend, by which she had the art of conveying the idea of as much pride, as her usual stiff erectness, she said, 'Now, Lord Strathallan, you have acted indeed as / becomes you, and as I always expected you to act.'

The ladies then retired again, and Lord Torrendale, faint with the exertion he had made, fell back in a state of complete insensibility. Strathallan, falling upon his apparently inanimate body, exclaimed 'Oh, my father, could not even that preserve you? then I must follow you!'

In a few moments, however, his father revived. 'Do not leave me, my dearest, my noble-minded son,' he said. 'I fully appreciate the value of the sacrifice you have made.' He then complained of fatigue; and Strathallan hoped, that if he could obtain a few hours sleep, he might recover from the harassing effects of his preceding anxieties. During the night he often appeared restless and perturbed; still he sometimes slept, and at each uneasy interval, the idea that his affectionate, his devoted son, watched by him, seemed to be a refreshment to his wearied soul, a cordial to his anxious heart. Towards morning he appeared desirous to talk with Strathallan, of the satisfaction his conduct had given him; of the new hopes and cheerful views, with which it inspired him. 'It infuses a delight into my soul,' he said; 'a feeling of pleasure, which seems to reinvigorate my whole frame, and to whisper I shall not so soon be parted from the blessing I enjoy in you.'

By the time his medical attendants usually met, most of the unfavourable symptoms, that had alarmed them in Lord Torrendale, had given way, and proved how potent a physician the happiness of the mind is, in restoring ease to the body. They now ventured to flatter his family with the most sanguine hopes of his lordship's recovery, though they acknowledged it must be tedious, and would require change of air to perfect it.

From that moment Lord Strathallan's marriage was universally talked of, as a thing decided upon, and which was to take place immediately; and Matilda, / though she mixed so little with the world, was soon informed of it by Lady Emily Fitzroy; who found it impossible to leave her friend long in ignorance of an event, that caused such joy to the family, as her father's recovery. Matilda now, in her own mind, fully accounted for the strange and powerful emotion she had experienced at the first mention of Lord Torrendale's illness; an agitation, which, she often afterwards declared, more resembled the solicitude excited by that which most nearly concerns our dearest interests, than the share, however lively, which we can be supposed to take, in what merely affects another. During this short period, the anguish and misery of mind Strathallan endured was extreme. He often unconsciously exclaimed, And is it indeed irrevocable? have I thrown that hope for ever from me? Have I, can I have consented? Lord Torrendale, however, seemed desirous to leave him as little time as possible for such reflections, and to shorten as much as it was in his power, any interval that might give his son an opportunity to retract or repent of the consent he had yielded. Strathallan himself no longer started any difficulty; but, with a kind of desperate resolution, appeared equally eager to hurry on the preparations for his inauspicious nuptials. He made no farther attempt to see Matilda; but, that this neglect was not caused by recovered tranquillity, she might judge by the contents of a letter, which Lady Emily put into her hands, at the conclusion of a visit she paid, a few days subsequent to that in which she had come so eagerly to announce Lord Torrendale's recovery. As she presented her with the packet, 'There are verses inclosed, I believe,' she said; 'which my brother tells me you left by mistake at our house some time ago, and which he has kept, always intending to return them to you.'

Matilda, who easily guessed the allowable stratagem, by which Lord Strathallan, in making her his ambassadress, had yet respected the innocence and candour of / Lady Emily, thought the moments too long in which she bade farewell to her once loved little friend. As soon as she was alone, she hastened to her chamber, and devoured rather than read these lines, traced by that beloved hand, which was now for ever to be devoted to another.

'I have accomplished my destiny. I have sacrificed to filial duty what nothing, not even Matilda's command, could force me to resign; but I dare not see you; one look would make me retract all the engagements of years; and madly vow at your feet, to live or die devoted to you alone. I think I may claim your approbation; I ask it as the solace of my life; I know I have relinquished all right to demand more; yet, if indeed our passion had a purer source, a more exalted aim than that which lower souls conceive, prove it to me by continuing your friendship; and then I shall not think you wholly lost. Do not imagine that I mean to ask it now; long, long must be the period that shall intervene ere the time comes, (should it ever arrive) when I can hear without a thrill of transport that voice, when I can gaze upon that form without emotion; but then, (Oh God! how calmly have I brought myself to write of that which is to rob my existence of its sweetest charm!) then, oh my loveliest friend, suffer me to hope I may address you by that tender name. Your sex is formed for friendship, and you are formed for it above all your sex; will you then deny me this sweet consolation? Perhaps at some future time – I know not what I would say: all before me is gloom and desperation, which darkens as I contemplate it, a misery without limit, end, or measure. Adieu, dear, too dear, Matilda. Oh, how faint are these words, to express the feelings that now rend my heart; again farewell. Forgive, and – may I ask it? do not quite forget – the wretched STRATHALLAN.'

'Dear, lost Strathallan! forget you! / would I could! it would be happy for us both,' cried Matilda, as she deluged with tears the letter she held; she heeded not the lapse of time, while she stood with her eyes fixed upon that name, in which every letter seemed to speak to her heart, and to represent in a degree the presence of Strathallan. She had nothing with which to reproach herself; yet in her distracted state of mind, every line of conduct, for a moment, seemed preferable to that she had pursued; and something like remorse accompanied the idea, that perhaps had she not willed it otherwise, she would have now been free. Reflection soon placed her own conduct in its true light, and reconciled her to herself. At all events, this was no moment for the indulgence of such reflections, for she expected her friend Miss Ferrars to spend the day with her; and in no circumstance of her life had Matilda, by betraying the least outward sign of feelings which she thought it her duty to repress, put it in the power of the indiscretion of her friend, to wound her peace of mind, by imprudent disclosures, or even inconsiderate sympathy. Though truly glad to see Arbella, Miss Melbourne was rather surprised to find she had brought Mr. Spring with her; and however unwelcome the intrusion, Matilda received them both with her wonted smile of benevolent hospitality.

'I have brought this poor lad in my train,' whispered Arbella, 'for we really know not what to do with him at home. After he has looked at a book of prints, opened and shut the doors and windows, and pulled the blinds up and down, the poor boy is utterly at a loss how to find employment for himself.'

'And am I to have the charge of all the idle youths in town, Arbella?' said Matilda, with a languid smile.

'No. Yet still you cannot but improve him, as you do every one except me; you know I am incorrigible.'

At dinner George Spring thought it necessary to be very entertaining: when he had come up from the country, having been told by Arbella that his manners were not quite the thing, he began by / imitating her cousin Sam Stockwell; but he soon found, as he told Matilda in confidence, and shaking his head with an air of mystery, that poor Sam 'was little better than a fool; a thing, which of all others he detested.' So, dropping the Stockwell solemnity, he attempted to assume a tone of airy gaiety and raillery, that altogether formed a most comical embroidery, upon his plain surface of sincere but blundering good-nature. He had heard of intentions of a marriage in the Torrendale family, and had no doubt but Matilda was the expected viscountess, as he had noticed the visible partiality of Strathallan at Woodlands. He had heard him afterwards talked of, for his gallantry towards her at the Opera; he remarked the intimate connexion between the families, and some confused reports had reached his ear, of her last interview with him, and of his having returned from the country, purposely to obtain it.

All this George had spelt and put together, till he thought himself sure of the facts, and was very glad when Arbella gave him an opportunity to indulge in some facetious hints upon the occasion. Happening to ask him if he had picked up any news in Bond-street that day, he answered he had heard enough if he could remember it; 'but plague take their fine names and titles, I never can retain them; yet there is a marriage talked of in the great world, I know, and Miss Melbourne knows it too, perhaps.' Then, observing that Matilda kept her eyes fixed upon her plate, and appeared not to hear him; he continued 'Dear heart, how close some people are; but for all their concealments, some people may know as much as other people; do you know, Tom Touchit asked me to-day, when we were to have the new viscountess introduced. But I said nothing, and looked very wise!'

'Really, George, how did you possibly contrive that?' said Arbella, with affected surprise.

'Oh, let me alone for that; you don't think I can keep a secret; but I can be as close as other folks. All I say is, that the queen will not have a lovelier face / to compliment next drawing-room, than a certain person, that shall be nameless.' This was said with such a significant wink at Matilda, that thinking herself obliged to take it as addressed to her, she said 'Really, Mr. Spring, you are hinting at affairs in the fashionable world of which I am perfectly ignorant; so suppose we change the subject of the conversation, to something more generally amusing.'

'Admirably turned off! Who says a woman can't keep a secret? but you won't take me in; no, no – I know better.' All this, and the preceding hints, had been uttered in a kind of whisper, leaning across Arbella to reach Matilda; and Miss Ferrars, who perceived how much her friend suffered, repented more than once having imposed upon her complaisance the task of enduring such ridiculous and teazing importunity. More serious trials had, however, inured Miss Melbourne to bear the needle smart of these lilliputian darts with equanimity and patience. Perhaps it was not with equal philosophy that she read, some short time afterwards, in a fashionable morning paper, the following paragraph.

'Yesterday Lord Strathallan, eldest son of the Earl of Torrendale, led the amiable and beautiful Miss Mountain, sole heiress of Hugh Mountain, Esq. of Vinesbury in Derbyshire, to the hymeneal altar. The ceremony was performed at Lord Torrendale's house, Fitzroy-square. The bride was entirely attired in white lace, and looked most delicately lovely, and interesting. Immediately after the ceremony, the happy pair set off in a barouche and four, on the first stage of their journey to Lord Strathallan's seat in Scotland, where, it is reported, they are to spend the honeymoon: an elegant and sumptuous collation was provided, of which many characters of the first distinction partook; among whom we noticed Lord and Lady Lyndhurst, who had come up from their elegant mansion of Rose Villa in Surrey, to be present at the celebration of this happy event.' /

CHAPTER IV.

Praise, of which virtuous minds may boast,
They best confer who merit most.
WORKS OF SIR WILLIAM JONES. Epistles.[29]

Un alma grande
E teatro a sè stesso. Ella in segreto
S'approva, e si condanna.
METASTASIO. Artaserse.[30]

THE remembrance of Strathallan, which prudence had long condemned, duty now joined to forbid; and it was Matilda's new and painful task, to eradicate it as much as possible from her bosom. She experienced, for the first time, what charms are attached to the indulgence of a cherished passion, even though nourished almost without hope; and how much more difficult it is to banish from the heart an attachment encouraged so long, than even to deprive it of its food in the sight of the object beloved. Many a soft dream of bliss, many a tender and unreproved contemplation, had in former days plunged her soul into a pleasing, and luxurious melancholy, and beguiled the real severity of her fate. But these must be now resigned, as affording a dangerous and no longer innocent relief; and in the bitterness of this total resignation, she felt that none can be called completely wretched, but those who are forbid to love. She in part succeeded in obtaining an outward calmness; but the less her mind appeared to sink, the more visibly her health declined.

Mrs. Melbourne beheld the alteration with an anxiety, to which she hardly dared to give words. The too brilliant eye, the flushing cheek, excited her wildest apprehensions. She had lost a beloved partner by slow and undermining decay; was she also to see the only child of her hopes, sink under its dreaded and blasting power?

Fortunately for her, the inclinations of Sowerby (who fretted daily at the increased / expense, and decreased satisfaction he experienced in the town residence, which he had only taken to be near his fair friends) coincided with her own, with respect to the necessity of change of air for Matilda. Though truly liberal, whenever any act of beneficence or generosity was to be performed, Mr. Sowerby was one of those petty economists who cannot bear to see the smallest sum unnecessarily spent; or rather who, as Lord Chesterfield expresses it, lose their character by giving four shillings, where a crown would have established their credit for generosity.[31] Unused to the habits of a London life, lodging-houses, theatres, taverns, were equally and indiscriminately the objects of his indignation, as scenes of imposition and deceit. He abused his servants, beat down his tradespeople, and regularly quarrelled with his landlady upon every charge she made him. Another of his maxims was, that the village poor were all honest, diligent, and worthy of encouragement; but the whole race of porters, waiters, and servants, in town, were so many sharpers, spies, and ruffians in disguise. In consequence of this prejudice, while he would in the country have bestowed his money liberally on an industrious tenant, or distressed domestic who applied to him for assistance, – in London, the smallest additional expense irritated, the slightest proposed gratuity, offended him.

Unwilling to allege his real motives, from the dread in which he stood of Mrs. Melbourne, who frequently rallied him on these peculiarities, he found in his apprehensions for Matilda's health, an ostensible cause for his wish to return to the country. And he pressed his friends, with a vehemence equal to his desire of success, to visit him in the retirement to which he was about to return.

To his remonstrances were added the entreaties of his sister, the gentle Clara, who had experienced her full share of the disagreeables attached to her brother's impracticable temper in town, and who languished for the freshness of mountain breezes, and sylvan verdure again. /

'This close confinement don't agree with you, Matilda,' said Sowerby; 'we must get you into the country to recover your looks a little.'

Mrs. Melbourne joined in the opinion of the necessity of the change, and such being the dispositions of the whole party, their removal would have been speedily resolved upon, if Matilda, with whom *self* was ever the last object of concern, had not opposed to this scheme, her wish that her little Julia might continue to attend some lectures which an eminent professor was at that time giving in London; and which her brother, who was desirous to cultivate in her a taste for natural knowledge, had desired she might be permitted to hear. She at length yielded so far, as to agree that the end of June should be the period for their migration to Clifden-Down: and in the mean time the amiable sufferer endeavoured by a constant, and unremitting attention to her usual avocations, and a gaiety, assumed indeed, but bewitching, to banish from the minds of those most dear to her, all painful apprehensions, respecting her health or tranquillity.

But when released from all her self-imposed duties, her heart stole an hour, to devote to solitude and regret; it was then that she felt indeed the whole weight of the loss she had sustained; and found that nothing could wholly replace the sentiment which had become the habit of her soul. She would often feel as if searching for something; and then, forlorn and wretched, find it was the forbidden image of Strathallan. Hardly sufficing to herself, she seemed to have lost her better part, and tried, often in vain, to check the rising feelings of disgust and impatience, excited by the presence of others, while HE was banished, was lost, was irreparably lost to her, who alone could interest her heart; to recal the wanderings of her thoughts, of her eyes, of her soul, when addressed by her other friends, and when her person indeed was present, but her mind was fled far away, to the secret object of its involuntary and most dangerous meditation. 'I must conquer this last weakness,' she / said, 'or I am not worthy of the mother, whose every exertion and precept was applied to form my heart to virtue. She would not admit of temporizing: she would not approve of the imperfect virtue of an *Estelle*,[32] who, content with being irreproachable in action, allows herself to nourish in secret an unhallowed passion, in the vague hope of its ultimate reward.'

Looking over the few monuments she possessed of their past tenderness, with a resolution to destroy them, she found the letter of Strathallan, the last address despairing love had dictated. She tried to tear it, but her hands refused their office; and she could only look at it, lay it down, and burst into tears. 'Rest there,' she said, throwing it from her: 'Ah! what would its destruction avail me, when every word is engraven on my heart? Rather let me engage, thus solemnly engage (it is all that is in my power) never to reperuse its dangerous lines.'

The brooch which she had won from Miss Mountain happened to be in the same drawer with the letter. Matilda remembered the night she had received it, and a thousand overwhelming recollections rushing upon her mind, she stood in apparent contemplation, but real forgetfulness of what she held, when suddenly an accidental movement touched a slight spring, – the back opened, and discovered a miniature of Strathallan. What language can describe her feelings, as with an exclamation of involuntary joy, she bathed with tears of tenderness, this unexpected treasure; and gazed upon it as if she would have 'looked it into life.' Her eyes raised, her hands clasped together, in speechless, painful extacy, she appeared the enraptured discoverer of some lost, precious jewel, which its possessor had despaired ever again to behold. At the moment that she had resigned every hope, it seemed sent to recal her back once more to the sweet illusions of happiness.

This ornament, intended for Miss Mountain, had been for that reason enriched with a portrait of her future husband, of the most striking resemblance. On a more attentive / survey, Matilda observed that the whole countenance bore the impression of that pensive cast of feeling which he had lately habitually indulged. The general aspect was more calm, but the eyes spoke to her heart with all that melancholy impassioned softness, which in their last interview they possessed; while fancy whispered 'When this image was traced, his thoughts were fled to you.' She hastily closed it, hurried it back into its place, and with the most anxious precautions secured against the possibility of its being discovered or lost. 'Yes, dear Strathallan,' she exclaimed, 'when I gaze upon those features, you seem restored to me again. I have now an unsuspected treasure; – a secret, undisturbed, delicious source of joy. I shall not waste life entirely in the languor of privation and regret; but when the tedious duties of the day are done, when moonlight solitude invites my soul to peace, and, withdrawn from the world, I vent to the calming breath of dark, silent night, the long-suppressed, impassioned sigh, then – then – Whither, unfortunate Matilda, does your fatal attachment hurry you? You would THEN, in a forbidden and fearful delight, spend hours in the alternate indulgence of too tender contemplation and of criminal despair! Hence with that image which, too suddenly presented to your unguarded soul, unnerved your best resolutions, and left it the prey of every wind of passion.' Her determination was instantly made; and no sooner made than executed. Raising to heaven her eyes, swimming in other, but more blessed tears, than those which rapture had lately made her

---

* The heroine of Florian's admired novel.

shed, – 'O thou,' she said, 'who delightest only in the pure in *heart*, and who hast left us the command to keep it with all diligence, assist the efforts of a frail and wretched creature, who would fain preserve its innocence unspotted; that, amidst the wreck of worldly happiness, she may look to its testimony as her sole reward.' With the brooch and letter in her hand, she hastened to Mrs. Melbourne. 'Keep them, my mother,' she said, 'keep them out of my power, out of my sight, till – Oh! would I could tell you *when* you might restore them. / Name them not, withdraw them not from the oblivion to which I consign them. But do not, oh! do not destroy them.'

This temporary effort of resolution was rewarded by a tranquillity exceeding even what she had hoped it would have procured her; and in the tearful embraces of Mrs. Melbourne, and the heart-warm encomiums she bestowed, Matilda experienced if not perfect consolation, at least that tender and lasting satisfaction, only to be appreciated by those delicate and well-formed minds, to whose existence the testimony of a self-approving conscience is even more essential than the possession of happiness itself.

CHAPTER V.

Quì nessum raggio di beltà si mira;
Rustico è fatto e co' bifolchi amore
Pasce gli armenti e'n sull' estivo ardore
Or tratta il rastro, ed or la falce aggira.

Tasso. Sonnets.[33]

ARBELLA TO MATILDA.

Woodlands.

'You saw me last, a poor, pining, discontented thing, tired of town, sick of smoke, noise, and cousin Stockwell. We part, and hey! presto! before you have time to inquire after me, the London-bred Arbella is transformed into your faithful shepherdess. How I have come here you will wonder; but wonder on, for the steps that led to my present situation were so painful I cannot yet bear to recal them; so they shall be made the subject of another letter when I am possessed / of more spirits than I can boast at present. My task is, at this moment, to try to enliven Lady Torrendale, who is very solitary and very cross; and his Lordship, who is a little better, being very well satisfied with himself for having contrived to whirl her into Derbyshire so soon after Strathallan's marriage. But, even in his best humour, such a *wet blanket* (if the elegant Matilda will forgive the familiar expression) my conversation never coped withal: with his air of immense condescension in making some trifling inquiry, the answer to which he never deigns to wait for; his silent sneer and affected stare of astonishment if one ventures of oneself to address his gravity; and the delightful self-satisfaction with which he delivers some common-place saw, as if it were one of the most irrefragable dictates of human wisdom – Oh, my dear! you may call him a "worthy character," or a "respectable character," or any of the other of your long *et cetera* of apologies for dullness; but if the man has any merits, they are so hedged in, over-grown and smothered with his pomposity, and his solemnity, and his absurdity, that I find them quite impervious to my research. For some reason or other, he has lately been entertaining, I believe, the whole county. Such conversations as we have had at dinner and supper, about roads, and dykes, and parish and borough business; with sometimes a redcoat or two to enliven us; and then we have the whole story of a dispute on a point of precedence between an Ensign of the Local, and a Lieutenant of the Additional Provisional Supplementary Militia.

'Heigho! I find myself very ill, and out of spirits. Remember, Matilda, if any thing should happen to me, I leave you my whole fortune in my will. – We had last night an Assembly (I think they call it) in the village of Woodlands. But not even the patronage of the Lady of the Manor can absolutely create men, or make them spring up, as Cadmus did, by sowing dragon's teeth.[34] I wish you had seen the few we had there, hanging together like a little black cluster of bees, till dispersed by the noise of the music, which is indeed not very unlike a frying-pan or candlestick. Then dancing / away, with looks so determined, and yet so grave, one would suppose, they were thinking the whole time, that they had paid at the door for so many shilling's worth of dancing, and that they would not, for the world, lose one penny-worth of their due. In the house we are nearly the same domestic circle, as you remember, except poor Miss Langrish, who went away, you know, in a sort of disgrace for a few *lapsus linguæ*.[35] Lady Torrendale never enquires what is become of her. I think her wrong; we have also a great diminution of gaiety, in the absence of Spencer. Dear Spencer! Why cannot those little letters, convey any idea of what thou art? Seriously, I esteem it a fault in language, that the names of persons and places do not, like other words, contain in themselves a specific meaning, to convey to those who may have not seen their owners, an idea of the qualities they possess. What think you of a treatise upon the subject? My motto will be certainly good, for it is borrowed from Campbell, and shall run thus:

"Who hath not owned, with rapture-smitten frame,
The power of grace, '*the magic of a name?*"[36]

And it shall be by the Signora "Arbella Ferrara, Female Professor (if you please,) of the Academy of the *Oziósi*, or the *Addormentáti*," if she stays here much longer.[37]

'I will give as an example, that when one says the name of Spencer, nobody who does not know him, perceives BY the name thus uttered that one means the most captivating, wicked, dear, bewitching creature in the world. I remember, at a remarkably stupid ball Lady Torrendale gave, in London, I observed to a young lady, *as* stupid, that we should have been gayer if Captain Fitzroy had been in town. She looked at me: I perceived she annexed no more idea to the words "Captain Fitzroy," than she would have done to those of "Sam Stockwell!" In this dearth of conversation, and news, my chief amusement used to be, the little bickerments (as Shenstone has it,)[38] of Sappho and Alcæus. At first, they were not unwilling to give us the amusement of seeing them dispute; but suddenly the most cautious silence and reserve, succeeded to their mutual vivacity. I was quite at a loss to divine the cause, 'till / I discovered, by the whispering round, that Alcæus was unwilling to throw his precious wit away, ever since he had accidentally given words to a very bright thought, which he meant to expand into a tragedy; but which Sappho snatched up and transplanted, into one of her Odes, at the same time so spoiling it, that he declares no one would know it. The same Sappho accuses him of acting in a similar manner, by one of her ideas, which she unfortunately dropt, before she had worked it into a Sonnet; when to her great surprise and dismay, she found it the next day, hitched into an Epigram. Since that time, when Alcæus is going to astonish the company, the reflection suddenly stops him, that what he is about to utter is too good to be thrown away upon Saph; whom he fancies upon the watch to catch it. While Saph, equally afraid her enemy Alcæus will take advantage of her bright conceptions, and make them his own, suddenly prims up her mouth, when intending to utter some brilliant simile, or impassioned sentiment; and looks the very picture of Fatima in Cymon,[39] going to sing "Tax my tongue, it is a shame." These, with haymaking, herborizing, and occasional moralizing – melancholy, melancholy, moralizing, are all the amusements of my dear Matilda's disconsolate

A<small>RBELLA</small>'

As Miss Ferrars may not immediately find time to follow up this, with another letter, we will beg leave to go back a little, in order to relate a scene which had recently passed at Mrs. Stockwell's, and which ultimately caused the very extraordinary step the young lady had taken. Mr. Stockwell had at length, with the consent and advice of his mother, requested an explanation with his fair cousin Arbella, in which, after stating in a very methodical manner, what he thought due for the amount of his services, he plainly told her, he wished to know her final intentions: for that he would be trifled with no longer. When he had finished speaking, 'Bless me cousin,' she cried, with a start of affected surprise, here is a very serious accusation laid to my charge; I suppose you mean to bring me in debtor, to a considerable / amount; and I shall have a bill duly sent up to me, very much in the manner of an attorney's letter, with,

'To dancing two sets with you at a ball, 6s. 8d.

To saying three sentences to you, during said dances, *ditto*.

To keeping in good humour two hours and a half, wholly, and solely, with the view, and intention, to have and to hold your good graces, thereby, 10s. 6d.

To absenting myself from home, to attend you to lectures, exhibitions, panoramas, and so forth, £50.

To taking six lessons from a *maître de graces*, with the intention in the third article aforesaid, £6 6s.

To laming a horse, pretending to ride it a *la houssard*,[40] £30.

To – .'

While thus she rattled on, with a rapidity which her cousin endeavoured in vain to interrupt, he at length contented himself with shaking his head, and saying very well Madam, very well; but give me leave to repeat to you, that, you may go farther and fare worse.

'Not easily,' replied the lady, with a disdainful toss of the head. 'But as to going farther, I chearfully accept your permission.'

'And I give it you with equal pleasure; but at the same time, I must tell you cousin, that after all the expence, trouble, and loss of time, you have cost me, your behaviour is most unhandsome, ungenerous, and base.'

'But Sammy, dear Sammy, do not let passion blind your noble reason. To treat the matter seriously, in what respect have I given you trouble, or made you neglect your business?'

'You *did* make me neglect my business,' replied Sam sulkily, 'you made a man of fashion of me.'

'No, Mr. Stockwell,' returned Arbella, curtseying with the most provoking politeness, 'that is a thing of which you cannot accuse me. For the rest, my affections are mine to give; my person and fortune are at my own disposal; and now I am of full age, I insist on your accounting to me for it, and / resigning the management of my property into my own hands.'

'As to your person,' answered the gentleman, 'those may take it that will; it is not so fine; for your fortune,' he added, with a grin, 'you may find reason to repent of withdrawing it so suddenly out of my hands; and may not find it so considerable as you imagine.' To an exclamation of surprise and alarm that escaped Arbella, upon the intelligence thus darkly hinted at, he replied in contination, 'that while her fortune had remained in his possession, to be increased for her during her minority, he had ventured a portion of it in certain speculations in the stocks, which had not had the success he originally expected. But,' he added, softening his tone, for upon reflection he thought it a pity so good a fortune should be lost to him, on account of a little imprudence, 'If once you and I is friends, my pretty cousin, all may go on right again, I'll manage your business friendly for you.'

'Friendly indeed! Do you think that if your person and addresses were equally odious to me, before I knew this last instance of your conduct, you have recommended yourself as a protector, and friend, by such an acknowledgment of the unworthy manner in which you have taken advantage of my unprotected, orphan state!' A flood of tears succeeded this animated reproof, and rising sobs prevented her utterance, while Sam repeated, with the most perfect composure,

'Take your redress, Madam. You are, I know, of old, clever in business. I should like, of all things, to hear Miss Ferrars talk of accounts, and arrears, and scrip, and omnium, and annuities.'

The entrance of Mrs. Stockwell put an end to this dispute, and she, who was evidently already acquainted with the merits of the cause, immediately began the apology of her dear boy. 'Coom, coom,' said she, with that affected whine which she always employed, when she endeavoured to sooth; 'Surely you do not expect my poor Sam of being capable of embellishing your fortune.'

'No Madam,' said Arbella, who, chagrined as she was, could not resist noticing / this ridiculous mistake; 'you may depend upon it I do not suspect him of that.'

'Why then make up your little petty quarrel; lovers quarrels, as the poet says, is but the beginning of love.[41] There's a dear, give him your hand, and – '

Enraged to see herself the dupe of both mother and son, Arbella abruptly quitted the room, without allowing her aunt to finish the sentence, and not giving herself time for a moment's reflection, hastened to the Countess of Torrendale, whose house was at no great distance; and who, she persuaded herself, would willingly afford her countenance and protection. She was not mistaken in the first instance: She received from her noble friend the most flattering welcome. For, independent of a dear love of a little mischief, her Ladyship had been just that morning alarmed with the dreadful prospect, of another approaching *téte-a-téte* in Derbyshire, with Lord Torrendale; and perceiving, with that admirable *coup d'œil*,[42] which selfish cunning sometimes lends to folly, how completely the imprudent Arbella had put herself in her power, loudly applauded her spirit, while she secretly rejoiced in the idea of taking with her to that solitude, an agreeable girl, whom she could ride with – walk with – talk with – and occasionally, torment.

'My dear soul,' said she, 'I admire your resolution, more than I can express; but are you not afraid, should I openly protect you against your aunt, that she will go about every where complaining of my behaviour, and saying, like Madame De Sevigne's country friend, 'I have used her like a barbarity – like a horror.'

To this Miss Ferrars could only reply, 'that she relied entirely on her Ladyship's generosity; for that she would rather endure any persecution than stay any longer with persons who were capable of treating her with such baseness.' 'Well, *passe cela*,'[43] resumed the lively Countess, 'whatever I may have to fear from Mrs. Stockwell's wrath, I do feel my knight-errantry rise in your favour, dear Arbella; and I don't care if for once, I act female Quixote in your favour.'

In consequence of this conversation Lady Torrendale, still preserving the greatest politeness, / contrived to affront her old friend Mrs. Stockwell, beyond all possibility of reconciliation. She then made a few faint overtures towards an accommodation between the aunt and niece which she was sure would be rejected; and afterwards, loudly declaring she had made every effort the sincerest friendship could suggest towards healing their unhappy misunderstanding, professed that since they were rendered vain by Mrs. Stockwell's impracticable temper, she could not 'in honour,' refuse her protection to Miss Ferrars, who had so 'nobly' and 'generously' relied on it. This conduct succeeded exactly as she expected. The old lady protested every where, 'As she was excessive ill-used by'em *all*,' and the intercourse between the houses of Stockwell and Torrendale was completely at an end.

CHAPTER VI.

And sleep, which obeys me,
Shall visit thee never;
And the curse shall be on thee,
For ever and ever.

SOUTHEY – CURSE OF KEHAMA.[44]

SHORTLY after the receipt of Arbella's rambling epistle, Matilda, with her mother, accepted the invitation of their friend to Clifden Down, and found in its pure air, and the change of scene it offered, the best balsam to her injured health, and wounded feelings; while little Julia delighted to have escaped from smoke and noise to Derby's heathy hills again,

'Wove their blue-bells into garlands wild.'[45]

And, with the happy innocence of childhood forgot, in the enjoyment of the present, the / threatenings of future calamity. Her visible health and improvement afforded the highest delight to her brother, Sir Harold; who did not let the arrival of his fair relatives, pass long unmarked by his visits. Though his mind had evidently not recovered is tone, the sight of Matilda, seemed for a moment to calm the perturbed spirit in his breast, and he spoke with animation and interest of his meditated improvements, which he pressed both ladies soon to visit. Mrs. Melbourne, who dreaded to approach a scene which must recal, in their liveliest colours, those images that for the sake of her peace, she most wished to banish appeared unwilling. – He then turned to Matilda, and urged her with still greater earnestness to comply; using, in his own favour, some of those enthusiastic and fanciful arguments, which were suggested to his disordered imagination by what his memory and reading supplied.

'You know not the appearance,' he said, of my castle of the Rocks – it resembles now the golden palace of the Roman emperor. From the ivory roof, showers of roses descend and greet with their perfumes each entering guest. You will be surprised to think how I have contrived it. The mechanism is upon the plan of Nero's ivory palace at Rome.[46] And when Matilda appears, then will my good genius return, and beat away the busy meddling fiends that now sometimes grin and laugh from their dark nooks, at the changes I make around; cover my pearl woven hangings with sepulchral black; and convert my stately residence into a shrieking wilderness. When Matilda returns, all the good spirits, who sighed at her departure, and said, 'let us depart,' will return with her.' He fixed his eyes on her as he uttered these words, with such a wild yet mournful expression, that his cousin felt her heart melt with regret, and compassion, while for reasons similar to those of her mother, she intimated her refusal. Struck with the manner of it, Sir Harold suddenly dropt the wild vehemence with which he had urged his request, and seemed at once to enter into the feelings that might cause her reluctance. Mrs. Melbourne and Matilda had often observed / in him that amiable peculiarity, that whatever were the occasional wanderings of his mind, they never prevented his attention and consideration for others, however they might interfere with his observance of the forms of life. Except where his ill-fated passion was concerned, to hint to him that this perseverance in any particular object would give pain to those he loved, was always sufficient to make him renounce his most favorite intention. This disposition, while it increased the interest they felt for him, so far induced his fair relatives to give up their own inclinations, as at length to promise him, at some future time, the visit he desired.

At the time they made it, they found Sir Harold deeply engaged inspecting the labours of his workmen, who were employed in digging up the earth, in search of remains of antiquity, which it was hoped would be found beneath it. 'The cloud-capt towers,' and 'Gorgeous palaces,' which had existed only in Sir Harold's own imagination, were no longer the subject of his boast. The rage of improvement had, with him, given way to that of antiquarianism. Some old coins, and a small part of a very beautiful tessalated floor having lately been discovered near that spot, he was persuaded, that many remains of Roman magnificence lay concealed there; which, if those employed would use proper diligence, might be brought to light, and his whole conversation now ran on nothing but medals, urns, vases, and inscriptions. The planted walk, and twisted bower was dug up, with equal indifference, in hopes of discovering some treasure below; sometimes a trifling success rewarded the attempt; but more frequently the lovely scene was defaced, without affording, in return, any gratification to zeal, or curiosity. 'I have been thinking, my lovely cousin,' said Sir Harold, (seizing an opportunity when no one was observing them to address Matilda), 'that if we could once discover some secret retreat, some place under ground where we might live away from them all, we might then be happy; for while you are here, some one always comes between us to prevent your staying with me. It is for this that I am searching / among the ruins, in hopes at last to find a subterranean city; why should we not?' he continued, pursuing, with vivacity, the course of his first idea; 'why should we not discover one similar to Herculaneum, or Pompeii, buried in the eruption of Vesuvius?'

'Because,' replied Matilda, who knew that in his wildest flights he always expected to be answered rationally, 'we have no volcanoes here as in Italy.'

'No, not now,' resumed Sir Harold, 'but you know, my fair cousin, when the Romans were here, it might have been different. For,' he continued, speaking very fast, 'it is well known it was their policy to impose their laws, customs, and usages, upon the vanquished nations. Now, as nothing was more customary abroad than a convulsion of the earth, or the eruption of a volcano, no doubt, during their stay, they introduced the fashion of earthquakes, and volcanoes into England.'

Here was a specimen of the ingenious reasoning upon acknowledged facts, in which the Baronet sometimes indulged. In general he ended with giving up the theories so raised, as mere sports of fancy. On this occasion, however, he was serious, and Matilda could not refrain from at once pitying and admiring, the misapplied subtlety by which he united his present rage for antiquities with the ruling passion of his soul. Unwilling, however, to prolong so singular a conversation, and unable to resist an habitual terror inspired by his manner, when she for a moment found herself alone with him, she suddenly turned into one of the winding paths, with the intention of meeting her mother from whom they had strolled to a little distance; but missing her way she found herself in a part of the garden, which had once been Mr. Melbourne's favourite retreat; where, sheltered from the noon-day sun, he had spent many an hour in study, in a little arbour raised by her hands. A piece of water, clear as crystal, where golden fishes formerly sported, was near it, and used with its fairy banks, made rough with moss, bright pebbles, and aquatic weeds, to increase / the beauty of the little spot. This had not escaped the general devastation; the pond was filled with earth and rubbish, thrown up from the neighbouring excavations, and some of the roses and honey-suckles that had flourished over the bower, now torn up by the roots, lay extended along the ground: one rose-tree, however, still bloomed in matchless beauty and luxuriance, and wafted its rich fragrance over the scene, which had often witnessed the mild dictates of wisdom, falling from a father's lips; which had often cherished in her secret soul, visions bright as the beam of noon-day sun, of the beloved Strathallan. How changed had all become! That father was dead – his possessions the heritage of another – and Strathallan! – At this moment of torturing recollection, the wind conveyed to her in their full force, the odours that breathed around her; she felt their overpowering sweetness, but it conveyed no gladness to her heart: tears started into her eyes; she had never before experienced so perfect a conviction, that the period for simple and innocent pleasures, was completely flown.

Following the course of the stream which had once supplied this little reservoir, she came in front of the rock, from whose dark bosom it derived its source; and beneath whose hanging brow, a rustic retreat was formed, which, by its wild and savage appearance, melancholy herself might have selected for her chosen seat. It was new to Matilda, and she recognised in it the work of Sir Harold. She smiled, but it was in bitterness, to see the pleasing seats of peace and innocence overthrown, and the fantastic erections of a wild disordered mind, supplying their places. 'We will see,' she said, 'what taste adorns Sir Harold's favourite retreat – Oh, how unlike my father's! A meeting cypress and willow, formed the front; the entrance of it was overgrown with night-shade, and no ornament adorned it, save a little recumbent figure, lately discovered among the excavations he was daily making. The sedge with which it was crowned, announced it for a water-deity; and a chaplet composed of some beautiful imitations of aquatic plants, which it held in / one hand, added to the classic elegance of its appearance; within, a kind of rude altar, dim descried in the recess of the rock, was hung around with apparently votive garlands, for within one were inscribed the words 'Peace! Peace! Peace!' and below was written, 'In vain I invoke her from the genius of this retirement – she flies at my approach.' Immediately under that was added from Petrarch,

> Ma pur sì aspre víe nè sí selvagge,[a]
> Cercár non so, ch' amór non vénga sémpre
> Ragionándo con me, ed io con lui.[47]

These then had been the employment of her unhappy cousin, during the voluntary solitude to which he had condemned himself, since his absence from her. She was tempted to look at some of the fragments which lay scattered in profusion upon and around the altar. They all breathed the passionate enthusiasm of his soul, they all spoke of hopeless love and Matilda. On one paper was written fragments of a Persian Ode.

> 'Thou hast a heart, like summer hail,
> Marring the beauty thou bearest.'

*****

> 'Wound me, but smile, O lovely foe!
> Smile on the heart, thou tearest!'
> And again,
> 'See at thy feet, no vulgar slave,
> Frantic, with love's enchanting wave;
> Thee, ere he seek the gloomy grave,
> Thee his best idol styling.'[48]

'Oh, Matilda! Oh, my *soul's* idol! how can these chosen words, these measured lines, express the boundless passion with which my bosom glows? Ardent, immense, eternal. Even as I write, I think that as I trace *her* name it brings me nearer her! Vain thought! I look around, and find vacuity and misery. Drear, empty, dark, as this deserted breast! Oh could this sigh express the intense, the heart warm wish that prompts it! Its force would bear me to her. – Often, as I sit within this bower, her form, brightly smiling, suddenly flashes before me; then vanishing leaves me in double darkness. What sighs / what silent tears, are witnessed by the silent night! Oh, Matilda! lamp of my life, light of my lonely path,

> 'My friend, my goddess, and my guide,'[49]

I am dead to life, but I live to thee. Alas! 'tis in vain to struggle in the toils. I feel, I feel it is so. In vain I still repeat,

> 'Fond love, farewell! unfettered given to range
> To other breasts, your airy throne remove.
> Here Pride resumes her seat – the welcome change,
> Alike my reason, and my heart approve.
> Think not to win me now, with former wiles,
> My soul is proof 'gainst those seducing eyes;
> Those blushes soft; sweet terrors; dimpling smiles;
> Looks that betray; half words; and feigned sighs.<?>
> Fond love, farewell! say, must I bid again?
> Has Fancy's picture, roused a latent flame?
> Sure danger lurks beneath my parting strain,
> There is a magic in the liquid name;
> And while I boast me from thy fetters free,
> Enchanting Love! still, still I sing of thee!'[50]

Some of the chaplets of flowers which hung round the altar, adorned with inscriptions in the Greek manner, were inscribed, 'To the virtues of Matilda.' They were chiefly composed of those plants to which were ascribed some real or fanciful attribute. A crown of lilies denoted her candour. A wreath of intermingled moss and violets expressed her modesty; and so real was that quality in her, that she blushed to contemplate her own praises, even when no witness was near; and was leaving the retreat which she had been thus tempted to disturb, when she was prevented by the reappearance of Sir Harold, who had sought her anxiously all over the garden; and who, delighted that she had discovered of herself his favourite spot, began with his wonted wild romantic earnestness to expatiate on its beauties. 'This is,' said he, 'the seat of my repose whenever *they* threaten to torment me, I have only to reach this bower, and I am safe as in a sanctuary. Observe how calm it is! For, do you know,' he continued, in a whispering tone, 'however bright the sun may shine, it is here eternal star-light. Observe them gleaming through the roof,' he continued, pointing to the luxuriant flowers of the jessamin, which were intermingled with the cypress / green, 'other light is there none, save the emerald lamp of the glow-worm; the night-sparkling flowers of the nasturtium*; and the clusters of the shining medusa; the friendly insect, which, with its milky ray illuminates the dark bosom of the ocean, and cheers the heart of the midnight mariner. Here I remain whole days in repose of body, but with thoughts flitting thick round Matilda. When beside the softly murmuring stream, the owlet arises flapping her light wing; it is then I know that I may rest indeed, for then even the busy world is at repose: this, and this only, is the sign by which I can discover night from day, in this dusky bower. Nay, do not leave me yet,' he added, perceiving Matilda's impatience to be gone, 'or at least look once, but once again as you did just now, and it will be a ray of light to my heart.' As he spoke, he had caught hold of her gown, and fallen at her feet in a supplicating posture, to prevent her departure, when suddenly a loud noise, as of persons gaily talking and laughing together, struck upon their ears, and a moment afterwards a party of ladies and gentlemen issued from a neighbouring walk, and suddenly stood in front of the bower. Lady Torrendale, who seemed the conductress of this 'rabble rout,' gaily rallied Sir Harold on his desertion of the ladies, whom he had summoned to view his recent discoveries. Sir Harold, who had risen at the first sound of strange voices, approaching them, defended himself with equal grace, and almost made his unhappy forgetfulness, and absence of mind, be forgotten in the natural politeness and spirit with which he could atone for it.

The poet Alcaeus, struck, or pretending to be struck with the savage simplicity of the scene, stood, with his back against the rock; a silver pencil in one hand and his pocketbook in the other, to write down some golden lines his fancy, or, more probably, his / memory suggested: while the Countess apologised for the apparent rudeness of their previous mirth. 'We have been listening to that worthy old gentleman, Mr. William Anstey, who has been doing the honours of the tesselated fragments in your absence, my dear Sir Harold,' she said, 'till our gravity could resist no longer. There was a very elegant figure of a Roman Knight that particularly called forth his eloquence.'

'Look, your Ladyship, that is reckoned, I can tell 'e, a very well done thing, of an *ancient thing* – excessive nat'ral – as nat'ral as life – and that there lion and boy, with

---

*   A phenomenon observed by Elizabeth Christina, one of the daughters of Linnaeus, who remarked, that the flowers emitted spontaneously, at certain intervals, sparks like those of electricity, visible only in the dusk of the evening.[51]

wings like a bird, is not amiss; and them borders are nearly as pretty as our oil-cloths, as I tells my master; but nothing nigh so comfortable to my thinking. Them brick carpets must have been special cold, and unless the Roman gentlemen –'

While her Ladyship thus proceeded in her mimicry of the grey-headed steward, Matilda had time to recover from the slight confusion into which her sudden appearance had thrown her. She could not avoid remarking, however, that though the Countess, purposely abstained from any observation on Sir Harold's particular attention to her; she had noticed her embarrassment with a malignant joy. She had scarce time for these reflections; for, from an adjoining walk, she at this moment observed her friend Arbella advancing with open arms to meet her. After the first expressions of their joy were over, she affected, in the presence of Lady Torrendale, to turn the conversation on trifling topics; and shewing some slight sketches she had made; 'I want your correct eye, my faultless nymph,' she said, 'to tell me, whether I have not diminished the likeness in the copies I have taken from these fragments, by making the squares too regular – like a chess-board – hey? How do you like this gorgon-headed lady? Perhaps I have succeeded better with her – I assure you I took great pains with the snakes – or that little figure carrying a basket of flowers at a sacrifice – or a nuptial procession – "the same thing," Lady Torrendale would say; the hag! I mean *la belle dame*. I can no / longer trifle when I speak of her,' Arbella continued, in a whisper: and gradually drawing Matilda away from the party, she began to unburthen her heart on more interesting objects.

Meantime Lady Torrendale, wholly occupied with herself, or rather for the time being, with the interesting young baronet, whose romantic melancholy, and fanciful peculiarities, were perhaps an additional recommendation, in the eyes of a woman accustomed to the every day sameness of fashionable characters, was alternately making a judicious display of her vivacity, beauty, and pretty becoming simplicity. She asked if Roman brick was not stone: then laughed at her own ignorance; said Sir Harold must be her master, for that she idolized antiquities; took up a medal covered with earth in her pretty white hand, then wondered to find it dirtied her – extended her neck for a moment to watch with eagerness the progress of the workmen: then shuddered in affected terror, 'lest the next thing they turned up, should be an ugly head, or jaw-bone of somebody.'

Sir Harold for some time kept up the conversation with a fluency, a politeness, and a display of antiquarian and travelled knowledge, which made it doubly to be regretted, that a mind so elegant and so well-informed, should not be always equally well-directed. But when Matilda delayed to return, his anxious countenance and roving eyes soon shewed where his thoughts had flown; and Lady Torrendale, unwilling to own to herself, that the unassuming beauty of his fair relative, outweighed in the opinion of the gentleman whom at that moment she wished to captivate, all that gaiety, dress, and fashion could do in her own favour, used various efforts, but in vain, to recal his attention. 'She had several books at Woodlands,' she said, 'of "*antiquarian*" engravings, or "*anti-something*," she was not *learned* enough to say exactly what: Miss Melbourne who was so *clever*, if she was here could probably tell.'

'Miss Melbourne,' interrupted the Baronet, only catching the last word, 'Where is she? do you see her?'

'Really no,' resumed the Countess, / greatly piqued, 'I was going to say, that if Sir Harold Melbourne would condescend to look over those volumes, I should esteem it a great favour. You must soon expect another visit from us,' she added, recovering her good humour, and rattling on with her usual freedom. 'I feel a perfect enthusiasm, Sir Harold, for your discoveries; and you may soon see me, like the French ladies in the *Champ de Mars,* turning up the earth with my fan, in my zeal to assist your labourers.'[52]

At this moment, Matilda and her friend, were seen coming arm in arm up the walk, and the flash of Sir Harold's dark blue eyes, as she approached, was not lost upon the Countess.

'There Arbella,' said she, in a voice of evident ill-humour, 'throw away those scrawled sketches of the tesselated fragments which would disgrace a school-boy, it is time to prepare for our return. I forgot,' she added, as if recollecting herself, 'I should say *tasselled* pavement, as Mrs. Stockwell calls it, poor, dear soul!'

'Her Ladyship has been seized, I believe, with an unsuccessful *accés de coquetterie*[53] this morning,' whispered Arbella to Matilda, 'and she thinks it time to take her alterative, *viz.* a dinner with Lord Torrendale. Heigho, Matilda; remember your promise!'

'I assure you Miss Melbourne,' said the Countess, 'your friend does not pretend to find any thing in your absence, that can supply your place; I hope you will not delay long to give her the satisfaction she so much desires.'

To this faint invitation to Woodlands, Matilda only replied by a bow; and Lady Torrendale soon after took leave: observing, to all Sir Harold's entreaties, that she would prolong her stay, 'that he could not possibly want her company, when he was already so well engaged.'

The departure of the fine ladies, was indeed in spite of his politeness, that led him to conceal it, a real relief – and during the rest of the day, he conversed with his amiable cousins, with such cheerfulness and freedom, that Mrs. Melbourne flattered herself, still / more than Matilda, that his powers of mind were greatly restored. The time passed so agreeably that they forgot themselves, 'till twelve o'clock had struck. At that moment Sir Harold starting, and fixing his eyes earnestly on a small door, which they had not before observed, exclaimed, mournfully, but without any appearance of terror, 'Could you not wait *one* night?' then rising, 'I must leave you, my amiable cousins,' he said, 'I see my vigil cannot be dispensed with: but will you not give me hopes, that I may soon enjoy such sweet hours again? Adieu! may the repose that flies my pillow, shed all its roses upon yours.'

CHAPTER VII.

It is not friendly, 'tis not 'WOMANLY,'
Our sex, as well as I, may chide you for it,
Though I alone do feel the injury.
SHAKESPEARE. MIDSUMMER NIGHT'S DREAM.[54]

LADY TORRENDALE, finding that Mrs. Melbourne was settled for some time as her neighbour in the country, with all the promptitude, and decision of a woman of the world, at once took her resolution. On the day that followed their accidental meeting, at Sir Harold's, she visited her; conversing with the same ease, as if there had been no previous coolness, or cause of complaint. Mrs. Melbourne, who could not retain resentment, where her feelings were so nearly allied to contempt, thought a renewal of intercourse with Arbella, might be of benefit to Matilda's spirits; and therefore did not / retreat from the advances of the Countess: while Sowerby, who rather liked Lord Torrendale, from some points of resemblance in their characters, consented at times to endure her Ladyship, as a necessary evil.

The first morning Matilda visited at Woodlands, Lady Torrendale had not yet made her appearance, though it was three o'clock. She was dressing for a dinner party; and Arbella seized that favourable opportunity, to pour forth to her friend, the complaints her Ladyship's conduct every day and hour excited.

'No, no,' she repeated, in answer to Miss Melbourne's expressions of belief and sympathy, 'it is not for you to conceive, it is not for you to imagine, the torments she inflicts on me. With you at least she is polite; but with me she is – herself. Every day she makes me feel, how dependant I have made myself upon her, since I have broke with my family. Sometimes, when her Ladyship is in good humour, some plan of *mystification*, as they call it, is proposed: and then, I am to assist in playing off those, who are invited to the house with apparent kindness; but really, to afford her and her favoured few, an unfeeling amusement. If any compunctious visitings of remorse seize me at these guest-baitings, or if, when after their departure, she laughs and boasts how successfully she has concealed her contempt, and led them on to expose themselves, I look a little grave; 'I am the most disagreeable girl in the world; and mean to set myself up as a censor of the company.' When no such diversion offers, I, myself, am to be played off, to enable her delicate nerves to endure the *ennui* of the country: sometimes it is by grave, yet extravagant praises, bestowed upon some dowdy, and recommendations to me to endeavour to be like Miss Such-a-one, who is admired exactly for what I do not value. Now I am not envious, but I do not like to hear another, maliciously *be-praised* for hours, for the very thing, in which I least excel. That is the game when she visits the Crossbrooks. I am not over-fond of work. They never have the needle out of their hands; work, work, work – company / – meal-times – still it goes on. I hate those working-women. Don't you? I mean,' continued Arbella, without pausing for an answer, 'those who pride themselves upon a spider-like minuteness of touch, and delicacy of finish; and can do nothing else. They never have any souls. Say what you will to them, enter into the most interesting argument, it is "pray don't interrupt me, I'm counting my stitches" – or, "be so good as to stand a little out of my light." Hem! very true, Lord, how unlucky! "I have broke this thread." Oh! I would rather a thousand times have my poor Sappho, who is as awkward at her needle as ever Queen Christina[55] was, and does not know muslin from gauze, nor lace from leno. I cannot bear a woman who does not let her work insensibly drop out of her hand, as any subject arises that interests her heart, or engages her attention.'

'Now Lady Torrendale never takes up a bit of work, by any chance, and would laugh at those people the moment she turned her back; yet, when she is there, it is, "Oh how clever, how ingenious; what an œconomist of time Miss Lavinia Crossbrook is! What a happy art she possesses of always employing herself," as if one was never employed, but when one's fingers were engaged! Then at the Heathcotes; they are dashing fine people, as Mr. Sowerby would call them. There it is, "that I am not fashionable enough;" and when I ask her in what my deficiency consists, and what I must do to be fashionable enough, she intrenches herself in some unintelligible phrases, about certain forms, certain circles, certain sets, certain opinions, which she will never go beyond. Upon occasion of some slight inadvertence, that would not have been noticed in Helen De Courcy, she said to me, in her provokingly calm, languid manner, "Arbella, my love, surely you had the same tutor as Henry the fourth of France." Every one, being in the precious secret I suppose, laughed. And I, not knowing whether to look pleased or vexed, asked her what she meant. "Oh you will find it," she replied indolently, "somewhere about in Sully's Memoirs[56] – is it not, / Mr. Spring?" I looked at the passage pointed out me, and found that the name of one of the young king's first instructors was *La Gaucherie*. Well, while I stood overwhelmed with confusion, and my cheek burnt to ashes with shame and vexation, what do you think she advised me to do? why truly, to compose my features as fast as I could, and say *plum*. She said the pronouncing that word was sufficient to restore the mouth to a pretty smiling expression, after any irrition, and that she made it a rule to repeat it softly before she went into company, after a *tête-a-tête* with Lord Torrendale. Did you ever hear of such matchless impudence and ill-nature? I flung from her crying I could not say plum; and, I doubt not, furnished the subject for a fine disquisition, with her select circle, on the necessity of keeping one's temper. But I must bear it all, for I am sold – yes, I have sold myself to a proud, malignant being, who grudges me even the transient *eclat* her protection was to afford me in return.'

'But with pretensions, with attractions like yours is there no resource? no means of escape? you have broke with Mr. Stockwell, but have I not heard of another admirer of yours, a Major O'Hara?'

'Oh! Major O'Hara, Major Madcap,' interrupted Arbella impatiently, 'I never thought seriously of that, nor he of me, I dare say. – For,' she proceeded, (giving the best reason last, as young ladies generally do,) 'to say the truth, since my return to the country I must confess I think he has relaxed a little in his attentions – and as to Stockwell – no – I proudly protest that even in my most miserable moments I never repented the resolution I took with regard to him. In our best days Sam's loves and mine somewhat resembled the Sussex courtship, between the farmer's hind and the dairy maid, which my maid, who was a girl from East-bourne, used to amuse me with describing. You are to suppose the lady and gentleman seated *téte-a-téte,* by the kitchen fire. After the youth has sat for some time in silence, with his back turned to the damsel, she begins / to shake him, and says, "Well John – be'est asleep? say something." "Why, what shall I say?" returns John, "Why say you love me John." "So I do sure," and then they relapse into edifying silence. – And now that he has proved himself not only a stupid but a base wretch, would you have me – '

'And do you mean to let such injustice as your cousin's pass unnoticed?'

'Not if I could help it, I assure you, my dear – but setting raillery apart, what can I do? The truth is,' Arbella continued, casting her fine dark eyes on the ground, while a sudden thrill of anguish changed the tone of her voice and the expression of her whole countenance, 'I am a deserted orphan, without a human being that loves or pities me. I might indeed now have found protection, but I wilfully deprived myself of it. My uncle, Charles Stockwell, who is in Sam's line, but a much genteeler, more liberal spirited man, has broken off with me since I slighted his wife on some occasion for Lady Torrendale. Sometimes I consider that his Lordship ought to protect me, as I am now become one of his family. I think his countenance seems to say, "he on-ly waits 'till Miss Fer-rars will fa-vor him with the hon-or of her com-mands." But then the recollection of his habitual hatred to my whole family, comes across me. I remember the cold worldly maxims, by which he is probably guided; one of the first of which you know is, not to interfere in other people's affairs: and whenever I would approach the antarctic region that surrounds him, I am stopped by the ice, before I can get near enough, to penetrate to the *terra incognita,* (if such there be) of his sensibility. As for her Ladyship, if I ever venture to turn the conversation from Floss to what is more interesting to me, she yawns with affected weariness, or stares haughtily at me, with those insolent eyes! Heavens! that any one should call them fine! Never bright, but when sparkling with envy, malice, or some bad passion; and half the time dead and glassy, as the panes of a window in a hazy morning. I would defy the most skillful physiognomist to determine whether / pride, indolence, or discontent, be the prevailing expression, that

"Freezes o'er their lifeless blue."[57]

I used to complain of her behaviour last summer, but it is nothing to what she allows herself now; for then at least I had friends – '

'And still shall have them,' exclaimed the kind-hearted Matilda – 'Trust me, my Arbella, Heaven itself will raise up friends, who will interest themselves in your fate.'

'Oh! let me have no cant from you, Matilda. I thought you were above it. Yet sometimes I am half tempted to envy the different state of your statue nun; and to think, that if I could, like her, elevate my mind above the present scene, and do every thing with a view to please a superior Power, living in and for him alone, I might, in religion find a resource against all the crosses and accidents of life; but still, there is a something to which my disinterested spirit cannot bend: for after all, you must own, that the generally received notions, make it an interested sort of affair: a matter of traffic, in which you do so many good works, in hopes of so many blessings in return.

'Have we not a higher incentive,' replied Matilda, 'in the certain satisfaction that attends the consciousness of being well-pleasing in the eyes of that Being, who is at once the source of our every virtue and every blessing. He knows our limited powers, and that we are neither capable of conceiving infinity, nor endued with feelings lively enough to love, as we ought, the idea of his abstract perfections. He is therefore graciously pleased, that every exertion of goodness below, should be accepted as an active proof of the grateful affection we bear to him, should be in reality the same.' Yet, she continued, kindling into a beautiful enthusiasm, while her clasped hands, and eyes raised up to Heaven, evinced how sincerely and deeply she was interested in her subject; 'were this world to bound my hopes, were no future and higher reward extended to me, still, still it would be my happiness to obey him, serve him, love him: still nothing would equal the joy, / (a joy which is in itself sufficient reward,) of proving, as far as my imperfect nature would allow me, my gratitude to the sacred source, from which has flowed all the blessings I already possess.'

'Would I could feel like you! but you have set the matter before me, in a new point of view, and that is what I like. If you can once prove to me, that my devotion is not interested – I cannot bear in any thing to be thought interested – you will then find me open to conviction. But when I apply to one of your elderly, cold, stiff, dogmatical people, who stop all questions they cannot answer, with an "It is so because it is so;" "nothing farther can be said upon the subject," (now that always gives me a mind to say more upon a subject,) "that cannot admit a doubt" (which always tempts me to begin doubting,) "Young ladies pretend to ask for a reason indeed!" "now in my time," and so they go on, prozy, dozy. Ah Lud! why will your very good people think it incumbent on them sometimes, to be so very insupportable?'

'Rather say,' said Matilda, with a sigh, 'why will your amiable and ingenuous spirits ever consent to resign the sweetest consolations of our nature, to wander into a labyrinth of errors, from which they can gather no fruit but disappointment and despair.' Matilda said this with an earnestness of manner, perhaps increased by perceiving that her friend, when deceived in some of her hopes and views of life, she had turned to reading as a resource, had found in Lord Torrendale's extensive library, (where poison and its antidote lay side by side,) food for doubts and conjectures, which were sooner to be roused than laid asleep again. Anxious for the future as well as present welfare of Arbella, Matilda's uneasiness was the greater, as her modesty did not allow her to suppose herself capable of combating her opinions, or convicting her of her errors. Yet, to leave her in them was dreadful.

While she stood revolving these ideas in her mind, Miss Ferrars suddenly looking at her watch, exclaimed, 'See how enchanting your converse is my Matilda; it has actually / made me forget I had to dress to dine at Lord Heathcote's. This will be a fine theme for Lady Torrendale; though I believe she would really rather I always went neglected, than drest tolerably; for whenever I look well she seems to envy me. Oh here comes REAL BEAUTY; you'll see how finely she'll show off;' and Arbella, such was the happy versatility of her disposition, seemed in the idea of Lady Torrendale's 'showing off,' ready to anticipate an enjoyment, and to forget it must be at her own expence.

'Not drest yet Miss Ferrars,' she said, with a haughty survey of her person, as she entered the room; 'perhaps you intend to go in that charming deshabille, and certainly,' she continued disdainfully, 'for one possessed of such striking and undisputed advantages of face and person, nothing can be more becoming.'

On perceiving Matilda, she appeared almost ashamed of having indulged before her, in such an open display of temper; and approaching her with one of her most fascinating smiles, 'You see how I am hurried, dear Miss Melbourne,' she said, 'but I hope I shall be able to spare one half hour to you. How are all at home, and how is Mrs. Melbourne and her dear nun?' Now the dear nun Matilda knew to be the object of Lady Torrendale's most unqualified aversion, whether it was, that in the saint-like meekness and purity of Clara's aspect and manners, she read a tacit reproach to her own; whether the serene happiness, that inhabited the bosom of the gentle recluse, and shone forth on her countenance, contrasted too painfully with the tumults of hers; certain it is she had been heard to declare, 'that Mrs. Melbourne would be tolerable to visit, if it were not for her wearisome shadow:' for her dislike of whom she gave one of her usual unanswerable reasons: 'she had a something about her that somehow how she did not like.' Matilda, however, replied with her customary frank urbanity; and regretted the circumstance that prevented her from having more of her Ladyship's company. Lady Torrendale recollecting a new manner by which she could indulge, unsuspected, the malignity of her disposition, continued with / a look in which, though her eyes retained their wonted 'azure languish,' triumphant demons of pride and approaching vengeance revelled in her smile.

'I ought to apologize to you Miss Melbourne for not having sooner sought you out. But, since our last meeting in town, such changes have happened that – you will excuse me, people will take things in their head you know; I could not help thinking an interview would excite painful recollections in both. I am glad to find myself undeceived; I was happy upon a recent occasion, to be convinced that other views already completely occupy your heart and thoughts.'

These words, which plainly alluded to the obvious partiality of Sir Harold Melbourne, threw Matilda into the most painful confusion. She was unwilling Lady Torrendale should take up the belief, that she approved and encouraged her cousin's addresses; yet she knew not how, consistently with prudence, completely to undeceive her. She ventured to say, 'If you allude, Madam, to a circumstance, most disagreeable and distressing to my feelings, that took place lately at the Rocks, I must beg you will not, on that account, give any credit to reports, that are I assure you equally silly and groundless.'

'I understand you,' replied the Countess, with a glance of intelligence and mystery; 'I see you are anxious the affair should not be misrepresented to him, and your fears are reasonable. I give you my word *he* shall know, that whatever the world may say, you still retain the same sentiments. Poor Strathallan! I would have served him; and still, still I pity him.'

Here was an unforeseen perplexity, in which the arts of the Countess had involved the too-innocent Matilda. If she continued to deny her supposed engagements with

Sir Harold, she gave occasion to the mortifying conjecture, that she was actuated by a desire not to lose her hold upon the affections of one, who ought to be considered as dead to her for ever. If she admitted it, she authorized a falsehood; and one which it would be most unpleasant to her to have circulated. She replied, therefore, with an exertion of / spirit which the occasion rendered necessary: 'Lady Torrendale, there are circumstances, in which affected delicacy becomes weakness. I must speak openly to you. You surely cannot mean to insinuate, in the presence of my friend, that I still continue to cherish a hope, which would make me in my own eyes, the lowest of the low; because I contradict an idea which was founded upon misconstruction, and in which I thought it my duty to undeceive you.'

'Good Heavens! how warm. I did not say any thing so very shocking, did I? I am sure all I meant was, that disagreeable reports might alarm the jealousy of that watchful friendship, is not friendship the word? which a certain gentleman professed he would ever retain for you. There is surely no harm in friendship, platonic friendship,' she repeated; dwelling on the words with a sneer.

'I thought it particularly well suited to the refinement of Miss Melbourne's ideas; and I am sure half my acquaintance preserve it for each other, without any manner of scandal. Ask the beautiful Miss Piers, if the purity of her attachment to my Lord Heathcote is ever questioned, because she had not quite as much fortune as a humpbacked ugly heiress, he lately married: or Lady Barbara Montravers, if the match made by her FRIEND the Duke of Arran, has diminished the "tender interest she takes in his fate," or the "pleasure she derives from his conversation."'

While Lady Torrendale continued these malicious remarks, which derived their origin from the disappointment of her own views, in not having been able, by making Matilda her tool, to hurry the envied and hated Strathallan into a blameable step, Matilda continued in cool and silent dignity to gaze upon her, in such astonishment at her baseness, that at length she compelled those haughty eyes to seek refuge on the ground; and that cheek, albeit unused to the '*blushing*' mood, to acknowledge the innate superiority, of insulted virtue.

'Oh, my dear, I shall pay for your having mortified her thus,' Arbella whispered; as Miss Melbourne put an end to the discussion / by seizing the first opportunity that afforded her a pretext, for taking leave.

'I foresee a dismal half hour in the carriage. Heigho!' she continued, following her friend with grievances as she went down stairs; 'I am sure I go to dress with a heavy heart. One of Lady Torrendale's complaints against me, when we were first acquainted, was that my spirits were so high, I was unable to weep at sentimental novels, or tragedies. In that at least I am reformed; for *now* I am ready to cry any hour of the day or night she pleases. I go abroad, but I no longer feel the pleasure I used to do. The novelty is over; yet the worst of it is, I could not now give up this way of life, though it so tires me. But thank God we have got you among us again! Come to me often, to help me to support it. What are you afraid of here? – any vestiges of the past? – any –'

'Peace, trifler! Lady Torrendale calls you.'

'Oh, you need not fear them; your mildly-looking hero, your blue-eyed Strathallan, is not yet returned from his stormy isle.'

'Mine! Oh, Arbella, this is too serious a subject to be sported with, and by you!' Matilda unwilling to show how deeply she was hurt, or to add to the distress of her well-meaning, but unthinking friend, found it still necessary to check a levity which, spite of the subduing power of sorrow and mortification, was ever tottering on the brink of indiscretion.

'True, true,' said Arbella, recollecting herself; 'I shall always be the same absurd, imprudent creature; and almost deserve my fate. Adieu! bright faultless Matilda! you leave one, whom your persuasive reasoning has consoled, to go to friends that esteem and love you; I leave a home I hate, to meet abroad with – misery!' /

CHAPTER VIII.

Si spande al sole in faccia
Nube talor così
E folgora e minaccia
Su l'arido terren
Ma poi che in quella foggia
Assai d'umori unì
Tutta si scioglie in pioggia
E gli feconda il sen.

METASTASIO. IL RE PASTORE.[58]

THE interest Matilda took in her friends was not of that kind, which spends itself in words. She felt the injustice, the wrongs Arbella had experienced, as her own; and wished, vainly wished, to afford her more effectual assistance. While she was relating to her mother, with all the earnestness and animation of youthful friendship, the peculiarly distressing circumstances in which Miss Ferrars now found herself placed, she did not notice the attentive sympathy, with which Sowerby, leaning on one end of his great knotted stick, listened to the recital; now and then striking it with vehemence against the ground, as the story proceeded, and exclaiming at times, 'Poor thing! poor thing! it is plain she is an orphan. Is that the Miss Ferrars, Matilda, who one morning looked over the volume of Philosophical Transactions I was reading?'

'The same.'

'I think she used to be with you at the Rocks; but I never much minded her till that day – very pleasant she was. I remember her coming another time to talk to me about conchology. She made no great hand of that; but on the whole, she was a very clever, smart, sensible, young woman: and she, you say, is now in a very unpleasant situation; and all, originally, on account of that pitiful rascal, Stockwell.'

'It is so; and she does not know how to get that part of her property out of his hands.' /

'And Lord Torrendale, cannot he speak for her? Does not he know how?'

'He has not yet offered. People are unwilling to interfere in affairs of that kind; he is not her guardian, and – '

'That is so like your fine people. That man, I'll answer for it, has no more feeling than a stone post; and I protest, Matilda, I believe you are learning his prate. I am not her guardian either, and I am not so young as I have been; yet I should not mind the distance from this to London, when the question was to defend an innocent woman,

– 338 –

and restore her right to her. I think I know law enough, at least, to frighten such a whipper-snapper as Mr. Sam Stockwell. Do you suppose (for after all I would not affront the fellow), that Torrendale would take it ill, if I, a comparative stranger, were yet from mere good-will, to offer my services to a young lady who had placed herself in his family.'

'Lord Torrendale, except where his family interests are concerned,' replied Matilda, 'is that cold, absent, abstracted being, that he would probably know and understand nothing of the matter, till he was told some day, that he had to congratulate Miss Ferrars, upon a happy turn in her affairs.'

'Then I'll go,' said Sowerby; 'I'll get the necessary information. But I must not go to Lady Torrendale's yet; the constant rioting, in which these ladies of fashion, as you call them, indulge, does not permit them to suffer themselves to be disturbed early, after the orgies of the preceding night.'

'Oh, you may go, my dear Sir; I hope Lady Torrendale's midnight revels, will not prevent her having the pleasure of seeing you,' said Matilda, endeavouring to give him gently to understand, that the tremendous terms of reprobation against fashionable levities, with which he came armed from his closet, would be better replaced by the middle style.

Sowerby, notwithstanding his deep-rooted aversion to what he emphatically styled fine people, and among them, super-eminently to / fine ladies, got the better of it so far, when there was a kind action to be done, as actually to dress himself, shave himself, and make his bow at Lady Torrendale's. It was a circumstance sufficiently remarkable in the character of this gentleman, that, in spite of his long-indulged antipathy to the habits of the great world, and the severe terms in which he never failed to speak of it, in company with his private friends, yet he never was so inattentive as to hurt the feelings of any body, from a neglect of the established customs and ceremonies of life; and on the few occasions in which he appeared in general society, always conciliated respect and good-will, by the propriety and dignity of his demeanour.

Arbella received, with some of her best smiles, the knight-errant, who thus proposed to espouse her cause. He soon was master of every particular relating to her affairs; and thus prepared, put himself in readiness to set off for London, with as much alacrity as if it were only the distance of a morning's ride; or, as if he had not yet numbered five and twenty years. Before he had gone one stage, he had the satisfaction to learn that Mr. Stockwell was arrived at his house in the town of W— , in Derbyshire; so that he was not obliged to pursue his journey any farther. Mr. Stockwell was very civil, the moment he heard a man of such consequence in the county, as Mr. Sowerby, of Cliffden-down, wanted to speak to him; and the lady, his mother, whispered him 'as she was sure he was come to consult about standing the next county election against Sir Harry Hairbrain; and advised him to seize the *importunity* of assuring him of his vote and interest, and so securing a friend.' Sam's face lengthened, however, when he found that Mr. Sowerby was come not to talk about political business, but upon the affairs of a certain cousin of his, named Arbella Ferrars. He attempted to turn the interest in his own favour, by representing himself as a very ill used man, to whom his cousin had given every encouragement, and had then jilted him, in the most unprovoked and cruel manner. Mr. Sowerby, however, giving /

him to understand that he was empowered by the lady, to take what steps he thought proper towards the final arrangement of her affairs, immediately brought him to the point, by asking him, if he had not been entrusted with certain sums of hers during her minority, which still remained to be accounted for. Seeing that Stockwell turned pale, and was preparing an evasive answer, he, assuming his most authoritative tone and brow, assured him that all shuffling would be vain; and that if he did not immediately give him an account of that part of the young lady's fortune, which remained in his hands, he was determined to proceed with him to the utmost rigour of the law.

'I have my proofs, Sir,' added he, 'and you know I neither value trouble nor expense; what I think, I'll say; and what I say, I'll do:' continued he, striking his thick club stick with increased vehemence into the ground.

Overcome by the eloquence of Mr. Sowerby, or his stick; and recollecting that his knowledge of law exceeded that of most country gentlemen; and that he was not more remarkable for his pertinacity, in pursuing whatever scheme he had once entered upon, than for the discernment and ability by which he provided for its success, Sam's countenance softened in exact proportion as that of his opponent's grew gruffer; and he declared in his mildest tone of voice, 'that he had never intended his pretty cousin the least harm; that he was engaged in some commercial speculations, which, to be sure, would have made it convenient to him to retain a small sum, belonging to her, for a short time in his hands; that such trifles were no great matter between friends and relations; but since she was in a hurry for it, and no doubt she had her reasons,' he continued, glancing at Sowerby, 'I am ready this moment to settle with you, Sir, and account for every penny that ever passed through my hands.'

This was exactly what Sowerby wished; and he concluded the desired settlement without delay. And now, as anxious as Mr. Stockwell to dismiss the business, he returned / pleased and triumphant at the success of his mission to Woodlands. The very important service he had rendered her, made him a most welcome visitor to Arbella, who felt her restored consequence, in the manner of every individual around her. Even Lady Torrendale condescended, kindly taking her by the hand, to say, 'she was truly happy matters had been settled somehow, to Miss Ferrars satisfaction;' while Arbella, delighted with the present, could already laugh at her past uneasinesses; and, speaking of her cousin's bad conduct with more than foreign levity, 'hoped, that poor Sam had not been obliged to sell out stock at a great loss, on her account.'

The interest with which this affair had inspired Sowerby, brought him insensibly to abate of his dislike to visiting at Lady Torrendale's. He was sure there to meet the agreeable Miss Ferrars; and, as their conversation often turned upon serious topics, Matilda hoped her respected friend might contribute to wean Arbella from those vain and dangerous speculations which she had originally adopted, rather from too little than too much examination. No one could be better qualified than Mr. Sowerby for such an undertaking, as he joined, to faith unshaken, confirmed by reason, and enlightened by philosophy, argument that convinces, and eloquence that persuades. Armed with such weapons, he easily led back the fair wanderer to that upward path she had quitted; and, in return, the grateful smiles and large Circassian eyes of the lovely orphan,

'Negri, vivaci, di dolce fuoco ardenti,'[59]

sometimes recalled his thoughts to that world which he had, in spleen and resentment, renounced.

'Well, it is not such a bad world after all,' Arbella exclaimed, 'I am not near so much out of humour with it since I have recovered my fortune.'

'Did I not tell you,' said Matilda kindly, not to despair,

'For friends in all the aged you'll meet,

And lovers in the young.'[60] /

'Aye, and lovers in those who are not young too; for my ancient Damon nibbles the bait most delightfully.'

'Have a care how you indulge yourself at the expence of Mr. Sowerby,' Miss Melbourne resumed, 'I will not suffer my friend to be trifled with.'

'Why, there's unreasonableness! She will neither have him herself, nor let others try. This dear creature is always in such terrible alarm lest I should metamorphose an F.R.S. into an A.S.S. and really an air and figure like Mr. Sowerby's, is a serious temptation to an exercise of the transforming powers in a young lady verging on the desperation of – two and twenty – but to set your mind at rest, I assure you I mean him no harm: only, after the signal service he has rendered me, it would be very ungrateful, you know, not to repay him with one of my best curtsies!'

Matilda had viewed with pleasure the beginning of Sowerby's partiality for her friend, as believing it might contribute to encrease his happiness. It was only an intimate knowledge of that friend's disposition, and a fear that he might be led into a painful error by her thoughtless vanity, that induced a wish in her to obtain a knowledge of the real intentions of one, whom she justly considered as a pleasing and generous girl, but as a dangerous and finished coquette.

Her real intentions! Arbella scarce knew them herself. Forced, at length, by the neglect and silence of months, unwillingly to admit the conviction of Spencer's indifference; mortified at home, and uneasy abroad, she had sought that admiration, which was now become necessary to her existence, even in her intercourse with Sowerby: just as her feelings had been grated by the desertion of the Major, whose suit was agreeable to her vanity at least, he had stept in, and by the interest he had taken in what concerned her, had restored her, in a degree, to that self-complacency she had lost: but she had reflected little upon the probable consequences of her present behaviour; when she was roused from this state of supine indifference, by the / more watchful Countess. She was sitting with her at work, humming

'Un peu d'amour, un peu de soin,

Mene souvent un cœur bien loin,'[61]

her thoughts, perhaps, far distant from the object on which she was engaged; when she was awakened from a deep reverie, by Lady Torrendale's carelessly observing,

'Sowerby is grown very attentive to you; I declare his visits are quite pleasant. He is so conversable, and comes in and out so familiarly, and so sociably – and so – like a tame cat!'

Her Ladyship tossed back her head as she finished this anticlimax, in a drawling indolent manner; and smiled as if she thought she had said the most obliging thing in the world. Arbella laughed.

'Now be so good as to *un*-laugh all that again; for I never was more serious in my life.'

Another long silence – at length Lady Torrendale exclaimed,

'Well, Miss Ferrars, when is it to be?'

'When is what to be, Madam?'

'Your marriage with Mr. Sowerby, to be sure; you don't suppose, child, that you are to read Paley,[62] and drink coffee with him all your life, without proceeding any farther.'

'But why such hurry, Madam, what foundation have you to suppose – ?'

'I have very good foundation,' her Ladyship replied, 'here is what I received,' she continued, holding out a letter from Mr. Sowerby, 'this morning. I am sure nothing can be more handsome than his proposals; and if you are not of the same opinion, this is the last time I shall ever trouble myself in your affairs.'

'Bless me how sudden, what have I brought myself to?' exclaimed Arbella, clasping her hands in amazement, 'I am sure I never thought I gave him the least encouragement: will your Ladyship be so good as to tell him so, and to – '

'Indeed I shall tell him no such thing; your behaviour is growing the conversation of all circles. Miss Ferrars, I shall not / assist you in treating another gentleman dishonourably; I thought to have had that affair of Mr. Stockwell forgot, by establishing you handsomely from under my protection; I cultivated Sir Harold Melbourne solely, positively solely on your account; and you let his little cousin (who is nobody now) carry him off.'

'Not my fault, not my fault,' replied Arbella, who, in snip-snap dialogue, had become quite a match for her Ladyship, 'if things were as I wish, all the men would worship me, and me alone.'

'Well, now you have a better opportunity, and if you let it slip, I shall think myself very unfortunate in producing a young lady who is so much her own enemy. What is it you dislike in Sowerby? Perhaps you'd prefer a gay officer! How long do you think this game is to last? I am already quite weary of taking you out; last night, at Lord Heathcote's, you cannot think how much you were found fault with.'

'In what Madam?'

'Oh, in every thing! you want a certain something, an indescribable *tact;* your petticoat was too long; your body was too short; you had on one of those vile narrow trains seven miles and a half long, of the last century; in short, you were looked upon by the whole circle with disdain.'

'Very probably, Madam, very probably,' said Arbella, composedly going on with her work; for she was not so ignorant of her Ladyship's manners, as not to know that this insulting discourse was all a manœuvre, by which to provoke her to declare she would accept any proposals that would separate them.

'If it were a beautiful girl, indeed, like Miss Mullins, or Miss Piers, for instance,' pursued the Lady, vexed that her remarks had not produced a more passionate answer, 'one might overlook little errors of behaviour, for the credit of producing so lovely a creature; but in one who would not be fit to be show girl in a milliner's shop; yet still beauty one would not insist upon; few, few indeed,' continued her Ladyship, drawing up and glancing at the mirror, 'possess real / beauty; but then, the graces, which every one might command – you want taste – you want air – you hardly know how to come into a room.'

'Perhaps not, Madam,' replied Arbella, rising with a quiet dignity, 'but you shall at least see I know how to go out of one: so leaving your Ladyship to recover your temper at leisure, I have the honour of wishing you a very good morning.'

'And so Miss Ferrars, after all her fine schemes of blue ribbons and coronets, is going to take up with Mr. Sowerby, the virtuoso, at last. A fine ending, isn't it Miss Hautenville?'

The Lady who made this remark was not very distant from the truth. Arbella found herself entangled in a net of her own weaving; from which it was difficult with honour to extricate herself. She shrunk from the imputation of wilful deceit, which the Countess had so maliciously attempted to fix upon her. She compared the possession of splendour and independence at Clifden-down, to the unpleasantness, and comparative insignificance of her situation at Woodlands. She feared to be ungrateful; she wished to be just. At length, her resolution was taken: and she hastened to confirm the report, Matilda had already heard, of her intentions. Perhaps, such was her surprise and agitation at moments, in contemplating the alternative to which she was reduced, to hear Matilda confirm the reality of those intentions to herself. 'Your predictions are verified,' she said, 'you see your friend at length caught in the labyrinth of coquettes; but what could I do?' she continued, replying to Miss Melbourne's silence; and, as if trying to reconcile herself by every argument, to the projected change. 'The slave of circumstances, birth, and consideration, are of absolute necessity in my choice. It is still more circumscribed, from the character attributed to me by the malice of the world, which has already accused me of deceiving Major O'Hara, as well as my cousin, though you know it was not I who first – and now if I dismiss a third gentleman – besides,' she added, still interrupting herself, 'such is / my peculiar way of thinking, I could not marry a man with the temper, the manners, and the person of an angel, on whom Lady Torrendale, and her set, might think they had a right, from the difference of situation, to look down. Now Clifden-down is a charming place, and has capabilities, as Whistler, the upholsterer, used to say, fully equal to Woodlands; which, under the direction of a clever woman; – Heavens! if a prophet had told me a year ago that – well, after all, Mr. Sowerby is a man of worth – a man of sense – a man of reading – Heigho! I wonder where is Spencer Fitzroy all this time?'

CHAPTER IX.

The rock untouched was hard and cold,
The stricken flint its fires betrayed.

LORD STRANGFORD'S CAMOENS.[63]

SPENCER Fitzroy was, at that moment, at no great distance. He had been for some days quartered, with a small detachment, in a town in the neighbourhood. They were on a recruiting expedition; a business for which he was always selected; to win over every man, and to subdue every woman, by his eloquence, or his arts, being alike the object of his ambition. Having now nobody that interested him at Woodlands, and being besides engaged in the prosecution of some designs, which he knew Lord Torrendale's / pride, or his principle, would lead him to disapprove, he had not deemed it necessary to announce his arrival to the family; and it might have continued unknown to them, for some time longer, if an accidental meeting had not led to the discovery he was most desirous to prevent.

It happened, that as the usual party was assembled around the breakfast table, consisting of Lord and Lady Torrendale, Miss Ferrars, Miss Swanley, the two Springs, and Major O'Hara, who had again become very assiduous at Woodlands, the poet Alcæus replied to Lady Torrendale's incessant demand for news, that Sir Harold Melbourne was now the happiest of men; for that he had just discovered the whole of the precious tessellated pavement, of which he had shewn them a part. 'Your Ladyship may, therefore, soon expect an invitation,' he continued, 'and a grand breakfast at least.'

'I hate a grand breakfast; then he will have time to collect the Saplings – and the Crossbrooks – and the Musgraves – and the Evertires, and all the quizzes[64] within ten miles of him; had we not better surprize him?'

'With all my heart,' resumed the Bard; as if he were the only person to be consulted on the occasion; 'and I'll tell you how we will have it: Lord Torrendale and the three ladies in the barouche, the Major and I will drive, and the gentlemen, not so engaged, can accompany the ladies on horseback. What say you, my Lord, how do you like that?' clapping Lord Torrendale familiarly on the shoulder to awaken his attention.

His Lordship looked at the Poet in some surprise, but contented himself with removing, in silence, the hand thus unceremoniously placed upon him.

'What say you, Contessa,' continued Alcæus, no way disconcerted, 'To morrow! Next day! *"Eccomi á cenni suoi."'*[65]

'Dear heart! how pleasant it *will* be;' cried George Spring, 'I'm sure I'm ready, horse or foot, what you will; and I do flatter myself with being a pretty good horseman, though I never was at the *menagerie*.'

'There's[a] nothing on earth I like so much,' / said the Major, 'as those rural parties and that sort of thing. I remember in Ireland, I mean, I have been told, in that country, they make the pleasantest excursions from Dublin on jaunting-cars.'

'And in jingles and noddies,'[66] interrupted Alcæus.

'No, Mr. Spring, neither in jingles nor in noddies, but on jaunting-cars to the waterfalls at Powerscourt, and to Carton, and to the Dargle, and to the rocks of Bullock, and – '[67]

'The rocks of Bullock,' Alcæus slowly repeated, as if he had a great mind to be impertinent.

'I will try to give your Ladyship an idea of one,' continued Major O'Hara, turning his back on the Poet; and, addressing himself solely to Lady Torrendale, he began very busily building up, in toast, the form of this singular carriage; but, after arranging and deranging several pieces, without being able, even with the assistance of a spoon for a trowel, to give an idea of the equipage he wished to describe, he suddenly threw down the whole, exclaiming, 'Oh faith, I'll never make you understand it, if I set about explaining it to you; but I'll try, by and bye, what I can do!'

At dinner, the Major, after the cloth was removed, produced a model of an Irish jaunting car, so perfect in all its parts, that Lady Torrendale, who had never seen any thing of the kind before, was quite enchanted with it. She was never tired running it up and down the table. Alcæus compared it to Madame de Montespan's fillagree equipage, drawn by mice, which bit her pretty white fingers, as she led it along.[68]

'Dear! how delightful! here is a place for the provisions, and every thing. Positively,' cried Lady Torrendale, 'I will go to the Rocks on a jaunting-car. Do you not think, Major, that such a thing as a jaunting-car could be procured?'

'Possibly not; but if your Ladyship will honour me with your commands, I will engage to make them understand what I mean; and to get one finished for you in a very / short time – Miss Ferrars shall assist us with her opinion.'

Arbella bowed coldly – 'I am a very indifferent judge of equipages, Sir.'

But Lady Torrendale seized the idea with avidity. 'Dear Major let it be begun tomorrow, I long to form the party, and we will make it a pic nic.'

'Or, as they call it here, a gipsey party!' said Sappho, 'The very thing! ours shall be a gipsey party.'

'If so,' returned Alcæus, 'how shall we adore our Gipsey Countess?'

'No, no, flatterer; you know youth is necessary to become such scenes and costume, as that character requires.'

The expected compliment was not omitted in return to this observation. 'Lady Torrendale going on a gipsey party in a jaunting car!' repeated the Earl, with accent ominous.

'And why not, my Lord? it makes no difference in our arrangements; there will be room for you too.'

'Oh, for a dozen if you please;' interrupted the Major.

'Not for me, Lady Torrendale, you know my opinion upon such sort of excursions is unalterable.'

'I know it is; and that if you would sometimes alter a little, I should like you much the better for it.' Lady Torrendale looked round unconcernedly; careless of the opinion of the circle, upon this open declaration of her indifference for her husband: while Arbella, perceiving her Ladyship incapable of blushing, looked down and blushed for her.

'Do you think, Lady Torrendale,' resumed his Lordship, 'that such an expedition is exactly suited to the dignity of your character?'

'Dignity of character!' This expression seemed the signal for universal gaiety among her Ladyship's favourite groupe. Lord Torrendale, having given his opinion, said no more. 'I will go,' said her Ladyship, whose first ebullition of spirit had subsided into sullen resistance: 'and it shall be in the manner / first proposed. I will go,' she continued, fixing her eyes obstinately on the table, to avoid meeting those of her Lord – 'I'll go, I'll go, I'll certainly go.'

'You SHALL go, Madam,' said Alcæus, bowing with obsequious devotion to – the mistress of the house. The resolution was carried.

Major O'Hara, empowered by the Countess, immediately begun his pleasing task; and, it was not to be doubted, but that the happy combination of Hibernian ingenuity with English patience, would soon produce a vehicle such as the roads of Derby had not lately witnessed. When it was finished, Lord Torrendale was found the only seceder, and his place was well supplied by some lively damsels, who had been added to the party, all eager as goddesses could be to mount a car; but as the happy moment approached, the Countess began to indulge in some of her usual misgivings and apprehensions. 'Do you really think, Alcæus, it will hold up. Heavens! if it should prove wet! and we have nothing to defend us against it as in a barouche – do not you see a little cloud? no, now it is fine again – no, there is the cloud. It is[a] a delightful morning, a perfectly Italian sky, replied Alcæus. You remember Major, Virgil's beautiful description:

"Evandrum ex humiles tectus lux suscitat almâ."[69]

The Major bowed, and smiled assent in silence; while Arbella answered for him in a whisper,

'Ma foi, s'il m'en souvient, il ne m'en souvient guère.'[70]

'It was just such a day,' resumed the poet, 'that I once took an excursion to some of the charming spots in the environs of Naples. Being a tolerable Italian scholar, and no disagreeable companion, I was recommended to my Lord Stare, in his last little continental trip, (it was just before the war broke out, and though so very young, my lord honored me with the preference,) I remember we had Prince Pappagallo with us. The sun had just risen above the sea, and illuminated the bay of – . /

'There, Mr. Spring,' exclaimed Sappho, 'settle the order of march, and that will save us a great deal, about "gilding the eastern hemisphere."'

The Major took this trouble off his hands: indeed ever since the car had been completed, so elegantly, under his inspection, every thing was referred to his management and controul. It was to be a complete gipsey party; they were to take their dinner in some romantic spot, near the Rocks; and then to proceed to examine the antiquities at Sir Harold's. They had a gipsey jack;[71] and the Major, in order to diversify the entertainment, by adding to their dishes, had besides undertaken to show them how to make the 'most famous dish in the world,' which Alcæus declared he had certainly the best right to understand, as it was commonly called "Irish stew," but to which the Major would only prefer his claim, under the appellation of "soldier's harico."[72]

Arbella lightly jumped into one of the seats of this novel vehicle, and declared she had never felt herself so pleasantly situated in her life. Yet, as she took a second survey of the whole, she could hardly forbear a whispered 'What would Spencer say?' An attempt was made to put Sappho and Alcæus back to back, but, though the poet instantly protested, he thought it a much more advantageous situation for any one with Miss Swanley, than being placed *vis-a-vis*, he could, not be brought to relish even this degree of proximity; and Miss De Courcy having taken his place, it was at length agreed, that as the ladies were sufficient to occupy the seats of the carriage, the two gentlemen should take their horses; while the post of driver, of which no one seemed very ambitious, was conceded to George Spring. With this, Lady Torrendale declared herself quite satisfied. Arbella said something about Governor Thickness's monkey postillion, but George cracked his whip, and was, perhaps, the happiest of the whole party.

Her Ladyship, though drest with apparent simplicity, to suit the title she at present assumed, had yet taken care to set off as much as possible the attractions she still possessed. / The large hat, that on one side completely shaded her face, served to soften her faded features; while a bunch of poppies and corn flowers, disposed with taste upon it, prevented its having that unadorned appearance, which is only favourable to extreme youth and beauty. She was, however, scarcely seated on the vehicle, when she exclaimed, 'What is to defend us from the heat! Mr. Spring, run in directly and fetch us parasols, or I give up the party – Heavens! who would think of going without parasols such a day as this.' Every thing being procured, according to the desire of the Countess, they at length set forward. Mars and Apollo, in the shape of Major O'Hara and Alcæus, bearing them company on horseback, and seeming determined to be very entertaining, and to relieve the tediousness of the road, by agreeable discourse. The fineness of the day produced remarks upon the country.

'I doubt Major,' said Alcæus, 'if in any part of Ireland, even in the delightful county of Wicklow, you have finer prospects than these.'

'I,' said the Major, 'I never was in Ireland; that is to say, not since I was quite a little boy.'

'How then do you take care of your estate?' said Alcæus, maliciously. 'Oh! I leave every thing to be managed by the agent,' he replied; and quickly turning the conversation to the object of their present expedition, this led to a discourse on ruins, and antiquities in general; the Major had once visited Italy, and seen the ruins of Rome. 'They were very neat, faith,' he said, 'I saw them in company with a very pleasant set of fellows, that were among the English, resident there at that time. We had the luck to be there, after the tombs of the Scipios had been discovered; those famous fellows – so we made a party to go and see them – there were five of us; Lord Row, and Lord Riot, Jemmy Ferguson, and Colonel Reginald Lionhart, and myself.'

'Scipio's tomb! delightful.' cries the enthusiastic Arbella; 'do tell me, Major, about Scipio's tomb.'[73]

'It was a broiling hot day like this,' continued / the Major, 'and when we had got to it we were cursedly tired; so I made them all sit down in a little green spot, at some distance from the vaults; and we took out our provisions, among which was the finest Westphalia hams; but afterwards – '

'Go on,' said Arbella impatiently.

'Afterwards, when we had feasted on the hams, we found ourselves confoundedly thirsty; so Lord Riot produced some of their mawkish Italian wine, from Tarentum, or Brundusium, or some such place I think he said; which he wanted to persuade us was the finest in the world.'

'Well, well,' pursued Arbella.

'Well, when I had let them surfeit themselves with that flat stuff, at length I produced some bottles of fine genuine claret, such as they drink in Ire – , such as is drunk at Bourdeaux, I mean, and I made them all confess, in full bumpers to the memory of the Scipio gentlemen, that good, neat claret, was worth all the Tarentine, and all the Falernian, that ever was tasted, by Jove.'

'But the tombs – did not you visit the tombs,' asked Arbella, who had expected a different termination of the account, and thought the merits of the claret might have been decided elsewhere.

'Oh the tombs were not worth seeing – a parcel of rubbish – we did not go in – besides it was growing late, and we began getting together our horses and mules, for we were engaged in the evening to a concert, at Prince Belmontes.'

Alcæus, who, according to good custom, instead of listening to what was said, had been waiting for a pause, in order to put in something which he thought better, of his own, observed, 'the tomb of the warriors, after all, creates[a] an interest much allayed by painful feelings of regret; it is to that of the poet, without whose aid all their honors would crumble into dust, that posterity approaches, with unmingled reverence and delight, such were my sensations, when, during my residence at Naples, I visited Virgil's tomb! 'twas evening, for you know the words of our enchanting bard, /

'If thou would'st view fair Melrose right,
Go visit it by the pale moon-light.'[74]

'Yes, Mr. Spring, but remember you are at Naples, not at Melrose now, said Sappho, and pray spare us quotations from your favorite poet, *a propos de bottes.*'[75]

'It was by moonlight,' pursued Alcæus, 'that to visit this awful ruin we scaled the heights of Pausilippo. You know, ladies, that the edifice which was once Virgil's tomb, is now often converted into a place of retirement for banditti; it was a scene well suited to their dreadful purposes; the uncertain light, broken by great masses of shade, faintly showed the moss and ivy, with which the ruin was overgrown; the bat flapped his wings – the owl screamed – and it seemed as if the spectre of the poet was wandering about the deserted abode – suddenly we noticed a confused noise of voices, and lights within the tomb – as we advanced a flash of steel – '

'Oh my God,' cried Sappho, clasping her hands together, and gasping as if struck with sudden dismay.

'You conceive my situation,' continued Alcæus, delighted with the idea of having made even his fair enemy acknowledge the force of his descriptive powers.

'Oh gracious,' added Sappho, heedless of his remark; 'after all, we have forgot the ginger-beer.'

'I see how wrong I was, in supposing it possible to interest a female mind in any thing touching or elevated,' said the poet, darting a glance of rage at Miss Swanley: while Arbella, who knew that Sappho had affected a want of enthusiasm on this occasion, to vex her brother poet, sat silently enjoying the scene. For some time after, Alcæus continued sullen, leaving the field clear to the Major; or only interrupted him with some snarling remark.

'We lived very pleasantly at Rome,' continued O'Hara, 'and often made excursions to Tivoli to breakfast, and see the waterfalls.'

'But did you never go to visit the fountain of the nymph Egeria?' interrupted Alcæus, 'Then you lost a thing much better / worth seeing; every one knows the waterfalls of Tivoli.'

'Have you seen, Lady Torrendale, the model of the Pantheon,' resumed Major O'Hara, affecting not to notice him. 'I assure you it can give you no idea of the original – nor of the Coliseum! we were delighted with the Coliseum.'

'But I dare say you did not visit the convent Cuiet, within-side,' observed the tetchy poet.

'No, what the the devil did we care for convents?'

'Then you saw nothing,' resumed Alcæus.

'Saw nothing; I saw the Vatican, before it was stripped by the French; saw the Apollo, the Torso, the Laocoon.'

'But you did not go into the library.'

'No, we did not care much about that – what was there to be seen? nothing but books!'

'Then you saw nothing.'

'We went next to St. Peter's.'

'But did you go to San Pietro in Vincola?'

'No.'

'Then you saw nothing.'

'We had the good fortune to be there on Good Friday night, when it was illuminated.'

'The illumination of the churches at Naples,' resumed the obstinate Alcæus, 'are much finer – if you did not see them you saw nothing.'

'Yes, I saw something,' replied the Major, whose Hibernian determination to 'keep never minding,' was at length shaken by the pertinacious buzzing of this little importunate gad-fly of Parnassus.[76]

'I saw an impertinent whipper-snapper, who, wherever I went, wanted to persuade me I had better have been some where else.'

'Oh probably some French Abbé, or Italian Cicerone; they are very troublesome,' observed Alcæus, who, whether he possessed talents, had at least the same regard for personal safety, as his namesake of ancient renown, and therefore prudently chose, not to understand the insinuation thrown out by the man-of-war; from that period he let him finish his narration unmolested: he continued, /

'I assure you Miss Ferrars, it is the very grandest ceremony in our – in their religion I mean, when the dome of the Vatican church appears one cross of light, and when we – when they kneel down, and the Pope bestows his benediction. Oh, by Jove it is the finest, most impressive thing. Oh, by Jupiter you can have no idea.'

'No idea,' muttered Alcæus, 'what a very convenient figure in a description, for people who have no ideas themselves. It saves them such a quantity of trouble.'

How much farther he would have ventured to push his animadversions is uncertain; for they were now arrived at a pretty romantic spot, sufficiently near 'The Rocks,' where it was unanimously agreed, the party had better alight, and spread their rural meal, on the verdant carpet beneath them. A cottage at a very little distance was inhabited by an old couple, who could supply them with whatever was wanting, for the complete comfort of the meal. The scene, a little hollow, formed beneath the shaggy brow of a hill, overhung with coppice wood, was sufficiently sylvan and picturesque, and was declared by Alcæus, first to remind him of the Sybil's cave, and then of the grotto of the nymph Egeria;[77] and by the Major to be 'the very thing.'

'One may perceive Alcæus's intercourse with the nymph Egeria,' said Sappho, 'by the wisdom that penetrates through the most trifling observation he utters.'

'And Sappho proves her relationship to the Sybil,' Alcæus retorted, 'for if most of her works were burnt, shoot me if any odd volume of them would not, like that lady's, be of equal value, with the whole.'

'How insufferable that young pedant grows,' Sappho whispered to Arbella, 'always bringing in his reading, or his travels, without minding whether any one cares for either.'

'I am never placed by him,' that young lady replied, 'without envying Petrarch's art, by which he professed himself able, when in company with the most disagreeable person, by the mere force of imagination, / to transform him into the one, whose presence he most desired.'

'Then would the poet shine a bold dragoon, I fear,' resumed Sappho.

Scarcely were the words uttered, when a noise of horsemen was heard near the spot; and a moment afterwards, three gentlemen in officers uniform rode up, the foremost of whom gracefully acknowledging the fairer part of the company with a military salute, was immediately recognized by them to be Spencer Fitzroy. These gentlemen had set out that morning from the town of – , about ten miles distant, to see the famous tessellated pavement. One of the officers, having undertaken to shew his two companions a short cut to the Rocks, had brought them about half-a-mile out of their way, and seeing a party of ladies and gentlemen assembled beneath the shade of the wooded hill, that overhung the side of that wild and romantic road, they ventured, without knowing of whom it consisted, to approach them, in order to enquire the nearest way of regaining their lost route.

Neither Lady Torrendale, nor her son were without some slight uneasiness at this unexpected rencontre: a confused idea, that the elegant Fitzroy might not perfectly approve her 'gipsey party,' prevented in the Countess that pleasure, with which his presence otherwise always inspired her; while Spencer, who had his reasons for desiring his arrival should be some time longer unknown to his family, devoutly wished the whole party at that moment at – a distance; and whispered to himself, 'Hardy shall pay for taking us this pretty round.' Concealing his chagrin, however, under an appearance of the most perfect ease, he continued, half leaning along the back of his horse, with the same careless *nonchalance*, with which his mother would have stretched herself upon a chaise lounge, to answer sometimes in unsatisfactory monosyllables – sometimes more fully, the various questions, her anxiety, or curiosity, induced her at once to propose.

'Heavens, Spencer! who would have thought of your being so near us! why the last news we had of you was from the Lakes.' /

'Very extraordinary, that a military man should remove from one place to another, as his services happened to be required.'

'Have you been long in Derbyshire?'

'Only a few days, I believe – can't exactly recollect – never keep an account – come on recruiting service.'

'On recruiting service? Are you likely to stay long?'

'Impossible to tell – depends entirely upon orders from head-quarters – disagreeable business – worried to death.'

Arbella had not seen Spencer since he had recovered from the effects of his fatigues in the Peninsula. He now looked most brilliantly handsome; and she was surprised to find time, absence, and neglect like his, insufficient to prevent her former flutters from reviving.

'And now,' resumed Fitzroy, addressing himself to the Countess, 'let me ask you a few questions, Madonna. Are you too for the tessellated fragments, or is this interesting solitude the boundary of your excursion?'

'Oh no, certainly; we are to proceed to Sir Harold's – but we were tempted – we, I proposed a kind of rural party, and since you are here, you shall not run away from us so soon.'

Spencer suffered himself to be entreated some time, before he would alight and join the rustic group: perhaps fearful of being intrusive, perhaps desirous of exhibiting to advantage, for the greatest length of time possible, the beauties of his fine spirited horse, inlaid sword, and shell-bridle. At length he yielded. 'I think I must do as you would have me,' he said, 'Hardy and Leyster, (aside to his two companions, who, though they had received the desired information, still loitered near,) you may get along.'

The latter, a mild, delicate looking youth, seemed disposed to obey his summary order, but Captain Hardy riding close up to him, whispered 'upon my word Fitzroy it would be both more kind, and more sociable in you too, if, instead of sending us away, you were to introduce us to your ladies, particularly (looking at Miss Ferrars) as the thirty thousand is in the wheel.' /

'And if you were to hear him talk sometimes, you would think he did not much care if she were under the wheel,' whispered the mild-looking Leyster.

Spencer, though he had no great inclination at this moment to introduce these two gay young men, either to his mother or his *ci-devant*[78] fair lady, yet seeing no alternative, complied with a good grace; and begged leave to present to the Countess, and her party, his military acquaintances; who were officers of different regiments, he said, 'dispatched, like himself, on the unpleasant business of recruiting.'

The gentlemen were received by her Ladyship with an engaging politeness, which put them at once completely at their ease. It was seldom necessary to apologize to her for an addition of beaux to her circle.

In the introduction of Major O'Hara to Fitzroy, which took place in return, the two heroes eyed each other with looks of mutual defiance and dislike; Spencer immediately perceived, with the quick eagle glance of jealousy, or rather of wounded vanity, that he also made pretensions to Arbella. However disposed to undervalue the claims of any other gentleman, and, above all, of any other officer, who was not 'of our's,' Spencer could not but perceive, in the easy confidence, the handsome shewy person, and the glow of health and spirit diffused over the fine, though not very expressive, features of the Major, enough to alarm his reigning passion. Arbella suddenly became an object of value in his estimation; and the desire of pleasing, strong as it ever reigned in any female breast, usurped every faculty.

Meanwhile, the gipsey Countess seemed to have quite entered into the spirit of the scene in which she had engaged; and to be perfectly happy, while employed in laughing, talking, and flirting with every man around her.

Spencer, though nature had not in him a very enthusiastic adorer, yet found so many objects in the prospect before them, which it was convenient to point out, with his beautiful sabre, that it was seldom it was not flourished in his hand, or flashing in the ladies' / eyes. 'How lovely this surrounding scene,' he said, 'it only requires the addition of a few cork trees to the landscape, and that the verdure of those hills should be a little more rich, and the blue of the sky of a tint more warm, to make me fancy myself again at Cintra; where I once spent a fortnight, the happiest I ever passed in my life. Here is a spot,' turning to Arbella, 'for the pretty country girls, with their neat little jackets and dark braided hair, to meet their faithful shepherd lads, and trip beneath the moon-beam to the sound of the light seguedilla.'[79]

'Here is a place for people to talk nonsense in, I think,' said the Major, stalking away in evident displeasure.

'You see you have deprived me of my cavalier,' said Arbella, in a tone of affected reproach – 'what amends can you make me?'

'Any in my power, most gladly; but that is little, I perceive – and I perceive it with a pain which I am surprised I still can feel.'

For Spencer to turn accuser, rather startled Miss Ferrars; yet she continued in the same strain of affected indifference – 'You were really too hard upon the poor Major, with your foreign allusions, I confess; I myself am almost too little of a Portuguese, or Spaniard, to enter into them.'

'No doubt – you never took the trouble of recalling the lessons I gave you since last I saw you; you must have quite forgotten your Spanish.'

'I have had time to forget it,' replied Arbella, rather indignantly.

'That, young ladies seldom, require to forget their old friends,' resumed Spencer, with an offended air; then turning on her his eyes, that melted with liquid softness, 'you could not, I dare say, repeat the list of phrases, I once transcribed for you, yet they are simple, nearly resembling the French and Italian; for instance, "My life, *Mi vida.*"

'*Mi Alma*,' returned Arbella, 'that is my soul – is it not?'

'*Cielo miò*' – '*Estrella mia*'* – '*Lumbre / de mis ojos†*' – '*Hija di mi Corazón‡*,' were repeated in lively alternation by the animated pair.

'Excellent – charming,' continued Spencer; 'but they have one expression – I can hardly remember it – Moore has something like it – I know it means 'child of my soul,' in which the pronunciation of the *n* is remarkably difficult. Now, if you were to try a hundred times, I doubt you could not say, '*Nina de mi alma*.' '

'*Nina de mi alma*,' Arbella softly repeated, in a tone, in which the soul of present, and remembered tenderness, seemed blended – their eyes met. Poor Mr. Sowerby! where was he at that moment?

While Spencer and Arbella were thus engaged, apparent satisfaction and hilarity seemed to reign among the gipsey party: the laugh, the song went round, and they seemed so well satisfied with the novelty of the entertainment, and the scene, that the principal object of their expedition was in danger of being forgotten, if Alcæus had no remarked, 'well, good people, if you mean to give Lord Torrendale an account of the wonders you have visited to-night, you had better think of proceeding to the Rocks, and striking tent, as the Captain would say.'

The gipsies rose from off the grass, the gentlemen took to their horses, and they soon arrived at Sir Harold's, where several strangers, attracted by the same motives of curiosity and amusement, were already collected. Here was Mr. Sowerby, to whom the Baronet was haranguing, very learnedly, on the discoveries he had made, and expected to make.

The countenance of the philosopher of Clifden Down brightened as Arbella approached; but turned black as Erebus,[80] on perceiving the Major and the train of officers that followed. While O'Hara, on his part, was equally disconcerted, on recognizing him to be the person, who had met him on his first visit to the Rocks; and exclaimed, half aside, 'Oh, the Devil! here is old Caliban again!' /

He was soon, however, recovered from these disagreeable reflections, by the cheerful politeness of Sir Harold's reception. Wholly intent upon pleasing his guests, he undertook to conduct their unsteady footing through the various excavations he commanded to be made; and, first, produced fragments of pillars and friezes – and porticos, adorned with heads of owls and bats, and ivy wreaths, and gorgon shields, till at length he came to the famous tessellated pavement, which was supposed to have formed part of the floor of some room of state. He seemed visibly gratified by the expressions of wonder and praise, which the admirable contexture of the various parts (though individually so minute, yet contributing to the perfection of a finished whole) excited. Every one admired the variety and richness of the colours, and the ingenuity displayed in the manner in which they were blended, alike in the figures of men and animals, and in the lighter ornaments that bordered each compartment.

At length, the weary looks of some of the party and the whistling of Major O'Hara, convinced Sir Harold the fine arts could not interest every mind as long as his own;

* My guiding star.
† Light of my eyes.
‡ Girl of my heart.

but, before they separated, he entreated them so politely, yet so earnestly, to rest, and allow him to order some refreshment, that they could not refuse his request.

The Countess found several of her acquaintance already assembled in the saloon, and soon entered into conversation with them. While she was thus employed, Spencer and Arbella were no less intent on an animated discussion upon the beauties of the tessellated pavement. So much indeed had they to say upon the subject, that it is supposed they did not chuse to favour the public with all they thought; certain it is, that while the rest of the company divided into little knots, they fell into a whisper at a distance from all. Never had Spencer looked to such advantage, and as his spirits rose always in exact proportion to that circumstance, never perhaps had he been so entertaining. Such at least was the opinion of Arbella, who continued / engaged with him in a *solto voce* conversation, heedless of the animadversions and remarks of those around her.

'Do you mind that vile fellow?' said Sowerby, in a half whisper, to Sappho; 'one cannot tell what he is saying, but he makes as many gestures as a clown in a pantomime. There, now he has her ear – now he is reaching across her, and now he is drawing back in an affected half laugh – and now – hang him! I wish he was pinioned. – There – would you not swear they had their heads together, upon some subject in which the interests of the whole nation were concerned; though if you were to enquire into it, you would find it something too frivolous, even for them to repeat to you: and then how he is drest! – What is the meaning of all those fringes, and chains, and tassels?'

'Oh, I believe Captain Fitzroy would not give up that pelisse and tasselled sash, for the Strathallan estate,' replied Sappho.

'He is said to be remarked for the grace with which he ties it – and you, ladies, are remarked for the good sense with which you admire it, I suppose.'

'We, ladies! no, no, you do us injustice.'

'Yes, but you do – don't deny it; – and then you expect a man of sense to seek, to chuse you as a companion. What man of sense would think twice of a woman?'

'Dear Sir, do not think us so frivolous,' said Sappho.

'I protest to you, that is what you like, and why should not you?' pursued Sowerby,[a] following the course of his own ideas, without deigning the Poetess the least reply; 'young ladies should have what they like; and if it is a hateful coxcomb, why, in the devil's name, let them have a hateful coxcomb.'

'I am quite of your opinion, Sir,' said Major O'Hara, as Sowerby concluded these words in his most tremendous tone of voice; for he felt almost equal pique on perceiving Captain Fitzroy likely to supplant him with the heiress. 'Above all things, I hate a cox-comb, / and that gentleman seems to me a very complete one.'

'He is, indeed,' said Sappho, 'an inferior character to his brother Lord Strathallan; I never think of that young nobleman, without applying to him the words of your admirable countryman, Burke, in praise of another person: 'he was something high; it was a wild stock of pride, on which the tenderest of all hearts had grafted the milder virtues.' '[81]

'Faith, I know his was a wild stock of nobility, upon which he has grafted a very fine fortune, which is more to the purpose,' observed the Major, 'and that without any great pretensions – at least not superior ones, to those of many men who have not been equally favoured.'

As Major O'Hara concluded these words with a general and pleased survey of his whole person, he remarked, 'that he did not see any reason, why they should not beat up the quarters of the horse officer;' and Sowerby having assented to the proposal, the *tête-a-tête* was broken in upon by the two gentlemen, in whose countenances appeared a jealousy, in one repressed, in the other openly declared.

Arbella saw that they both feared Spencer, and that Spencer disliked them; the idea of this feeling existing in the breast of him she once had loved so tenderly, raised her spirits to the highest pitch of animation; and seized with the most violent and dangerous fit of coquetry she had ever experienced; she played Spencer against the Major, and the Major against Spencer, and Sowerby against both; but in this last effort, successfully to raise the jealousy of him she secretly preferred. She failed as usual, from proceeding upon false premises; as it was all done upon the supposition, that Captain Fitzroy had a heart. Fitzroy, who looked with great contempt upon a major of militia, and of Irish militia too, continued a description he had been giving his fair lady, of manners and customs in Portugal, enforced by appropriate action, and intermixed with a proper quantity of foreign words and military phrases. Major O'Hara, if he could not cope with / him in talking of 'the Peninsula,' or repeat *bon mots* said at the great Lord's table, had yet a sufficient quantity of topics in his Tipperary estate; the good and bad quarters he had respectively visited, and the variety of pretty girls he had seen. Hardy and Leyster, who had remained at an awful distance, fearful of interrupting the operations of the formidable Fitzroy, now ventured to join the conversation party at that end of the room; and the circle thus extended, became every moment more enlarged; still the greater part of the discourse was engrossed by Spencer, and Major O'Hara.

Arbella was astonished at the various and accurate knowledge this gentleman displayed, not only of the anecdotes of their more intimate circle, but of the secret history, and tittle tattle, of almost every family, and country town, within fifty miles of their vicinity. To explain this, it may be necessary to observe, that besides those great leaders of fashion, whom he adored as the principal deities, whenever he was within their influence; the Major had a set of subaltern divinities, who presided over every town, village, or hamlet, in which his quarters, be they in the form of encampment, hut, or billet, happened to be fixed. With these charmers (*the ladies*, when he was in their presence, and *the girls* every where else) he laughed, flirted, and coquetted away, the tedious time of his absence from those more worthy of his vows; and while he was with them, would never have been supposed to have moved in another sphere, but for an occasional anecdote of Lady Caroline, or Lady Julia, to show these rural belles, how well he was every where received among the fair; but woe be to them if meeting Major O'Hara with any of more elevated rank, or in any more fashionable scene, they expected more than the notice of a sliding bow, from the man who had lounged whole days, and danced whole nights with them, in winter-quarters. That the Major was a polytheist must, we fear, be acknowledged; but for this, the long and forced absences caused by his profession, from fanes,[82] where the more exalted objects of his sincere adoration were / worshipped, will surely be admitted as a sufficient apology.

While Spencer was endeavouring to please his fair, every thing he said, was enforced by the eloquent language of the most expressive, if not the most brilliant eyes, in the world; and Major O'Hara, who was much too modest ever to raise his quite so high as a lady's face, was aspiring to the same end, without the aid of those advantages. Arbella listened to each with that easy and pleased attention which was sure to convey the satisfaction she appeared to receive. When very young, and just entered upon the scene of life, her eagerness to please sometimes militated against the designs she had in view, by the extreme and obvious pains she took to secure her object; now all was apparently free and undesigned, though the result of study, and repeated observation. It might also be remarked, that the extreme turbulence and vivacity which sometimes led her into those inadvertences of expression, which did not pause to consider the feelings of her own sex, was now always restrained in the presence o that whom it was the study of her life to please: her air and gestures were as well as her conversation, planned with the utmost care; not a look, not a motion, but what was calculated to set off some beauty, and palliate or conceal some defect; a passing, and apparently unintended compliment, to the particular situation, profession, or character of the person who addressed her; that air of unconstrained, yet marked attention, which showed, in the most flattering manner, the value she set upon the speaker; that bright glance of intelligence, which proved that the slightest play of wit, or exertion of fancy, was perceived and applauded by her; and that smile of grateful acknowledgment, which appeared to confess the pleasure she derived from it, these were some of the means she used, and used with success, to enchain, without beauty, those whom she wished to captivate.

'I remember a very pleasing custom which I first observed at the little fort of Villaverde, in Portugal,' said Spencer, 'when I was presented to Donna Laura / de Lourinha, the governor's lady; it was after she had taken her *siesta*; and she was surrounded by cavaliers, conversing with her and offering her refreshments; but instead of sitting round her, as we do now, each cavalier knelt before her; and with a kind of respectful homage, presented her with coffee, flowers, or sweetmeats.'

'And why should we be more rustic,' exclaimed the Major, and instantly threw himself, with inimitable gallantry, at the Lady's feet; his example had an instantaneous effect; it was immediately followed by the elegant Spencer, and in a few moments Arbella found herself surrounded by admiring and kneeling cavaliers, while they poured forth to her that complimentary sort of conversation, which seemed to be suggested by the novelty and romantic circumstances of the scene. Arbella closely dissembling the extreme gratification her vanity received, answered with all the ease of a French woman, and all the modesty of an English one; while in an indolent attitude, as if almost wearied with the incense offered up to her, she kept her beautiful eyes half closed, that when she spoke, she might gradually open them again, and pour with the greater effect, their full brilliancy upon the beholder, the charms of every thing she did, being rendered resistless by the adherence to that admirable rule,

L'arte che tutto fa nulla si scopre.[83]

This, which is the perfection of coquetry as it is of gardening, was well understood by Arbella, who never at the same time lost sight of the reigning motive, which influenced every change in her apparently thoughtless conduct. She enjoyed the homage she excited, the competition, of which she was the object; but it was chiefly, that Spencer might perceive her notice was disputed by others, that Spencer might acknowledge she was ready to sacrifice an admiring croud to him. Vain as she was of her own attractions, she was still vainer for him; and while she seemed to listen with equal pleasure and attention to all, artfully contrived to turn the discourse to those subjects on which he could most shine, or which / exhibited his advantages, in their most prominent light.

While thus engaged upon her own plans of operation, she did not remark the sarcastic glances of the female part of the company, on the triumph of her charms. Lady Torrendale was the first to observe the effect produced upon the gentlemen, by the graces or the conversation of Miss Ferrars; and turning from the table at which she sat, exclaimed in a tone of mingled gaiety and pique, 'Upon my word! Miss Swanley, Miss de Courcy, pray look there – 'tis the Lady Arbella, I protest, in all her glory!'

If it was so, poor Arbella was doomed to experience that glory was indeed 'a circle in the water;' and that her's had at this period, reached its outmost ring: for from that moment the number of her court began to decrease, at the same time that the ill-will which had been gradually augmenting, and which she had, by her manner, unthinkingly fostered, between Spencer and the Major, was exasperated to its height, by the easy complacency with which the former, encouraged by his mistress, related anecdote after anecdote, of the officers mentioned in the last engagement which he had been in, till Major O'Hara, who found himself shut out of this conversation, no longer able to conceal his impatience, exclaimed, at the end of a very remarkable circumstance Fitzroy had been relating, 'It is very odd that honest Jack Rainstorth, who served in that very brigade, never mentioned a syllable of so extraordinary a thing to me.'

'Do you mean to insinuate, Sir,' said Spencer, turning very quick upon him, 'that Mr. Rainsforth's relating, or not relating the circumstance, is to make any difference in the credit of my narrative?'

'Oh not in the least, Sir,' the Major replied, 'on such a subject, I presume, every one is permitted to have his own opinion.'

To this Spencer assented; still observing drily, that it was impossible to form one, with any degree of accuracy, without having been upon the spot. The Major, who had himself almost bid adieu to the fascinating twenties, uttered some reflections upon the / vanity of 'boys, who were never tired of talking of their first campaign.' Spencer, intoxicated with success, elated by the obvious partiality and the presence of his mistress, and in that buoyant state of spirits which never left him perfectly master of himself, retorted with interest, and in the heat of altercation, thoughtlessly made use of an expression, which Arbella felt assured O'Hara would not pass over. The Major, who had with difficulty, through the evening, smothered the feelings of an injured rival, replied with a degree of resentment that justified Arbella's wildest alarms; still attempting to conceal her anguish and apprehension under the appearance of gaiety, she raised her fan between the disputants, in the manner of a staff of office, exclaiming, in a tone of playful authority, 'in the name and on the behalf of his Majesty, I command you both to – ' She caught Spencer's eye, and while the vindictive determination of its expression made the unfinished sentence die away upon her lips, she felt that the moment for sportive interference was past. Terrified at the angry looks, and still more at the warm expressions that had passed between the gentlemen, she lost in anxiety for his safety all prudence[a] and discretion, while losing all reserve, and turning to him with a pleading accent, she exclaimed, 'Oh! Fitzroy, if you have any pity, any affection for me – '

'Affection, my dear Madam,' interrupted the Major, with well assumed irony, 'that is quite out of the question with a gentleman, who seemed almost a stranger to you this morning.'

'He is no stranger to my heart,' returned Arbella, unguardedly.

'Then he shall make his way to it through mine,' cried O'Hara, with an ardour, in which resentment had full as great a share as love; 'For, by heavens! I will not suffer any man to – '

Arbella wrung her hands, she looked round for Lady Torrendale, and perceived, with dismay, that Lady and her train had already risen, and most of them left the room; and that she must, in the hurry and alarm of the / moment, have neglected the repeated summons of the Countess to depart.

As the gentlemen followed her out of the room into the hall, where Sir Harold was taking leave of the ladies, and, with his usual urbanity, giving directions with respect to the jaunting car, which he feared was hardly a safe conveyance for his visitors at night, Spencer pressed his fair one's hand, muttered something about, 'Inviolable respect,' and 'heedlessly alarming herself;' and whispered her, 'that flights of Hibernian gallantry need not always be attended with the serious consequences she seemed to apprehend. Arbella tried to believe him.

'You return with us to-night, Spencer,' said Lady Torrendale.

'Excuse me, Madam, I fear it is not in my power at present to be any time absent from D – ,' he replied, in a tone where she thought she perceived ill-disguised emotion.

Major O'Hara was to return also that night to his quarters, at a town not very distant from the Rocks. Her Ladyship, perhaps, engrossed with the idea of her loss, and busily employed in wrapping herself up to brave the dangers of the night air, seemed hardly to attend to her son's reply: but it sunk to Arbella's heart. She wished to make the Countess notice it; to make her acquainted with what had passed; but an insuperable awkwardness and confusion, that Lady's cold and repelling looks, Spencer's recent assurances, all tended to restore her to a degree of false security, and, at least, apparent composure. Meanwhile, most of the ladies had seated themselves in the car; Spencer would have offered his hand to Arbella, but was prevented by the Major, who stepped before him, and helped her to her seat. She shrunk from him, with a foreboding and a fearful shuddering, she tried in vain to conquer. He remounted his horse, Spencer did the same, and directing his eyes with a last look to Arbella, gracefully kissed his hand to the ladies, and rode off in an opposite route from the Rocks. /

CHAPTER X.

Sweet is love, and sweet is the rose,
Each has a flower, and each has a thorn,
Roses die when the cold wind blows,
Love is killed by lady's scorn.

AUSIUS MARCH.[84]

AGONIZED by apprehensions which the vivacity of her disposition, only served to present to her imagination, in a greater variety of torturing forms, without being sufficiently powerful, as she had formerly found it, to diminish the force of their impression, Arbella woke haggard and unrefreshed after a miserable night, in which her fancy had pictured to her every possible danger to which her beloved Fitzroy might be exposed. She now saw him pale, bleeding, sinking beneath the Major's sword; now, turning unhurt to receive the embraces and congratulations of his family; but in both scenes, repelling her eager affection, with an accusing look, and an action that marked, he considered her as the cause of the hazard which he had encountered. On her first arousing from this state of painful stupor, all she experienced was a confused consciousness, that some evil was impending over Spencer; but she too soon recovered a full and distinct apprehension of the cause she had to experience uneasiness on his account. The remembered gaieties of the preceding day, only added to the anguish of the present moment. She recalled the part she bore in them, with shame and regret. How poor the pleasure, how paltry the triumph, purchased perhaps with the blood of Fitzroy; the thought was misery.

She started up – she listened if there were not any appearance of stir, and bustle in the house, which might give her hopes of being able soon to make some enquiry; all was still. All seemed yet to partake of the blessings of / repose. But for Arbella there was no repose. She was in that state of mind, which renders inaction a real evil, and which can only find relief, in spending a part of its violence on outward objects. She dressed herself in haste; opened the shutters, and perceiving the first white glimmerings of dawn, streaking the horizon, ventured to descend the stairs. The sight of a slip-shod, grumbling, under-housemaid, who was beginning to dust and arrange the furniture in the great parlour, imparted a degree of comfort to the heart of Miss Ferrars, for it flattered her with the hopes of soon finding people ready to attend to her wishes; and some time after, the appearance of Lord Torrendale's gentleman *en papillottes*, gave her courage to enquire 'if the groom might not be sent to D – , as soon as a horse could be got ready.' She had hardly obtained an answer of assent, when she was obliged to retract her order. On what pretext could she send to D – ? Fitzroy was quartered there; but she had neither letter nor message to give from Lady Torrendale. Her own extreme anxiety to know whether he had returned there, after taking leave of them the preceding night, and whether any thing farther had passed between him and the Major, though extremely valid reasons in her own mind for such a step, it was to be feared would not pass in the rigid courts of custom. Blushing at her precipitance, and the curious, enquiring looks that it had already attracted upon her; distracted, irresolute, she had just thought of the ingenious expedient of sending some message, or billet in the name of Lady Torrendale, when the sound of her Ladyship's bell gave a sudden revulsion to her thoughts and feelings. She was ready to sink to the ground when she heard it; yet felt irresistibly impelled, with an eagerness that anticipated any servant, to approach the door of the apartment. She already thought she heard the reproaches of a justly incensed mother: and experienced a momentary reprieve, on observing that her Ladyship either had not remarked what had passed the preceding night, or that her senses were still too much dulled, to present it again distinctly to her mind. Her first words / were 'let me have some chocolate.' She complained of fatigue; and peevish, and half asleep, seemed yet dissatisfied with the remembrance she retained of her expedition; and inclined to quarrel with her companion, whom she now accused of having 'put her upon it.'

Before poor Arbella could command sufficient courage to enter upon the subject nearest her heart, a note was brought in by Lady Torrendale's woman, directed in a strange, and to her Ladyship an unknown hand. The Countess languidly desired Miss Ferrars to read it to her; she obeyed with a feeling of sick and giddy trepidation; for she saw danger in the ominous pot hooks, which she recognized for her aunt Stockwell's. This lady seldom, but on very great occasions, wielded the pen, an instrument she was much less accustomed to than the rolling-pin. She had now taken it from her secretary, Miss Hautenville, having a tale to relate to which she believed nothing but her own unrivalled powers of sentiment, pathos, and description could do justice. These were the contents of the billet.

'Least you Ladie Ship shod bee in any sort of a tostication or flustration respecking the fête of your feverite and only son Captain Fitzroy, I have the plesure to inform your Ladie Ship he receeved a very bad wound in an a Fair of honnor with Major O'Hara this mourning. A Captain Hardy was Captain Fitzroy's Second, and Captain Lionhart the Major's. As wel as i can understand the mater, Lionhart who was always a good-nater'd creeter, wanted to aggust it Amy Cably, and say'd if so be Capt. Fitzroy wold make an Apologue the Major wold be sattesfied. The Captain say'd as he could not by no means make an Apologue, it being a thing as he was never in the habit of doing, nohow; but as he could and wold give any sattesfakshon mite be demanded for the past. He had the first fire, witch mist; the Major[a] then fired; and Oh Moll and Colly to relate! hit Captain Fitzroy's eye. Oh why will not jentlemen larn from this most lamentable / case to constrain there hangers before they break out in crewel words or still more crewel sordes! – not that it was sordes as did the Captain's bizness – but that's neither here nor there – Oh why will Huffy sirs go for to seek red dress in harms! – Well, the Major say'd as he was quitt sattesfied very genteel – and helped to have Captain Fitzroy supported to a shay. He fainted twise he had lost so much blode, and they toque him to my ouse as the most contagious, being at the end of the tone nerest the comon ware they fit. Now I have sent your Ladie Ship a Count of the Hole; and tho' you no lady Torrendale you've beaved very ill to me, I thank heven i never was wanting in Xtian charity or General Phil Anthropy. So here he lies bad enuf heven he nose. And you may weset him without fear of any mad version or discrimination of the past; and if this is not rit quitt so leggable or genteel as ushual, contribute it i begg to the sincare griffe with witch i sine myself.

your servant to command,
M. STOCKWELL.'

Amazed and distressed beyond expression, by this strange and unexpected epistle, Lady Torrendale's grief was the more violent as the cause of it was unexpected. She overwhelmed the unfortunate Arbella with questions, wondered at her own blindness, in not before remarking the agitation of Spencer's manners, when he refused to accompany her back to Woodlands; recalled a thousand particulars of Arbella's conduct and conversation during that fatal evening, and imputing wholly to her, the pique that had at length arisen between the two gentlemen, to the height of a quarrel, finished by loading her with a torrent of reproaches. She could not add to the sufferings of Miss Ferrars; that unhappy girl on the contrary found a relief in the violence of her Ladyship's expressions, from the more intolerable stings of self-condemnation. Had Lady Torrendale said less, Arbella would have felt still more. But when that lady, recovered from the first paroxym of her grief, talked of instantly flying to her beloved son, poor Arbella felt that she was still to be envied, in comparison to herself. / The terms on which she was now with her aunt, would not allow her any pretext for accompanying her Ladyship; and with a heart that bled in every fibre for Spencer, she had no ostensible plea to justify her intrusion on his account. 'Now, now,' she exclaimed, with her characteristic mixture of levity and vehemence, 'for the first time I regret I ever quarrelled with my aunt.' Regrets were vain. Her Ladyship drove off alone to S – . Arbella could only weep, and pray that Fitzroy might be restored to her.

The receipt of a billet, which was brought in by the same woman who had carried Mrs. Stockwell's, turned the channel of her thoughts to a less interesting, if a less painful subject. She could not repress a sensation something resembling shame and remorse, on recognizing the hand-writing of Mr. Sowerby. Blushing, though alone, and with a trepidation, that anticipated the contents, she hastily perused the paper.

'Convinced by your yesterday's conduct, of the egregious error into which I suffered myself to fall, in believing you ever could feel the least regard for me, I did not wait for the distressing news of to-day, to take my final resolution. You are free, Miss Ferrars, as far as I can make you so; nor do I reproach you with the hopes in which you had indulged me. I have only myself to accuse, in listening at my time of life, and with my experience to the delusions of a practiced coquette. What I have farther to urge, wholly concerns yourself. Respect the advice of a friend, who will never cease to take an interest in your welfare. Correct, if it be possible, with the assistance of your excellent understanding, that inordinate thirst for admiration, which has already caused such fatal dangers. This time it has not, I hope, occasioned murder. Shudder at the narrowness of your escape; and recede in time from the dreadful precipice, to the verge of which it has been your delight thus wantonly to approach. Thus though you have lost the affections, you may still preserve some place in the esteem of your truest friend,

THEOPHILUS SOWERBY.' /

As Arbella concluded this billet, her bosom swelled with an emotion, of which it was difficult to say, whether the predominant feature were repentance, regret, or pleasure. 'He throws me from him,' she said; 'it is his own act, and be the consequence his own.'

'Spite of some mortifying feelings of self-reproach that would intrude, her heart on the whole felt lighter; for now its every pulse might throb, unreproved, for Fitzroy. Anxious for the present, wretched on account of what might be his future fate, it beat in anguish indeed, but still it beat for him. Her busy fancy had already begun to present her a brighter scene, when happening to cast her eyes again on the paper, the dreadful words 'it has not, I *hope*, occasioned murder,' were what first met her eye; at once each gay pulsation of her heart was chilled; the flattering ideas it had begun to admit, melted away, and she spent in the alternate paroxysms of anxiety and remorse, the time that intervened till Lady Torrendale's return. She almost feared to ask the Countess the result of her visit; it was painted but too plainly upon her Ladyship's expressive features.

Spencer's wound was accompanied with fever, which was dangerous, though the hurt in itself was not, and the idea of personal disfigurement, preying on his vain mind, increased every unfavorable symptom, and almost precluded hope of recovery. What would not Arbella have given in these momentary afflictions to have had recourse to the usual balsam for her wounded mind – Matilda's consoling society. But this, while her friend remained at Mr. Sowerby's, her late conduct had put it out of her power any longer to seek; and Matilda, wholly employed in performing the duties of friendship to Clara, the interesting nun, who had for some days past had a return of the dangerous illness for which she had been advised to quit her convent, watched with the affectionate solicitude of a sister, every turn of her complaint; and could not be prevailed on, while the danger continued, for any time to quit her chamber.

The illness of Fitzroy assuming a more alarming appearance, it was deemed advisable / no longer to delay sending for his brother; and the days that must still pass, before his arrival from his seat in the north of Scotland, were spent by Arbella in a state of mind, in which the lapse of time was unheeded, except that it was marked by misery. 'Can they hope his presence will work miracles? and yet I wish he were arrived. I wish he were arrived,' she repeated, as alone and wretched she sat watching the decline of a melancholy evening, in gloomy and undetermined meditation. 'Another day must yet pass, of grief unavailing, unshared, unpitied; he cannot possibly come before to morrow night, I think' – She imagined she heard a slight noise at the door of her chamber – she turned round – it softly opened, and she saw Strathallan. His countenance was pale, indicative both of fatigue and suffering, but more touchingly, more expressively beautiful than ever. 'Miss Ferrars!' he exclaimed, in evident surprise; but the voice was so soft, so unlike the usual tones of resentment and recrimination, the only language she had been lately used to hear, that those accents, though so few and unimportant, dropped like balm upon her despairing heart. 'Can you tell me,' he said, 'which way I shall find my brother?' She now perceived that he had not been informed that Spencer's situation rendered it dangerous he should yet be removed, and that he had arrived at Woodlands in the hope of immediately seeing him. A few broken words from her explained the mistake. 'Then some time must yet intervene before I see him,' he resumed, with an expression of anxious disappointment. 'Unfortunate oversight! – My dear Sophia,' he continued, turning to Lady Strathallan, who this moment entered from giving directions in the hall about the disposal of trunks and packages, 'poor Spencer is not here – I must go on to S – to him; but you will probably prefer remaining with Miss Ferrars, who will be so kind as to make tea for you. Do rest yourself,' he continued, tenderly; 'you indeed look fatigued.'

'Not in the least, not in the least, my Lord,' replied the Lady, with a sharpness which, appeared to Arbella, little merited by / the observation that gave rise to it; if you are for S – , I am for going there too. Lady Strathallan had, or thought she had good reasons for not approving of her husband's determination to go farther. It might really be anxiety to see Spencer, or it might be a wish to be welcomed on his return, by some more of his friends. At all events he could not reasonably object to her accompanying him, and with the pride of the Viscountess, united to the pertinacity of Miss Mountain, she insisted on adhering to her first proposal.

Arbella waited their return in breathless impatience. She could not resist indulging in a faint hope that the unfavorable symptoms might have been exaggerated by the maternal tenderness, or, premeditated malice of the Countess, in the bulletins she was in the habit of daily bringing back from Mrs. Stockwell's. It was almost dark when she heard the carriage drive up the long avenue leading to the mansion. She flung open the window, leant half out of it, saw Strathallan, but had the mortification to hear him run up stairs past her apartment to Lady Torrendale's – he remained closeted with his mother-in-law for some time.

Though extremely unwilling to have recourse to Lady Strathallan, Miss Ferrars still preferred it to the dreadful alternative of remaining any longer in doubt with respect to Spencer's real situation; but this lady, who now confessed her fatigue, was in no humour to talk; she had travelled at such an incredible rate she said, Strathallan made her go on day and night, without the least consideration for the fragility of her frame, and the delicacy of her constitution; and now she had got a newspaper, and some coffee, and seemed the farthest in the world from being inclined to be communicative. Arbella's disquietudes, however, were not of a nature to allow her to attend to a trifling repulse.

'Did your Ladyship find Captain Fitzroy?' she said, hesitatingly, 'did you find him quite, quite in as much – quite as ill, I mean, as you expected?'

'Quite,' returned the lady, with laconic composure, 'and oh, Lady Strathallan, do not deceive me – have they indeed fears – / have they hopes? – tell me what is the real opinion of the medical men?'

'Hey!' cried her Ladyship, raising her eyes from the paper, and haughtily fixing them, in unfeeling interrogatory, upon those of Arbella, which, however accustomed to their gaze, always sunk beneath them, resuming her former attitude and occupation, 'so, so,' she said, reading half aloud, 'disturbances in America apprehended, I find great uneasiness excited by the disaffection at fort Michelamickawhackachickasaw, Miss Ferrars were you never tempted to learn the Mohawk language?' Receiving no answer, she turned again to her paper, 'if this should be really the case, she murmured, Strathallan may chance to put one of his fine plans, the visiting of America, into execution. But I'll accompany him; what a melancholy prospect for England! already engaged in a European war – you smile Miss Ferrars – you wonder at the interest I take in what does not appear very nearly to concern me – you forgot that I have more reasons than you, for this generous participation in the anxieties of others. Beside the axiom of the immortal Pope, that the solicitude of a generous mind, extending beyond the claims of friendship and kindness, should embrace,

'Its country next, and next all human race.'[85]

I, as an Englishwoman, and a woman of rank, particularly, feel a near and dear interest in every thing that touches the security and honor of my country – how many lives are lost in each fatal quarrel? how many hundred, or, as king Henry says,

'How many thousand of my poorest subjects.'[86]

For you will surely allow his majesty's foot soldiers to be some of his poorest subjects.'

'True, Madam,' interrupted Arbella, mournfully; for, with her, deep dejection and self-condemnation had got the better of her accustomed irritability; 'but is it indeed thought probable that? – that Captain Fitzroy's sufferings may terminate fatally.'

''Tis probable,' said Lady Strathallan, who had now laid down her newspaper, and / was employed settling her curls, and renewing her colour at the glass.

'Yet his wound was not at first considered as dangerous – as mortal.'

'No, not mortal;' I cannot help fancying, resumed Arbella, thoughtfully, 'that if he were once removed here, he would have a much greater chance of recovery. Will you propose it to Lady Torrendale, dear Lady Strathallan. If it could possibly be managed – I do not doubt my aunt's attention, but indeed her house is not a fit place for a wounded man – all the noise of town and country about it – carriages and carts perpetually passing and repassing. Oh how can he have that quiet that is so absolutely necessary? – how can he sleep?'

'Sleep!' repeat her Ladyship, turning round with a complacent air,

'How sleep the brave who sink to rest,
By all their country's wishes blest?'[87]

Then presenting a little case, something resembling a book, that she held in her hand, 'you know this, without doubt,' she said, 'it is "*rose a l'usage des dames*,"[88] it is not quite so beautiful as the powder, but I always carry it with me when I travel, it is very convenient.'

However she might appear at that moment to need it, Arbella turned from her Ladyship with an impatience she could no longer disguise or restrain, as with a low curtsey she presented the book and brush to her; she could not, however, leave the room soon enough to lose the last consoling words of the Viscountess, pronounced in her most solemn and sententious tone.

'You seem in need of consolation Miss Ferrars. Consolation I think at length I have discovered for you. In the various accidents and crosses of life, some accuse their enemies, some accuse the stars, some accuse their fate; but you have, by all I hear, the singular and agreeable reflection that you can only accuse yourself.' – She closed this sentence, which she thought admirably rounded, with a smile, in which satisfied vanity, but not a spark of the Torrendale malice appeared, and Arbella convinced, by long / knowledge of her character, that she did not mean, in what she said, to hurt her, felt almost angry with her strange companion, for not allowing her, with justice, to hate her as much as she 'ere felt inclined to do.

She closed by a sleepless night a day, marked by no satisfactory circumstance but the return of Strathallan. From him, and him alone, she hoped a portion of that sympathy, which rendered her now lost Matilda's intercourse so endearing. She felt more bitterly than ever, that this amiable girl alone, of all her female acquaintance, possessed the power of completely forgetting each private feeling, in a generous interest for others; while, on recapitulating the unnecessary sufferings she had for many days endured at the hands of different characters, from the Countess, to Lady Strathallan, she found that the conduct she complained of, originated in all, from the same cause, from that 'plenteous fountain of selfishness,' which, however differently modified, must still be acknowledged as the source of every false estimate that is made of the vast importance of our own pursuits or opinions, when put in comparison with the feelings or concerns of others. 'Gentle Matilda! invaluable Friend,' she exclaimed, 'Oh let me, in sleep at least, see you restored to my wishes, since my deplorable folly has deprived me when I most wanted it, even of this last support.' Vain were her prayers; vain her aspirations for repose; and morning had already dawned, before she could banish the hateful thoughts that were now the only mementos, to remind her of her lately joyous gipsey party.' /

CHAPTER XI.

My lover's blood is on thy spear;
How canst thou, barbarous man, then woo me?

HAMILTON.[89]

'ARBELLA, my dear,' said Lady Torrendale, with one of her softest looks, 'I have ordered the carriage for S – , would you not like to accompany me? I am surprised you never go. My son must feel truly grateful for the flattering partiality with which you honor him, and to which he may almost entirely attribute his present situation; and there's your aunt who would, of course, be glad to see you, you know.'

Besides her daily visits to Mrs. Stockwell's, messages constantly passed between the Captain and Lady Torrendale, who desired to hear of him long before she was in readiness to ascertain in person how he was; for she could not, even for a son so beloved, put any restraint upon her settled habits.

Major O'Hara, from a different motive, was almost as constant in his enquiries, and was greatly relieved by hearing that a favorable turn had taken place in Captain Fitzroy's illness.[a]

As for Sowerby, his disappointment with regard to Arbella, seemed only to increase the value and regard he felt for his fair guest; with whose more praise-worthy conduct, on a similar occasion, he did not fail to contrast, the levity and coquetry of her friend. 'Matilda refused me indeed,' said he, 'but her whole behaviour was marked with that candour, that nobleness, that fair-dealing, which a woman, with a truly well-born mind and soul, feels it as much required of her from a man, as in any intercourse with her own sex. I was wrong to expect the same from her friend. The Stockwells are a bad breed – her uncle a mere trader, without expansion of heart, or ability of head. In any branch of such a stock, improve it by culture how / you will, a certain want of nobility of heart, a lower tone of mind will betray the inferior source from which it sprung.' So pleased did the good gentleman appear with this illustration of his favourite system of hereditary worth and honour, and so satisfied with his sagacity, in having his observations on the family failings of his mistress thus justified, that it was hard to decide, whether he was, on the whole, most angry or pleased, with the event which thus confirmed his repeated predictions.

Mr. Sowerby was seated at table with his sister, who was that day, for the first time, able to enjoy the company of her friends, Matilda and Mrs. Melbourne, to whose society, now their tempers no longer clashed, he became from day to day more attached; when the door was suddenly thrown open and unattended, unannounced, in rushed

– 366 –

– Arbella! Her eyes sparkling with transport, her cheeks glowing with animation; the ærial lightness of her figure scarce allowing her to touch the ground. She ran with open arms to Miss Melbourne, and sinking on her neck, exclaimed in tremulous extacy, 'Oh, Matilda, he's out of danger!'

The quickness with which this scene had passed, prevented any one from anticipating, or endeavouring to prevent it. Clara was the first to remark the dreadful change in the countenance of her brother, who too well guessed the person to whom this expression must allude; and a moment more recovered the thoughtless Arbella, from the delirium of joy, to make her sensible of the excessive indiscretion of which she had been guilty. Mrs. Melbourne, with ready presence of mind, turning to her blushing guest, said, 'I suppose Lady Torrendale was desirous I should have the very earliest information, and from good authority, of the cessation of her uneasiness, and I thank her for it; but you and Matilda must have many things to say to each other, so if you are for a turn in the garden, I will soon join you there.' Arbella did not wait to have the permission twice repeated: but glancing something of the look at her former admirer, / which the little mouse may be supposed to do to pussy, when she had just escaped from her claws, she tripped towards the garden followed by her less light-hearted friend. 'And now,' said she, drawing Matilda towards her by both her hands, 'no cross looks or grave words I insist upon it; for I have absolutely lived upon nothing else for this week past; never was a poor pill garlic so baited and 'be-thumped with words"[90] as I have been, and all for a little indiscretion. The revulsion of joy was too much for me. Just now, the tedious prosing doctors sent in word of what I suppose they knew an age ago, that dear, dear Fitzroy was safe; and I ran down, according to my old custom of sharing every pleasure with you, not immediately recollecting that your dear old friend had lately considered me in a light – a – sort of a light – of which I was quite unworthy; and which might make my presence, as a visitor, not so acceptable. But now, since I have committed this terrible breach of decorum, I will take advantage of it; for I want to tell you a great many things. What do you think of Major O'Hara? the ruffian! well, he is to be ordered away soon, thank God! they have staid an unconscionable time: he has had the impudence – assurance, I suppose he would call it, to send me this morning a written proposal; but I gave him such an answer as will, I think, put an end to the ardour of his pursuit for the present. I do not recollect exactly what I said; but I know there were several things pretty home; and I concluded with observing, that if I thought myself obliged at all to dispose of my hand, in consequence of a recent affair, it should certainly be in favour of that gentleman who had suffered the most for me in the contest. Yes, yes, Spencer, dear Spencer, is the man – I owe him that reparation – I can and I must – though I resign Clifden-down house, and all its splendours, for a tent, and Fitzroy's arm – that is to say if he will – Oh, should he repent his promises – determine to escape

'That dangerous thing a female wit[91] /

and regret that he ever met her – but no, he cannot; he knows my heart, and will not mind the cruel insinuations of others. Only this morning Miss Piers called to tell me Helena de Courcy said yesterday, before a large party at the Evertires, that if Fit-

* Shakespeare.

zroy lost his sight, (oh, cruel thought!) I must lead him. That girls can be so flippant! but I repeat it to you, to give you an idea of the general opinion. Yes, I must give up Mr. Sowerby; I must, I must, and resign the hope of being united to the most worthy, the most virtuous, the most respectable of men.'

Matilda perceived her friend was determined to consider her quarrel with Sowerby as a 'very pretty quarrel as it stood,' and that any attempt to interfere in it would be rather unwelcome, than grateful to her. She, therefore, forbore to press Arbella on this subject; Miss Ferrars continued, 'it would almost tempt one to believe there was something like retribution in this world; to think of the manner in which this duel was managed. That it should be Lionhart who carried the challenge.'

'Lionhart!' cried Matilda, with a start, while various recollections crouded on her memory, with the name.

'Yes, Lionhart, who was, you know, his sworn "*amigo*," has lately become his greatest enemy, and for the most silly reason. There was a beautiful young lady, (I am sorry for you Matilda) that the gallant Captain lately paid his addresses to, but having a modest opinion of his own talents, he requested his more engaging friend to speak for him – You know Fitzroy – you know the rest – "Eyes" (oh, why do I call him "Eyes" any more) remembered his cue, but forgot the words of his speech. He took care love should be still the subject, but he furnished from himself the expression: which, though found equally agreeable by the lady, was not at all approved of by honest Frank. Spencer, without availing himself of the favourable dispositions of his mistress to press his suit, lost his friend, the sensitive hero; who, without love or friendship expires, happened to contract a great intimacy with that vapouring insolent Major. He asked him to / be his second. Lionhart, I understand, did what he could to accommodate matters, but what did it avail! Oh! that he had never returned from the Peninsula, where he has been ever since our last year's party broke up! and there lies my charming Fitzroy; and I, oh grief of griefs, am not permitted to fly to his relief! Oh, Sam, Sam, Stockwell, "art thou not the wickedest worm that ever walked upon two legs*." Excuse me, my dear, but I must for this once trace my sorrows to their spring. If I had not quarreled with Aunt Stockwell, I might now see poor Spencer. If my cousin Sam, had not used me so like a rascal, I should not have quarrelled with Aunt Stockwell! so you see it is originally the fault of that cursed booby Sam, the beginning and end of all mischief, that my poor dear, little, *elegant* Fitzroy, is *ennuing* himself to death, with only my poor aunt, as vulgar as – well, she *is* my aunt, and so I won't abuse her. And Miss Hautenville, that most stiff, odious, and abominable of all frights. The Countess tells me, she finds them alternately "perched on his couch," like the phantom of "Distemper," in Hastings' Ode.[92] My aunt must be quite in her element, documenting the young officer; a thing she fancies she does 'most pathetically,' as she calls it, though her kind offices lately received a check. Last Sunday, on there being some appearance of greater danger than usual, she had him prayed for in church, "without saying nothing to nobody;" it, however, some way reached the ears of my gentleman, who was so incensed – What! was he to be treated like a mechanic, or day-labourer! – He to be prayed for – a man of his consequence indeed; it brought

* Sir Philip Sidney's Arcadia.

on his fever with redoubled violence, while poor auntie, who was closely questioned by the doctor, could only say, with uplift hands, and rolling eyes, that she had done all for the best; and did not know what upon earth ailed the Captain; but that for sure since ever he'd come to himself, he was for ever-lasting in one tantarum or another. When / he is tired of her on one side, he has the gentle Miss Hautenville on the other; who really, I begin to think, must have given him some philtre, to make him endure her phiz, for she is constantly about him, reading or talking to him. She tells his mamma she is giving him advice upon future good conduct, regularity, economy; and this being to the taste of the Contessa, she has found out her dear son cannot do better than attend to it; for that Miss Hautenville is a very sensible *young* woman, and has seen a vast deal of the world. This will be all soon ended, I trust, by his removal to Woodlands. Now he is on the mend he will rapidly recover: do you know he began to grow better since the day his brother returned; is not it very odd?'

'No, I think not,' Matilda replied with great *naïveté.*

'Oh, no, I had forgot – but I was telling you about Spencer. Dear fellow! during the intermissions of his disorder he thought on me, and has sent me a dozen sweet messages, at least as sweet as they can be after Lady Torrendale has murdered them; and this morning (suspecting her tricks, I suppose), he contrived to write me a note with his own hand, though he has a bandage over one of those sweet eyes; here is the little gaudy scrawl – how strong it smells of roses! You smile – well, I own it is a little coxcomb; he had once the impertinence to tell me he used such paper for *all* his *amourettes.* But now I've time, I think I'll read you some of it – hem, hem – he feels "truly grateful for the kind interest I have condescended to express for his fate." Grateful – hem – when did Spencer ever write three lines, or speak three words without the terms "grateful," or "gratitude," being either expressed or implied. He is 'too well acquainted with the tenderness of my disposition,' – the tenderness of my disposition! Deuce take his impertinence! "not to feel assured," – Oh, yes, he has assurance enough, a saucy fellow! – "that I must compassionate his feelings, their immensity and intensity," – that is so exactly Spencer, or rather so exactly his mother, "is such, that / he should in vain exert himself to give me the least idea of them; let it suffice, that Mrs. Stockwell is his monitor, and Miss Hautenville his nurse." He has "taken advantage of their absence to steal a gleam of light to write me these few lines, but he fears they will not be legible. If he should become wholly blind, he will only regret it, as it prevents his gazing on his Arbella." How nicely he brings in his misfortune, poor fellow! he need not remind me of it – hem – "adieu, my Arbella; if you knew all, you would pity me. – Pity him! who does not – His situation has excited a great sensation; I learnt more of that, than even I knew already, by the perusal of a little scrawl, I found on Lady Torrendale's dressing-table. It was not very honourable to be sure; but it was only a "bit of a note" as the Irish call it, from Aunt Stockwell; and I am of the opinion of Charles, in the School for Scandal, that it is very hard if one may not "make free with one's own relations."[93] I must read it you,' continued Miss Ferrars, laughing, 'if it be only to afford a contrast to the last. It was sent to Lady Torrendale one morning that she was sick, or idle, no matter which – stay – it is such a crabbed hand I can hardly make it out; and the dancing light, as we walk up and down, blinds me. We will sit down upon that bench – now for it – '

'Your Ladyship ma deppend upon every attenshon been ped to the Capten inn your abstinence Toby Shure. Yett still itt must bee a grate dishapointment to hymn not to sea his one deer muther, ass it wood bee too me sun Sam, in Simmy ler Sir Cumstances. Heed bee wel ennuf if hee cou'd get rid of an ugly favor, witch he cant in any wise get quit off. The sa stuf a cold an starf a favor; but I no better. I no it is allways the best whey to giv young gentlemen what tha like. Soe i hav shock o'late, and 2 letel fresh loves for him evvery morning, becase he says if any thing can doe him good it is a letel fresh love. This is the trew Bullykin of his healt. Its unknone the No. of Ink-wiry's I'm oblieged to anser aboat him. / No latter tan yesterda Kitty Kindly, as was yr Ladship's made, and was married last yere, to the big man that lives att the grate wight howse a 'tother side of the hill, his Lordship's Baliff as was kailed; and assed for to see him, and brote a fine cake, mad with her own hands, and full of allemandes and comforts, and several other young vimen of the nayberhud, besides a Jew; for the pressent.

P.S. You ma tell my nice Arbell, as – '

'Oh now we are come to "nice Arbella,"' pursued Miss Ferrars, 'you must excuse my going on, my dear, for it proceeds in a strain of Philippic rather mortifying to my vanity.' Perceiving Mrs. Melbourne approaching at this moment the seat where they were conversing, 'we have been talking, Madam,' she said, as she huddled her papers into her pocket, 'of Sir Harold Melbourne. Is it true that the rage for antiquities has given place to the passion for music; and the part of *Il Fanatico per la Musica*,[94] is enacted every night at the Rocks, by the Baronet in *propria persona?*'

Mrs. Melbourne had hoped, that, by giving Miss Ferrars plenty of time to 'talk over' her affairs, as she called it, with her daughter, she might find Matilda alone when she entered the garden; that however not being the case, she replied with her wonted urbanity to the questions which Miss Ferrars proposed, in their usual number and variety. 'Is it true that he has invited down Lorenzina and Marionelli for the summer? and is it true that he lavishes such immense sums upon them? and is it true that – '

'True, true, all true, my dear young lady, and I regret to think that it should be so.'

'Regret, nay, why regret it; let him ruin himself as fast as he likes; that is his affair you know; so we have concerts and company what do we care! I am sure such a thing was quite a desideratum in the neighbourhood. But I had forgot he is your relation. I am dying to hear this Marionelli,' she continued, turning with great unconcern to Matilda, 'have you heard her? how does she sing? They tell me she resembles Catalani / in some of her higher tones, particularly in that fine note which she held so long in the song of "Gratias Agimus Tibi;"[95] were not those some of the words? You remember the Oratorio; and how much we admired the clear full sound, that without stunning the ear, filled the whole house, and seemed more like the swell of some fine instrument than an exertion of the human voice. And can Marionelli equal that?'

Matilda, without any other reply, immediately ran through the passage alluded to, in the manner of the Signora Marionelli; giving to the higher parts the wonderful strength and beauty for which she was celebrated; imitating her in all her mazy evolutions, her artificial graces, and even her defects: then, as if wearied with this exertion of momentary spirit, she ceased, declined her head, and like a bird that droops its flagging wing, seemed to seek, in silence, relief from the momentary effort she had been tempted to make.

'Bravo! charming!' cried the enthusiastic Arbella, who though herself an indifferent musician, ever took the most unfeigned delight in the excellence of her friend. 'Why this would make your fortune at Lady Torrendale's – I mean with the *gen-tle-men,* as poor Miss Langrish used to drawl it out. Only let me give out some night, that Miss Melbourne will indulge the company with her celebrated imitations of Marionelli.'

'Ah, my dearest Arbella, when will you know me enough to conceive the dislike, the terror I feel at any thing that bears the appearance of pretension. If I have occasionally, and to oblige you, imitated for a moment, the manner of Grassini[96] or Marionelli, do not, I intreat you – '

'True, true, *"la petite Violette;"* but we must not have you a *la Valliere*[97] in every thing, must we Mamma Melbourne?'

'Arbella,' said Matilda, with an air the most deeply hurt, 'I will try to think you ONLY inconsiderate.'

'Dear, so I am, shockingly so; and always contriving, without intending it, to hurt my friends.' /

'Your female friends,' resumed Matilda, gravely.

'Well it is all your fault, why do you leave me to my folly? You have not come near me this twelvemonth; I have lost all the good I acquired in your society. You are turned nun, like Clara, I believe. You go no where. You have not been even to see the tall woman. But it is time I should take my departure,' she continued, answering Mrs. Melbourne's involuntary smile, at this ludicrous allusion to Lady Strathallan. 'I have staid too long already; for if I do not greatly mistake, yonder comes my late sighing Strephon, to growl, (I beg pardon) to call you in to tea. I think I should know his stride. But what's the matter, he stands still?'

Matilda directed her eyes to the point where Arbella was looking, and perceived nothing but a stuffed figure in a blue coat and a flapped hat, placed among the trees to frighten the birds; and that was occasionally moved backwards and forwards by the wind. Mrs. Melbourne's countenance expressed serious displeasure. 'Ten thousand pardons,' cried Arbella, 'I now perceive my mistake; and I vow and protest to you it was made in innocence of heart; am I to blame, if he chuses to make that stationary gentleman the inheritor of his cast dress suits, instead of his valet. Oh now if I have really offended my Mamma Melbourne, it is fit indeed that I should go; and here the dear man comes in good earnest. Haste, let me get out of his way, Matilda. Which way is the best? through the shrubbery? By my love; I must fly like 'the startled cushat dove,'[98] though I assure you, no pretty billing and cooing, awaits me at home. Heigho! But will not you forgive me, Mamma Melbourn?'

'Yes, yes, go you madcap, or he will see you.'

Arbella disappeared among the trees; and Mrs. Melbourne hastened up the walk to meet her respected friend, and sooth by her attentions, and those of her daughter, the disorder of his spirits, ruffled by Miss Ferrars / unexpected and most unpardonable intrusion. 'She is a pleasing creature,' said Mrs. Melbourne to Matilda, 'what a pity that so much spirit, vivacity, and good humour, should not be tempered by a single grain of discretion!'

CHAPTER XII.

So tuned in unison, Eolian lyre
Sounds in sweet symphony thy kindred wire;
Now, gently swept by Zephyrs' vernal wings,
Sink in soft cadences the love-sick strings;
And now with mingling chords and voices higher,
Peal the full anthem of the aërial choir.

DARWIN.[99]

MATILDA began to indulge a hope that Sir Harold's mysterious threat respecting Strathallan, 'I wait him at the Rocks,' was one of those vague suggestions of momentary frenzy, to which she had annexed an unnecessary and ideal importance. While the mansion resounded with the plaintive languish of Æolian harps, and voices worthy of a place in the cherub choir, filled up the intervals between, could she believe the master's breast the seat of desperation and revenge? The knowledge that Lord Strathallan had already / appeared at one or two of those performances which now took place almost every evening, encouraged her to adopt this consolatory idea. To these concerts, which afforded the most exquisite treat to the real lovers of musical science, combining the exertions of the most distinguished theatrical talent, with whatever the amateur could contribute, of taste and native grace, the neighbouring gentry were made welcome, with a generous and universally extended hospitality, which made the unhappy Baronet, noble even in his eccentricities, universally popular, if not universally admired. If his design was by this to draw a perpetual crowd around him, it must be confessed that he succeeded admirably. Some accepted his invitations, to judge, by their own observations, if report spoke too favorably of the dispositions he had made for their entertainment; some went merely because they heard others did so; and some, and, by far the smallest number, from real taste for the pleasures of harmony, offered under their most attractive form. Of this last number was Strathallan. Since the commencement of his brother's gradual amendment, he had sometimes beguiled a languid hour, among the enchanting harmonies of the Rocks; and had thus been led to renew the acquaintance the Baronet had formed with him, at Tunbridge. Of Matilda he had seen nothing; a formal visit, which had passed, when he was from home, was the only one she had lately made to Woodlands; and this visit, had not yet been returned by Lady Strathallan.

Sir Harold had just completed his new concert room; and was so anxious to have the opinion of Mrs. and Miss Melbourne upon it, that, though rarely a visitor at

Clifden-down, he called to request their presence at the next musical performance at his house; and, by one of his singular caprices, entreated Matilda to contrive, that the beautiful nun should be of the party. Clara, at first, started with horror, at the idea of joining any thing that bore so much the appearance of a public assembly; but entreated Matilda would not constrain herself for her. Miss Melbourne, who had discovered the passion of the fair recluse for music, and had a mind / for once to cheat her into a little blameless recreation, declared that her assent depended upon that of her friend. 'Going with us you will be surrounded only by those you know,' she said; 'it is an amusement of a perfectly private nature, and I own I can see no reason for your depriving yourself of a very high and innocent pleasure.'

'I have vowed to renounce all pleasure,' said Clara, looking down, 'and a concert – '

'It is not a regular concert,' replied Sir Harold, 'I have music every evening, and besides, my fair friend,' he continued, speaking very fast, as he usually did when he thought he had found an argument very much in point, 'what you assert about renouncing all pleasure is not literally true; as you do not wholly renounce the higher pleasure of friendship and society: now you would give me your society in that room, another evening, when music was not going on; and where is the culpable difference, in sitting there to hear strains that might prepare your soul for its blissful passage. You nuns are fond of music; the solemn harmony of the anthem, and the organ, is not banished from your community; and to-morrow we shall have some sacred pieces; so come with your friend, and fancy yourself in your convent again. Ask her, my fair cousin, and tell her we begin early, and cannot, dare not end late.'

'I think Sir Harold has too well argued the point, for me to add any thing to it,' said Matilda.

'Perhaps as you are a party of friends I should not refuse to hear your Handel,' said Clara; 'but to attract remark, and in this dress,' looking at her nun's habit, which she never had, and which she was determined she never would, put off.

Again the timid recluse was going positively to refuse, but Matilda's declaration that she would not go without her, the recollection of the confinement and privation this kind and generous friend had endured on her account, operating perhaps with a little curiosity to hear some of the compositions of him, who was said to embody in music the sublime ideas, in the contemplation of which her / mind had so long solely delighted, concurred to shake her resolution. After a short silence she then, with a smile and a soft sigh, said to Miss Melbourne, 'you are to blame if I sin in this.' Sir Harold joyfully accepted her reluctant consent, and the party was arranged without any farther difficulty.

Though the visitants from Clifden-down arrived at the Rocks, at rather an early hour, a considerable number of persons, considerable at least to Clara's unpractised eye, were already assembled; the saloon, appropriated to the performance of music, was fitted up with considerable taste; lightness, and an elegant simplicity, were the prevailing characteristics; ornaments consisting of lyres, harps, and other emblems of music, disposed in graceful groups, formed the chief decorations of the walls. They were raised in a white stucco, upon a stone-coloured ground; and Sir Harold, in rendering this apartment complete, omitted not to call in the aid of sculpture in many suitable designs, expressive of the triumphs of the art. The Baronet was soon discovered giving some directions to the musicians; he had a roll of music in his hand, and was surrounded by a bevy of fair aspirants, mostly amateurs, who were engaged in a dispute, loquacious, and apparently obstinate, which he was endeavoring with a gentle urbanity, and easy gaiety, to decide. 'You see me in my greatest glory,' he said, turning to Mrs. Melbourne, with a smile and a playful versatility of manner; but it was a smile and a playfulness which made the sympathizing heart of the too well-informed Matilda, ache for him more than the most settled melancholy. 'I am giving the law to youth, beauty, and talent. No arbiter of pleasure at any of her most favorite haunts; not the king of Bath himself,[100] with the loves and graces traced upon the medallion at his bosom, could be prouder of ushering in his "*belle Jeunesse*" to partake of her privileges, than I – what say you ladies? Will you abide by my decision? or shall this fair stranger's be the casting voice? Indeed I believe we must begin with Handel. There is one,' casting his eyes upon Clara, 'to whom we have half promised it.' /

Sir Harold addressed himself to Clara, but his wish to distinguish her was evidently as Matilda's friend; and both throughout this dispute, and in the course of the evening, he seemed, by every delicate, but not painfully marked, attention, to give his cousin to understand that she was the queen of the fête. He was particularly desirous to hear her sentiments respecting the style of the decorations, and the merits of the performers; while she contemplated with involuntary solicitude, his slight, spirit-like form, leaning against a rose-wreathed harp, which seemed to give him the support he almost needed; the classic elegance of his figure, and Roman beauty of his features, now animated with the glow of social pleasure, only increasing the regret, at the slow, but sure decline, his general appearance announced; while these lights, these tapers, and flowers, the choirs of virgin beauty, and the mingled stream of perfumes and harmony, seemed less the decorations of a triumph than the honors that fancy would decree to blooming youth devoted to the tomb.

Such thoughts, however, were happily strangers to the majority of the guests; who had already alternatively gratified others, and received pleasure themselves in hearing and performing several vocal and instrumental pieces, when Matilda was requested, by Sir Harold, to give her aid, if it was only by a single song, to the concert. To this effort she found herself unequal, but it was obvious no little jealousy mingled with her refusal. Miss Melbourne had none of that envy, from which the possession of the most distinguished talents, does not always exempt the amateur. She delighted to acknowledge merit, even when she imagined it surpassed or equalled her own. Carried away by the full tide of harmony that now burst upon her ear, the pleasure she enjoyed was of a double kind; a pleasure excited by the real superiority of the performance; a pleasure arising from the soft melancholy into which music ever plunged her mind. She was only roused by the name of Strathallan, repeated by several voices. As he advanced every eye was involuntarily turned towards him – / and the eye that had once rested on him, could, with pleasure, have rested on him for ever. But for his lady, how is it possible to describe the glance of mingled triumph and pleasure with which she passed on; swimming, writhing, yet still preserving something of her native unwieldy crocodile stiffness; and apparently unable to decide whether earth, air, or sea were most worthy of supporting 'Lady Strathallan.' Their appearance could not fail of exciting a momentary emotion in Matilda, but the change in her countenance was so slight that Mrs. Melbourne alone or perhaps Clara, could remark it sufficiently to give her credit for the perfect self-command with which she in a moment rallied her fluttered spirits. We must except Sir Harold, who secretly noticed her emotion with the watchful eye of jealousy. Matilda felt anxious to know how Strathallan would conduct himself in a first meeting, which chance had rendered such a public one; but with that graceful and noble politeness which above all men he possessed, he soon put her completely at her ease, by neither avoiding her nor seeking her with an air of too impatient attention. Approaching the ladies, and addressing himself more particularly to Mrs. Melbourne, he regretted that his absence from home, at the time of her visit, had prevented him from seeing friends he so much valued, and pleaded the numerous engagements of Lady Strathallan, which had alone hindered her performing a duty, which, with those she so much valued, she wished might not be considered as a mere formal call; and had therefore delayed till she could have some hope of really enjoying their society. This statement Lady Strathallan, happy and secure, and, in imagination at least, '*triomphante adorée*,' was sufficiently willing to confirm.

As his face was turned from her, when speaking to Mrs. Melbourne, Matilda could remark, without fear of being observed herself, the change a very few months had wrought on his manly and interesting countenance; and in the traces contending passions had left there, she could read how little his apparent calmness was the effect of insensibility. / Lady Strathallan, who had waited with impatience to the end of a bravura of Signora Marionelli's, paid her some formal compliments upon the delight she had received from it; and then flew from her to rattle away a thundering concerto, upon the grand piano, in which all time, tune, feeling, and expression were sacrificed to unmeaning noise, and tasteless execution. Of these compliments, which cost her little or nothing, and which never imparted pleasure to the receiver, her Ladyship was very profuse. That she was a goddess, who, moving in a superior sphere, performed every thing by inspiration, better than any others could by imitation, was, in her opinion of all incontrovertible facts the most incontrovertible; but then she considered it as very proper that humbler mortals should endeavour to follow her, and even condescended to look down with pleasure on their efforts, and reward them with a proportion of praise.

Such at least was the satirical remark of Arbella, who, with Sappho, Alcæus, and the rest of Lady Strathallan's worshippers, accompanied her to the concert. Her friend had hardly replied, when the entrance of two gentlemen made Miss Ferrars start, and change colour, for though she certainly could not be assured of not meeting them at the Rocks, she had flattered herself that harmony had but few attractions for them. These were Captain Lionhart and his friend Major O'Hara, handsomer and haughtier than ever; who, since his successful duel with Fitzroy, had been graced by his fair and considerate friends, with the additional title of the conqueror, an honour to which he seemed determined by his demeanour, to maintain his claim.

After perambulating the room arm in arm, with his friend, whispering and laughing, to the great disturbance of the musicians, and having sufficiently quizzed the company, with his eye-glass; and exhibiting his fine person for their admiration, he suddenly made a dead stop opposite to the sofa where Arbella, and her pretty little friend Helena De Courcy, were sitting engaged in deep conversation. He gave Arbella a stare which was sufficiently / insolent, and then casting a cursory and supercilious glance over the whole figure of her young friend, who had put on one of her sweetest smiles, expecting him to address her, he seemed suddenly to recollect himself, and turning completely away from both ladies, introduced himself to the fair nun, with a profusion of compliments equally unwelcome and unsought for. The circle which her beauty and singular appearance had by this time drawn around her, rendered it hopeless to attempt to obtain a seat near her, but this was no impediment to the gallant Major, who, with his leg resting on the bar of a music stand before him, and his back turned full upon the disconsolate damsels on the sofa, bent forward to whisper a thousand extravagancies to the lovely stranger; whose ear he seemed desirous of wholly engrossing, and not perceiving or pretending not to perceive, how much he fatigued and distrest her, visibly enjoyed the mortification of the fair Helena, whom he left to converse with her friend or to listen to his discourse as she thought best. It did not require the Major's predetermination to mark his displeasure against any one who should countenance his obdurate fair, to make the spot in which Clara presided the most attractive one to every admirer of unsophisticated beauty. The simplicity of her appearance, only added, by the charm of novelty, to the effect she produced. Her fair skin, of a snowy whiteness, and the deep vermilion, with which her cheeks were dyed, were only set off by the severe restrictions which forbade the aid of any adventitious embellishment. No art could wholly conceal, the beautiful turn of her face, or rob her eyes of that sacred fire, which they had stolen from Heaven; and the mantling confusion with which the attention she excited, every moment overspread her countenance, heightened to a degree of angelic beauty, the lustre of her native charms.

'The fair nun – the lovely nun – did you ever see so enchanting a creature? She will become quite the rage! Nobody will be ever able to bear flowers, or feathers, or gold and silver again!' /

'Why, Captain Lionhart,' said the little poet, 'you will soon be fit for the waxworks,' pointing out to the attention of his companion the ruined state of the hero's shoulder and brilliant epaulet. Seated exactly under a lustre in an inconvenient corner, into which he had squeezed himself to get near the beautiful Clara, he had not perceived the melting wax which had been dropping profusely on him for a quarter of an hour; during which he had indulged, almost without intermission, in the longing gaze of enraptured admiration.

'Oh, never mind him,' replied O'Hara coolly. 'It is only a love-fit coming on; I'll manage him when we get home.'

'Is the Captain often subject to those fits,' resumed Alcæus pertly? 'The gentleman seems indeed *bien* ÉPRIS. What a sublime unconsciousness to every thing that surrounds him! What a vacancy of eye is there!

Not the poet in the moment,
Fancy lightens to his e'e,
Kens the pleasure, feels the rapture,
That thy presence – [101]

A propos, I have seen too many fine women, and those of the highest rank and station, and of every country too, to be easily dazzled by their attractions, or to consider them as any thing more than a fine study, for a tolerably happy and versatile muse; but as a study, may I be shot if she does not supply me with a hint for a nun, that shall make the Constance in the Marmion, be quite despised and forgotten.[102] Be so good as to turn a little that way Madam; truly your fair friends are injudicious, who regret your appearing among us 'kerchieft in a comely cloud.'[103] For shoot me if there is not more art and coquetry requisite, to attain to the killing perfection of simplicity, which is displayed in pinning on that unpretending veil, than in adjusting the most brilliant tiara ever affixed to beauty's brow. Aye, and there is more vanity concealed under it, will you deny me that? the charming Gresset justly observes,

'Il est des modes pour le voile.' '[104]

'Gresset deserves the honour of being quoted by Mr. Spring,' observed Miss Swanley, / 'from the fortunate circumstance of his having chosen for his hero, a character that so much resembles his.'

In this allusion to the poem on the Parrot, Ver, Vert, Sappho, who had observed the lovely Clara, quite overwhelmed, and ready to sink to the earth with confusion, at the ill-timed raillery of Alcæus, enjoyed the double pleasure of making her hated rival ridiculous, and rescuing the persecuted stranger from his attacks. She was, however, almost equally distrest with Major O'Hara's efforts to entertain her, and the frequent loud laughs and vehemence of voice and gesture, by which, if he did not completely succeed in commanding her attention, he at least obtained his point, of directing that of the whole room to the spot where they were engaged together. His conversation, consisting entirely of the whispered anecdote of the fashionable circle, or the loudly spread report of general society, was the more interesting to her, as it turned upon subjects to which, from the secluded nature of her life, she was necessarily a perfect stranger. Upon these topics the Major poured forth a variety of commonplaces, of which he appeared to have a large assortment ever ready at his command. Every story he told was 'a good thing,' or 'a famous thing,' every man was 'a good fellow,' and every lady a 'beautiful creature.' He had found, by experience, the advantage of this liberal use of common-place, or describing things in the lump, with those set and received phrases, which fashion has appropriated to designate them. The favourite resource of those unfortunate minds, which are incapable of conceiving any thing, but in a gross and general manner. Those ready-made phrases being, to the varied expressions which convey the minuter shades of meaning, what hieroglyphics formerly were to words. Useful in the infancy of language, and for the purposes of common life, but too arbitrary and indistinct when conceptions grew more various, and ideas more refined.

So thought the poet Alcæus, who never liking that any one should too long usurp the conversation, 'entreated the Major to be / silent, and to listen to Signor Cavatina, who was just going to begin a fine oratorio song.'

'I wouldn't care,' cried O'Hara, angry at the interruption, 'if all the oratorios were at − ,' then suddenly correcting himself, on observing the expression of surprise and displeasure visibly painted on Clara's beautiful countenance − 'That is to say,' he added, 'those parts of the oratorios where you hear nothing but the rough voices of men and recitative. I am fond of all sacred music, and that sort of thing, as I have heard it in churches abroad; I have listened in Italy to the sweet voices of the nuns, 'till I have fancied the forms of all the dear angels behind the curtain, and actually thought myself in Mahomet's Paradise. Oh, by all that's beautiful! if ever I fall in love (that is to say seriously,) it will certainly be with a nun.'

'Abroad they are truly enchanting creatures,' interrupted Lionhart, 'I remember one – '

'Aye, was not there one,' cried the Major, interrupting him in his turn, 'who fell in love with Lord Strathallan, and rode along the lines, or did something extraordinary; faith I don't remember it very well now, but I know at the time I heard something of such a story.'

'Nor I neither,' said Lionhart, 'I was not upon the spot, and I believe it was all nonsense; though, to be sure, when I last was out I heard the great lord say – '

'No, by Jove,' cried the Major, 'it was a great lady.'

'No, but I mean the great lord would not have allowed such a thing, nor Sir John either, for it was in his time I think.'

'No, but the great lord could not help a lady's falling in love.'

'No, but give me leave to tell you my dear Major – '

'And give me leave to tell you, my dear Captain Lionhart – '

'All I know is that – '

'And all I know is that – '

While these two heroes were growing every moment warmer and warmer, in a dispute of which it was impossible to foresee / the conclusion, as each declared himself equally ignorant upon the subject, and its being necessarily carried on in an undertone, did not seem in the least to lessen its vehemence. Arbella, who had lent a most curious and attentive ear to it, affected to be solely engaged in bewailing the loss of her 'dear Zulistein,'[105] a performer who was not among those at Sir Harold's, and who, of course, 'transcended all who were present.'

While endeavouring to make the Major remark how wholly she was engrossed by this important loss, she did not advert to the ungenerous use her friend Miss Hautenville was making, during the intervals that were not devoted to offering incense to Lady Strathallan, of her affected exclamations and exaggerated expressions of regret. 'Hem, hem – of course Miss Ferrars means nothing, but it is really shocking to hear any one talk of a public performer in the manner she does of this Zulistein; and to hear her praise his excellence on the German flute; his fine *embouchure;*[106] his brilliant execution. One would really almost imagine – hem, hem – and they say she has his picture in a ring; and last, winter she declared she would go on her knees only to persuade Lord Torrendale to take tickets for his benefit. She ought to be spoken to about it; yet I am persuaded it is only her silly way: she is always 'distracted' (as she calls it) about any public person she admires. One should never judge harshly of a young person, but really, hem, hem – '

While Miss Hautenville was thus kindly and intelligibly giving her opinion of poor Arbella's behaviour, a commanding hush from some of the female amateurs startled her into unwilling silence. The Signora Lorenzina was going to favor them with a 'scena' out of Mitridate.[107] The noble air of the Italian, her deep commanding tones in the song, and clear, full, distinct utterance in the recitative, contrasted most unfavorably with the performance of Miss Helena De Courcy, who, blushing, trembling, and giving every apparent sign of unwillingness, was next led to the instrument, / and after much entreaty was at length prevailed upon,

> In low sweet tones to sing,
> Her unintelligible song.[108]

The connoisseurs cried bravo; but whether it was an Italian song Englished, or an English song Italianized, they seemed among themselves at a loss to determine.

'Charming,' cried Lionhart, 'that's Robin Adair.'

'Nonsense,' said the Major, 'you are always thinking of Robin Adair; don't you perceive its a little Venetian Canzonet? Gad there's nothing I like so much in the world as the Venetian music.'

'Excuse me sir,' said Miss Hautenville, who had been listening very attentively on the other side, 'I certainly coincide with your opinion, when the piece is Italian, but this happens to be a little Fench air, from the opera of Gretry's.'

'tis an air of Mozart's,' observed Miss De Courcy, rising with great solemnity, 'and the words are German, from the Zauberflôte.'[109]

'I thought so all the time,' resumed Lionhart, 'I am sure I heard it near a village where we bivouacked when – '

'Aye, Lionhart can tell you about Holland and Spain too, and all the rest of it,' said Major O'Hara, looking ruefully at his friend in humble acknowledgment, how far he surpassed him in knowledge; but Lionhart, who was of all men the last to speak of his travels, had already checked himself, and seemed to have perfectly lost all inclination to tell 'the rest of it.' The Major, however, appeared to be seized with an inclination to show off his friend; and whispered Miss De Courcy, to 'ask him about the beautiful nun of the convent of Santa Fé.'

Captain Lionhart was at first very modest, but he at length suffered himself to be persuaded. 'There was a convent that we were obliged to pass through,' he said, 'and at first we thought we should see nothing of the nuns, for they pretended to be afraid of us; but afterwards we saw them, and – ' /

'You liked them very much,' interrupted Alcæus.

'Yes, they liked us.'

'And one of them was particularly fond of Lionhart's pretty face,' added the Major, in a whisper, between laughing and earnest; 'Lionhart, tell Miss De Courcy the story of the perfuming box, or I'll tell it.'

'Oh, no nonsense – I won't allow that,' cried the Captain, with well-timed discretion. 'You know I told you they liked us all, and the old nuns gave us permission to kiss their hands through the grate. To be sure we made it a condition that the young ones should do us the same favor; and, by Jove,' continued Lionhart, roused by the subject from his usual taciturnity, 'I never saw so many beautiful hands, as I did that day: there was one I never saw equalled, but – but by that which is at this moment so gracefully beating time' (turning to the unconscious Clara, who had again become totally absorbed in the performance.) 'And I took a vow that I never would marry till I met with a face to match that hand.'

'Well done, Lionhart,' cried Major O'Hara, laughing, 'and a fortune, I suppose, to match that face.'

'And a mind,' added Alcæus, 'to match that fortune.'

'A mind!' repeated the Major, and began to whistle.

'The Spanish women have all white hands and fine eyes,' resumed Lionhart; 'I remember observing so to a beautiful Spanish woman, who once told me – '

'Captain Lionhart,' interrupted the impatient Alcæus, 'Did a beautiful Spanish woman ever tell you to let somebody speak besides yourself?'

Lionhart, who had been with the greatest difficulty induced to depart from his usual military conciseness, was silenced; and actually started at this unprecedented accusation; but '*the Shears*,' who had been fretting during the whole of his Spanish narration, on perceiving the moment to be irrecoverably gone, in which he could have slipt in a good thing, or what he imagined was a good thing, did not think it the less founded. /

'There, I told you,' said Major O'Hara to Miss De Courcy, 'if you wished to please Lionhart, you must ask him for the story of the nun of Santa Fe.'

'If I wished to please Captain Lionhart!' repeated Helen. 'Really the gentlemen now take it upon rather an extraordinary tone.'

'Faith Madam,' said the Major, 'It is you ladies, I think, who give the key note, and then quarrel with us for singing the tune.'

The sharpness of this dialogue was interrupted by Sir Harold's proposing the party should adjourn, for refreshment, into the gardens, where he had had seats placed and the whole illuminated for that purpose. This nocturnal promenade, and the *fête champetre*, was an unexpected addition to the pleasures of the evening; but had been secretly longed for by many of the younger part of the company, who finding the heat of the concert room oppressive, had ventured to peep through the falling draperies of the window curtains, and to wish that the glass, which, reaching to the ground gave a perfect moonlight view of the scenery beyond, might be no longer interposed between them and a balmy summer ramble. Greatly was the agreeable effect then heightened, by the surprise, when a thousand lights were perceived to start up, as if by magic, among the trees, and every gentleman, gaily offering an arm to his fair one, proposed to conduct her through this luxuriant wilderness of sweets. Alcæus was ready with a compliment to the Baronet upon the tasteful disposition of his decoration; which he compared to the oriental fairyism of Vauxhall. 'If in aught I have succeeded,' said Sir Harold, turning with a melancholy smile to Matilda, 'your approbation must pay me for what your taste alone suggested. On your first visit to this scene, in my company, you observed how susceptible its savage wildness, its picturesque rocks, its natural cascades, were of having their beauty heightened to the magic of romance, by the calm of night and the effect of lights judiciously disposed among them; and while you still deign to embalm by your presence the air around, it is indeed / a Paradise. Oh that you would descend to be the Houri, and reign for ever there!'

'No, my dear whimsical Nourjahad,[110] we are not fond enough of seclusion,' interrupted Mrs. Melbourne, perceiving how much her daughter was distrest; 'you shall not bribe us even with your feast of tulips, to grace with the constant presence of such divinities, the residence of a voluntary Anchorite; come a little more among us, and we will see if we cannot invent something equally good, to make it worth your while to stay.'

Lord and Lady Strathallan who had with difficulty from complaisance to Sir Harold, prolonged their stay a little after the entrance of the hated O'Hara, now seized this opportunity to take leave; but Sir Harold reminded them of the earliness of the time, which, though the performance had lasted nearly three hours, was still hardly ten, and insisted on knowing her Ladyship's opinion of his arrangements.

Flattered in her vanity, Lady Strathallan took Miss Melbourne's arm, and while giving her fairly to understand that she ascribed the honors of the fête to herself, continued a long and desultory dissertation upon the unreasonableness of pride, which was only, at length, interrupted by an exclamation of 'My God! where is Lord Strathallan?' Matilda started – she had caught Sir Harold's eagle glance, as it was fixed upon them the only time, during the evening, that Strathallan had addressed her. She remembered his threat that he 'waited his rival at the Rocks;' was it to immolate him there, after having confirmed his mad suspicions, by observing them in the very scene, which had beheld the commencement of their, then blameless love. – Sir Harold, having succeeded in hurrying his guests from the house, had taken the opportunity of drawing Strathallan into particular conversation, and led him imperceptibly from the cheerful and ornamented parts of the grounds, to one of their most solitary and savage recesses.

Lady Strathallan, to account for her apparent uneasiness, at length confessed her fears lest he should by any chance find himself one / moment alone with Sir Harold, whose violence and caprices were now but too generally acknowledged. Alas! she need not have apologized to Matilda, who more than shared her feelings: a heavy sickness seemed coming over her; every object swam before her eyes, and the lights, the cheerful hum of voices, instead of reviving her, seemed in varied, indistinct, but all terrible sounds to murmur forth the fate of Strathallan. Trembling like a leaf, she was obliged to accept the support of Lady Strathallan to one of the arbours, prepared for the reception of the company. Ignorant that the anxiety of Matilda proceeded from a similar cause with her own; she, with the same insensible, unmoved, illuminated countenance with which she had expressed her solicitude respecting her husband, ran over some exaggerated demonstrations of uneasiness on Miss Melbourne's account. Matilda's distress was not of a nature to admit relief from such discourses. Hers was not a guilty perturbation! The fear of having to answer for *his* death, over whose days, though no longer to be devoted to her, she would willingly have watched, with the generous solicitude of the purest friendship, was what pressed upon her heart with all the nameless horrors of unutterable apprehension. Meantime Sir Harold led his fearless companion through briery ways, and over precipitous paths, now giving him his assistance, now beckoning him to follow which Strathallan did, with a mixture of wonder, curiosity, and interest, as if he really imagined his conductor one of those wandering creations of the element, that rise and disappear, lure, promise, and destroy. At length he had ascended, with incredible swiftness, the highest point of the rock, that overhung the favorite sylvan stream. And here Strathallan perceived, for the first time, that Sir Harold was armed, who suddenly stopping, and taking out a case of pistols, stood for several moments in a musing manner, pointing them first at the tree that was opposite to them, then to the ground. Strathallan enquired if he might know the reason of such preparations. 'I want to bring down a bird,' Sir Harold murmured / in return, 'a bird, bright and beautiful – didst thou mark it, Strathallan? It perches on that tree, and kills me with its note; for its note is of love and happiness; light, life, and joy, roll in floods from its sparkling eye, and reproach my desolate breast. It rises in its pride, it shakes its radiant plumage to the air; but I see its eye droop, I hear the whirring of its flagging, fluttering wing. Its glory is past – it falls, it falls, it falls. Dost thou know its name, Strathallan? the bird that is unmatched in the world; the bird that has its bed among spices, and its tomb in the city of the sun; it has an English name too, but I cannot name it – the sound of it grates harsh upon my ear – you must help me to quell his youthful pride. Strathallan, that weapon is yours.'

Lord Strathallan could not doubt of the intentions of Sir Harold, from the whole tenor of this wild address; but deeming it worse than weakness to oppose his life against that of a madman, he contented himself with wrenching the pistols from his hands, and throwing them over the cliff, told him that another time, and when he should be more calm, he would give him whatever satisfaction he might chuse to demand; but at the same time, asked him what offence he had committed that could only be expiated with his life. 'What offence that, as a man of honor – '

Sir Harold started and shuddered at the word – 'honor!' 'I knew her once and adored her; but she has fled my abode. She said, after a bloody sacrifice, she would return to my house. 'Twas completed – but, as in mockery, she left me only guilt in her stead.'

'I must know my crime,' repeated Strathallan, who only saw in this exclamation a new evasion.

'You love Matilda,' cried Sir Harold, his voice trembling, with increased fury; 'nay deny it not – to-night the lynx lent me her eye. Something has always stept in between me and my gentle love, and the last was your glance of fire. I must quench it in blood, and then I shall be happy. Strathallan, thy sun must set in darkness. Survey this blasted / oak: 'tis thus that proud form must be laid low. Cast thine eyes on that withered plant: 'tis thus those bright locks must inglorious kiss the dust. Dost thou not fear my power? Knowest thou not that jealousy is cruel as the grave?'

Strathallan looked at him in disdainful silence; 'Nay, turn not on me those beautiful eyes of mingled scorn and pity. Dost thou not think me born to bear their glance. Strathallan, I was once like thee. Bright, proud, and prosperous, in fearless innocence, I began my glorious course – I looked up to a partial world, and challenged its applause; but my day was short – a dark fiend rushed across my path, and bade the clouds of sorrow compass round it, but its end shall not be unmarked.'

Rushing on the unguarded youth, he attempted to throw him from the rock into the stream below, but Strathallan, eluding his violence, extricated himself, with a trifling effort from his grasp; and equally anxious to preserve himself, and the unhappy Sir Harold, from the effect of such fatal rashness, he even condescended to expostulate with him, and to represent to him, the too late repentance that would follow a violence that only exposed his own weakness, and endangered the reputation of another. Sir Harold smiled disdainfully in his turn. 'Vain temporizing wretch; Dost thou think by once, by twice foiling my attempt thou hast deprived me of the power to harm thee? We are alone; none but the howling night-winds hear our parley; and here I swear, that Harold and Strathallan shall not descend this cliff in safety together. Cast away then all thoughts of mercy, for thou art happy, and the happy are my enemies; but ask for death, and I will give it in whatever form thou wilt. The death of the wasting fire; the death of the running stream: chuse, for thou art surrounded by its dangers. It frowns from the pointed rock; it yawns from the gulph below; it trembles on the moon-beam of the lucid wave. Speak quickly, which death shall be thine?'

While Sir Harold hurried over this awful interrogatory with a rapidity which formed / the most striking contrast with the calm determination that appeared in his death-pale countenance, Strathallan, unmoved by the circumstances of the scene, turned to the unhappy being, with whom, in night and solitude he held this fearful colloquy, and coolly said, 'Do you think by threats like these to detach me from a pursuit my heart was engaged in, if it indeed harboured a design so base? Mistaken man! look at that angel purity, which to suspect is to question the existence of virtue's self; you render her only justice in wholly acquitting me: but if warped judgment, or unhappy passion, so far blind you, as to make you still capable of harbouring suspicions injurious to my honour, remember, that the hour in which you dare me to a contest, you inflict a wound in HER peace, who but for you might have ever lived happy as she is virtuous. Respect, respect her spotless fame; not for my own life, it is valueless, but for Miss Melbourne's sake I descend to – .'

'Yet still you love her,' resumed the half convinced Sir Harold.

'As mortals love a dear and sainted spirit; not otherwise, as I hope for heaven,' replied the enthusiastic Strathallan, while the ingenuous fire which glowed in his countenance, ever the faithful interpreter of the feelings of his heart, carried evidence resistless as persuasion, convincing as truth. But conviction here was misery, and Sir Harold once more forced to ascribe to himself alone, the indifference and terror of Matilda, seemed unable to bear the added pang that consciousness inflicted on his heart. 'I am then alone the wretched one,' he said, 'and it is fitting that the wretched should suffer.'

Taking advantage of a moment in which he fancied Strathallan's eye turned from him, he now turned all his rage upon himself, and desperately attempted to cast himself from the top of the rock; but Strathallan, darting forward with the swiftness of lightning, succeeded in preventing his purpose. The unhappy man struggled, with a strength increased by his distemper, but Strathallan never letting go his hold, by prevailing and superior force succeeded, at length, in mastering / him, and dragging him, almost by violence, from the fatal spot. Indeed, Sir Harold was not long able to contend with him; exhausted by the violence of the exertion he had made, the superhuman strength with which he had seemed for a moment to be endued, soon fled from his languid and wearied frame; and the change, which had taken from his powers of resistance, seemed to have restored those of recollection. He already repented of his former transport, and bitterly reproached himself with having at once violated the rights of hospitality, and injured her in the opinion of others, for whose peace and security he would at any time have sacrificed his own. 'Oh! pardon me, thou brightest, bravest, thou only worthy of her,' he said, turning his moist eyes, full of the trembling effulgence of gratitude and recovered reason upon his preserver; 'I was not always the wretch I seem to you; even now the acts of outrage upon which my fatal transports force me, are at variance with my nature, and therefore tears my frame with frantic violence. But erring or collected, I must be a wretch indeed, if I ever again attempted aught against my deliverer.'

Looking on him with the mild pity of some superior being, whose breast overflows with compassion, unmixed with frailty, for the wanderings of a mortal heart, the gentle Strathallan caught his hand, and hurried him from the rock; then exerting all his soul-subduing powers to compose the agitated mind of the unhappy sufferer, he succeeded at length, at once, in calming his fears for others, and in reconciling him to himself.

Strathallan was, of all men, the most persuasive with the least art; for with him, the power of persuasion had its rise in sensibility, and it was the corresponding flow of his natural tenderness alone, that lent to his arguments their prevailing force. With that happy power, which he so eminently possessed, of placing himself in the circumstances, of actually throwing himself into the soul, and assuming for a moment, the sentiments of the person he addressed; he had almost unconsciously suited the language of his expostulations to the frame of mind of his unhappy / auditor, so that the victory he gained must have long before been complete, could any thing but passion's voice have been listened to by Sir Harold. They turned into a narrow walk which led to the more cultivated part of the gardens; the moon, which had looked down upon them a few moments before, in unclouded lustre, was now only visible through the dark trees which on each side lined their walk, and whose leaves were alternately visible and obscured, as the lines of quivering radiance were withdrawn, or streamed upon them. 'Mark that pale orb,' said Sir Harold, with an accent solemn and emphatic, 'soon shall it set behind those distant hills! 'tis thus my course is near run out; thus time is setting with me: but time itself shall be no more,' 'ere I forget the obligations of this night.'

Strathallan looked at him in pleased acknowledgment; a smile of inexpressible sweetness and benignity hovered on his lips; he saw it was but to touch the string of gratitude, and his wayward and misguided companion became calm as infant innocence, tractable as the new shorn lamb, to the direction of its feeder.

It was at the moment that Lady Strathallan, however disposed to maintain a dignified calmness, had discovered she must renounce, at least in the eyes of Matilda, the character of a wife of exquisite sensibility, or keep up to the uneasiness she had at first expressed respecting the disappearance, and long-protracted stay of her husband and Sir Harold together, that they entered the bower arm in arm, where those two ladies and many others were assembled, and Matilda beheld Strathallan safe, as her wishes had hardly dared to represent him; his countenance yet glowing with his recent exertion; and the consciousness of having rescued a fellow creature from destruction, still imparting its warm and delicious pulsation to his heart. Matilda would not venture to raise her eyes, nor give a second look, lest that look might unconsciously convey too much expression; while Lady Strathallan, determined not to be deficient in feeling, started up and embraced him, lamenting, at the same time, his absence, in a / regular mechanical tone, and describing how dull every pleasure had been in which he had not participated. Strathallan rallied her anxiety and the over-rated solicitude she expressed for his society, in such an agreeable manner as still increased, by the versatile gaiety he could at moments assume, the soft impression, which the winning tenderness of his address never failed to excite in his favor.

'Sir Harold wished to shew me,' he said, a fine effect of moon-light upon the great cascade, and after that we began to talk of gardening and planting, and the modern improvements from Kent to *Capability Brown*,[111] 'till we forgot – no, we could not forget there were ladies in the world; but we had the modesty, or the negligence to think that it was impossible we could be missed by them.'

This, Lady Strathallan thought but an indifferent excuse for not making her the exclusive object of his attention in public. She however thought proper to take the apology as it was meant; and whether from caprice, vanity, or to excite the envy of the other despairing belles during the short time she remained in the gardens, directed her sole attention to her amiable husband; catechizing him most minutely, and apparently forgetting the whole world, to be absorbed in exclusive admiration of him alone. This did not last long: while the rest of the company were attending to a beautiful piece performed upon wind instruments, whose responsive sounds by 'distance made more sweet,' floated upon the ear, with charms heightened by the calm around, and soft moonlight scenery, a faint cry attracted the attention to Sir Harold. Exhausted by the violence of his previous emotions, he had sunk down in a fainting fit, in the very moment that, surrounded by social pleasure and festivity, he had seemed most anxious in promoting it. All thoughts of farther gaiety was in an instant given over, and all were eager to administer assistance to the unhappy Baronet. None but Strathallan could guess the cause of his sudden illness; but Matilda, who heard from the clock of the Chapel adjoining the hermitage of the Rocks, the still dreaded notice of midnight, / given, guessed another, which had not ever occurred to his imagination.

With that habitual tenderness for her cousin, which the assurance of Strathallan's safety had revived in its wonted force, she flew to his side; but the odoriferous waters she sprinkled over him, and all the efforts of the surrounding attendants, that had been called at the alarm of their master's danger, were, for some moments, unequal to rouse him. Heart-sick with gaieties, that so ill accorded with her terror and anxiety, every guest seemed importunate – the music seemed a dirge that announced, in mournful strains, his fast approaching fate. She at length succeeded in having him removed to the saloon. Then he opened his eyes, and gazing wildly around, he soon fixed them towards one particular spot, exclaiming 'There, there! have me removed there; tis only there I can breathe – sweet soul, did I forget thee? – but thou pursuest me amid the entrancements of pleasure, and remindest me I am no longer my own.' He seemed distrest by the officious glances and whispers of those visitors, who still remained; and calling Matilda near him he caught her hand – 'Angelic sweetness, tis thine alone to witness, thine to console agonies like mine.'

The company had by this time dispersed, and Sir Harold was left alone with Mrs. Melbourne's party; and Mrs. Carlyle, the housekeeper who had hastened in, at the first alarm. That respectable woman appeared rather disturbed than relieved by Matilda's presence, and prolonged stay; 'heaven's, Miss!' said she, 'you should leave my master to me, when he is in these fits and takings. It is not for you to conduct him to *that* room.

However desirous of asking an explanation of the strange mystery, which grew every day more perplexing, Matilda was too much concerned about her cousin's actual state, and too anxious too see him restored to tranquility, to question the good woman farther: and perceiving that he was indeed in safe hands, and with one who, from long habit and experience, knew how to soothe and manage his distemper better even than she could / do, she yielded to her mother's entreaties that they should retire; but before they withdrew, she received an assurance from Sir Harold, which amply rewarded her for the forbearance she had practised; grasping her hand, he whispered in a hoarse and hurried voice; 'Be satisfied, your conduct has calmed my doubts – subdued my rage. Neither the dagger that was suspended on high, nor the abyss that opened beneath his feet, any longer shall harm him. The spell is taken off, or rather changed into a talisman of safety; no evil, no danger, by air, fire, or flood, shall, in future, have power to reach the charmed life of Strathallan.'

CHAPTER XIII.

Sing, gentle maid, reform my breast,
And soften every care,
So shall I be some moments blest,
And easy in despair.
The power of Orpheus lives in you,
You can the passions of my soul subdue,
And calm the lions and the tigers there.

LADY M. W. MONTAGUE.[112]

Six weeks had now elapsed since his duel, and Spencer was still a prisoner at Mrs. Stockwell's; a voluntary one it should appear; for every symptom of illness, and suffering, had left him; and he seemed to have recovered every thing of his former self, but beauty; he at length condescended to rejoin the society at Woodlands. The meeting between him and Arbella was, on her part, sufficiently tender. Resolved to / shew, that no personal change could effect an abatement in her sentiments, she ran into the opposite extreme, and professed, almost unasked, an ardour of affection, that seemed only to revive in his weak bosom the fluttering sparks of vanity, even at a moment when he ought to have been aware, that gratitude would have been a more becoming sensation. This observation was one, however, which his mistress would hardly make, even to herself; and though she was rather surprized and mortified at an occasional constraint and reserve he assumed, she was content to asscribe a good deal of the remissness of her 'Poor wounded hussar,' as she tenderly called him, to the languor of confinement and the fretfulness of recent mortification; and to trust to time and favourable circumstances for the rest.

From the time his brother shewed decided symptoms of amendment, Strathallan had become rather anxious to leave a scene, towards which he had been only drawn by the claims of a duty he considered as indispensable; but which he would otherwise have carefully avoided visiting, at least till Mrs. Melbourne and Matilda had quitted it; but here; as usual, Lady Strathallan's prevailing tastes interfered. A passion for field-sports, which had been checked, not eradicated, during the lifetime of her father, now she was possessed of consequence and independence, broke out with boundless extravagance. She was at the head of a certain set of dashers, who affected to give the *ton*, and to lead, on every occasion, in the county; and she found so much delight in the glades and copses of Woodlands, that it seemed now as hopeless a task to attempt to detach her from them, as it would have appeared, a short time before, to try to substitute them for the more elegant amusements of a town life. Of Matilda, she had no fear, and she was right. Strathallan, as the husband of another, had become, to a mind regulated like her's, a different being; and that consciousness not only influenced her feelings, but diffused itself over every circumstance of her countenance, manner, and behaviour. Her's was not that constrained and obvious coldness, more flattering, / perhaps, than the most marked partiality; as it points out, in its fullest extent, how dangerous the object must be, that is avoided with such painful circumspection. It was rather that easy air of noble self-possession, which shews passion to be annihilated; or, if a spark of it exist, to be so entirely merged in principle, as to have changed its nature; and only to give life and energy to the determinations of virtue. The bleeding struggles it had cost that noble and tender heart to arrive at the point where weakness ceased, and perfection took its date, was not the question; it was attained, and carried with it a consciousness of happiness, which well repaid every previous effort to arrive at it. Above the disingenuousness of wishing to be regretted, where she could no longer, with innocence, be beloved; Matilda denied herself the most harmless exertion of her powers of pleasing, as much as she would have avoided the most open and avowed encouragement. She saw the wounds of his heart were not sufficiently healed to make it safe to accord him that friendship, he had once ventured to demand; and every thing that could tempt him to recal the charms of an early tenderness, she considered as an intrusion upon the rights of another. All those ingenuous sallies that form the charm of conversation, by marking the free reciprocation of sentiment congenial to both; the interchange of thought, the mutual glance of received and communicated pleasure, all that the prudish and censorious might deem bordering on the 'flirting;' or the coarse-minded and ignorant, might sneeringly term sentimental and Platonic; in short, all that Lady Strathallan might not herself have dictated, or heard, (had she formed a third) with pleasure, was rigidly banished from their conversation. That was, indeed, the standard; and it was surely the safest she could have chosen; to which Miss Melbourne, when in company with Lord Strathallan, referred every look, word, and action.

There was one circumstance, of which, before he quitted the country, Strathallan would gladly have informed himself. Had Miss Melbourne, at length, given Sir Harold / any right to resent the supposed admiration or attention of others? or was his late conduct to be attributed solely to one of those starts of blind fury to which he often so unhappily yielded himself? Matilda was the last person from whom Strathallan could expect the least elucidation of this painful secret. Her manner was the most remote from that which invites to confidence. The declining state of Sir Harold's health (which had suffered severely since his last attack at the fête) was the real reason that induced her to bestow more time on him than formerly. The suspension of his concerts and splendid entertainments, had driven away those guests that afforded at least a temporary diversion to the course of his mournful thoughts; and, in this interval, he felt the incalculable advantages of the attentions of a relative such as Matilda. In the melting pathos of her voice, when she sung, her unhappy cousin seemed to find his only respite from suffering. His passion for her vocal talent every day increased. In it he found that very soul he had vainly sought for, in the most brilliant exertions of his paid performers. His taste for his former amusements, however, revived with

returning health; and the Baronet's hospitable mansion became again a scene of perpetual noise, if not of perfect harmony. Vain was it to hope to catch any other sounds
than those of harps and pianos, under the hands of the tuner or performer; or the still
more difficult exertions of vocal ability, running through the difficult evolutions of
musical science, previous to the renewal of the anticipated exhibitions. From these
Matilda promised herself but little pleasure; and, as for Clara, nothing could tempt
her to venture into a mixed company again. More fondly wedded than ever to the
even tenor of her calm and tranquil life, she returned to it, with renewed relish; even

As a child, when scaring sounds molest,
Clings close and closer to the mother's breast.[113]

However unwilling to share in Sir Harold's amusements, his amiable relatives continued to give him proofs of a sincere and tender / participation in his sufferings;
that best cordial to the neglected and miserable. These attentions now became the
more necessary, as Sir Harold, by a sudden start of caprice, most unexpectedly, at once
deprived himself of any advantage, or amusement, he might gain from the abilities, or
exertions, of those who had so long awaited his orders.

It happened one morning, that Mrs. Melbourne and her daughter called so early
that Sir Harold was not yet risen. Anxious to know how he had passed the night, they
resolved to stay till he should make his appearance in the music room. Here, Mrs.
Melbourne sat, too soon absorbed in painful reflection; while Matilda, to prevent
the intrusion of the same unwelcome visitant, found employment for herself, in looking over some of the many new musical publications, that were regularly sent down,
on their first appearance in London. Impatient for the moment of seeing her cousin,
and much wondering that he still could sleep, amidst the noise and bustle excited
through the house, by the reigning heroes and heroines, Matilda, who had often been
unable to suppress a smile at the airs of supreme importance, their supposed professional excellence induced them to assume, though those illustrious personages were
this morning more than usually noisy, in asserting their claim to exclusive attention.
The sound of bells ringing, and servants running different ways, to obey various and
contradictory orders, was only interrupted by that of some sharp reprimand from an
offended Signora, or some hurrying exhortation from a superior to an inferior domestic, to redouble the diligence with which he executed her commands. – Chocolate for
the Signor Marionelli; raw eggs for the Signora Lorenzina; Jack tell the groom to ride
without delay to S – , and tell Wyerby the musical instrument maker, if he does not
send Signor Trombone his trumpet, by this evening, he will never pay him a farthing;
'One farthing! not one maravedi; tell him I will send him to one twenty million of
Diavalones,' cried the Signor at the stair-head; who deemed his orders had not been
enforced with sufficient energy. /

As Matilda sat, immersed in the difficulties of some figured music, which she had
imposed upon herself the task of decyphering, she was startled by the entrance of
Signor Cavatina, one of the principal performers, who, engrossed in his own importance, strutted in, without immediately perceiving the modest form, which bent over
a music-desk at the other extremity of the room; he was in his morning dishabille,
a short flannel jacket, which made him appear like a hair-dresser, or gentleman's
gentleman, in his worst attire; but this did not diminish in the smallest degree his self-

complacency, and advancing to the glass, in the attitude of a *heros de theatre*, he began in the character of Tridates,[114] a passage in one of his best bravura songs, studying, as he went along, the various distortions, and gesticulations, which he thought gave it more force and pathos, before the faithful mirror; as he turned round at the conclusion, like a peacock in a transport of self-admiration, he, for the first time, perceived the two ladies; but his confusion, if he was likely to feel any at the discovery, was prevented by the sudden entrance of his beloved friend Signora Lorenzina; who, with dishevelled hair, and sobbing, exclaimed, 'dis is de last l'ultima volta I vil trust myself in de house of one English boor; I did tink he was a gentleman; *homme comme il faut;* but he is von Englishman; von Hottentot: I did but tell him, I should have Burgundy at my luncheon, as well as my supper and dinner; and dat my servants shoud have same, and he fly in von rage, put me in fear of my life; oh! he is von Englishman, von Hottentot;' then turning to Matilda, as if to answer the expression of surprize and curiosity, painted on her countenance at this representation of her cousin's conduct; 'Why Miss,' continued Lorenzina, who, though Sir Harold gave a bad account of her temper, was a pretty delicate looking little woman, with a soft voice, and insinuating address, 'I am not unreasonable; but yesterday, at dinner, he trow von glass of wine in my face; von glass of wine, and den he shake his fist at me, as if he tink to beat me: I can't bear such insults as dat; I cannot, you know, dear Miss.' /

'*Corpo di Bacco,*' cried Signor Martilino, who at that moment entered the room, with the air of a Grand Vizier, 'dere is no living vid dis man, he kick a me down stairs, because I simply tell him he should new lay his floors; and put oder cielings, as dese rooms have now an echo dat is unfit for music.'

'*Pazzo matto,*' cried Cavatina, 'I guessed he was growing so de tother day, when I was teaching him de violincello; an ungrateful wretch; I who did teach him de taste, de emphasis, de accent, de expression. When I take him in hand, he no able to draw out one sound, and every one know dat he sing like one table; yet when I make him de most reasonable request, of one carriage to go over these rough English roads, he,' – How long this harangue might have continued is uncertain, had it not suddenly been cut short by the appearance of the Signora Marionelli, whose presence was alone wanted to fill up the chorus of complaints. 'Where are my people?' she cried, 'dis instant I take my departure; I have had de eclaircissement with Sir Harold; I ask him only five thousand pound for my residence for two months; I might have had six from my Lord Flauto's; he treats me as one extravagant, one ingrate.'

Here these literally enraged musicians began all talking together, comparing their ill-treatment, and recapitulating their wrongs in the shrillest tones of ultramontane eloquence, till the ladies, quite terrified by the unusual din, were meditating a hasty retreat, when it was prevented by Sir Harold, in boots, and armed with his whip, as if he was prepared for riding; 'furies, vampires, harpies!' he exclaimed; 'you prey upon me, you make my house your den, and when I think to satisfy you liberally, you fill it with murmurs, and discontent.' Not satisfied with these words, he accompanied them with actions, and flourished the little instrument in his hand, with such grace and effect, that the affrighted musicians did not find harps, or pianos, a sufficient screen, but gladly took refuge in a different apartment. The sight of Matilda in an instant calmed his rage; not sooner did the lion crouch to / Una, than Sir Harold to this lovely maid: beneath her 'mild reproving eye,' gentleness and reason instantly returned:[115] he even seemed ashamed of his late excess, into which he declared he had been surprised, by finding that his ill-judged munificence, had only drawn on him the most extravagant proposals, and insolent demands. With the advice of his more judicious friends, he now soon came to a moderate and reasonable agreement, with these haughty and dangerous gentry; in which they were obliged to own, that the Baronet had treated them, on the whole, very handsomely. The Rocks were thus cleared of their presence, and became once more a pleasing solitude; but it required weeks to restore every thing to its former order, and repair the waste and confusion caused by the ruinous residence of of the heroes and nymphes D'Opéra.

END OF VOL. III.

STRATHALLAN.

BY
ALICIA LEFANU,

GRAND-DAUGHTER TO THE LATE THOMAS SHERIDAN, M.A.

IN FOUR VOLUMES.

VOL. IV.

Quando scende in nobil petto
E compagno un dolce affetto
Non rivale alla virtù:
Respirate, alme felici
E vi siano i Numi amici
Quanto avverso il ciel vi fù.
METASTASIO. – DEMETRIO.[1]

London:
PRINTED FOR SHERWOOD, NEELY, AND JONES,
PATERNOSTER-ROW.
1816. /

CHAPTER I.

Ah! perdona at primo affetto,
Quest' accento sconsigliato,
Colpa fu del labbro usato,
A chimarti ognor così.

Metastasio. La Clemenza di Tito.[2]

'Why need you venture your health and your life in that infected air, amidst that mingled mass of houses and graves called a great city; surrounded by the smoke and pestilent vapours of every different trade and manufactory; when, here, you can have leisure, independence, solitude, or society as you will?'

Such was Sowerby's abrupt exclamation, on Mrs. Melbourne's first hinting the necessity of her returning to London. He then / proceeded, 'You know that pretty little box called Woodbine Lodge, which you admired so much for its situation: it is mine, I lent it to young Mendlesham, who is just quitting it; so that I can let you have it, and I am sure if you would take it, it would be a blessed exchange. I obliged him with it, because his father was an old chum of mine, and I never ceased fretting, and wishing him out of it from the moment he got in it. He used it as a hunting lodge, but it would not be too small for two ladies; and there Matilda might have her harp, and you might have your books and drawings; it is only a walk across the park, so that I should be near enough sometimes to drop in upon you, and forget, in your society, the miserable forlorn condition of solitary man.'

Mrs. Melbourne easily saw into Sowerby's real motive for wishing her and Matilda to give up London; which was, by fixing them near him, to secure some compensation for the loss of Clara's society, whom he had vainly hoped to induce to live with him. The gentle nun, now her health was reestablished, considered every hour she spent away from her convent as a crime; and Sowerby saw himself about to be deprived, at once, of the little female society that had chased away the gloom from his solitary hearth, just as he began to acquire a taste for its charms. Could Mrs. Melbourne behold this constant and active friend of her adversity sinking under the gloom and depression induced by desertion and disappointment? She read his feelings; and, without taking counsel with any one, or communicating the conflicts that rent her heart, she, with unpretending greatness at once made her election. ' 'Tis but one pang more,' she said, 'and surely I who have endured so many may easily learn to bear it.'

To fix herself in the neighbourhood of the Rocks was to tear open the wounds of her widowed heart; yet still, the idea of its being a sacrifice, a sacrifice too for a man, whom it was impossible a mind perhaps, perhaps, to a degree of artificial refinement, could regard with partiality, added, perhaps, a secret charm to her resolution, in the opinion / of a woman firm and energetic in all her decisions as Mrs. Melbourne. However defective in manner, his late conduct had evinced the sterling goodness of his heart. To make the widow and child of his friend forget, in his attentions, the loss they had sustained, seemed the chief object of his life; and a remembrance of Melbourne, that shone in almost every word he addressed them, and in his most indifferent actions, imparted to them an interest that a more courteous and polished deportment might have failed to inspire. These circumstances Mrs. Melbourne represented to Sir Harold in the communication she made to him respecting her wish to give up the house in town. To speak of the obligations of friendship and gratitude was to speak conviction to the amiable Baronet. He highly approved of the motives that determined her conduct. And as for Mr. Sowerby, when once he had arranged her removal, he was so anxious to secure the house for her, and seemed so eager to prevent his friend Mendlesham from changing his mind, that he might have appeared to an indifferent observer, already weary of the long abode she had made at his own. Clara entreated she might have every moment of the company of her friends till the hour arrived for her departure; but Sowerby would have hurried them immediately into the new house, though he confessed himself it was in want of some repairs; and when they objected to the smell of paint, or the feel of damp mortar, flew into as great a passion with the weakness and fastidiousness of the sex, as if they had proposed the most unreasonable objection in the world.

Mrs. Melbourne good-humouredly rallied him on his impatience to turn them away; 'I understand your friend,' said she, 'made a kennel of every room in the house. You will not surely have the inhumanity to move us 'till those holes are stopped up that his canine favorites gnawed through the doors, or rather 'till you have put up new ones.'

'There are no holes,' muttered Sowerby, and, when obliged to confess there were, he still would not allow it as a sufficient reason for delay. 'The doors are mended, the / shutters are fast, the rooms are painted, the paint is dry, there are no dogs, and now will you take possession?' Who would have imagined that this obliging requisition was only the singular manner in which this mixture of misanthropy and benevolence endeavoured to secure the company of two most valuable women, whom he wished for life as his neighbours. Mrs. Melbourne knew it, and while she smiled at his uncourtly demonstrations of anxiety, felt that they proceeded from sincere solicitude for her comfort and convenience. And when he roughly reproached her for not hastening the removal of various articles to her new house, or vented his spleen in some of his usual exclamations against the procrastination of women, she ceased to complain of his whimsical peculiariarities, when she recollected the motive for all this bustling impatience. He was a friend, whose generosity and kindness were not to be questioned; although, from some strange caprice or absurd notion of petty œconomy, he might give his guests black tea instead of green; or wear his favourite old black coat till it was necessary, for his respectability, that he should be as well known as he was throughout the country, for rich Squire Sowerby, of Clifden-down.

The parting between Clara and Matilda was affecting to both. Matilda acknowledged, in Clara, the blessed instrument who had first roused her from the torpor of selfish despair; she loved her society as much as she respected her character; for, to the serenity attendant on her complete and absolute renunciation, such native sensibility was added, that the tranquillity of manner, which was the result of the former, partook rather of the nature of heavenly calm, than of that cold indifference, which sometimes marks a recluse.

Matilda had often asked herself why the same quality which displeased her in Lady Strathallan should be found so attractive in Clara; it was that the perfection of tranquility, the prevailing feature in the minds of both, was in the one the result of softness, in the other of hardness of character.

Sowerby was not long in paying his promised visit to his neighbours, and, after every / fresh call appeared to have imbibed an additional relish for social and domestic pleasure. Though fortunate in his researches, and enjoying respect and admiration for his talents, those pursuits that had been his pride and pleasure he found insufficient to gild the evening of his days; and he now seemed to envy every one who, surrounded by friends on whom nature gave him a claim, was not obliged to look abroad for the amusement of a heavy hour. 'It was well that pert, smart girl, your familiar, changed her mind in time,' he said, in speaking to Miss Melbourne of Arbella; 'for when I go back to that old house I feel so queer and dismal, I verily believe I should still be tempted to make her mistress of it; but it is better as it is, for you, Matilda.' That it should be the 'better for her,' was a circumstance Miss Melbourne never suffered to enter into her calculation; and she sincerely wished her friend reconciled to Mr. Sowerby for both their sakes. Notwithstanding the sanguine hopes of the young lady herself, she thought she saw Arbella's fate drawing towards no very pleasant crisis, and wished to snatch her, if it was yet possible, from the sneers of those who had first drawn her into folly; if it is said that she wished for her friend a fate which she would not have chosen for herself, let it be remembered that Arbella had, by her own imprudence, restricted herself in the power of choice: that she had given Matilda ample reason to believe love was not essential to her happiness; and every other sentiment her respected friend was capable of inspiring.

Julia Melbourne, who divided her time pretty equally between Woodbine Lodge and the Rocks, was at once the solace of her brother and Matilda; her gaiety was now encreased by the frequent society of Lady Emily Fitzroy, who, whenever she could escape from the ostentatious kindness of her mother, or the sententious reprimands of her sister-in-law, hastened to secure an hour of ease, confidence, and real instruction at the Lodge. Hither she was often followed by Strathallan, who did not like Mr. Sowerby, of Clifden-down; but who, now he could see / his amiable friends without that unwelcome addition to their society, seemed to think it his duty to pursue his little truant sister to the covert where he was always sure of finding her concealed. He wished to encrease in Lady Strathallan a taste for society, which, to him had so many charms. Often in his gayest hours he had been heard to declare that he preferred Mrs. Melbourne's conversation to that of the youngest or most beautiful woman of his acquaintance; and he thought it impossible but that a female mind, must be still more sensible of merit so distinguished, when discovered in her own sex. Lady Strathallan's passion for him was so great, that had not her mind been as unbending as her body, she would really, in compliance with his inclinations, have endeavoured to like the society that was most congenial to his taste; but though a *belle-esprit* by profession, she was far from finding the solace and amusement she wished for in private, in the intercourse of minds so much superior to her own. She soon civilly withdrew herself from a scene so little suited to her usual pursuits and habits, leaving her husband to the enjoyment of a dangerous pleasure, of which he seemed to have lost the salutary dread, which had, till now, alone secured his peace of mind, without acquiring that indifference which would have been its safe and desirable substitute. As more frequent opportunities of intercourse allowed Matilda to observe the change that the recent circumstances had wrought upon his character, she could not help surveying, with regret, the complete dejection into which a mind so noble seemed plunged, and asking herself if the sacrifice made to the welfare of his family, were not perhaps too much. His manners retained all their fascinating sweetness, but the varying graces of his conversation, from the proudest bursts of a noble and impassioned spirit, to tenderness the most seductive, or gaiety the most enchanting, were lost, or hid under an habitual pensiveness; calm, settled, and unchanged. A sadness soft, but ever-during, and soul-felt, that modulated every accent, and unconsciously pervaded every look and motion, constantly reminded / those who remembered his former self, that he had bid farewell to happiness, and that his future life was a blank. By degrees this settled sorrow began to give way, and transient flashes of his former animation to return. Matilda did not know whether she should most desire or fear the change.

One evening that she had been requested by Emily to indulge her in a lesson of music, to which she promised to apply herself assiduously, she had proposed removing her harp to the garden, the weather was so fine. The parlour windows opened upon it; the air was so rich and balmy, the flowers around them so fresh, that the young lady, who never too much liked application, soon changed her request, for a lesson, into one for a song, accompanied by Matilda. In this request she was warmly joined by Julia, who really idolized music, and Matilda, in complying with the wishes of her young friends, soon gave the reins to fancy, and forgot she had begun in compliance with their request; when, throwing her arms carelessly over the strings, she indulged in the strains most dear to taste and memory, till the evening was declining, and the 'crimsoned West' was illuminated with the last parting beams of day before she thought of retiring. While thus engaged, Lord Strathallan stole in upon the domestic group, pleased to find Matilda so employed, he gave the young ladies a sign not to interrupt the harmony; and taking his station in silence by the harp, seemed for a few moments lost in the delicious emotions suggested by the scene. Whether remembrance had some share in his pleasure, and the vernal airs, the low accompaniment of birds now flitting to their nests, the fragrance, harmony and bloom around, which reminded him of a former evening so spent, or whether it owed its enchantment to itself alone, was uncertain. Matilda, her whole soul given up to song, appeared for once almost insensible of his presence; and was only recalled to a painful consciousness of it, by his exclaiming as she concluded, in the words of the impassioned address to Imoinda,

'Sing, sing again,
And let me wonder at the many ways

You have to charm me.'[3] /

She started, and with an air more cold and constrained than she had ever before assumed, called her young friends and turned towards the house. They had left her and were at the other end of the garden.

'Nay, I will have that poor request complied with,' cried Strathallan; 'you see Emily and Julia are too wise to give up the pleasures of this enchanting evening so soon; one more song,' he continued, playfully taking hold of her hands, while she suffered herself to be reseated, in order to end the importunity of his solicitation; she excused herself, however, from singing more, and assured him she really had a cold, which made such an exertion unpleasant to her.

'You have always a cold, I think when I ask you to sing,' said Strathallan, with a discontented air. She was distrest at his manner. The expression of pique is so nearly related to that of partiality, that to avoid giving it the consequence it might otherwise have assumed, she complied; yet it was with no blush, no conscious terror, but rather with a gravity, which convinced Strathallan of what he never before would believe, that it was possible for Matilda to perform an action with an ill-grace. Her voice was low, her playing languid, spiritless, almost tasteless.

At the end of the song she rose abruptly.

'I think, my Lord, you cannot find it necessary to detain me any longer.'

'Unnecessary indeed,' murmured Strathallan, and though he spent an hour with the ladies in the house, before he took away the 'little truant,' the evening, for the first time, passed heavily, and they parted with a formality which had lately been banished from their little circle; from that moment the frank ingenuousness of Matilda's manner was no more; and, though she carefully avoided any reference to the past, she often availed herself of any pretext to be dispensed from joining the party when he was there. Weary of this constraint, Strathallan resolved to attempt an explanation with Miss Melbourne, or at least entreat she would restore to him the confidence which had imparted the greatest pleasure to his existence. The next declining sun-set saw him at the low green gate, / which, opening upon their unpretending garden, led to the small white house where the mother and daughter dwelt. He found the fair one alone and busied with her vegetable cares, reminding him of the poet's Isabella, when intent to

'Bind the straggling pink;
Cheer the sweet rose, the lupin, and the stock,
And lend a staff to the still gadding pea.'[4]

After a moment's common-place enquiry on both sides, Strathallan, in a slow hesitating manner, said, 'I fear, Miss Melbourne, I have unintentionally done something to offend you.'

Matilda knew too well the harmony in which a conversation generally ends, which begins with 'I fear I have offended you,' to risk listening to dangerous reproaches, or specious apologies; therefore raising her blue eyes, with a sweet smile of innocence, and candour, which would have instantly restored peace to a mind that had entertained such apprehensions, and no others; she replied, 'Lord Strathallan can never offend me, but in imagining me so capricious and unreasonable, as to feel displeased without a cause.' Strathallan was rather confused at this reply; he would have preferred a complaint, which might have afforded him an opportunity of justification: and turning his discourse from his own embarrassment, to the flowers, he continued, 'this is an elegant amusement; but you who possess so much real botanic science, ought not to content yourself with rearing a few plants just to please the eye. You must have a green house. I know Mrs. Melbourne loves one, and I should have such pleasure in adding to your collection any rare plant out of Lady Torrendale's conservatory, which she never enters. How I shall like to see you, like another, and a purer, Eve, marshal them in their ranks, "and give them names," and then watch, as they bloom again beneath your forming pencil.'

'Fortune, my Lord, that has put it out of our power, to indulge in many innocent pleasures, has, at the same time, taught us a lesson / of content and resignation to whatever may be her allotment.'

'Oh would she could teach it to us all,' Strathallan whispered: but there was something in Matilda's eye, that, he knew not how, checked the utterance even of this apparently simple wish; and, glad to recur to the first subject of conversation, he continued, 'perhaps you are weary of that trifling style of drawing; I have some views taken in this neighbourhood, and some representing the most bold picturesque spots near – near Strath – allan: they are by a very deserving young artist, and were intended by my father, who thinks she has a decided talent for drawing, as a present for Emily. But I think she is quite unequal to them, and if you would wish to sketch them, I will call with them to-morrow. I think they would please you, and I shall delight to correct and watch your progress.'

'Excuse me, my Lord, I never attempt landscape.'

'Now are you in that provoking humour,' resumed his Lordship, half laughing, to dissemble his pique, 'that if I were to ask you to read, work, sing, or what you will, you would answer, 'excuse me, my Lord, I never read, I never work, I never sing. Those delightful reading parties! indeed I miss them – you know what an idolater I was of Mrs. Melbourne's voice.'

'You may hear it now – she is reading in the parlour with Julia – she will be glad of the addition of your Lordship's company, and I will follow.'

She waved her snowy hand towards the house – Strathallan stood disconcerted – 'bewitching trifler!' Then resuming his former argument, 'is not this disingenuous, Miss Melbourne? What cause have I given you to mistrust me, that you will not say at once, "Lord Strathallan, you have displeased me:" there is no reparation I am not ready to make; but instead of that, you content yourself with shewing that I have done so, by every minute word and action.'

'I am quite unconscious of deserving / these reproaches,' Matilda murmured, while her complexion, as she bent over the roses, gradually assumed a more animated hue than their glowing cups.

'Then do not again,' resumed Strathallan, in a persuasive tone, 'let me see that I am a restraint upon your occupations, a damp upon your pleasures. Prove I am not that formidable being, by letting me hear you and Julia resume your charming harp duetts this evening. I had brought her some lessons of Kozeluch's,[5] to try yesterday morning, but, as usual, the ladies were out. Will you let her favour me so far this evening?'

'Mere children's play, my Lord, such as could not be interesting to you. I may surely give Julia's performance literally that name.'

'It is such children's play,' resumed Lord Strathallan, energetically, 'as angels might lean from their spheres to listen to. When I see your little Julia, with her miniature harp by your side, catching from your lips the inspiration of those heavenly strains, I think I see an already beatified spirit, training an infant cherub for the skies. So sweetly does she in her genius, her soft serious deportment, and already perfect beauty, resemble – almost resemble you. And shall Emily, who is a sweet amiable girl, but who has no soul for pathos, no susceptibility to the charms of music, be admitted to share a gratification, form which I alone am excluded? indeed it is shewing the sister too much partiality, and too much severity to the brother!'

'Heavens! what a comparison!' exclaimed Matilda, who now raised her eyes, in which perturbation, distress, and alarm, were visibly pictured.

'Then may I hope,' continued his Lordship, who mistook her agitation for conviction, 'that, in future, our former pursuits shall be resumed, and that we shall sing, and read, and draw, and ride out, with our former delightful freedom; and – '

He spoke so fast, that Matilda found it difficult to interrupt him; but, at the first pause, she, with a deep drawn sigh, and a look that chilled all farther hope, replied, 'Ah, no Strathallan, it must not be.' /

'Strathallan!' he repeated, with a change of colour, and an emotion, which shewed that the pain her refusal gave him, was swallowed up in the pleasure, which hearing his name thus uttered, once again communicated to his heart.

'You remind me of my error, my Lord,' said Matilda, while self-reproach crimsoned her cheek, with a glow which passion would have vainly endeavoured to call up. 'It must be my care to avoid it in future: you will not, I am sure, tax me with caprice, if I say that this evening, I am unequal to the exertions you did me the honor so much to praise; and that my spirits require solitude, or the presence of my own family, only till they can recover the tone in which but a short time ago you found them.'

Strathallan remained as if transfixed to the spot. 'She is gone!' he exclaimed, 'admirable creature! but she has left me her image, her example. Henceforth I shall learn to mistrust my own heart, and to think virtue's mild radiance poured from Matilda's eyes, a still safer guide, a more disinterested monitor.'

CHAPTER II.

Nè men del vero
L'apparenza d'un fallo
Evitar noi dobbiam; la gloria nostra
E geloso cristal è debil canna,
Ch'ogni aura inchina – ogni respiro appanna.

METASTASIO. ZENOBIO.[6]

'UPON my word it is too bad! Lady Strathallan should be informed of it – she really should!' Such was the decision of a discreet old lady, at a card party at Mrs. Stockwell's, consisting of all the Bourgeois gentry of the town and neighbourhood, while the mistress of the house, affecting rather to pity, and defend the persons mentioned, than to blame them, artfully contrived to draw out the whole of the articles of accusation.

'Why you know, Madam, Lord Strathallan is entirely engaged with them people at the Lodge; he is always there reading and singing, and talking and laughing, with that / Miss Melbourne, who is the most artfullest creature breathing; sometimes he has been shooting, so he must lounge on the sofa all day to rest himself; and sometimes he has not been shooting, and so he has the more time to spend with her, and his dear sister Emy; oh such sisters! for he makes her little runaway pranks, the pretext for his, and all to the neglect of his fine Lady wife.'

'But are you sure it is quite so bad?' said Mrs. Stockwell; 'Miss Melbourne was very coquettish, I'll grant you, and had such a way of drawing the gentlemen after her, I thought her rather a dangerous companion for my niece, when I had a niece; and his Lordship was reckoned very gay, and resistible; but as to any thing approaching to such absolute turpentine, moral turpentine; excuse me, Madam, I can't believe it of them: to be sure he married Miss Mountain, rather to please his father, and – '

'For my part,' said old Mr. Spring, the hop-merchant, (father of the two hopeful youths we have so often mentioned,) 'I think there is no love lost if he married Miss Mountain for her fortune; she married him for his title. If I had been my Lord Strathallan I would no more have taken a woman who – '

While this little dapper hero, was stretching himself, and deciding how he would have rejected her, with whom Strathallan had consented to share his title; a young lady who professed to be better informed, as to the affairs of the great, reproved him for the injustice he did her. 'I assure you,' said she, 'I have been told, and I have reason to credit my information, that during their engagement, they were the fondest lovers, till he met with this deceitful Miss Melbourne; then he was so anxious to return to her when abroad, that he got leave to come home, they say, at a time, when he could not be well spared; but he wrote to her; "my dearest," says he, "let the old folks say what they will, (he meant Lord and Lady Torrendale, who were rather against the match) I shall be happy, so I can breathe my vows at your dear feet before a month be out." Well then he came to Woodlands, and there he / met that artful Miss Melbourne, who spared no pains to win his affections from her, and – '

'O Ma'am,' said the old Lady, 'tell the story of the hysterics and the picture.'

'Ma'am I was going TO – . Miss Melbourne never ceased keeping on, till she had got a promise of marriage from him; and some letters passed between them; and he gave her his picture; it was in a brooch, but it was not the less his picture for that; but after all, my Lord felt some little touch of compunction, and thought it was more honourable to marry Miss Mountain; and so when the ceremony was performing at my Lord Torrendale's, (I had it from an eye witness) in bounced Miss Melbourne, and said as he was her's, and produced the picture and letters; and upon the parson insisting on going on, went into strong hysterics.'

'And then you know, my dear,' said the discreet matron, concluding the story for her, 'Miss Mountain, then Lady Strathallan, fell on her knees, and with tears entreated of her not to expose to the world, how her husband hated her; and so it was hushed up, on condition that Lady Strathallan, out of her large fortune should buy them Woodbine Lodge, as Mrs. Melbourne had taken a great fancy to, and settle it upon them for ever: and that Lady Emilia Fitzroy, should spend part of every year with them, under pretext of a visit, to do away the report of misunderstanding between the families.'

'Why as to that,' said Mrs. Stockwell with an oracular nod, for she loved to appear to act the part of moderator, 'your story may be as it may; but I do know as Lady Strathallan was very jealous of him, from the first moment he came down here, and for that reason would always accompany him, even in his visits to his brother at my house, for fear he should turn off to Clifden-down, which lay in the same road, and which was the place where them people lived then; but afterwards when I heard the programme of the whole affair, I thought I must make my incantation, and that Lady Strathallan must have very little feeling; by then, she could / bring herself to let her husband go amusing of himself in that sort of style without her.'

'Feeling!' cried an over-dressed farmer's daughter, whose blooming cheeks and sparkling eyes belied the compassion affected in her voice; 'oh poor dear creature, she has only too much of it; I know she is distracted about him; but what can she do? well I would not be a countess to be so treated, poor dear little soul, I know her well: at least, I know a friend of her's in town, whom she consults on every occasion, (this intimate friend being no other than Lady Strathallan's fancy dress-maker, was one with whom she indeed held frequent and confidential consultations) and Mrs. – hem – this lady, her particular friend, writes me word, the poor little creature has been distracted ever since she was married; and does not know which way to turn herself with jealousy.'

'Then she is such a poor mild soul,' said a young man, who had not yet spoken; 'she knows not how to right herself: I may judge of her disposition as have known her from a child; I was her play-fellow, and was welcome to her father's any time when at Vinesbury.'

The young gentleman did not think it necessary to mention the manner of his forming this noble acquaintance; his having been in the habit of calling to pay the rent for his father, who was a rich tenant; a circumstance which always made his visits particularly welcome to old Mr. Mountain: he had also, when younger, sometimes come with apples, or eggs, or chickens to the mansion, from the farm, and had been occasionally honoured by Miss Mountain, in her juvenile and romping days, by a game of play at Christmas, or an invitation to stand up in the dance. 'I do not know,' he continued, 'what has hindred my calling since her marriage; but I have such loads of business; I hope she don't take it ill.'

'Oh no,' said Mrs. Stockwell, sentimentally, 'that is the way friendship's finest fiddle strings will break, as they say: now who would have thought that Lady Torrendale and I, AS was such friends, would grow so cold all of a sudden; and to see her bounce / in and out, as she used to, when he was sick; I only wants to see my son, then after sitting with him an hour, home again, without a word; not but she behaved to me in the politest of manners,' continued Mrs. Stockwell, retracting a little, for fear this representation might diminish her consequence in the eyes of the rest of the company; 'but it is not politeness, 'tis friendship I want. Now to think that woman used to come so free, and lie down on the sofa, and ask what was for dinner, if I was out, and stay and tumble all the things, not treating me stiff as if I was a stranger indeed, but with the kindest familiarity; just as she would shew to any duchess. Oh dear to think how the world changes.'

'But, Madam,' said little Mr. Gros the attorney, 'as I hear her Ladyship's son, Captain Fitzroy, is shortly to make part of your family; I should think that would not only be the means of reconciling you to Lady Torrendale, but through her you might inform Lady Strathallan of what – '

'If you mean by the marriage of my ungrateful niece Arbella,' said Mrs. Stockwell, drawing herself up with dignity; 'you may depend upon't, Mr. Gros, you was misinformed. Captain Fitzroy will never, by that means, be allied to our family; Miss Ferrars, after refusing half the county, jilting 'squire Sowerby, Major O'Hara, and super-eminently my son Sam, would be glad enough to snap at the Captain; but her name's up, and he won't have her; I think I know it from pretty good authority, for 'twas he told me so; and I believe, if there is a creature in the world, poor dear little Spencer has a love and confidence for, it is myself.'

During this conversation, in which Miss Hautenville had taken no share beyond her favorite and dubious hem! hem! she had not, however, been an inattentive listener; crouched in a corner, every limb drawn up into an attitude of watchfulness; her long lean arms skewered to her sides; her eyes alone every now and then, expressed the envenomed delight of her heart; and as each character was, in turn, given up to slander, a suppressed laugh indicated her fiendish joy, / which seemed to exult over the ruin, and triumphantly to mutter, 'Lost! lost! lost!'

While she thus indulged in her truly diabolical pleasure, and Mrs. Stockwell in the more innocent one, of believing herself the sole object of the love of Captain Spencer Fitzroy; Stephenson, the young farmer, who had spoke with such interest of

Mountain, exclaimed, snapping his fingers with evident satisfaction, 'I have it, the way she shall be informed of it is this, somebody may write an anomalous letter (I shan't say who) but I believe every one knows who is the best spoken Lady, and finest scribe in this good company; it may be signed by her unknown friend, as shall be nameless; and that will make her mistress of the whole transaction.'

With this laudable resolution, which was much applauded, the whole of this scandalous and well-informed crew separated, resolved (at least as far as in them lay) that there should not long be peace between Miss Melbourne and Lady Strathallan.

Unsuspicious of these machinations, the innocent Matilda had risen in unusual spirits, and was employed in her favorite amusement of painting, when she was surprised by a visit from the Viscountess; she requested to see her alone; and there was an uncommon affection of ease and pleasure in her looks, and of airy gaiety in her appearance; she had a large sash tied behind, *a l'enfant*, and looked more immense and disagreeable than usual; a smile of assumed benignity sat on her lips, and her countenance glowed with more than its wonted enamelled brightness; yet there was something inauspicious in the whole, like the appearance of those red clouds in a sultry evening, which promise a stormy morning. Looking down (which Matilda's height rendered unnecessary) and smothering her little hand in both her own, 'you seem pale, my dear,' said she, with her usual affected condescension; 'I hope you do not apply too intently to your work, or that the absence of those roses is not to be attributed to any more tender and latent cause.' Observing that Matilda did not seem to take the application, 'I am come,' she continued, 'my / little dear, to have some serious conversation with you. The honour of our sex is, you are aware, of that slight texture, that delicate substance, that at the least breath of censure it flies away, like a gossamer gauze, as it were, and you find it – a broken reed; now do not suppose that I care for the hum of the general voice, *auram popularem*; 'tis something, nothing, as Hamlet says, caviare to the multitude;[7] the mere echo of their vain and foolish imaginations; the shadow of a shade. For imagination itself I take to be a very nothing – a vague thing – a vain thing – a mere matter of moonshine – you smile – 'tis true I love to envelope my ideas in the gauze of metaphor, which sometimes renders them not tangible to ordinary capacities; but I trust, Miss Melbourne, you take my meaning.'

'I confess I do not perfectly comprehend your Ladyship's intentions.'

'I will endeavour to explain myself; remarks have been excited (not that they have reached any of the upper circles, but are merely confined to the most vulgar and ill-informed) by the frequent visits made by Lord Strathallan, and his supposed preference to Woodbine Lodge: now do not imagine that they could make me uneasy; no, I am not vain, (surveying herself complaisantly in a pier glass) there are few women, indeed, who could excite my apprehension; and were it excited, it would not be by you, my little dear; but for your own sake, my love, as there was once a report of a *tendre* between you – '

'I understand you now, Madam,' interrupted Matilda, with a look, in which surprise, indignation, and the noble candour of injured innocence were equally blended. 'I did not believe that malice itself could find food for employment in a destiny so obscure, a character so harmless and unpretending as mine; but you shall be satisfied at least of its injustice.'

She spoke these words with spirit; but overcome by the sense of the new and unforeseen ills which attacked her; ills against which she thought she had guarded by the strictest propriety, the most apprehensive delicacy / in her own conduct, her voice soon failed, and her sinking courage dissolved into a shower of tears. 'I am young,' she continued, 'and still ignorant, very ignorant of that world with which I have to contend. In the presence of my mother, of your amiable sister, and in that of my cousin Julia Melbourne, I little thought that an occasional visit, where every word that passed, your Ladyship might have said, would give rise to a calumny which has aimed at my peace, a blow, from which I feel it will never wholly recover. But the pretext, slight as it is, shall occur no more; be assured that Lord Strathallan shall never again, unaccompanied by your Ladyship, enter these doors.'

'Nay, my dear soul, that is not what I mean,' cried Lady Strathallan quickly, 'such a sudden change would wholly defeat my intention, which is, to contradict the report – that I – that you – nobody can be so silly as to suppose me jealous,' she continued, affecting to laugh; 'I believe no woman has less reason, no woman receives more decided, more daily proofs of the constant, the devoted attachment of the man she has honoured with her preference; yet still were it suspected, that by my interference his visits suddenly ceased, they would say, therefore – you understand me – my intention is only to hint to you, that you can, by gently breaking it off, prevent the world from talking; gradually let the habit decrease – let the chain be lengthened but – you remember the rest of the quotation.'[8]

'Lady Strathallan,' said Matilda, firmly, 'this is no time for half measures; if Lord Strathallan's attentions to me are not perfectly innocent, they are criminal; there is no medium – and since it is possible the world can look on them in the latter light, our intercourse is at an end.'

'I had mistaken you, Miss Melbourne,' said the Lady, rising in great perturbation, 'I thought you had the good sense to have received my caution as it was meant; and to have joined with me in prudently smothering those reports, so derogatory to my dignity, my delicacy, the only circumstance of the whole which makes me uneasy; and now, / by your own imprudent violence, you will make a scene; and only confirm what was said before, with added and ridiculous imputations.'

She walked about, and seemed in the highest irritation of spirits; but Matilda, who saw that this passion was as much assumed as her former benignity, and assumed with an intention to terrify her into acquiescence in her plans, remained firm, till her Ladyship thinking the storm had lasted long enough, thought proper, by degrees, to become appeased; and taking her hand, with a smile of apparent kindness, said, 'You are a charming girl, and I believe I must take you on your own terms. Will you then suffer us to visit you together sometimes.' With this request Matilda readily complied; and the lady being so far satisfied, curiosity, the next prevailing passion took possession of her mind. 'Will you tell me truly,' she said, 'if this renunciation does not cost you some pain? nay, don't fear to speak to me (smiling, and fixing those eyes on her, which always distressed by a look, confident to excess, and yet not absolutely bold) does not there still lurk about your heart a slight wish, a struggling hope.' –

She repeated this searching address in a slow measured tone, which evinced she was more delighted with her own eloquence and penetration, than anxious about its effect on her hearer.

'I believe, Madam,' replied Matilda, 'I can answer your question;' and retiring for a moment, she returned with the pearl brooch she had received at Lady Torrendale's lottery, and which contained the picture of Strathallan, 'this is the only memorial I possess,' she said, 'of him, who this morning has caused us such unpleasant discussion. Take it, Madam; chance made it mine; but a more sacred right confirms it yours – and may you find the attachment of the original as unchanged as it has been my wish that' – Here her voice again had nearly failed, but Lady Strathallan embracing her with transport, loaded her with eulogiums, while Matilda indulged upon her bosom in those tears, which to the virtuous is luxury to shed. /

'A thought has occurred to me,' said her Ladyship, carefully wiping her damask cheek; 'to-morrow evening I go to a ball at Buxton, which I am worried to death to patronize; will you appear with me? nothing will so effectually put an end to any silly reports that may have gone abroad, to your disadvantage or mine.'

Matilda, grateful to Lady Strathallan for this attentive care of her fair fame, joy-fully promised compliance; and generous to excess herself, did not perceive that it was the same pride that dictated every thought, wish, and action of the Viscountess, which made her desire, for her own sake, that she, whom the public had given her as a rival, should appear to that public in the light of her friend. This consideration did not, however, render the circumstance itself less pleasant. On the following evening they were seen at the Buxton Ball; Lady Strathallan was adorned with all the elegance that fashion could bestow; but Matilda looked as if all the graces had presided at her toilet; and while, during the evening, they were observed engaged in friendly conver-sation, or arm in arm with her lovely rival, the stately Viscountess swept the length of the ball-room, the scandalous chronicle and its abettors were totally disappointed of a month's expected food, in whispers, glances, and inuendoes; and sincere and general satisfaction was experienced by all those, who feel for beauty, virtue, and innocence, the interest they ever desire to excite. /

CHAPTER III.

Che non si può su generoso cuore
Con generosi modi?

ALFIERI. ORESTE.[9]

MATILDA, who, from an object of dislike, was become a sort of favorite with Lady Strathallan; received frequent invitations, (which she did not always refuse) to join the party at Woodlands. An innocent plan to turn the partiality of the Viscountess to the advantage of Strathallan, and thus in an indirect manner, contribute to his happiness, was the cause of this compliance. 'Oh! could I be but the instrument to reconcile him to the choice my well-intended disinterestedness, in part, induced him to make,' she exclaimed, 'I should be repaid for all! – more than repaid.' She endeavoured to discover if Lady Strathallan had not some points of character in sympathy with that of her Lord, and thought she at length perceived that congeniality in a certain elevation of sentiment, which often broke forth from amidst the cloud of absurdity, and romantic affectation with which it was surrounded, and a disinterestedness, amounting almost to a contempt of money, which she not only professed, but acted up to, on every occasion. She was not destitute of greatness of mind, if she had not been too conscious of the possession of that advantage. Her's was not, indeed, that unaffected and almost unconscious heroism which springs from the heart, and may be termed, the sublime of tenderness. She was not an Arria, to draw forth the dagger and cry 'Pœtus, it is not painful;'[10] but she was fully equal to the answer of Lewis the Fourteenth's consort, when questioned if her heart had ever entertained a former preference, '*Il n'y avait point de roi à la cour de mon père.*'[11] 'Sydney's sister, Pembroke's mother,'[12] she would have deemed far inferior titles to that of the wife of the matchless / Strathallan. Was it hard with a woman of such dispositions to suggest the means of deserving him? Still referring to Strathallan's wishes, Matilda gradually led her, not contented with being the promoter of the ball, or the patroness of a play, to stand forth the encourager of every thing that had the happiness or advantage of those within the sphere of her influence, for its object.

Such conduct could not fail of producing its effect upon a heart like Strathallan's; and as Matilda had foreseen, the attractions of one common interest, drew closer the bands of union between him and his lady; her name was united with that of Lady Strathallan, and repeated with blessings wherever it was heard; while that of Lady Torrendale was scarcely remembered, or remembered only to be marked by an expression of indifference or disapprobation.

One evening as, arm in arm, the ladies strolled out upon a ramble, which was much too long for the delicacy of the Countess, but which Strathallan promised his wife and Miss Melbourne, would reward, by the grandeur of an uncommonly beautiful prospect, their deviation from the usual route, they struck into a shady lane, which led to a row of buildings that was appropriated for the reception of the aged poor of the village; and that had lately received, from the bounty of Lady Strathallan, many additional conveniences.

One of its rustic inhabitants had ventured out to taste the freshness of the evening. He leant upon a staff for support, and was, in all respects, like Crabbe's description of the Aged Villager;[13] but, oh, how unlike him in his fate; he had found an asylum where his wants and infirmities were relieved, and where even the comforts and indulgences he could still enjoy, were not neglected. He drew back respectfully to make way for the ladies, but on perceiving who they were, the mechanical reverence that only marks the difference of station, at once gave way to the much more pleasing tribute to the heart. Fixing his eyes on them, as if the sight was a cordial to his faint and exhausted spirits; 'Bless you both!' he fervently exclaimed, / while tears of gratitude ran down his furrowed cheek, 'and heaven *will* surely bless you! for you are young and great, and yet you remember the destitute!'

Even Lady Strathallan appeared affected – Matilda gave her a sweet expressive look, which seemed to say, 'Is not this worth all the triumphs of vanity?' While Strathallan, indulging in the effusions of a manly, graceful tenderness, beheld them with admiration almost arising to enthusiasm, and 'smiled with superior love.' 'Be ever thus united,' he said, 'and praise, and adoration will follow wherever you turn.'

It was in moments like these, he felt his heart was not wholly without employment: that expansiveness of mind prevented it from shrinking into itself, however deprived, by circumstances, of the exercise of its most grateful feelings. Passion was, with him, only a centre from which every other amiable affection diverged with different but proportioned force; and it was not hard to trace them up to their source, from the first generous sigh for the happiness of mankind, to the stronger and more determined impulses of pity – generosity – benevolence – tenderness – love. He found the compensation for that painful blessing, a feeling heart, in the happiness it still enabled him to taste. The rose of life, indeed, was withered; but its perfume was not gone. That he acknowledged Matilda as the author even of this imperfect satisfaction, she could not deny; but she no longer dreaded his gratitude, should either distress or offend her; it was a gratitude which ever feared to wound, by appearing too impassioned, the delicacy and generosity that at first excited it.

While such was the conduct of Miss Melbourne, Lady Torrendale appeared as if anxious to detach Strathallan from his bride, by employing all her little power of ridicule, in pointing out her absurdities, and exaggerating her follies; yet even that wayward temper was gradually weaned by Matilda, from this gratuitous love of giving pain. She represented to the Countess so strongly, that it was her interest to keep well with her daughter-in-law, who was making rapid advances / in the favour of Lord Torrendale, that her Ladyship was induced to treat Lady Strathallan, in general, with outward attention, if not with real kindness. The Earl suddenly found his house a more agreeable residence, without being able exactly to determine to what he should attribute the change. It was impossible, however, for him long to continue blind to the influence of that angel of gentleness, who had breathed into it the spirit of harmony, and love, and joy. All his former injustice arose to his mind with added pangs of self-reproach. As the circumstances relating to his son's past attachment to Matilda had never been discussed between him and Mrs. Melbourne, it might have been supposed easier for him to slide again into that friendly unaffected behaviour, which he had formerly maintained towards her daughter. But that generosity of disposition, which he concealed under the habitual reserve of his manners, and the dignity of his age and station, rendered him unhappy, while conscious of an injustice he had not acknowledged; and an accidental interview of a few moments, that he had alone, with this amiable girl, put to flight all the resolutions he had often formed, of preserving an inviolable and prudent silence. Observing, that her presence had now again become rare at Woodlands, he entreated she would appear oftener in a scene, which was always so much improved by her presence. Matilda surprised at this alteration of manner, excused herself with a blush, saying, 'That her domestic occupations did not allow her so much time, as formerly, to spend with her friends, and share their pleasures.'

'Say, rather, their happiness!' interrupted Lord Torrendale, with emotion; 'and surely none have so great a right to witness happiness, as those who are themselves the authors of it. Miss Melbourne, I did, I own, think Strathallan influenced – violent – absurd – but were he free, and had he to chuse out of a thousand women, his choice could not be fixed more worthily than – but it was impossible;' he continued, 'you have, yourself, too much penetration, too much native delicacy, not to perceive, how / impossible it is for us to follow the dictates of inclination, and fulfil all the obligations imposed on us.' Then, as if fearful of having said too much, and resuming all his wonted dignity and self-importance, his Lordship concluded; 'All I meant to say, Miss Melbourne, was, that I think I owe you, in common with my whole family, an acknowledgment for the uniform dignity, propriety, and decorum of your conduct, in a trying, (I will allow it), a very trying situation.' With his usual, perhaps more than his usual formality, he took leave; but the first effusion of a feeling heart had been expressed, it could not be recalled; and Matilda saw in it a tribute the most grateful, to the difficulty and the merit of the distressing conflicts she had had with herself.

Thus surrounded by those she had contributed to bless, loaded with daily and most flattering marks of the esteem of every individual of that family, with which she had voluntarily declined a closer connexion, was it possible for the sophistry of passion itself to persuade her, that in becoming a part of that family against their interest and wishes, making use of her influence over her lover's heart, to make him disappoint, instead of fulfilling the object of his father's life, and involving his name and her's in one common censure, she could have hoped to taste a purer satisfaction than that, which now descended to gild the serene tenor of her days, and minister a tempered joy to her subdued and chastened spirit. /

CHAPTER IV.

Let not that devil which undoes your sex,
That cursed curiosity, seduce you
To hunt for needless secrets.

ROWE'S JANE SHORE.[14]

'Upon my word,' said Arbella, to Matilda, 'I think our different stories might make the subject of a pretty moral dissertation entitled, "Advantages of Circumspection, or Dangers of Coquetry." Here have you, after the most distressing reverse of fortune, transformed into an adorer, the relation whom at first you feared to meet! converted into the warmest friend, the man you refused, (for you will not deny that you refused Sowerby), and obtained the friendship and esteem, even of your rival, in the most difficult and trying circumstance of your life. While I, with as flattering prospects as ever opened to the vanity of woman; after thinking I had my choice of three, each in their way, let me tell you, valuable admirers, may as well, I think, go and make my best curtsey to my cousin Sam, and beg of him to forget the past, and take me for pity; for I really begin to believe, after all, that Spencer won't have me. Well, we must confess, in the manner you have conducted every thing, you have been extremely fortunate.'

'Do you not recollect the correction made to that title by the lucky Saladin, in the Turkish Tale?'[15]

'Saladin the Prudent? well then, if you will not allow luck to have any share in it, you are assuredly more prudent than I am; or, as a certain great legal character was said to have replied, when some one observed to him, he had been through life a most fortunate man, "you might say, with much more truth, I have been a most laborious man," and laborious it would certainly be, to show ones-self, on all occasions, so very good as you are." /

'I do not find it so; I leave to you entirely the support of a much more laborious character, and yet one from which you own, yourself, you have as yet derived neither pleasure, nor advantage.'

'Why no, you are not a professed coquette as I am; but you have greater success in your own quiet way, and must, therefore, have greater art.'

'I have no art; I resign to you all the honours of the science.'

'What does that signify,' resumed Arbella, with a playful petulance, that was becoming in her, and in her alone; 'while the deuce of it is, that if I have most science, as the musicians say, you have most execution. Then what a miracle have you performed for your faultless lord – behold his huntress bride,

"That bouncing Amazon,
His buskined mistress, and his warrior love."[16]

has given up (I beg pardon) *almost* given up,[a] "Tray, Blanch, and Sweetheart,"[17] for the pleasures of reading, friendship, and the conversation of the beloved Strathallan. Is it that; or is it the terrible fall she got that reformed her? By the bye, before we say a word more on any other subject, I must communicate to you a discovery I have made, respecting a subject I once before mentioned to you, that will, perhaps, surprise you. We will allow a great deal for the exaggeration of common report; yet still I must say I did think, if he had a preference – however, I find we were all mistaken, and that he has found consolation quite independently of you.'

'How, what do you mean?' enquired Matilda, much disturbed.

'There is a certain fair lady, whom he brought with him from abroad, who is the real object of all his attentions, and in whose company he forgets – '

'Impossible! Miss Ferrars,' said Matilda; her mild eyes flashing for the first time with indignation, 'Lord Strathallan is incapable of so unprincipled a conduct; the rules of honour alone – '

'Lord Strathallan! good heavens, my / dear, where had your thoughts wandered. I was speaking all along, you know, of your crazy cousin – you will excuse me for thus mentioning your relation. I will tell you the first cause of my suspicion,' continued Arbella, sparing her friend the confusion of an apology. 'When we were in the library, looking at some of the marbles which he had removed there for ornament, my ears were suddenly struck with the sound of a harp, the sweetest music I ever heard – you smile; now you are going to say it was some of the musicians practising, or as George Spring says, practising; no such thing – it was from that side of the house where the musicians never went; that part which only contains the rooms appropriated in your – in former times to a museum, and conservatory, and so on; and which, since Sir Harold has taken possession, have never been opened to view. I said, 'Sir Harold, I believe you have got an invisible lady in those forbidden apartments; I declare I have heard sweeter sounds than ever proceeded from the little crystal cage of the real one,' he looked a me – Oh, my dear! I shall not attempt to describe his look – then saying there was nothing farther worth detaining us in the library, he hurried us out of it. I afterwards questioned the servants if my suspicions were not just, but could get no satisfaction.'

'You could not!' said Matilda, with a smile of pretended surprise, 'amazing.'

'No, indeed. Lady Torrendale said it was wrong to ask, but I think I did well, for how is one to learn any thing but by asking questions? and at last, I did get some satisfaction – the housekeeper told me, under the seal of secrecy; but I entrust it to you; that it was true her master had brought over a beautiful young lady from Italy, whom he was distractedly in love with, and very desirous to marry. He had been instrumental in delivering her from the imprisonment of a convent, where her friends had placed her, with the intention that she should take the veil: this had thrown her into his power, and instead of restoring her, as she had expected and conditioned, to a relation who would have received her till she could make terms with her other connexions, he had forcibly / conveyed her away to England, and then endeavoured to persuade her she had no other alternative but becoming his wife. The difference of religion, however, and the want of her parents[a] consent, formed an insuperable bar, in her opinion; and she did nothing but weep and sigh during the daily visits of Sir Harold, who, though he kept her under close confinement, studied every thing that could make that confinement agreeable to her; and her constant resistance was the cause of that unhappiness, and those occasional starts of fury, which may be observed in your cousin. You may suppose, my dear,' pursued Arbella, 'I was anxious to see the sweet creature after this account; but the housekeeper, a very discreet woman, told me it was impossible for her to procure me that gratification; and begged I would rest satisfied with the information she had given me; but I am determined it shall not be long before I, in some manner or other, indulge my wish.'

Matilda now called to mind a former idle report about Sir Harold, which did not disagree with this statement; still, as she thought the whole story extremely improbable, and most likely, related by the woman to amuse the curiosity of Arbella, she used her utmost endeavours to dissuade her from her wild intention; but Arbella's was not a mind to be so easily governed; whenever a subject interested her, she was apt, as the French term it, à *se passionner*,[18] and a singular peculiarity in her character was, that these *passions* were sometimes taken, for objects, that should have been the most absolutely indifferent to her, whilst she manifested a coldness, amounting almost to insensibility, for many that might be supposed to touch her much more nearly; the beautiful Italian nun, 'who could not speak English, poor dear soul, and had no friend in England to right her,' became the subject of her nightly dreams and daily cogitations. She raved of nothing else to Matilda, who, considering the whole as a fable, was rather weary of her constant sighs, tears, and plaints, on the subject. She soon had reason to repent having indulged her curiosity.

About half a mile beyond the Rocks there / was the ruins of an ancient priory, which had also once belonged to the Melbourne family. One fine evening that the Melbournes spent at Woodlands, Lady Torrendale observing there were many young people in company, proposed an excursion to it. The carriages were ordered, in which they were to proceed as far as the Rocks, where they intended to alight and walk to the Priory. Returning from their ramble, the Countess, who had not forgot her old *penchant* for flirting with and 'surprising' the Baronet, proposed they should look in upon the 'hermit Sir Harold,' and carry him off *vi et armis* [19] to sup with his relations at Woodlands. Miss Ferrars, delighted with the idea, led the way. She was just then relating the history of the Italian nun to Miss Sagely, a stony damsel of the neighbourhood, who always thought Arbella 'odd,' and congratulating herself on her superior wisdom, because, too dull to commit the errors of vivacity, imagined she must indubitably be right, as she made it a rule on all occasions to say nothing and do nothing: her statue-like calmness, and the difficulty with which she at length brought out a 'really ma'am,' or 'very singular indeed,' formed the best contrast with the varying countenance, and eyes of trembling lustre, with which Arbella related the improbable and romantic tale; but when she came within sight of the gothic door which led to the (supposed) uninhabited wing of the mansion, her transport knew no bounds. 'Look Madam,' she exclaimed to Lady Torrendale, ' 'tis open – left open by chance – I will see her once before she dies!'

'Not for your life, Arbella,' cried Matilda, stepping forward and seizing her arm.

'Miss Ferrars, have you forgot all propriety?' cried Lady Torrendale.

'Propriety Madam,' said Arbella, 'when sensibility, when justice is in the cause!' she darted forward, passed the broken arch, which was overhung with moss and ivy, and was out of sight in a moment.

'Dear heart! she is a spirited young lady,' cried George Spring, jumping for joy, 'Gad I'd like to have a peep myself.'

Lady Torrendale followed, under pretence / of wishing to overtake and prevent Arbella, and Miss Sagely looking at her mother, they exchanged glances of mutual regret at the indecorum of her young companion; while they perhaps secretly exulted in the eccentricities of one often superior to them, and were not sorry to find themselves, by a lucky chance, thus in at the death – of her discretion. Crossing a large and empty hall, they entered a room into which Arbella had already penetrated; but, as if struck motionless at the scene that presented itself, she no longer offered to lead on her companions: she stood with clasped hands, and a countenance in which horror was deeply painted, exclaiming, 'That Sir Harold was addressing a spirit.' The sun, which was just setting, shed, from its parting rays, a gloomy richness over the large and magnificent apartment. The crimson curtains of a huge gothic window were partly drawn, and discovered Sir Harold in an attitude of fervent supplication, addressing a figure, which, though partly shrouded in the gloom, yet, from the aërial transparency of that part of the outline which was visible, and the fleecy whiteness of the vestments that enfolded it, might well pass for an inhabitant of the other world. A single beam, that darted through the dim pane, fell on Sir Harold's countenance, and discovered it to be more pale and haggard than usual; his lips moved with earnestness; and the few words that could be caught of what fell from him, appeared those of invocation; but the silence of the mysterious being he addressed was not to be moved. Yet she bent over him, in an attitude of Madonna tenderness. Those features, though wasted almost to spiritual transparency, could still boast the line of beauty; but the pale, wan tint with which they were overcast, their fixed, waxlike regularity, had something that appalled the mind, as being too lovely to belong to death's dominion, yet no longer varying or animated by the breath of life. Lady Torrendale, the moment the figure met her view, uttered a piercing shriek, and fell senseless to the ground – it was some moments before she could be recovered, and, when she was, she continued to exclaim, in a piercing accent, / 'She calls me, she calls me, I shall not long survive her – take, take me from this chamber of horrors.' She repeated these words so unceasingly, and with such vehemence, that, fearful of her being attacked with hysterics, her female friends hastened to have her conveyed back into the air – but Sir Harold, turning with solemn earnestness to Mrs. and Miss Melbourne, and laying a hand on each, said, 'You do not go.' Arbella terrified, shocked, and ashamed of what she had done, still lingered in a kind of irresolute curiosity; and the same motive tempted those who could be spared from Lady Torrendale, to prolong their unwelcome intrusion. The presence of so many strangers produced a visible effect upon the fair incomprehensible being, whose sanctuary they had invaded. Advancing towards them with a courteous but hurried accent, 'I thank you good ladies,' she cried; 'Thank you, thank you, good ladies and gentlemen – you are come to rescue me, but this is not the hour! The clock has scarce struck seven – one, two, three, four, five,' she reckoned over the numbers with inconceivable rapidity, 'five hours of liberty still remain. At twelve I shall require your assistance.' And, with a sweet earnestness, and in the attitude and tone of a Belvidera, she repeated, 'remember twelve.' A smile of angel brightness for a moment illumined her faded features; but the eyes that should have spoken the language of the soul, vacant and wandering, shewed that the nobler faculties, which distinguish and exalt the intellectual nature, informed no more their lovely mansion.

Sir Harold, who had appeared extremely disturbed during the whole of this address, which he had been unable to prevent, now turned to the intruders with added fierceness, 'away, away, officious meddling beings,' he cried, 'do you not fear to break in upon the sacredness of a solitude like this?' But his endeavours were rendered ineffectual by the emotion of the lovely sufferer, who, on observing his menacing tone and gesture, clung terrified to his arm, exclaiming, in a plaintive accent, 'Oh Harold, oh my son, not, not again for me; remember I have none / now left but you, my Harold – let no more blood be shed – let not – '

'Heavens! Lady Julia Melbourne, has she not been dead some years ago,' exclaimed several voices at once. 'Lady Julia Melbourne – is it possible?'

'Yes, it *is* possible,' cried Sir Harold, with a sternness, and in a tone that thrilled every heart with horror. 'You have at length torn from me my secret, discovered the wreck of all that was great and lovely. That wreck which I would have mourned in secret. This *is* Lady Julia Melbourne. This is my only parent, she, who, snatched from the gay thoughtless scene which she adorned, was regretted a moment, pitied, and forgotten; but she did not die. The cruelty which destroyed her nobler part, sanctioned that falsehood too.' At this moment the most violent agitation seized Lady Julia. 'They are come to take me,' she cried, 'they will again hide me from you – do not, do not again leave me to the mercy of my enemies.'

'Fear it not,' cried Sir Harold, kneeling and pressing, in filial anguish, the hand he held, while grief and anxiety at the sight of her sufferings, seemed to suspend in his soul every other feeling.'

This was then the true secret of the unhappy Baronet, who had, a moment before, been considered as a tyrant, a merciless oppressor of beauty and innocence. – An awful pause succeeded, which was only interrupted by the shrieks of Lady Torrendale, distinctly heard at intervals; for she had fallen into strong hysterics, and could not, for the present, be removed home. One fit succeeded another, and she only recovered to repeat, with incessant violence, 'I have seen her – she has returned to the world – I have seen the spirit of Julia!'

Mrs. Melbourne, who knew the Countess to be of a disposition which was seldom affected by any circumstance that did not immediately concern herself, but who also knew her to be particularly liable to the attacks of superstition, was, from motives of humanity, most anxious that she should be removed, as soon as possible, from a scene / so painfully irritating to her feelings. Upon the first symptoms of returning composure she had her carriage ordered round, and Lady Torrendale was lifted into it, being still unable to support herself. Arbella was preparing to accompany her, and the rest, who had expected the evening to close so differently, to return, much discomfited, to their separate homes, when Sir Harold, turning to his fair relations, said, with an air, tranquil and composed, even to a degree of melancholy dignity, 'To those who could, (from whatever motive,) wantonly intrude upon the sacred source of all my sorrows, I have no desire to appeal, or to justify myself – No, let them triumph in having accomplished their purpose – In having deprived me of the sad privilege of being a wretch in secret! I asked no human being to share my sorrows. I invited them to the sound of the dance and song; and strewed with flowers the grave beneath my feet: but they were not satisfied. To you, my lovely cousins, who, led by some motive of angel pity, and benevolence, to restrain others, not indulge yourselves, find yourselves thus unexpectedly in this melancholy scene, shall all the past be opened. It is fair you should be satisfied, that he who has shared so much of your friendly care and kindness, is neither a demon of cruelty nor a monster of caprice and injustice.'

'I am ready, my dear sir,' said Mrs. Melbourne, with a melancholy firmness, while she could scarcely restrain a glance of indignation at those around her, 'to hear any secret of which you may wish to unburthen your mind, though persuaded, you can have none, which can lessen you in my esteem.'

As she spoke, she led the way into another apartment; but Sir Harold, forcing her to be reseated, exclaimed, 'No, no, here, and only here, can I relate my tale of woe. The scene that daily witnesses the effects of too late repented cruelty, is alone fitted to hear the progress of that cruelty revealed.'

Matilda looked timidly around her; her spirits already exhausted by repeated sufferings, could not boast the steady equanimity / of her mother's, and a heavy convulsive sigh spoke her shuddering alarm.

'Happy girl!' whispered Arbella, as unwilling, and dying with curiosity, she slowly retreated towards the door.

'Happy!' Matilda repeated, looking up, with an accent that thrilled her friend with horror.

'Why then, miserable – I know not whether most to envy or deplore you; Heaven send you safe out of the Blue Chamber,' replied her friend,[20] shuddering in her turn. Amen, seemed to be expressed in the countenances of the other visitants, as, casting a hasty glance of pity on the mother and daughter, they closed, with as much precipitation as possible, the vast and creaking door. The sullen sound it returned, the every moment increasing gloom of the apartment, struck Matilda to the heart; but in her mother, solicitude to obtain an explanation of the late extraordinary events, had swallowed up alarm, and even for the moment, the expression of regret and pity. The fair sufferer had retired into an inner chamber; and Sir Harold, seating his cousins on a sofa, and affectionately taking a hand of each, prepared to unfold to them the clue to his singular and mournful destiny; while they listened in mute attention, as he, for the first time, displayed to them the darkest page in the eventful history of the family of Melbourne. /

CHAPTER V.

O speak no more, my heart flames in its heste,
I once was Ælla – now am not his shade;
Had all the fury of misfortune's will,
Fallen on my baned head, I had been Ælla still;
This alone was unblurred of all my spryte,
My honour, honour frowned on the dulce wind
That stealed on it. –

CHATTERTON – ÆLLA.[21]

HISTORY OF SIR HAROLD MELBOURNE.

'My father, Sir Reginald Melbourne, had virtues; but they were of a cast so gloomy and severe, that even where his character raised esteem, it failed to excite love; and the first impression I recollect receiving from him, was that of fear. My mother, (Oh! how does fancy bleed upon recalling her sweet excellence,) joined to the most enchanting form, each nobler quality of heart and mind. We were one – I loved her with a tenderness, a *companionship* of affection, far beyond what is usually felt, in a relation such as ours. I seemed to her, born to enable her to bear the load of domestic tyranny; a tyranny which, while it rendered her home insupportable, made her appear to an ill-judging world, given up to its pleasures – they called her gay, unthinking – I knew her heart; 'twas all softness; 'twas what I fear Julia's will be; and while I witnessed the tears she often shed in private, could feel how much she was formed for a different scene. To me was unveiled the elegance of her mind, the sensibility of her heart. She delighted to form my youth to something beyond the general routine of public studies; and the similarity of our tastes, a resemblance to her, that was said to exist in the manners and way of thinking of her dearest blessing, as she often fondly called me, served more strongly to cement our union. The first long separation I endured from her, was when I left my paternal mansion for the University. The tears she shed at parting were prophetic; my grief I carefully concealed, that her's / might not be increased by beholding it. –

'Who will now screen me from severities,' she said, 'that I am ill able to endure. Who will now be my solace, when, with a mind bowed down by domestic anguish, I seek in society for relief in vain!'

'Her attention was not, indeed, wholly undivided. My sister Julia, now just emerging from infancy into childhood, shared her cares; but the confidence, the feelings that conceived and doubly suffered for her sorrows, could not exist between them. I spent the period of my exile in my allotted studies, which afforded me, at least, at times, a compensation for the privations I endured, till – I hardly dare to recollect the day, a fellow student – no, I will not call him so, a wretch, a coward, ventured in public, to utter some expressions that reflected upon the fair fame of her who commanded all my reverence and affection. I scarcely remember the words that afterwards passed between us; I only know I called him to an explanation, and he insultingly replied, that what he said, alluded to a circumstance too well known to need from him a particular apology. I insisted upon one, or to be satisfied with the blood of his dastard heart. We fought – he fell. I cannot paint my horror at the moment; I felt not that I too was wounded. The wound was in my head, and rendered me incapable of attending to my own safety: the first thing I remember was the consciousness that my own life was endangered by having sacrificed his. I know not whether it was the goodness of my cause, and the provocation I had received, or the ability of my legal defenders, but by the laws of my country I was acquitted. Not so by my father, who reproached me for making more public what he confirmed as true – HER error. But I charge you, my cousin,' continued Sir Harold, his eyes lighted up with sudden fury, 'believe it not – no, though yon bright star, that in its listening silence starts and trembles as I relate, were to descend from its orbit and attest it true; believe it not, *she* could not err. Some vile jealousy deceived him; still, considerate for his daughter's sake, he said, he would not farther divulge her / disgrace, but banish her to some distant country, where the public might be deceived by a report she had gone in search of health. Agonized by this intelligence, I forsook my studies, I forsook every thing, and hastened to Mosscliff Abbey, to take a last long adieu of a parent so beloved – rather, perhaps, to offer to accompany her in her exile, preferring sorrow and obscurity with her, to all the bright prospects I left behind. But I came too late. I was told she had set out upon her pilgrimage of woe, and when I declared my resolution to seek and console her, my father opposed himself in the strongest manner to what he considered as a rebellion against him; a shameful dereliction from the precepts that should be cherished by his only son, and he would not inform me what route she had taken.

'Distracting as must have been the events that led to this catastrophe, I yet felt surprized and pained that she had not, by a few brief lines, informed me where I might seek her out. Enraged, however, at what I deemed in my father the height of injustice, I departed, without any other clue to guide me than what my own memory and probable conjectures afforded. I knew she had relations, who had educated her, at Florence, and an uncle who had a *chateau*, in the south of France; to one of these places she might have been spirited away by the same power that had forced her from her home.

'After taking the necessary precautions for my personal safety, precautions that I took more for her sake than my own, I traversed countries convulsed with the flames of war – their distracted state assimilated to the tortures of my mind. I passed through every scene unharmed, for I had a stronger safeguard than that of authority. Who would injure a son in pursuit of his lost parent? I visited courts, saw churches, palaces, theatres – '

'And did not that variety of objects afford your mind relief,' Matilda, in a tone of compassion, enquired.

'No,' replied her cousin, 'for about that time spirits began to torment me, and allowed me no repose. Sometimes, at a / crowded assembly, they would come up and whisper me that SHE was just passing through another part of the city, and then I hurried to the place, but found her not. Another time at the theatre, when gazing on a beautiful young lady, they told me not to think of such a bride, for she would ask to be conducted to her mother, and I had none to lead her to. Then would I quit in haste the brilliant scene, which offered to my view, happiness I must never hope to enjoy.

'Again, from court or from some country palace these spirits would hurry me away, and bid me seek her among the tombs, yet was she not there. In spite of their persecutions I had contrived to visit every scene where it was possible she might be found; had visited Sicily, Cadiz, Lisbon. My recollection, which began to grow confused and dim, though my heart was ever the same, sometimes presented the reason my father gave the world for her absence, as a reality, and I sought her wherever health was to be found, with renewed ardour, and hope of success.

'In the midst of this new pursuit, a letter arrived from my father, abruptly acquainting me with my mother's death, but without indicating the spot where her pale remains were deposited. Yet this, by the few faint lights I possessed, I resolved to discover, when a second letter, in a different hand, was delivered to me, urging my speedy return to England, if I wished to receive the last commands of my father, who was not expected to live. Though I travelled with incredible speed, and did not a moment defer my embarkation, I had been too late had I landed one day beyond that in which I hailed my native shore.

'I found my father fully conscious of his situation; the sternness and gloom of his nature struggled with the weakness of death. 'I have a secret to confide,' he said, 'which is for your ear alone.' After dismissing his attendants, he took from his pillow two massy keys, and delivering them to me, 'These,' he continued, 'constitute you the guardian of a prisoner, who must fall to your care. To my family and the world she has been / dead above two years, but I dreaded your greater penetration, and therefore banished you for a time, till weary of your protracted stay, I announced her death also to you. In both these accounts I deceived my son, as well as the world, by a false report. She who dishonoured the name of Melbourne is not suffered to enjoy its pleasures at a distance from me, and to revel with impunity on the fortune which she does not deserve to possess. The west wing of this ancient building has been her prison. In the wilds of Northumberland I was secure from prying curiosity and intrusion, and by changing all the servants at the time of her confinement, and well-securing, by the power of interest, the fidelity of the one who was entrusted with the secret, and attended upon her, I knew how to baffle even the anxiety of filial partiality like yours. It is now in your power to set her free. Perhaps, exulting in the possession of your newly acquired rights, happy with your favorite parent, you will rejoice over the extinction of that which you will, no doubt, term an unjust and barbarous tyranny, and restore to light those graces which were your pride, while on your house they brought shame, reproach, and ruin. But if you listen to the counsel a dying father gives, trust not the first emotions of your heart; be firm, as I have been, and yield not uncontrolled freedom to a spirit that will abuse it, to bring on you accumulated repentance.'

'I cannot express to you, my amiable friends, the mixture of my feelings at this discourse. Joy that my mother yet lived; surprise and pity at the cruel and long imprisonment she had endured, combined, with compassion for my father's situation, and horror at his latest counsel, agitated my mind with an overwhelming contrariety of emotions, such as I had never before experienced. I forbore to reproach him, but scarcely had I waited to close his eyes, when I hastened to the western wing of Moss cliff Abbey, to the prison-house of my mother; enraptured with the idea of being the means of releasing that dear parent, of restoring her to life, to liberty, and happiness, I determined / to offer my fortune to her disposal, and promise to devote my future life to make her amends for her past sufferings. For an instant I felt nothing but delight, wild, pure, unmingled. No – all I have felt since has not obliterated the remembrance of that scene.

'When the massy^a doors, which kept her from me, gave way, I once more found myself at her feet, and in a transport of filial tenderness, told her she was free! Delicious moment! succeeded by sufferings so long and bitter. She looked at me, but knew me not for her deliverer. The pressure of misfortune had sunk too deep on a mind too finely formed, and reason had given way under the ills she had endured. She thanked me, but as a stranger, told me she had no wish to depart; that had she experienced such, she had no obstacle to prevent her, for she had always been at liberty. Sweet sufferer! the spacious apartments she occupied, and the gloomy and sullen gardens annexed to them, had long been the world to her. I endeavoured to recal to her remembrance a son who had loved her with such devoted attachment, and who had long sought her, with anguish, through the world, in vain; and tried, with every soothing art, to lead her to enjoy the present, and to make her sensible of the difference of her situation. My efforts were fruitless, and I found that any attempt to remove her from her present abode, excited in her the most painful emotions. When I urged it, she mistook me for my father; thought herself at liberty where she was, but that he was coming, with his former violence, to force her into confinement.

'Obliged to leave her, for the present, under this impression, I withdrew from a sight, which tore my heart, and passed the greater part of the night in an anxiety and perturbation little inferior to that with which I had seen her agitated. Being determined not to place myself far from her, I had a bed made in the apartment adjoining to hers, and had at length sunk to a disturbed and uneasy repose, when, in the middle of the night, I was awakened by the most plaintive and heart-piercing cries; they evidently proceeded from my mother's apartment. I hastily rose / to her assistance, but was encountered in the passage by the woman who guarded her.

'It is nothing Sir,' said she, 'but my Lady's usual way. Every night at twelve she thinks old Sir Reginald and a band of men are come to take her back to prison – because it was at that hour that he laid wait for her at the eastern gate, and had her carried to these apartments, when she had appointed to meet Lord – '

'I stopped her audacious discourse, and hastening to the dear mourner, with assurances of safety, staid with her till I had soothed her into repose. But these terrors, nightly repeated, while no gleam of reason seemed to repay my efforts, were near reducing me to a state like her own. In such distraction of mind, I know not how I was able to attend to the multitude of affairs that pressed upon me in consequence of my father's death, or the care of the estates that devolved upon me. I shut myself up almost entirely with her, and the only gleam of consolation I remember feeling, was upon observing nothing had been neglected in her mournful prison, that could contribute to her convenience and health; and the assurance from the mercenary who attended her, that Sir Reginald had always been ready to grant her any indulgence she might request within its precincts, so that the pangs of inward regret, had not been aided by any outward severity, to bring her to the state I deplored. To disclose that state to the world I still felt myself unequal. In this one caprice I indulged. Her once numerous acquaintance believed her dead. I let them believe so still. I suffered them to attribute my voluntary seclusion, and my almost constant residence in one wing of my gloomy paternal mansion, to what singularity they chose, rather than allow the hard-hearted, and the fool, to rejoice at the overthrow of grace, talent, mind, like hers. At midnight she always required my presence to guard her from her returning terrors. One night – Oh! how deeply engraven on my memory is that moment. After I thought I had soothed her into something of repose, she looked at me earnestly, and her eyes suddenly beaming / with that intelligence, which in former times rendered them so beautiful, 'I believe,' she said, (she spoke with sweet hesitation) 'I need no longer fear – you are, you are my son!'

'Matilda, you, a few like you, can feel how well the transport of this recognition repaid whatever I had suffered. To hear her thank me; to see her grateful smile in acknowledgment of all my efforts for her relief; to tell her all I had endured; to mark her kindling eye that felt and understood all I related, and hear her once more call me her son, her Harold, returned from a distant world to defend and protect her! but I had more to suffer. From the moment that she knew me, I formed hopes of her complete recovery; they were too sanguine. Nothing could persuade her of Sir Reginald's death, or that she had leave to venture beyond the mansion. I, however, persuaded her to visit those parts of it which she had formerly inhabited; and thus enlarged the sphere of her enjoyment, while I restricted my own power of receiving society. To general society I was indeed every day becoming more indifferent, or to speak truly, I felt at the idea of it, a growing fear and disgust. The mournful events that had taken place in my family I thought I saw written on every countenance. My father's cruelty – my fatal duel – and (what they would impiously call) my mother's – frailty. It was not for me, whose fate renewed the tale of stern Thebes and Pelop's line,[22] to mingle in scenes of thoughtless gaiety and dissipation, where I might accidentally hear the circumstances of my life recalled to mind, where, in the silly fable of the day, each erring female might be, at least in thought, compared to her in whom my soul's respect and love were centered. I devoted what time I could spare, from my newly-imposed duties, to agriculture and the improvement of my estates. The bowers I raised, the trees I planted, did not reproach me with my parent's errors, the whispering woods around me did not echo to the voice of calumny or complaint.

'Before the period of my misfortunes, I / have heard it said that I was gay, and attached, even to a fault, to those fashionable societies, of which I was often the soul and spirit. But I am inclined to think;' and here Sir Harold's voice and countenance assumed the expression of one who related a narrative of an indifferent person, with whose fate he is not perfectly acquainted, 'that it was never so; and again I charge you, my fair cousin,' still addressing Matilda, 'believe not those who say it was. An additional tie which attached me to solitude was, the attraction of my dear mother's company. When she knew me again, her conversation, by degrees resuming all its former charms, was to me, more delightful than the intercourse of any one I met with in society. She was again capable of enjoying the pleasures of reading. We again turned over those authors that had delighted us in former times; again discussed those subjects, now rendered doubly dear, by the mournful and heart thrilling recollection of the different period in which we formerly found pleasure in them; when, with me, life and hope were new, and SHE was the world's idol, applauded and adored. Taste, and sensibility, had thus with her survived the use of reason. Is it not a proof, sweet cousin, how much those qualities should be ranked above it? For her little Julia alone, she never enquired; and I had not the courage to reveal to my sister the sad truth of her mother's fate. The child of sensibility, beautiful, but sad in the gay opening of life, she seems formed for love and melancholy alone. I tremble for her future happiness, and I trust you will not now reveal to her a secret that might destroy her.' After this caution he resumed:

'My time was now fully employed; my gentle mourner demanded from me every exertion; for, oh! my beloved friends, how much should we, who enjoy in its full power the use of reason, endeavour to alleviate the sufferings of those who labour under its temporary alienation! The addition to my former fortune, of the estate of the Rocks was, to me, rather a source of perplexity than of satisfaction. I was obliged to go down there, and I could not bring myself to part, for any / time, from the object of my mournful, yet pleasing cares. I soon wrote to Mrs. Carlyle, who had succeeded on the death of the woman that attended my mother to that delicate trust, to hasten to me with her. Julia and one attendant had accompanied me already to the Rocks. Mrs. Carlyle and her lady travelled together in a close carriage, and I took care to be apprized of the hour I might expect them. Having sent all my servants out of the way, on different pretexts, I met them myself on their arrival, which was towards night, and conducted Lady Julia and her companion to the apartment I had allotted for her, and which I had fitted up and adorned with every thing that could make her life tolerable. She was completely muffled up, from head to foot, in a wrapping pelisse and hood, and was mistaken by the driver, a north country lad and servant of my own, for another of the female domestics of the Abbey. I however dismissed him, and sent him back to his own country, that he might not afterwards remark in this neighbourhood upon the arrival of an additional stranger, when he found out I had retained none of my former establishment but Mrs. Carlyle, and the domestic who attended Julia. By means of these precautions the existence of my mother was, till now, only known to myself and to Mrs. Carlyle, to whom I gave power to divert the curiosity of others, by inventing whatever tale she pleased, even though it were to my disadvantage. One satisfaction I thought I should have at the Rocks. When at Moss-cliff Abbey

I had lately been distressed by an appearance which, added to the sufferings I had before sustained, contributed to drive me almost to distraction. At twelve, if I delayed one moment hastening to my mother, to allay her nightly returning terrors, I was reminded of my neglect, by the spirit of the murdered stripling, whose temerity had cost him his life. He too had a mother; a mother who had fondly doated on him; and now he came, and pointing with his thin transparent hand to the door where mine reposed, he besought me in plaintive accents, since he had died for her, that at least I should not desert the / duty to which I had sacrificed every other; then pointing to his ghastly wound, he would depart and vanish into air. I thought, perhaps, to lose this apparition; but the first night I was at the Rocks, exactly at twelve, he appeared to me, and asked me why I had left Lady Julia behind, a prey to anxiety and stronger alarms than ever?

'From the hour of her arrival she singularly attached herself to her new abode, which made me give up all thoughts of leaving it, or dividing my time between the Rocks and Moss-cliff Abbey, as I had at first proposed. Another reason drew me by stronger ties towards my other residence, even before she came to fix me in it, by the preference she gave it. An angel had once hovered there, and hallowed the spot by her presence. It was in a journey to London, which necessity obliged me to make, I learnt that secret. Reluctantly I went, but I soon wondered at the unwillingness I had felt to go; I arrived; I was blest with a vision; an angel,' turning to Matilda, ' 'twas you. A new life seemed instilled into my veins; I had been in a long and burning fever; you came upon me like the breeze in the desert, like the refreshing stream to the parched lip of the traveller. I began a new course of years; my life became one dream of love; I moved in the magic of beauty, of harmony, and grace. But I have no recollection of this new life; you must retrace it to me, my cousin, for you know it; nay, help me to remember it, for the memory of those days is pleasant to me as a soft stream flowing, wave after wave, over one oppressed with the heats of summer, as the earliest, sweetest, most art- less music of spring, to one just escaped from the bed of death. Tell me then of this new life, Matilda; recall it, for you know it.'

'Would we could recall you to peace, to tranquillity, to every happiness,' replied Mrs. Melbourne, with a look in which unutterable compassion was expressed.

'Do you indeed desire it,' he eagerly exclaimed, 'I thank you for that wish, and for your sake I will let myself be recalled. I thought that no one cared for me, for the last time I was in London they looked cold on me, / and told me so. I was the world's favourite, but the world has cast me off; and will you indeed assist me to bear the load of woe you have discovered, and will you soothe the sorrows that I so long have endured alone?'

'We will, we will,' exclaimed Matilda, affected by the preceding scene with a vari- ety of the most painful and contradictory sensations.

It was not until his cousins had repeatedly reiterated the promise he had required of them, that they were suffered by the Baronet to depart, which they did, hardly knowing whether they ought most to deplore the sad fate of Lady Julia Melbourne, to compassionate the unfortunate Sir Harold, or to regret Arbella's imprudent and ill-timed curiosity.

CHAPTER VI.

Fumi di fasto, ed ombre d'onor sono;
Ed amor proprio quei, che v'han tenuto
Tanti anni, e tengori fuor, del cammin buono.

TANSILLO. LA BALIA.[23]

THE shock that Lady Torrendale's spirits had received from the recent scene at Sir Harold Melbourne's, was such that she declared it absolutely impossible she should ever completely recover while she remained in that neighbourhood. Lord and Lady Strathallan were invited to spend a week at Lady Lyndhurst's, after which they were to proceed on a visiting tour to several friends. This scheme would fill up the time till the period returned for enjoying the pleasures of London; but as Lady Torrendale was not included in it, she got her physician to prescribe Cheltenham as absolutely necessary to restore her shattered / nerves to their tone. Matilda rather rejoiced in the departure of Strathallan and his bride, as withdrawing from her sight, an object, that was in danger sometimes of exciting recollections, painful, if not fatal to her peace. She had promoted their happiness as much as was in her power, and did not fear that the newly implanted taste for benevolence which she had encouraged in the bosom of Lady Strathallan should wither amid scenes that might present so many more objects worthy of real compassion. One dear remembrance she wished to keep of both. Emily, even if she had not been the sister of Strathallan, would have always been a favorite with her; but this partiality was greatly increased by the pity and interest with which she had lately inspired her.

During the course of the last six months, Miss Melbourne had been shocked and distressed to observe the roses that had glowed on the cheeks of her young favorite, already exchanged for the paleness and sickly langour of fashionable life. The latter part of the time Lady Torrendale had spent in London, had been fatal to Emily's health and improvement. About the period of Miss Langrish's dismission, her Lady-ship suddenly was heard to declare, that she could enjoy no pleasure of which her dear little Emily did not partake. She could not bear to appear in society, without acting some prominent part; and that of an interesting mother, she thought would be equally new, and attractive. One of her beaux, after seeing them together, having observed that the finished beauties of the charming mother never appeared in greater lustre than when grouped with the unfolding attractions of the blooming child; Lady Torrendale never afterwards made her appearance in any scene of amusement, unaccompanied by her attendant cherub: satisfied if, while the gentlemen crowded round the youthful stranger, or admired the diamonds that prematurely sparkled on her pretty white hand, they remarked, that hand, though lovely, equalled not her mother's. On Lady Strathallan's arrival at Woodlands, she had undertaken to remedy the effects of the dissipation in which her young sister-in-law had lately indulged; / and, with her usual pedantry and presumption, prosecuted her design with so much zeal and so little judgment, that the wearied and tormented girl was often heard to implore in vain for any intermission from the severity of perpetual application, if it were even being employed upon the plainest and homeliest needle-work. From this Scylla and Charybdis, Matilda designed to rescue her young friend, by requesting she might spend the time of Lady Torrendale's excursion to Cheltenham, with her. She urged her request in the last visit the Countess paid her, and found her Ladyship in a humor to grant it. The idea of departure always raised her spirits; her adieus partook of the hurry and bustle in which she found herself: 'I can never repay your kindness and attention to Emily,' she said; 'adieu, my dear Miss Melbourne – we are all in the greatest confusion you see, and I hope that will apologize for this short farewell.'

'A concise farewell may suit with your Ladyship's feelings,' said Lady Strathallan, who had accompanied the Countess; 'but,' she added, turning on Matilda, a countenance more than usually solemn, and which had, in its style and expression something even beyond its common appearance, impressive and *grandioso*, 'I have debts to this young lady which cannot so easily be acquitted.'

Her air, her look, her motion, all showed that she meditated *quelque grand coup*,[24] but what it might be, surpassed her young friend's faculty of guessing; at length, taking the opportunity (while Lady Torrendale was making her parting speeches to Mrs. Melbourne) of continuing her address. 'This,' said she, offering a case that seemed to contain jewels, 'will serve sometimes to remind you of an hour, in which you displayed a greatness of character that can never be remembered without admiration. I have meditated how to reward it. On that day you gave me a portrait. I now insist on your accepting one in return.'

Not doubting that the case contained Lady Strathallan's picture, Matilda was near mentally exclaiming, 'Ah what an exchange!' but instantly checking the unguarded feeling, / she thanked her Ladyship with warmth for this proof of affectionate attention, and assured her she should ever consider it among the most valuable of her possessions.

'Then you promise me sacredly,' resumed the Viscountess, 'to keep it, and that nothing shall tempt you to part with it.' Matilda readily gave the desired promise.

'Then take it,' said Lady Strathallan, looking earnestly at her, 'for now you deserve it; and may it prove,' she continued embracing her with more warmth than she often betrayed, 'the pledge of the perfect confidence that from this moment shall subsist between us. I have only one more favor to ask,' she added, 'will you write to me?'

Miss Melbourne having willingly agreed to keep up an intercourse already so pleasantly established, felt herself affected by these proofs of sincere attachment in the Viscountess, and had mingled something more of tenderness in her farewell, than she had ever expected to do on parting with Lady Strathallan and Lady Torrendale; but the former, in whose character Miss Mountain might for a moment be suspended, but could never be forgot, had already resumed her wonted formality of manner and deportment, and as she sailed out of the room with her usual stately grace, left her young friend more full of curiosity to examine her present, than of regret for her departure, which afforded an opportunity for doing so. She hastily opened the shagreen case which she expected would contain the portrait of Lady Strathallan, nor could she forbear internally smiling at the supposed vanity which had dictated the remark in presenting it, 'you now deserve it.' How was the course of her feelings changed in a moment, when, instead of the expected portrait, she beheld the brooch that some months before she had confided to the care of Lady Strathallan, as containing her husband's picture. Her first idea was that there must be some mistake, but then recollecting the precautions her Ladyship had taken against her present being returned, and the tenor of the whole discourse she had previously held to her, she saw the whole circumstance at once in its / true light, and perceived this was the manner in which this eccentric and generous spirit chose to prove to her the esteem, the confidence, her recent conduct had excited. She also observed that the brooch had been reset for her with small diamonds, instead of pearls, and that the case contained besides, an elegant set of ornaments in pearls and diamonds, to match it. Lady Strathallan, who, with her strange solemnity of deportment, possessed a fund of romantic exaltation of ideas, that would have enabled her well to support the character of the Lady Blanche's, and Lady Belerma's of former days,[25] and who gloried in being above the little jealousies and weaknesses of her sex, had thought this was a method truly sublime, to convince her noble-minded young friend that she had a nature as unsuspicious, a 'spirit as proud as her own.' What was to be done? Still, to attempt to return it, would appear a tacit confession on Matilda's part, that the present was not as completely without danger, as Lady Strathallan wished to suppose it. This Lady's overtrained heroism, which made her overlook the seeming impropriety she forced her young friend to commit, placed her in a truly awkward and perplexing predicament. All Miss Melbourne's consolation was to look, literally, at 'the bright side of the picture;' and accept this as the most grateful acknowledgment of the success of her unremitting efforts to promote the happiness of her friends, and to forget the sacrifice she had made of her own. She could not but be proud of such a distinguished tribute to the purity of her intentions; but as Matilda's confidence in herself, the result of a modest, yet firm consciousness of internal rectitude, was of a nature totally distinct from wilful presumption, she contented herself with restoring the much disputed portrait to its original place on Mrs. Melbourne's bureau, which terminated the consequences of a step, which Lady Strathallan, in the self-complacence and pride of her heart, called a 'magnanimous;' but which Matilda, perhaps more truly, considered as a distressing action. /

CHAPTER VII.

'Tis an old maxim in the schools,
That flattery's the food of fools;
Yet now and then your men of wit
Will condescend to take a bit.

SWIFT.[26]

AND now the bustle of servants and tradesmen, the various preparations that precede the departure of greatness, announced the secession of the Torrendale family from the Derbyshire neighbourhood. Already had Emily, with moist eyes, taken a tender farewell of her brother, and wept at parting with him, because he was going for some time; and at bidding farewell to Lady Strathallan, because it was possible, she said, she might soon return.

Lady Torrendale was to set off in a few days for Cheltenham; Spencer, to whom the waters were recommended as conducive to his perfect recovery, was to be of the party. Though suffering little from the effects of his quarrel, except the mortification of having one eye still covered, there was evidently a weight that hung upon his spirits at times sufficient to alarm the watchful tenderness of his mother; and though she was pretty well satisfied that she had little to fear from the partiality he had once professed for Arbella, her Ladyship was determined, before she left the country *d'en avoir le cœur net,*[27] as she phrased it, upon the subject. We must then imagine the mother and son seated on opposite sofas; her Ladyship employed in her new and favorite amusement of plaiting chips;[28] Spencer, indolently lounging, sometimes returning, and more often neglecting, the caresses of Floss, who most ambitiously raising himself on his hind legs, sought the honor of licking his hand. After a silence of some continuance, the Countess began the conversation, observing, 'You look uncommonly well to-day, Spencer; you will only / require a month at Cheltenham completely to recover your former self. But I had forgotten – the rooms and walks may not present the same attraction; for I tell you candidly I shall not take Arbella with me. She has made herself talked of, without attaining celebrity. I do not know whether you clearly understand me; but I am perfectly satisfied there is no other expression that would exactly convey my meaning; in short she has played her cards ill, and made it disagreeable to me to have any thing farther to say to her, beyond the civility of a common acquaintance; but with you it may be different; I do not inquire into your secrets. She may still have a tyrannic influence, a kind of habitual sway, and in trying to break the spell you may only find each scene recal, in livelier colours, your former intercourse

– 427 –

with the dashing *belle* of Cheltenham. Have I guessed it? and will it indeed be *le plus loin, le plus serré?*[29]

'Certainly, madam, if you like.'

'If I like! what a strange answer! you have long had my opinion on the subject.'

'Why then mine is, that it would make a very pretty motto.'

'A pretty motto! what do you think I am talking of?'

'Are you not asking my opinion, madam, about that seal with two doves each holding in its bill an end of a true lover's knot, one that Lady Honora means to send to Captain Seabright?'

' 'Tis true I alluded to it, but I was asking your opinion of Arbella.'

'Oh, Arbella!'

'Yes Arbella, Captain Fitzroy; and I must tell you I am tired of this trifling.'

'So am I (yawning and stretching himself) very tired, I assure you.'

'I am glad to hear you say so; then I am to suppose the alteration in my plans, with regard to her, makes no difference to you?'

'None in the least, madam.'

'I am then to conclude the silly affair that once gave me some uneasiness quite broken off between you?'

'If you please, madam.'

'"If you please, madam!" there is something / strangely unsatisfactory in your manner of giving a satisfactory answer,' resumed her Ladyship, with a half laugh; 'I insist upon knowing what is the matter with you, Spencer, you seem half asleep?'

'Would I were asleep indeed,' cried Fitzroy, suddenly throwing off his apparently listless calm – that I were in a long, long sleep; or that the occurrences of the last three months were but a frightful dream.'

'What is it has annoyed you to such a degree, my dearest boy, and damped your charming spirit. If it is that ugly black patch, consider that while you continue to wear it, you look more like a hero than ever, and when you leave it off, the contrast will be more striking, than it otherwise could possibly be. Don't you remember the lines Alcæus composed when your accident was recent, in which he contrived to bring in your attentions to Miss Rachael Adonijah, the beautiful one-eyed Jewess. Under the figure of a brother and sister he pourtrays a much tenderer relation. They say the little wretch adapted it from a Greek epigram, but I believe it is his own. Stay, I think I have it written out some where.'

'Of his right eye young Æcon was bereft,
His sister Leonilla of her left.
Give her thine eye, sweet boy, so shall ye prove
The goddess she, and thou the god of love.'[30]

'Confound Alcæus and the whole tribe of scribbling impertinent poetasters!' exclaimed Spencer, starting up and striking the table with a vehemence which startled her Ladyship. 'To what end, madam, do you thus needlessly torture my feelings? Though to be sure,' he added, in a lowered voice, and resuming something of his former languid calmness, 'to be blind would be perhaps the only way to be reconciled to my present situation.'

'To be blind! you alarm and distress me, child, by these mysterious expressions. I assure you if you think your affair has been a disadvantage to you, you are wrong; it has produced a very favourable sensation among a certain set, and wherever you go / you are looked upon with rather more interest than less; there is your former flirt, Helen, who regrets nothing but that it was not in her cause you engaged yourself; you might have your choice of her, or the die-away Lavinia Crossbrook, who was in fits when she heard what had happened; but I would advise you to let them both wear the willow,[31] and think seriously of our dear little Peruvian Princess, Miss Bullion Ingoldsby, who has mines of wealth at her own disposal, with the possible prospect of a peerage in her own right, and and who said very lately in my hearing, that instead of being disadvantageously altered, you would now make more impression than ever.'

'"More impression!" do I indeed?' said Spencer, looking up languidly, and 'lighted up his faded eye'[32] for a moment, with that expression of satisfaction, which coquettes, whether male or female, experience in the gratification of their reigning passions; but soon recollecting himself, with a deep sigh, he added, 'it is useless to think of it now; it is all over – yes, in short, madam, I am married.'

'Married! and without consulting me,' said her Ladyship, hastily, and in a tone of evident pique and disappointment; but, changing almost immediately to one of mingled reproach and tenderness, 'you need not have feared me, Spencer,' she added, 'for I believe you have not a friend more zealously attached to your interests; but come,' (a little recovering her good humour) 'let us see what this sudden affair is. I must know all about it, the when, where, and who; is it the sentimental Miss Crossbrook, who has insisted upon a private marriage? well that is no great harm, the girl has a good fortune at present, and will have a better at the death of her brother, who is going off, dear complaisant soul, in a most obliging consumption.'

'Madam, you need not distress yourself: it is not Miss Crossbrook,' replied Spencer.

'Perhaps the Scotch heiress, Lady Margaret Maclean; though her high stiff relations would not approve of such unceremonious / courtships I should imagine; or is it her sister, Lady Georgiana? or perhaps one of the Miss Kingstons, our rich nabob's daughters; I remember you were a great favourite there.'

'True,' observed Spencer, 'I might have had any of them, but – '

'No, I am not right yet? I am certain it is not Miss Ferrars; it cannot be Miss Melbourne,' added her Ladyship; and a look of angry suspicion glanced over her features, as she pronounced the name.

'I wish it were,' resumed Fitzroy, with a sigh, 'it is – what use is there in longer concealment, since it must out; it is – Miss Hautenville.'

'Now Captain Fitzroy,' said the Countess, with a look of the most serious displeasure, 'you are pleased to jest with what, I suppose, you term, among your more favored intimates, my silly maternal anxiety; yet it is not the less real. Miss Hautenville! that is very likely to be true indeed!'

'Upon my soul I wish it were not.'

'Married to Miss Hautenville at three and twenty! with your person, advantages, and expectations, thrown yourself away upon a woman ten years older, and so every way unworthy of you?'

'True, Madam, as you say, with my person, advantages, and expectations,' repeated Spencer, surveying himself with complacency, yet with a sigh, 'but what could I do! She was always with me, and – a – I saw nobody else; when she was not reading, we were of course sentimentalizing, or flirting, or that sort of thing: there is no other conversation you know; and so – by Jove I don't know how it was – I believe she has a devilish deal of art: she took up some foolish thing I said in the way of gratitude, (for while she was devoting herself to me, I could not tell her she was old and ugly) and said I had made her a promise; and when I wanted to be off, I thought she would have died; for, with all her faults she loves me to distraction. At last I told her to keep it a secret, and that I would; for to say the truth I thought at that time it was all over with me, and that I might as well take pity: so you see how it / was, and how impossible it was for me to help myself.'

'And I see what an elegant creature I have to present for my daughter-in-law,' added her Ladyship, with an affected contempt, which concealed the smothered anguish of disappointed ambition. 'Oh, Spencer, how shall I endure it?'

'You shall not have it to endure,' replied Fitzroy, in a more natural tone than he had in the latter part of the dialogue employed; 'for, by Jove, though she has taken advantage of my cursed folly, I will not expose myself farther, by ever acknowledging her as my wife.'

'Spoken with a spirit that becomes your blood,' exclaimed Lady Torrendale, a little revived by this assurance. 'The creature will not gain much by her arts and her canting: whenever I came to the house – "I am giving Spencer a little advice; I am repeating to Captain Fitzroy what your Ladyship says" – Oh, my Ladyship! – If ever I believe in disinterested female friendship again! – There is no way of breaking this marriage,' continued her Ladyship, after a pause of painful reflection; 'unfortunately you are of age, and so is the Lady.'

'That she is, twice over, I believe,' replied Spencer, with a bitter sigh.

'Well then, all that can be done for the present is, to preserve the same prudent silence you have hitherto maintained; and above all things to keep this dis – ' she had nearly said disgraceful affair; but changing the term in compliment to her son's feelings to one of milder import, the Countess continued, 'all you have to do, my dear Spencer, is to keep this disagreeable affair from your father's knowledge, who is apt to be at once violent, refractory, and old-fashioned in his notions, and we will see what can be done for you. Marriage, though the commonest and the easiest speculation, is not the only way of rising, with interest, and family talents like yours. Some way or other I am persuaded, you are intended to surpass that Strathallan. It is my *presentiment*, and you know I have great faith in *presentiment*.'

'Strathallan may be after all our best / friend on this occasion,' Spencer murmured; but his mother did not hear him, and after consoling herself with the reflection that at least he had disappointed 'that jilt Arbella,' she left him, in order to have the pleasure of being the first bearer of these agreeable tidings to a young lady, whom she had often told 'in confidence,' that 'could she chuse among the various young women to whom her volatile Spencer had, at different times, devoted his attentions, she knew no person to whom she could so willingly resign him as her charming self.'

Her Ladyship anticipated in the rage and despair of her young *protegée*, at least one delicious treat, but she knew not, or she chose to continue wilfully ignorant of Miss Ferrar's superiority over her, even in that art on which she prided herself, and forgot that a degree of dissimulation and self-command, if it may be acquired by the fine lady, is natural to the coquette of every rank.

The communication was not new to Arbella; Miss Hautenville, or, as she must now be called, the Honourable Mrs. Fitzroy,[a] hearing some talk of a removal in which she was not included, and being too good a military wife not to be willing to accompany her husband in his campaigns, had immediately announced her intentions to Mrs. Stockwell, and dropping the veil of secrecy (which she considered as not only inconvenient but impolitic) announced to her former patroness, in very peremptory terms, the necessity of providing herself with another companion, as she, for her own part meant, in future, to be the constant one of the amiable and passionate Captain Fitzroy. Mrs. Stockwell, after repeatedly blessing herself, exclaiming to more stars than she knew the names of, mingling reproaches and congratulations, began at length to express her doubts of the accuracy of the lady's statement, or at least her wonder that such a transaction should take place in her own house, 'unknown to her.' Miss Hautenville coolly reminded her of a little 'excrescence' she made early one morning to spend the whole day with a friend three miles off; in which propitious moment (a licence having been previously secured) the / enamoured youth had been bound in those chains which secured him her's for ever, by the aid of a young Clergyman (whose literary attempts Miss Hautenville had patronized) in the presence of no other witnesses than that lady's own maid, and Spencer's man, and in the very parlour in which she had now the honour of making the communication to her. The question to which Mrs. Stockwell returned was, how to supply Mrs. Fitzroy's place? To be left alone was shocking; it was besides so very unfashionable; yet she could hardly hope again to meet with a companion so well-drest, so 'so well-read,' and 'comed of so good a family' as Miss Hautenville. The two first qualities her long neglected niece Arbella possessed to admiration; and, for the last, her youth and various attractions might amply compensate.

On the very evening, therefore, previous to the discovery made by Lady Torrendale, this prudent lady dispatched, to her niece, a long epistle, explanatory and apologetical, telling her that if she was really tired of fine airs and fine company, she would feel herself most happy again in her society. The intelligence of Spencer's marriage with Miss Hautenville was a thunder stroke to Arbella, and prevented her at first from attending to, or even understanding the rest of the contents of this epistle; hearing, however, that an answer was expected, she rallied her spirits, took up the letter again, and smiled as she looked at it; then perceiving, upon a reperusal, the only part that remained for her to act, if she wished to preserve any degree of dignity, the duped, despised, every way disappointed Arbella prepared, with her usual admirable presence of mind, to go through the last act of her tragi-comedy with spirit. The place where Spencer resided was no longer an abode for her; accordingly, with a frankness and grace which distinguished every thing she did, she at once accepted her aunt's proposal; for the air of ease and candour that ran through Arbella's reply, she was, perhaps, very much indebted to that natural openness and generosity of disposition, which really hardly permitted her to / harbour, for twenty-four hours, a serious resentment towards any one who had injured her, particularly in a matter she considered so much beneath her attention, as money.

After a night of agony, the dreadful details of which she wisely resolved should remain buried for ever in her own bosom, she prepared, with a smooth brow, and a countenance of apparent openness and gaiety, to encounter the scrutinizing glances of the Countess of Torrendale; they met on the landing-place, for that lady had just retired from the distressing interview with Spencer, that has been related. Her separation from her young friend, she had long determined upon; and, without busying herself about the possible arrangements of Miss Ferrars, she resolved to put it upon the uncertainty of her stay at the place to which she was now going, indifferent accommodations, probability of making a visiting tour, and several more excuses which she was to convey in language as polite as possible. Composing her countenance to its most benign expression, 'I declare I was looking for you, my dear Miss Ferrars,' she began; 'I am truly mortified to think – .'

'I hope nothing disagreeable has happened, Madam,' interrupted Arbella, with an air of assumed concern, 'I thought I was to have wished your Ladyship joy.'

'Joy,' reiterated Lady Torrendale.'

'Yes, Madam, for the happy event that has taken place in your family; may you and Captain Fitzroy – ' Lady Torrendale coloured extremely.

'So, Madam,' she said, 'you have been listening.'

'No, Madam,' replied Miss Ferrars, with unaffected dignity; 'I have not been listening, but this letter,' presenting Mrs. Stockwell's billet, 'will inform you how I came acquainted with the event.'

'You will be so good, Miss Ferrars,' resumed her Ladyship, 'as to step into my dressing-room, this is no place for discussions of such a nature.'

Arbella obeyed, and then added, 'I wish. Madam, to communicate to you a circumstance / in which my happiness is very much concerned. My poor aunt has expressed in this note a great desire to have me as her companion for the winter. Her wishes coincide with mine, yet still, if you wish me to accompany you, I would not, for the world – '

'Make yourself quite easy on that head, my dear Miss Ferrars,' replied Lady Torrendale, sarcastically; 'it is never my way to come across the inclinations of young ladies; my carriage and servants are at your command, whenever you chuse to order them. I never aspired to be the rival of Mrs. Stockwell, nor ever shall.' In these last words the Countess had endeavoured to throw all the mingled bitterness and scorn of which her nature was susceptible, and she paused triumphantly to notice their effect.

'This generous and unreserved compliance was almost beyond my hopes; and overwhelms me with gratitude,' exclaimed Arbella, 'particularly as I know it must be at the risk of a temporary inconvenience to your Ladyship, for when one's plans are arranged – '

'None, in the least, and I beg – '

'I feel your Ladyship's goodness, and I know what you would say, indeed I should have been miserable without your permission – '

'Oh! you have my full permission,' with a smile of contempt.

'How good you are, how kind it is, thus to put yourself out of the question; yet believe me Madam, nothing but the consideration of my poor aunt's solitary situation – '

'Ah! now I have at length found the way to vex her,' thought Lady Torrendale; 'Is Mrs. Stockwell going to lose her companion? then you must have no doubt been surprised, my dear Miss Ferrars, at the reason your aunt gives for parting with Miss Hautenville.'

'Surprised, Madam? I own I could hardly have believed it of Captain Fitzroy. Few young men, at his age, have sense and courage to despise the world, and make merit alone the object of their choice. May they both be as happy as they deserve to be. Miss Hautenville (I can speak it from a long acquaintance) though not possessed of / brilliant accomplishments, is a sensible well-informed – ' Her Ladyship bit her lip. 'This is past bearing, sure she cannot be truly indifferent, and yet how otherwise could a woman, and so young a woman, preserve such perfect self-command.'

The Countess forgot, during this short argument with herself, that she had no longer to deal with the open, ingenuous, affectionate Arbella, who, but a summer before, had flung out of that very dressing-room, and vowed never to re-enter it, in all the heat of passionate resentment; that giddy Arbella, who was equally open in avowing her indignation, and imprudent in betraying her partiality.

Since that time these finished actresses had assisted in perfecting each other, and Arbella now surpassed her mistress, by as much as a person of sense (whatever be the undertaking) always excels a fool.

Finding it, at all events, absolutely necessary to change her battery, if she wished for any gratification in her favourite passion; her Ladyship instantly bade her eyes exchange their former forbidding expression, for that look of tender interest, of kind concern which, when Fitzroy assumed, it was so irresistible, and which, even with her, was bewitching. 'I know, my dear Miss Ferrars,' said she, kindly taking her hand (a trick she had, whenever she meditated mischief, as if she feared her victim should escape her) that you speak as you feel, and are above all disguise; but now tell me truly, and do not fear you shall ever have to repent your confidence, are you not a *little* disappointed; do you not think WE HAVE BOTH a right to be a little disappointed at Spencer's thus throwing himself away? I will myself candidly own to you, that I am not much pleased with the match. Come, I see by your eyes you are of my opinion; charming sensibility! acknowledge the truth to me, my dearest girl, and do not fear to meet a rigid monitor. Spencer is, indeed, a young man who would more than justify – '

Miss Ferrars looked down, blushed, hesitated; a tear of sensibility seemed to tremble in her eye; and all that spirit which she had / summoned up against the haughtiness of the Countess, appeared ready to give way before the melting force of her unexpected kindness. For a moment she stood irresolute, then throwing herself into the arms of her noble friend, 'Your Ladyship's generosity overcomes me,' she said, 'and merits, on my part, a return of similar frankness. To you I will then venture to acknowledge those feelings which, though they might be termed by the world an excess of absurd and romantic weakness, yet – '

Lady Torrendale's cheeks glowed, her eyes sparkled, and, as she listened in panting exultation to this exordium, she was ready to exclaim with Sir Peter Teazle, 'Aye, now I believe the truth is coming out!'[33] she however deferred her triumph, in order to render it more complete. Arbella continued.

'From the time of Captain Fitzroy's being wounded in a duel, in which my name was unhappily brought forward; honour, compassion, pleaded so strongly for him – '

'Compassion!' exclaimed her Ladyship starting.

'Yes, Madam, it may be a weakness, but it appeared to me, I had no choice left; and though inclination no longer seconded his claim on my heart, I resolved to sacrifice it entirely, to what I considered as my duty.'

'Duty! humph – '

'Hear me, Lady Torrendale. Captain Fitzroy's and mine were never congenial characters; and his capricious unfeeling conduct had long ago conquered any little girlish partiality which your Ladyship might formerly have observed. I anticipated with him nothing but a life of frigid indifference; the hardest for one of my temper to endure with patience; but I had chosen my lot, and was determined,' and here Arbella assumed an air the most theatrically grand, 'to submit heroically to my destiny. When thus engaged, in what I thought an inextricable entanglement, the discovery of Captain Fitzroy's more prudent choice, came at once to satisfy my honour, and relieve me from the self-imposed obligations to which I had devoted myself. I feel now like a bird released from the – ' /

'Well, Miss Ferrars, I have not time now to listen to a detail of your feelings,' interrupted her Ladyship, abruptly, while her countenance expressed the bitterest disappointment; 'if you are in haste to leave me, the carriage shall be ordered at whatever hour you think fit; and, as I have many letters to write, and matters to arrange, which will engage me till night, I will take this opportunity of expressing my sincere wishes for your health and happiness, with Mrs. Stockwell; and my regret, that it was not in my power to make my house any longer an agreeable residence to you.' With these words she flung out of the room, leaving Arbella clearly mistress of the field; and not aware that that young lady had already acquired the difficult art of masking a breaking heart under the appearance of gaiety; and that Arbella took hours, after this temporary exertion of spirit, to recover breath, voice, power, in short, to support with tolerable patience, the load of hated life; her Ladyship continued, through the day, to indulge her wonder how her young friend could by any means, have been brought to become insensible to merit so shining as Spencer's, when she ought rather to have lamented that she had not herself followed the Spartan rule, of never exhibiting her tactics too often to the same enemy. /

CHAPTER VIII.

Oh Lady! since I've worn thy gentle chain,
How oft have I deplored each wasted hour,
When I was free – and had not learned to love!

Lord Strangford. Camöens.[34]

Mrs. fitzroy, in so formally notifying to Mrs. Stockwell her intention of leaving her, had forgot that a small circumstance was necessary in order to put her plan in execution – her husband's consent. The moment he understood her design, Spencer assured her that 'though nothing could mortify him to such a degree, he held himself bound, in honour, to give her warning. If she attempted to follow him to Cheltenham it would not[a] be in his power to take the least notice of her, as he did not wish to be made the subject of conversation at that place – that he was also unable to supply her with money for her appearance there, and that he therefore advised her, as a friend, to stay, till they could arrange some future plan of life, with a lady whose company she had till now found so agreeable. Lady Torrendale seconded the sentiments of her son; and finding herself despised by her husband, and discountenanced by his family, poor Miss Hautenville reaped but few advantages from her unworthy artifices; and was but too happy to accept the offer of the same accommodation she had formerly enjoyed with Mrs. Stockwell. This poor woman, still the dupe of that lady's pretensions to lineage and literature, asked nothing in return for her hospitality, but the privilege of deploring, wherever she went, in terms properly pathetic, the hard fate of her dear friend, the hon-o-ra-ble Mrs. Fitzroy; who, 'though she was wife to a captain of horse, and, what was more, daughter-in-law to an Earl, was reduced for to put up with her poor accommodations, and be her companion still, poor thing!' But the good lady was obliged to decline this *comedie larmoyante*,[35] wherever the 'Ho-no-ra-ble / Mrs. Fitzroy' made her appearance, who seemed to find, in the pleasure of lording it over her friend, more completely than ever, some compensation for the pain which the conduct of others made her experience.

Not so Arbella – when the bustle occasioned by the departure of the Torrendales, and the momentary self-possession she was forced to assume, no longer kept up her spirits; she looked in vain, on every side, for any circumstance to mitigate her regret, or diminish her mortification. The prolonged stay of Mrs. Fitzroy, filled up the measure of her vexations. They had always hated each other, and to be forced perpetually to endure the presence of her, who, if she did not possess Spencer's heart, had at least received his vows, was perhaps the severest suffering Arbella's tortured bosom had yet endured. She sunk into a dejection the more alarming, as it was totally at war with her general disposition and character. She had loved sincerely, tenderly, passionately, as she was capable of loving: and she found all these soft feelings in a moment scorned and outraged, in a manner the most mortifying, the least to be anticipated. As if it had been decreed that his image should, in every circumstance of her life, be associated in her mind with that of his mother, whom he so strongly resembled, she felt, at the same moment, cruelly hurt at Lady Torrendale's abrupt desertion of her. That it would be followed by that of many of her former gay friends, she plainly foresaw. After having been, from her first entrance into life, in constant chase of an illusion, the bubble burst, and she found herself, while yet in youthful bloom, a wreck, the sport of every malignant blast upon the shoreless sea of fashion, on which she had so carelssly ventured all her hopes. She became gloomy, retired, and was with difficulty drawn from her home. Matilda sometimes made use of the attraction of Miss Swanley, who was to have been of the Cheltenham party, but for a fit of abstraction which made her in the place of a Birth-day Ode on the Countess, put into her hand the plan of a tragedy, for which it appeared the scenes she had recently / witnessed had furnished some hints – these are a few of the notes:

'*Plan for the Tragedy of the Rival Brothers.*

Orthon, (the jealous gloomy tyrant,) Lord Torrendale – his character – particularly afternoon conversation – furnish fine hints.

Artainta, (the ambitious artful step-mother,) the deceit, malice, faded charms of the gypsey Countess can furnish *un beau canevas* – [36] how suitable to her present appearance, the scene in which the declining Artainta opens the play, singing,

Faded beauty, waning charms,

Where are fled your conquering arms?

In the first scene to be gorgeously apparelled – in the trial scene, (where she is to be called to account for strangling the sultan,) disshevelled, pale, haggard – Lady T – 's exact morning face. Lady S – stands for Phedyma, the young Sultana, as Lady T – does for the elder one, or sultana validi. Mem. to make a scene between them in the style of the Rival Queens – [37] an excellent study – great pity I was not present at their grand quarrel yesterday – Alcæus said it was as good as a comedy – no genius – I would have made a tragedy of it – must endeavour to keep in the way, and if they don't soon begin again, foment a little dispute, in which to study their character – at the end we will overthrow the machinations of the step-mother – hang the worthless Ariamnes, (Spencer) and poisoning the other interlocutors, establish on the throne the virtuous Artazires, who (like Lord Strathallan) shall be constellation of talents, virtues, &c.'

'Upon my word! study my character! – hang my son Spencer! – I shall take care how I admit such ingenious young ladies as inmates!' Such were the exclamations of Lady Torrendale, upon perusing the fatal scroll; and poor Sappho, deprived for ever of the sunshine of her favor and protection, had time to lament, in the most melodious strains, her not having remarked how a paper was docketed before she delivered it. There was, in Sappho's character, an inconsistency for which it was long before Matilda could account. / That she was averse to solitude and obscurity was evident; yet so *distrait*[38] was she in the ordinary intercourse of life, that where once she received applause, she ten times met with mortification.

The first symptom Arbella gave of a dawning interest in the world again, was an enquiry relative to Sir Harold and the lady who had once been an object of such lively solicitude to her. 'I hope you never told him it was I, and I alone that planned and effected the forcible entry, which produced so unexpected and painful a scene,' she said, 'otherwise much as I feel relieved by visiting you, I must indulge in the pleasure less frequently, for fear of meeting him.'

'You may be sure,' replied Matilda, 'that I have not communicated to him any thing that might increase his vexation and uneasiness. But as the discovery did not really tend to my cousin's disadvantage, I think he has, on the whole, been happier since it has been made; his manner has been more tranquil, since he has not laboured under a load of conscious concealment.'

Arbella asked many more questions respecting Lady Julia Melbourne, and hinted a desire to be admitted to see her; but this curiosity Matilda always repressed, conscious that though she had unlimited access to this unhappy lady, the extending the privilege, but for once, even to the dearest intimate, could be productive of no advantage, and might renew sufferings she dreaded to contemplate.

At other times the unfortunate Miss Ferrars would appear perfectly indifferent to all that passed, and mournfully rapt in former scenes, recapitulated, with a melancholy satisfaction, pleasures so short, so delusive, so fatal to her peace. Then would Matilda mingle tears with hers, 'till what appeared at first the tribute of sympathy, became, at length, an almost dangerous indulgence – for sometimes her treacherous heart would whisper, 'she weeps for the dispersion of an illusion; I, for the destruction of real happiness.'

The first interview Matilda had with Lady Julia after the late painful discovery, was productive of unexpected and distressing effects. / Sir Harold had been desirous to try the power of her soothing conversation, from which he had himself experienced such beneficial effects, upon one who, at least when discoursing with him, almost always evinced the power of thinking justly: but he was disappointed in his hopes of giving her pleasure. Examining with anxious scrutiny, the downcast lovely features of Matilda, Lady Julia suddenly turned to her son, and said, 'That is the lady without a fault;' then sighed, and with a kind of convulsive shudder, motioned her to withdraw, while the dejection in which she was usually plunged, appeared, for the rest of the day, visibly increased.

She often amused herself touching the harp, and it was from her those sweet plaintive tones had proceeded which Arbella formerly noticed. By degrees she became accustomed to, and even fond of, Matilda's society. Lady Julia's sufferings, her melancholy situation, her delicate and interesting appearance, that had prepossessed even strangers, increased to a degree of fondness, the compassion with which Mrs. Melbourne and her daughter beheld her. To vary Sir Harold's amusements, Matilda often read to him; for she had adopted, from her mother, the idea, that it is to lose half the advantages of a voice that can render the feelings of the poet, not to be able to convey pleasure by the modulation of its tones, in speaking, as well as singing. This gave a variety to her powers of pleasing, while mere shewy accomplishments, by constant repetition, fatigue and disgust.

As he listened, one evening, delighted while she read to him part of the fifth book of Milton, which opens with the vision of Eve, he stopt her at the words,

'My fairest, my espoused, my *latest* found!'[39]

And repeating the line, in a low voice, with a marked emphasis on the last epithet, he inwardly murmured, '*That* were bliss indeed! but found *too* late' – the sigh and melancholy pause which followed this broken sentence plainly marked his meaning. The idea of the loss, the voluntary loss he had, for so many years sustained, was never absent from his mind. To secure to himself this treasure, / for the remaining years he had to live, he had recourse to an expedient which, for the time, awed and terrified Matilda. It was after one of those sallies of violence, which always made him, when recovered, fear she would detach herself wholly from him. On this occasion it was, perhaps, more than usually excusable. He had surprised his friends of Woodbine Lodge, conversing in Matilda's favorite arbour. Arbella endeavoured to smile at the amusing sallies of Sappho. Julia read at their feet, and Emily was busily cultivating her little garden. A kind of dejection soon stole over the whole party. This was the very spot in which Strathallan had, on the renewal of their intercourse, listened with such dangerous rapture to the music of Matilda; and the remembrance of the pain he had, on that occasion, given her feelings, imparted a sad and pensive shade to her contemplations. Yet, perhaps, the secret uneasiness that dwelt in every bosom, was a bond of union as powerful and sympathetic, though not so visible, as the most active and successful desire to please; for certain it is that they passed the time in desultory converse, 'pleasant, but mournful to the soul,' 'till the resplendent moon,

'Peeped through the chambers of the fleecy east,
Enlightened by degrees, and in her train,
Led on the gentle hours*.'

Oh! what a group was there to sit and weep,

'Beneath the trembling languish of her beam'.'[40]

Not a heart but had bled from the stings of ill placed passion – not a mind but was attuned in harmony to the solemn scene, and felt the magic influence of the hour.

'What a lover's light!' exclaimed Sappho, as she remarked the strong line of brilliancy that fell upon the seat on which they reposed.

Sir Harold raising his eyes to the beautiful planet above them, half murmured, 'Hast thou thy hall like Ossian, dwellest thou in the shadow of grief?'[41] /

'I would fain answer thy question, Sir Knight,' resumed Sappho, with affected solemnity; 'thou whose distinguished encouragement alike of music and the muse, entitles thee to rank with the glorious chief who patronized the bards that celebrated a night such as this:

'The Roe is in the cleft of the rock. The Heath-cock's head is beneath his wing; no beast, no bird is abroad, but the owl and the howling fox. She on a leafless tree. He in a cloud on the hill†*.'[42]

---

*   Thomson.
†   Song of the Five Bards.

'Would it not be just the hour,' continued the fair enthusiast, who, when once possessed by the genius, or rather perhaps the demon of illusion,ᵃ was not easily interrupted in her career, to address one's favoured swain with some lay like those Shakespeare declares worthy to be

'Sung by a fair queen in a summer's bower,
With ravishing division to her lute.'[43]

'Miss Melbourne could do so,' said Sir Harold.

'If you wish it I will,' replied Matilda, 'though you know the lute is wanting,' and, after musing a moment she begun the song of

'Too plain, dear youth, these tell-tale eyes.' – [44]

'I know that song,' exclaimed Julia, suddenly turning from her book, 'there was a Lord Arlington, who used to come to our house, and listen to mamma singing it, when papa was out. I remember she new set it to please him, and used to accompany it with her harp. Poor mamma! she sung it very sweetly before she died.'

There was something so touching in the manner in which these words were pronounced by the poor little 'more than orphan,' as her brother had once emphatically called her – her innocence and total unconsciousness were so affecting, that Matilda, as she drew her tenderly towards her, felt a rising tear steal, unbidden, down her cheek: but their effect on Sir Harold was dreadful, and left her no doubt, if she could before have entertained one, that his sister had named the disturber of his family's honour / and peace. His eyes flashed fury, but then, as if endeavouring to command himself, he checked the muttered exclamation that seemed ready to escape his lips, and taking his sister's trembling hand, 'poor innocent,' he said, 'the error was not thine!' Then darting away left the astonished group, and was soon seen pacing at a distance among the trees that partly shaded his hurried and unequal steps.

Matilda, vexed to have been, though unintentionally the cause of his emotion, and desirous to draw off the attention of the other ladies from it, attempted some general conversation, in which she was well seconded by Sappho. They again reverted to the beauty of the surrounding scenery; talked of the pleasure of social intercourse; and Miss Swanley, though she had not much reason, at this moment, to do it, congratulated herself on the sensible and animated circle to which she could always retire, when desirous to escape the impertinent curiosity and malicious dulness of a country village. Then sighing, recurred, (as she now almost always did,) to the still greater gaiety she might have enjoyed, but for her own unpardonable inadvertence; which often, she observed, led her into errors, that the most pack-horse DULNESS, (to repeat her favourite expression,) would have avoided.

At length Matilda, who had lost sight of Sir Harold, grew so uneasy, she determined to return to the house, with the faint hope of finding him there. Abruptly rising, she exclaimed, 'we should quite forget ourselves, talking by this soft moonlight, if it were not for those OTHER lights that stream so reproachfully, (to remind us of our neglect,) through the brier-bound casement.'

Both ladies prepared, with alacrity, to obey her hint; and found Mrs. Melbourne surrounded by Sir Harold, and the children, whose playful gaiety, united to her solid good sense, seemed to have restored him again to reason and chearfulness. She felt disposed to rally her daughter a little upon her stay; but readily guessed that it might be attributed, as usual, to Sappho, who often possessed much of the fascinating talent attributed in / the Allegory to Pity, and was fond of stealing upon the sports of the village maids, and captivating them with her 'tales full of a charming sadness.'[45] As for Sir Harold, he abstained from all remark, and seemed only desirous his own singularity and abruptness should be forgotten. By the resumed mildness and composure of his manner, which was dejected, but gentle in the extreme, he endeavoured to obtain Matilda's forgiveness, for what he deemed an unwarrantable violence and indiscretion. He often looked in her eyes, as if endeavouring to read her secret thoughts; could he have penetrated them, he would have only discovered the softest compassion and regret. Almost unable to tear himself from her, he took occasion to whisper her at parting, 'I am very unfortunate, my sweet cousin; at times I still am not master of myself, and then I alienate from me even those, whom I might otherwise interest; but you can command me; you can recal me from my wildest wanderings – do not refuse the power I delegate to you; 'tis all I have left to give.' He uttered these words with more than his usual mournful earnestness; but it was not till after his departure, that Matilda perceived, with a perturbation caused by the most painful surprize and emotion, that he had taken that opportunity to slip a ring on her finger. It was a hoop of gold, with the Italian word '*sempre*,' raised in the middle, upon a ground of black enamel.

'What have you got here?' said Arbella, '"*sempre*," for ever! That was the motto of the Medici family!'

Alas! it was the fatal pledge that bound Matilda to the most wretched of all the descendants of a family, distinguished also, for genius, for misfortunes, and crimes. /

CHAPTER IX.

Why need I launch into the praise of friendship?
Friendship, that best support of wretched man,
Which gives us, when our life is painful to us,
A sweet existence in another's being.[46]

ARBELLA, though she had recovered from the first surprise produced by learning Spencer's unaccountable infatuation, yet the more she reflected, felt it the more impossible to find a clue to such strange inconsistency. It might, perhaps, have been discovered in the principle that ruled his life; that vanity, which had long led him to set so high a value on his own merit, that the most elevated rank, the most finished beauty, was deemed hardly worthy to aspire to his notice, had received a sudden and mortifying check. Deprived of his usual resources, and dreading to become an object of mere compassion in those scenes where he had formerly been regarded with the tenderest interest; he readily accepted the intoxicating draught of flattery from the first hand that presented it. In Miss Hautenville there seemed nothing to fear; but Miss Hautenville surpassed him in his own arts. She had ingenuity to persuade him he was the object of a sincere and ardent passion, of which his then alarming situation at length forced from her the avowal. Her sensibility immediately made her of consequence in his eyes, and when we add, the advantage of their perpetual *tête-a-têtes*, we must only refer to her ability, and Captain Fitzroy's inveterate habit of coquetting, to explain the rest. As for his former *bien-aimée*,[47] she began to derive consolation both from the flexibility and elasticity of her mind; it could bend to pleasures that afforded no gratification to Matilda, and it could rise against undeserved injury with a spirit, which, if it bespoke a smaller portion of sensibility, and had its source rather / in self-opinion than self-respect, yet, ultimately, answered the end of consolation as effectually as if it had derived its origin from a nobler principle. Matilda, without possessing the romantic extravagance of either, was the connecting link that united the fair enthusiasts; [a] and tempered the vivacity of their sallies. Arbella was ready, at length, sincerely to subscribe to the superiority that she had formerly, amid the fancied triumphs of coquetry, rather insidiously allowed her unaffected and artless young friend; and Sappho, who might be said to possess the frankest vanity that ever woman had, used often to declare Miss Melbourne was the only beauty whom she did not envy for her charms; and who did not, in return, hate her for her talents.

Nothing now occurred to disturb the even tenor of Matilda's life, till the arrival of a letter from Lady Torrendale, in which, after slightly mentioning Emily, (about whom her Ladyship seemed to feel no farther anxiety, but rather to be desirous she should remain an unlimited time at the Lodge), she proceeded to inform her friend, that Strathallan, who was now with them, had most generously stepped forward on the occasion of Spencer's marriage; and not only effected a complete reconciliation between him and his father, but prevailed so far with Lord Torrendale, by his earnest entreaties, and the representation he made of Spencer's embarrassed situation, as at length to obtain his consent to bestow on him the long withheld estate of Strath-Allan; her Ladyship could not refuse her praises to her son-in-law, who, in the moment that his brother's former prospects were blasted, had proved himself such a generous friend; and Matilda, delighted at this new *trait* of fraternal affection in Strathallan, communicated that part of the letter to Arbella. Miss Ferrars seemed sincerely rejoiced at Fitzroy's good fortune. 'I like that,' she said, 'that is magnificent – worthy of the stately youth, the lovely Lord of Colonsay; and as for his *less* worthy brother, take my word for it, he won't share this windfall with that withered broomstick – / no, no – now he can dash again and not grow pale with *meditations* upon it; which, however they might suit the Dean, were by far too dull for the Captain of horse. That he should ever have thought of her! there was surely some witchery in it: with her age and *vis*-age, the creature must have had Agatha's ring, to deceive him into any thing like the semblance of an attachment:[48] but she has not been yet sufficiently punished. Should I ever, by any chance, meet with him again, let her beware, and not lay that 'flattering unction to her soul,'[49] that I shall spare her a heart-ache, after the many she has caused me. Nay, no reproofs,' she continued to Matilda, who, however pleased with her returning chearfulness, was always the first to discourage her levity. 'I must and I will teaze Miss Hautenville a little.'

'You remember she is *not* Miss Hautenville now.'

'I do but too well; and, for that very reason am resolved to plague her: it is but renewing our old flirtation; and, as for the dear soul himself, *la douce habitude*[50] is so natural to him, that he will slide into it again, almost without perceiving it.'

'I am sure, Arbella, you do not mean what you say.'

'If I know myself, Matilda, I certainly do. I know no pleasure so soothing, as to punish those who have had the audacity to encourage similar hopes to my own: reversing the song of Delia, I thus half revenge the perfidy of Spencer, on others; and

"All that I *endure* inflict"'[51]

Oh, well-imagined line! in future be my motto!'

Matilda lamented to see how much this fatal passion had altered a character once mild, generous, and amiable. She wished to give her friend some more grateful subject of reflection; for she saw that, after all, it was neglect which most preyed upon the spirits, and hurt the formerly sweet and lively temper of Arbella. She spoke to her of the returning admiration of Sowerby; but was answered with that careless indifference, / which spoke, either utter repugnance, or hopelessness of success. 'Attempt again to be Aspasia to that Diogenes![52] oh, your humble! as George Spring says, when he means to be witty; if I had your patent, indeed, for converting lovers into friends, there might be some temptation to try *that*; and I should really request it, if I thought it worth while learning how to change gold into lead; but I am equally obliged to you; you are such a good creature – so superior! now that is quite unlike me; I own, I could not bear to see a pug, that had once followed me, in the train of another mistress. Oh, you are all disinterestedness, you live for others.'

Matilda did, indeed, live for others; her friendly wishes for Arbella formed but a small portion of the extensive plans of that benevolent heart. In the days of her prosperity she had been adored, in the vicinity of the Rocks, for her judiciously distributed charities; and now that her purse could not afford 'to misery,' all she wished to give, she turned to Miss Ferrars as to one who had the power, as well as the will, to relieve it; and it was never without discovering an answering fund of sympathy, in the heart of the good-natured and generous heiress.

'Make me your banker, my Matilda,' she said, 'it is little, in return for your being my consoler, instructress, and guide.'

Matilda, however, availed herself but moderately of her friend's unlimited confidence; preferring the idea of inspiring her with a wish, to enjoy those pure and permanent pleasures, to that of alone receiving the thanks, that in part were due to the liberality of her companion. Arbella soon convinced her, that she only wanted opportunity to be actively, as well as speculatively benevolent. It was in one of the rounds that Matilda took, according to the promise she had given to Lady Strathallan, to visit the poor of Woodlands, that Miss Ferrars, who accompanied her into some of the cottages, was particularly struck with the appearance of one, which had a neatness that might have done honour to a drawing-room; / though every thing in it bore evidently the appearance of the greatest poverty. A numerous family of little boys and girls, were playing round the room. Arbella, who though not really fond of children, was too much of a coquette not to desire to be popular, took very distinguished notice of them; and having delighted the mother of the family by a number of questions, which it cost her no trouble to make; she was taking leave, with a handsome present, when struck with the beauty of the youngest of the female children, she stopped to caress her; and taking her on her knee, promised her a fine book the next time she should see her: the little girl hung down her head, and said, she did not want a book; 'bless me,' cried Arbella, in her precipitate manner, 'what's the meaning of that? can't the ape read.'

'Lord love you, Miss, how should she?' replied the mother, 'we have no time to send her to school: indeed we wants our children, as soon as they are big enough, to help ourselves a little to work in the fields, to go a casing, or at least to take care of the young ones, and carry them about: besides what good would she learn at school, as I say, only to be made rude among boys: if the girls were taught to use their needle, indeed – '

'And are they not taught to work at the new school?' said Arbella, with an absent air, and as if in haste to get away.

'Oh dear, no, Miss; last week, at the vestry, they did talk of another superscription, I think they call it, that the girls might be teached knitting, and sewing besides; but, lack-a-day, the poor little parish of Woodlands, couldn't make it out among'em, though the grocer's lady did give a pound note: if it had been thought of when Lady Strathallan was here, it might, I reckon, have been brought to bear; for she was always free hearted, and ready to give her money: I never saw such a prodigious lady.'

'I wish, indeed, it had occurred to us *then*,' observed Matilda, struck with the utility of the plan. /

'We *must* think of this,' said Arbella, with an air of interest; and recovering from her temporary fidget, (which had been occasioned by unexpectedly observing a party of light horse, galloping at a distance); 'I myself will be among the first to subscribe; and I am sure I can command names enough, among the young ladies of my acquaintance, to make the little sum we want; and then, my good woman, when they are taught something that you value, won't you promise me to send your little angels to school; for it is a terrible thing, upon my word it is, to have them running about like little rabbits, as ignorant as the rocks they climb. Come here, Nanny, my dear,' she continued, 'you would like to read, would you not love; well, to-morrow, I will call with the book I promised, and give you the first lesson.'

'Arbella, you will never persevere,' said Matilda; but Arbella was determined to persevere, and actually did so; the subscription for additional instruction, in the more useful parts of needle-work, was soon filled up to their highest satisfaction; and Arbella, whose active mind always continued to work on whatever object was presented to it, opened to Matilda her more extended views.

'I'll tell you what, Matilda,' she said, 'you want such a school near the Rocks, as there is at Woodlands: now, though I know what you are going to say, that I am an heiress, and all that, I really have not sufficient command of money to attempt such a thing without assistance; though I should be very happy to promote it; could you not apply to your crazy – I beg your pardon – he shall be your *wise* cousin on this occasion.'

'I will,' said Matilda, 'and to Mr. Sowerby.'

'Hum – I have no great hopes of him; between you and I, *Square* Sowerby (as the country folks call him, meaning Squire) is very narrow; you know how he grumbled on being asked to be one of the stewards for the subscription balls at S – ; and in little things he is most ridiculous, You remember / his breaking off all correspondence with an old friend and schoolfellow, because he made him pay postage too often for his letters?'

'I do – yet this man is the promoter of almost every charitable scheme around us; besides contributing large sums to various public institutions.'

'Indeed! then do you manage him; for to say the truth, I am afraid; though he has reconciled himself to seeing me sometimes, I perceive, since that fatal duel, I have never recovered his good opinion; I fear he thinks nothing of me.'

'I rather fear he thinks too much of you – ' replied Matilda.

'Well then, since you will have it that he his generous, and tender, and all we wish; do go to your *bourru bienfaisant*,[53] and tell him, like Lady Teazle, I want him to be in a monstrous good humour, for I wish him to lend me a hundred pounds.'[54]

'Matilda intended to execute her friend's commission; but before it was in her power to do so, Arbella had an opportunity of speaking for herself. One morning, on entering the cottage, which belonged to the mother of her little favourite Nanny, she was sorry to find the poor woman keeping her bed with some feverish symptoms, which had long hung over her, and which were occasioned by working too long during the late harvest: Miss Ferrars, however, did not let this prevent her from giving her usual lesson to her little girl; and she was so intent upon her employment, that she did not perceive the entrance of a stranger; this was no other than 'Squire Sowerby;' whose benevolence, often secret, though extensive, led him to acquaint himself, personally, with the wants of all the distressed who surrounded him: his knowledge of medicine which he had acquired in the course of his philosophical studies, enabled him often to do good, and to prevent expence; and he now came to renew a simple prescription, which had already benefited his poor patient, when he was struck, as he approached the door, with the figure of Arbella, bending over the little / girl, whom she was teaching to read an easy lesson. The patient sweetness with which she corrected, and endured the various blunders of her little scholar; and the bright glance of intelligence, and delight, with which she hailed any dawning of improvement, were not lost upon Sowerby; and he stood for some moments yielding to the pure pleasure this contemplation inspired. Soon recollecting, however, what was due to his age and character, he blushed at thus mysteriously stealing on the occupations of the fair one, like an enamoured boy, watching the steps and actions of his beloved; and advancing into the room, discovered himself, and said, his eyes beaming with benevolent pleasure, 'to see you here thus employed, Miss Ferrars, was, indeed, an unexpected satisfaction; these are not scenes in which a fine lady delights.'

It was impossible for Sowerby to say even a gracious thing, in a perfectly gracious manner; still Arbella took the compliment as it was meant. 'My heart, I trust, is not that of a fine lady;'ᵃ she said looking down, while her cheeks glowed with the long-forgotten pleasure of pleasing.

Mr. Sowerby was melted, struck, delighted. Perhaps he wished to encourage any gleam of right-feeling in the imprudent and giddy Miss Ferrars; perhaps he thought with the Archbishop of Granada, '*a tout peché misericorde*;'⁵⁵ especially when the sinner was agreeable, and young, if not extremely beautiful. Certain it is, he never found himself in a more forgiving disposition; and the amiable Arbella, did not discourage the propensity. She seized this opportunity to mention her plan of a school near the Rocks, to which he gave his most cordial approbation. The numerous consultations these arrangements required, rendered their meetings, at Woodbine Lodge, still more frequent; and they were, perhaps, additionally pleasing, from the contrast they afforded, to his now solitary home; where he was no longer welcomed by that gentle being, who seemed to make every place she inhabited a sainted shrine. He took an opportunity / of more particularly questioning the poor woman, at whose cottage they had met; and every thing she said confirmed him in his opinion of Arbella's mildness, sweetness, and perseverance.

'Oh, Sir,' she cried, 'you have no idea what a good young lady she is; she not only teached my little girl her book, so that she now can read it quite fluidly; but gived my master money when he was bad with the ague; and bought us clothes and firing against Christmas.'

Her poor neighbours were no less eloquent in Sowerby's *praises* to Arbella; till she forgot the difference of years, in the glowing benevolence of his heart; and he was piqued by her spirit and generosity, to shew himself even more than usually liberal. 'I hate giving my money,' he said, as he put down his name to a very large sum; 'but you shame me by your munificence. Yet, after all, I doubt not, you find more pleasure in thus laying it out, than in all you ever threw away in feathers and flounces, and gimcracks,[56] hey?'

Arbella accepted the gracious compliment, as it was intended; and even, by degrees, once more accustomed herself to the prospect of becoming mistress of Clifden-down. /

CHAPTER X.

On such a night
Stood Dido with a willow in her hand
Upon the wild sea-banks, and waved her love
To come again to Carthage.

SHAKSPEARE. MERCHANT OF VENICE.[57]

SHORTLY after reading Lady Torrendale's letter, Arbella called upon Matilda at Woodbine Lodge, but her air was so wild, her countenance so pale and exhausted, that her friend anxiously demanded the cause of her evident agitation of spirits. She threw herself into a chair and after asking for a glass of water, 'Oh my dear,' she exclaimed, 'I have had such a shock; no wonder I look pale; the sight of that man gave me such a turn.'

'What shock? What man? You look indeed as if you had seen a ghost,' said Matilda, endeavouring to rally her.

'True, true, indeed, 'tis but the ghost of his former self; yet still interesting. The wretch! I hardly knew him. When just returning home from a long walk with dear Sowerby, who you know is a preacher of exercise in all weathers, a dashing carriage and four, drove furiously past us, and a man bowed to me with the greatest *nonchalance:* 'don't you know Captain Fitzroy,' said Sowerby. He must have perceived by the change in my countenance how much I hated him. He was at my aunt's before us; Sowerby took leave at the door, and my first emotion was, to run up and hide myself, till he should be gone; the sight of him is now become so odious to me; but curiosity, or some other devilish motive, restrained me, and I went into the parlour; I found my aunt so triumphant, and so *affairée,* and Miss Hautenville (I won't call her Mrs. Fitzroy) so satisfied, and so detestable; and I have been so sick of their servility, and their nonsense, and his affectation, that I / have at length escaped to steal a quiet half hour with you.'

Matilda could not but observe that ill-humor had a great share in this slight and satiric sketch of the family party, and begged her friend to be composed, and to detail the scene as it had happened.

'When I came in,' resumed Arbella, after a long pause to take breath, 'I found my aunt, who had just laid down her knitting and her spectacles, overwhelming the gentleman with enquiries and compliments, but he put them all aside, and advancing to his delightful bride, he told the creature, the Fitzroy, that the sudden change in his affairs rendered his presence at Strath-Allan necessary; but that he could not

– 447 –

think his good fortune complete, without the additional pleasure of her company in the journey; he then continued something in a lower tone, which I suppose was an apology for his previous neglect. She seemed to take it in very good part. Oh when Spencer whispers, 'tis hard not to forgive; and at the end if you could have seen the look she gave me; may all the – but she is still too happy, is she not, *with him?* My aunt would hardly let him finish what he had to say; but overwhelmed him with a torrent of the most vulgar and impertinent questions: "Was that carriage really his? and was he really Lord of Strath-Allan? and did that make him a Lord of the Manor, or a Laird." Oh! when I saw the lurking smile, that hovered round those traitorous lips, I could, with such pleasure, have snipt off a little bit of the good lady's tongue. Spencer, as full as ever of idle business, and important insignificance, had hardly a moment to stay; could hardly be prevailed on to taste the elegant collation that, by this time, was served up; his wife must make her arrangements in less than half an hour, or he must leave her behind. Aye do, my dear Mrs. Fitzroy, said I, and I will help you. Meantime aunt went on, as if determined to set me distracted: "do ye go, my dear honorable Mrs. Fitzroy, into your own elegant, honorable new carriage. Didn't I say it would come to this; and didn't the fortune-teller say it would come to / this. Now you are indeed the honorable Mrs. Fitzroy, and your husband is the honorable Captain Fitzroy, for he has behaved as I always said he would, like a man of honor. And nobody as I take it (assuming her dreadfully sentimental tone) is truly honorable, but who behaves themselves honorably;" then embracing her with tears in her eyes, she ran on, "and now do ye write to me, and remember, though I scorn to remind you of it, dear Mrs. Fitzroy, I was your good friend in your diversity, and 'twould break my heart if you was to forget me in your influence, for I never loved you so well in my life as I do at this blessed minute. Now for the love of goodness sake, do ye look out at the four beautiful pye-bald horses, as is prancing and pawing just before the door; pretty creaters; all your own: I never loved ye so well as this minute." Well, my dear, he is seriously determined to take his wife away with him, and what can be his intention, it goes even beyond me to discover, though so long accustomed to read all the movements of that vain, weak, wavering heart. To rusticate with a Hautenville, and live upon love at Strath-Allan would be too ridiculous, even for Spencer Fitzroy.'

Matilda found herself as unable as her friend, to solve the difficulty; and the two young ladies after wearying themselves with conjectures, parted at length, unable to come to any conclusion, but that Captain Fitzroy had always the art of surpassing expectation, however high it might have been raised by his former extravagancies. When Arbella returned home, she found the Fitzroys gone, as she had expected. It was not till some time after, that she learnt, by the laughing and whispering round, the *dénouement* of this strange adventure, and when she thought of it, was no more 'in amazement lost.'

Scarcely had Strathallan silenced the murmurs of Fitzroy, (who lamented with true pathos to Lady Torrendale, that while his brother by the merest luck in the world had the enjoyment of two fine estates, men of merit, like himself, remained poor and neglected) / when the gay capricious Spencer, struck out the bright plan which he resolved that moment to put in execution. Strath-Allan was too retired a spot ever to be an agreeable residence to him; he however, on learning his brother's unexampled generosity, squeezed his hand, muttered some hasty expressions of gratitude, said he would have acted exactly in the same manner, if placed in similar circumstances; and then hastened to take up all the money he could command, upon his new estate, part of which he employed in paying his debts, and the rest in purchasing an equipage, which had made such an impression on Mrs. Stockwell, and Mrs. Fitzroy. On this occasion Lady Torrendale, who had been the only person formerly to listen to her son's complaints, was obliged to own herself satisfied; and Strathallan, delighted to see contentment once more restored to the domestic groupe, could hardly persuade himself he had been once the object of so much envy and ill-will. 'I never intended, my dear fellow,' said he to Fitzroy, 'so far to avail myself of the favours of fortune, as to suffer so great a disproportion to exist between us; you know too well accumulation never was my pleasure; and that you may find this a relief adequate to all your present exigencies, is my most earnest desire.'

From the moment of Spencer's arrival at S – , Mrs. Stockwell, who could hardly believe her eyes, ran out and called from the bottom of the stairs; 'come down, my dear Miss Hautenville – Mrs. Spencer – pooh, Mrs. Fitzroy, I mean; would you believe it, here's your own dear husband come to see you – come quickly: Lord bless me, if I was ever so surprised in my life.'

'Why surprised, Madam?' said the Lady, who had, by this time, made her appearance to this unexpected summons, and who still maintained her dignity, though the visit was indeed to her equally unexpected and agreeable. What followed has been already detailed by Arbella. Mrs. Fitzroy thought all the sufferings of her life compensated, as the elegant, the animated Spencer handed her into his splendidly blazoned / barouche. The infatuation lasted the whole of their journey to Scotland, nor was it dissipated by the appearance of the mansion at Strath-Allan, though little calculated to inspire chearful ideas in any but the happy Mrs. Fitzroy, we may suppose, saw it only with a lover's eye. The house though *un peu delabrée*,[58] was *so* venerable. The trees (though now brown and shedding their leaves) would, she was sure, in spring, burst forth in the most enchanting beauty, and then the winding walks would be *so* delightful with a book, or Fitzroy's arm! This was not exactly the Captain's intention; and she was not quite so much enchanted when, on the third day after his arrival, he mentioned his design of returning to London; but gave no hint of a desire that she should accompany him: 'I have not taste,' said he, 'for rural beauties, but as you, Mrs. Fitzroy, have probably not yet examined half the romantic scenes around, you may wish to have time to explore them more accurately, and give me an account of them – when I return.'

Mrs. Fitzroy, who saw through Spencer's design, which was indeed to keep her at a distance from him, (a design which had made the present of a house and estate in a remote part of Scotland peculiarly acceptable) replied, with some spirit, that she preferred accompanying him wherever he went. 'There can be no objection to that now, I suppose,' she added.

'None in the world, my dear creature, but that it is impossible,' he answered, with the greatest *sang froid*; 'I have been obliged to take up all the ready money upon my estate, in the discharge of honorable and necessary demands: you must be aware you cannot appear in the world without *appointments*,[a] such as are suitable to my wife;

when it is in my power to give them to you, you shall hear from me; till then, your taste and literature (he dwelt upon this last word with a sneer) can, I am satisfied, make this abode, *un sejour enchanté*,[59] and one of which I shall leave you undisturbed possession.'

Mrs. Fitzroy, unable to restrain her indignation, was going to reply, but Spencer begged of her not to be *emportée*,[60] and, politely / bowing, and wishing her all health and happiness, stepped into his carriage, and left this disconsolate Ariadne to deplore her sad banishment, while he prepared (sinking, as much as possible, the title of a married man) to assume, once more, the envied character of an *elégant* at every scene of fashionable amusement.

It was not till the evening of the day following that of Spencer's abrupt and cruel departure, that poor Mrs. Fitzroy found courage to walk out, and survey her now solitary domain, which, deprived of the adventitious charms, that Spencer's presence had lent it, now appeared in all its real bleakness and nakedness to her view. Before her was the sea, tossing its foaming billows for ever among dreary and barren rocks; behind the house were lofty mountains, that frowned in terrific and savage grandeur; and though the cascades that burst down their sides, glittering through the various diversities of green, that were mingled in the plantations around, might altogether furnish in the summer a scene of picturesque beauty: the whole view presented, at the moment, nothing to the forsaken fair one, but the image of solitude, gloom, and despair. The night was dark and dreary; lurid clouds hung low in the air, and threatened every moment to burst in torrents on her head; but this was nothing to the storm that raged in Mrs. Fitzroy's breast. She was followed by a young Scotch girl, the daughter of the bailiff and his wife, who lived in the house, and had the care of it during the absence of its owners. 'Heavens! what a desolate looking place this is!' she exclaimed, turning, in utter despair to her companion.

'Why yes, my Lady,' answered Janet, 'it be reckoned an unco pretty place as you shall see.'

'I mean forlorn, deserted, girl,' reiterated Mrs. Fitzroy, who discovered that Janet mistook the word desolate, for some fine 'Southron' term of commendation. 'Oh 'tis a dismal sight! not a neighbour of any distinction for ten miles round; nothing but a few straggling huts to be seen upon a common.' /

'Truly, my Lady, 'tis but a strolling sort of a village, yet still Strathallan Castle is sure a bonny wonder; and for the kirk, ayont it has nae peer.'

'He may truly say,' resumed Mrs. Fitzroy, who had not listened to the latter part of this observation, 'that he has left me without appointments? – Pray are you and your father,' turning disdainfully to the girl, 'the only servants in the house.'

'The only servants, my Lady, except Brownie.'

'Browne! who the deuce is Browne?'

'Oh, my Lady, ye manna talk o'the de'il when ye mention Brownie. Ye mun ha mair respect. Indeed! This Mr. Brownie is a very ceremonious gentleman. Do ye na ken he is a spirit?' resumed the girl, with added solemnity; 'and what is more remarkable he has kept awa' sin ever ye hae been here. He'd do half the work before I was up, and leave me sixpence too, if I remembered to set his milk for him.'

Mrs. Fitzroy now called to mind her little poetical and black-letter knowledge,[61] which her own distresses had before quite driven away, and remembering Brownie was a guardian sprite, attached to many northern families of distinction, did not doubt but that of Strathallan was included in the honor. She cast a rueful look upon her attendant, who seemed by no means more delighted with the beauty of her mistress, and muttered, 'surely my graunie had the second sight of this laidly Lady coming to Strathallan, when she made me pray wi' uplift hands against aw witches and warlocks, and lang-nibbed'* things.'

'Perfidious, ungrateful Fitzroy!' the Lady at length exclaimed; 'are these the vows of eternal love, which you promised to renew beneath the renewing verdure, while the conscious stars, or the nightingale should be the only witnesses to our love?'

'Gif an ye are fond of nightingales, my Lady, ye may hear 'em every night aneath your chamber window.' /

'Indeed! that may, in time, be soothing to my heart-sick grief.'

'Oh then, this place be famous for nightingales. Bonny creatures wi' the horns and staring eyes, that do cry hoot! hoot! by night.'

Mrs. Fitzroy shuddered, clasped her hands together, and, for once, with a natural expression, cast up her eyes to heaven, while Janet continued to set forth the beauties of the chamber. ' 'Tis the room where the last Lady Strathallan died; and sometimes her ghaist do walk about at night. But don't be frightened, my Lady, 'tis only on All hallowe'en or the night she died.'

Such stories amused the time till total darkness came on, and poor Mrs. Fitzroy with no choice but to listen to Janet's tales of witches, fairies, banshis, or death-lights, or to the mournful sighing (sighing her companion called it) of the wind among the trees, had full time to regret the hour, she exchanged the obsequious attentions, and substantial comforts of Mrs. Stockwell's fireside, for the barren privilege of comparing herself by turns to every heroine, ancient and modern, celebrated in mournful story as a victim to the perfidy of man. /

---

*   Long-nosed

CHAPTER XI.

'Matilda' lost! I woo a sterner bride;
The armed Bellona calls me to her side:
Harsh is the music of our marriage strains!
It breathes in thunder from the western plains.

Miss Seward.[62]

Spencer was not long returned from his northern excursion, when the papers informed him of Arbella's marriage with Mr. Sowerby. It piqued his vanity; yet ever equally ready at disguising what he really did feel, or assuming what he did not, he declared, in all companies, his satisfaction at finding, that a girl who had aimed so high, had at length made such a prudent, tolerable, decent sort of a match. Mrs. Stockwell's satisfaction was of a warmer and sincerer nature. Having every cause of discontent removed by her son being, at that time, in pursuit of another lady, she congratulated her niece Arbella with unmingled cordiality, and even went so far as to say that 'as she was but young at house-keeping, she would not only be happy to give every assistance and advice in her power, but would (provided dear little Mrs. Sowerby was agreeable) spend the first months of her marriage with her.' This, Arbella, though she continued on perfectly good terms with her aunt, civilly evaded. Not so the advances of her other relations, who were greatly induced, by the wealthy and respectable connexion she had, at length, formed, to overlook her previous slights. Thus divided between the duties she owed her husband, and the attentions required by her new-made friends, Mrs. Sowerby found her good humour and self-consequence return together, and had no longer any room for that gnawing discontent that had wasted her spirits, and preyed upon her peace.

Matilda continued, during the winter, to keep up a regular correspondence with Lady / Strathallan, who flattered her with hopes of seeing her the ensuing summer. To this prospect Miss Melbourne looked forward with serenity, if not with any very lively anticipations of delight; and as the gay season of spring returned, was far from being guilty of that 'sullenness against nature,'[63] which refuses to appear sensible of its charms. Summer however passed without bringing the promised addition to her society; and as the sporting season approached, Matilda felt sensible she could not hope for the presence of the amazonian dame, till she had taken every hunting lodge in her way that belonged to any one who was of her acquaintance. The letters now began to be less interesting; details of murdered hares, for details of Strathallan's pursuits, his plans and amusements, appeared, to her little friend, an indifferent exchange. An

– 452 –

interval of greater length than ordinary had elapsed since the receipt of the last letter from Lady Strathallan, when Mrs. Sowerby, who was come to spend the morning with her friend, happening to take up the paper which was just come in, startled the assembled group, by exclaiming, 'bless me, this woman is always breaking her neck!' and on an explanation being demanded, read aloud the following paragraph:

'We regret much to have the painful task of announcing an accident, which has excited the most serious alarm in the breast of every person connected with the amiable individual to whom it has arrived. The beautiful Lady Strathallan, who it is well known delights in uniting the crescent of Diana, to the Ægis of Minerva,[64] was thrown from her horse, with violence, while in ardent pursuit of a fox, and fractured her arm in two places. The limb was instantly set, but we are sorry to say, a violent fever was the consequence, and all the symptoms since have been unfavourable. Every one who has the honor of this Lady's acquaintance, must unite with us, in ardently hoping, that the world will not be deprived of a character, in whom at once, distress found a friend, taste and pleasure a support, and science a patroness.'

'There, now you have it in the flourishing way *that* paper always gives things,' added / Mrs. Sowerby, 'was it not better as I told you, in two words, that she had broken her neck?'

'No, not quite so bad as that,' interrupted Mrs. Melbourne, benevolently; 'she recovered from the effects of a very serious accident before, and I trust this will not be found of such fatal consequence as was at first imagined.'

Begging her young friend to excuse her, she, with these words, left the room to address a few lines instantly to Lady Torrendale, to enquire into the exact truth of the report. The Countess did not delay her answer, but on pretence of the intimacy that had subsisted between Matilda and Lady Strathallan, chose to address it to her.

' 'Tis true *ma chere petite*,' she said, 'that her Ladyship's horse chucked her rather impolitely over a six-bar gate; and it is also true that, instead of thanking him, and saying, 'dat is a good horse, but how will *you* get over?' (as the Frenchman did when in a similar situation, imagining the English hunters were trained to convey their masters clear over gates in that manner) she lay crying out, with all her might that her arm was broken. However, there is no reason for any immediate fear about our Hippolita; at least it is by no means impossible but she may recover. Should it turn out differently, my only consolation would be, that a certain dear little friend of mine, might stand a chance of being rewarded according to her merit; and a certain gentleman, whom her prudery long ago forbade to hope, might at length find the recompence of all his forbearance. But where am I wandering? Is it possible to live in a court, and not to learn the necessary caution, with which it teaches us to disguise our thoughts and feelings? – yes, for, Matilda, I was not *bred* in a court; and now, while giving way to the fond flatteries of a too friendly and susceptible heart, run the risk of incurring your grave looks and rebukes in return. Oh spare them this time, and – *should it really be so*, allow me to console *his* mind, with the idea that you will not always ways be inexorable.'

Shocked at the mixture of unfeeling levity / and insincerity this epistle betrayed, Matilda could yet scarcely forbear a smile, at the Countess's still supposing her so much the dupe of her arts, as to give into a snare so gross; one that supposed a conduct so unlike the whole tenor of that held by the refined, the humane Strathallan.

'Ah! little does he suspect,' she said, 'the commission her Ladyship insinuates she has received from him. Insinuates for no visible purpose, but the gratuitous pleasure of making me odious and contemptible in the eyes of all, to whom she would show the unworthy avowal she solicits!'

As she had not originally addressed Lady Torrendale, Matilda did not conceive an answer to this strange epistle necessary; but understanding that Lady Strathallan's head was not affected by her present illness, she dispatched a letter full of the real tenderness and sympathy, she felt for her situation; and entreating her, if it were only by the hand of an amanuensis, to send her a line soon, respecting her state of health. The letter she received by return of post, in the handwriting of her Ladyship's woman, though more grateful and affectionate than usual, was of a most gloomy cast. It appeared intended as a kind of farewell. In it Lady Strathallan seemed fully sensible of her danger. At the beginning of the week that succeeded the eventful one, in which Lady Strathallan's accident had been first announced, Matilda happening to take up the newspaper, turned very pale, and handed it, in silence, to her mother. ' 'Tis over, then,' exclaimed Mrs. Melbourne, 'poor Lady Strathallan has paid with her life, the forfeit of her unfeminine temerity, and Strathallan is free!'

'Still Penseroso,[65] my little lonely beam,' said Arbella, as, several days after the last mournful intelligence, she stole upon Matilda's solitary stroll in her garden; 'if Strathallan himself were gone instead of his lady, you could not be more sad; hang melancholy reflections. You must know Papa Sowerby is gone to a county meeting, and I am come to billet myself upon you, and intend to be as gay as he is grave, till his return; indeed / you should go out with your mother; she met me and sent me home to enliven you.'

'You are always welcome, my Arbella, but who can be gay, that reflects on the frail tenure by which we hold all that makes life desirable. What a little space it is since poor Lady Strathallan's lot appeared the most enviable! possessed of youth, health, riches, and united to the most amiable of men.'

'Ah there it comes! little self must mix with the best characters; the most amiable of men! well, *Le plus amiable des hommes se consolera*,[66] we must suppose, or if he will not of himself we must help him.'

'Forgive me, Arbella, but really my spirits are not in a tone to keep pace with your — '

'Levity, you would have added; forgive me, Matilda, but really my desire to see you placed as high as your merit deserves, sometimes makes me overstep the bounds of propriety. Besides, I was put into this train of thought by seeing the most amiable of men just now.'

'Seeing him, where, when? how did he come?'

'On the back of a griffin, my dear, to be sure; so valiant a Knight of Spain could chuse no more common conveyance. There, I said I could bring back the rosy colour into her cheeks.'

'Are you sure it was Lord Strathallan?'

'Sure that it was either he or his wraith,[67] as the Scotch call it; but I am almost certain a wraith could not have looked half so handsome. I will not positively say he spoke to me, he rather flashed on me like a sun-beam, as your Saph's favourite Scotch prose-poet has it,[68] while I was walking among our woods at Clifden-down. You may be certain it was a sun-beam from a very dark cloud. It seemed hastening rapidly away; and to say the truth, I thought it must have been here by this time, so came to have a little gossip with you, and to hear about the proposals, and when – '

'Oh Arbella, why will you imagine him capable of a conduct that would at once rob me of the only mournful delight I ever permitted / myself to taste? esteem for his character.'[a]

'Because, my dear, I thought such conduct might make said mournful delight a very lively delight, by changing esteem for his character into love for himself.'

'His presence in Derbyshire might be necessary,' resumed Matilda, thoughtfully. 'Now I recollect, poor Lady Strathallan had desired her remains might be placed by those of her father (to whom she had ever conducted herself with exemplary duty) at Vinesbury. Business might have induced him to proceed to Woodlands, but he would never, no never seek to force himself into my presence before time had – '

'Very probably, my dear, very probably,' replied Arbella, coolly, 'you know best; but as I perceive sunbeam is advancing due west, and rests at this moment at your garden door, I must beg leave to be off, and postpone, to another opportunity, the pleasure of passing the day with you.'

'Stay, stay, Arbella,' exclaimed Matilda, convulsively grasping her hand.

'Not for the world, my dear; am I not a wife and a lover, and do I not know the value of a tender uninterrupted *téte-a-téte?*'

Matilda made another effort to detain her. 'No, no,' exclaimed her lively friend, 'it shall never be said that the witty and agreeable Mrs. Sowerby, a title I begin to value as much as I once did the honourable, was ever Madame De Trop.[69] So you must act "She would and She would not," as well as you can, without a prompter.' She darted through the gate as she finished this sentence; and even had she delayed, Matilda was no longer in a state to entreat her stay. Strathallan stood before her.

Hardly justified in his own eyes, he could scarcely endure the surprise and displeasure that appeared in her's; without design or wish, the day before, to break in upon her solitude, a tormenting idea had haunted his mind from the moment he found himself near her abode, with renewed and redoubled force. He had long, long been obliged to be silent, with respect to the sentiments she had formerly / inspired. He had an enemy, busy, restless, assiduous, that had the advantage of being ever near her; one who had a hand to offer, when he, alas! durst not even own to himself his heart was her's; he feared to think of the influence that constant importunity, opposed to involuntary neglect might, in his absence, and without his knowledge, have acquired; he feared to think of the force of the united claims of blood and fond affection, on a heart like Matilda's. These, and a thousand other arguments he was prepared to address her with, in excuse of his unexpected intrusion; but, once in her presence, a secret feeling told him, the mention of such suspicions would only add to his offence; and he was content to await, in silence, the decree, which should declare, whether her coldness proceeded from displeasure or indifference.

'His heart unhushed, although his lips were mute.'[70]

She reproached him for the little regard to her feelings this unexpected intrusion shewed; but with these reproaches was mingled a degree of tenderness that inspired Strathallan with a hope they were not meant to convey.

'You teach me what I ought to be; yet how difficult it is to remember it, and remain with you! Believe me, I harboured not a thought of offending that purity, of hurting that sensibility, on which I build my highest hopes of happiness; 'twas but to reclaim my interest, too long dormant, in that heart, to tell you mine is yours, and to entreat you not to forget me in the moment I am free again to love you, that I ventured on this imprudent – this, perhaps, blameable step. You yourself could not have a deeper sense, a greater desire, to relieve the sufferings of the unfortunate being, to whose virtues we both did justice, than I felt during every hour she was with me; and the most soothing thought I experience is, from the grateful consciousness she expressed at her latest hour, of the devotion of my life to her. We were sacrificed to the interested views of our parents; with another she might have been happier. It cannot, surely, offend you, to say / that your name was one of the subjects on which she seemed to dwell with the greatest pleasure. True to the last to her prevailing passion, she expressed herself in acknowledgment of your conduct, as having relieved her mind, and saved her PRIDE, in a manner the most unassumingly noble, flattering, and generous.'

Matilda's tears flowed at this tribute to her virtues, paid by a rival whom she had endeavoured, with such success, to convert into a friend. Strathallan seized this moment of softness to request an intercourse, by letter, till time should remove the barrier that still existed between them. 'Is this small boon,' he said, 'too much for me to ask, for you to grant?' He watched Matilda's lips, and hailed the answer in the relenting smile, that hovered round them once more. Softened by this concession, she began to think she had shewn, perhaps, an unnecessary severity. All these variations of sentiment, though hardly distinguished by herself, were marked by the penetrating eye of Strathallan with the fondest rapture. The cold suspicions that had darkened all his prospects, vanished at this dawn of returning love. There was no need of words to assure him he still saw his own Matilda, artless, as she was lovely, fearful, as kind. He pleaded their approaching parting, as an excuse for the long forbidden pleasure of expressing his sentiments. In that very scene, amid those fair flowery arbours, where she had once so coldly checked the fond admiration she inspired, he renewed the confession of a passion, now authorized by heaven and by her. All the tenderness of his nature so long repressed, or diverted into another channel, flowed at that moment in its charming and genial current. Equally formed to feel and to inspire love, it was only when yielding, without reserve, to the influence of that gentle, generous passion, that Strathallan could appear in all his power, resistless as amiable. The silence of his mistress was as eloquent as the language which painted his love; there, every delightful feeling, only heightened by the veil her delicacy still interposed, could be by him / but too distinctly traced; their hearts were, for a moment fully disclosed to each other; and they mutually exchanged in secret, but deep felt rapture, the conscious vow that made their future fortunes one. The world – Sir Harold – every thing was forgot – she lived but to gaze upon Strathallan, to repeat, he is mine for ever, ever mine! Her lover reminded her of her promise to write to him.

'I must waste a year in insipid idleness, or still more irksome business. But while I am believed far distant from you, you will know my heart and soul are here; farewell! then most beloved – till – '

'Till then I'll think of you.'

'My own Matilda!'

'My dear Strathallan!'

Enchanting sounds! but they were lost to him for whom they were intended; breathed in too low a tone, by his charmer's timid tenderness, for even the ear of love to catch them; unless, indeed, he guessed them by the fondness with which her eyes overflowed.

'Surely you are now content, Strathallan,' resumed Matilda, with a bewitching smile, 'why then prolong this painful moment, for indeed, indeed we must part.'

'I go then!' he exclaimed, as with a lightened heart he bade farewell; 'but oh! may every power to whom innocence and loveliness are dear, watch over my treasure till I return – and I will think of this parting as an hour more sweet and sacred than that in which many lovers meet.' As he spoke, he raised Matilda's hand to his lips, a freedom which, for the first time, during their long intimacy, he permitted himself. What was then her surprise, to perceive his countenance, so lately beaming with tender transport, suddenly overcast with the gloom of resentment and despair; as, hastily renouncing the hand till now so dear, he exclaimed,

'Is it thus you would again deceive me!'

It was the ring, placed as if the symbol of her engagement to Sir Harold Melbourne; an engagement which the inscription seemed but too fatally to verify, that had struck his eye, and dashed his late glowing hopes to the ground. Matilda felt she had been allowed / to taste a moment of happiness, never, perhaps, to be succeeded by another. In the transport of that hour the lovers had forgot the malignant destiny, which was not weary yet of persecuting them. She shuddered when she recalled the emotion, the fatal foreboding with which she had received this ill-omened gift. A gift of which her cousin was too apt to remind her, with expressions that shewed it was the tacit compact, on which the life and safety of the best-beloved of her heart still depended. It was vain to remind him of his former obligations to Strathallan; of his having once declared, when that obligation was recent, his enmity to his preserver was at an end. Alas! was it possible to reason with madness, to combat unbridled love? ' 'Tis true,' she said, in a voice scarcely articulate, from hopeless dejection, 'while that unhappy being lives, I dare not venture to unite myself to any other.'

But it was useless to renew her former arguments with one, who never admitted them to be of any force. Strathallan treated her fears with slight, with resentment, even with contempt: but finding he had only offended where he had failed to convince, he soon resumed all the softness, which she ever found so much more dangerous than his anger, and abjured her, by their past tenderness, by their present joys, not to defer his happiness to such a distant, such an indefinite period, nor to let evils so imaginary, trouble their promised bliss.

'Strathallan,' resumed Matilda, mournfully, 'they are *not* imaginary. Seek not to change my resolution,' she continued, 'for it is unalterable. – Cruel, cruel wayward fate!'

Strathallan stood gazing on her for a moment, as if expecting she would have added something to the sentence it cost her such anguish to pronounce, and then broke from her in silent desperation; but soon returning,

'One word more Matilda: how cruel is your imagined kindness? – to what a life do you condemn me, from a false idea of preserving it from a possible danger – say – will / you not change this harsh, this unnecessary determination?'

'I will not, I cannot,' she replied, in a low but steady voice; for, in the moment that he was most dear to her, she felt, in its most fatal force, the dreadful threat of which her ring reminded her.

'You will not?' she was silent – he paused, as if struck with some new and important idea. His mind seemed engrossed by it. 'Then farewell, Matilda!'

An emotion, like presentiment, induced her to think she had been, perhaps, too hasty. Distracted, irresolute, she felt an inclination to recal him, to consult if no other course could possibly be taken, consistent with his safety: but he was gone, and as her strained eyes followed the last glimpse of his form, she felt that her heart, that her whole being went with it.

But a few hours before this meeting, Strathallan had congratulated himself, that from the nature of the service in which he was engaged, his exertions would be immediately demanded in the field: and that he could charm the languor of expectation, by knowing himself to be near her, and perhaps by some interviews which, however rare, would shorten, by the magic of anticipation and recollection, the gloomy period that must elapse before he could call her wholly his. Upon the cruel blow given to his hopes, inaction seemed worse than death; and being informed that he could obtain a command which would require his presence abroad, he directly took the necessary steps to facilitate an arrangement for that purpose, though, at the time, one extremely disadvantageous to him. Repenting already of the abrupt and precipitate manner in which he had parted from Matilda, he wrote to inform her of his resolution; and only requested, in return for his devoted submission, that she would not withdraw the promise she had given him, of her correspondence, but sometimes express that generous sympathy in his fortunes, which alone could make him, for a few moments, forget, that happiness had been once more / presented to his grasp, perhaps to elude it for ever.

'You will not have a Verdinha to detain you this time; so we may hope, unless ill-fate pursue us, for regular communications and a happy return.' Such had been the half sneering, half tender farewell of Lady Torrendale. Strathallan started – the forgotten name, for a moment, brought a glow still richer to his cheek, and distant scenes crowded to his remembrance with vivid and painful force. But he had just lost – had renounced, a dearer than Verdinha – and the remark, that curiosity perhaps had dictated, was, the next moment, banished from his mind.

CHAPTER XII.

E, in atto di morir lieto e vivace,
Dir parea: s'apre il ciel io vado in pace.
D'un bel pallore ha il bianco volto asperso
Come a' gigli sarían miste vïole
E gli occhi al cielo affisa:– in questa forma
Passa la bella donna, e par che dorma.

TASSO. – GERUSALEMME LIBERATA.[71]

MATILDA's attention was soon called from her own sorrows, to those of her unhappy cousin; for such was her wayward fate, that duty, compassion, every sentiment, urged her to give up her time and thoughts to him, who had most cruelly blasted all her hopes of happiness. His situation now called more imperiously than ever for her active pity; for it was evident that Lady Julia, long the victim of illness and calamity, drooped from day to day, and as evident, that the ill-fated / Sir Harold drooped with her. He himself appeared sensible of his gradual decline, and contemplated it with a feeling of melancholy satisfaction. 'Why should you wish,' he would say to Mrs. Melbourne and Matilda, 'to prolong my days? My life was attached to hers – every thought, every feeling of it interwoven with her existence. Ask the blasted and sapless branch, if it can bloom when dissevered from its parent tree? No – as we have lived, let us be laid to rest together.'

His kind relatives, however, judged otherwise; and thought that however violent the shock of grief might be at first, the removal of an object that afforded a perpetual irritation to his mental malady, was the only chance Sir Harold had of cure.

He sometimes would flatter himself with hopes that his beloved parent betrayed symptoms of amendment. At length Lady Julia's weakness increased so much that she was completely confined to her bed: it was then Sir Harold gave up all expectations that her life could be much prolonged, and from that moment he never quitted her: the nights he spent in praying by her: that she could not join him in prayer, was the circumstance for which he expressed the most constant regret. 'Do not think,' he would say, 'that I fear she has ought to repent of. No, but how blest were that pure soul, to be able once again to prefer its humble wishes, and to know that they were accepted.'

At length the constant desire of his heart was accomplished. One night, performing his now almost hopeless supplication, he knelt beside his mother; the sinking lamp and increasing gloom around, scarcely allowed him to distinguish her fading form; while contemplating the lovely ruin time had made, his anxiety for her future welfare, added to the wonted fervency of his mental orison. 'Oh gracious power,' he cried, in hopeless anguish, 'I ask not her life – grant her but one moment the returning light of her soul; let her but know she is accepted – hear my prayers, not for myself they rise, they are for *her* – let not my mother / pass in darkness, let her not leave me in utter despair.'

At this moment a beam of intelligence illuminated the fine features of Lady Julia. She turned her eyes upon the agonized countenance of her son, who still kneeling, gazed anxiously, yet fearfully, to watch the returning ray. That son who had ever loved her with more than filial reverence – who had been firm to her, when forsaken by the world – had sacrificed health, fortune, reason, to her cause. 'My dear son,' she said, in a calm tone of voice, 'I have long been very ill; and yet have been strangely insensible to my danger. I now feel its extent. I have but a few moments to live, join me then in employing those moments to implore forgiveness for the past – if I dare ask it, to hope for mercy.'

An instant before, Sir Harold did not venture even to wish for more than what he now hailed with transport – his mother's restored reason. Yet, with this restoration a faint hope now rose in his breast, that she might not yet be lost to him. But the hope which flattered for a moment, soon sunk into despair, as he marked the death-like hue which occupied the place of the former clear paleness of her features. Lady Julia repeated her earnest and solemn entreaty, that he would join her in the last act of her life.

'And must you be torn from me,' cried Sir Harold, 'at that moment when consciousness is restored, must life be denied to our prayers? – life, now so doubly precious!'

Lady Julia did not answer him – absorbed in the concerns of a superior state, the world, its interests, it sorrows, even its affections receded from her sight.

Struck with awe and admiration at the divine expression which now illuminated her countenance; 'Oh stay,' he cried, 'and let me, breathing my soul in orisons like yours, with you, as I have lived, expire.' His wish seemed granted – for as he uttered it, Lady Julia tenderly pressing the hand she still retained, resigned a soul purified by / suffering, and long fitted to be received within the mansions of eternal rest: and her unhappy son, overcome by the anxieties, the vigils, the fears, and even the hopes he had alternately experienced, sunk by her side into insensibility; deep, motionless, and apparently complete as her own.

CHAPTER XIII.

Véggio, ed ódo, ed inténdo: ch' áncor víva,
Dì si lontáno a' sóspir miéi risponde.
Deh! perch' innánzi témpo ti consume?
Mi dice con pietáte: a che pur vérsi
Dágli ócchi Trísti un doloróso fiume?
Di me non piánger tu.

PETRARCA.[72]

THE first symptoms of recovery that Sir Harold evinced, appeared in the gratitude he expressed towards his active and sympathising friends, who had scarcely ever quitted him during the late period of suffering: and who were still unwilling to leave him, dreading the effects of the first transports of his grief; its violence shewed itself, however, only in a fixt and immoveable determination not to quit the body till the hour of twelve had passed; an hour at which he appeared to have still some confused idea that / his late loved parent might desire his presence.

In anxious and mournful suspence, Mrs. Melbourne and her daughter waited, in another apartment, the expiration of that awful period. How much was their minds relieved to see Sir Harold, the moment it was elapsed, re-enter the room, with a comparatively chearful countenance. Adverting with sensibility, but composure and resignation to the past, he affectionately thanked his cousins for all their kindness to him; but intreated them to consider their health, and not to risk it any longer by needless solicitude; he promised to be careful of his own, and requested they would let him soon see them again. 'You find me,' he added, (as if desirous to the utmost, of calming their apprehensions,) 'not only satisfied but thankful; I feel indeed there are still some pleasures worth living for.'

A little comforted by these assurances, though not exactly comprehending the purport of the last sentence, Mrs. and Miss Melbourne returned to Woodbine Lodge, where they kept Julia a kind of prisoner, lest the affecting secret should reach her. They did not find, during the ensuing melancholy week, any reason to entertain apprehensions that Sir Harold's feelings would lead him into any extravagance. They continued, however, their affectionate attentions, well-knowing how much the presence of a friend, however intimate, is a restraint upon the destructive ebullitions of sorrow, without preventing its more soothing indulgence. Still they remarked that it was seldom they could see Sir Harold. He now absented himself more than ever, and frequently his domestics were at a loss to direct where he was to be found. His compassionate visitants were too well accustomed to his peculiarities to be much alarmed by this conduct, till their attention was roused by an unexpected and affecting communication.

One evening the ladies had called, and received the usual answer from the servants: Observing the old gardener look up from his work, and shake his head significantly, they could not forbear asking him after his master. /

'Master's in a bad way, sure enough,' he replied sorrowfully; 'indeed Miss I wish you and Madam would come and sit a little with him of an evening now and then.'

'We never find him at home,' said Matilda; overlooking, in her anxiety for her cousin's welfare, the oddity and familiarity of the old man's manner.

'No ma'am, that's the worst of it – and at first we thought it no harm to let'n have his way. I knew that he spent his days in the thick woods, and I thought he might as well have his fancy; only sometimes I followed him when it began to get damp, and begged of him to go home; but when he would turn home, and when I used to think I had him safe in the drawing-room, and lit the candles and every thing to make it look a little chearful and comfortable to him; he'd disappear, and for a long time we could not guess where he used to go; and where do you think we found him at last? in the vault under the old chapel – he was sitting there talking away, as if he had somebody to answer him; and when I begged of'n to leave it, he said it was cruel to force him away, for that he never was so happy as when he was there, and if he left her she would so grieve. Now who *she* was, that he was talking of, is best known unto himself, unless it was my late lady, yet surely her death was a blessing; so I take it 'tis some new fantasmagory or other, as is disturbing of his honor's poor head.'

'And is he there now?' enquired Matilda, in trembling agitation.

'Yes, madam, and will stay there till the great clock have gone twelve.'

'I will go to him,' she exclaimed, 'the voice of a friend might yet recal him.'

'Oh no!' said Mrs. Melbourne, while she trembled at an idea that had not before struck her, 'go not to that vault.'

But Matilda, alive only to the active energies of friendship, was for once deaf even to her mother's voice; and had already advanced several paces towards the chapel, accompanied by the gardener, whom she forced, unwillingly, to lead the way. Having procured lighted torches, to descend into the vault, she soon arrived at the mournful scene / of her cousin's devotion. At the door of the vault the old man again paused. 'Indeed you had better not go in Miss,' he said, alarmed at what he had done, which had produced in Matilda an exertion so much beyond any he meant to have required of her.

' 'Tis such a cold damp place you may catch your death, and you can do no mortal good; for as to thinking of moving *him* before the hour is expired, you might as well think to move a rock.'

'Proceed,' said Matilda, in a firm voice, though her heart was wrung. The servant was forced to yield. The door was opened. Leaning, in the silence of filial anguish, over a coffin, which bore the name of Melbourne, they discovered the unfortunate Sir Harold. His air, his attitude, his piercing grief, the relation which he bore to the object of his regret, all struck the trembling Matilda, for the first time, with a heartbreaking recollection. She now guessed the reason of her mother's parting entreaty, and almost feared her own courage would fail her in executing the task she had undertaken. Equally unable to advance, or to recede, she stood, for a moment, absorbed in these painful contemplations; till the reflection, that the object now before her, had a still greater claim to compassion than herself, arose to arm her with resolution to go through with her benevolent purpose.

The night-air blew her white garments to the wind, and her fine eyes were raised as in prayer for her cousin: he directed his towards her; 'Angel of consolation,' he cried, 'come you then sooner to my prayers?' But turning from her, with a look of grief and disappointment, 'Ah no,' he said, 'a fairer, not a dearer spirit is there.'

'Oh, that I could be a spirit of peace to you,' said Matilda, in a voice of the tenderest compassion. 'Dear Sir Harold, suffer me to tear you from this spot. Why will you distress your friends – all those who love you, by thus indulging a fatal grief?'

'Have I friends? no, she who loved me is here; you, Matilda, never loved me – you have told me so; why, then, should I quit the living for the dead? That night, when / she appeared to you to have left us for ever; that night, in which I watched by her mortal remains, she returned to me, beaming in all that angelic beauty with which she was adorned before oppression crushed her; and she promised to see me each night at that hour, if my affection remained unchanged; if I suffered not its devotion to be disturbed by sharing it with any outward object. I have complied. Buried in retirement, I have not even suffered you to share my soul with her; and she has, in return, rewarded me with interviews which have repaid – '

Here Matilda, interrupting him, endeavoured to reason him out of this new illusion; but in vain. 'Do you think,' he replied, looking at her with disdain, 'that the attachment of lovers, of two mortals united by chance, by vanity, or caprice, is to be supposed to survive the tomb; and yet that an affection, the earliest, the purest, the most ardent, cannot resist its power? No, my mother,' he continued, throwing himself upon the mournful pall, 'not even death itself shall part us more.'

'Will you not hear me?' exclaimed the distressd Matilda. 'I, too, have wept in agony over a parent's cold remains; a parent, whose remains these walls enclose. I will weep with you, if you will give me but a hope, that at some future time, your soul may admit of consolation. Then do not, oh, do not, if you ever valued my peace, give way to such destructive grief.'

'You have wept?' Sir Harold repeated, looking on her with an air of incredulity. Poor innocent! do you think you loved your parent with a love like mine?' But perceiving that the words she had uttered were indeed from her heart, and that her tears flowed involuntarily, and in great abundance, the reality of her emotion produced an instantaneous change in his manner and feelings. 'Oh, spare these tears,' he said, 'I am not worthy of them; do they, indeed, fall for me? I will obey them. Matilda wishes it, I will obey.' Rising, he followed her from this scene of desolation; thus showing the empire she still maintained over his mind, and the habitual submission / he paid, even in his wildest or most gloomy hours, to any wish she sincerely expressed.

Having extorted from him a promise that he would not revisit the vault till she saw him again, she no longer opposed herself to her mother's anxious entreaty; and was taking leave, when he said to her, with a smile, 'You think now you have preserved me from the effects of a vision, which you weakly imagine might be injurious to me;

but you are mistaken; you have only changed the scene from that where it usually appears. At twelve, when you are gone, she will issue from that door,' (pointing to the one which led to the apartments where Lady Julia Melbourne formerly lived,) 'and bless me with her conversation. It now gives me added delight, as she has all the faculties, which in life were suspended, restored in tenfold lustre; but what is strange,' he added, whispering, 'is, that she retains her dread of the hour of twelve, and could not spend it without my society. She tells me it was necessary she should be withdrawn from me for a space, to be restored to the full exercise of her powers, but that she will soon return and – ' he paused for a moment, then rapidly resumed, with an expression of exulting confidence, 'she will return, and live with me for ever. You see I have prepared all things for her reception.'

The apartment in which they conversed had indeed been adorned with studied elegance, since the death of Lady Julia Melbourne; and every day Sir Harold employed himself in making some addition of whatever was most pleasing to the eye, or gratifying to the taste and fancy; then, surveying with complacency the silent scene, he would often repeat, ' 'Twas thus she loved it living – her presence now alone is wanting – nor shall it be wanting long.'

This infatuation was not made to last. Ever the sport of some new illusion, Sir Harold Melbourne contrived, (without infringing the promise given to his relations, of not returning to the vaults); to find out for himself another equally melancholy occupation. He determined to erect a magnificent mausoleum to his mother; to which, / as soon as it was finished, her remains were to be removed. The spot was marked out; it was one already planted with yew, cypress, willow, and many other trees of mournful shade. In the midst of a circular space, that had been cleared by Sir Harold's direction, he resolved the monument should be erected. In that part of his grounds, and in that alone, Sir Harold might be seen every morning before sun-rise, encouraging his workmen, and assisting, with his own hands, in the prosecution of the work. The first time Mrs. Melbourne found him surrounded by his plans and marbles, she endeavoured to dissuade him from an undertaking so calculated to revive every painful sensation; she remonstrated against his being himself employed in forwarding it; but counsel or reproof he rejected, with equal disdain. 'Kings have found pleasure in the occupation,' he said, 'and what king ever could boast a parent like mine? Guide of my youth – indulgent friend of my maturer years – in infancy my guard, support, consoler; when she instructed, her words were wisdom, when she approved, her looks were love.'

How detach him from an employment, calculated only to nourish the most melancholy and fatal ideas? How draw off his attention from it, when the unhappy man remained under a firm conviction, that his lost parent appeared to him every night to urge the completion of the work! What charm could again soothe his spirits to peace! – For some time he had lost his usual pleasure in music; yet Matilda determined once more to try its effect on him.

One night, at the hour in which he usually expected his awful visitant, his fair friend, who had engaged him in an animated conversation, took up her harp, and, without apparent premeditation, striking some chords, began a song, to which he had often, in former days, listened with delight; then, as if inspired by her own exertions, she continued, for some time, to shew, in different airs, the powers and pathos she possessed. Sir Harold listened, in breathless attention; the hour passed on, and for that night he seemed to have forgot the vision that generally engrossed him. When she found the / power she had thus obtained, she habituated herself to repeat, at the same hour, the same experiment. Its success was beyond her expectations. Sir Harold, dead to every other pleasure, could still listen to that voice; and it seemed to restore his cheerfulness, if not his health. He now could talk with composure of quitting the Rocks, the scene of all his sorrows; and his former passion for travelling seemed to have revived again. Yet still true to the principle that now influenced all his actions, he managed to unite this newly returned taste, with the desire he had to render the tribute of affection he constantly meditated for his mother, every way worthy of her. 'He would defer its completion,' he said, 'till he had himself procured the marbles and bas-reliefs abroad, that were destined to form the pillars, and to adorn the compartments of her tomb.

CHAPTER XIV.

Fare thee well, thou first and fairest!
Fare thee well, thou best and dearest!
Thine be every joy and treasure,
Peace, enjoyment, love, and pleasure.

BURNS[73]

SIR Harold, since his taste for travelling had returned, was become very inquisitive respecting the affairs of the continent; and as every thing yielded before the warm creations of his fancy, the peace of Europe was soon settled. Italy was restored among its rightful owners, and travelling was rendered equally commodious and secure. To see how far the public accounts promised in time to realize these sanguine plans, Matilda was / constantly required to read him the news of the day; and the uneasiness and constraint she endured, when so employed, became every moment more insupportable. Whenever the name of Strathallan met her eye; that name which spoke such volumes to her heart; that name, which seemed to stand apart from all others, and to irradiate, with the single light of the characters which composed it, the page in which it was found; she was obliged to assume a composure the most foreign to her feelings, to check the blush, to curb the sigh; if possible, even to restrain the start of sudden anguish when his danger was the theme; for still, as she read, the eyes of her cousin were fixed on her, with a scrutiny so severe, that she dreaded his penetration, and the starts of phrenzy that were too often the consequence of it.

Yet this terror was again subdued and melted into pity, when she listened to the delusions in which her ill-fated relative indulged; and which seemed to promise him years of variety and amusement, while his exhausted health refused to ratify the flattering hope.

'Your songs ever delighted me, my lovely cousin,' he said, 'but when I have been in Italy, I will bring you back so much music from that land of witchery and Syren strains, that you will be forced to own the powers of your voice lay dormant till then. From Venice, the light song of the Gondolier, and the evening chaunt of the enamoured maid of Palestrina's opposing coast, shall woo your taste, when she sings, to the responsive voice of her love, upon the Laguna, the strains of the Bard of Salerno.[74] 'Tis thus Matilda's voice shall charm me to return – it is thus, when I am gone, she will watch and weep for me. From Sicily, the song of the mariner, or the rich harmonies that float along the bay of Naples and its proud and beauteous city. Whatever is sweet, whatever is lovely, I will lay at your feet; that you may improve it by your talents, that you may endear it by your charms; but what shall I bring *her*,' he resumed, with a fearful and altered look, 'round whom / every one once pressed eager to render homage, for whom I would brave death, would wander through the world? What is all I can offer, all she can receive? – a tomb.' – Then turning his eyes with renewed interest on Matilda, 'To your mother,' he said, I entrust, during my absence, the guardianship of my treasure; and I need not fear your inconstancy,' he continued, with a glance of conscious security and satisfaction at the fatal ring.

An acuteness and intelligence, together with a wonderful degree of memory, was always mingled with his wanderings; a circumstance, which made it impossible, on any subject in which his heart was concerned, to hope, for a moment, to lull or deceive his vigilance. The idea of visiting Italy, which Sir Harold had been prevented, by the peculiar circumstances attending his travels, from viewing in any other than a cursory and partial manner before, was now his most favourite speculation. Matilda only replied to the plans he communicated to her, by a look of tender apprehension and pity, as she cast her eyes on *his* flushed cheek and emaciated form, who talked of traversing continents, when his existence appeared, from day to day, as if, by miracle, prolonged. Of this he soon himself became fully sensible.

One evening, at the close of an air he had particularly desired to hear, he continued gazing for some moments upon the beautiful animation of her countenance, never so lovely as when she sung, and then earnestly exclaimed, 'Thus listening, thus beholding, surely I ought not to complain.'

'You think so now, but on your return from Italy, you will find much to correct in my wood-notes wild;'[75] said Matilda, affecting a gaiety and ease she did not feel, to conceal how much she was confused by the suddenness and warmth of his address.

He shook his head – 'Matilda,' he resumed with solemn emphasis, 'I shall never go to Italy; this sylvan scene contains my mother's remains, and will contain mine. It / was decreed, that in this spot we both should fall.' Then, as if endeavouring more completely to collect his thoughts, 'My lovely cousin,' he said, 'I had something to say to you, before my final preparations for a long, long separation. I have, perhaps, committed many errors, but nothing weighs so heavy on my heart as my conduct to you. It has been unjust, it has been cruel; but remember, I was lost to myself before I even knew your charms. Honour was my idol. The whisper, that it was attained in the very sanctuary where I had fondly conceived it enshrined, overthrew that reason, it had not power to convince; converted that affection all to bitternesss, which it was unable to destroy. Then over my already suffering heart came too, too powerful love. I do not excuse myself. What did I wish? I had only misery, reason impaired, health blasted, hopes destroyed, to wed you to – and these I would have had you share – but patience – yet a few brief moments, and the black thread I would have interwoven in the golden tissue of your days, will break – love, joy, and youth, will woo you to possess each pleasure, which I have alone opposed. I rejoice in your approaching bliss. Yet, will you forgive me, cousin, the contradiction of a heart too fondly doating. I go to the grave with added bitterness, from the thought you will then be Strathallan's. I envy his felicity, and still, were it in my power – '

'Do not anticipate,' said Matilda, who had not heard him for some time past indulge in this melancholy strain, 'Life, I trust, may yet have its value for you and – '

'Never so much as at this moment,' he replied, bending forward as he uttered these words with fervent and encreasing energy – 'Oh! looking thus, to die were still unequalled bliss!' He fixed his eyes on that adored countenance, and seemed to drink, in every beauty, happiness restored. At length his gaze became less earnest – still it was turned with tenderness on her – still his eyes sought her's, and seemed to express a languid pleasure, in a presence so beloved. / Gradually, and gently, they closed, as if unwilling to shut out those beams of beauty, on which they so long had lived; and at length letting fall the hand he had fondly clasped, he, in a sigh, soft, deep and tremulous, expired.

CHAPTER XV.

Se mai senti spirarti sul volto
Lieve fiato, che lento s'aggiri
Di': son questi gli estremi sospiri
Del mio fido che muore per me.
Al mio spirto dal seno disciolto
La memoria di tanti martiri
Sarà dolce con questa mercè.

METASTASIO LA CLEMENZA DI TITO.[76]

ON examining Sir Harold's papers, two articles in his will more particularly demanded the attention of Mrs. and Miss Melbourne. By the first, he bequeathed to Matilda the whole of his personal property, which amounted to about ten thousand pounds, as a small return, he said, for the attention she had bestowed upon his sister, and the hours of delight he himself had known in her society. He mentioned her merits and amiable qualities in the highest terms; and then added / a wish, that Julia Melbourne might spend the three first months of her mourning at the Rocks, under the care of her most respected relative, to whose guardianship he, in the most solemn manner, consigned her. To spend any time, however short, entirely at the Rocks, was a circumstance the most painful to the feelings of his relations, but they were determined to observe the last requests of the amiable, unhappy being they had just lost, as religiously as a law. A sealed paper, addressed to Mrs. Melbourne, more fully explained his reasons for expressing this desire, by which he seemed to extend his gentle, yet cruel tyranny, even beyond the grave.

'Before you will have opened this writing, the Rocks will be my Julia's,' he said, 'I wish her ever to consider that scene as her home, and to be known and beloved in the spot she has inherited. Where she lives, you will be – for, has not Matilda given me her most solemn promise, never to forsake her. But another, and a stronger reason, urges me to desire she may make no delay in taking possession of her inheritance. It is her right; but recollect she is a female infant; alone, unprotected, an orphan, doubly an orphan, from her tenderest years; mystery and slander have rested on them. Believe the last dying dictates of a brother's anxious love, a brother who, during life, ever watched her with the fondest affection; and think not that the wanderings of the head have, in this instance, misled the heart. Relations I have; distant relatives whom I esteem not. But what then? they can sting, though incapable of reflecting honour on us. Me they have traduced; they might more fatally traduce her. Haste and anticipate them, before they can afford you the shadow of disquietude. Claim they have none; but who can answer for the attempts of grasping avarice? To you, my dearest cousin, I continue to recommend my only treasure. Possessed of riches, beauty, and a sensibility deep and alarming, how can I hope she will escape the various dangers that will surround her. My best, my only security is in confiding her to you; but what precaution can ensure happiness? The sage boasts that the goods of fortune are all that / fortune's self can rob him of? But are not peace, virtue, reason, almost equally in the power of fate?'

On this mournful reflection, the best comment was his own wayward lot. Behold then Matilda, once more reinstated in the scene that had cradled her infancy; but oh, how different from the artless child of solitude! who peeping, for the first time, with fawn-like timidity from behind her native rocks, seemed hardly to know that there existed a world, in which misfortune, cruelty, and deceit, were at every moment to be found. No two persons could be more dissimilar to each other, than she was to her former self. Yet had Matilda rather gained than lost by the alteration. Sorrow, in distinguishing, had added beauties to her mind as well as countenance. She had known the passions, but it was to resist them with courage; had become acquainted with affliction, but it was to receive it with resignation. The playful, almost infantine innocence and grace of early youth, were exchanged for a dignity, a firmness, a deep, but constantly repressed sensibility, that lent its impression to all her features, its majestic and touching beauties to her gestures, air, and countenance. In person and mind she was now all the fondest lover could wish, or the most anxious parent hope to see accomplished; purified from every girlish foible that could diminish the lustre and effect of so many united excellencies.

Surrounded by objects that perpetually reminded her of the unhappy friend, whose death alone could set her free, in every dusky walk and twisted bower she seemed to meet, in pensive musings, *his* pallid shade, whose life had been devoted to her idea. His spirit seemed to breathe along the groves – the rocky seat, the winding, silent stream, now turbid from neglect; the altar, still strewed with inscriptions of his cherished passion, all spoke to her pitying heart; all seemed, in plaintive murmurs, to recall the memory of him who had loved so long, so well; still these were not her constant thoughts – sometimes the image of Strathallan would cross her solitary walk, invested in all that / radiant glory, beaming with all that blooming beauty, in which her partial tender love had so often anticipated his return; and then he passed

> 'Before her fancy's eye,
> Like some delightful vision of the soul,
> To soothe, not trouble it!'[77]

But stern reality too oft disturbed these fond illusions; a few months had entirely changed the face of her destiny; and, when she reflected how soon the tie that bound her to Sir Harold had been broken after his departure, she was ready, with fretful impatience, to accuse her lover of cruelty, of precipitancy; then, soon repenting, 'let me not blame thee, Strathallan!' she cried, 'MY evil star prevailed even in that fatal hour when I refused your love! Oh surely, surely 'tis decreed none of our wretched, our divided family should ever taste of happiness! should it prevail once more!' She remembered, with horror, the wish one of his letters had expressed, that a glorious death might terminate his sufferings at once; 'if it should come now – now that life is, in his eyes, I hope most valuable! let me endure,' she exclaimed, 'in trembling anguish, each various torture yet reserved by fate – but spare, Oh heaven, the dear presumptuous one! – the loved, the too dearly, fondly loved offender!'

In the habits of sincere and ardent piety, that Matilda had ever cultivated, she now found her best consolation and support. With parents the most deeply impressed by all the sublime truths of religion, she had been left upon this head, very much to the workings of her own mind; and this, which in a disposition less excellent, might have been of dangerous consequence, with her only tended to improve her knowledge, and to confirm her faith.

Mr. Melbourne, from the peculiarity of his habits, and latterly from his state of health, had been, in general, too negligent of the forms enjoined by religion. Accustomed to see the Creator in all his works, God was in his heart and in his thoughts; but, naturally silent and contemplative, he seldom / gave words to the overflowings of a truly pious and benevolent nature. Mrs. Melbourne on the contrary, while scrupulously attentive to the observances it requires, was, from a different cause, habituated to check every expression of that conviction, which was the rule and the reward of all her actions. Educated in the bosom of a gay, mixed society, accustomed to touch, with the light spear of ridicule, every thing that passed its comprehension, or warred with its pursuits, a modest silence, and constant refusal of all controversy, had, alone preserved her own belief from shipwreck, in a scene, where venturing to defend it, might have exposed it to the overpowering, though not convincing, arms of learning, eloquence, and dangerous sophistry united. But that world which had spared her principles, had a little influenced her taste; and, by perhaps too great an excess of refinement, she was apt to view, with alarm, as symptoms of enthusiasm, affectation, or hypocrisy, the least mention of that sweet hope, the least allusion to those sacred truths, which the works of the inspired writers contain, except when authorized by the express purpose of the moment, when introduced at the hour of worship, thanksgiving, and prayer. To Matilda, whose ardent mind was ever demanding more than the present scene can afford, the knowledge of these opinions often occasioned a painful constraint. She had sought, by turns, with her younger friends, to communicate the feelings of an ingenuous and grateful spirit; but then Clara, she considered, professed an erring faith; and Arbella, when they were first acquainted, professed no faith at all. Thrown back to the resources of her own mind, she had read, she had reflected, she had decided. And that belief, which solitude had, in infancy a little tinctured with local superstition, had brightened into the clearest, purest flame of rational piety. One favourite, though fanciful conviction of all her former illusions she still fondly cherished. It is that which inculcates the belief of guardian spirits, appointed to assist the virtuous, and convey them, with honour and safety, through the terrors and temptations of their mortal career. /

On this subject Mrs. Melbourne rallied her most unmercifully; and thought herself sure of the assistance of Mrs. Sowerby, who, though no longer an *esprit fort*, three thousand a-year had rendered more than ever (in the opinion of the world) a *bel-esprit*.[78] 'Yes,' she said, 'Matilda will not deny it; when she was yet but a very little lady, she pleased herself with imagining every grot and hill, the seat of an aërial power; with fancying the air itself inhabited by invisible but beneficent beings, busily employed in providing for our happiness, or defending us against every possible danger. She has wept at finding my tales of sylphs and genii were not true, and to this day, she believes that a certain noble youth, who has all our wishes, is followed on the Continent by an angel *'tout à lui,'*[79] who will guide him, like the Duke of Marlborough, to all sorts of honor and glory – is it not so, Matilda?'

'I do not see,' replied the young Lady, raising up her modest eyes, 'what there is absurd, or fantastic in the belief; other nations trust in guardian angels of kingdoms; and why should not – '

'Others!' interrupted Mr. Sowerby with more asperity than he had lately allowed himself to show; 'those, perhaps, whose national religion, frivolous and false as their manners, only deserves to be what our immortal Dryden, in the plan of his noble poem, wished to make it, the basis of our national mythology.'[80]

'Come, come, Monsieur Anti-gallican,' exclaimed his wife, playfully silencing him, 'I had some thoughts of joining with you, but a passage I read last night, pleased me so much, that it has almost made me a convert to Matilda's opinion. It is the farewell of an amiable wife, whose name, I am sorry, is not preserved, expressing the last wishes of a heart, which, even approaching death, could not render indifferent to the object of its fond affections. Her husband was an officer, who had a command in Spain; she wishes for the power of following him, as a protecting spirit, when released from her present suffering frame. Arbella then read from / a collection of letters, the passage she had alluded to.

'To be present at all the adventures to which human life is exposed: to administer slumber to thine eye-lids, in the agonies of a fever; to cover thy face in the day of battle; and go with thee, a guardian angel, incapable of wound or pain, where I have longed to attend thee when a weak, a fearful woman. Oh, best of men! I cannot figure to myself a greater happiness than – '[81]

Arbella had read thus far, when the audible sobs of Matilda, and the streaming tears that she could no longer suppress, shewed her friend, that she had dwelt too long on a subject so painfully interesting. Yet though it led to anticipations that too often harrowed her feelings, it was only when the conversation could be thus brought round to the object of her secret meditations, that Matilda could take any interest in it. At other times, even in the midst of those animated discussions of which she used to be the charm and soul, her vacant look and wandering eye, shewed that her thoughts were with him, who was far distant from her sight, but ever present to her heart. Though she had written to inform him of the late melancholy events, and to express the half uttered wish of modest, fearful love, that duty might not long detain him from her, he was, now, alas! no longer master to declare when its call should cease.

As Strathallan had made his father the confidant of all that latterly passed between him and Matilda, his Lordship took an early opportunity of expressing, by letter to her, the complete satisfaction he now felt in the prospect of their union.

'In his former choice,' he said, 'my son sacrificed the dearest affections of his heart to my interest, my peace, and honor. It is time I should, in my turn, consider his wishes.

They are indeed become my own; and experience has taught me justly to value the blessing I now venture, Madam, to hope at your hands. Do not reproach yourself for the past. Strathallan, with his apparent mildness, is like his father, sometimes impetuous in his resolutions, and must consent to abide by their consequences. I have only to / request that if you are not very angry with him, you will continue sometimes to cheer the poor wanderer, by epistolary communications. I shall have a pleasure in forwarding them, together with our own, as there is now, I flatter myself, but one wish respecting Strathallan's return, in our re-united circle, from Mrs. Melbourne and her fair daughter, to Emilia, Laura, and

Your very faithful and obedient,
TORRENDALE.'

Though still unable to discover, that resemblance between Lord Torrendale and his son, which his Lordship flattered himself existed, Matilda was delighted with the familiar, and friendly tone in which this letter was written; one which he had indeed taken the greatest pains to assume, in the place of his usually formal manner, and which, it may be observed, did not yet sit entirely easy on him. She accepted, with eagerness, his proposal of conveying her letters to Strathallan; flattering herself, that by keeping up a correspondence with his family, she should receive both more frequent, and more copious intelligence, respecting him. She little imagined that she was only unthinkingly giving into a snare laid for her by Lady Torrendale, who had herself suggested to her Lord this proposal, with the secret intention of revenging herself for Matilda's want of confidence, when she proposed her insidious question, on the supposed danger of Lady Strathallan. How little she was deserving of trust, or how unbecoming it would have been in Matilda to place it in her, the Countess never paused to consider. Miss Melbourne's not replying to that letter, she vowed she would never forgive. 'I would have contributed to the *denoüement* of her novel again,' she said, 'as I endeavoured to forward its progress before; but since she thinks she can carry on her plans independently of me, we will see if I cannot mange a little arrangement without consulting her. It is no matter how long Strathallan remains in the Peninsula, there are others besides him to support the name of Torrendale.' Pursuant to these laudable resolutions, her Ladyship, / under pretence of saving Lord Torrendale the trouble of making up the packets, suppressed his letter to his son (which he had shewn her) containing an account of Sir Harold's death, and only transmitted one of inferior importance which had been written some days before; Matilda's letter also she destroyed; resolved to do the same good office, by all that should arrive from her, at Fitzroy square. She allowed some of Strathallan's to be sent to the Rocks for fear Miss Melbourne might otherwise suspect some treachery, and have recourse to other means of hearing from him. 'Now Miss Melbourne will be gay,' Emily would say, 'for to-day she expects a letter from – '

Matilda smiled; and no longer, as in former times, defended herself from the accusation. The letter arrived. It was full of tenderness; still she thought it strange that his reviving hopes were never touched upon by Strathallan; but soon consoled herself with the reflections Lady Torrendale foresaw she would make, on the difficulty and irregularity of communication with the army abroad. Again, and again, she wrote.

Many were the days, the weeks of heart-sick anxiety she often endured, while public rumour was all that reached her ear; and while spring passed away in this miserable manner, she sometimes sighed, 'Oh Strathallan, can even a future hour of tranquillity and happiness with thee, repay the long protracted sufferings of a life of lingering suspence? were he but returned – returned, though war and toil had obscured those dazzling and captivating distinctions that biassed, perhaps, my youthful choice; were he but safe, my heart would rest contented, nor ask my eyes if aught without were changed!' Sometimes his letters a little calmed her mind. Towards the close of summer, after an interval of more than usual length she opened with eager joy a packet from Strathallan; but it was far from conveying the balm to her heart, the former ones had done. It spoke of an expected engagement; it complained of her silence – her neglect.

Absorbed in more important cares, Matilda scarcely remarked that it did not acknowledge / what she last had written. Still then, 'upon the hazard of a die,'[82] hung all her hopes of future happiness. She could not contemplate the prospect before her with steadiness; she only saw Strathallan too brave, herself too tender, to survive it. If for a moment, she ventured to indulge the idea that, this one peril past, he might be restored the sooner to her wishes, she soon feared again, with the solicitude of a lover, that it was impossible those wishes, so strong, so ardent, could be granted; and she would often exclaim, 'no, I never shall see him again. I love him too much. I never shall see him more.'

Observing how much this situation affected her daughter's health, Mrs. Melbourne proposed a temporary absence from the Rocks; as the best means of diverting her mind from continually dwelling on one painful topic. Mrs. Carlyle, who had been continued, by Sir Harold's recommendation, in her place about Julia, promised in every thing where only care and affection were demanded, to be the most able representative of Mrs. Melbourne, and some dispute respecting the Baronet's disposal of his property, in favor of Matilda, rendered this journey as necessary, as desirable. The relation to whom Sir Harold had alluded, in his letter to Mrs. Melbourne, and who was not in England at the time of the Baronet's decease, had immediately, on his return, taken advantage of his cousin's occasional alienations of mind, to question the validity of his will, and though Mrs. Melbourne was certain she could produce incontestible proof of his being in full possession of his powers of intellect, at the time he made the disposition which excited so much contest and envy, she did not chuse to neglect, in its commencement, a circumstance that might occasion her, or her daughter, future vexation.

During the short period that Mrs. and Miss Melbourne staid in town, Emily was, of course, to remain with Julia; as the only answer Matilda had received to her letter, requesting to know Lady Torrendale's pleasure respecting her daughter, on the removal of the family to the Rocks, was to desire the / change might make no alteration in their former arrangement. 'Keep her, my dear Miss Melbourne; she cannot be better than with you. The same instructors that attend Miss J. Melbourne from **** are quite sufficient for her, till the time of finishing masters arrives.'

Such were the replies of the dissipated Countess, who seemed now as well pleased with a pretext to get rid of all domestic trouble, as she had formerly been with an

excuse for taking her daughter out with her every where. Matilda viewed the preparations for her journey with that torpid indifference, that indolence which arise from
despair, that sickness of the mind which made her dislike the scene in which she lived,
and yet feel a strange reluctance to the effort required to leave it; in these moments,
the company of Sappho was more grateful to her than that of the livelier Arbella. The
romantic enthusiasm of the poetess gave her an appearance of still greater sensibility
than she really possessed; it also inclined her more readily to discuss those fearful
and lofty topics, which now alone were pleasing to Matilda, as being identified in her
mind with the image of Strathallan. 'Shall I repeat to you, my friend, the little poem
I composed upon the subject of our last night's conversation,' said Sappho, (after a
long *tête-a-tête* silence, which had arisen during a visit of Matilda's to her at the village, which, like the ancient seat that adjoined it, bore the name of the Rocks); Lady
Lyndhurst has not yet seen it – you shall have the first copy.'

'Is it about Spain?' enquired Matilda, with an absent look.

Matilda, who had been hitherto accustomed to welcome with the most winning
affability every production of Sappho's muse, enquired, with an absent look, 'Is it
about Spain?'

'It is. [a] The subject is its vile usurper, and the contrasting glories of your hero, my
hero, every body's hero. I do not mean your lover: but while I repeat it you may think
of him, or dream of him, which ever you like best.' /

THE HOPE OF IBERIA.

> With tresses wild, by golden Tagus' side,
> Stood a bright maid, in sorrow's graceful pride;
> Her slender form hung o'er the wave below,
> Her voice, sonorous, spoke of war and woe,
> In her dark eye, a thousand passions rolled,
> While thus her heart's impassioned griefs she told.
> 'A thousand wrongs this bleeding breast have torn,
> Stabbed by domestic guile, by foreign force,
> The Goth, the Moor, on wings of rapine borne,
> By turns have track'd their desolating course;
> But now! Oh, knighthood's shame, oh, ruin worse,
> Than every pictured woe remembrance brings,
> No princely victor reigns – a splendid curse!
> A traitor's breath the tyrant mandate wings,
> And treason treads the courts, and mocks the voice of kings.'
>
> She ceased – a gathering vapour slowly rolled,
> In curling rings along the river-side,
> The mist dispersed, a voice her heart cousoled,
> She bowed, and knew the genius of the tide.
> 'Weep not Iberia, soon shall knighthood's pride,
> Wipe the foul stain that blots thy burning brow,
> Thy bold avenger comes! Whate'er betide,
> To thy racked state of after weal or woe,
> Maid of the dauntless eye! my faithful wave shall show.'

Then, oh! when first the rapt Sicilian spies,
(And yields to famed Morgana'* praise, how due!)
On the smooth waters, towers and fanes arise;
And arches now of gold, now purple hue,
Melting, in gay confusion, to the view;
While, with delight, immingles soft surprise,
Knows he the joy the blest Iberia knew,
When the clear mirror of the crystal wave,
In bright prophetic tints, her brighter glories gave?

And first, directed by the Western star,
Whose beams, beneath the waters, trembling play,
She hails a lovely island, distant far;
Its emerald beauties mild, the fount of day,
Illumines with its last, its parting ray.
There, sheathed in glittering panoply of war,
Her champion first, her wondering eyes survey;
Bright round his crest, young Hope, and Fortune smile,
And urge their favoured chief, son of the verdant isle.

A warrior chief he seemed; but soon the brand,
Drawn but for justice, conquering but to save;
To olive-branch was changed, at heaven's command.
And flowers, and blossoms, fruit and perfumes gave; /
As when 'twas given to Israel's Priest to wave,
The sterile rod – with almonds bloomed the wand,
Fair, like the youthful spring, with blossoms brave,
Such mighty change, shall sad Iberia see,
Conqueror in virtue's cause! when cheered, when raised by thee!

With speechless extacy, the virgin sighed,
Closed her bright eyes, as if no longer waking;<?>
Oh, for a long, long night of sleep, she cried,
Time, still unfelt, his slow departure taking;
Till I salute the day-spring from on high,
The loved, the rising star of dawning liberty.

'Hark!' exclaimed Matilda, who would scarcely give Sappho time to finish reading her verses, 'what was it I heard then? – a shout! – Oh, surely yes? – and hark! 'tis there again!'

'And listen to the bells,' cried Sappho, 'surely there must be some reason for their bursting forth in that merry peal! Some news is perhaps arrived this moment – a great advantage gained over the enemy!'

They were not kept long in suspense, for at this moment, the entrance of one of Sappho's officious neighbours; an old lady, who always liked to be the first with any good news, informed them of the victory gained over the French at Salamanca, which

---

*   The phænomenon called in Calabria, the Castles of the Fairy Morgana.

was just announced to the delighted inhabitants of the village, with the entrance of the herald of the morning's intelligence. 'They say now,' she pursued, 'that the Spaniards will soon drive the French quite out of their country; and that they may thank us for that, as for every thing else.'

'I said so,' exclaimed Sappho; her countenance kindling with sudden enthusiasm, while she lifted, in pious gratitude, her tearful eye to heaven. 'He lives but to conquer, and conquers to save!' and, as she spoke, the animated expression of her face and figure, which, for a moment, assimilated her to one of the prophetic, tuneful daughters of Antiquity, afforded the most striking contrast to the pale drooping form of Matilda; in whom one sole idea checked the current of rejoicing, and turned every smiling prospect into gloom.

'If you were to have seen the postman,' / continued the good lady, 'as he passed through the village, to go on to S***; and how the little urchins hallooed when they saw he had a branch of laurel in his cap; and then they must all be gathering laurel too – and such shouting – you must have heard it – hark! they are at it again!'

Sappho, who perceived her friend's emotion was much increased by the presence of a stranger, soon contrived, under some pretext, to disengage herself from her; and then endeavoured, in the most gentle and soothing manner, to reason with the lovely mourner. 'Why should Lord Strathallan's danger be greater,' she said, 'only because he is the most amiable, and most beloved of men? In a very short time, perhaps to-morrow, all the particulars may reach us – Heavens!' she continued, observing Matilda heard her, cold and trembling, and unable to derive any consolation; almost unable to understand the import of the words that were addressed to her; 'Could you be worse, if report had committed that fatal error it did on the occasion of a former engagement, in which he bore a part?'

'Could I be worse?' Matilda repeated, in a hollow tone, while she started with horror at the idea suggested, 'The error that then gave my heart the first throb of pain for Strathallan, would now, if repeated, soon make it cease to beat.' /

CHAPTER XVI.

Come then! again your laurel-wreaths prepare!
Bring every sweetest flower that scents the air!
In festive troops around the victor throng;
And greet the triumph as it sweeps along!

POEM OF BONAPARTE.[83]

It was come – it was gone – that eventful day, dreaded, with such anxiety, by the trembling Matilda – wished for with such heroic ardour by Strathallan – escaped, escaped, with glory, from its carnage. Was he happy? Had public success left his heart nothing more to desire? The preparations for war, the tumult of battle might have drowned, for a moment, the murmurs of that heart; but, in the intervals of the mighty struggle of an empire, it flew back, with trembling fondness to Matilda. Conceiving his services could, for a short period, be dispensed with, he determined, (giving up the pleasure of entering the capital of Spain with the army that had so nobly avenged her), to obtain permission to absent himself, that he might judge, by his own eyes, if there were yet, beyond the proud rewards of valour, any object worth living for. Matilda's unaccountable silence struck his heart, by turns, with every painful suspicion. Fears for her health – doubts of her fidelity, alternately racked his mind. Yet, when he thought of the whole tenor of her conduct, he was ready to reproach himself for sullying the image of that angel brightness enshrined in his heart, with even the momentary imputation of inconstancy.

Landed in England, his impatience to behold her was such, that, without seeing Lord and Lady Torrendale, he immediately proceeded into Derbyshire, after dispatching to Matilda a letter, informing her of the day she might expect his arrival; but not even Matilda could conceive the speed that love imparted to the wanderer's approach. It / was with 'wonder, great as her content,'[84] that she learnt his arrival at Woodlands; within four miles of her abode! She wished that others might share in her delight, and had sketched the plan of rural festivity that was to mark the day. She now thought she had hardly time to hasten her few and simple preparations. What could delay Strathallan? Had they still pangs to suffer, before they at length should meet? Obliged to pass through the village of Woodlands before he reached the residence of his mistress, for once the good, the benevolent Strathallan, had urged his horses with such excessive speed, that when he arrived near his family mansion, beyond which the small country town of Woodlands lay, he would have been obliged to allow them a little rest, even if they had not been stopped by the delighted villagers, who, on perceiving their dear

Lord, surrounded him with acclamations and welcomes. He thought his small stock of patience would fail, when they entreated he would alight and take refreshment; but when he perceived the intended compliment designed by these honest people, it was not in his nature to let them see how much their ill-timed gratitude distressed him. Passing by the house, he observed the steps lined, on both sides, with young damsels, clad in white, and crowned with garlands. A pair of colours exquisitely worked, and surmounted with laurel, adorned the centre. Strathallan cast an anxious hurried glance around; a faint hope lurked at his heart, that, among those wild and blooming flowers, he should discover the lovely rose on which all his affections were fixed. But no, these colours were an offering from the young maids of the village, to the hero, whom they so justly and proudly claimed as their own. They had heard that the colours of the regiment led by Lord Strathallan, after having been the rallying point for actions the most brilliant, had been taken and retaken, pierced through with bullets, torn into stripes, and, at length, reduced to a fragment, glorious indeed; but which, while preserved, with anxious care, as a trophy of the past, could hardly lead to future scenes / of danger. They, therefore, had resolved, to employ that industry, of which they had so lately been taught the value by his charming Matilda, in fabricating a pair of state colours, which they entreated him to accept, as a memorial of the gratitude and affection of every class over which his goodness had extended. The youngest of the country girls took from her head her chaplet, which was so ingeniously contrived as to change into a nosegay, when she presented it to him: it had some heath flowers, mingled with laurel, myrtles, and roses; and, in a few words, which she addressed to his Lordship, with a pretty hesitation, and a modest blush, she expressed a hope, of the assembled group, that the rose, the laurel and myrtle, which were to crown his days, would never make him quite forget the wild heath of their native mountain, nor the place he held in the hearts of the simple inhabitants. Strathallan, with a grace, which was only his, thanked the assembled group; and, saluting the pretty speaker, assured her, that their interests were interwoven with the dearest wishes of his soul; and that he should always recal, with gratitude, this testimony of their regard. The cheeks of his pretty rosebud now glowed with the radiance of the full expanded flower, at this unexpected compliment, while pride, shame, and fear, alternately struggled in her innocent breast; but Strathallan telling her he considered her as the representative of the kind and long regretted friends, whose remembrance showed the goodness of their hearts, added, he trusted she would forgive his thus confirming the promise he had made them, that they should ever retain the nearest and dearest place in his memory.

'Sure you are not going yet, my Lord,' said some of the country people, 'we are to have lights and bonfires, and what not, by and bye.'

'Aye, sure your honor,' interrupted a woman, 'we intended, by the blessing of God, to set the whole village in one conflagration.'

'I hope not – I think we are surrounded by fires enough already,' replied his Lordship / gallantly, as he glanced his eyes round the fairer part of the assembly; and then disguising, as much as he could, his impatience to break from them, 'I am obliged,' he said, 'to proceed farther to-night, my worthy friends, but I hope you will not let that prevent you from drinking my health as if I was still among you.'

'Bless your kind heart! you were always the same. Something like my old Lord – yet still, so much more affable, as I may say.'

'Oh! husband,' continued the woman who had just spoken, 'I never can help thinking how sad we were three years agone, and better; and if it had so been, that our dear young Lord had really not returned, then – '

'Why then, if he had not, dame,' replied a hoary-headed sire, sagaciously shaking his head, 'he would not have been among us now – but don't let's think of sorrow, now my Lord has given us wherewithal to be joyful.'

With some difficulty Strathallan disengaged himself from the well-meaning group, who still surrounded him with huzzas, congratulations, and blessings; the men pressing round him, the children anxious to obtain a sight of him; and the women still more desirous to be distinguished by a nod, or a glance of approbation. At first his rustic friends would not suffer the horses to be restored to the carriage, but insisted upon drawing him, at least through the village. But Strathallan at length succeeded in dissuading them from this mark of attachment, distressing to his feelings, though meant by them as a proof of the heart-warm wishes, with which they once again welcomed their beloved warrior to his native land. And then, with a hand to each, and a kindly breathed prayer for the happiness of hearts so honest, simple, and affectionate, he bade them, for a while, farewell; and urging his people to redoubled speed, was soon out of sight of the villagers, leaving them at a loss which most to admire, the sensibility, the spirit, or liberality, of their darling hero.

All these unavoidable delays had conspired to render Strathallan later than he / intended, in meeting his beloved; but after having given so much to others, he now felt that he owed something to his own feelings, and to himself. The kind master, the benefactor, and friend, had enjoyed their turn; now the man and the lover resumed their place in his heart. 'In a few moments I shall see her,' he whispered to himself, as the carriage drove down a winding path, overhung by a lofty steep, which led to Woodbine Lodge. 'In a few moments I shall read in those sweet eyes the joys which overflows her heart; for even Sir Harold shall not prevent her from conceding one hour to rapture unconstrained.' Alas! how happy had he been if he had known the long-dreaded Sir Harold was no more.

He now drove rapidly below a romantic ridge of mountains, and the pure breezes that blew from their healthy summits came to his sense, with added fragrance, as it brought with it the remembrance of many an enchanted ramble with Matilda. At length he reached the humble scene where last he had left the spotless mistress of his affections, under the care of her mother, and his heart beat higher as he approached,

'The lovely, lowly dwelling.'[85]

How did remembered joys rush at this moment, with redoubled force, to his mind! how did the noisy plaudits of assembled numbers, the voice of welcome, though pleasing, the voice of gratitude, though sweet, sink before the anticipated praises of blushing, faithful love! But the greater his preceding elevation of spirit, the higher the wild tumultuous throb of hope, had arisen in his bosom, the more sudden and chill struck the damp of disappointment, on finding the beloved spot deserted; the garden run wild, and no one to reply to his anxious enquiries respecting the absence of those, whose residence had alone converted it into a paradise. Though a thousand reasons might render a change of residence eligible, Strathallan's vivid imagination, instantly created a presentiment of danger to his love, of misfortune to Matilda. At length, he perceived an old man, moving home slowly / under the weight of wood he had to carry; and, hastening to him, asked in a voice, scarcely intelligible from emotion, where Matilda then was?

'At the Rocks, at her own home again,' replied the old churl, with an appearance of surly impatience at the interruption.

'The Rocks – and where is, where is Mrs. Melbourne?'

'Gone to live with her daughter to be sure.'

'To live with her daughter – to live with her – Oh! tell me,' Strathallan continued, gasping for breath, while all his former dark presentiments returned with redoubled force, but his informant was already gone; and, resolved to clear up all his doubts at once, he, instead of returning to his carriage, hastily walked on toward the Rocks.

On approaching the rustic hamlet that adjoined the ancient and romantic dwelling of the Melbourne family, he was surprized to remark, as at Woodlands, the signs of rejoicing, and every appearance of a village festival. Anxious to know the reason of this entertainment, which he could not avoid connecting, in idea, with Matilda, he asked a woman, among the by-standers, the cause of this universal holiday; and being recognized by her, was answered by numerous blessings and congratulations, intermingled with praises of Matilda.

'What! your honor don't know that its my young Lady at the Rocks have ordered it all! – she do like to see folks chearful and happy; and she do a power of good besides; God bless her Ladyship.'

What a thrill did these ominous sounds convey! – What a welcome for Strathallan to his native land! the title he had heard, though commonly enough given by rustics to their superiors, struck his mind (already prepossessed with the idea of the probable success of Sir Harold,) with all the force of conviction. From that moment all seemed darkness and confusion; unable to arrange his thoughts, he lived but to the one torturing idea, that Matilda was another's – irrevocably another's; and the very means his gentle mistress had taken to celebrate her innocent love / for him, proved to his distempered imagination a snare that convinced him of her devotion to a different object: 'Perfidious woman!' he cried, 'in the moment that, determined to sacrifice life itself to your dear idea, I could scarce pronounce an agonized farewell, you coolly sent me to a distance from you, that you might fulfill, uninterrupted by a single plaint of mine, the base, the impious vow you made.'

The jealousy of years, a jealousy that had never been wholly laid asleep, spoke in these hasty exclamations of Strathallan, purposely kept in ignorance, by his mother-in-law, of Sir Harold's death; and believing Matilda silent, when she had repeatedly written to assure him of her unchanging love, the present circumstances rather confirmed than created the conviction of her inconstancy. Still some demon seemed to urge him not to return till he had viewed the scene that contained his heart's lost treasure; and, as he approached it, an object struck his eye that would have been sufficient to have dispelled prepossessions not so deep-rooted as his.

The lovely Matilda was walking arm-in-arm with her mother, upon the lawn; her features illuminated with pleasure at the remembrance of happiness she had dispensed, and beaming with a softer joy at the anticipation of that which was in store for herself. As she turned to Mrs. Melbourne the name of Strathallan often hovered on her lips, and a half-uttered wish, of which he was the subject, seemed to employ her thoughts, when a joyful cry, from that Lady, announced that the object of all their solicitude was in sight. Hastily advancing towards him, it is impossible to describe the mingled dignity and grace with which the tender, the lofty Aspasia, as she welcomed the young warrior to his home, blended the grateful thanks-giving she uttered for his return, with the name of hero and of son!

The mist that had obscured them, fell in an instant, from the eyes of Strathallan. Ashamed of his precipitancy, he now rejoiced that it was concealed from Matilda; he paused not to retrace the steps that led to / his error, was it not already sufficiently punished? his suspence, though short, included an age of suffering.

Throughout the evening the moments flew with that delighted swiftness which may be imagined in the intercourse of hearts so fond, so long divided. Strathallan pressed his suit with a vehemence he had never dared to use before. He endeavoured to engage Mrs. Melbourne to second his arguments against all Matilda's objections to an early day; and even made use of his sister's persuasions to determine her resolution. – 'Consider, my best love, that life is short, and now it trembles on the wing of danger! Can I again leave England without calling you mine?'

A thousand endearing, yet fearful ideas were recalled to Matilda's mind by this appeal: she scorned to torture with suspence the bosom of her noble lover; and her eyes had said, even before her words confirmed it, 'Strathallan, I am yours!'

CHAPTER XVII.

– Those whom Love cements in holy faith,
And equal transport, free as nature live,
Disdaining fear – What is the world to them,
Its pomp, its pleasure, and its nonsense all,
Who in each other clasp whatever fair
High fancy forms, or lavish hearts can wish?

THOMSON'S SEASONS.[86]

Though formed by nature, and refined by art,
With charms to win, and sense to fix the heart,
Content in shades obscure to waste her life,
A hidden beauty and a country wife!

TICKELL.[87]

THOUGH Mrs. Melbourne declared it impossible farther to delay her London journey, Strathallan entreated that if the scene of his felicity must be changed, the duration
of his uncertainty might not be prolonged.

He easily prevailed on his father to join in this request, and a most pressing
and obliging / letter from Lord Torrendale, accompanied by one from the Countess, insisting that they should have no other home but her house, during their stay,
determined the ladies to consent to that arrangement. Her Ladyship was, if the whole
truth must be acknowledged, at the moment of writing this letter, in a most terrible
alarm. She saw plainly that Strathallan's first interview with Matilda, on his return,
must have brought all her past misdemeanours to light; and she hoped, by civility,
to ensure silence, if she could not revive esteem. Not that she had to reproach herself, in her original scheme, with any intention deeply culpable. To produce between
the lovers some misunderstanding, that it would be difficult to clear up, had been
the extent of the ambition of her plotting Ladyship. Had she been a dramatist, her
conceptions would never have proved dark and atrocious enough for the horrors of
tragedy. The embarrassments of a farce, or tragi-comedy at most, would have bounded
her attempts. She was far from a female Catiline: but her talents would perhaps have
made no contemptible figure in the ridiculously intriguing court of a Duchesse Du
Maine.[88] Disdaining to resent her conduct, Mrs. and Miss Melbourne affected not to
perceive the forced air of this invitation, and, preceded by Strathallan, bade a pleased

adieu, for some time, to the Rocks. Emily accompanied them, and Julia, without whom Emily now declared she could enjoy no pleasure completely.

The reception Lord Torrendale gave Matilda was truly paternal; but the Countess, who had been influenced in her concessions by fear alone, found it impossible, in her presence, any longer to feign an interest she was so far from feeling. Concealing her mingled grief, shame, and disappointment, under the appearance of languor and indisposition, she apologized for not rising from the couch on which she lay, indolently extended. She 'had been very ill, and kept her bed for several days.' This, in a degree, excused the alteration in her manner to her once 'dear, delightful' Matilda; it was indeed sufficiently sullen, but the happy are / not extreme to mark the conduct that, to the diffident and the wretched might give offence. Matilda, with her usual soothing attention, condoled with her Ladyship on her indisposition: while Lord Torrendale, never tired with contemplating the health which glowed in the cheeks of his darling Emily, and the improvement in every respect which time and instruction had, during the interval of their separation, produced in her mind, expressed his obligations to her invaluable friends, with a grace, a warmth, and energy, of which they had, till then, thought him incapable.

'You confer on us an obligation,' he said, 'to which fortune is poor in comparison. You have restored to me a daughter; for every opening merit Emily now possesses is your work.'

Touched and delighted, Matilda, while he spoke, felt, for one instant, reminded of Strathallan; after a long and animated conversation, in which it was almost forgotten that the Gipsey Countess, (as she still continued to be styled by her familiars,) lolled discontentedly on a sofa in the room. The Earl suddenly turning to Julia Melbourne, kindly exclaimed, 'Shall this be another daughter?'

The little girl who, in silent but deep emotion, had remarked the tender reception Emily met from her parent, replied with a piercing accent, 'No, I am no daughter – I have neither father nor mother – and to-day I have lost my mamma a second time.'

'I am your mother,' said Mrs. Melbourne tenderly embracing her, 'you shall now, dear Julia, be all my pleasure.'

'But my most loved, my little mamma,' said Julia, unable any longer to suppress her tears, 'she will love me no more – no,' continued the interesting child, sobbing, while she threw her arms round Matilda's neck, 'from the moment *he* came, I saw you had no longer any affection to spare for me – I saw you would forget your poor Julia.'

'Heaven forbid that I should part you!' cried Strathallan, touched and charmed with a jealous delicacy of affection, at her age so rare; 'Will you forgive me, Julia,' he continued, 'the involuntary pain I have inflicted / on you, while I thus engage, for my Matilda, to adopt you as our own.'

Matilda, with tender and joyful readiness, ratified the promise, and harmony was restored among the happy circle.

Mrs. Melbourne having received from her legal friends the most satisfactory assurances respecting the validity of her daughter's claims to Sir Harold's legacy, and the impossibility of their being disputed with success, had, now, leisure to attend to those, at once trifling and important subjects of dress and decoration, without which, even a Matilda must have appeared, to the world of fashion, as a star shorn of its beams. She had long ago satisfied her pecuniary debt to her friend Arbella; but there was a debt of the heart, which she thought kindness alone could pay, and therefore wished much to request her presence at the important change in her situation, that was now approaching. But Arbella, though her reply marked the exultation she felt at her friend's good fortune, was not at liberty to attend to the invitation her letter contained. She was a mother; and, absorbed in the pleasing cares her little boy required, found, in them, at once the cause and compensation for many sacrifices.

A present, from Lord Torrendale to his lady, of a dress of the most surpassing elegance, for the expected nuptials, revived, in the bosom of the Countess, her half-extinguished love of display. And wisely considering it would be rather awkward not to recover her health till the very day on which she wished to appear to such advantage, she immediately exchanged her chaise-longue for an Ottoman; discovered that airings were particularly beneficial to her, and kindly accompanied Mrs. and Miss Melbourne to make all their purchases, till her attentions were in danger of becoming as troublesome, as her previous neglect had been pointed. Proud of her accurate knowledge in dress, the only science she professed, her Ladyship insisted on deciding upon every article; and it was almost ludicrous to see the importance she assumed, and the seriousness of countenance with which she examined, re-examined, took up, and laid down every piece of silk, / muslin, and lace, submitted to her inspection; and, at length, in a slow and hesitating voice pronounced – not 'that she was satisfied,' for she never was so, but that, 'perhaps if nothing better could be got it might – possibly do,' and then the rich bales, and elegant patterns were to be sent home to be looked at, criticised, folded, unfolded, and at length frequently sent back with a message, that there was nothing in them which would exactly suit. Besides the length of time these protracted negociations necessarily took up, another inconvenience, attended her Ladyship's shopping with them. She piqued herself not only on getting every thing the best, but the cheapest that could possibly be procured; and these desires being often contradictory, she made her companions blush at her meanness, in insisting upon a price below the value of the article for which she bargained, when, if she had not interfered, they could have arranged every thing to their own satisfaction. One morning, that in pursuance of this plan, for which the Countess thought herself entitled to the eternal gratitude of her friends, she had not only completely tired *their* patience, but that of half the milliners in town, she was attracted by the showy appearance of a milliner's and dress-maker's shop, that had lately been opened in a fashionable street; and remarking, 'that new beginners were apt to be reasonable in their demands, in order to tempt people to go again,' she pulled the check, and alighted with Mrs. and Miss Melbourne. Two girls were in the shop, already engaged with other ladies: a plain young woman, genteelly drest, who appeared to be the mistress, asked her Ladyship's commands. Lady Torrendale had run in without looking at the name over the door, but Matilda thought it impossible she should not recollect the face. While she was examining lace head-dresses and veils, the Countess, who began to grow impatient, and who had a happy knack of saying obliging things to her inferiors, exclaimed, 'Lord, you know we can never guess how these caps would look, unless they were tried upon a pretty woman – are / not either of your young Misses

disengaged?' then turning to Matilda, 'Pray recollect Miss Melbourne that it is growing late, and that we have promised by four to meet Strathallan at Gray's.'

A faint blush, which tinged the sallow cheek of the young woman at the name of
Strathallan, changed the doubt of the fair bride-elect into certainty; and Miss Langrish, though awe-struck and distanced by the haughty and unacknowledging stare
of Lady Torrendale, was not afraid to meet with a look of recognition, the soft and
encouraging smile of Matilda. 'Common report then does not this time err,' she said,
'and I have to congratulate your Ladyship,' turning to the Countess, 'on the addition,
which the beauty, and amiable qualities like Miss Melbourne's, must make to the happiness of your family.'

'It is to that Lady your congratulations should be addressed,' replied Lady Torrendale, coldly designating Mrs. Melbourne.

Miss Langrish, though somewhat disconcerted, ventured to mention her having
lately entered into business, with the patronage and liberal assistance of her constant
friends, Lady N. and Mrs. Murray; and to hope, that she also might have to boast of
her Ladyship's encouragement. 'I had something to struggle with at first,' she said,
'but have now the fairest prospects of success; and am, as I ought to be, thankful, and
extremely happy.'

'Humph,' cried the Lady, as who should say 'What matter whether *you* are happy
or not,' and hurried to her carriage, while Matilda, bestowing upon her one of those
angel smiles which raise the humble and doubting heart, assured her of her good will,
and every kind assistance in her power; and received with a graciousness, which quite
restored the spirits of the *ci-devant* governess, the card that she humbly presented.

Leaving Miss Langrish in a situation that suited her talents so much better than
that of an instructress of youth, we will return to Lord Torrendale, who, one morning,
rather surprised his son by abruptly proposing 'He should spend his honey-moon at
Rose-villa. /

'Rose-villa!' exclaimed Lady Torrendale in a tone of ill-disguised resentment;
'when I wanted it you said it was sold to Lord Lyndhurst.'

'So it was, but now Lord Lyndhurst wants it no longer, and has sold it again to
me. His lady has lately found out that one cannot be a *bel-esprit* for nothing; whoever
applauded her muse obtained ready access not only to her ear but her purse; and having, like some others, assumed a character which she wanted both discernment to
exercise with usefulness, and ability to maintain with dignity, she has been the dupe
of flattering dedicators and necessitous poets, till poor Lyndhurst has found himself
necessitated to part with a substantial brick-built, modern residence, (to speak in the
style of the Advertisers,) which I believe he greatly preferred to the air-built castles
of her Ladyship's inspired favorites. I hear there is much required to restore it to the
state in which I parted with it, so as you never approved of my taste, Lady Torrendale,
I shall appoint Strathallan my chief surveyor, with unlimited powers to knock down,
or raise up; and if he is able to hit upon additions suitable to his taste, he may put
them into execution, and take it for his pains. When tired of considering the beauties
of Rose-villa he may join us in Derbyshire, you know.'

Strathallan was delighted with the kind solicitude with which his father strove
to make him amends for the sacrifice he had always lamented, and endeavoured to

prevent; but the abode once so dear to him of the estate that bore his son's name, on account of its recalling the memory of his mother, was now profaned and altered; and could a sigh have obtained it back again, he would not, to obtain it, have given that sigh. His departure for Rose-villa, and all the other arrangements, were therefore settled with that facility and delight which is ever taken in forming plans of happiness. As for Lord Torrendale, his prediliection for his native seat had its origin in a singular circumstance.

Walking one day upon those hills that formed an amphitheatre around, a breeze had suddenly sprung up, which inspired his heart / with a vivifying sensation, an enjoyment of life, more complete and delightful than he had ever before or afterwards experienced. No wonder than that the scene became endeared to a man, whose natural habits were melancholy and contemplative. He declared that now he saw his son once more restored to his wishes, and at length secure in the possession of happiness and honours, equal to his high deserts, he no longer felt those anxieties which could lead him to mix any more in the tumults of the gay or the great world; he held to no party; and his absences, for the future, should be but of rare occurrence, and short duration, from his favourite seat. This resolution did not agree at all with the inclinations of his Lady, who protested that another autumn passed in Derbyshire, would be destruction to her nerves; but Lord Torrendale saying he wished it might be so, and that if she were to be carried in a horse-litter she should go, her Ladyship found it better to submit to what she knew to be irremediable, and contented herself with inviting Mrs. Melbourne, whose wit, at once amused and terrified her, and as many more agreeable people as she could collect, to share her dreadful solitude.

For a short time before her marriage, nothing was talked of but the beauty of the young bride, the splendour with which her nuptials would be celebrated, and the impression her first appearance must undoubtedly create. She alone, insensible to all that passed around her, was alive only to the happiness of soon confirming her claim to the undivided care, the fond affections of Strathallan. On the day which gave her to his wishes, every surrounding object seemed to vanish before the delighted pair; too happy to be gay, Strathallan, when for the first time he embraced his own Matilda, and all the past rushed to his memory, enhancing the present joy, could only by a silence, deepfelt, and well understood by his beloved, indulge the feelings which oppressed his heart. Mrs. Melbourne, as she returned her daughter's embrace, her cheek still wet with the tears Matilda shed on quitting a mother's care, though even for a protector so dear; / said to her amiable Lord; 'I give you in my child, a treasure, which I hope will ever constitute your happiness; not from that beauty that now enchants your eye, or the graces that so long have captivated your heart, but because in her, the affections have ever superseded the passions; while passion, pure, generous, and elevated, held in its turn a place above the petty interests and vanities of life. Such should be ever the gradations of feeling in the well-regulated mind of woman; and must not such a character excite in those that can best appreciate it, more than common tenderness, more than common regret?'

Rose-villa and its surrounding wilderness of ground, laid out in the most pleasing, yet fanciful and romantic taste, was a charming solitude, just suited for the reception of lovers who had fled from the world, to taste, unmingled, that cup of happiness it never could bestow. There, in the enjoyment of a bliss, pure as their virtues, great as their deserts, Matilda and her Strathallan at length found themselves permitted to yield, without reserve, to that tenderness, for which both were equally formed; from which both had been equally excluded, which they had resisted so nobly; and now indulged without one self-upbraiding recollection to mingle its corrosive bitter with their present happiness. Often when wandering, supported by her Strathallan, she tasted the cool evening breeze beneath the moon-beam that streamed along their silent path, and seemed formed to light their love; Matilda secretly sighed, with pensive, timid gratitude. 'Oh! when I would remember that life is but a vain and fleeting shadow, I must not call to mind those soft delighted hours when I bend to hear *him* whisper again the enchanting vow that he is mine, that he will be ever only mine; when, unreproved, I at length drink from those eyes, sweet draughts of added love, and hear him, in return, breathe the deep, long-drawn sigh of tender, conscious happiness.'

She compared the security and fulness of bliss she now enjoyed, to the moments of uneasiness and embarrassment she had experienced three years before, at Woodlands, when she blushed at being even suspected of / an involuntary interest in the then unknown warrior's safety; and, while retracing all her former anxieties, she blessed heaven those hours were past, never to return; but, perhaps she was wrong; for, could she have recalled, at will, in all its vivid charms, the first dawn of infant passion, the first bright, kindling glance of full requited love, she would have owned, that the vow which confirmed her ever his, conveyed scarcely more pleasure to her heart, than the sweet, struggling tumult of hope's earliest sigh.

A letter, from her mother, informed Matilda that Mrs. Melbourne had, as she styled it, actually taken compassion on the unhappy Countess, and was, for the present, established, with Julia, at Woodlands. As she was a professed enemy to every kind of *gossip*, her letter contained little farther news; and it was reserved for Mrs. Sowerby to inform her friend of the wonderful changes that had lately taken place in her neighbourhood, by the last letter we shall communicate from

ARBELLA TO MATILDA.

Clifden-down.

'From the Eden of happy lovers, can Matilda, Strathallan's Matilda, attend to the voice of friendship, in the congratulations of her Arbella? I will believe she can; and, therefore, rejoice with my friend, rejoice with her sincerely, to see her add to the number of those happy and distinguished fair ones, who have spirit and courage enough to reward our beloved heroes, on their return from their glorious toils. But have a care, Matilda! bind him fast with chains of roses, or, at the fantastic call of honour, the dear creature will again escape you. Surely she, who, in these times, unites her fate to that of a warrior, has need to be more or less than mortal! You see I am kindly endeavouring to mingle a few imaginary evils with your sum of real bliss; and am I not right? for 'fear and sorrow fan the fire of joy;' and we must still clasp, with the fondest transport, *that* treasure to our / breast, of which, the next moment may, for ever, deprive us. I, too, have my joys; and not small ones they are. Silence, master Theophilus, you little monkey! am I never to do any thing but play with you? I think you might suffer me to write to my friend, particularly when it is in praise of you. I beseech you to believe, Matilda, that the boy already promises to have, "All his father's sense," united to "his mother's beauty!" so you see he bids fair to be a little prodigy. And now, while thus supremely happy in the society of each other, I dare say you imagine, as all lovers have done before you, that no fond pair can live and love like you. How much you are mistaken! Believe me it requires neither the heart, the soul, nor the face of a Matilda, to inspire a passion, ardent, violent, sincere; and of course, prevailing; and this I shall undertake to prove, by opening my Buxton Chronicle: for my good man being willing to give me every reasonable pleasure, and determined that, "Verily-a, he and I should be first in the throng," forced me, notwithstanding my protestations of indifference to gaiety, to spend last month there. That you may completely understand the adventure, which has made so much noise, that hardly any thing else is talked of; I must remind you, my constant swain, and cousin of my heart, was on the point of marriage, when you left us, with a rich, "West stingy widow," as my aunt calls her, "a sweet pretty creeter, as he had been courting of a long time, with balls and suppers, and what not." You surely must recollect the little widow Cypress, who was so much admired last season, because she was pretty, rich, and, for the rest, as, Pope describes it "no character at all;"[89] the widow of a man, who adored her while living, and had shown, that his regard extended beyond the grave, by bequeathing to her, without reserve or limitation, the whole of his property; she had yet become, before she left off her mourning, the gayest of the gay. In short, a mere drest and painted doll, only that Miss Dolly knew how to sit up and behave itself at a ball; good-tempered, without effort; good-natured, because / it would have given her trouble to be otherwise. And good-natured she must have been, to have admitted the suit of my cousin. He had, however, a formidable rival to encounter; no less a one than my heroic admirer Major O'Hara, who last summer made some progress in the affections of the kind-hearted widow, which he did not lessen by taking the trouble of returning from Ireland, a month or two ago, to remind her of his claim. What chance had the uninviting exterior, frigid reserve, and inelegant pride, of poor Sam, against the continued fire kept up by military ardour, and Hibernian gallantry, like the Major's. Being determined to give the neighbourhood something to talk of, and, accordingly to render my cousin's mortification more complete, they, (I can hardly help laughing when I think of it,) agreed to go off together from a public breakfast at Buxton, given by the poor duped lover, in honour of his charming widow. The company was distributed in *Marquées*, snow-white as the lady's innocence, gay as her smiles of love. A band of music attended – every thing was harmony and good-homour. Mrs. Cypress rolled her eyes, smiled on one, complimented another, talked of love and poetry, till Sam, betrayed into the expression of more than usual pleasure and complaisance, thought of nothing but looking in the fair widow's eyes, and beating time to the air she had commanded. When, at that critical juncture, the lady suddenly complained of illness, and left the tent, followed by Major O'Hara; who had conducted her, in a few moments, to a chaise and four, which had been previously ordered near the spot, and, before their intentions could be suspected, they were on their way to London. Since their return, they have taken the most elegant house, and sported the finest carriage and liveries that can possibly be imagined; they give the greatest entertainments; and, in short, the Major seems determined to prove, by the noble manner in which he spends the fortune of the fair widow, how deserving he was "to win her and wear her."[90] The worst of it is, as my poor aunt told me almost sobbing, that / a *puradox* (as she calls it) of "Shepherds I have lost my love,"[91] has come out entitled, "The beau tossed in a *blanket*," or, 'Kidderminster no match for Tipperary.' So that I really think my poor cousin would have gone mad with vexation, if he had not immediately set off for London, by his mother's advice, upon a commission to fall in love with the Widow Molosses. The husband of this Widow Molosses was an eminent sugar-baker, (whom you know nothing about,) I shall, therefore, just inform you, that the saccharine fair one, (very unlike the other) shows herself already so grateful for Sam's tender partiality, that I doubt not she will soon consent to sweeten the mortal cup of mingled bliss and woe for him, "And make the bitter draught of life go down."

'Before I leave off the article of Buxton, I must tell you, that Spencer acts at present the most prominent part among the *elégants*. He drives a dashing equipage, not always alone; and exhibits, to advantage, his-graceful figure – *that*, at least, is not injured, poor fellow! and flattering himself, I suppose, that if not quite so handsome, he is more *interesting* than ever, has resumed, with renovated spirits, his old amusement of breaking hearts. Yet some there are, who since the wound in his eye, scruple not to say he is sadly altered. "Ah, Lindor!" change how you would, there *was* a time when one faithful heart would have still – but no matter. I am now my dear Sowerby's, and it shall be the ambition of my life to justify his choice. Poor Eyes! for what farther mortifications may he not be yet reserved! perhaps at this moment, notwithstanding these transient reliefs, he envies the fate of his former friend Lionhart; who, after exposing himself often, in a manner that made it a miracle he escaped so long, fell, gallantly bringing up his troop at Salamanca. We have been greatly disappointed since the arrival of Spencer's lady-mother, instead of the expected balls and fêtes, she has taken entirely to her couch, and can hardly be prevailed on to see any one. Poor woman, she labours under a complication of disorders, to which I believe / it would puzzle the faculty to administer relief: decaying beauty, and blasted ambition; to the former she still fondly clings, but, alas! as my old courtly favorite Castiglione says, in a style rather uncourtly,

> "Si spoglian i serpenti la vecchiezza
> E rinovan la scorza insieme e gli anni
> Ma fugge e non ritorna la Bellezza
> In noi per arte alcuna, o nuovi panni."[92]

But surely she deserves all she can suffer; for did she not plot against you, and endeavour to break my heart? Sappho and Alcæus have both composed epithalamiums upon a late happy event. If I can procure copies in time I will enclose them. These formidable rivals have at length – I will not absolutely say, embraced; but seriously they had a formal reconciliation last Thursday at Lady Lyndhurst's. Alcæus promised never again to libel Sappho, and Sappho engaged, on the word of a poet, not to say any thing malicious, more than ten times a day, to Alcæus. Yet, under this hollow truce, I fear, still lurk the embers of many a fierce dissension; at least if I may judge by the dispositions in which I found Sappho the very day after the treaty. She called, I believe, on purpose to tell me a smart thing she had just said to Alcæus. It seems the unlucky bard prides himself greatly on having planned the fêtes at Woodlands for the return of your heroic Lord, and on having suggested the working the colours that were presented to him. Lady Lyndhurst called him *le petit glorieux*,[93] and said she doubted not he expected his name to go down to posterity in company with that of Lord Strathallan.

"If so," observed Sappho, "we may indeed apply to that pair the epitaph originally made by Piron on Turenne and Marshal Belleisle,

'Ci git le glorieux a coté de la gloire.'"[94]

'My sister in-law, as I would now call Clara, if she had not renounced all human ties, notices your marriage in her usual sweet affectionate manner. In the last letter I received from her, she asked if a poor nun could be still remembered by you; and then / after many praises which I shall not transcribe, that I may not encrease your vanity, she adds, "different are the paths by which we seek the palm of virtue. Your friend has, in the possession of all those blessings her tender and amiable disposition could wish for, perhaps, even in this life, a foretaste of the joys that are in store for her: mine are all in the future, but are not the less consolatory, nor the less sure." The dear saint always takes care, in the letters, to mingle such counsels as from my peculiar disposition I may most stand in need of, and seems to be endued before her time with a divine prescience, to judge exactly of those dangers to which I may possibly be exposed; her advice is accordingly invaluable, and if ever I neglect it – but I will make no engagements, lest, from the mere spirit of mischief, I should be tempted to break them. Sowerby and I have made a very fair exchange – I persuade him to wear a better coat, and cut his hair a little more fashionably, and he trains my mind to knowledge, and my heart to virtue. The difference between our years is not so considerable as to prevent my feeling for him the tenderest attachment; and this disparity is, in appearance, considerably lessened, now he has left off that fur cap and strange *roquelaure*,[95] which used to make him when botanizing and herbarizing about in the morning, look really more like a bear in a brown study, than a man. Now when he is shaved and drest, and I have by some innocent rattle attuned his spirits to their happiest pitch, he really looks – not quite a Strathallan, you know. Sowerby bids me say a thousand kind things to you, which I repeat with the more pleasure as you are not here to excite my jealousy. Seriously my best, my earliest, and truest friend, I know not how such a fiend as jealousy can dare intrude upon the pure and exquisite pleasure of contemplating such endearing, unobtrusive, mild perfection. Who shall in future lament her being born a woman, as contracting the sphere of her influence, or diminishing her power of doing good, when your own family furnishes two examples, that on the conduct of our sex, depends the happiness or / misery of all connected with them? The follies of the ill-fated Lady Julia, embittered a husband's days, shook the reason of a son of affections too tender, yet of a spirit too lofty and refined, either to endure a reflection on his honor, or to tear himself from the unhappy cause of that aspersion, and tinctured the young mind of her deserted daughter with that deep-toned melancholy, which may fatally influence the whole future tenor of her existence, while a Matilda's steady persevering virtues restored a widowed mother's heart to joy, compelled the admiration of a family too slow at first in acknowledging her merits, and at length made that heart her own, which she rejected as long as duty did not sanction the choice. But who am I, who thus dare to deal out praise and blame, as worthy to judge and decide on the conduct of others? alas! was I not once in danger of plunging into follies as ruinous, though not errors so great, as those which I now condemn? Never were the decrees of fate more truly equitable, than in that sentence she has passed upon us both. With advantages in some respects superior, I neglected many duties; but my intentions were ever innocent. I am rewarded beyond my deserts; perhaps not quite according to my earlier wishes. You resigned a lover, such as woman never had, only to bind him in the bonds of fond esteem, more truly, more lastingly yours. When I consider the mournful and strange events, which so fast followed upon each other before your final re-union could take place, I think I see you, like Balsora and her lover, in the beautiful Eastern tale, two pure and lovely spirits, passing hand in hand, through the glooms of death, to the opening gate of Paradise.[96] Go, happy pair, and and may never the rude blast of misfortune disturb the Eden, of which your hearts are the centre. Go, blest Matilda, and taste, without fear, the happiness you so well deserve, with your long-lamented, your twice-restored Strathallan.'

THE END. /.

ENDNOTES

Volume I

1. *Quando ... Metastasio. – Demetrio*: These lines are taken from the final act of the libretto, *Demetrio*, by the Italian librettist and poet, Pietro Metastasio (1698–1782). The piece was first set in 1731, with further compositions throughout the period until 1840. John Hoole translated *The Works of Metastasio* in 1767, though a later bilingual version of the text, including these lines as printed, provides the following translation: 'Love, that to noble breasts extends,/ Is not a rival to controul / Fair virtue's sway; but mutual friends / To gen'rous deeds they raise the soul. / Rest, happy pair, in peace secure; / Henceforth may ev'ry fav'ring pow'r, / To you, that happiness ensure, / Which Heav'n averse deny'd before.' See *Demetrio: An Opera, as performed at the King's-Theatre in the Hay-market. The music by Signor Pietro Guglielmi, [...] The poetry by the celebrated Metastasio, altered by Giovan Gualberto Bottarelli. Most of the translation by Mr. Carara.* (London: W.Griffin, 1772), p. 36.

2. *Meglio ... cale. Alfieri*: from *Saul* (I.iv), by the Italian tragedian and poet, Vittorio Alfieri (1749–1803), which was first published in the Paris edition of tragedies (1787–9): 'It is better to die than to pass a savage's life in solitude – where you are dear to nobody and you care about no-one.'

3. *'my coachman ...fog'*: from a poem entitled 'Country and Town' which was included in *A Collection of Political and Other Songs* (London: T. Lewis, 1797) by the Whig army officer and contemporary of R.B. Sheridan, Charles Morris (1745–1836).

4. *For sanctity ... above. LORD STRANGFORD'S CAMOENS*: The British diplomat Percy Clinton Sydney Smythe, sixth Viscount Strangford (1780–1855), included notable translations into English of the relatively little known lyric poetry of Luís Vaz de Camoëns in *Poems from the Portuguese of Camoens, with Remarks and Notes* (London: J. Carpenter, 1803). This is taken from 'Sonnet I', 9–11.

5. *Deh!... TASSO, GERUSALEMME LIBERATA*: from Book XVI of the epic poem commemorating events of the first crusade by the Italian poet Torquato Tasso (1544–95). John Hoole's 1763 translation of the poem ran to several editions in the eighteenth and early nineteenth centuries. These lines in the 1797 edition read: 'Behold how lovely blooms the vernal rose, / When scarce the leaves her early bud disclose: / When half inwrapt, and half to view reveal'd, / She gives new pleasure from her charms conceal'd.' See *Jerusalem delivered: an heroic poem. Translated from the Italian of Torquato Tasso,* trans. John Hoole, 2 vols (London: J. Johnson; T.N. Longman [and nine others] 1797), vol. 2, p. 124.

6. *'Or for ... reason'*: from *The Critic* (1779), II.i.33–4, by R. B. Sheridan (1751–1816).

7. *Duchess of Northumberland*: Elizabeth Seymour Percy, Duchess of Northumberland (1716–76).

8. *the* Hommes des Champs *to have been*: The poem, *L'Homme des Champs, ou les Geórgiques Françoises* ('The Rural Philospher, or French Georgics') by Jacques Delille (1738–1813), was published in 1800.

9. *I thought myself ... grotto of Antiparos*: Lady Torrendale refers to the Leverian Museum of natural history acquired by James Parkinson (*c*. 1730–1813) in 1786 and reopened by him the following year at London's Rotunda. Her familiarity with current tourist attractions takes her from the Hebridean island of Staffa, renowned for its spectacular basalt columns, to the limestone caverns of Antiporos, an island in the Aegean Sea.

10. *Huber I believe*: The English translation of *Nouvelles Observations sur les abeilles* by the naturalist François Huber (1750–1831) was published in 1806.

11. *But ... SHAKESPEARE*: *The Life and Death of King John*: I.i.205.

12. *'How many ... calls idle!'*: These lines are slightly modified from those included in *The Task* (1785) by William Cowper (1731–1800): 'How various his employments, whom the world / Calls idle, and who justly, in return, / Esteems that bu[s]y world an idler too!' (III. 'The Garden', 352–4).

13. *Rosina*: Aspasia appears as the eponymous heroine of the successful comic opera *Rosina* by Frances Brooke (1724–89). First performed in 1782, it remained popular for the remainder of the eighteenth century.

14. *'Mark ... sound'*: from the poem *The Pleasures of Hope* (1799) by Thomas Campbell (1777–1844), I.131–2.

15. *'Soon as ... her hair'*: from Campbell's poem *Gertrude of Wyoming; or, The Pennsylvanian cottage* (1809), II.viii.68.

16. *bilboquet*: 'the plaything called cup and ball' (*OED*).

17. *'Now ... repose'*: 'The Descent of Odin. An Ode' by Thomas Gray (1716–71), first published in *Poems* (London: J. Dodsley,1768), 57–8.

18. *'Awhile ... chuse'*: The greater men to whom these lines allude are Jonathan Swift and Alexander Pope in Swift's poem, *Dr. Swift to Mr. Pope, While he was writing the Dunciad* (1727), 5–6.

19. *Non sai ... TASSO. GERUSALEMME LIBERATA*: Hoole condenses the spirit of these lines from Book II into one couplet: 'An artless negligence compos'd her dress, / And Nature's genuine grace her charms confess' (I. p. 49).

20. *Mais ... que le frere. RACINE. BRITANNICUS*: from Act II.iii. of the tragedy of 1669 by Jean Racine (1639–99): 'But let us not delude ourselves, and drop the pretence;/The sister, in this instance, moves you much less than the brother.'

21. *'A' misteri ...eletto'*: *Gerusalemme Liberata*, Book XVI in which the lover, Rinaldo, rises to hold a crystal mirror to his mistress. Edward Fairfax's original translation of 1600 is more literal than that of Hoole – 'A noble page, graced with that service great' – and more usefully demonstrates in this instance how LeFanu anthropomorphises the mirror itself into the subservient lover.

22. *'Padrona'*: A comic intermezzo, *La Serva Padrona or, The Maid Turned Mistress* (1733), by the Italian composer Giovanni Battista Pergolesi (1710–36).

23. *Madame Recamier ... Persian Prince*: Lady Torrendale's 'predilections' reflect her familiarity with social events and figures popularized by the British press. The famed Parisian salon hostess, Madame Récamier (1777–1849) entertained significant literary, political and artistic figures throughout the 1790s and early years of the nineteenth century before being exiled by Napoleon in 1805. Thaddeus Kosciusko (1748–1817), anglicized from

the Polish Tadeusz Kosciuszko, also antagonized Napoleon; refusing to be recruited to his cause after a life spent devoted to liberation movements in his native Poland and in America during the Revolution. At around the time of Kosciusko's retirement from public life, in 1804, the child actor William Henry West (1791–1874), known as 'the young Roscius', was making his debut on the London stage. His four-year celebrity status followed that of the so-called 'Persian Prince', Mīrzā Abū Ṭālib Khān (1752–1806), who published accounts of his travels from India across Europe, Britain, and Ireland at the turn of the nineteenth century.

24. *une de ces figures dont on ne dit rien*: 'one of those nondescript faces.' (French).

25. *Steibelt ...Von Esch*: Daniel Steibelt (1765–1823) and Louis von Esch were composers, the latter primarily for the pianoforte. Since renowned for his operatic compositions, Steibelt was, for contemporary readers, also a successful concert pianist and had played to a London audience in advance of his European tour of 1799 to 1800.

26. 'Ah perdona a primo affeto': 'Ah! Forgive my first emotion', from Metastasio's libretto *La Clemenza di Tito* ('The Clemency of Titus'), which, as set by Mozart, was first performed in London in 1806. As a duet in that opera it is an unusual and poignant choice for the solitary Miss Langrish, though as an example of Mozart's late style it might indeed have been considered less complex.

27. 'Felice ...d'amore': Though untraced the lines read 'Happy the heart / that pines for love.'(Italian)

28. Innocenza's, Veneziana's ... Francalanza's: Possibly a reference to collected operatic numbers, which, as distinct from those of Beethoven, were not at all 'learned'.

29. *Avea Bionde ... METASTASIO*: A conflation of lines from *L'Olimpiade* ('The Olimpiad', first set 1733), I.iv: 'Fair were his shining locks, his eyebrows dark, his lips / of ruddiest hue [...].' The next line quoted, 'un arrossir frequente', is construed by Hoole as a frequent 'smile' rather than the more literal 'blush'. See *The Works of Metastasio*, trans. J. Hoole, 2 vols (London: T. Davies, 1767), vol. 1, p.136.

30. *Bruno ... TASSO*: from Tasso's lyric, 'O con le Grazie elette e con gli Amori'('O! by the Graces, by the Loves design'd'), construed by Hoole as: 'Though brown thy hue, yet lovely is thy frame; / (So blooms some violet, the virgin's care!) / I burn – yet blush not to confess my flame'. See *Jerusalem Delivered*, vol. 1, p. xxxiii.

31. *L'AMITIÉ disparait où légalité cesse*: This should read 'l'égalité': 'Friendship disappears where equality ceases.' This originates in 'Fanfan et Colas' from the collection of *Fables* (1756) by the French dramatist and poet known as L'Abbé Aubert (1731–1814).

32. *One is never so much alone as in a croud*: This sentiment of Jean Jacques Rousseau is echoed by Byron in *Childe Harold's Pilgrimage* (1812), although the lines as quoted are nearest to those included in his *Stanzas to a Lady, on Leaving England* : 'I look around, and cannot trace / One friendly smile or welcome face, / And ev'n in crowds am still alone, / Because I cannot love but one'. See E. J. Lovell, Jnr., 'Byron and *La Nouvelle Héloïse*: Two Parallel Paradoxes', *Modern Language Notes*, 66: 7 (1951), pp. 459–61.

33. *Madame d'Arblay*: The married name of the author Frances Burney.

34. *Corvée*: 'a thankless task.' (French).

35. '*Let Bourbon ... higher*': The phrase, slightly modified, originates in the epitaph Matthew Prior composed for himself: 'Nobles and heralds, by your leave, / Here lie the bones of *Matthew Prior*; / The son of *Adam* and of *Eve*: / Let *Bourbon* or *Nassau* go higher.' By the late eighteenth century it was in use as a form of acknowledging good breeding but, in the 1720s, the epigram had been the object of Swift's parodic lines, supposedly written when in company with LeFanu's great-grandfather, Dr Thomas Sheridan. See D. Chan-

dler, 'Swift's "Violent Hatred" of William III: The "Paraphrase of Prior's Epitaph" and its Provenance', *Notes and Queries,* 46:3 (Sept. 1999), pp. 348–50.

36. *From worldy ... Simplicity*: Not identified.

37. *'Et les graces ... beauté'*: from the poem 'Adonis' (1658) by Jean de La Fontaine (1621– 95): 'And charms are more beautiful than good looks.'

38. *Burke ... on the principles of taste*: Following on from her recommendation of Joseph Addison's *The Spectator*, Miss Hautenville alludes to various engagements with issues of Taste such as: Edmund Burke (1729/30–97), *A Philosophical Enquiry into the Origin of our Ideas of the Sublime and Beautiful* (1757); James Beattie (1735–1803), *An Essay on Poetry and Music, as They Affect the Mind* (1762); Hugh Blair (1718–1800), *Heads of the Lectures on Rhetoric and Belles Lettres, in the University of Edinburgh* (1767); Samuel Johnson (1709–84), *The Rambler* (1750–52); Henry Home, Lord Kames (1696–1782), *Elements of Criticism* (1762); Archibald Alison (1757–1839), *Essays on the Nature and Principles of Taste* (1790), and Richard Payne Knight (1751–1824), *An Analytical Inquiry into the Principles of Taste* (1805).

39. Lettere d'una ... *Miss Melbourne, I presume*: Lettere d'una Peruviana was the title of the Italian translation of the French novel, *Lettres d'une Péruvienne* (1747), by *Françoise de Graffigny* (1695–1758).

40. *St Pierre ... Florian*: This reference to French literature ranges from early writers such as the dramatist Pierre Corneille (1606–84), and the poet and pedagogue, François Féne- lon (1651–1715), to the enlightenment thinker Jacques-Henri Bernardin de Saint Pierre (1737–1814) and the fabulist Jean-Pierre Claris de Florian (1755–94).

41. *Collins's Ode, is the divinest thing*: 'The Passions. An Ode for Music', by William Collins (1721–59), was published in *Odes on Several Descriptive and Allegoric Subjects* (1746).

42. *Piron ... Pastoral Letters*: A reference to an incident involving the Archbishop of Paris, Christophe de Beaumont (1703–1781), and the French poet and dramatist Alexis Piron (1689–1773). Upon being asked by de Beaumont if he had read his pastoral letter, Piron reputedly replied, 'No, my Lord ... Have you?' See John Aiken, *General Biography; or, Lives, Critical and Historical of the Most Eminent Persons*, 10 vols (London: G. G. & J. Robinson; G. Kearsley; R. H. Evans; J. Wright, 1799–1815), vol. 8, (1813), p. 184.

43. Tant pis ... Mademoiselle: 'What a pity.' (French).

44. *Many books ... for choice matter*: This is a misquotation from John Milton's *Paradise Regained*, IV. line numbers 318–26. The text of 1671 reads: '[...] However, many books, / Wise men have said, are wearisome; who reads / Incessantly, and to his reading brings not / A spirit and judgment equal or superior, / (And what he brings, what needs he else- where seek?) / Uncertain and unsettled still remains, / Deep-versed in books and shallow in himself, / Crude or intoxicate, collecting toys, / And trifles for choice matters, worth a sponge'.

45. *Dryden ... affability and pride*: This list testifies to the enduring significance of the sev- enteenth-century dramatists, John Dryden and Nathaniel Lee. In the same period, both Gaultier de Coste, seigneur de La Calprenède, and the Irish Parliamentarian, Roger Boyle, First Earl of Orrery, combined military careers with the writing of romance novels, a genre particularly associated with the French socialite, Madeleine de Scudéry. Pyrocles, Musidorus, Pamela and Philoclea are characters in Philip Sidney's *The Countess of Pembroke's Arcadia* (1593).

46. *'did you ever read David Simple?'*: Arbella makes an ironic if not wholly inappropriate comparison between herself and the guileless hero of *The Adventures of David Simple* (1744) by Sarah Fielding (1710–68). David Simple determines to seek out a real friend,

although it is the allusion to Fielding which is perhaps more pertinent: LeFanu recognising in the similarly well-connected author, a financial dependency upon writing which prefigured her own.

47. Cet air distingué: 'gentlemanly' or 'distinguished.' (French).

48. *A me ... METASTASIO*: Possibly a typesetting error as lines elided in the previous quotation from *L'Olimpiade* (see note 29 above) – 'Lenti e pietosi' and 'Il soave parlar' – are incorporated in a quotation otherwise derived from *Semiramide Riconosciuta* ('Semiramis Recognised'; first set 1729).

49. Quintas: Fitzroy is referring to the Quinta: 'in Spain, Portugal, and Latin America: a large house or villa in the country or on the outskirts of a town; a country estate' (*OED*).

50. '*Then his crest ... conquered wing*': from Plutarch's *Parallel Lives*, 'Alcibiades'

51. *This was about the time ... towards Corunna*: Sir John Moore took command as Lieutenant General of the British forces during the Peninsula War. Forced to retreat by Napoleon's army, he was fatally wounded at the battle of La Coruña on 16 January 1809.

52. *D'Amori .... IL NIDO DEGLI AMORI*: from Metastasio's cantata ('The Nest of Love'): 'The heart of Irene is a strangely fertile nest of Loves; one had just begun to carry itself up on its wings; another was eagerly bursting forth from the husk [...] It contained ones of each colour – one the colour of violets; it seemed to be spreading its pinions; another was of the colour of lilies, brown and red.'

53. '*Tis all ... prunello*': from Pope, *An Essay on Man*, epistle IV (1733–4), in which the line reads: 'The rest is all but leather or prunella' (203). Derived from plum or prune, prunella is also 'a strong stuff, orig. silk, afterwards worsted' (*OED*).

54. *Sterne ...pleasantry of thine*: from Laurence Sterne's *The Life and Opinions of Tristram Shandy, Gentleman* (1759–67): 'Trust me, dear *Yorick*, this unwary pleasantry of thine will sooner or later bring thee into scrapes and difficulties, which no after-wit can extricate thee out of' (vol I. chapter XII). Arbella soon matches this warning with a quotation from Shakespeare: 'I'd rather hear you chide than this man woo' (*As You Like It*, III. v.65).

55. 'La fatuité ... la jeunesse militaire': 'silliness suits no-one so well as the young soldier' ; a variation of '*la fatuite ne sied qu'a la jeunesse militaire*' from the *Contes Moraux* ('Moral Stories', 1761) by the novelist, dramatist and contributor to the *Encyclopedié*, Jean-François Marmontel (1723–99). Inspired by Voltaire, Marmontel became the historiographer of France in 1771. His autobiographical *Mémoires d'un Père* was published in 1804.

56. *Non ere ... SPANISH SONG OF PERAZA*: a fifteenth-century *endecha* or song of mourning for the young Governor of the Canary Islands named Guillen Peraza, who was killed attempting to take Palma for Spain. This extract reads: 'Thou fatal isle, art not Palma, a name significant of victory and joy; thou art a bramble; thou art a cypress of melancholy branch; thou art a misfortune, a dreadful evil. Where is thy shield? Where is thy spear? A fatal rashness destroyed all!'. See John Pinkerton, *Letters of Literature* (London: G. G. J. & J. Pinkerton, 1785), pp. 7–8.

57. '*Her fancy ...what a 'SOLDIER' suffers*': from Cowper, *The Task*, with the substitution of 'soldier' for the original 'sailor' (I. 'The Sofa', 539–41).

58. *Hercules wielding the distaff of Omphale*: Following his murder of the Iphitus, Hercules was enslaved to the Lydian Queen Omphale, whom he served for three years. During this time he is supposed to have undertaken the conventionally female duty of spinning, and is depicted in François Le Moyne's painting, *Hercules and Omphale* (1724), holding the distaff of the Queen, while she is adorned by a lion's skin.

59.   La guerre de la Fronde, *in France*: Meaning 'sling' *la Fronde* refers to the French civil wars, the *Fronde Parlementaire* (1648–9) and *Fronde des Nobles* (1650–3), in which *parlement* and then members of the nobility attempted to resist the respective powers of Louis XIV, and the chief minister of France, Cardinal Jules Mazarin.

60.   *'They drink … the fair Imogine'* : a reference to Matthew Lewis's 'Alonzo the Brave and Fair Imogine' (1796). Miss Mountain elides the second line of this, the seventh stanza – 'Dancing round them the spectres are seen', – and in the last describes Imogine as fair rather than 'false' (83–7).

61.   *Lenora, Donica … evening's entertainments*: LeFanu begins her list of popular Gothic writings with three ballads: the German Gottfried August Bürger's 'Leonora' (1774), Robert Southey's 'Donica', published in his *Poems* (1797), and Matthew Lewis's, 'The Grim White Woman'. This had appeared along with a reprint of 'Alonzo' in his *Tales of Wonder* (1800) to which Walter Scott also contributed 'The Eve of St. John'. The list includes Scott's later poem 'The Lay of the Last Minstrel; a Poem, in six cantos' (1805), Mary Robinson's 'The Haunted Beach', published in her *Poetical Works* of 1806, and *The Castle of Otranto* (1764) by Horace Walpole, *The Mysteries of Udolpho* (1794) by Ann Radcliffe, and an early novel by Charles Maturin, *The Fatal Revenge; or, the Family of Montorio* (1807).

62.   *With eyes …world obey. J* : Not identified.

63.   *'Ghosts of my fathers … his presence'*: LeFanu elides the line which bids the supplicant ghosts to 'lay by the red terror of your course' in a passage from 'Dar-thula', one of several poems supposedly written by the third-century Gaelic poet Ossian and brought into the public domain by his self-styled translator James Macpherson in the 1760s. See *The Poems of Ossian*, 2 vols (Edinburgh: J. Elder and T. Brown, 1797), vol. 1., p. 160.

64.   *'Rock'd … on the wild'*: Not identified.

65.   *Sulpicius to Cicero … human being*: a reference to the letter sent from the Roman jurist Sulpicius to Cicero in which he consoles the orator on the death of his daughter: 'Remember then, oh my heart! the general lot to which man is born: And let that thought suppress thy unreasonable murmurs.' The letter had been included in manuals on elocution and letter-writing. See George Seymour, *The Instructive Letter-Writer, and Entertaining Companion: Containing Letters on the most Interesting Subjects in an Elegant and Easy Style*, 3rd edn (London: W. Domville, 1769), p. 46.

66.   *Iberians … Viriatus*: Miss Mountain's evocations of battle from ancient history begin with the resistance to the Roman domination of the Iberian Peninsula in the second century BC. Viriathus successfully led a group of Celtic federals, known as the Lusitani, to a number of victories against the Romans and, a generation later, an allegiance with the Lusitanian people enabled the rebel Roman statesman, Quintus Sertorius, to establish independent rule in Spain.

67.   *'A lonely traveller on the moon-light sea'*: Robert Southey, *Madoc* (1805), I.xiii.2774. In this poem Southey recounts the adventures of Madoc, son of the King of North Wales, who leaves his country for America following his disputed line of succession to the throne.

68.   *Guerrier … au Prince Henri de Prusse*: 'Fearful warrior, / In the heat of the battle, / Although invincible, / Often his heart beats / Because his sensitive heart / Feels for the soldier.' Stanislas Jean, Chevalier de Boufflers (1738–1815) pursued a military and literary career and, as Governor of Senegal, disapproved of the iniquities of the slave trade. During the French Revolution he sought refuge with Prince Henry of Prussia.

69.   'Les Graces … l'Amour': 'the alluring Graces.' (French).

70. *Zimmerman upon Solitude ... amusement*: Originally published in German, an English version of *The Advantages and Disadvantages of Solitude*, by Johann Georg Zimmerman (1728–95), translated from the French of J. B. Mercier, was published in 1791.

71. *Krumpbh*: Possibly the French harpist and composer, Anne-Marie Krumpholtz (1766–1813). Published *c.*1810 her 'fashionable harp arrangements of well-known tunes and themes and variations [...] found a ready market as domestic music for young women' (*Grove*).

72. *'Mine's the prettier ... thine Matilda'*: a reference to Dryden's *King Arthur; or, The British Worthy* (1691), a dramatic opera set to music by Purcell.

73. *'Quick ... as those'*: Pope's *The Rape of the Lock* (1714) was dedicated to Arabella Fermor: 'Her lively looks a sprightly mind disclose/Quick as her eyes, and as unfixed as those' (II. 9–10).

74. *O thou ... COLLINS. ODE TO PITY*: the first and fifth stanzas of William Collins's 'Ode to Pity' which was published in *Odes on Several Descriptive and Allegoric Subjects* (1746).

75. *'Truth Complete'... pensive pleasure*: from 'Ode to Pity': 'Thy temple's pride design / Its southern site, its truth complete, / Shall raise a wild enthusiast heat / In all who view the shrine' (27–30). The river Arun runs across William Collins's home county of Sussex.

76. *'There pictures ... bliss prevail'*: 'Ode to Pity', 31–3.

77. *'Sky-worn robes ... light'*: 'Ode to Pity', 11–12.

78. *'That seem'd ... look'd upon'*: from Campbell's *Gertrude of Wyoming; or, the Pennsylvanian Cottage*, II.vi.31.

79. *'To him ... was bent'*: Walter Scott, *The Lady of the Lake: A Poem, in six cantos* (1810), VI.xxvi.20–1, LeFanu replacing 'courtiers' with 'warriors'.

80. flacon: 'scent bottle.' (French).

81. Une assez jolie mine fantaisie *at most*: 'a rather fanciful look.' (French)

82. *'Enough for me ... fates assign'*: from Thomas Erskine, first Baron Erskine (1750–1823), *The Barber*, IX.131–2.

83. *'Whilst I ... Mable thine'*: Thomas Parnell (1679–1718), 'A Fairy Tale in the Ancient English Style,' 71–2. The poem was published in a posthumous collection by Pope in 1758.

84. *Slow melting... approach declare'*: from Thomas Gray (1716–71), 'A Progress of Poesy. A Pindaric Ode' first published in *Odes, by Mr. Gray* (1757), 36.

85. *A page of Baxter's!... I presume*: Of the many and diverse writings by the theologian Richard Baxter (1615–91), his evangelical *A Call to the Unconverted* (1658) was reprinted throughout the 1790s and early nineteenth century.

86. *'Le plaisir ... LA BRUYÉRE*: lines taken from *Les Caractères de Théophraste traduits du grec avec Les Caractères ou les moeurs de ce siècle* (1688) by Jean de La Bruyére (1645–96): 'The pleasure of being critical denies us the pleasure of being touched by very beautiful things.'

87. *'Want ...valour clung'*: Samuel Rogers (1763–1855), *The Pleasures of Memory, in two parts* (London: T. Cadell, 1792), I.351.

88. *'The Old Woman behind the Fire'... set*: *The Old Wife Behind the Fire* was an eighteenth-century country dance tune.

89. *push-pin ... brother*: Push-pin is 'a child's game, in which each player pushes his pin with the object of crossing that of another player' (*OED*). Coronella is possibly derived from the card game, colonel.

90. *Sir John Mandeville*: Fourteenth-century compiler of *The Voyage and Travels of Sir John Mandeville, Knight.*

91. *Bacon* ...sang froid: Miss Mountain's appetite is for Francis Bacon (1561–1626) and possibly the scientist Thomas Young (1773–1829), both of whom at various times have been designated 'the last man to know everything'.

92. Melopée *...as she called it*: She is referring to Melopœïa, 'the part of dramatic art concerned with music' (*OED*).

93. *'Have you nothing new ... from Gay?'*: These lines are taken from Pope's 'Imitation of the Sixth Satire of the Second Book of Horace' (93–4; published 1738), and refer to Swift and his patron, the first earl of Oxford and Mortimer, Robert Harley.

94. *'Who hath his fancy ... dies'*: The first lines of a poem included in *Certain Sonnets* by Sir Philip Sidney, first published in 1598.

95. *the Portuguese bard for his mistress*: a reference to Luís Vaz de Camoëns (*c.* 1524–80).

96. Vous ... déviné: 'You have seen through me.' (French).

97. *'Cease! Nymph of the Danube!' he exclaimed*: The reference has its origins in Friedrich de la Motte Fourqué's German tale *Undine* (1811), in which the eponymous water spirit pursues her mortal lover after he has married another. Arbella refers to this later on. See p. 113.

98. *'Exulting, trembling ... painting'*: Sappho begins to recite from William Collins's 'The Passions. An Ode for Music', 5–6; lines 19–20 follow.

99. *the true Zoilus curl ... twas wild*: a reference to an early critic of Homer, whom Cervantes had discredited as 'saucy' in his preface to *Don Quixote*. Alcæus then resumes the recitation from the 'Ode': 28.

100. *'But thou ... eyes so fair'*: With the exception of Alcæus's vague allusion to 'a notable poem on the death of a great person' this line and those which follow are also taken from Collins's 'Ode': 29; 38; 61; 71–2; 80; 81–3.

101. *Euterpes excelled on the viol*: a reference to Euterpe, muse of lyric poetry and music.

102. *'Pour ... sound'*: The context of this, slightly misquoted, line from Collins's 'Ode', explains Alcæus's reference to 'Mrs. Melancholy': 'With eyes up-raised, as one inspired / Poor Melancholy sat retired; / And from her wild sequester'd seat, / In notes by distance made more sweet, / Pour'd through the mellow horn her pensive soul' (57–61).

103. *the pitcher of Danaides*: a reference to Greek mythology, in which, as a consequence of killing the husbands to whom they had been forcibly married, the daughters of Danaeus were condemned to the perpetual task of carrying water from the Styx in leaking pitchers.

104. *PAPILOTTES for her ladyship's hair*: a reference to the French name for the papers used to curl hair.

105. sabot: 'a clog.' (French).

106. *Robin Adair*: a ballad of the 1750s by Lady Caroline Keppel which refers to her husband, Robert Adair, who became Surgeon-General under George III. Adair earned notoriety when forced to flee Dublin upon being discovered in the bedroom of Laetitia Pilkington by her husband.

107. *PASSIONCELLI of his friend*: a derisory reference to his poor little passions.

108. beaux esprits: 'wits.' (French).

109. *it seems to have 'touch'd you nearly!'*: from Sheridan's *The Critic*, II.i.391.

110. *With thee conversing ... PARADISE LOST*: John Milton, *Paradise Lost*, IV.639–40; 650–6.

111. Tous les genres sont bons, hors le genre ennuyeux: 'All kinds are good, except for the boring kind.' (French).

112. *Gray's opinion ... voice of a Spirit?*: derived from a letter written by Thomas Gray to Richard Stonhewer in which he echoes sentiments he has seen expressed in the 'Song of the Five Bards' (see below, vol. IV n.42). Gray had been sent the manuscript of the ancient poem subsequently transcribed in James Macpherson's Ossian collections: 'Did you never observe (*while rocking winds are piping loud*) that pause, as the gust is recollecting itself, and rising upon the ear in a shrill and plaintive note, like the swell of an Æolian harp? I do assure you there is nothing in the world so like the voice of a spirit.' See W. Mason, *The Works of Thomas Gray. Containing his Poems, and Correspondence with Several Eminent Literary Characters*, 3rd edn, 2 vols (London: Vernor, Hood & Sharp [and five others], 1807), vol. 1, Letter xxxvii. p. 164.

113. *seraph's wing*: The anecdote is derived from Anna Seward's *Memoirs of the Life of Dr. Darwin, Chiefly During his Residence in Lichfield* (London: J. Johnson, 1804), and refers to Darwin's answer when asked the colour of the then newly imported Kalmia plant.

114. La cour et la ville: 'The Court and the Town.' (French).

115. *'There seemed a glory ...vision'*: Matilda's name replaces that of Teresa in a line from Samuel Taylor Coleridge's tragedy, *Remorse* (1813), I.i.

116. *Sybil Gray ... bason below*: a reference to Walter Scott's poem, *Marmion: A Tale of Flodden Field, in six cantos* (1808): '[...] behold her mark/A little fountain cell,/Where water, clear as diamond-spark,/In a stone basin fell./Above, some half-worn letters say,/Drink. weary. pilgrim. drink. and. pray/ For the kind soul of Sybil Grey/Who built this cross and well' (VI. xxx. 18–24). What follows seems to be a conflation of images possibly derived from *Tales of the Genii* (1757), a collection of ostensible 'translations' from the Persian by the pseudonymous Sir Charles Morrell.

117. *But if ... THOMSON*: James Thomson (1700–48), 'The Lover's Fate', 21–4.

118. *Calypso, surrounded by her Nymphs*: the sea nymph with whom Odysseus lived for seven years after he was shipwrecked on her island.

119. *Leyden's 'Lovely Lord of Colonsay'*: a reference to one of the ballads John Leyden (1775–1811) contributed to Walter Scott's collection, *Minstrelsy of the Scottish Border*, the first two-volume edition of which was published in 1802. Appearing in the third volume as 'The Mermaid', it focuses on the titular heroine's seduction of the island's laird, MacPhail, the 'lovely chief of Colonsay'.

120. *Sacharissa*: The woman addressed as Sacharissa in several poems by Edmund Waller (1606–87), and by whom the speaker is rejected, was Lady Dorothy Sidney, daughter of the Earl of Leicester, and the wife of the Earl of Sunderland.

121. *Prosers*: derogatory term for aspiring prose writers used by Anna Seward in her literary correspondence. LeFanu alludes to Seward's comments on the prosers's unimaginative and uninspired technique: 'It is not the rhymes or measures of poetry which are either unintelligible or disgusting to the tribe of the prosers; but it is the imagery [...] It is the resemblance between objects, which, when shadowed forth in metaphor, they cannot trace.' See W. Scott (ed), *The Poetical Works of Anna Seward. With Extracts from her Literary Correspondence*, 3 vols (Edinburgh: J. Ballantyne, 1810; London: Longman, Hurst, Rees & Orme, 1810), vol. 1, p. lxxiv.

122. 'Les jeux ... les ris': 'Play, graces and laughter.' (French).

123. *'Lungi ah Lungi ite O profani'...Tasso's Aminta*: This is also Tasso's rendering of a line from Book VI of Virgil's *Aeneid*, in which the Sibyl warns Aeneas: 'Keep far, far off, all who are profane'.

124. *Leonora of Estes*: one of the two sisters of Duke Alfonso II d'Este who acted as patrons of Torquato Tasso.

125. *Madame de Maintenon ...intimate friends*: The Marquise de Maintenon was a title given by Louis XIV of France to Françoise Scarron (1635–1719), the widow of the French writer Paul Scarron. Maintenon later became the second wife of the king.

126. '*What is good ... not good*': the response of the German poet, Gottold Ephraim Lessing, to Christoph Nicolai's speaking of Voltaire as amongst the few writers to 'have produced so much that is new and so much that is good.' The anecdote subsequently appeared in William Taylor's *Historic Survey of German Poetry*, 3 vols (London: Treuttel and Würtz, Treuttel Jun. and Richter, 1828–30), vol. 1, p. 349, although LeFanu's source could have been one of the periodicals to which Taylor, as a reviewer and translator, regularly contributed.

127. secundem artem: meaning, in this sense, 'as befits his art.' (Latin).

128. *the Blue Chamber*: an allusion to the tale of Bluebeard and his wife Fatima's discovery of the ghastly contents of the forbidden closet.

129. *Pythia*: the medium of the oracle of Apollo at Delphi.

130. Les noces Persanes, *at the Opera*: 'The Persian Wedding.' (French).

131. nulleté *of character*: 'Nothingness' or 'emptiness' of character. (French).

132. '*De mon Berger ... l'objet*': As Matilda will point out this is misattributed to Jean-Jacques Rousseau's *Le Devin du Village*, first performed in 1752 at Fountainbleau. These lines are instead taken from the song 'Le Depit de la Bergère': 'I hear the flageolet of my inconstant shepherd, [and] am no longer the object of his treacherous compliments.' LeFanu's source is uncertain but the piece was subsequently set by the composer Hector Berlioz in 1819.

133. '*L'amour croit ... constant*': Le Devin du Village, I.ii: 'Love grows if it is worried, it sleeps if it is happy, and the coquettish shepherdess makes the shepherd constant.'

134. *Bernis ... La Fare*: The librettist Jean-Pierre Bernard (1708–75), and French ambassador Louis-Jules-Barbon Mancini-Mazarini (1716–98), were, as society poets, better known as Gentil-Bernard, and the Duc de Nivernois. Others in this group include Claude Emmanuel Luillier [La] Chapelle (1626–86), L'Abbé de Guillaume Amfrye de Chaulieu (1639–1720), and Charles Augustus, Marquis de la Fare (b.1644).

135. *Quinault:* Phillippe Quinault (1635–88) was a librettist and Academician whose collaboration with the composer Jean-Baptiste Lully led to the development of the *tragédie en musique*, an innovation which is considered to have influenced the development of French opera.

136. '*Jardins*' *of Delille ... Deshoulieres*: It is in keeping with her mock flattery of Alcæus that Arbella should associate the French poet Jacques Delille with an earlier writer of enduringly popular verses on nature, Antoinette du Ligier de la Garde Deshoulières (1638–94). Her remarking upon Delille's *Les Jardins* (1782) conspicuously overlooks the more scholarly translations of Virgil and Milton to which the more discerning might attribute his reputation.

137. '*For ne'er ... poet's ear*': from Scott, *The Lay of the Last Minstrel*, IV. xxxv.33–4.

138. *As she ... SHAKESPEARE. WINTER'S TALE*: The Winter's Tale, V.iii.14–17.

139. consolez vous: 'rest assured.' (French).

140. '*That still ... himself alone*': from an air in R.B. Sheridan's *The Duenna* (1775), I.iii.25–6.

141. *Cicerone*: Guide.

142. '*A sigh ... not to restrain*': an adaptation of lines originating in James Beattie's *The Minstrel*, the first book of which was published, anonymously, in 1771. LeFanu appropriates for

Matilda lines relating to the shepherd swain Edwin: 'A sigh, a tear, so sweet, he wish'd not to control' (I. xxii.198). The poem had resonance throughout the Romantic period and Ann Radcliffe had used this verse as an epigraph in *The Mysteries of Udolpho*.

143. *'every want and every woe'... benefactor and friend*: an oblique if not unlikely allusion to the poem *Eighteen Hundred and Thirteen* (1814) by Anne Grant (1755–1838) in which, envisaging the increased stability of Britain, the Scottish-born poet surveys a land which had in recent political history suffered 'every want and every woe' (II.750).

144. *'O nól ... s'avvéde'*: from Book II of Tasso's *Gerusalemme Liberata*, the sense of which LeFanu has herself anticipated: 'either she didn't see, or she didn't attend to its progress.'

145. *'Fidus Achates'*: the faithful companion of Aeneas in Virgil's *The Aeneid*.

146. *the legend* 'elle fut aimée': 'she has been loved.' (French).

147. *'By the side ... was his hat'*: these and the lines following are from 'The Elderly Gentleman', attributed to George Canning (1770–1827).

148. *life of Alfieri ... of music*: The autobiography of Vittorio Alfieri entitled, *di Vittorio Alfieri scritta da esso*, was published posthumously in 1804. An English translation appeared in 1810.

149. *Celia ...Rosalind*: characters in Shakespeare's *As You Like It*.

150. *the female Pretender mentioned in Hume*: Considered as second in line to the English throne after James IV of Scotland (James I), his first cousin, Arbella Stuart, is mentioned in David Hume's *The History of England Under the House of Tudor* (1759). Subsequently developed and extended, editions of the work were published throughout the nineteenth century.

151. *'One should ... injures me'*: Lines spoken by Achilles in Pope's translation of *The Iliad*, IX.127–8.

152. *L'onda ... METASTASIO. SIROE*: from Act I.ix. of the libretto 'Siroe re di Persia' ('Siroes, King of Persia') first set, 1726: 'The wave which murmurs from bank to bank, the breeze that trembles from leaf to leaf, are less inconstant than your heart.'

153. 'La jeunesse ... resolution': 'The young sleep well on a mind made up.' (French).

154. *'Zephyr ... False as fair'*: from a lyric written by Charles Leftley (d.1797) for a glee composed by his friend, William Linley (1771–1835). Linley was the younger brother of Elizabeth Linley, who married LeFanu's uncle, R.B. Sheridan, in 1773. See *A Selection of Favourite Catches, Glees, &c. as sung at the Bath Harmonic Society*, 2nd edn (Bath: R. Cruttwell, 1799), pp.133–4.

155. *Atala ... soit bien puissante*: One of the foremost writers of Romantic literature in France, François-Auguste-René, Vicomte de Chateaubriand (1768–1848) published his epic tale of the romance between a Christian girl and an Indian chief, *Atala*, in 1801. The quotation reads: 'Our walk was almost in silence. I was walking next to Atala. [...] I was looking sometimes to the sky, sometimes at the ground, listening carefully to the birdsong; gesturing toward the sunset; [...] my heart sometimes beating, sometimes quiet. The names Chactas and Atala softly repeated from time to time. Oh! Love's first outing, your memory is of course engraved on my mind.'

156. *Paul et Virginie ... would like better*: Bernardin de Saint-Pierre's short romantic tale, *Paul et Virginie* (1788), was first published as part of his *Études de la Nature* (1784). *Caroline de Lichtfield, ou Mèmoires d'une Famille Prussienne*, published in London in 1786, was the first novel of Swiss-born author and translator Élisabeth Jeanne Isabelle Pauline de Montolieu (1751–86).

157. J'ai été épris ... pour la vie: 'I was enamoured of Louise; I adored Caroline; but I love Matilda and I feel it is for the rest of my life.' (French).

158. *'Odi ... d'amor'*: Metastasio's 'Odi l'aura che dolce sospira' was set by Beethoven and published in 1811, Op. 82. no. 5: 'Hear the wind that breathes so sweetly as it rushes past, stripping the leaves – if you pay heed to it, it speaks to you of love; see the wave that raises itself hoarsely up as it wails striking its banks – if you pay heed to it, its plaints to you are of love.'

159. *Oh maraviglia! ...GERUSALEMME LIBERATA*: Book I. Hoole captures the spirit of the lines in 'O wondrous force of Love's resistless dart,/ That pierced at once and rooted in his heart,' (Vol.1, p. 31), although a more literal translation might be: 'Oh miracle! Love that is new born already flies full-grown, and triumphs in full armour'.

160. *The keenest ... unemployed. LORD BYRON; THE GIAOUR*: from Byron's *The Giaour: A Fragment of a Turkish Tale* (1813), 957–60.

161. *Werter or Oberon*: a reference to Johann Wolfgang von Goethe's *The Sorrows of Young Werther* (1774; English trans. 1779) and Christoph Martin Wieland's *Oberon* (1780; English trans. 1798).

162. *'Palter ... our hope'*: Macbeth, V.viii.20–2.

163. *'Sir Archy's Grandmother'*: This idiom has its origins in Charles Macklin's *Love à la Mode; or, the Amours of Florella and Phillis* (1779). Sir Callaghan O Brallaghan dismisses the puerile and fantastically inaccurate dispute he is having with Sir Archy M'Sarcasm on the preminence of the Scots over the Irish as being 'about Sir Archy's great-grandmother' (I.i).

164. *'Young ... bloom?'*: from 'Specimens of Translation from *Medea*: Antistrophe I' by Thomas Campbell, in *The Pleasures of Hope, in two parts. With Other Poems* (Edinburgh: Mundell & Son, 1799; Longman & Rees, and J. Wright, 1799).

165. *d'une noble inutilité*: A 'noble futility', from *Corrina, or Italy* (1807) by Germaine de Staël (1766–1817).

166. *Two maxims ... to disguise. SWIFT*: Jonathan Swift, *Cadenus and Vanessa* (composed, 1713), 625–8; 631–6.

167. *Arabian Nights*: In this, 'The Story of the Sleeper Awakened, or The Dead Alive,' the Caliph and his wife bet against each other, though they are unaware that the facts upon which they stake their respective claims are equally without foundation.

168. *de fond en comble*: 'from top to bottom'; that is, 'utterly'. (French)

169. *crescendo ... morendo*: markings used on musical scores to denote changes in tone and volume. *Crescendo* and *forte* refer to increases in volume of a phrase, and *rinforzando* the volume of a note. The other markings involve weakening, fading out, or slowing down.

170. *'Slept ... darkness furled'*: Replacing 'sleep' with 'slept', LeFanu borrows from Thomas Moore's 'Silent O Moyle', a lyric composed to the tune of an Irish air and published in *Irish Melodies* (1808). Later in his own career Moore acknowledged the 'highly gifted' Alicia LeFanu for her assistance in his biographical study, *Memoirs of the Life of the Right Honourable Richard Brinsley Sheridan* (1825).

171. *Ecco ... dirò METASTASIO*: from the Canzonette, 'La Partenza' ('The Departure'; 1746): 'See, I shall tell of how (she) this fountain burst forth in disdain, but then, as a pledge of peace, gave me her fair hand.'

Volume II

1. *Quando ... METASTASIO. – DEMETRIO*: These lines are taken from the final act of the libretto, *Demetrio*, by the Italian librettist and poet, Pietro Metastasio (1698–1782). The piece was first set in 1731, with further compositions throughout the period until 1840.

John Hoole translated *The Works of Metastasio* in 1767, though a later bilingual version of the text, including these lines as printed, provides the following translation: 'Love, that to noble breasts extends, / Is not a rival to controul / Fair virtue's sway; but mutual friends / To gen'rous deeds they raise the soul./ Rest, happy pair, in peace secure;/Henceforth may ev'ry fav'ring pow'r, / To you, that happiness ensure, / Which Heav'n averse deny'd before.' See *Demetrio: An Opera, as performed at the King's-Theatre in the Haymarket. The music by Signor Pietro Guglielmi, [...] The poetry by the celebrated Metastasio, altered by Giovan Gualberto Bottarelli. Most of the translation by Mr. Carara.* (London: W.Griffin, 1772), p. 36.

2. *Je n'examine ... RACINE – Bajazet*: Jean Racine, *Bajazet* (1672), III.i: 'I am not concerned with my own joy or sadness / I care enough for my lover to let him go.' (French).

3. intriguante: 'a woman who schemes or plots.' (French).

4. veilleés de chateau: Meaning 'evenings at home' here rather than more literally, 'evenings at the castle,' this is also an allusion to the *Les Veillées du Château* (1784) by Madame Stéphanie Félicité de Genlis (1746–1830).

5. *'Giant statue fell'*: from William Collins's, 'Ode to Liberty' (1746) in which the 'giant' Rome is overthrown, l.19.

6. *Roxana and Statira, in ancient story* : Roxana was the first wife of Alexander the Great who, after his death, ordered that his second wife, Statira, be killed. Their story is the subject of Nathaniel Lee's tragedy *The Rival Queens* (1677).

7. *Hæphestion ... I would be Fitzroy*: Hephæstion was the closest friend of Alexander the Great, and once mistaken for him by the Persian Queen, Sisygambis. Neither this, nor the indifference of the cynic philosopher Diogenes, affronted the king who, in admiration of the latter, purportedly claimed: 'If I were not Alexander, I would be Diogenes.'

8. *Octavia ... Titus*: Having brought troops and reinforcements to Mark Antony in Athens, Octavia was denied the company of her husband by Cleopatra. The shadow of the eastern queen also fell on Berenice (b. AD 28) the Jewish mistress of the Roman Emperor Titus Vespasianus Augustus (AD 39–81) who was given up in the face of public antipathy.

9. *Playful ... COLERIDGE.* Remorse: The probable source of these lines as quoted is a review of *Remorse* by J. T. Coleridge in the *Quarterly Review* (April 1814), xi, 177–90. See *Samuel Taylor Coleridge: Volume I, 1794–1834,* J. R. de J. Jackson (ed.), The Critical Heritage (London & New York: Routledge, 1995), p. 180.

10. *The heart ... to fly. LANGHORNE*: John Langhorne (1735–79), *Owen of Carron* (1778), XXIV. 489–96.

11. catalogue raisonné: 'a descriptive list.' (French).

12. *The morn ... BURNS.* Lament: Extracted from two stanzas of Robert Burns's 'The Lament, Occasioned by the Unfortunate Issue of a Friend's Amour', in *Poems, chiefly in the Scottish dialect* (1786), VII. 49–52; VIII. 61–4.

13. *I'll beg ... SHAKESPEARE*: Richard to Bolingbroke in *King Richard II*, IV.i.302–4.

14. *'And her mild ... pity'*: from Robert Southey, Sonnet V 'Hard by the road, where on that little mound', 7–8, in *Poems*, 2nd edn (1797).

15. *Pysche ... already possessed*: According to mythology, Cupid defied the instruction of a jealous Venus and, rather than making the mortal beauty Psyche fall in love with contemptible men, placed her in a remote palace. Enthralled, he visited her under cover of night, but fled when Psyche disobediently lit a lamp and discovered his identity.

16. *'Rather chuse ... a lie'*: LeFanu replaces 'I' with 'you' in lines taken from Jonathan Swift, 'Verses on the Death of Dr. Swift, D.S.P.D. Occasioned by reading a Maxim in Rochefoulcault' (composed 1731–2), 148–9.

17. *Portia*: a reference to Shakespeare's *The Merchant of Venice*, in which Portia and her maid Nerissa disguise themselves as a doctor of law and his clerk in an attempt to prevent Shylock's taking his pound of flesh from Antonio. Bassanio, Portia's husband, does not see through the disguise and, albeit reluctantly, rewards the 'doctor' with the ring entrusted to him by his wife.

18. *'la lame use le fourreau'*: 'the mind is wearing out the body.' (French).

19. *Maiden ...than I. SCOTT.* – Rokeby: Walter Scott, *Rokeby: A Poem in Six Cantos* (1813), III. xviii.1–4.

20. un peu plus prononcé: 'a little bit more pronounced.' (French).

21. *Envy ... POPE*: from Pope's *An Essay on Criticism* (published, 1711), 466–7. LeFanu replaces 'as its shade' with 'like its shade,' and replaces 'But' with 'And'.

22. *'When ... native bowers'*: from *Amusement. A Poetical Essay* (1790), 316–19, by Henry James Pye (1745–1813).

23. *the Loves of the Plants ... papa selected*: Erasmus Darwin's verse, *The Botanic Garden* (1789–91) is comprised of two parts: 'The Economy of Vegetation', and 'The Loves of the Plants' (1789). This second, four-canto part is, as the first, extensively annotated, incorporating explanatory material and discourses on botany, natural philosophy, and poetry. Following on from his translations of Carl Linnaeus's taxonomic classifications, Darwin's 'The Loves of Plants' is informed by an interest in the interrelation of plant and animal reproductive systems. The French naturalist Georges-Louis Leclerc, Comte de Buffon (1707–88) was a contemporary of Linnaeus, and the first part of his *Histoire naturelle* was published in 1749. Alcæus perhaps deliberately misconstrues this as a reference to the philosopher Claude Buffier (1661–1737). As he expects, this does not prompt a query from Miss Hautenville and so exposes the limits of her understanding.

24. Nascosta ma dolce: 'hidden but sweet.' (Italian).

25. devise: 'motto.' (French).

26. sortes Virgilianæ: 'divination, or the seeking of guidance, by chance selection of a passage in Virgil' (*OED*).

27. épris: 'in love.' (French)

28. *Sir Ashton Lever's museum was sold*: Mr. Melbourne's interest in birds, shells and fossils was reflected on a much larger scale in the natural history collection of Sir Ashton Lever (1729–88). Transferred from his own home to Leicester House, London, in 1773, the collection was sold, first wholesale by lottery in 1786, and then piecemeal by auction in 1806. O'Hara does not recognize Sir Nicholas Gimcrack as a fictional character in Thomas Shadwell's satire *The Virtuoso* (1676), albeit one based upon the Royal Society's first curator of experiments, Robert Hooke.

29. par hazard: 'by accident.' (French)

30. *lady Pekuah*: a character in Samuel Johnson's *The History of Rasselas, Prince of Abissinia* (1759).

31. *Tycho Brahe*: Swedish astronomer (1546–1601) who significantly revised earlier understandings of the planetary system.

32. *'Sweet ... adversity'*: Shakespeare, *As You Like It*, II.i.12. This line is also quoted in another of LeFanu's sources, Anne Grant's *Eighteen Hundred and Thirteen*, Part I. 809.

33. *Sweets to the sweet*: Shakespeare, *Hamlet*, V.i.237.

34. *'For earthly ... blessedness'*: a slight misquotation from Shakespeare's *A Midsummer Night's Dream*, the lines beginning 'For earthlier happy is the rose distill'd' (I.i.76–8).

35. *'Her eyes'... auburn hair'*: a misquotation from William Collins's *Eclogue the Fourth: Agib and Secander; or, The Fugitives* (1742). This line, spoken by Agib on the impending ruin of fair maidens by war reads: 'Their eyes' blue languish and their golden hair! / Those eyes in tears their fruitless grief must send; / Those hairs the Tartar's cruel hand shall rend' (56–8).

36. *'hushed in grim repose'*: from Thomas Gray's *The Bard. A Pindaric Ode* (1757), 76.

37. *Tu que ... JUAN DE TARSIS*: from 'A una gran Senora que dexo el siglo', by the Spanish baroque poet. The poem was included, with the following translation, in Robert Southey, *Letters Written During a Short Residence in Spain and Portugal*, 2nd edn (Bristol: Biggs and Cottle, 1799), pp. 358–9:

> You Lady! who in early youth have fled
> The pomp of courts to tread the narrow way,
> And for the Nun's coarse garb and flinty bed,
> Have left the couch of down and silk array,
> You wisely from the world's deceitful train
> To the holy port resolved your course to bend,
> As the wise pilot would the haven gain,
> Who sees the gathering storm of night impend.
> Pour you to heaven the grateful song of praise,
> With hymns of joy your full of glory boast,
> Your full content; for if the sailor raise
> The exulting cry to view his destined coast,
> What shouts of rapture should by her be given,
> Escaped the storms of life, who sees the port of Heaven!

38. *'pure ... blood'*: from John Donne's *The Progress of the Soul: The Second Anniversary* (1612), 244.

39. *I wander ... MISS BAILLIE*. Ethwald: from the tragedy *Ethwald* (1790), by Joanna Baillie (1762–1851), V.ii.40–3.

40. *'Toutes les ... ressemblait'*: The daughter of Charles I, Princess Henrietta (1644–70), later known as Henriette Ann, married the younger brother of Louis XIV, Phillipe, Duke of Orléans. She was reputedly poisoned, possibly on her husband's authority, but an official post-mortem concluded that she died of natural causes. The lines read: 'All the women were imitating her, and none were looking like her.'

41. *'Combien ... cherchais toujours'*: from Racine, *Britannicus*, III. These lines, spoken by Junia, read: 'How many times, alas! Because you have to know, / Was my heart going to tell you of its confusion? / With how many interrupted sighs / Have I avoided those eyes, which I was constantly seeking!'

42. *Mrs Barbauld's ... Pity*: Included in *Miscellaneous Pieces in Prose* (London: J. Johnson, 1773) by Anna Laetitia Aiken (later Barbauld) and her brother John, 'A Tale' of Love, Sorrow, Joy and Pity reappeared throughout the remainder of the eighteenth century in others' collections of works designed for the improvement of young minds. Pity is the daughter of Love and Sorrow and is described as having 'a dejected appearance, but so soft and gentle a mien that she was loved to a degree of enthusiasm' (p. 217).

43. *Persepolis*: Persepolis is the setting for Voltaire's tale *Le Monde Comme Il Va* (c. 1748).

44. *Un beau … LA BRUYERE*: from Bruyère's *Les Caractères de Théophraste traduits du grec avec Les Caractères ou les moeurs de ce siècle*: 'A fine face, is the finest of all sights; and the sweetest music is the sound of the voice of the one you love.'

45. *Hookham's*: Thomas Hookham's circulating library, situated on Bond Street, London, was fashionable amongst the gentry and affluent classes.

46. *Missionary … Lady of the Lake, as soon as you possibly can*: a reference to *The Missionary, or; An Indian Tale* (London: 1811) by Sydney Owenson (1783–1859) and Walter Scott's *The Lady of the Lake* (1810).

47. *Cornelia … as good*: a reference to a Roman story in which the poor and unadorned Cornelia, upon being asked by her wealthy friend if she herself owned any precious gems, declared that her two sons alone were her 'jewels'.

48. Demetrio … *pace. METASTASIO*. Antigono: from the libretto 'Antigono', ('Antigonis'; first set, 1743): Dem: 'Ah, in your face I see a lantern of Love, oh you my fair torch – / Ber. 'What do you want from me? – leave me in peace.'

49. *O entre … fidèle? BOETHIUS'* Sonnets: An extract from Sonnet VIII of Etienne de Boétie's *Vingt et Neuf Sonnets*. Michel de Montaigne published Boétie's works, and included the sonnets in early editions of the *Essais*. The lines read: 'Of your beauties, how fine is your constancy!/It is this assured heart, this steadfast courage / That, of your virtues, we prize the most/And what is more beautiful than a faithful friend?'

50. personnage muet: 'mute.' (French).

51. *Vestris*: This roll-call of performers begins with the Parisian-born dancer Gaetano Vestris (1726–1808), who was the most celebrated soloist of his generation, and includes the soprano Angelica Catalani (1780–1849) who made her London debut in 1806, and the Italian opera singers, Carlos Rovedino (d.1822) and Giuseppe Viganoni (d.c.1823).

52. Begli astri d'amor: 'fair stars of love.' (Italian).

53. *Mrs. Hill … 'Limerick Gloves'*: In her repeated use of the word 'since' in this way Arbella mimics Mrs Hill in Maria Edgeworth's short story, 'The Limerick Gloves' in, *Popular Tales* (1804).

54. *Ajut …Greenland Tale*: 'Anningait and Ajut; A Greenland History' and 'The History of Anningait and Ajut Concluded' had appeared in Samuel Johnson's *The Rambler*, numbers 186 (28 December 1751) and 187 (31 December 1751).

55. *Un Prince … eut point*: Idiomatically these phrases correspond with the sense that the first prince in the tale is 'quite proper', the second 'too good to be true' and the third, regrettably, one of whom we might say, 'it would have been better had he not been born.'

56. *Jaques … Malvolio*: characters in *As You Like It* and *Twelfth Night*.

57. *worthy Old Fuller*: The cleric and historian Thomas Fuller (1608–61) was the author of two important biographical studies. *The Holy State, The Profane State* (1642) included character portraits of historical and literary significance and anticipated the more extensive *History of the Worthies of England*. Published posthumously in 1662, this account of the country's modes, manners and notable individuals has since been regarded as the first dictionary of national biography.

58. *Conde*: a Portuguese title of nobility.

59. bien imposans… très prévenans: Miss Mountain consistently misapplies words in French which resemble the English word she is aiming for. Here she compliments people as generally deserving of respect when she means to disparage, and proceeds to use the verb 'to unearth,' when she means 'decourager', to deter. She concludes her criticism of the lack of consideration shown to one's friends by affirming that such people are indeed 'very considerate.'

60. très ingénu ... effrontée: As before, Miss Mountain mistakenly describes French toys as unsophisticated when she intends the opposite, and her parting shot, which at least ought to express the hope that she herself has not outstayed her welcome, succeeds in further insulting her hostess: I am sure, she claims, 'that you have not been insolent.'

61. 'Voilà le monde! *Matilda,' said she*: a rather ironic, 'There goes the world.' (French).

62. *Love ... SIR WILLIAM JONES*: The sentiments expressed by the Orientalist, translator, essayist and poet, Sir William Jones (1746–94), in a letter to Lord Althorp, dated 5 January 1782. It was included in John Shore, Baron Teignmouth's *Life, Writings, and Correspondence, of Sir William Jones* (London: n.p., 1804).

63. *landaulet*: a smaller, two-seater version of the four-wheeled landau, having the characteristic folding hood.

64. les entrées libres: 'free access.' (French).

65. *Bond-street*: The quality shops established throughout the eighteenth century along London's Bond Street continued to serve the fashionable elite.

66. *'The little ... flying maze'*: from James Beattie's *The Minstrel*, I.xxxv.309.

67. *'If few ... are but few'*: from Oliver Goldsmith's, *The Traveller* (1764), 212.

68. *Lawrence*: probably the London-based portrait artist Thomas Lawrence (1769–1830).

69. galanterie: 'compliment.' (French).

70. *Dear ... ROSCOE'S* Translation of Lorenzo de Medici: extracted from a transcription of a poem William Roscoe (1753–1831) included, along with other selected translations of the writings of Lorenzo de Medici, in his biography, *The Life of Lorenzo de' Medici; Called the Magnificent*, 2 vols. (Liverpool: J. M'Creery, 1795), vol 1., p. 271.

71. *True ... HERVEY*: The use to which LeFanu puts these lines belies the notoriety of their context. Included in *A Letter from the Hon. Thomas Hervey, to Sir Thomas Hanmer, Bart.*, they were first published as part of the politician Thomas Hervey's attack on his godfather Hanmer, with whose wife Hervey had conducted a scandalous affair. The letter was published after her death in 1741 and occasioned not only further public scrutiny, but also Hervey's taste for pamphleteering. See William R. Jones, 'Hervey, Thomas (1699–1775)', *DNB*.

72. éloquence du cœur: 'words from the heart.' (French).

73. *La Volubile ... a niente*: 'The Fickle One', this is possibly derived from the song included in I.vi. of the comic opera *I Bagni d'Abano* (first set, 1753) by the Italian dramatist and librettist Carlo Goldoni (1707–93): 'I want to carry on cheerfully, / I don't want to think about anything.'

74. *Philosophical Transcations*: a serious professional journal published by The Royal Society of London which reported on scientific investigations.

75. *cerulean symbol ... crucible*: Arbella's part in an earlier conversation between Alcæus and Sappho would explain what is perhaps her reference to learned women (in terms of the 'bluestockings') and to the aquatic nymphs of Darwin's *Botanic Garden* (1805). Both topics informed the poets' earlier debate on the likelihood of Mr Sowerby's marrying Matilda.

76. *'Più ... speranza'*: 'I no longer have any sweet hope.' (Italian).

77. *'Eyes, like ... the morn'*: Lines derived from a song in Shakespeare's *Measure for Measure*, IV.i.3–4. The lines also appear in the song included in V.ii. of the tragedy, *Rollo, Duke of Normandy; or, The Bloody Brother*. The original date of publication of this play is uncertain but, in addition to John Fletcher, authorship is variously ascribed to Francis Beaumont, Philip Massinger, George Chapman and Benjamin Jonson.

78. le Desiré, le Bien-aimé: 'the desired one, the beloved one.' (French).

79. *Claire d'Albe* ... ma Bien-aimée: Sophie Cottin's first novel, a tale of a childless woman's adulterous relationship with her husband's adopted son, was published in 1799. 'Love in the Deserts' is the name Arbella gives to *Mathilde, ou Mémoires tirés de l'histoire des croisades* (1805), an English translation of which, entitled *The Saracen; or, Matilda and Malek Adhel*, was published in the same year. In reading this, Cottin's third novel, Arbella encounters further representations of female sexual awakening and the religious and cultural tensions which disrupt and, finally, destroy the happiness of the eponymous English princess and her noble Muslim lover. The line as quoted from this novel read:
    'What do you fear my love?'
80. prôneurs: 'flatterers.' (French).
81. *Who aims ... MISS MORE. Search after Happiness*: from lines spoken by Urania, one of several characters exploring the proprieties of a female education in *The Search After Happiness* (1762), a short pastoral drama by Hannah More (1745–1833).
82. *Cabinet des Fées*: *Le Cabinet des Fées et des autres contes merveilleux* (1785–9) was a multivolume anthology of fairy tales edited by Charles-Joseph de Mayer.
83. comme a l'ordinaire: 'as usual.' (French).
84. *'For to ... unkind'*: Shakespeare, *Hamlet*, III.i.101.

Volume III

1. *Quando ... fù. METASTASIO.* – *DEMETRIO*: These lines are taken from the final act of the libretto, *Demetrio*, by the Italian librettist and poet, Pietro Metastasio (1698–1782). The piece was first set in 1731, with further compositions throughout the period until 1840. John Hoole translated *The Works of Metastasio* in 1767, though a later bilingual version of the text, including these lines as printed, provides the following translation: 'Love, that to noble breasts extends, / Is not a rival to controul / Fair virtue's sway; but mutual friends / To gen'rous deeds they raise the soul. / Rest, happy pair, in peace secure; / Henceforth may ev'ry fav'ring pow'r, / To you, that happiness ensure, / Which Heav'n averse deny'd before.' See *Demetrio: An Opera, as performed at the King's-Theatre in the Hay-market. The music by Signor Pietro Guglielmi, [...] The poetry by the celebrated Metastasio, altered by Giovan Gualberto Bottarelli. Most of the translation by Mr. Carara.* (London: W.Griffin, 1772), p. 36.
2. *'Tous... MOLIERE. Misanthrope*: from Act V of the tragi-comedy (*The Misanthrope*, 1666) by the comic actor and dramatist Jean-Baptiste Poquelin, known as Molière (*c.*1622–73): 'The defects of human nature afford us opportunities of exercising our philosophy, the best employment of our virtues. If all men were righteous, all hearts, true and frank and loyal what use would our virtues be? Their use lies in enabling us to support with constancy the injustices others inflict upon us.' See *Molière: The Misanthrope and Other Plays*, trans. & intro., John Wood (London: Penguin, 1959), p. 68.
3. *Colonsay*: name of hero enthralled to the mermaid in Leyden's 'The Mermaid' (1811).
4. *Aurora*: Roman goddess of the dawn.
5. *polacca*: Although derived from the Italian 'Polonaise', by the early nineteenth century the term was used more generally to denote an audibly striking if not typically Polish instrumental piece. (*Grove*).
6. *Melmoth maketh honourable mention*: possibly a reference to William Melmouth, the younger (*c.* 1710–99), principally a translator of classical writing including that of Pliny and Cicero.

7. *Tales of the Castle*: Thomas Holcroft's English translation of *Les Veillées du Château* was published in 1785 and, along with De Genlis's *Theatre of Education* (1779–80), was recommended as suitable reading matter for young women.

8. *Lady Wortley Montague*: Published in 1763, the letters of Lady Mary Wortley Montagu (1689–1762), including those addressed to her daughter Mary, Countess of Bute, reflect on her earlier travels in Europe, Asia and Africa. A five-volume collection of her *Works* appeared in 1803.

9. *'Answered ... not what'*: spoken by Hotspur in Shakespeare's *Henry IV. Part I*, I.iii.52. Charlotte Smith quotes the same, likewise replacing 'I' with 'she' in her novel, *The Banished Man* (1794).

10. *Musidorus*: Prince of Thessalia in Philip Sidney's *Arcadia* who, together with his cousin, the prince of Macedon, uses disguise to pursue the princesses Pamela and Philoclea.

11. *scarlet buccinum*: *Buccinum Undatum* is the Latin name for the Common Whelk, which Arbella may be confusing here with the Red Whelk, *Neptuna Antiqua*.

12. *'Ye woods ... sadness'*: lines spoken by Lady Randolph in the tragedy, *Douglas* (1756) by John Home (1722–1808), I.i. The solemnity of the passage being somewhat at odds with the cheeriness of Helen's interpretation of it, Arbella responds with a compliment which is then perhaps quite intentionally compromised by the context of her own choice of quotation.

13. *'She ran ... hill'*: It is with this description that the character Anna announces the suicide of Matilda, Lady Randolph, to her husband: 'nor halted till the precipice she gain'd, / Beneath whose low'ring top the river falls / Ingulph'd in rifted rocks: thither she came, / As fearless as the eagle lights upon it, / And headlong down – '. See *Douglas: A Tragedy. As it is Acted at the Theatre-Royal in Covent-Garden* (London: A. Millar, 1757), V.i.

14. *Thickest ... BURNS'* Strathallan's Lament: the first half of Robert Burns's song of 1787 which commemorates the fall of William Drummond, the fourth Viscount of Strathallan (1690–1746) at Culloden, the decisive battle in the defeat of the 1745 Jacobite uprising.

15. *Melpomene*: the classical muse of tragedy.

16. *'moving ... this languid tête-à-tete:* Possibly an allusion to Byron's 'She Walks in Beauty' (1815), the opening lines of which read: 'She walks in beauty, like the night / Of cloudless climes and starry skies; / And all that's best of dark and bright / Meet in her aspect and her eyes.'

17. *Werter's Charlotte*: a reference to the heroine of Goethe's *The Sorrows of Young Werther*.

18. *in* prise: from the French, *prise*, meaning 'capture': in chess the term *en prise* refers to a piece which is undefended and so in a position to be taken.

19. *'Long meditating ... do'*: Not identified.

20. *cicisbeo*: in Italy, 'the recognized gallant or *cavalier servente* of a married woman' (*OED*).

21. *Piron's* Metromanie: a reference to the comedy, *La Métromanie* (1738) or 'The Poetry Craze', by the French dramatist Alexis Piron.

22. rôles de suivante: the character of the waiting maid.

23. *Robertson's Charles the 5th or 6th*: a reference to the *History of the Reign of Charles V* (1769) by the Scottish minister and historian, William Robertson (1721–91).

24. *'light summer cloud'*: Refrain in a poem also entitled 'Love's Light Summer Cloud' by Thomas Moore.

25. *huntress, she carried in her hand*: Matilda's costume is that of Diana, goddess of the hunt.

26. *let into the baby-house*: Baby houses, or doll's houses, had become increasingly popular by the end of the eighteenth century. In appropriating the term to her conduct, Lady Torrendale thinks twice about giving a false account of herself or, in other words, acting childishly.

27. *'O married … LANGHORNE*: from John Langhorne's *Owen of Carron*, XVIII. 417–24.

28. *'want the generous tear she paid'*: possibly an adaptation of a line from Elizabeth Moody's 'Parody, On the Death of a celebrated Physician, written in the Character of a Brother of the Faculty', published in her *Poetic Trifles* (London, Cadell Jun. and Davies 1798). In Moody's poem it is the doctor who, upon his own deathbed, 'shall shortly want the generous tear he pays' (4).

29. *Praise … WORKS OF SIR WILLIAM JONES* Epistles: lines 11–12 from 'Extempore Opinion on Native Talent, In Answer to Lines from a Friend'. The expanded, thirteen-volume *Collected Works of Sir William Jones* was published in 1807.

30. *Un alma grande … METASTASIO*. Artaserse: from Act II of the libretto 'Artaxerxes' first set, 1730: 'A great soul is a theatre in itself. In secret it approves and condemns itself.'

31. *Lord Chesterfield … credit for generosity*: The letters written by the Right Honourable Philip Dormer Stanhope, Earl of Chesterfield, to his son, Philip Stanhope, were first published in 1774, with further additions and selections appearing throughout the period. The advice alluded to here had been included in, for example, *Lord Chesterfield's advice to his son, on men and manners: or, a new system of education*, 3rd edn (London: Richardson and Urquhart, 1777): 'The reputation of generosity is to be purchased pretty cheap; it does not depend so much upon a man's general expence, as it does upon his giving handsomely where it is proper to give at all. A man, for instance, who should give a servant four shillings, would pass for covetous, while he who gave him a crown would be reckoned generous: so that the difference of those two opposite characters turns upon one shilling' (p. 111).

32. Estelle: a pastoral romance by Jean-Pierre Claris de Florian, first published in 1788.

33. *Qui … TASSO. SONNETS*: A literal translation of this unidentified sonnet reads: 'Here no ray of beauty was to be seen; he is become a peasant and with a ploughman's love he feeds the herds and, in the summer heat, he at one moment guides the plough, at another whirls the scythe.'

34. *Cadmus … dragon's teeth*: The son of the king of Phoenicia, Cadmus is credited in Greek mythology as the founder of the city of Thebes. The city's first noble families were established by the surviving members of the Sparti, armed warriors who sprang from the ground in which Cadmus, having killed a dragon guarding his only source of water, had sown the creature's teeth.

35. lapsus linguæ: 'slips of the tongue.' (Latin).

36. *'Who … name?'*: from Thomas Campbell's *The Pleasures of Hope*, II. 5–6.

37. Oziósi *… here much longer*: an allusion to aristocratic literary academies such as the Academia degli Oziós of Naples, although Arbella playfully invokes the sense of *Oziósi* ('Idlers') and Addormnetáti ('sleepy heads').

38. *Shenstone has it*: William Shenstone (1714–63), writing to Richard Graves on the death of their close friend and fellow poet, John Whistler, referred affectionately to their former 'little strifes and bickerments.' Graves included some correspondence in his *Recollections of Some Particulars in the Life of William Shenstone, Esq.* (1788), although Arbella may be considered to have come across the phrase in the letter as it is included in *Elegant*

Epistles: or, a copius collection of familiar and amusing letters, selected for the improvement of young persons (Dublin: Chamberlaine and Rice [and eight others], 1790), p. 648.

39. *Fatima in Cymon*: In David Garrick's dramatic romance *Cymon* (1767), Merlin allows Fatima to answer only in the negative or affirmative.

40. a la houssard: 'in the manner of the Hussars' (French), and so an allusion to either the recklessness with which the regiment was sometimes associated or the splendid ornamentation of their uniforms.

41. *as the poet ... love*: The line is attributable to the comic dramatist Terence (Publius Terentius Afer, *c.* 190–159 BC), and appeared in his first play, *Andria*, as 'Amantium irae amoris integratio est' or, 'Lovers' rows make love whole'.

42. coup d'œil: in this context, 'the action or faculty of rapidly taking a general view of a position, and estimating its advantages and disadvantages' (*OED*).

43. passe cela: 'go on.' (French).

44. *And sleep ... SOUTHEY – CURSE OF KEHAMA*: minor variation of vengeful lines spoken by the Hindu Rajah, Kemah, to Ladurlad, the murderer of his son and the hero of Robert Southey's epic poem *The Curse of Kehama* (1810), II.166–9.

45. '*Wove ... wild*': Line 3 of 'Sonnet V. To the South Downs', included in Charlotte Smith's collection of *Elegiac Sonnets, and other Essays* (1784).

46. *Nero's ivory palace at Rome*: Built on extensive grounds in Rome after the devastating fire of AD 64, the Emperor Nero's palace, or *Domus Aurea*, overlaid in places with gold-leaf, boasted amongst its many other splendours fretted ivory ceilings through which the rooms could be infused with fragrance or showered with flowers.

47. *Ma pur ... con lui*: the final tercet of Sonnet 35, 'Solo et pensoso i piú deserti campi,' from Petrarch's *Il Canzoniere*: 'But still, I cannot find paths so rough, or so strange but that Love will always come on them with me as I with him.'

48. '*Thou ... styling*': minor variation of the final stanza of William Jones's 'A Song, From the Persian, paraphrased in the Measure of the Original' included in the 1810 edition of the *Poetical Works*.

49. '*My friend ... guide*': from Lady Mary Wortley Montagu's love poem 'Hymn to the Moon', 8.

50. '*Fond love ... thee*': Not identified.

51. *A phenonomenon ... evening*: This note is derived from William Curtis's periodical, *The Botannical Magazine; or, Flower Garden Displayed* (London, 1787), vol. I. p. 23.

52. Champ de Mars ... *your labourers*: Arbella alludes to the events of the Fête de la Fédération, an organised civic declaration of allegiance to mark the establishment of the Constitution, which was celebrated across France on 14 July 1790. In Paris, men and women of diverse ages and social backgrounds reportedly gathered to dig the earth on the green of le Champ de Mars, located behind the present site of the Eiffel Tower.

53. accés de coquetterie: 'a fit of coquetry.' (French).

54. *It is ... SHAKESPEARE.. MIDSUMMER NIGHT'S DREAM*: LeFanu replaces 'maidenly' with 'womanly' in lines spoken by Helena to Hermia, III.ii.217–19.

55. *Queen Christina*: Queen Christina of Sweden (1626–89), who notoriously abdicated her throne in 1754, had been educated to the standard usually reserved for the male heir and became a significant and influential patron of the arts.

56. *Sully's Memoirs*: Maximilien de Béthune, later the Duc de Sully (1560–1641), was a pre-eminent statesman in the service of Henry IV of France. His memoirs, the *Économies Royales*, first appeared in 1638.

57. *'Freezes ... blue'*: slight modification of a line from Byron's *The Giaour*, 774.
58. *Si ... METASTASIO. IL RE PASTORE*: from Act I. iii. of the libretto ('The Shepherd King'; first set, 1751): An eighteenth-century prose translation of these lines reads: 'Thus does a cloud spread itself, and intercepting the rays of the sun, send out lightnings and threaten the arid ground. But when it has collected sufficient waters, it dissolves in rain, and renders that ground fertile.' See *Il Re Pastore Dramma Musica. Pel Teatro di S.M.B.* (London: G. Woodfall, 1757), p. 10.
59. *'Negri ... ardenti'*: the first line of a sonnet by Vittorio Alfieri, which reads: 'dark, lively, burning with sweet fire.'
60. *'For friends ... young'*: from an Air in Sheridan's *The Duenna*, I.v.138–9.
61. *'Un peu ... loin'*: 'A little love, a little care / Can often lead the heart far away.' (French).
62. *Paley*: The scholar and cleric William Paley (1743–1805) was the author of several theological and moralist texts, including his counter-evolutionist *Natural Theology* (London: 1802).
63. *The rock ... LORD STRANGFORD'S CAMOENS*: not traceable to a particular poem, although Strangford's collection of poems by Luís Vaz de Camoëns is one of LeFanu's sources. See vol. 1. n. 4.
64. *quizzes*: from 'quiz', 'an odd or eccentric person, in character or appearance' (*OED*).
65. *Eccomi á cenni suoi*: The line *Eccomi á cenni tuoi* 'I attend your commands' appears in Act II of Metastasio's *Siroe*.
66. *jaunting cars ... noddies*: These lightweight two-wheeled carriages were more particular to Ireland, a jingle differing in the main from the other two in being covered.
67. *Powerscourt ... Bullock*: Attractions in Ireland included the impressive eighteenth-century gardens of Powerscourt House which, located above the Dargle river, is the site of the country's highest waterfall. In the first two decades of the nineteenth century, the first Duke of Leinster's Carton House estate would have retained much of its eighteenth-century character; the gardens in particular having been landscaped during that period under the supervision of his wife, Lady Emily Lennox. Bullock Castle presided over the small fishing village of that name, which was also notable for its rock.
68. *Madame de Montespan's ... led it along*: This whim of Louis XIV's former mistress, Françoise-Athénaïs, Marquise de Montespan, is referred to in the published letters of his second wife. At thirty-three years old, the Marquise was yet amused by 'six mice harnessed to a little Coach of Filligree, and suffered them to bite her fine Hands.' See *Letters of Madame Maintenon. Translated from the French*, 2 vols (London: L. Davis and C. Reymers 1759), vol. 2., p. 289; M.de la Baumelle, *Memoirs for the History of Madame de Maintenon*, trans. Charlotte Lennox, 5 vols (London: A. Millar, and J.Nourse; R. and J. Dodsley; L. Davis, and C. Reymer, 1757), vol. II. p. 55.
69. *'Evandrum ... almâ'*: a misquotation from *The Aeneid*, Book VIII. The lines should read 'Evandrum ex humili tecto lux suscitat alma' : 'The kindly morning light raised Evander from his humble dwelling.' (Latin).
70. *'Ma foi ... guère'*: 'Upon my word, if my memory serves me right, I hardly remember it.' (French).
71. *gipsey jack*: a colloquial reference to a carriage, in this case, one capable of carrying four passengers with two on each side seated back to back.
72. *'soldier's harico'*: Haricot beans made for a substantial proportion of the dried vegetable rations of soldiers.
73. *Scipio's tomb*: The tomb of the family of Roman generals descended from Cornelius Scipio is on the Appian way just outside the city.

74. *'If thou ... moon-light'*: from Walter Scott, 'The Lay of the Last Minstrel', II.i.1–2.
75. a propos de bottes: French phrase meaning, 'to change the subject'.
76. *Parnassus*: Mount Parnassus is the classical home of the nine muses.
77. *Egeria*: The water spirit Egeria shared the prophetic powers of the goddesses of Roman religion, the Camenae, and lived with them in their grove.
78. ci-devant: 'aristocratic.' (French).
79. *seguedilla*: 'a Spanish dance in 3/4 or 3/8 time; also, the music for this' (*OED*).
80. *Erebus*: in Greek mythology, pertaining to the son of Chaos and embodiment of darkness, as well as to a 'place of darkness between earth and Hades' (*OED*).
81. *Burke ... virtues*: The person is Lord Keppel in Edmund Burke's, *A letter from the Right Honourable Edmund Burke to a noble lord, on the attacks made upon him and his pension, in the House of Lords, by the Duke of Bedford and the Earl of Lauderdale, early in the present Sessions of Parliament* (London, n.pub., 1796), p. 31.
82. *fanes*: temples of idolatry.
83. *L'arte che ... scopre*: Tasso, *Gerusalemme Liberata*, Book XVI. Hoole renders the sense of this as: 'art conceal'd / With greater charms the pleas'd attention held' (II. p. 123).
84. *Sweet ... AUSIUS MARCH*: The verse of the fifteenth-century Valencian-born poet, Ausiàs March (*c.* 1397–1459), was written in Catalan.
85. *'Its country ... race'*: from Pope, *Essay on Man*, IV.368.
86. *'How ... subjects'*: Shakespeare, *Henry IV, Part II*, III.i.4.
87. *'How ...blest?'*: first lines of Collins's, 'Ode, Written in the Beginning of the Year 1746' which was included in his *Odes on Several Descriptive and Allegoric subjects* (London, 1746).
88. 'rose a l'usage des dames': a pink cosmetic for women.
89. *My lover's blood ... HAMILTON*: from the ballad 'The Braes of Yarrow' (1730) by the Scottish poet, William Hamilton (1704–54), 87–8.
90. *'be-thumped with words'*: Shakespeare, *The Life and Death of King John*, II.i.466.
91. *'That dangerous ...wit*: This phrase can be traced to manuscript variations of the line 'more a Dupe than Wit' (368) in Pope's 'Epistle to Dr Arbuthnot'. See *The Poems of Alexander Pope*, 3 vols (London, n. p., 1779), II, p.164. The phrase was later taken up by Byron who, in a letter of 1810, used it to describe the renowned traveller to the East, Lady Hester Lucy Stanhope (1776–1839).
92. *Hastings' Ode*: from *An Imitation of Horace* (1785), by the governor of Bengal, Warren Hastings (1732–1818), which was written shortly after his resignation: 'Perch'd on his couch Distemper breathes, / And Care like Smoke, in turbid wreathes, / Round the gay ceiling flies' (Book II, Ode 16).
93. *'make free ... relations'*: a reference to Act III of R. B. Sheridan's *The School for Scandal* (1776), in which Charles Surface prepares to auction the family portraits in order to pay off his gambling debts.
94. Il Fanatico ... Musica: from the comic opera *Che originali* (1798) by Johann Simon Mayr (1763–1845).
95. *'Gratias Agimus Tibi'*: a line from the Latin Mass: 'We give You thanks.'
96. *Grassini*: Italian opera singer Giuseppe Grassini (1773–1850).
97. 'la petite Violette' ... la Valliere: Arbella refers to Louise-Francoise, Duchess de La Vallière, the shy, unassuming mistress of Louis XIV who was, at her own behest, finally allowed to enter a convent in Paris where she lived a penitent until her death in 1710. Madame de Sevigne apparently compared her to a 'little violet [...] which hid amid the herbage, and which blushed alike to be a mistress, a mother, and a duchess.' See Julia

Pardoe, *Louis the Fourteenth and the Court of France in the Seventeenth Century*, 2 vols (New York: Harpers Brothers 1847), vol. 1, p. 291.

98. *'the ... dove'*: from Walter Scott's *The Lay of the Last Minstrel*, II.xxxiv.9.

99. *So ... DARWIN*: from *The Loves of the Plants*, Canto I.

100. *king of Bath*: a reference to Richard 'Beau' Nash who became master of ceremonies at Bath from 1705 until his death in 1761, rather than to Bath's other reputed king and founder, Bladud.

101. *Not ... presence*: Robert Burns's 'Fair Eliza' (1791), the completed line reading: 'That thy presence gies to me' (21–4).

102. *Constance ... despised and forgotten*: a reference to Constance de Beverley in Walter Scott's *Marmion* (1810), 'whom the church number'd with the dead, / For broken vows, and convent fled' (II.xx.19–20).

103. *'kerchieft ... cloud'*: from John Milton's 'Il Penseroso' (1645), 125.

104. *'Il est des modes pour le voile'*: a reference to the eponymous 'hero' of the comic poem, *Ver-Ver, or, the Nunnery Parrot* (1734), by Jean-Baptiste-Louis Gresset (1709–77). The line quoted reads: 'There is a fashionable way to wear the veil'.

105. *'dear Zulistein'*: Not identified.

106. embouchure: 'The coupling mechanism, during the playing of a wind instrument, between the air supply of the player and the instrument. Embouchure is a matter of such vital importance that its nature will influence the wind instrument player's progress and ultimate capability as a musician' (*Grove*).

107. *Mitridate*: possibly a reference to Mozart's 'Mithridates, King of Pontus' (1770).

108. *In low ... song*: from Robert Southey's, *Thalaba the Destroyer* (1801) Book VIII.332–3.

109. *Zauberflöte*: Mozart's *The Magic Flute* (1791).

110. *Nourjahad*: an allusion to Frances Sheridan's oriental tale *The History of Nourjahad* (1767), in which the hero, having wished for a kind of earthly Paradise, believes himself granted immortality and perpetual enjoyment of inexhaustible riches.

111. *Kent to* Capability Brown: William Kent (*c.* 1686–1748), artist, architect, furniture and garden designer under whose supervision at Stowe the renowned landscaper Lancelot 'Capability' Brown (*c.*1716–83) initially worked.

112. *Sing ... LADY CH. W. MONTAGUE*: This is Montagu's 'Impromtu, To a Young Lady Singing.'

113. *As a child ... breast*: from Oliver Goldsmith's, *The Traveller*, 205–6.

114. *Tridates*: The Armenian king Tiridates is a character in both Reinhard Keiser's sing-spiel, *Octavia* (1705), and Giuseppe Maria Orlandi's tragedia per musica, *Nerone* (1721).

115. *the lion crouch ... instantly returned*: an allusion to Spenser's *The Faerie Queene*, in which a lion, poised to attack Una, is subdued by her beauty and innocence (Book 1, Canto II).

Volume IV

1. *Quando ... METASTASIO. – DEMETRIO*: These lines are taken from the final act of the libretto, *Demetrio*, by the Italian librettist and poet, Pietro Metastasio (1698–1782). The piece was first set in 1731, with further compositions throughout the period until 1840. John Hoole translated *The Works of Metastasio* in 1767, though a later bilingual version of the text, including these lines as printed, provides the following translation: 'Love, that to noble breasts extends,/Is not a rival to controul / Fair virtue's sway; but mutual friends / To gen'rous deeds they raise the soul. / Rest, happy pair, in peace secure; / Henceforth may ev'ry fav'ring pow'r, / To you, that happiness ensure, / Which Heav'n

averse deny'd before.' See *Demetrio: An Opera, as performed at the King's-Theatre in the Hay-market. The music by Signor Pietro Guglielmi, [...] The poetry by the celebrated Metastasio, altered by Giovan Gualberto Bottarelli. Most of the translation by Mr. Carara.* (London: W.Griffin, 1772), p. 36.

2. *Ah! ... Metastasio. La Clemenza Di Tito*: See note 126 to Volume I. 'Ah! Forgive my first emotion; that rash tone was the fault of lips that are used to naming everything as it is.' (Italian).

3. *'Sing ... me'*: from Act II.ii. of John Hawkesworth's *Oroonoko* (1759), his dramatic adaptation of Aphra Behn's *Oroonoko or, The Royal Slave* (1688). The work had been previously dramatized by Thomas Southerne, and in each case it is the governor of the plantation who speaks these words to Oroonoko's lover, Imoinda, and refers to the ways in which she might 'ravish' rather than 'charm' him.

4. *'Bind ... pea'*: from *The Village Curate* (1788) by James Hurdis (*c.* 1763–1801), 1267–9.

5. *Kozeluch*: a reference to the published music of the Czech composer and piano teacher Leopold Kozeluch (1752–1818).

6. *Nè ...Metastasio. Zenobio*: from Act I of the libretto first performed in 1740. Metastasio's drama of forced marriage, filial obligation and forbidden love focuses on the divided loyalties of its eponymous heroine: 'No less than stating the truth, we should avoid the appearance of a fault; our glory [or reputation] is a crystal of ice dimmed by every breath; a slender reed bent in every wind.'

7. *caviare to the multitude*: an allusion to Hamlet's description of the player's speech as 'but caviary to the general' (II.ii.432).

8. *let ... lengthened*: Not identified.

9. *Che ... Alfieri. Oreste*: from the tragedy of 1778: 'What is impossible when a generous heart and generous manners join?' (Italian).

10. *Arria ... painful*: Martial's epigram XIV on Arria, the wife of Claudius, had been translated by earlier writers such Richard Lovelace and Charles Sedley, and was published in translation in the mid- and late-eighteenth century by William Hay. Versions of Arria's story were also, however, included in instructive manuals for young ladies such as *A Mirror for the Female Sex. Historical Beauties for Young Ladies. Intended to Lead the Female Mind to the Love and Practice of Moral Goodness* (London: Vernor and Hood and sold by E. Newbery, 1798), by Mary Pilkington (1761–1839).

11. *Lewis ... pére*: a reference to Marie Thérèse of Austria (1638–83). The lines read: 'There is no place for kings in my father's court.' (French).

12. *'Sydney's ... mother'*: from the epitaph of the Countess of Pembroke. See, for example, *A Select Collection of Ancient and Modern Epitaphs, and Inscriptions: To which are added some on the decease of eminent personages. Collected by Thomas Caldwall* (London: The Compiler, 1796), p. 163.

13. *Crabbe's ...Villager*: a character in *The Village: A Poem* (1783) by George Crabbe (1754–1832): ' For yonder see that hoary swain, whose age / Can with no cares except its own engage; / Who, propt on that rude staff, looks up to see / The bare arms broken from the withering tree' (I.182–5).

14. *Let not ... Rowe's Jane Shore*: from II. ii. of the tragedy first performed in 1714.

15. *Saladin ... Tale*: an allusion to Maria Edgeworth's 'Murad the Unlucky', from *Popular Tales*, a story in which the eponymous hero and his brother, 'Saladin the Lucky', are brought to realize that their experiences are determined by prudence rather than by fortune.

16. *'That ... love'*: derived from Titania's description of Hippolyta to Oberon in Shakespeare's *A Midsummer Night's Dream*, I.ii.70–1.

17. *'Tray ... Sweetheart'*: the names of the dogs Lear imagines he sees in III. vi. of Shakespeare's *King Lear*.

18. á se passioner: 'to be carried away by [her] passions.' (French).

19. vi et armis: 'violently, forcibly, by compulsion' (*OED*).

20. *Blue Chamber ... her friend*: see note 128 to Volume I.

21. *O speak ... CHATTERTON – ÆLLA*: from Cantos CXLI and CXLII of the dramatic poem 'Ælla' (composed, *c.* 1768–9) by Thomas Chatterton (1752–70).

22. *Thebes and Pelop's line*: This phrase from Milton's *Il Penseroso* conjures images from ancient tragic drama. Thebes was the setting for the tragedy of Oedipus, and both Sophocles and Euripides dramatized the fate of members of the Pelopid dynasty, including Agamemnon, his son, Orestes, and daughters, Electra and Iphigenia.

23. *Fumi ... buono. TANSILLO. LA BALIA*: from the first canto of *La Balia*, or 'The Nurse', by the Italian poet Luigi Tansillo (1510–68). William Roscoe's translation of these lines reads: 'Shades of false honour, darker mists of pride,/ Touch'd by the beam ethereal quick subside./ Self-love his long prescriptive rule foregoes.' See William Roscoe, *The Nurse, A Poem. Translated from the Italian* (Liverpool (printed); London: Cadell and Davies, 1798), p. 31.

24. quelque grand coup: 'some grand coup.' (French).

25. *Lady Belerma*: Although the particular Lady Blanche to whom Lady Strathallan refers is uncertain, Lady Belerma was a character in Cervantes's *Don Quixote*.

26. *'Tis ... SWIFT*: from *Cadenus and Vanessa* published in 1726. George Crabbe quoted the same lines and attribution in his 'The Birth of Flattery,' in *Poems* (London: J. Hatchard, 1807).

27. d'en avoir le cœur net: 'to get to the bottom of it'. (French).

28. *plaiting chips*: weaving together of thin, fibrous, woody strips which could then be used to make ladies' hats.

29. le plus loin, le plus serré: 'the further [away] the tighter [the grip]' (French); the phrase is akin, in this context, to the English 'absence makes the heart grow fonder'.

30. *'Of his ... love'*: Alcæus shares his name with the Greek lyric poet (620–580 BC) who was a contemporary of Sappho, as well as with the earlier, though more obscure epigrammatist, Alcæus of Messene.

31. *wear the willow*: Lady Torrendale suggests that the two be left to lament their loss.

32. *'lighted up ... eye'*: The phrase is quite possibly derived from 'Distress and Relief', included in *The Rural Minstrel: A Miscellany of Descriptive Poems* (Halifax: P. K. Holden, 1813) by Patrick Brontë (1777–1861).

33. *Sir Peter Teazle*: an allusion to Peter Teazle's exclamation upon discovering his young wife's attraction toward another man: 'Now I believe the truth is coming indeed' (Sheridan, *The School for Scandal*, IV.iii.435).

34. *Oh Lady ... to love! LORD STRANGFORD CAMOËNS*: from Luís Vaz de Camoëns's Sonnet 1, as included in Strangford's *Poems from the Portuguese of Camoens*; the lines (12–14) consecutive to those quoted in volume 1. n.4

35. comedie larmoyante: A term principally associated with the plays of the eighteenth-century French dramatist Pierre Claude Nivelle de La Chaussée is here appropriated for the more general purpose of suggesting sentimental, moralizing comedy.

36. un beau canevas: 'a good story.' (French).

37. *Rival Queens*: Nathaniel Lee's tragedy, *The Rival Queens; or, Alexander the Great* continued to be performed throughout the eighteenth century.
38. distrait: 'distracted.' (French).
39. *'My fairest ... found'*: from *Paradise Lost*, V.18.
40. *'pleasant, but mournful ... languish of her beam'*: The first phrase, 'pleasant but mournful to the soul', is derived from James Macpherson's Ossian poem, 'The Death of Cuthullin'. See *The Poems of Ossian* 2 vols (Edinburgh: J. Elder and T. Brown, 1797), vol. 1, p. 140. The ensuing lines are taken (with minor, syntactical modification) from James Thomson's *The Seasons: Spring* (1728), 1032–7.
41. *'Hast thou ... grief?'*: LeFanu resumes her reading of Ossian here, quoting from Macpherson's 'Dar-thula' (*Poems*, vol. 1, p. 148). Her source may, however, have been the 'Dissertation by Dr Blair' appended to this edition, as both this and the previous quotation from Ossian, were included in that essay as examples of the bard's excellent phrasing.
42. *'The Roe ... on the hill'*: As LeFanu notes, this is taken from the 'Song of the Five Bards', an ancient poem 'a thousand years later than Ossian,' to which Macpherson refers in his footnote to the poem 'Croma' (*Poems*, vol 1, p. 224). In this song, each bard is invited to make an extempore observation on night. Macpherson includes their responses in his note, and Sappho recites, in part, that of the first bard.
43. *'Sung by ... lute'*: Shakespeare's *Henry IV, Part I*, III.i.209–10.
44. *'Too plain ... eyes'*: The first line of 'Chloe to Stephron' by Soame Jenyns (1704–47), which was first published in Robert Dodsley's *A Collection of Poems in Three Volumes by Several Hands*, 3 vols (London: R. Dodsley, 1748), vol 3.
45. *Allegory to Pity ... charming sadness*: a further reference to Barbauld's allegory which, in later publications, was variously entitled 'A Tale' or 'Pity'. The *New Novelist's Magazine* (vol 1., 1786), for example, has it as 'Pity. An Allegory,' and it this title which is adopted by LeFanu's contemporary, Felicia Hemans (1793–1835), for an early composition along the same lines. Signed 'F.D.B. aged 11,' Hemans's poem, 'Pity. An Allegory', appeared in her first published volume, *Poems* (1808).
46. *Why ... being*: lines taken from II.i. of Torquato Tasso's pastoral play Aminta (1573) as translated by Percival Stockdale. See his *The Amyntas of Tasso* (London: T. Davies, 1770), p. 22.
47. bien-aimée: 'beloved.' (French).
48. *Agatha's ring ... semblance of an attachment*: possibly a reference to the marriage ring of the Virgin Mary preserved at the Cathedral of Peruglia. Exhibited every St Agatha's Day, it was considered to have the power to cure ailments in mothers and, by implication, older women. See George Frederick Kunz, *The Curious Lore of Precious Stones* (Philadelphia & London: J. P. Lippincott, 1913), p. 316.
49. *'flattering ... to her soul'*: derived from Shakespeare's *Hamlet*, III.iv.145.
50. la douce habitude: 'sweet habit or practice.' (French).
51. *'All ... inflict'*: This seems to be derived from 'The Reply' to 'Song, To the Tune of I Loo'd a Bony Lady', both of which were included in the poet Allan Ramsay's *Tea-Table Miscellany; or, A Complete Collection of Scots Sangs*, 3 vols (Dublin: E. Smith, 1729), as well as in several later collections. Arranged as a two-part dialogue, the speaker of 'Song' appeals to the object of his unrequited love. She regrets his pain, but in her reply can only suggest that he find a restorative 'for the Ills I cannot cure' in the knowledge that 'I drag a hopeless Chain / And all that I inflict endure' (vol. 1, p. 49).

52. *Aspasia ... Diogenes*: Aspasia was courtesan to the Athenian general, Pericles, in the fifth century BC. Arbella's comparison of Sowerby and Diogenes, the philosopher renowned for his asceticism and frugality, is meant unfavourably.

53. bourru bienfaisant: 'rough diamond.' (French).

54. *Lady Teazle ... hundred pounds*: In Sheridan's *The School for Scandal*, Lady Teazle, the country wife of the one-time sworn bachelor Sir Peter, demands (and gets) all the luxuries he and the town can afford. See III.i.

55. 'a tout ... misericorde': from lines spoken by the vain and dismissive Archbishop of Granada in Alain-René Lesage's novel *Histoire de Gil Blas de Santillane* (1715–35). This translates as, 'There is mercy for every transgression.'

56. *gimcracks*: 'small ornaments' (*OED*).

57. *On such ... SHAKESPEARE. MERCHANT OF VENICE*: lines spoken by Lorenzo, V.i.9–12.

58. un peu delabrée: 'a little ramshackle.' (French).

59. un sejour enchanté: 'an enchanting place to stay.' (French).

60. emportée: 'quick tempered or carried away.' (French).

61. *black-letter knowledge*: in this context, an allusion to Mrs Fitzroy's awareness of the gothic mode and its traditions.

62. 'Matilda' ... *MISS SEWARD*: an adaptation of lines taken from Anna Seward's *Monody on Major André* (Lichfield: J. Jackson, 1781) in which 'Honora' is the name replaced by that of LeFanu's heroine (p. 9).

63. 'sullenness against nature': This originates in Milton's pamphlet, *Of Education* (1644): 'in those vernal seasons of the year, when the air is calm and pleasant, it were an injury and sullenness against nature not to go out and see her riches, and partake in her rejoicing with Heaven and Earth.'

64. *crescent of Diana, to the Ægis of Minerva*: Although goddess of the hunt, Diana's association with the moon is here invoked to indicate that chastity was a trait Lady Strathallan combined with the wisdom and, it would seem, with the ardour, which is represented by the breastplate worn by the warrior goddess Minerva.

65. *Penseroso*: 'contemplative man' (Italian).

66. Le plus amiable des hommes se consolera: 'The most amicable of men will get over the loss.' (French).

67. *wraith*: 'a phantom or ghost' (*OED*).

68. *like a sun beam*: probably a reference to Macpherson's Ossian, the phrase being used in Book II of *Fingal*, for example. See *Poems*, vol. 1, p. 31.

69. *Madame De Trop*: possibly the name given to a woman excessive in her manner.

70. 'His heart ... mute': from Byron's oriental tale, *The Corsair* (1814), the line reading: 'My heart unhushed, although my lips were mute' (I.xiv).

71. *E, in ... TASSO – GERUSALEMME LIBERATA*: a conflation of lines from two consecutive stanzas of Book XII. Hoole renders the whole in the third person, conveying the sense of the lines as: 'Rejoic'd in death, she seem'd her joy to tell, / And bade for Heav'n the empty world farewell. / A lovely paleness o'er her features flew; / As vi'lets mix'd with lilies blend their hue. / Her eyes to Heav'n the dying virgin rais'd. [...] her lips their music cease. / So life departing left her lovely breast; / So seem'd the virgin lull'd to silent rest!' (vol. 2, p. 45).

72. *Véggio ... PETEARCA*: Petrarch's Sonnet 279. A late-eighteenth-century translation reads: 'That she yet lives each sense assurance brings, / E'en now from far she answers to my moan. / 'Ah! Wherefore thus,' I hear her as she cries, / 'In fruitless anguish waste thy prime away? / What cause this swelling stream of tears supplies? / Weep not for me [...]'.

See Thomas Le Mesurier, *Translations Chiefly from the Italian of Petrarch and Metastasio* (Oxford: J. Cooke, 1795), p. 35.

73. *Fare ... Burns*: from the last stanza of Robert Burns's 'Ae Fond Kiss, And Then We Sever' (*c.* 1791).

74. *From Venice ... Bard of Salerno*: derived from Isaac Disraeli's comments on the song of the Venetian gondoliers, to which he adds: 'I was told that the women of Libo, the long row of islands that divides the Adriatic from the Lagouns, particularly the women of the extreme districts of Malamocca and Palestrina, sing in like manner the works of Tasso to these and similar tunes. They have the custom, when their husbands are fishing out at sea, to sit along the shore in the evenings and vociferate these songs, and continue to do so with great violence, till each of them can distinguish the responses of her own husband at a distance.' See *Curiosities of Literature. Consisting of Anecdotes, Characters, Sketches and Observations*, 4th edn, 2 vols (London: Murray and Highley, 1798), vol 2, p. 148. Disraeli is referring to Torquato Tasso, although it was Tasso's father, Bernardo, who enjoyed the patronage of Ferrante Sanseverino, Prince of Salerno.

75. *my wood-notes wild*: The phrase is inspired by Milton's 'L'Allegro', which was composed between 1632 and 1638: 'Then to the well-trod stage anon, / If Jonson's learned sock be on, / Or sweetest Shakespeare, Fancy's child, / Warble his native wood-notes wild' (131–4).

76. *Se mai ... Metastasio. La Clemenza Di Tito*: 'If you have ever felt a light breeze blow gently on your face, such are the last sighs of my faith, which is dying with me. To a soul torn from my breast, the memory of such sufferings shall, with this reward, be sweet.'

77. *'Before ... trouble it!'*: minor variation of lines from Joanna Baillie's 'Count Basil' (I.ii.), a tragic drama included in the first of a three-part *Series of Plays: in which it is attempted to delineate the stronger passions of the mind. Each passion being the subject of a tragedy and a comedy.* (London: T. Cadell, jun. and W. Davies, 1798).

78. esprit fort ... bel-esprit: no longer 'a freethinker', but 'a brilliant wit'. (French).

79. 'tout à lui': 'entirely his.' (French).

80. *Dryden ... national mythology*: Sowerby is possibly referring to Dryden's Preface to *The State of Innocence* (first printed 1677), in which the likes of sylphs and genii, if not those 'immaterial substances authoris'd by Scripture', are considered the stuff of poetry: 'And Poets may be allow'd the like Liberty, for describing things which really exist not, if they are founded on popular belief: Of this Nature are Fairies, Pigmies, and the extraordinary Effects of Magick: For 'tis still an imitation, though of other mens fancies.' See *The State of Innocence, and Fall of Man: An Opera. Written in Heroic Verse* (London: J. Tonson, 1721), p. 13.

81. *'To be present ... than'*: Though this letter was included in several letter-writing manuals published throughout the eighteenth century, it is likely (and fitting) that Arbella is reading from *The Complete Art of Writing Love Letters; or the Lover's Best Instructor* (London: W. Franklin, *c.* 1800), p. 38. Published at the turn of the century, this volume, like others, has Arbella's last line at the beginning of the quotation, but is otherwise distinctive in focusing on love letters and in identifying the correspondent as a dying wife.

82. *'upon the hazard of a die'*: In his final speech Shakespeare's Richard III declares, 'I have set my life upon a cast, / And I will stand the hazard of the die' (V.iv.9–10).

83. *Come then! ... Poem Of Bonaparte*: *Bonaparte, A Poem* (London, 1814), by Stratford Canning, Viscount Stratford de Redcliffe, was admired by Byron, who makes mention of it in his letters.

84. *'wonder ... content'*: a slight modification of lines with which the moor greets Desdemona in *Othello*: 'It gives me wonder great as my content / To see you here before me' (II. i.181–2).

85. *'The lovely, lowly dwelling'*: from Robert Southey's 'Botany Bay Eclogues: Elinor', which was published in *Poems* (1797), 26.

86. *Those ... THOMSON'S SEASONS*: from 'Spring' (1728), 1132–7.

87. *Though ... TICKEL*: a conflation of lines taken from the poem, 'To A Lady Before Marriage' by Thomas Tickell (1685–1740). LeFanu can claim a family connection through the poet's son, Richard Tickell (1751–93). He was the brother-in-law of Richard Brinsley Sheridan, having married Mary Linley, the sister of Sheridan's wife, Elizabeth. Many of Tickell's writings, including this poem, appeared in collections dating from the mid-eighteenth to early-nineteenth centuries.

88. *female Catiline ... Duchesse Du Maine*: a reference to Lucius Sergius Catiline (*c.*108–62 BC), the aristocrat who attempted, unsuccessfully, to overthrow the Roman republic. Married to the illegitimate son of Louis XIV, Anne-Louise-Bénédicte de Bourbon-Condé, Duchesse du Maine (1676–1753) was renowned for her distinguished literary salon and less successful intervention in court politics.

89. *'no character at all'*: derived from the opening lines of Pope's *Moral Essays. Epistle II. To a Lady. Of the Characters of Women* (1735).

90. *'to win her and wear her'*: Arbella is quite possibly quoting O'Hara here, but the eponymous heroine of Frances Sheridan's *Memoirs of Miss Sidney Bidulph*, 3 vols (London: R. and J. Dodsley, 1761), uses the phrase with similar contempt: Sidney is exasperated by her mother's giving permission to a then unwanted suitor to 'win and wear me. I could cry for very vexation, to be made such a puppet of' (vol. 1, p. 179).

91. *'Shepherds I have lost my love'*: This song was composed, in his youth, by the Irish MP George Ogle (1742–1814). Though it remained popular throughout the eighteenth century, it inspired several burlesque pieces, the like of which are alluded to here.

92. *'Si spoglian ... panni'*: The Italian soldier, diplomat and courtier, Count Castiglione Baldassarre (1478–1529) composed his pastoral *Egloga Tirsi Intitulata* ('Thyrsis') for Guidobaldo da Montefeltro, Duke of Urbino in 1506. The sense of these lines may be summarized: 'Though the snake can shake off its old age and renew its skin and its years at once, in me Beauty flies away; neither artifice nor clothing enables its return.'

93. le petit glorieux: 'the little glorious one.' (French).

94. *'Ci git ... gloire'*: Piron's epitaph for the French military leaders and statesmen Henri de la Tour d'Auvergne, Vicomte de Turenne and Charles Belle-Isle, Duc de Gisors, reads: 'Here lies the glorious one beside the Glory.'

95. roquelaure: 'cloak.' (French).

96. *Balsora ... gate of Paradise*: In this oriental tale, the king's physician feigns the death of his daughter, Balsora, and that of her admirer and heir to the Persian throne, Abdullah, with a sleeping potion. Interred in the tyrant king's heavily guarded Black Palace the two are able to emerge, disguised as spirits, and live in a mountain Paradise until the king's death.

TEXTUAL VARIANTS

The first edition of *Strathallan* is used as the copy-text. Substantive variants between this and the second (*1816b*) and third (*1817*) editions are given below.

Volume I

2a

PREFACE
TO THE
SECOND EDITION
OF
STRATHALLAN.

On a second edition of Strathallan being called for, the Author has been requested to supply a short preface; on which occasion, she experiences the embarrassment natural to one who dreads alike the imputation of ingratitude on the one hand, or presumption on the other. The favorable notices in British and Foreign Prints and Journals that have met her eye, induce her to hope, that her first attempt has been received with some indulgence by an enlightened and generous public. Should she ever venture again to appear before its tribunal, such indulgence in exciting her gratitude shall redouble her diligence to deserve it.

The present edition of Strathallan she has endeavoured to render as correct as possible, and trusts that her absence from London will apologize for any remaining errors.
FAREHAM,
Nov. 29, 1816

In the second and third editions this preface is printed in addition to the original.
13a   It was rather small, the roof arched, which was] The roof was arched, which was *1816b, 1817*

14a   natricles] watricles *1816b, 1817*

16a   Clever! no -- I only] 'Clever! -- I only *1816b, 1817*

39a   "done" me] done me *1816b, 1817*

63a   He knows I make myself very easy about him.'] He knows that seriously he
        has very little influence with me, as well as I do -- and better --" *1816b,
        1817*

68a   memorable day. Never] memorable day; and the arrival of our troops
        only gave the last blow to the faint hope that still lingered in the bosoms
        of his anxious relatives, respecting some possible error in the first com-
        munications.-- Never *1816b, 1817*

92a   To the waltzing, Spanish dances had succeeded;] To the German, Span-
        ish waltzing had succeeded; *1816b, 1817*

92b   and the gay ...brother's return.] *1816b, 1817 omit.*

130a   a laugh against Joseph)] "a laugh against Joseph") *1816b, 1817*

123a   SPIRITS] spirits *1816b, 1817*

166a   *perceive*] perceive *1816b, 1817*

Volume II

252a

Jaques.
Why, 'tis good to be sad and say nothing.
Rosalind.
Why, then 'tis good to be a post.
                                SHAKESPEARE.-- AS YOU LIKE IT.

1816b, 1817: additional epigraph

253a   *agréable*] agreeable *1816b, 1817*

253a   parodizing] parodying *1816b, 1817*

260a   *très ingénu.* Then,] *très ingénu.* "They are made," she said, "*à un boutique
        auquel j'ai promis ma coutume.*" Then, *1816b, 1817*

Volume III

326a   nè sí selvagge] nè selvagge *1816b, 1817*

345a   *menagerie.'* 'There's nothing] *menagerie'* 'the manége, you mean," said
        Alcæus. 'There's *1816b, 1817*

346   cloud. It is] cloud.' 'Tis *1816b, 1817*

348a   the tomb of the warriors, after all, creates] the tombs of warriors, after all,
        create *1816b* the tombs of the warriors, after all, create *1817*

354a   said Sappho. 'I protest to you, that is what you like, and why should not
        you?" pursued Sowerby,] said Sappho, --'I protest to you.' 'That is what
        you like, and why should not you?' pursued Sowerby, *1816b, 1817*

358a   gentlemen, she lost in anxiety for his safety all prudence] gentlemen, she forgot, in anxiety for his safety, all prudence *1816b, 1817*

360a   past. He had the first fire, witch mist; the Major] past. It was deranged by the seconds to leave it to the De Termination of chans witch shoud have the first fire; and so it happened the Captain had the first fire, witch mist; the Major *1816b, 1817*

365a   Major O'Hara ... Fitzroy's illness.] *1816b, 1817 omit.*

Volume IV

410a   beg pardon) *almost* given up] (I beg pardon *almost* given up *1816b*; (I beg pardon *almost* given up) *1817*

411a   parents] parents' *1816b, 1817*

418a   scene. 'When the massy] scene; when the massy *1816b, 1817*

429a   the Honourable Mrs. Fitzroy] the hon. Mrs. Fitzroy *1816b 1817*

433a   warning. If she attempted to follow him to Cheltenham it would not] warning, if she attempted to follow him to Cheltenham. It would not *1816b, 1817*

437a   demon of illusion] demon of allusion *1816b, 1817*

439a   principle. Matilda, without ... enthusiasts;] principle. In the company of Miss Swanley she now began to find a real resource, while Matilda, without ... enthusiasts; *1816b, 1817*

443a   lady] Lady *1816b, 1817*

447a   *appointments*] appointments *1816b, 1817*

453a   taste? esteem for his character.'] taste – esteem for his character?' *1816b, 1817*

474a   Sappho's muse, enquired, with an absent look, 'Is it about Spain?' 'It is.] Sappho's muse.' 'It is. *1816b, 1817 omit.*

SILENT CORRECTIONS

Volume I

4 don't] dont
12 house"] house
14 'A truce] A truce
15 doubt;] doubt,
15 Torrendale.] Torrendale.'
15 Rocks] rocks
15 faces.] faces
15 Lady] lady
16 'Yes] Yes
25 looking] look-
28 contemporaries] cotemporaries
28 Rocks] rocks
32 synonymous] synonimous
33 'I trust] I trust
34 *protegée*] *protege*
35 ventured] venture
40 moment] moment'
40 Stockwells] Stockwell's
40 Arbella's'] Arbella's
43 first.] first'
43 hers'.] hers
45 life,] life,'
45 commonplaces] common places
47 Albermarle's'.] Albermarle's
49 daughter-in-law] daughter-in law
53 favorite sitting] favorite-sitting
53 right?'] right?
56 *Quintas*] *Quinta's*
57 that – '] that –

62 Mr.] Mr:
64 Ladyship] ladyship
66 fire, it] fire. It
67 Horoscope.'] Horoscope.
69 mine' he said] mine he said'
71 resembles his] resemblesh is
74 war.'] war.
77 studies.'] studies'
79 disposed] diposed
79 sworn it.] sworn it.'
79 amusement.'] amusement
80 after] 'after
80 'He] He
81 so.'] so'
83 Matilda*."'] Matilda*.
84 called] call
85 couldn't] could't
87 Rose-villa] Rosevilla
88 Is] "Is
89 Ferrars] Ferrar's
93 tonight, I think,'] tonight," I think,
94 supper-room] supper room
95 about] abut
95 Ferrars's] Ferrar's
95 don't] do'nt
96 'Pretty!'] Pretty!
96 *fantaisie*] *fantaisce*
96 heroes, he proceeded] heroes, proceeded
98 Ferrars's] Ferrar's
98 'Perhaps] Perhaps
99 partner!'] partner!
108 Euterpes] Euterpes'
109 is a fine] Is a fine
109 Joy] joy
116 of] of of
119 don't] dont
121 varied. Above] varied; above
125 Ferrars] Ferrars'
126 letters] letlers
126 Estes's] Estes
129 Bergère] Bergére

135 rosy cheek'] rosy cheek
135 Forgive] forgive
135 this] This
141 and] and and
145 SIROE] SIROC
149 Melbourne's] Melbourne
150 again?'] again?
150 *vie;'] vie;*
151 GERUSALEMME] GIERUSALEMME
169 from] form

Volume II

203 mention] menrion
212 Major] major
221 grandfather] grandfeather
255 Aunt] aunt
269 strict watch] strictwatch
279 this scene] thisscene
281 sight of] sight o

Volume III

295 Melbourne] Melbonrne
325 that] tha
354 what they] whatthey
359 blessings of] blessings o
362 the verge] theverge
375 ÉPRIS] E'PRIS
378 unfavorably] unfafavorably
386 LADY M. W.] LADY CH. W.
389 Tiridates] Tridates
389 ingrate.] ingrate
390 of] of of

Volume IV

400 should!] should?
406 *père] pére*
412 Madonna] Madona
441 couldn't] could'nt
443 *peché] pechè*

448 Castle is] Castleis
452 be] he
456 An emotion] A nemotion
465 when] whem
466 solemn] solmn
472 Torrendale.'] Torrendale
476 gloom.] gloom.'
476 a part] a a part
481 sight.] sight
482 Its pomp] it's pomp
482 TICKELL] TICKEL